# Financialization and Strategy

This book analyzes the impact of capital market pressures on giant-firm strategy in the US and UK since the early 1980s. It explains how classical strategy, including Porter and Prahalad & Hamel, has been preoccupied with the product market so it cannot engage with how financialization has changed what giant firms say and do.

An extended introduction presents compelling evidence which shows that the pressure for 'shareholder value' in the 1990s did not lead to any great improvement in performance in groups of giant firms like the FTSE 100 or the S&P 500. The beneficiaries were not shareholders but managers who used corporate governance reforms and the bull market of the 1990s to claim large pay increases.

More fundamentally, the book argues that giant-firm strategy has been transformed: the narrative and performative elements of strategy, along with corroborating financial numbers, have become much more important. This point is developed and demonstrated through case studies of three companies (General Electric, Ford and GlaxoSmithKline) which use long run financial data and analysis of company and industry narratives to explore these themes.

The result is an innovative account of the limits of management action in a corporate world where managers find it easier to put together narratives than to deliver improved performance. It offers innovative business analysis which uniquely combines and counterposes empirical evidence on firm trajectory and financial results with new kinds of cultural analysis.

*Financialization and Strategy* offers a distinctive, critical account of what corporate management has become in large UK and US corporations. It will be an invaluable resource for practitioners and academics with interdisciplinary interests in management and cultural economy. It is already being used as a course text in MBA and Masters teaching at Manchester Business School and Royal Holloway.

The authors are all researchers at the ESRC Centre for Research in Socio Cultural Change (www.cresc.ac.uk) where **Karel Williams** is co-director. **Julie Froud**, **Adam Leaver** and Karel Williams all teach at Manchester Business School, University of Manchester and **Sukhdev Johal** at the School of Management, Royal Holloway, University of London. They have set up the International Working Group on Financialization (www.iwgf.org) and edit the journal Competition and Change (www.maney.co.uk).

# Financialization and Strategy

## Narrative and numbers

Julie Froud,
Sukhdev Johal,
Adam Leaver and
Karel Williams

LONDON AND NEW YORK

First published 2006
by Routledge
2 Park Square, Milton Park, Abingdon, Oxon OX14 4RN

Simultaneously published in the USA and Canada
by Routledge
270 Madison Ave, New York, NY 10016

*Routledge is an imprint of the Taylor & Francis Group*

Transferred to Digital Printing 2010



Typeset in Perpetua and Bell Gothic
by Keystroke, Jacaranda Lodge, Wolverhampton



*British Library Cataloguing in Publication Data*
A catalogue record for this book is available from the British Library

*Library of Congress Cataloging in Publication Data*
Strategy and financialisation : narrative and numbers / Julie Froud . . . [et al.].– 1st ed.
p. cm.
Includes bibliographical references and index.
1. Conglomerate corporations–United States–Management. 2. Conglomerate corporations–Great Britain–Management. 3. Conglomerate corporations–United States–Case studies. 4. Conglomerate corporations–Great Britain–Case studies.
I. Froud, Julie.
HD2756.2.U5S77 2006
658′.046–dc22
2005015415

ISBN10: 0–415–33417–9 ISBN13: 9–78–0–415–33417–4 (hbk)
ISBN10: 0–415–33418–7 ISBN13: 9–78–0–415–33418–1 (pbk)

# Contents

# Exhibits and tables

## EXHIBITS

## TABLES

# Acknowledgements

We could not have written this long, difficult and radical book without the support and encouragement of various sponsors who believed in our capacity to execute this project and gave us the time and stimulus to develop the ideas:

1 The John Lloyd Huck Institute for Management Science Research funded research leave for Julie Froud to work on a twenty-year case study of General Electric from which the whole idea of the book developed. We are grateful to David Leslie-Hughes of the John Lloyd Huck Institute who had the imagination to back an exploratory project.
2 The European Socio-Economic Model of a Knowledge-Based Society (ESEMK) project, under EU Framework 6, funded research leave for Adam Leaver in autumn 2004 to work on adding finance to industrial companies which gave us the chance to work on the Ford case and the broader issue of adding finance. We owe a considerable debt to Yannick Lung who, as the coordinator of successive EU funded projects, has created a space in which we can work on financialization along with European colleagues.
3 The Economic and Social Research Council (ESRC) has funded the new Centre for Research on Socio-Cultural Change (CRESC) where Karel Williams is co-director. Since autumn 2004, the centre has given us the time, space and active stimulus to develop our ideas on cultural economy in dialogue with other academics, and the result is a different kind of book. Our special thanks to Mike Savage who, from the beginning, saw the potential of a distinctive CRESC approach to business analysis; as co-director Mike also willingly took on more administrative work so that others could research and write.
4 Our editor Jacqueline Curthoys at Routledge responded immediately and positively to our book proposal, then helped us develop the concept of the book and was humorous but firm about the need to deliver. We are particularly grateful for her patience when final delivery of the manuscript was delayed by the serious illness of a young child.

We also owe a series of debts to key individuals without whose practical support and help we could not have done the research and completed the writing up:

1 JP Morgan Chase supplied hard copies of all the accounts for the twenty-year case studies, including all the historic 10-K returns for Ford Credit. We thank Paul Bateman, CEO Asset Management, JP Morgan Chase for giving us access to the resources of his organization and thereby making the case studies possible.
2 Steven Kay, Business Data Specialist at the Manchester Business School (MBS) Library, University of Manchester guided us through all the complexities of using the available databases on S&P 500 and FTSE 100. Steven's assistance was invaluable when we wanted to go beyond what was straightforward in working up twenty-year comparisons from databases.
3 Peter Folkman and Steve Francis, the two businessmen on the CRESC advisory board, have encouraged our business analysis and provided practical advice and criticism of drafts which were never an easy read. We are also indebted to several business and practitioner readers, including an experienced stock-market analyst, who gave us feedback on drafts.
4 Wei Zhang, an intending doctoral student, worked as our research assistant on this project in the final three months before the manuscript was delivered. She played a major role in working up exhibits and tables as well as formatting the manuscript text and thereby saved the four authors weeks of work at the end of the project.

It should also be noted formally that we have worked and published with two other individuals who have played a major role in developing the general ideas that went into the introduction of this book. All our early work on financialization from 2000 onwards was jointly authored with Colin Haslam of the University of Hertfordshire; our more recent work on governance has been jointly authored with Ismail Erturk, another CRESC researcher. Four authors appear on the title page but our stock of ideas has been jointly developed with Colin and Ismail so we cannot easily say what is ours and theirs.

We began writing the book at the end of 2004, a year that was completely overshadowed by the death from leukaemia of our oldest collaborator John Williams, who was in every way the founding and senior member of the team which wrote this book. In the early 1980s a conversation at his kitchen table led to the book *Why Are the British Bad at Manufacturing?* and two decades of innovative work on present-day capitalism. In a last conversation in the same room, John talked only about future projects and the need to develop every member of the team so that they fulfilled their potential. This book is dedicated to the memory of John and expresses our determination that his values will prevail.

JF, SJ, AL, KW

# Abbreviations

| | |
|---|---|
| ABPI | Association of British Pharmaceutical Industries |
| AHP | American Home Products |
| ANDA | Abbreviated New Drug Application |
| BA | British Airways |
| BCCI | Bank of Credit and Commerce International |
| BLMC/BL | British Leyland Motor Corporation/British Leyland |
| CEO | Chief Executive Officer |
| CFO | Chief Financial Officer |
| CFROI | Cash Flow Return on Investment |
| CPI | consumer price index |
| DoH | Department of Health |
| DTC | direct to consumer |
| EBITDA | earnings before interest, tax, depreciation and amortisation |
| EMEA | European Medicines Evaluation Agency |
| ESEMK | European Socio-Economic Model of a Knowledge Based Society |
| ESRC | Economic and Social Research Council |
| EVA™ | Economic Value Added |
| FDA | Food and Drug Administration |
| FTSE | Financial Times Stock Exchange |
| GAAP | generally accepted accounting practice |
| GCC | global commodity chain |
| GDP | gross domestic product |
| GE | General Electric |
| GEC | General Electric Company |
| GECAS | General Electric Capital Aviation Services |
| GECS | General Electric Capital Services |
| GERPISA | Groupe d'Études et de Recherches Permanent sur l'Industrie et les Salariés de l'Automobile |
| GM | General Motors |
| GMAC | General Motors Acceptance Corp. |
| GSK | GlaxoSmithKline |

| | |
|---|---|
| IMVP | International Motor Vehicle Program |
| IPO | initial public offering |
| LBO | leveraged buy-out |
| LSE | London Stock Exchange |
| M&A | merger and acquisition |
| MBS | Manchester Business School |
| MHW | Ministry of Health and Welfare |
| MOSS | market-oriented sector selected |
| MSF | Médicins Sans Frontières |
| MVA | Market Value Added |
| NASDAQ | National Association of Securities Dealer Automated Quotation |
| NCE | new chemical entity |
| NICE | National Institute for Clinical Excellence |
| NYSE | New York Stock Exchange |
| OTC | over the counter |
| P/E | price/earning |
| PAG | Premier Automotive Group |
| PCB | polychlorinated biphenyl |
| PhRMA | Pharmaceutical Research and Manufacturers of America |
| PPRS | Pharmaceutical Price Regulation Scheme |
| R&D | research and development |
| RBT | resource-based theory |
| ROCE | return on capital employed |
| ROE | return on equity |
| ROS | return on sales |
| S&P | Standard & Poor's |
| SEC | Securities and Exchange Commission |
| SIC | standard industrial classification |
| SPE | special-purpose entity |
| SUV | sports utility vehicle |
| TSR | Total Shareholder Return |
| UAW | Union of Auto Workers |
| VBM | value-based management |
| WL | Warner Lambert |

Part I

# Giant-firm strategy and present-day capitalism

## General argument and evidence

## Chapter 1

# Overview

Through a long general introduction and three substantial historical cases, this book describes, analyses and explores what management strategy has become for giant US and UK firms under pressure from the capital market since the 1980s. This first chapter introduces the book and its revisionist argument in two ways. The first two sections provide an overview by explaining the book's object and its approach to analysing the intrusion of the capital market, as well as summarizing the book's argument about the capital market's impact on strategy after financialization. The second section also explains how the argument and evidence is organized into two major parts with a five-chapter general introduction in Part I, complemented by three extended historical case studies of Glaxo, Ford and General Electric (GE) in Part II. The third and final section of this chapter provides some context on giant firms in the US and UK by considering size, sectoral affiliation and other characteristics of the giant firms whose market capitalization puts them in the S&P 500 and the FTSE 100; it also sets these groups of firms in the context of the US and UK economies.

## OBJECT AND APPROACH OF THIS BOOK

Readers may find that this book mixes literatures, styles of argument, concepts and use of evidence in ways that are probably disconcerting and certainly challenging. The authors' response is that our object is management strategy in giant firms and this object now requires an innovative approach which starts by reflecting on why the existing discourse of strategy is unsatisfactory and then tries to do something different by constructing a frame that is broader and deeper than the firm in industry of current strategy study. Thus, we discuss two groups of giant firms in the UK and USA in the introduction before shifting to three historical case studies based on multiple sources including twenty years of financial results. This section explains the rationale behind our approach.

If this book's object is management strategy in giant firms, our starting point is both dissatisfaction with existing strategy literature and curiosity about aspects of present-day capitalism which barely figure in the field of the visible for mainstream strategy discourse. The literature on strategy is voluminous and includes work within many different problematics whose intellectual assumptions and practical objectives are diverse. Whittington's (1993) short, serious book on strategy is self-consciously different from the popular management texts that offer recipes for success and transferable lessons. Our argument focuses on what we construct as the mainstream lineage of 'classical strategy' from Chandler through Porter to Prahalad and Hamel. These authors disagree about many things but share a common problem definition about the giant firm facing the product market. We have considerable respect for Chandler's historical case studies but less for his successors whose firm-in-product-market problem definition is now anachronistic.

The anachronism arises from the intrusion of the capital market, signalled by the increasingly vociferous investor demands for 'shareholder value' since the late 1980s in both the UK and USA. This book tackles the problem of how capital-market pressure has reshaped what American and British giant-firm management says and does. The problem turns out to be an interesting intellectual problem in itself which raises all kinds of political and social issues about social actors and who does what for whom. Shareholder value is a malleable social rhetoric used by investors with diverse requirements which does not, therefore, have one invariant set of consequences such as increased management distributions to shareholders. Instead, the intrusion of the capital market makes the narrative and performative more important because every giant company now needs a story of purpose and achievement that can be rendered more plausible by initiatives. Our work on this local paradigm shift around giant-firm strategy vindicates the importance of the socio-cultural, without endorsing over-ambitious epochal theories associated with terms such as 'network society' or 'economies of signs'.

If we do not start by pretending to know how a new and different kind of economy operates, we can learn more about the character of present-day capitalism by working on a problem such as giant-firm strategy under pressure from the capital market. We argue that the changes around strategy are part of a broader process that we understand as financialization, the term we use to denote the changes induced by the rhetoric of shareholder value. In our view, the process of financialization sets firms and households utopian objectives such as value creation by management intervention for giant firms or security through stock-market saving for households. On the evidence we cite, this corporate objective is almost certainly unrealizable in most firms most of the time, yet the world may be changed by management's attempt to achieve that objective. And the recognition of rhetoric and utopian projects takes us from political economy to cultural economy.

From this point of view, we are interested in discourse and narrative as a basis for rethinking strategy and explaining governance. Discourse analysis figures, first, through our critique of classical strategy since the early 1960s and second, through our commentary on corporate governance since the early 1990s. The preoccupation of classical strategy with the product market continues to the present day in a strategy literature that is unreflective about company and industry stories, over-reliant on confirming examples and vignettes and amnesiac about the unexpected transition from exemplary corporate success to failure. As for the new discourse of corporate governance, that acquired a high profile over the 1990s so that what began as a low-key response to corporate malpractice is now presented as a key technology for controlling management in the interests of shareholders. In its standard agency theory form, we argue that governance is a theoretically crude and empirically implausible set of propositions whose account of actors, motives and consequences nevertheless provides a kind of constitution for the market after Reagan and Thatcher.

Narrative figures in a variety of ways. In the general introduction we distinguish between company narratives, industry narratives and economic grand narratives, and we also observe that many of these narratives are collectively authored by stock-market analysts and business journalists as much as by giant company CEOs. Management is however responsible for the performative initiatives which signal that senior executives are 'walking the walk as well as talking the talk'. The narrative and performative are important parts of strategy after financialization. But we could not endorse overexcited commentators who credit the narrative and performative with a near miraculous capacity to format and frame action, understanding and consequences. On this issue, the British response to the French intellectual should echo that of Waugh's editor to his overbearing proprietor: 'up to a point, Lord Copper'.

Our starting point is that, if we consider company narratives, the promises of management can be backed by performative initiatives but often do not accord with subsequent financial numbers where outcomes at single firm level reflect constraints elsewhere in product market competition and suchlike. If we wish to understand how giant-firm strategy plays in this kind of world of disappointment, the financial numbers are crucially important because they are not a function of the tale that management spins (except in cases of fraud) and management's general dilemma is that it has many moves but few levers for improving financial performance. This observation does not take us back towards positivistic testing but forwards to exploratory single-company case studies as well as generalization about the value-creation records of the two groups of giant companies in the UK FTSE 100 and the US S&P 500 over the past twenty years. The survey of the group-value performance records incidentally changes our understanding of what corporate management did in the bull market decade of the 1990s. In retrospect the decade of the 1990s looks quite different because it provided an unprecedented opportunity for top managers to enrich themselves, though their actions did little directly to create value for shareholders.

The final chapter of our general introduction does develop some distinctive concepts such as 'sector matrix', but the introduction does not aim to produce a tool kit of new generic concepts for 'doing strategy' which are then mechanically applied to our three case companies on the assumption that these concepts are transferable to all firms. Rather, the general introduction provides a framework of argument and evidence that help us better understand what strategy has become in giant British and American firms under pressure from the capital market. These themes and issues are then explored and developed through three extended historical case studies of giant firms: Glaxo (now GlaxoSmithKline), Ford and GE. These cases add substance so that our approach combines forms of argument and exposition familiar from historiography as well as those of formalized social science.

While our emphasis throughout on the narrative and performative gives the analysis a faintly postmodern aura which echoes cultural turn academic analysis, the detailed analysis of accounting numbers in all three cases, as well as the introduction tables on the group performance of giant firms, represents an evidence-based form of analysis that echoes stock-market research by practitioners. Our book is an argument about and demonstration of how these two elements can be held in a relation of tension to create a new kind of business analysis which transcends the false opposition between the technical and the cultural that dominates current business research.

## STRUCTURE AND ARGUMENT

The first section of this overview provides a further explanation of how the five-chapter general introduction and the three historical cases on Glaxo, Ford and GE complement each other, before providing a brief chapter-by-chapter, case-by-case outline that follows the order of exposition in the book and explains how each of these major components contributes to the book's argument about the intrusion of the capital market and its impact on strategy after financialization.

At the very beginning of classical strategy, Alfred Chandler demonstrated that there is no good reason why authors should have to choose between writing history from primary sources about cases or presenting general concepts and evidence. With a problem such as giant-firm strategy after financialization, we have reached a point where it is necessary to construct both kinds of knowledge in a dialectic relation, which, in this book, is symbolized by the inclusion of the general introduction and historical cases as two distinct halves between one set of covers. The introduction serves two purposes as it aims to contextualize and direct the subsequent case histories: first, the introduction presents general evidence on issues such as the performance of groups of giant firms in the UK and USA so the reader has some understanding of average performance, dispersion and changes in trajectory over twenty years; second, the introduction provides discussion of organizing terms such as narrative and numbers as well as specific new concepts such as sector matrix for understanding management moves into related activities. Without this evidence base and some conceptual precision, the cases histories of Glaxo, Ford and GE would lack focus and direction. At the same time, the cases are not mechanical applications of some general a priori. The last chapter of the introduction focuses on the crucial issue of how narrative and numbers fit together in complex relations of corroboration and discrepancy, and these complexities are explored and illustrated in the cases so that the examples in this last section of the introduction are almost all taken from the cases that follow.

If the front and back parts of this book fit together, the general introduction and the cases both need separate explanation and justification. When most articles and monographs are about fairly narrowly defined objects, the most obvious peculiarity of Part I of this book is its range and scope. In 50,000 words it ranges over strategy and governance literatures, then tracks sideways to review secondary literature and primary evidence on value creation and distribution by US and UK giant firms; and incidentally then distinguishes between the rhetoric of shareholder value and the concept of financialization, as well as finally proposing new concepts for understanding strategy in the context of financialization. The scope of the introduction partly reflects the authors' temperamental preference for driving on the accelerator not the brake. But, the range of the argument also reflects a deliberate and considered choice about the balance of advantages and disadvantages of this approach given our objective of understanding more about giant-firm management in present-day capitalism.

Any text that ranges as broadly as our introduction is bound to frustrate specialists who will find, for example, that we cover employment in giant firms and labour as stakeholder in a few short pages. In our defence, we would note that standard political economy assertions and assumptions about, for example, increased distribution to shareholders after financialization rest on limited evidence; and on this key issue we are able to provide more sophisticated measures for the USA and UK that challenge the idea that financialization means increased distribution to shareholders. Furthermore, it would be wrong for readers to rest their judgement on our treatment of individual issues in an abstracted way because our aim was to put together information on several issues in the USA and UK into a preliminary Gestalt that challenges the conventional wisdom. On the evidence presented in our introduction, the top management of giant firms are not (as business apologists maintain) hugely creative and constructive social actors; nor (as leftist critics maintain) the agents who ensure capital gains at the expense of labour. Set against our evidence that giant firms grow no faster than GDP while CEO pay has risen much faster, top managers in giant firms appear to be an averagely ineffectual officer class who do, however, know how to look after themselves.

The attentive reader will note that the introduction includes many tables and graphs but does not use any systematic empiricist techniques to extract generalizable quasi-causal relations between variables. We are not fundamentally opposed to such techniques but systematic empiricist techniques are irrelevant to this book for two reasons. First, our basic argument is that, because shareholder value as social rhetoric can be appropriated and inflected by different social actors, financialization is not associated with one invariant set of consequences in terms of firm performance or management behaviour.

Second, the authors of this book are primarily interested in answering what and how questions. Why questions are much more difficult to answer because it is always difficult to move from correlation to causality and because causes can be regressed according to theoretical preferences. From this point of view, our approach is to try to escape the prison of an a priori by ranging broadly across evidence and explanations.

With these points made, it is now possible to explain the object and argument of each one of the next four chapters of this general introduction.

## Chapter 2 Giant Firms and Classical Strategy

The second chapter of our introduction does not provide a general history of strategy but instead focuses on the problem definition and mode of argument in many classical strategy texts. Classical strategy is manifestly diverse in so far as authors such as Porter (1980, 1985) and Prahalad and Hamel (1990) took very different positions on the sources of competitive advantage at business unit or corporate level and whether they were to be found inside or outside the firm. However, within what we call 'the classical tradition', all the different authors from Chandler (1962) to the Resource Based Theorists of the 1990s share a common problem definition in so far as strategy is always about the firm in industry facing the product market, which occludes discussion of the capital market and financialization. Moreover, in their use of evidence, most classical authors, with the notable exception of Chandler, rely on short company vignettes rather than historic case studies or large scale empirics. The unintended result is that many of those companies that figure as exemplars of success then experience unexpected reversals of fortune, which undermines confident claims that the principles of long-term success have been discovered and are easily transferable to other firms.

## Chapter 3 Shareholder Value: The Intrusion of the Capital Market

The third chapter of our introduction focuses on the demands of the capital market for 'shareholder value' in the 1990s and the claims of consultants and other commentators about how management should and could deliver shareholder value. The chapter's central argument is that 'shareholder value' was never a well-defined concept but a pliable rhetoric that was appropriated and inflected by different social actors. This chapter also introduces our theme of discrepancy between promise and outcome by observing how the consultancy product of 'value-based management' ended in disappointment, as recently acknowledged in the *Harvard Business Review*. It then goes on to consider proceduralized corporate governance as a 1990s control technology that promises to ensure managers act in the shareholder interest and ends with the Enron fraud and recrimination about the uncontrolled general enrichment of CEOs. The final section of this chapter reviews the evidence on giant-company CEO pay over twenty years and shows how top managers in US and UK giant companies were able to become rich through 'value skimming'.

## Chapter 4 Financialization and Corporate Performance

This fourth chapter turns to the social-science concept of 'financialization' which can be used to understand the rhetoric of 'shareholder value' and the impact of capital-market intrusion on giant-firm strategy. This chapter rejects the orthodox political economy approach to financialization which involves the search for invariant general consequences (such as increased distribution to shareholders) and proposes an alternative cultural-economy concept where financialization sets giant-company management on a utopian quest for growth and higher returns for capital whose uncertain consequences include a gap between saying and doing. The discrepancy between promise and outcome is explored by presenting evidence on long-run value creation by giant firms in the US S&P 500 and the UK FTSE 100, as well as on distributive shifts between capital and labour. If giant-firm management cannot take all the credit for the general increase in share prices during the 1990s bull market, they must, in their own terms, accept a modicum of responsibility for an otherwise mediocre long-term record. Maybe this is not a case of *tout comprendre c'est tout pardoner* but we would allow a plea of mitigating circumstances. The final section of this chapter explains this discrepancy by arguing that giant-firm managers typically have many strategic moves but few levers that will transform the financial numbers.

## Chapter 5 New Interventions: Sector Matrix, Restructuring, Narrative and Numbers

The central argument of this book is that the growing pressure from the capital market redefines company strategy and changes the work of management against a background of product market constraints in a world that does not usually take CEOs and giant firms at their own estimation. The general problem for managers in giant firms is that delivering the financial numbers that 'keep it going' is often difficult so that they must engage in new and different strategic moves from those conceived in the classical tradition. This fifth chapter introduces some basic concepts for thinking through the distinctive interventions of giant-firm management after financialization. The first section of this chapter analyses 'sector matrix' moves such as adding finance or selling services, while the second section considers serial restructuring in giant firms which elevates breach of implicit stakeholder contract into a guiding principle of management. The third and final section of this chapter outlines the narrative and numbers approach which frames our three historical case studies. Giant company CEOs now need a story of purpose and achievement for analysts and shareholders, backed by performative initiatives (for quality improvement, cost reduction or whatever) which establish that management is doing as well as saying. The practical problem then is to generate the financial numbers that corroborate the story.

Distinctive new concepts and a new problem definition are both necessary if we are to deliver something different from classical strategy. But, while we recognize the need for concepts and framework, we do not believe in putting concepts first and then moving to applications that reveal what we already knew. As a matter of record, the three historical case studies were written before the introduction and the most complex case on GE was written first of all in the form of a working paper which raised questions about narrative and numbers. The general introduction represents an attempt to create a context and framework for these three case studies that explore the limits on management action and the way in which discrepancies between narrative and numbers are identified and suppressed by stock-market analysts, media and business writers. Quite properly, the cases will in a disorderly way sometimes escape the categories and presuppositions of the introduction which reflects on them.

The most obvious peculiarity of the three cases is that they are all much longer than most business cases because each is around 25,000 words in length. The length is a consequence of three decisions: first, to extend each case to cover a twenty-year time span; second, to include twenty-year series on all the basic financial numbers for each company; third, to include multiple voices including stock-market analysts and popular business writers. The twenty-year time span was determined so that we did not fall into the classical strategy trap of sampling a short section of a much longer trajectory, only to be surprised (and undermined) by unexpected changes in corporate performance and market judgement. The appendix of tables in each case on financial and market performance gives a twenty-year series on the major financials so that unconvinced readers can check our storyline and construct alternative storylines. Accounting readers will also appreciate that it is not easy to get twenty years of original hard-copy accounts for any giant firm (nor to generate consistent series) and so the publication of these tables also represents a kind of public service. The aim here is to avoid the old business-case trap of presenting small quantities of confirming evidence so that it is simply not possible for a reader to disagree with the authors of the case study without undertaking research.

The final point concerns the voices that figure in our accounts of company and industry stories. The discussion here is based on analysis of business media, stock-market analysts, consultants, business-school and social-science academics, as well as popular management texts. The mix of texts considered varies according to the case. Thus, stock-market analysts figure quite prominently in the Glaxo and Ford cases, but not in the GE case where analysts do not have a high profile and a major role in explaining industry and company as in the other two cases. The case study on Ford includes discussion of texts by academics because cars have attracted business-school and political-economy commentary, whereas the case study of GE concentrates on popular management texts that package the brilliant success of Jack Welch and GE as so many lessons and transferable techniques that guarantee success for other companies. Attentive readers will note that we report interviews with CEOs but have not ourselves interviewed Welch, Nasser or any of the other CEOs. There are many research projects where it is helpful or necessary to talk to management, but that is not the case with this project of inquiring about strategy. We believed that interviewing CEOs such as Welch and Nasser about strategy would be no more informative than interviewing Tony Blair about the decision to go to war with Iraq. At this level, management is about what the CEO has to say according to a script; and just as most politicians memoirs are boring, we did not expect the retired Welch or Nasser to give us a candid retrospect on either Machiavellian self-knowledge or confusion about the conditions of business success.

Before turning to the cases, we can briefly note how and why the three companies were chosen. The three companies GE, Ford and Glaxo were chosen so as to illustrate three contrasting conditions or trajectories: GE illustrates brilliant success over twenty years where sustained profits and sales growth confirms the reputation of management; Ford illustrates the opposite condition of persistent failure: Glaxo illustrates the transition from brilliant success in the 1990s to disappointment when management could not keep it going. GE was chosen on the basis of its public reputation as the only US giant firm from the old economy that never stumbled or fell, and our initial aim here was simply to deconstruct that success. With Ford we were building on our own previous work on car assembly but broadening the scope of the analysis where we had previously been participants in academic debates about lean production and subsequently about adding finance. Glaxo was actually suggested by our editor at Routledge who had previously edited a medical booklist and wanted one British or European company to contrast with the two American ones; we would add that, on the basis of its share register, Glaxo is not much less American than GE or Ford.

## Case 1 GlaxoSmithKline: Keeping It Going?

This case nicely illustrates the importance of history. As a company, Glaxo has made the transition from brilliant financial success in the early 1990s to closely scrutinized disappointment in the early 2000s. In context, this is partly because the pharma industry has in the 2000s lost the latest round of a long-standing struggle with its critics who, from Senator Kefauver onwards in the late 1950s, have charged that pharma is not about research-driven, innovation but marketing-driven profiteering. Contested social accounts of the industry are then contrasted with narrower stock-market understandings of the pharma-company business model, where marketing is applied to create blockbusters so that future revenues can be predicted from information about patent expiry and product pipeline. As this business model now begins to falter for the major pharma companies, Glaxo has tried to keep things going in two ways: first, by defensive cost-reducing horizontal merger and, second, by a narrative that promises research productivity which has not as yet come through in the numbers. The Glaxo case explores how a firm keeps it going for the stock market in a world where multiple and contested narratives are as important as the financial numbers.

## Case 2 Ford: Effort and Reward

The Ford case is overshadowed by the persistent inability of Ford and other assemblers in the volume car industry to deliver sizeable and consistent profits. Despite the support of a credit operation which generates nearly half of its profit, the Ford Motor Company since the 1970s has lapsed into crisis whenever its auto markets turn down. Since the early 1990s, business-school authors and consultants have responded to problems at Ford and other assemblers by envisioning transformation and an industry-wide break with old production and business models. Such transformative visions do not impress stock-market analysts of car assemblers, who have learnt to live with mediocre financial results and cyclicality by focusing on profit opportunities arising from good or bad news that is not already in the stock price. Successive chief executives, such as Jacques Nasser and Bill Ford, must then promise to improve results through new strategies such as Nasser's post-2000 sector matrix move into services which are doomed to disappoint, in so far as they are symbolically enacted rather than coherently implemented. In a case such as Ford, there is a disproportion between management effort and the financial rewards from strategies which both buy time and create new problems, such as the depreciation burden arising from the leasing business that Ford credit developed in the later 1990s.

## Case 3 General Electric: The Conditions of Success

The GE conglomerate and its long-serving CEO Jack Welch are management icons whose reputation was secured by a nearly unbroken twenty-year run of earnings increases through the 1980s and 1990s. These financial results encouraged hagiographic business-media coverage and the production of many popular business books which confidently attributed the exceptional financial results to outstanding management in the form of the leadership of Welch as CEO and the internal culture and organization of GE. Our analysis of the accounting numbers over twenty years suggests a rather different set of conditions of success. GE's no-growth, blue-chip industrial businesses were run for profits and to maintain the AAA credit rating which was then used to expand GE Capital. This expansion of GE Capital in turn generated sales growth and earnings at the expense of declining return on capital employed. The undisclosed business model is interesting in several respects. It shows how Welch realized that a company narrative, plus performative initiatives such as Six Sigma were necessary but not sufficient conditions of success, which required financial results that would deflect difficult questions. Outside the company, a shallow world preferred congenial narratives of management success which falsely presented GE as a model for others and a source of transferable lessons of success.

If the cases are diverse and illustrate different articulations of narrative and numbers, that is how it should be because our aim is to encourage further historical explorations of this kind whose results would broaden our understanding. The cases are not written in any kind of 'myth and reality' framework. We do not assume that the numbers represent 'reality' whatever that may be. As we emphasize in Chapter 5 of the introduction and then demonstrate in the cases, the important thing is that the numbers have an independent life of their own and are not a function or epiphenomenon of whatever narrative the CEO and the business press jointly invent.

## US AND UK GIANT FIRMS

How and why are giant firms a distinct object of investigation? The answer to that question of course depends on the problematic within which the organization, behaviour and performance of these firms is constructed. Thus, as we shall see in the next chapter, Chandler (1962) considered US giant firms to be *sui generis* because they had organized divisionally to meet the challenge of diversification. Chapters 3 and 4 develop our own answer to these questions about object and rationale by focusing on the complex results of pressure from the stock market. Meanwhile, it may be helpful to give the reader some basic background information on the size and weight of the S&P 500 and FTSE 100 group of firms in their respective US and UK economies plus some basic information on the sectoral affiliation, average size and diversification characteristics of the individual firms within the group.

The FTSE 100 is the 100 largest UK firms by market capitalization on the London Stock Exchange (LSE), while the S&P 500 represents the corresponding list of the 500 largest US firms quoted on two exchanges: the New York Stock Exchange (NYSE) and the National Association of Securities Dealers Automated Quotation (NASDAQ). Strictly, the S&P 500 is not based on market capitalization because it focuses on 'leading industries' including financial services, technology, communications, capital and consumer goods; it is also 'market weighted' because the calculation for the index is made by multiplying the price of each stock by the number of shares held by the public. Our analysis of both groups of giant firms is based on data extracted from Datastream (UK) and Compustat (US), but with considerable reworking to construct a database that covers those 100 or 500 firms that were actually members of the relevant index in each year (i.e. the constituents). This was important to allow us to identify and understand differences that arise from the changing membership of these indices, in response to take-overs, buy outs, failure and reductions in market value that cause firms to lose their place.

Both the FTSE 100 and S&P 500 account for a small subset of all the quoted firms in their national economies because, in 2002, there were a total of 6,015 companies listed on the NYSE and the NASDAQ in the USA and 2,272 listed on the LSE (source: World Federation of Exchanges). Nevertheless these groups have some weight because they account for a sizeable volume of activity and output in relation to their respective home economies; though they do not by any means account for all or most national activity so the group of giant firms definitely represents the part not the whole.

Several scaling devices can be used to give some idea of the aggregate productive and financial weight of the S&P 500 and FTSE 100 firms. Measuring giant-firm share of domestic production is not straightforward because many firms within these groupings are global entities and hence have a sizeable proportion of their activities located outside their own domestic market. However, when taken together, the giant firms represent a tranche of (international) production activity which is significant in relation to the size of the home (national) economy in which they are financially embedded as Exhibits 1.1 and 1.2 show. The most stable and intelligible indicator is employment, where in 2002 the S&P 500 globally employed a number equal to 16.3 per cent of US civilian employment and the FTSE 100 globally employed a number equal to 16.1 per cent of UK domestic employment (Exhibit 1.1). Their international activity in relation to national sales or value added is even more important because here it equals one-third or more of domestic sales or value added. If the focus is shifted onto measures of financial weight and significance as shown in Exhibit 1.2, such comparisons highlight the considerable financial importance of S&P 500 and FTSE 100 firms because their pre-tax corporate profit accounts for a much higher but cyclically unstable share of all national pre-tax corporate profit. In the USA, the S&P 500 firms account for between 55 and 90 per cent of all US pre-tax corporate profit depending on the year. Meanwhile the FTSE 100 accounts for 25–45 per cent of all UK pre-tax corporate operating surplus.

If we move from profit to market capitalization, we can see that in both UK and US cases, the decade-long bull market of the 1990s hugely boosted the market capitalization of each economy's largest firms in relation to Gross Domestic Product (GDP). At the beginning of the 1990s, the market value of the S&P 500 and FTSE 100 accounted for no more than about one-third of domestic GDP. By the peak in 2000, the market value of the S&P 500 was equal to 129 per cent of US GDP and the market value of the FTSE

***Exhibit 1.1*** *A comparison of employment and sales/value added of FTSE 100 and S&P 500 companies against their national economies*

| | *FTSE 100* | | *S&P 500* | |
|---|---|---|---|---|
| | *FTSE 100 employment as a share of UK employment* | *FTSE 100 value added as a % of all UK (private non-financial and financial) corporate value added* | *S&P 500 employment as a % of US civilian employment* | *S&P 500 sales as a % of all US corporate business receipts* |
| | % | % | % | % |
| 1980–3 | 15.9 | n/a | 19.5 | 34.9 |
| 1985 | 16.6 | n/a | 18.0 | 34.1 |
| 1990 | 18.3 | 36.1 | 16.1 | 34.4 |
| 1995 | 15.1 | 39.1 | 15.1 | 32.7 |
| 2000 | 14.6 | 36.5 | 16.2 | 36.2 |
| 2002 | 16.1 | n/a | 16.3 | n/a |

*Source*: Compustat and Datastream

*Note*: FTSE 100 data begins in 1983 and S&P 500 in 1980

**Exhibit 1.2** *The relative weight and significance of the FTSE 100 and S&P 500 companies within their national economies*

| | *FTSE 100* | | *S&P 500* | |
|---|---|---|---|---|
| | *FTSE 100 pre-tax profit as a % of UK corporate pre-tax profit* | *FTSE 100 market value as a % of UK GDP* | *S&P 500 pre-tax profit as a % of US corporate pre-tax profit* | *S&P 500 market value as a % of US GDP* |
| | % | % | % | % |
| 1980–3 | 39.3 | 33.9 | 72.6 | 30.1 |
| 1985 | 29.9 | 45.9 | 75.5 | 32.1 |
| 1990 | 34.2 | 53.8 | 58.8 | 38.4 |
| 1995 | 38.7 | 82.5 | 60.6 | 55.6 |
| 2000 | 42.3 | 148.7 | 88.6 | 128.9 |
| 2002 | 23.3 | 91.3 | 58.5 | 86.7 |

*Source*: Compustat and Datastream, UK National Accounts and Statistical Abstract of the United States

*Note*: FTSE 100 data begins in 1983 and S&P 500 in 1980

100 was equal to 149 per cent of UK GDP, as Exhibit 1.2 shows. This remarkable rise in relative value and financial weight reflects two considerations: first, the vigour of the bull market where equity prices rose by 10–15 per cent each year, at a rate much faster than GDP; and, second, the way in which these giant firms account for a large and growing proportion of total stock market capitalization. In both the USA and the UK, investors in the quoted corporate sector now show much less interest in a second division of mid-sized firms. Twenty years ago the S&P 500 and FTSE 100 giant firms accounted for just over half of their national stock-market capitalization, whereas today they account for more than three-quarters of market capitalization in the USA and more than four-fifths of market capitalization in the UK.

Having establishing the collective weight and significance of the S&P 500 and FTSE 100 groups, it is also necessary to understand the size and activity of the typical giant firm. Exhibit 1.3 presents data on constituents, i.e. the firms in both groups, which give us a changing population of giant firms as fast-growing firms join the index and others leave. This table presents financial information on the FTSE 100 firms in both sterling and in US dollars (translated at a rate of 1.64 dollars per pound) to allow some direct comparison between these giant firms in the two countries.

The first and most obvious point is that in both the USA and UK, the average member of the S&P 500 and FTSE 100 is by any standard a giant firm. By the most intelligible productive measure of numbers employed, the average S&P and FTSE firm is very large and fairly evenly matched for size on both sides of the Atlantic, as Exhibit 1.3 shows. In 2002, the average S&P 500 firm and the average FTSE 100 firm employed almost exactly 44,500 workers. For that matter, the constituents had been fairly evenly matched twenty

*Exhibit 1.3 Average employment, real pre-tax income and real market value per constituent firm in the FTSE 100 and S&P 500 (in real 2003 prices)*

| | *Employment (no.)* | | *Pre-tax profit (income)* | | | *Market value* | | |
|---|---|---|---|---|---|---|---|---|
| | *FTSE 100* | *S&P 500* | *FTSE 100* | *FTSE 100* | *S&P 500* | *FTSE 100* | *FTSE 100* | *S&P 500* |
| | | | £m | $m | $m | £m | $m | $m |
| 1980 | | 38,777 | | | 822 | | | 3,749 |
| 1981 | | 39,139 | | | 766 | | | 3,749 |
| 1982 | | 37,752 | | | 627 | | | 3,504 |
| 1983 | 36,548 | 36,421 | 342 | 563 | 701 | 2,111 | 3,475 | 4,395 |
| 1984 | 38,592 | 38,771 | 406 | 668 | 771 | 2,735 | 4,502 | 4,267 |
| 1985 | 39,635 | 38,660 | 443 | 729 | 665 | 3,117 | 5,132 | 4,636 |
| 1986 | 42,955 | 38,125 | 446 | 734 | 604 | 3,874 | 6,378 | 5,584 |
| 1987 | 45,608 | 37,698 | 483 | 796 | 679 | 4,031 | 6,636 | 6,231 |
| 1988 | 47,280 | 37,679 | 631 | 1,039 | 806 | 4,099 | 6,749 | 5,686 |
| 1989 | 47,854 | 38,038 | 594 | 979 | 747 | 5,211 | 8,579 | 6,487 |
| 1990 | 48,185 | 38,239 | 546 | 898 | 678 | 4,284 | 7,053 | 6,280 |
| 1991 | 46,518 | 37,236 | 452 | 745 | 505 | 4,942 | 8,136 | 6,892 |
| 1992 | 40,735 | 36,830 | 463 | 762 | 564 | 5,616 | 9,247 | 7,627 |
| 1993 | 41,170 | 36,544 | 567 | 933 | 651 | 6,763 | 11,135 | 8,240 |
| 1994 | 39,176 | 36,162 | 672 | 1,107 | 890 | 6,091 | 10,027 | 8,362 |
| 1995 | 38,831 | 37,696 | 752 | 1,239 | 987 | 7,139 | 11,753 | 9,940 |
| 1996 | 38,747 | 38,550 | 837 | 1,378 | 1,101 | 7,985 | 13,146 | 12,230 |
| 1997 | 38,823 | 40,245 | 855 | 1,408 | 1,157 | 10,129 | 16,675 | 15,731 |
| 1998 | 43,129 | 41,923 | 788 | 1,298 | 1,119 | 11,485 | 18,908 | 19,752 |
| 1999 | 43,688 | 43,524 | 867 | 1,427 | 1,397 | 15,130 | 24,910 | 25,432 |
| 2000 | 40,123 | 44,415 | 898 | 1,479 | 1,465 | 15,068 | 24,807 | 27,049 |
| 2001 | 43,950 | 44,240 | 676 | 1,113 | 748 | 12,930 | 21,288 | 22,932 |
| 2002 | 44,741 | 44,517 | 526 | 866 | 907 | 9,808 | 16,148 | 18,576 |

*Sources*: Compustat and Datastream

*Notes*: The FTSE 100 total starts from 1983, the first year of this index. FTSE 100 market values based on fiscal year end and S&P 500 based on the average share price in the calendar year. FTSE 100 pre-tax profit and market value are converted into US$ dollars at a rate of $1.64 per £, which is the average £:$ exchange rate over twenty years

years previously when the average FTSE 100 company employed 36,500 against 38,750 for the S&P 500 constituent. By financial measures, taking pre-tax profit or market capitalization as the indicator, the US and UK giant firms are fairly evenly matched through the 1980s and 1990s, though there are timing differences in cyclicality. In 2002 an average FTSE 100 company had pre-tax profits of $866 million, compared with $907 million in the S&P 500; and in both countries the market value of the average giant firm has risen from around $4 billion in the early 1980s to around $24 billion at the top of the market in 1999/2000. If the size of the lump of profit is quite striking in the FTSE 100 (even in 2002 when profits were depressed, the average FTSE 100 firm has a pre-tax profit of £500 million), it should be remembered that these averages cover only 100 firms in the UK, compared with 500 in the USA: comparisons of the top 100 firms in each country would be likely to show much greater differences in terms of average size.

The activity characteristics of the giant companies in terms of industry affiliation are both similar and different in the two countries (and we should remember at this point that the FTSE 100 listings are adjusted to obtain industry representation). Nevertheless, Exhibits 1.4 and 1.5 show that the basic similarity is the growing importance of financial-services companies, which account for an increasingly large part of each index. Exhibit 1.4 shows that finance's share of total S&P 500 pre-tax income grew from just 6 per cent in 1983 to 39.4 per cent by 2002. The figures for capital employed and market value follow a similar trend, growing from just 9.3 per cent and 6.2 per cent in 1983 to

**Exhibit 1.4** *SIC breakdown of S&P 500 companies in 1983 and 2002*

(a) 1983

| | *Companies* % | *Employment* % | *Pre-tax income* % | *Capital employed* % | *Market value* % |
|---|---|---|---|---|---|
| SIC 1: mining, oil and gas | 4.4 | 2.0 | 4.4 | 4.1 | 4.4 |
| SIC 2: food, drink, tobacco, chemical | 27.8 | 26.5 | 41.9 | 30.6 | 33.1 |
| SIC 3: manufacturing | 29.6 | 34.5 | 14.7 | 19.1 | 23.5 |
| SIC 4: transport, utilities | 15.0 | 8.5 | 18.9 | 26.5 | 16.3 |
| SIC 5: retailing, wholesale | 9.0 | 16.4 | 6.6 | 5.8 | 6.7 |
| SIC 6: finance | 8.8 | 5.5 | 6.0 | 9.3 | 6.2 |
| SIC 7: computing and other services | 4.0 | 5.2 | 6.8 | 3.5 | 8.9 |
| SIC 8: medical and business services | 1.2 | 1.4 | 0.7 | 1.1 | 0.9 |
| SIC 9: conglomerate | 0.2 | 0.0 | 0.0 | 0.0 | 0.0 |

(b) 2002

| | *Companies* % | *Employment* % | *Pre-tax income* % | *Capital employed* % | *Market value* % |
|---|---|---|---|---|---|
| SIC 1: mining, oil and gas | 4.6 | 1.5 | 0.4 | 2.1 | 1.8 |
| SIC 2: food, drink, tobacco, chemical | 18.4 | 14.9 | 33.7 | 11.9 | 28.0 |
| SIC 3: manufacturing | 25.6 | 20.6 | 4.5 | 13.0 | 15.5 |
| SIC 4: transport, utilities | 13.0 | 11.6 | 7.6 | 16.6 | 10.9 |
| SIC 5: retailing, wholesale | 9.6 | 27.9 | 12.5 | 5.1 | 8.1 |
| SIC 6: finance | 17.4 | 10.1 | 39.4 | 42.8 | 21.5 |
| SIC 7: computing and other services | 8.8 | 8.7 | −3.1 | 4.4 | 9.9 |
| SIC 8: medical and business services | 2.0 | 2.0 | 1.2 | 0.5 | 0.8 |
| SIC 9: conglomerate | 0.6 | 2.8 | 3.8 | 3.7 | 3.4 |

*Source*: Compustat

42.8 per cent and 21.5 per cent respectively by 2002. Exhibit 1.5 shows the same trend in the UK, where finance's share of the FTSE 100 grows from 17.7 per cent, 23.5 per cent and 18.6 per cent in terms of pre-tax income, capital employed and market value respectively in 1983 to 41.7 per cent, 37.7 per cent and 27.4 per cent by 2002. One additional point that emerges from both US and UK exhibits below is that the impressive growing contribution of finance to the S&P 500 and the FTSE 100 in financial

***Exhibit 1.5*** *SIC breakdown of FTSE 100 companies in 1983 and 2002*

(a) 1983

| | *Companies* % | *Employment* % | *Pre-tax income* % | *Capital employed* % | *Market value* % |
|---|---|---|---|---|---|
| **SIC 1**: mining, oil and gas | 16.0 | 10.9 | 30.7 | 32.1 | 22.7 |
| **SIC 2**: food, drink, tobacco, chemical | 20.0 | 30.4 | 25.0 | 21.3 | 21.0 |
| **SIC 3**: manufacturing | 12.0 | 19.0 | 11.6 | 8.4 | 14.7 |
| **SIC 4**: transport, utilities | 7.0 | 6.0 | 3.4 | 3.1 | 4.2 |
| **SIC 5**: retailing, wholesale | 18.0 | 19.7 | 10.3 | 10.4 | 16.8 |
| **SIC 6**: finance | 24.0 | 11.0 | 17.7 | 23.5 | 18.6 |
| **SIC 7**: computing and other services | 0.0 | 0.0 | 0.0 | 0.0 | 0.0 |
| **SIC 8**: medical and business services | 2.0 | 1.7 | 0.7 | 0.6 | 1.0 |
| **SIC 9**: conglomerate | 1.0 | 1.4 | 0.6 | 0.5 | 1.1 |

(b) 2002

| | *Companies* % | *Employment* % | *Pre-tax income* % | *Capital employed* % | *Market value* % |
|---|---|---|---|---|---|
| **SIC 1**: mining, oil and gas | 9.0 | 9.9 | 36.8 | 13.6 | 19.7 |
| **SIC 2**: food, drink, tobacco, chemical | 19.0 | 19.3 | 38.0 | 9.8 | 23.0 |
| **SIC 3**: manufacturing | 6.0 | 5.9 | −1.6 | 2.0 | 1.4 |
| **SIC 4**: transport, utilities | 19.0 | 12.0 | −27.7 | 30.1 | 19.1 |
| **SIC 5**: retailing, wholesale | 15.0 | 22.3 | 10.3 | 5.6 | 7.1 |
| **SIC 6**: finance | 24.0 | 18.0 | 41.7 | 37.7 | 27.4 |
| **SIC 7**: computing and other services | 3.0 | 0.4 | 0.6 | 0.2 | 0.5 |
| **SIC 8**: medical and business services | 5.0 | 12.2 | 1.9 | 1.1 | 1.8 |
| **SIC 9**: conglomerate | 0.0 | 0.0 | 0.0 | 0.0 | 0.0 |

*Source*: Datastream

*Note*: SIC categories are derived from Datastream's industry sector codes

terms is less evident when looking at its physical contribution in terms of employment, which has risen only modestly in both countries.

Despite these similarities, there are also significant differences between the population of giant firms in both countries. The US index has a stronger presence of technology, media and telecoms companies, whereas the subaltern British capitalism has nothing that corresponds to Microsoft, Intel, IBM or Cisco, which together account for 8 per cent of market capitalization of the S&P 500. Also, whereas manufacturing has declined in importance on the stock exchanges of both countries, in the UK it has declined to the point of negligibility, with just 5.9 per cent of total FTSE 100 employment and 1.4 per cent of the FTSE market value accounted for by manufacturing in 2002, against 20.6 per cent of employment and 15.5 per cent of market value in the S&P 500.

One of the interesting points that also emerges from this comparison is the limited extent of diversification in most giant firms in the UK and USA, if diversification is measured conventionally in terms of a firm's revenue generated in different product markets, usually defined by Standard Industrial Classification (SIC) codes. Diversification figures prominently in the strategy literature. For instance Chandler in the 1960s represented diversification strategies as the driver of organizational change; while more recent resource-based approaches aim to explore the link between diversification strategies, internal resources and financial success (Goold et al. 1994, Montgomery 1994). However, for the past twenty-five years, so-called conglomerates have been out of fashion, with the US and UK stock markets having some preference for 'pure plays'.

In terms of our analysis of these giant firms, it is not very meaningful to measure changes in diversification in the UK where all we can say is that a small number of very large, undiversified firms increasingly dominate the FTSE 100 index. As Exhibit 1.6

**Exhibit 1.6** *Top 10 FTSE 100 companies by market capitalization in 1983 and 2002*

| *1983*<br>*Share of FTSE 100 market value*<br>% | | *2002*<br>*Share of FTSE 100 market value*<br>% | |
|---|---|---|---|
| Grand Metropolitan | 2.0 | HBOS | 2.9 |
| Beecham Group | 2.2 | Lloyds TSB | 2.9 |
| BTR | 2.3 | Barclays | 3.0 |
| Glaxo | 2.6 | AstraZeneca | 4.4 |
| BAT | 2.6 | Shell Transport & Trading | 4.6 |
| Marks & Spencer | 2.9 | Royal Bank of Scotland | 5.0 |
| ICI | 3.9 | HSBC | 7.6 |
| GEC | 5.0 | GlaxoSmithKline | 8.4 |
| Shell Transport & Trading | 6.3 | Vodafone | 9.0 |
| BP | 7.5 | BP | 11.1 |
| **Total/Share** | **37.4** | | **68.7** |

*Source*: Datastream

*Note*: Market value is measured at the fiscal year end

***Exhibit 1.7*** *Extent of concentration within S&P 500 companies in 2002, based on the share of corporate turnover within one (4-digit) SIC class*

| Share of turnover<br>% | S&P 500 companies within each class<br>% | Cumulative total proportion of all turnover (sales revenues)<br>% |
|---|---|---|
| 100 | 34.5 | 34.5 |
| 99–90 | 14.9 | 49.4 |
| 89–80 | 12.4 | 61.8 |
| 79–70 | 10.3 | 72.0 |
| 69–60 | 8.9 | 80.9 |
| 59–50 | 7.5 | 88.3 |
| 49–40 | 5.8 | 94.2 |
| 39–30 | 3.5 | 97.7 |
| 29–20 | 2.3 | 100.0 |

*Source*: Compustat

*Note*: The data from which this table is constructed is based on 429 companies. The remaining seventy-one S&P 500 companies are overwhelmingly within the banking and finance sector where it is not meaningful to measure turnover (sales revenues) in the same way as for a non-financial company. The table shows that 34.5 per cent of these S&P 500 non-financial companies generate all of their turnover from one SIC class; 49.4 per cent of companies generate at least 90 per cent of their turnover from one SIC class and so on

shows, by 2002 BP (integrated oil), Glaxo (pharmaceuticals) and Vodafone (mobile phones) alone accounted for 28.5 per cent of the total FTSE 100 market value. In the US case we can calculate some spot measures of diversification for US giant firms over the past decade and the results are quite striking. Exhibit 1.7 shows that some 88.3 per cent of S&P 500 firms have more than half of their turnover in one 4-digit SIC class, whilst over one-third are entirely within one 4-digit class. This makes them extraordinarily undiversified, if we recall the 4-digit classification is a narrow one which, for example, distinguishes between auto assembly and auto parts or between truck and auto parts.

The classic discussions of diversification are all set in a frame about firm and product market which leaves the capital market only partially visible as an inert recipient of a share of profit generated through productive strategies. In this book, we aim to redress this imbalance by focusing on the relation between firm and capital market, but first we must in the next chapter consider classical strategy and its enduring commitment to the firm in product-market definition.

Chapter 2

# Giant firms and classical strategy

The established social-science discourses are generally associated with a founding doxa; thus, mainstream economics believes in the market as an allocating mechanism, just as classical sociology believes that stratification can be read off the division of labour. Strategy is immediately more puzzling. It is a recently invented discourse which dates from the 1960s and lacks any clear founding belief. Instead, strategy manifests individual disagreements and collective changes of position about the sources of 'competitive advantage' which, from the 1960s to the 1990s, was successively attributed to giant-firm organization, engagement with the external product market and mobilization of internal resources.

This chapter analyses the consistent and enduring a priori that allows the discourse to survive such changes of position. The first section of the chapter sets up our discourse analysis by observing that, if the authors of strategy texts disagree about the levers of 'competitive advantage' inside and outside the firm, they can nevertheless share common assumptions and problem definitions as well as devices and forms of argument which provide a common discursive frame. With these points made, the second section of this chapter goes on to analyse the shared 'firm in industry' problem definition of classical strategy in 1960s Chandler, 1980s Porter and 1990s Prahalad and Hamel; while the third section goes on to discuss illustration and proof and to observe a form of argument which, from Porter onwards, relies on vignettes to corroborate principles of success. In our view, these assumptions and devices define the lineage of classical strategy, and the final section observes the consequent problems about refutation by events when exemplary success turns into unexplained failure.

This chapter is important because our concept of strategy and our form of argument is set up antithetically against the classical problem definition about firm in product market supported by vignettes of deserved success. In our alternative perspective, giant-firm strategy since the 1980s is as management says, does and delivers in response to increasing pressure from the financial markets. This is the complex object that we analyse in the later chapters of this introduction through argument, conceptualization and review of group performance in the S&P 500 and the FTSE 100 before turning, in the second half of our book, to explore the relation between promise and outcome, narrative and numbers in three historical cases.

## A CLASSICAL LINEAGE

This section opens the argument by reviewing the strategy literature since the 1960s and by noting the many confusing disagreements and differences about the sources of advantage. It then observes that texts with different conclusions may yet share the same problem definition; just as rhetoric, devices and forms of argument may be shared by texts that take different positions. This provides the basis for identifying a classical lineage of writing about giant firms in texts from 1960 onwards by authors such as Chandler, Porter and Prahalad and Hamel whose work is then analysed in later sections of this chapter.

The idea of management as a distinct activity or function within the firm is a relatively recent development which dates symbolically from the publication of Peter Drucker's (1955) book *The Practice of Management*. The *Oxford English Dictionary*, which records the first usage of words in the English language, puts the date slightly later. All the *OED* first usage examples are taken from texts published after 1962; and these include Ansoff's (1965) claim that the 'management of a business firm is a very large complex of activities which consists of analysis, decisions, communications, leadership, motivation, measurement and control'. This new language of management was associated with a reorganization of business discourse. The old discourse of 'business administration' had centred on operations and productive intervention, so that in a popular business-administration textbook like E. L. Jones (1916), eleven of the fourteen chapters were about production management and labour. Now this was displaced by a troika of new business discourses that finally included strategy, marketing and human-resource management. All the new discourses emphasized the proactive role of senior managers in organizational design and higher-level enterprise calculation, epitomized by 'strategy', a term hitherto applied to military staff planning.

If strategy was the would-be queen of these new management discourses, it arrived at maturity from the 1980s onwards by offering a diverse set of conceptual tools for thinking about enterprise calculation and action. The heterogeneity of the tools makes it difficult to generalize about the intellectual object or objects of the new strategy discourse, which begins in the 1970s with the Mintzberg (1973) and Quinn (1978) debates about the role of planning and continues into the 2000s with the current 'resource-based' orthodoxy which includes 'soft' core competence strategists like

Prahalad and Hamel (1990) as well as 'hard' industrial economists like Barney (1986) and Rumelt (1991). The tool kit also includes a set of techniques and measures derived from various consultancy firms including Boston Consulting Group on portfolio management in the early years, or Stern Stewart on value-based management in the 1990s. These different tools and measures are now very confusingly presented in most strategy texts for students, which either attempt a synthesis of different positions or simply take the side that is winning. Hence, the best-selling British strategy textbook from Johnson et al. (2005) tries to reconcile tools and concepts from different sources to give a broad overview of 'doing strategy'; while the strategy reader from Segal-Horn (2004) chooses a set of articles which represent strategy as an intellectual journey that culminates in the triumph of resource-based theory.

Against this background of confusion, what we want to do is to identify and to describe the classical lineage of strategy-writing on giant firms as it develops from Chandler, via Porter, to the current 'soft' and 'hard' variants on resource-based theory (RBT). For our purposes, the founding figure here is Chandler whose 1962 text *Strategy and Structure* focused on corporate organization and argued the advantages of the divisional form of organization for giant diversified firms operating across several product or geographic markets. The dominating figure of the 1980s was Michael Porter (1980, 1985) who broke micro-economics into pieces and used new concepts such as 'five forces', 'generic strategies' and 'value chain' to argue that the division could negotiate the external market environment and find sustainable advantage. In the 1990s, the seminal 'soft' RBT figures were Prahalad and Hamel (1990) who argued that firms could reinvent by tapping the internal competences or 'the collective learning in the organization' that were buried in the divisional silos, while from Rumelt (1991) onwards 'hard' RBT focused on internal resources such as property rights as the basis for superior divisional profitability.

There are obvious differences between these authors about the level and levers through which strategy supposedly creates 'competitive advantage'. Thus strategy is not a discourse that has a fixed a priori about the sources of advantage, as mainstream economics has an a priori about the merits of market allocation. Every decade or so, mainstream strategists have changed position on the sources of business advantage and strategy orthodoxies have been bewilderingly reversed so that readers who are not impressed by one statement of position have only to wait for its antithesis to become fashionable. The diversity of this discourse is typically rationalized by identifying themes and then positioning strategy authors or texts along axes of choice with a contrast between yin and yang, old and new, in a way that confirms the insight of the textbook commentary. Thus, one theme could be firm organization where the old literature of the 1960s was about control in the divisional organization and the new post-1990 literature is about breaking down organizational resistances to change and encouraging adaptability in the 'learning organization'. Another theme could be internal versus external sources of advantage, with the choice between the old 1980s view of strategy as adaptation to external environment and the new 1990s view of strategy as mobilization of internal resources which was represented as RBT.

Classical strategy can certainly be mapped onto this kind of textbook grid. Thus, Chandler (1962) is about how the head office can add value by the appropriate choice of organization, controls and planning which fits the rationalist frame of corporate strategy thinking in the 1960s. This emphasis on corporate organization changed in the 1980s with Porter (1980, 1985) who effectively shifts attention onto management at the divisional level where the generic levers of advantage are positioning in relation to the external industry and market. All this was turned upside down in the early 1990s in a collective exercise in differentiation that created RBT. Where Chandler saw divisional organization and capital-allocation controls as the solution, Prahalad and Hamel (1990: 81) saw it as a problem because the challenge was to 'consolidate corporate wide technologies and production skills into competences that empower individual businesses to adapt quickly'. Likewise, if Porter (1980) had emphasized industry environmental fit, by way of contrast the hard RBT economists emphasized firm specific internal resources.

At the same time, this development of strategy discourse can be constructed in a much darker way as an oblique commentary on the perceived success and failure of US giant firms. The trajectory of these firms is from exemplary success in the 1960s to reverses in the 1980s and struggle in the 1990s. Thus, strategy as commentary increasingly raises questions about the practical efficacy and relevance of its own nostrums. Chandler's celebration of divisional organization at GM and DuPont is part of a general 1960s triumphalism about US discovery of management best practice which was dutifully assimilated in Europe by authors like Channon (1973), who believed the answer was to improve European performance by adopting American-style divisional organization. The discovery of RBT in the 1990s comes after the Japanese had unexpectedly beaten the Americans in consumer electronics and cars in the 1980s. While Japanese success was being attributed to lean manufacturing techniques (Womack et al. 1990), US strategists and managers had begun to question the advantages of financially controlled divisional organization (Hayes and Abernathy 1980). The 1990s bull market and the new economy boom shifted the frame because they encouraged speculation about the disruptive impact of digital technologies on existing business models (Evans and Wurster 1997) and premature generalization about an epochal shift to a knowledge-based or network economy (Castells 1996). This environmental turbulence is increasingly accommodated within strategy by a new conservatism about what management can do to master the environment. After Reagan and Thatcher in the 1980s had inaugurated an era of market-led neo-liberal reform, our RBT strategists in the 1990s discovered that the abridgement of competition (through resources such as property rights) is the infallible basis for enterprise success.

The reputation of strategy discourse also suffers because of conceptual blur associated with increasing tautology and circularity that undermine any pretence to rigour. The problem of conceptual blur is long-standing and endemic. Porter (1985), for example, used the term 'competitive advantage' to denote firm profits higher than the cost of capital or the industry average. Subsequent strategists have used the term in a much looser, metaphorical sense without recognizing the difficulties about whether industry is defined broadly or narrowly. All of this has got more confusing since RBT introduced a new language about competences, capabilities and resources. Prahalad and Hamel (1990: 83–4) are explicit about the three criteria by which a core competence can be identified: access to a wide variety of markets, perceived customer benefits and the difficulty of imitation. For Collis and Montgomery (1995: 121–3), three becomes five, so that key resources should pass the tests of imitability, durability, appropriability, substitutability and competitive superiority. In each of these cases, unchallenged 1990s business success is then referred to its underlying conditions in firm competences, such as Honda's engine design or Marks and Spencer's superior brand and supply-chain organization. These assertive identifications only encourage the suspicion that a resource is tautologically defined as anything which is, *ex post*, associated with business success or higher profitability. On such points, strategists are manifestly less critical than their mainstream social-science colleagues. For example, the pioneering British sociologists interested in developing a capital, assets and resources approach to the question of social stratification have immediately highlighted the problem of circularity and tautology (Savage et al. 2004).

Thus strategy is a recently invented discourse with a credibility problem. The history of strategy is about the reversal of previously taken-for-granted positions, and the discourse of strategy is a series of attempts to reassert practical relevance which never resolves conceptual problems. In some ways, this makes strategy all the more interesting because here is a discourse that must struggle to secure suspension of critical disbelief. How can such a discourse continue to operate through institutions such as academic strategy journals and conferences or consultancy reports that presuppose a space for debate and dispute around shared assumptions and concerns? The answer is that the discourse is stabilized for the academic and business communities of strategists by two intellectual devices: the first device is a heavy framing of the basic problem definition which most or all strategists share; and the second device is a form of argument that makes limited use of empirical evidence, mainly to confirm prior identifications. These stabilizing devices highlight two issues that will concern us in the rest of this chapter.

## Device 1: the common elements, especially the frames, which recur in texts with very different positions/conclusions

This issue was first posed at the end of the 1960s in a structuralist way by referring the present in the text to an absent master structure such as Althusser's (1969) concept of problematic. That creates all kind of epistemological and practical problems about discourse as overdetermined ventriloquism and does not deal with more recent perceptions that discourse often involves many voices and polysemy. But, it is still possible to take away the idea that strategists who disagree (for example on internal or external levers of advantage) may yet share common assumptions and a frame of reference about problem definition. Hence, the discussion below of the 'field of the visible' in classical strategy, which presupposes the discourse operates as kind of framing device that includes a 'firm in industry' problem definition.

### Device 2: the rhetoric, the devices and the forms of argument that are shared by texts which take different positions

The importance of rhetoric was established by McCloskey (1986) who argued that, despite its scientism and emphasis on value-free research, economic research is an exercise in persuasion informed by certain rhetorical 'conversational norms' (McCloskey 1986: 24). Hence, economics or other discourses can be understood through the study of rhetoric, defined as, 'the study of all the ways of accomplishing things with language' (McCloskey 1986: xvii). Thus, strategy (like economics and any other academic discourse) has characteristic forms of argument, ways of using evidence and modes of proof. As such, we present a discussion below of how strategists whose conclusions diverge may yet share ways of using evidence, such as a reliance on vignettes.

If we invoke Althusser, we must recognize the great French tradition of history of science from Bachelard (1940) and Canguilhem (1966) onwards which, via figures like Latour and Woolgar (1979) or Callon et al. (1986), has now been anglicized by Law (2002), so that we now speak of a discourse called 'Science, Technology and Society'. We plan something rather different because the aim is not simply to observe classical strategy but to try to change concepts and methods, partly through the long historical cases on Glaxo, Ford and GE which demonstrate a different way of doing 'strategy'. We might observe, as Matthew 6:27 does, that it is not possible to take thought and add a cubit to one's stature, but it should be possible to take stock of a discourse's problem definition or mode of proof and then do something different. And, while we would now argue for a break with classical strategy, we would not disparage or abuse everything in that lineage. Indeed, this introduction shows our considerable respect for Chandler (1962) who brought the narrative skills of a historian to classical strategy, explicitly included a macro-context and produced extended historical cases, not vignettes. Forty years later, we would be happy if our readers accepted that the three extended cases in the second part of this book resume and update Chandler's project.

## FIRM IN PRODUCT MARKET

If classical strategy writers differ about the sources of advantage, they share a common problem definition about the giant firm facing its product market(s) at micro-level which largely leads them to neglect macro-processes. This can be briefly demonstrated by considering 1980s' Porter and 1990s' Prahalad and Hamel, preceded by some brief discussion of Chandler who in this, as in so many other respects, was a broader, more liberal figure than those who came afterwards. Nevertheless, for Chandler as for his successors, strategy is about the interaction between firm and product market in a frame where industry is defined in entirely orthodox economic terms as a group of firms using similar process technologies to produce products that compete in the same markets. Within strategy, this focus on management action at firm level has in recent years allowed engagement with the issues around globalization, but it has also encouraged neglect of financialization.

For Chandler (1962), giant-firm organization became a problem when great corporations in early twentieth-century America escaped industry boundaries by diversifying and thus competing in a variety of related and unrelated product markets. This development created problems about management control arising from increasing complexity and the work overload of senior management. For Chandler, such problems were in due course addressed by the organizational innovation of divisionalization which created 'quasi-firms' (or strategic business units, or even just 'business units') with all the necessary functions to meet demand across one geographic or product area, thus releasing head office from divisional duties and information overload (Chandler 1962: 8–9). Chandler's argument was that, after a lag, (divisionalized) structure followed (diversification) strategy in a way that created the space for head-office strategic planning and financial control (Chandler 1962: 14). This was all set in a definite macro-context as US national development and the opportunity of a huge internal market was the driver and initiator of diversification. The theme of market opportunity and development was later elaborated in Chandler's (1977) book, *The Visible Hand*.

Subsequent classical strategists had a much narrower and less historical vision which took divisional (or business unit) organization as given and focused on how the division or corporation could find product market success. From this point of view, 1980s' Porter and 1990s' Prahalad and Hamel simply come up with different answers to very similar questions about the conditions of business success. Porter (1980) emphasized how divisional management could negotiate an industry environment characterized by five competitive forces; the division should do this by applying one of three generic strategies: differentiation, cost leadership and focus. These product-market-oriented strategies were thus a set of guidelines for determining 'how a firm can actually create and sustain a competitive advantage in its industry' (Porter 1980: 3). Prahalad and Hamel (1990) and later Hamel and Prahalad (1994) differ in so far as they shifted the focus of strategy away from the strategic business unit and towards the corporation as a whole, so that strategy becomes about, 'senior management . . . developing a corporate-wide strategic architecture that establishes objectives for competence building' (Prahalad and Hamel 1990: 89). But, these authors' objective remained classical because 'top management's primary task is reinventing industries and regenerating strategy' (Hamel and Prahalad 1994: 19).

For all their differences Chandler, Porter and Prahalad and Hamel share a *firm in industry* problem definition and present firm-level micro-moves as the way to sustainable advantage. From Porter onwards, this is associated with the neglect of the external macro-environment, even though the whole period after the oil shocks of 1973 and 1979 was one of economic challenge and volatility. In 1980s' Porter on the giant firm, the macro-environment figures only tangentially in one-line throwaways that are not integrated into his analysis. For example: 'the environment of most of the developed world is one of relatively slow growth, coupled with growing global competition, a dramatic change from previous decades' (Porter 1985: 320).

Porter did address the bigger picture in his 1990s work, especially *The Competitive Advantage of Nations* (1990), which takes a Schumpeterian approach and forsakes the classical concern with the individual giant firm because it is about why some national industries prosper. While many academics then went off to discuss other things such as agglomeration and industrial districts, classical strategy metamorphosed into RBT and continued with much the same indifference to economic environment and government policy. Prahalad and Hamel clear such concerns away in the opening paragraph of their 1990 article or in the first chapter of their 1993 book, which argues that adverse environment is simply an excuse for bad managers:

> Despite the excuses about global competition and the job destroying impact of productivity-enhancing technology, the fact was that most of the employment contraction in large US companies [in the 1980s] was caused not by distant foreign competitors intent on 'stealing US jobs' but by US senior managers who had fallen asleep at the switch.
>
> (1993: 7)

This position on management agency at firm level is reinforced by the way in which globalization could be accommodated in strategy but financialization was much more of an awkward corner.

The literature on globalization of course starts with Levitt's (1983) *Harvard Business Review* article on the standardization of tastes, which is a classic of its kind in so far as it asserts epochal change on the basis of almost no evidence at all. However, it did open the space for a business-school debate about unrepresentative examples such as Levi's jeans and Coca-Cola. More fundamentally, if tastes were not being standardized, it was easy to assimilate globalization into strategy discourse. The old classical literature on the divisionalized firm had been about organizing so as to achieve the right balance between centralization and decentralization: here the divisions represented the decentralization of initiative for effective response to specific product market conditions, while head office added centralized planning and financial control. These concerns could be transposed into a new geographic context where giant firms needed to 'think global and act local', albeit without Chandler's one best way. This discussion could also be linked to political-economy debates after Hirst and Thompson (1996), who queried the extent of globalization when 90 per cent of production was still for the domestic market. Though authors such as Reich, Strange and Boyer do get noted in the more academic international business texts, understandably perhaps, such books have more difficulty with the work of radical authors such as Brenner (2001) who argues that globalization depresses industrial profits because low wage, Asian new entrants to manufacturing bring over-capacity and price competition. After all, classical strategy is all about how single-firm management organizes for success, not about how whole industries are doomed to failure by forces beyond the control of management.

From this point of view, financialization represents an altogether trickier problem for strategy because political economy quickly registered the point that most firms were failures, if the stock market's standard of success was returns on capital of 10 to 12 per cent or more (see Froud et al. 2000a). Within strategy, the response has been to assimilate the demand for shareholder value as the new financial goal and to avoid the problem of financialization, which raises difficult questions about whether and how most firms can deliver shareholder value and about what new capital market pressures mean. This conservative response is nicely illustrated by Kay's 1993 book, *The Foundations of Corporate Success*. The new financial objective is recognized when Kay proposes 'added value' or the lump of excess profit (over and above cost of capital) as the sole measure of business success (Kay 1993: 19). But the empirics then concentrate on a short list of Europe's most successful companies (Kay 1993: 28–9) and so do not engage with the many who fail to create value. Furthermore, Kay's explanation of how added value is created takes us back into the conventional product market-facing frame of classical strategy. For Kay, management's efforts should be invested in identifying or building distinctive capabilities. This is seen as vital because a 'distinctive capability becomes a competitive advantage when it is applied in an industry and brought to a market' (Kay 1993: 14). The product market-facing frame survives intact and the only real change is that the firm's goals have morphed from 'securing competitive advantage' to 'creating shareholder value' (measured by the 'added value' metric).

## ILLUSTRATION AND PROOF

Outside the world of mathematics, it is impossible to prove anything conclusively because other worlds do not have the same structure of necessary relations. Inconclusiveness turns into internal difficulties when discourses make large relational claims on the basis of limited evidence, as in classical strategy where vignettes and short cases are used to show how either business success or failure are the predictable results of following or breaking principles about positioning or competence-building. The problem here is not the vignette itself because it would be absurd to proscribe short illustrations that usefully supplement other evidence. The problem is the burden of proof that strategy invests in the vignette in the absence of (a) more general evidence about performance, (b) systematic empiricism that demonstrates that a general relation applies in many cases or (c) in-depth investigation through extended cases. We would not wish to put our trust dogmatically in any one method or kind of evidence, but it is perturbing to find that the general, relational and the extended are all absent in recent classical strategy which starts well with Chandler's extended historical case studies before shifting to vignettes with Porter in the 1980s and ending up with speculative predictions by Prahalad and Hamel in the 1990s.

Chandler was a professional business historian writing scholarly history of large industrial enterprises for an audience of his peers. His text is serious historiography which includes a discussion of methods and sources (Chandler 1962: 4) and tells the story of four giant companies (DuPont, General Motors, Jersey Standard and Sears) from primary sources. Thus, Chandler covers a relatively small number of companies in depth with argument that is well supported by evidence drawn from business correspondence, reports, memoranda, minutes of meetings and interviews. The backdrop of broader changes in the US economy is also drawn carefully from annual reports, government publications, articles in periodicals, business histories and biographies (Chandler 1962: 4). After a long general introduction, the central part of the text is taken up with in-depth historical case studies. Chandler's interpretation of strategy and structure was effectively immunized against short-run disproof because the cases could only be challenged by major historical revisionism of the kind that comes at most once in a generation. They also opened the way to a broader literature of 'testing' the performance consequences of divisional organization which was of course bound to be empirically indecisive given the many ways in which divisional organization could be operated by managers or measured and conceptualized by researchers.

Chandler's cases dealt with finished businesses where the combination of extensive archive research and historical closure created an aura of solidity enhanced by the low risk of immediate refutation. However, strategists in the 1980s and 1990s have increasingly moved into an area of greater vulnerability because they deal not in sustained historical case studies but in brief vignettes of glamorous success (or well-deserved failure). In 1980s' Porter and subsequently, these vignettes have taken an increasingly evangelical form, where they show how success follows the application of key principles recommended by the wise strategist, whilst dismal failure inevitably follows from their neglect.

Porter's mode of exposition is rather different to Chandler's because he is, on his own admission, targeting practitioners not academics (Porter 1980: xv) with a 'how to' guide that provides advice on techniques for analysing industries, followed by step-by-step advice on how to overcome problems in particular industry types. So Porter, for example, covers the different strategic moves possible in fragmented industries, merging industries, maturing industries, declining industries and global industries. He does this without a dense network of references: his 1980 book includes just fifty-seven references in just under 400 pages. Instead of extended historical cases, Porter uses vignettes or small illustrative examples, which are an important device for an author whose aim is to capture a broadly non-academic audience. For example, on generic strategies, Porter uses the case of Ethan Allen, who successfully employed a strategy of differentiation in the fragmented furniture business (Porter 1980: 208–9). On cost leadership, the success of firms such as Briggs and Stratton in small horse-power gasoline engines and Lincoln Electric's success in arc-welding equipment and supplies are also used to illustrate his concepts (Porter 1980: 36).

In terms of its assumptions, Porter's 1980s' argument was nuanced and included all kinds of caveats and qualifications. The reader was, for example, warned that cost-leadership strategies only work if there is one least cost producer, or that differentiation requires features consumers are prepared to pay for. However, he did sidestep discussion about the logic of his 1980s project, which was to construct an analysis of management calculation by breaking micro-economics into pieces. In our view, this was logically bound to yield indeterminacy under conditions of imperfect competition and oligopoly, where competitor reactions could not be predicted. However, this logic was artistically countervailed by 'just desserts'-style vignettes of success and failure through appropriate generic strategies. Here, for example, is Porter (1985) on focus strategy where Hammermill Paper was presented as an example of successful focus built on process technology, whilst Laker Airways, a pioneering British low-cost airline, was presented as a company that lost its focus and paid the price:

> Hammermill has increasingly been moving toward relatively low-volume, high-quality speciality papers, where the larger paper companies with higher volume machines face a stiff cost penalty for short production runs. Hammermill's equipment is more suited to shorter runs with frequent set ups.
>
> (Porter 1985: 15)

> Laker Airways began with a clear cost focus strategy based on no-frills operation in the North Atlantic market, aimed at a particular segment of the travelling public that was extremely price sensitive. Over time however, Laker began adding frills, new services and new routes. It blurred its image and sub-optimised its service and delivery system. The consequences were disastrous and Laker eventually went bankrupt.
>
> (Porter 1985: 17)

At one level it could be argued that Porter's use of vignettes is partly related to a desire to stay within a word limit, and he did also publish a now largely forgotten book of teaching case studies titled *Cases in Competitive Strategy* (Porter 1983). But this only serves to illustrate the gap between historical case studies of the kind that Chandler produced for historians and others, and the teaching cases that Porter and others have produced for their MBA 'case crackers'. Porter's cases on Raytheon, Kodak or GE represent the usual prepackaged material that focuses on business choice and crisis, which in the 1983 book are organized into sections around themes such as 'competitor analysis' and 'entry'. Such cases avoid overt direction but also inhibit independent analysis by the student who is presented with limited numerical information and who is also guided by a strong authorial voice that mostly endorses uncritically the management point of view. If these limits are sometimes transcended, it is more by accident than by scholarly design, because the cases are clearly based on too little research, particularly on primary sources. Thus, Porter (1983) includes an unusually informative case on GE versus Westinghouse in large gas turbines, but the critical reader will note that nine of the eleven exhibits on the turbine market and business financials are taken from one (outdated) source, a 1965 court case between Ohio Valley Electric and GE (Porter 1983: 109–18).

If Porter's vignettes are clearly illustrative, Prahalad and Hamel take things one step further by combining vignettes with speculative anticipations and predictions. Thus, Prahalad and Hamel offer vignettes that consist of upbeat tales whose moral is that 'strategy saves' in so far as companies who build and exploit their core competences are duly rewarded with success, as illustrated by their line on JVC (Matsushita) and its success with consumer VCRs from the 1970s onwards (Prahalad and Hamel 1990: 84–5). Prahalad and Hamel also critique Porter's concept of strategy, which is 'more concerned with how to position products and businesses within the existing structure than how to create tomorrow's industry' (Hamel and Prahalad 1994: 240). Thus, Hamel and Prahalad in their 1994 book cannot resist prophecy or speculative anticipations of how firms can build their competencies to capture the future. They list interactive television (along with genetically engineered drugs and multimedia publishing) as an area of emerging opportunity (Hamel and Prahalad 1994: 31) and observe that, 'in 1994 the dream of ubiquitous, fully interactive television was still a decade or more away from being a true mass market reality'; and one might add, it does not look much closer in 2005. Equally interesting is their fitful vision of the Internet and Silicon Valley in their 1994 discussion of 'digital industry'. Here, the Internet figures as 'the digital highway' which is going to be developed by big firms such as AT&T, MCI and BT (Hamel and Prahalad 1994: 38). They confidently claim that, 'a Silicon Valley without AT&T, IBM, Eastman Kodak and Motorola would create little wealth' (1994: 271); and in doing so completely miss the venture capital boom and the new-economy start-ups.

Ten years on and none of this prophecy looks convincing. At one level, this is hardly surprising because it shows only that Prahalad and Hamel are no more prescient than the rest of us in predicting the future, which usually turns out to be a surprise. The problem of course is that their 'building competences and competing for tomorrow' line requires them to be able to predict rather more, so that they end up hoisted on their own petard.

## SYSTEMATIC EMPIRICS AND REFUTATION BY EVENTS

After reviewing the use of vignettes in strategy discourse, we would conclude that strategists are as fascinated with business successes as show-business journalists are besotted with stars. The resulting problems are approached from another direction in this section which focuses on two further issues around the use of empirics. The first issue is the long-standing neglect of systematic empirics, i.e. the various techniques for exploring and extracting causal relations from large datasets. Strategists have generally not been much interested in the performance of average firms or industries and this neglect is only partly redressed by the recent 'hard' RBT work of applied economists who do use large datasets but focus narrowly on the variability of firm and industry profitability. The second issue concerns the problem of refutation by events as identified exemplars of corporate success falter and turn into unexplained failure. The pressure for up-to-date examples, complete with *ex-post* identification of competences, leads strategists to sample short sections of unexamined longer-term firm trajectories in a way that guarantees embarrassment.

Systematic empiricism should not be idealized when large areas of mainstream economics and finance have been laid waste by technicians whose use of such techniques demonstrates only that empirical results can be the enemy of understanding. Nevertheless, strategy has suffered from its neglect of systematic empiricism when, for more than twenty years, the only systematic evidence in most popular strategy textbooks was taken from the PIMS database (Profit Impact of Market Strategy). This dataset shows that across a large number of businesses, there is a positive correlation between market-share rank and return in investment (see de Witt and Meyer 1998: 367–82 or Johnson et al. 2005: 365–7) so that, on average, market leaders earn rates of return that are several times greater than businesses with a market share rank of fifth or worse. But this observation does not explain the nature and direction of the cause and effect relations underlying the basic correlation. On these issues, the textbooks can offer only interpretative banalities such as, 'a market leader with premium products has a strong competitive advantage' (Johnson et al. 2005: 366).

The increasing popularity of harder, more economics-based RBT leads to the recent inclusion of articles in generic-strategy readers by applied economists such as Rumelt and Barney who do use the techniques of systematic empiricism to explore causal relations. The problem here is that their work is very narrowly focused on the one question of whether profit varies more within or between industries; and their answers to this question are apparently inconclusive because they vary according to the tester's model and dataset. Hence, in response to Schmalensee (1985), Rumelt's classic 1991 article claimed that in terms of the distribution of economic rents, 'business units within industries differ from one another a great deal more than industries differ from one another' and added the point that only a relatively small part of the dispersion of business-unit or divisional profitability could be explained by size, industry affiliation or corporate parentage (Rumelt 1991: 182). McGahan and Porter (1997) produced an effective response using a larger dataset and a longer time span. Their conclusions from a study of manufacturing as well as services companies over fourteen years were that, 'industry effects are more persistent over time than business-specific or corporate-parent effects' (McGahan and Porter 1997: 29). This stimulated a flurry of papers on industry and firm variation in profitability which produced mixed results. Thus, Hawawini et al. (2003) found that only in the special case of a few dominant value creators or destroyers did firm-specific assets matter more than industry factors. This was countered later by Spanos et al. (2004) on Greek manufacturing who found the opposite.

Behind the variable answers to the narrow questions is an underlying problem. Questions about the variability of industry profitability are unlikely to have sensible answers because accounting 'noise' complicates any attempt to generalize about rates of return by industry from activity characteristics. Hence, if it is not easy to discriminate between inherently high- and low-return activities, then most other kinds of inference about business-unit profitability become very difficult. Thus, activities such as software or telecoms based on property rights, or immaterial activities such as tobacco, typically have lower requirements for physical capital, which generally makes it easier to generate higher rates of return on capital employed (ROCE). But, as in any business, the actual ROCE depends on the accident of when the business was last sold and fitted up with a new financial-capital base. Thus, utilities such as water are low ROCE companies for those who make the initial heavy investment, high ROCE companies for those who can buy bankrupt utilities cheaply, and finally moderate ROCE companies for those who buy from the state in privatization auctions, subject to the hazard of regulatory intervention. In these circumstances, systematic empiricism by the applied economists does not clarify basic relationships but becomes another authority that can be invoked selectively to impress those who cannot do algebra. Thus, the British strategy reader by Segal-Horn (2004) significantly reprints Rumelt (1991) but not his critics because Rumelt's results support RBT assumptions about the importance of firm-specific resources.

Most strategy writers continue to work by fielding corroborating examples or vignettes, after the style of Porter where success apparently comes from following sound strategic principles (and failure comes from neglecting those principles). This immunizes such writers from the challenges faced by applied economists who must defend their choice of datasets and econometric models. But mainstream strategists who use vignettes must live with the embarrassing possibility that identified corporate success does not last and turns into unexplained failure. This has become a public issue in the case of best-selling popular business books from the airport bookstand which go one step further than respectable academic texts in proposing recipes for success. The most vulnerable of these texts have been best-sellers such as *In Search of Excellence* by Tom Peters and Robert Waterman (1982) or *Built to Last* by Collins and Porras (1994), which promise to give readers the secret of sustained business success. In such cases, subsequent transition of case companies from success to failure has shock value and attracts media comment.

*In Search of Excellence* provides the classic example. Supposedly based on a systematic study plus consulting experience of what made firms excellent, Peters and Waterman came up with eight key attributes of the successful firm based on operating values: a bias for action; closeness to the customer; autonomy and entrepreneurship; productivity through people; hands-on, value-driven executives; stick to the knitting; simple form, lean staff; simultaneous loose–tight properties for internal organization. These attributes were all illustrated with company examples such as Delta, Hewlett Packard, 3M and Kodak, which exemplified excellence through operating values (which most readers would presume was a durable, rooted kind of internal advantage). Just two years after Peters and Waterman published their book, *Business Week* (5 November 1984) ran an article under the headline 'Who's excellent now?' which argued that at least fourteen of the forty-three companies identified by Peters and Waterman had slipped and lost their claims to excellence. Waterman responded limply in an article headlined 'Who said excellence was forever?' (*Business Week*, 26 November 1984).

The contrast between Peters' and Waterman's opportunist identifications of success and Chandler's meticulous historical case studies could not be more stark and closes our discussion of modes of illustration and proof in classical strategy. In the meanwhile, we would conclude that vignettes may illustrate but can never vindicate the principles of successful management as many strategy texts suppose. Those who recall Matthew 7:3 on motes and beams may be uneasy about our own form of critical exposition which constructs gobbet commentaries on very short quotations from strategy texts. To which our response would be that the texts from Chandler onwards are familiar to all our readers who teach or study strategy, and the originals are available on open shelf in any major library. Furthermore, we would be happy to put our argument to other tests. Why not an investigation of how examples of success are dropped and substituted in successive editions of major teaching texts or an extended case investigation of a significant episode such as the new economy where strategists got it wrong?

After the Netscape public offering in 1995, the new-economy hype was stoked in the *Harvard Business Review* by authors such as Evans and Wurster (1997) whose argument about 'falling costs of information' was supported by one or two good stories about the problems of Encyclopaedia Britannica. Even more interesting, Gary Hamel in his 2000 book, *Leading the Revolution*, praised Enron over ten pages because, 'as much as any company in the world, Enron has institutionalized a capacity for perpetual innovation' (Hamel 2000: 212). He did not check Enron's accounts, which showed recent profits collapse and a problem about declining ROCE (Froud et al. 2004: 893). Nor did he ask any questions about Enron's business model where its precarious credit rating was crucial because Enron was the counterpart in all its derivatives transactions (Froud et al. 2004: 895). Anybody who doubts our critique of classical strategy should read the 2000 edition of *Leading the Revolution* and ask themselves: if strategy is so smart, why did Gary Hamel get Enron completely wrong?

Chapter 3

# Shareholder value

## The intrusion of the capital market

The focus of our argument now changes from giant firm in product market to giant firm facing the capital market. From the 1960s onwards, classical strategy from Chandler, through Porter to Prahalad and Hamel was, in one way or another, an argument where academics took the leading role in analysing the firm facing the product market and made competing recommendations of divisional reorganization, positioning or mobilization of competences. Behind these differences was the implicit assumption that strategic action aimed at product-market advantage could generate enough profit. From the 1990s onwards, the demands of the capital market intruded and the insufficiency of profit became an increasingly important issue with non-academic actors such as business consultants and governance code-makers taking the leading role in explaining how management could deliver 'shareholder value' through value-based management (VBM) supported by corporate governance. This section of our introduction is about what the new actors (and their academic fellow travellers) promised.

While 'shareholder value' makes an appealing slogan, the difficulty is that various shareholders might want different things by way of share price or income that could not be easily fitted into one single scale and metric. Furthermore, the generic demand to safeguard shareholder interests or to seek higher returns for shareholders implies specific, different courses of action in different periods and sectors when, for example, stock prices are rising or falling. These are not roadblock problems in so far as shareholder value is not so much a defined concept as a kind of pliable rhetoric, appropriated and inflected by social actors. Thus, the consultancy firms concentrated on value metrics which gave each consultancy firm a differentiated saleable product and largely ignored the complications about shareholder identity and calculation. Indeed, it would be possible to write the history of shareholder value in terms of its capture and inflection by different groups, in the same way that Roberto Grun (2004) is writing the history of corporate governance in Brazil. On this basis, we would distinguish the social rhetoric of 'shareholder value' which is observed in this third chapter from the academic, social-scientific concept of financialization, which is analysed in the fourth chapter of this book.

Value-based management (VBM) is a management movement or fad that promised to deliver shareholder value and is, like world-class manufacturing or business-process engineering before it, very loosely defined by a set of techniques and a specific field of application. But in these other cases, as with VBM, the trajectory is crucial because there is usually a contrast between blithe promise and disappointing outcome. The promise of the 'how to do it' guides is that one approved set of actions always produces positive results. The outcome is the inevitable debunking article about how and why many companies find that the results are so often disappointing. Corporate governance has a rather different and more defensive political point of departure because the aim is to immunize the giant corporation and its senior management from external criticism by establishing management accountability. However, the trajectory of disillusion is much the same because the 1990s corporate-governance control technology promised to ensure managers act in the shareholder interest, but the outcome was egregious fraud in giant-company collapses such as Enron and social recrimination about the uncontrolled general enrichment of the CEOs.

This chapter develops these themes in four sections. The first introductory section deals with the definitional issues conventionally posed in terms of 'What is shareholder value?' The second section then surveys shareholder value as a consultancy product, emphasizing the banality of VBM which quickly ends in disillusion and new reform projects that promise to deliver what the old reform projects did not. The third section then switches to consider corporate governance and the 1990s proceduralized approach to controlling management in the interests of shareholders, before the final section reviews the evidence on giant-company CEO pay over twenty years and suggests that giant-company managers in the USA and UK were able to enrich themselves through value skimming. This observation provides an entrée into the next chapter on financialization which sets pay in context by including a systematic review of corporate performance and value creation in the S&P 500 and FTSE 100 since 1980.

## WHEN WAS SHAREHOLDER VALUE?

When the distinguished historian Gwyn Alf Williams (1985) turned from broader European themes to write a history of Wales, he titled his book 'When was Wales?' This question sidestepped more obvious *what is* essentialism and assumptions as it opened the way to an understanding of *how* Wales was put together at a fairly recent point in time, just like the grander European nation-states that Napoleon or Bismarck invented. The same argument applies even more so in the case of shareholder value in so far as it is not a mechanical assembly of discursive and non-discursive elements but a pliable rhetoric which can be borrowed, used and inflected. Questions about 'when and where was shareholder value' therefore provide the starting point, before we turn to consider the 'what is' question which, in the case of most rhetorics, seldom has one definite answer.

Sometime in the first half of the 1990s the term 'shareholder value' passed into general usage in the USA and UK so that, for example, business journalists such as Lex in the *Financial Times* began to judge management against the standard of whether they were creating value for shareholders. Corporate management also started to use the term 'shareholder value' as the all-purpose justification for everything they did strategically. The question of 'why' the language of shareholder value took hold in the UK and USA is a complicated one because it can be answered at several different levels using various assumptions about the relation between the ideal and the material. A rhetoric such as shareholder value gains credibility and currency in a specific socio-economic context, which helps us to understand why capital-market pressures affected US and UK giant companies more than their counterparts in Germany or Japan. As Faccio and Lang's (2002) detailed analysis shows, there are very considerable differences in ownership and control across western European corporations with the role of families, the state and networks of other firms providing a mainland European context for shareholder value pressures quite distinct from those in the UK and USA.

The context in the UK and USA included a long-standing corporate/company law system which established the primacy of shareholder interests through fiduciary duties enforceable by private rights of action. This principle was recently buttressed through a Company Law Review Steering Group (1999) paper in the UK which used the concept of 'enlightened shareholder value' to defend a shareholder-oriented concept of the company against more pluralist stakeholder concepts of the company. This Anglo-Saxon model contrasts sharply with neo-corporatist company-law structures such as those in Germany which have historically balanced the interests of capital and labour through devices such as the two-tier board, with employees represented on the supervisory board. The contrast is equally marked with statist structures in France and Japan which link banks, firms and suppliers and thus subordinate shareholder interests to corporate and state policy (Cioffi 2000: 578–9).

These differing legal contexts both condition and reflect the role of individual stock markets within national boundaries. Finance has often been stereotyped as rootless and cosmopolitan but, in the first half of the 1990s, the world's stock markets were still organized on an autarchic basis so that companies typically raised equity finance on their home market and investors preferred domestic companies. According to Henderson et al. (2003: 37) between 1990 and 2001 the value of firm equity issues in foreign markets relative to the value of equity issues in their home market was 5.4 per cent in the UK,

7.8 per cent in France, 4.7 per cent in Germany, 1.16 per cent in Italy, 2.6 per cent in Japan and just 0.6 per cent in the USA. Likewise, evidence on the domestic preferences of investors shows that there has historically been a home bias. Watson (1999: 60) observes that in 1989 US investors held 94 per cent of their stock-market wealth in their home country, Japanese investors 94 per cent and UK investors 82 per cent. This relation would also seem to apply at a sectoral level as Dupuy and Lung (2002) have demonstrated in their study of the car industry which shows that in 2000 German investors accounted for 97.6 per cent of all institutional holdings in German auto companies.

It should be noted that this situation is changing with arrival of American investors in other national markets. As Morin showed, by 1997 foreign (mainly US funds) held 35 per cent by value of the French stock market (Morin 2000: 41). The growing influence of US investors can also be seen in the increasing number of foreign-owned companies listing on the NYSE in the form of American Depository Receipts (ADRs), because whilst German investors might own the vast majority of shares on the DAX, not all German companies list solely on their domestic stock markets. Thus Glassman (2001: 2) has shown that American ownership of foreign stocks rose from $198 billion in 1990 to $1.8 trillion by 2000 and that Americans now own 20 per cent of the shares of publicly traded non-US companies that invest heavily in the USA. This has even impacted on some German firms such as Henkel KGaA and Great Atlantic and Pacific Tea Company Inc., where US investors own some 30 per cent of shares (Glassman 2001: 11).

Against this backdrop, the demands and pressures of the US and UK capital markets were more urgent than elsewhere for three reasons. First, the US and UK markets were much larger in terms of market capitalization relative to GDP and Exhibit 3.1 illustrates the contrast in size of the market. In 2002 there is a clear difference between two groups: the USA, UK and Australia, where stock-market capitalization is equivalent to the value of GDP (plus or minus 10 per cent); and France on 62.7 per cent with Germany and

***Exhibit 3.1*** *The significance of listed companies: stock-market capitalization compared with GDP*

| | *Market capitalization as a % of GDP* | | |
|---|---|---|---|
| | *1995* | *2000* | *2002* |
| USA | 95.5 | 152.7 | 105.0 |
| UK | 121.7 | 184.3 | 111.0 |
| Australia | 70.1 | 97.7 | 91.7 |
| France/ Euronext (for 2002 data) | 31.9 | 111.7 | 62.7 |
| Germany | 25.6 | 67.8 | 31.2 |
| Japan | 83.5 | 67.3 | 49.5 |

*Source*: World Federation of Exchanges (www.world-exchanges.org)

*Notes*: The 2002 data for the US includes the NYSE and the NASDAQ. The 2002 data for France is for Euronext, which includes Belgium, France, Netherlands and Portugal

Japan at less than half of GDP. It is worth noting that this is true even after the end of the 1990s bull market and the new economy bubble, when at the peak in 2000 the stock market appeared much more significant in all six countries in relation to national GDP.

Second, in both the UK and USA there was a clear shift in ownership from direct (individual or household) ownership to institutions, such as pensions and insurance funds. Exhibit 3.2 shows that in the UK in 1957, 65.8 per cent of shares were held directly by households, falling to 14.9 per cent in 2003; while for the USA in 1950 the proportion held by households and non-profit organizations was 90.2 per cent which was reduced to 36.7 per cent in 2003 (Exhibit 3.3). An implication of the increasing importance of institutional ownership in both countries is that management of share portfolios is delegated to professional fund managers who are often judged (and rewarded) on the basis of short-term performance. This not only adds pressure to perform on those companies whose shares are mainly held by institutions, it also influences the composition of share portfolios. For example, Golding (2001: 2–3) argues that small and medium-size firms in terms of their capitalization are relatively unattractive to fund managers because they cannot offer the required level of liquidity.

Third, on the US and UK stock markets, hostile take-over was permitted and thus offered a potential threat for under-performers. In other advanced capitalist countries such as Germany, capital market demands and pressures were damped because their network form of capitalism meant giant companies could (until recently) rely on long-term passive shareholding by banks and other industrial companies in markets where hostile take-over is virtually unknown (Lane 1992, Goergen et al. 2005).

These differing institutional conditions both reflect and constitute understandings of corporate performance and how it is measured. Lawrence (1980) long ago argued in

***Exhibit 3.2*** *Trends in share ownership in the UK*

| | *Ownership of shares %* | | | | | | | | |
|---|---|---|---|---|---|---|---|---|---|
| | *1957* | *1963* | *1975* | *1981* | *1990* | *1994* | *2001* | *2002* | *2003* |
| Personal (direct) | 65.8 | 54.0 | 37.5 | 28.2 | 20.3 | 20.3 | 14.8 | 14.3 | 14.9 |
| Pension funds | 3.4 | 6.4 | 16.8 | 26.7 | 31.6 | 27.8 | 16.6 | 15.6 | 16.1 |
| Insurance companies | 8.8 | 10.0 | 15.9 | 20.5 | 20.4 | 21.9 | 20.0 | 19.9 | 17.3 |
| Investment trusts | 5.2 | 11.3 | 10.5 | 5.4 | 1.6 | 2.0 | 2.2 | 1.8 | 2.3 |
| Unit trusts | 0.5 | 1.3 | 4.1 | 3.6 | 6.1 | 6.8 | 1.8 | 1.6 | 2.0 |
| Banks | | 1.3 | 0.7 | 0.3 | 0.7 | 0.4 | 1.3 | 2.1 | 2.2 |
| Other financial institutions | | | | | 0.7 | 1.3 | 9.9 | 10.5 | 11.1 |
| Overseas | 7.0 | 5.6 | 3.6 | 11.8 | 16.3 | 20.0 | 31.9 | 32.1 | 32.3 |
| Other (e.g. charities, non-financial companies) | 10.9 | 8.7 | 8.9 | 10.3 | 6.7 | 3.2 | 2.0 | 2.0 | 1.9 |

*Source*: National Statistics, *Share Ownership Report*, various years

*Note*: Ownership data is for the end of December in each year

*Exhibit 3.3 Ownership structure of NYSE shareholdings*

| | Ownership of shares % | | | | | |
|---|---|---|---|---|---|---|
| | *1950* | *1970* | *1990* | *1995* | *2000* | *2003* |
| Bank personal trust | 0.0 | 10.4 | 5.4 | 2.6 | 2.0 | 2.1 |
| Closed-end funds | 1.1 | 0.5 | 0.5 | 0.4 | 0.2 | 0.2 |
| Foreign sector | 2.0 | 3.2 | 6.9 | 6.0 | 9.2 | 10.9 |
| Households and non-profit organizations | 90.2 | 68.0 | 51.0 | 47.4 | 42.1 | 36.7 |
| Life-insurance companies | 1.5 | 1.7 | 2.3 | 3.6 | 5.3 | 6.4 |
| Mutual funds | 2.0 | 4.7 | 6.6 | 11.7 | 18.3 | 18.3 |
| Other insurance companies | 1.8 | 1.6 | 2.3 | 1.5 | 1.1 | 1.4 |
| Private pension funds | 0.8 | 8.0 | 16.8 | 14.7 | 12.5 | 12.9 |
| Other | 0.6 | 0.6 | 0.7 | 0.9 | 1.7 | 2.6 |
| State and local pension funds | 0.0 | 1.2 | 7.6 | 11.2 | 7.6 | 8.5 |
| *Share of equity held by* | | | | | | |
| Households and non-profit organizations | 90.2 | 68.0 | 51.0 | 47.4 | 42.1 | 36.7 |
| Institutions | 9.8 | 32.0 | 49.0 | 52.6 | 57.9 | 63.3 |

*Source*: NYSE Factbook, 2003

the German case that productive and market success in the form of *technik* was more important. These observations about national difference would appear to be supported by survey evidence from the 1990s which suggests that British directors attach considerably more importance to achieving financial results than their German counterparts (Jürgens et al. 2000).

Under US and UK conditions, the 1990s rhetoric of shareholder value connotes (more) pressure on management to create 'value' for shareholders. Yet what this implies or requires is unclear because shareholders often want different things or want the same thing for different reasons. This point was underlined by *Financial Times* commentator Lex in 2005, after hedge funds and US mutuals had taken a leading role in stopping the Deutsche Börse bid for the LSE: 'pity the poor executive. Creating shareholder value is one thing, but it is increasingly difficult to determine who these shareholders are and what they want' (*Financial Times*, 2 March 2005). The mutuals and hedge funds had made common cause around the demand that Deutsche Börse should return cash to shareholders rather than spend it on acquiring LSE. This implied either that these investors had a short-term time horizon and a strong preference for cash quickly or had made a judgement that merger to create a leading European stock exchange with a dominant market position would not create value for its shareholders in the longer term because national regulators would one way or another spoil its profitability. The hedge funds had a supplementary motive for blocking the Deutsche Börse take-over because they had shorted LSE shares and stood to gain from a fall in price that would inevitably follow the withdrawal of the Deutsche Börse offer. LSE shares had risen sharply on the assumption that both the French and German exchanges would wish to bid for the company and LSE shares could be expected to fall heavily if one of the two suitors withdrew. The mutual funds stood to lose from this share price fall if they had to sell quickly but meanwhile the mutual funds of course gained a turn from the fees that hedge funds paid to 'borrow' their shares for short-selling.

In this context, shareholder value denotes the artifice that everybody understands what shareholders want, just as VBM denotes the pretence that management has a course of action that can deliver value as measured by one simple metric. From this point of view it is the variability and inconsistency in value requirements that is most striking if we survey the history of shareholder value since the early 1990s.

For some academics and consultants, shareholder value meant a new and different earnings hurdle for giant firms. The objective was not the avoidance of operating loss achieved by a positive profit, but 'value creation' achieved by a rate of ROCE greater than the cost of capital. In the 1990s, this target rate of profit was estimated by consultants such as Rappaport (1998) at 10 to 12 per cent after tax for all firms regardless of sector. The 10–12 per cent is calculated in various worked examples, using a beta measure of stock volatility of 1.23 per cent and assuming that the risk-free rate was 6.6 per cent (Rappaport 1998: 140, 149). The peculiar assumption was that any and every firm should be able to meet this financial target, and this principle was implicit in public league tables and rankings by Stern Stewart, the consultancy firm whose Economic Value Added (EVA™) was a proprietary variant on standard residual-income accounting measures. But this hurdle was never consistently applied by the UK and US stock markets in their valuation of individual companies because stock-market investors remain cheerfully tolerant of firms that combine low ROCE with other desirable characteristics, such as growth of corporate earnings through organic growth or acquisitions. Our historical case study of GE shows that this stock market star of the 1990s had a post-tax ROCE of around 5 per cent through the 1990s (see Table C3.7, p. 376), which may puzzle some academics but did not deter institutional investors.

As for 'what the market wants', the problem here is that the stock market does not apply one universal valuation standard or adopt one single investor strategy to all companies and sectors. Thus, in an article on the new economy (Feng et al. 2001), we argued that after the Netscape initial public offering, the US market from 1995 to 2000 operated a peculiar double standard. On the one hand, old economy firms with low ROCE or cyclicality problems were viewed unsympathetically and their shares were valued low by shareholders because of the difficulty they had recovering costs from the product market. By way of contrast, for new-economy firms, the exuberant expectation of future earnings, boosted by a belief in a digital future and supported by growing sales revenue which represented a proxy for success justified a boom in new issues and sky-high price/earnings (P/E) ratios in the telecoms, media and technology sector. Such new-economy firms often had no profits because of high costs associated with set-up, advertising and so on. Thus ROCE had little relevance as a performance measure because, in effect, they were recovering their costs (in an unsustainable way) from the capital market via venture capital, initial public offerings (IPOs) and subsequent equity issues, rather than from the product market.

This episode also raises issues about how prophecies become temporarily self-fulfilling if enough investors believe them. Venture-capital commitments in the USA grew from $4.2 billion in 1995 to more than $100 billion in 2000. This investment was very narrowly concentrated: in the first half of 2000, Internet-specific investments accounted for 47 per cent of total venture-capital commitments; communications, computers and semi-conductors accounted for another 40 per cent of the total. IPOs ballooned slightly later with $174 billion worth of Internet IPOs offered between the second quarter of 1999 and the first quarter of 2000 (Feng et al. 2001: 494–5). When such huge sums are mobilized for investment in a narrow range of sectors, the momentum of investment has the capacity to realize and validate high share prices in digital stocks within a world where 'whatever looks good is good' and share prices (for a while) run on narratives of economic transformation rather than on the numbers.

In less extreme circumstances, share prices can relate to the financial numbers, where the price of the share reflects the present value of future earnings, as orthodox finance theory predicts. Thus, shares in successful ethical pharmaceutical companies with double-digit rates of sales and earnings growth and a healthy return on capital have traditionally traded at substantial premium to average P/E ratios. But, as our historical case on Ford shows, there is no general flight to quality and growth because the market can find value opportunities in the shares of companies whose precarious and cyclical earnings are unlikely to generate any sustained rise in share price. In the case of a company such as Ford, the opportunity arises for an individual investor who spots something, such as early signs of a market turndown, which is not factored into the price. This further complicates matters because it again hangs value on external perception which may have little to do with the management action and agency that many shareholder value propagandists present as crucial.

Investor strategies also vary according to whether share prices are going up in a bull market or down in a bear market. In a sustained bull market, as in the 1990s, when US and UK share prices generally rose by 10–15 per cent per annum, it is enough to buy and hold. Many institutional investors will then 'buy the market', that is, choose a portfolio of giant-company stocks, in ways that make the merits or demerits of an individual stock less important in a world where it is assumed that 'all boats rise with the tide'. All this changes in a bear market when share prices fall (as they did for more than two years after spring 2000) and investors, confronted with a choice of strategies, are forced towards different tactics. More generally, in recession and stock-market downturn when asset prices will usually be falling, the stock market acquires a new sensitivity to balance-sheet risks from pensions and health-care provision on the liabilities side as well as credit down-rating for highly leveraged firms. With equity finance shut off in the early 2000s, Merrill Lynch concluded, 'the name of the game is to avoid being downgraded' (*Financial Times*, 20 January 2003), and in early 2005 one of the biggest business stories was the threatened downgrading of General Motors (GM) bonds to junk.

This point about the variability in value standards and requirements is dramatized by the way in which the stock market can often change its shallow, collective mind much more rapidly than giant firms can change their strategies. Thus, in a first period, the market may encourage or even demand supposedly value-creating moves by individual firms which may then in a second period provide the basis for general condemnation of the industry and a call for strategy reversal. European telecoms provide a recent example. During the summer of 2000, telecom companies in the UK and most of Europe were encouraged to bid for 3G licences by the stock market, because market analysts and the media had convinced themselves that this technology represented the future for mobile telephony, even though nobody knew what the product would be or how costs might be recovered. After the telecom companies had saddled themselves with debt (and 3G handsets and content were only in the developmental stages), the market took fright and demanded debt reduction in businesses that were now seen to be boring utilities. In the UK, BT was forced to demerge mmO2, its mobile phone division, amid fears that 3G might be no better than other existing technologies and could struggle to yield adequate returns on the £10 billion spent on the purchase of the 3G licence (*Financial Times*, 13 September 2001; *Financial Times*, 15 September 2001).

In one of his later books, Michel Foucault observes the doctors and the lawyers quarrelling over whether the murderer Rivière is mad and deserves the asylum or just bad and fit to stand trial. Foucault (1975) then quietly adds the comment, 'maybe he was not always the same'. Much the same point needs to be made about shareholder value. As the next section demonstrates, different groups of social scientists debate whether its outcomes are bad without fully recognizing that the demands of the share-holder value rhetoric are confusingly variable.

## VALUE-BASED MANAGEMENT (VBM)

If shareholder value did not have any one definite meaning, this was both an intellectual problem for business-school academics and a practical opportunity for management consultants. Management consultancy, or the outsourced business of knowledge transfer, stood to benefit from pliable and changing definitions of shareholder value that fed the insecurity of corporate management and required expert interpretation, plus subsequent implementation through performative initiatives. Most major consultancy firms in the 1990s replaced strategy consultancy with VBM, which combined proprietary metrics, implementation packages and homiletic examples of success. On closer inspection though, many of the old 1980s' Porteresque concepts were retained behind a façade of novelty and differentiation so that the VBM offer included a new promise of financial transformation as well as the old, familiar strategy concepts.

In the mid-1990s, proprietary value metrics were being pushed by up and coming consultancy firms such as Stern Stewart and LEK/Alcar as well as by long-established firms such as Boston Consulting Group, which were previously identified with strategic consultancy but now developed a 'value management practice' (Myers 1996). Stern Stewart's Economic Value Added (EVA™) and Market Value Added (MVA) contended with LEK/Alcar Consulting Group's Shareholder Value Added (SVA) and Holt Value Associates' Cash Flow Return on Investment (CFROI). Not to be outdone, McKinsey had Economic Profit, while Boston Consulting Group had its own version of Cash Flow Return on Investment (CFROI) and Total Shareholder Return (TSR) (see Exhibit 3.4). The international accounting firms, such as PriceWaterhouseCoopers and Arthur Andersen, also joined in with their own metrics. Some consultants, such as Stern Stewart, adopted a 'one best way' approach and explicitly promoted one metric and its associated implementation package for all clients. Others, such as Boston Consulting Group, recognized a range of metrics and offered to use 'appropriate measurement' matched to individual clients (1996a: 11).

***Exhibit 3.4*** *Consultancy metrics for shareholder value: some illustrations*

**(a) Metrics from new value-based consultancies: Stern Stewart, LEK/Alcar**

**EVA™**: 'EVA™ is defined as the net operating profits after tax, minus the required rate of return on capital employed' (*Corporate Finance*, February 1991). 'Companies have a clear directive with EVA™ to improve returns earned on existing capital, to invest in projects that earn returns above the cost of capital and to sell assets that are worth more to others' (Milano and Schwartz 1998).

**MVA**: 'Market Value Added (MVA) [is] the difference between the current value of a company and the total invested capital. MVA reveals how well each company has performed over the long term in using its resources to create value . . . But it is hard to manage for MVA because of share price volatility, the difficulty in seeing the impact of decisions on MVA and the inability to measure MVA definitively at various levels within a company. That is why Stern Stewart invented EVA™' (Milano and Schwartz 1998).

**SVA**: According to Alfred Rappaport, a principal of LEK/Alcar, Shareholder Value Added (SVA) is 'the amount of value created by the forecasted scenario. While SV characterises the absolute economic value resulting from the forecasted scenario, SVA addresses the change in value over the forecast period. Recall that value creation results from corporate investment at rates in excess of the cost of capital rate required by the capital market' (1998: 49).

**CFROI**: 'HOLT calculates the CFROI (cash flow return on investment) in two steps. First HOLT measures the inflation-adjusted (current dollar) cash flows available to all capital owners in the company and compares that to the inflation-adjusted (current dollar) gross investment made by those capital owners. Next, HOLT translates the ratio of gross cash flow to gross investments into an Internal Rate of Return (IRR) . . . the CFROI is directly comparable to the shareholder return investors expect to receive, i.e. their cost of capital or discount rate' (HOLT Value Associates undated: 4).

continued

*Exhibit 3.4 continued*

**(b) Metrics from old general consultants: Boston Consulting Group, Arthur Andersen**

**TSR**: 'The individual investor's and professional fund manager's scorecard is the total shareholder return (TSR) of their portfolio. TSR is the combined capital gain and dividend yield of the stocks held in the portfolio and is usually judged in relation to the return of similar portfolios' (BCG 1996b: 1). 'TSR is the most useful summary measure of value creation' (BCG 1996b: 2).

**SVA**: Arthur Andersen calculate SVA as 'net operating profit after tax (NOPAT) less a capital charge . . . SVA can be enhanced by focusing on its four components: revenue and expenses (NOPAT), capital (value of assets), and cost of capital (adjusted for risk)' (1997: 5). 'The true power of SVA-based management is that it provides a single focal point for strategic decisions, resource allocations, and performance management' (1997: 3).

*Source*: Froud, J., Haslam, C., Johal, S. and Williams, K. 'Shareholder value and financialization: consultancy promises, management moves' 2000 *Economy and Society*, vol. 29, no. 1, pp. 80–110, by permission of Taylor and Francis (http://www.tandf.co.uk)

All the metrics were in technical terms, straightforward, even banal. The most widely used new metric, EVA™, for example, was a residual-income measure which showed whether the firm in one year earns more than its weighted average cost of capital. What each consultancy firm added to create its own proprietary product was a series of adjustments to accounting measures of earnings and capital plus an acronym that identified the product. Stern Stewart, for example, capitalized research and development expenditure and goodwill, which had the effect of inflating the value of the company's capital base and thereby reducing the lump of what it trademarked as EVA™. Other firms made different minor changes to standard ratios, added their own acronym and then promoted their product as the best definition/measure of shareholder value. This only serves to illustrate how consultancy firms prefer minor innovation backed by serious marketing and, in this respect, are little different from ethical pharmaceuticals whose research focuses on me-too products with just enough molecular difference to justify the patent and with product differences asserted through extensive marketing campaigns.

Considerable effort was put into boosting one firm's measure and knocking others as part of the process of differentiating (basically similar) products in a battle of the acronyms. Consider, for example, this tussle between Holt and Stern Stewart about the merits of their different measures: 'CFROIs are ideally suited to displaying long term track records, whereas a Stern Stewart-type EVA™ is in millions of dollars heavily influenced by asset size and unadjusted for inflation-induced biases' (Holt Value Associates partner, Bentley J. Madden in Myers 1996: 1); and '[CFROI is] a technology in search of a problem, as opposed to a system designed to be integrated into a company's culture in the way real people make business decisions' (Stern Stewart partner and co-founder, G. B. Stewart in Myers 1996: 1).

All the consultants insisted their offer included an implementation package which was much more than a metric and presented implementation as the key to corporate success with VBM. This is certainly what created the product and made money for the consultancy firms because this emphasis on implementation allowed them to charge out lots of hours for developing 'payment by results' incentives for managers. This was coupled with an insistence on using value as a universal language throughout the firm, so that VBM packages such as EVA™ were

> not just a performance measure. When fully implemented, [EVA™] is the centrepiece of an integrated financial management system that encompasses the full range of corporate financial decision-making – everything from capital budgeting, acquisition pricing, and the setting of corporate goals to shareholder communication and management incentive compensation. By putting all financial and operating functions on the same basis, an EVA™ system effectively provides a common language for employees across all corporate functions, linking strategic planning with the operating divisions, and the corporate treasury staff with investor relations and human resources.
>
> (Stern et al. 1995: 33)

But, if we turn from this vision of a shareholder-value-driven management system to actions and the specifics about what management can do to improve financial results, then we find a good deal of tautology combined with a fairly traditional 1980s concept of strategy. The tautology and circularity is clearest in the Stern Stewart concept of improvement because 'three principal ways of increasing shareholder value' are no more than arithmetical possibilities inherent in any profit ratio, which can be changed by increasing the numerator or decreasing the denominator. Thus firms can make existing assets work harder, invest in activities with positive EVA™ or retreat from activities with low ROCE (Stern et al. 1998: 482). A traditional Porteresque concept of strategy figures in the second edition of Rappaport's (1998) book which is promoted by LEK/Alcar with the claim that it shows, 'why competitive advantage and shareholder value should be regarded as synergistic rather than competing objectives' (LEK/Alcar 1997: Vol. V: 7). In a careful review and comparison, Ameels et al. (2001) categorizes six VBM packages by different firms (including Stern Stewart, LEK and McKinsey) and distinguishes different concepts of strategy development, which is variously either top-down or bottom-up, either centralized or decentralized. But such differences conceal a fundamental similarity arising from the old strategy concepts borrowed from Porter which lie at the heart of all these consultancy visions of new transformation. Ameels et al. (2001: 27) find that four of the six firms refer to Porter and another independently develops Porter-style concepts, demonstrating that behind the veneer of novelty lies some fairly old-fashioned ideas.

At the same time, the consultants make positive promises that are mainly (often only) illustrated by homiletic examples and parables wherein consultant, metric and implementation save the value-destroying company just as Jesus saves the erring sinner.

'The 1997 Stern Stewart performance 1000' for the USA opens with five 'recent success stories' which all take the religious form, as in the case of Harnischfeger Industries of Minneapolis:

> The top line was growing, the bottom line was growing, but the stock price was going nowhere [in 1993]. . . . EVA™ was first adopted as a performance measure, then in 1994 some 400 executives were put on a standard EVA™ incentive bonus plan . . . later 3,600 salaried employees were enrolled in a modified EVA™ plan . . .
>
> When the program began, Harnischfeger had a negative EVA™ and a share price of $18. Thereafter, year by year, the company's EVA™ grew until it was substantially positive in 1996 – the first year in which all business units posted positive EVA™ – and the stock reached $40 a share. Harnischfeger's improvement over the three years was so rapid that it was number two on Fortune's list of the fastest growing companies in the US.
>
> (Ross 1998: 117)

The effects of such parables are reinforced when corporate executives themselves endorse the product in their own words, as in LEK/Alcar's newsletter. Their fourth volume presented, 'three testimonials on the successful application of SVA and LEK/Alcar's Value Based Management system' in Question and Answer form, with senior executives from companies such as RJR Nabisco answering the questions. The associative chain connects the consultancy firm via metric and implementation with corporate success. The association is reinforced by reassuring lists of blue-chip corporate clients which constitute a kind of widely circulated appeal to authority. Since its foundation in 1982, Stern Stewart claims to have advised 250 corporations whose sales revenues total more than $400 billion. Its US client list includes Coca-Cola, AT&T, Eli Lilly, Trans America and Georgia Pacific, Briggs & Stratton and Quaker Oats (Myers 1996: 2). Boston Consulting Group similarly claims 100 corporate clients and by the late 1990s all the major consultants were having some success with European companies such as Siemens (Ross 1998: 120).

However, the time interval between the confident consultancy promises and their practically disappointing outcome was in this case no more than a few years. The consultancy texts so far cited date from 1995 to 1998, yet by 2001 INSEAD academics writing in the *Harvard Business Review* observed that many companies that bought VBM packages had difficulty in delivering value:

> As recent reports in the press indicate, almost half the companies that have adopted a VBM metric have met with mediocre success. Some have even abandoned the system altogether after three to five years, reverting to traditional performance measures such as earnings per share. Reportedly, they include household names like AT&T which launched a VBM program in 1992 and recruited Stern Stewart to help with the endeavour.
>
> (Haspeslagh et al. 2001: 66)

This side-swipe at Stern Stewart was perhaps unsurprising given the INSEAD academics were assisted by the Boston Consulting Group and also explains why VBM is not rejected outright. Rather than presenting systematic data on average firm performance (such as we provide in the next chapter of this introduction), the *Harvard Business Review* article jumps from the unsubstantiated 'reports in the press' about half the adopters failing to a speculative identification of the conditions of success in those giant firms that do succeed. Haspeslagh et al. argue that VBM requires 'fundamental changes to a big company's culture' and discerns, 'a striking similarity in the way successful VBM companies . . . went about achieving the desired cultural transformation' (Haspeslagh et al. 2001: 67). This experience is then distilled into five principles for the reader including 'an explicit commitment to shareholder value' and 'incentive systems that were closely tied to the VBM performance measures' (Haspeslagh et al. 2001: 67). Thus, it becomes clear that the consultancy offer of VBM is not discredited by the initial failure of VBM in many giant firms because, in the next phase of the value revolution, another consulting firm will explain the initial failure and recommend a new product that really works. In consultancy, as in Maoist politics, the revolution fails because it is incomplete.

## CORPORATE GOVERNANCE

Corporate governance and VBM fit together because they are both about ensuring managers act to create shareholder value and both end in predictable disappointment. VBM is the private consultancy product which from the early 1990s promises to harness management action inside firms for the creation of shareholder value. Corporate governance is the public regulatory regime which from the early 1990s promises to control and incentivize top managers so that they pursue shareholder value. We would argue that corporate governance, like VBM, turns out to deliver less than it promises. The collapse of giant firms such as Enron and WorldCom led to a major crisis of confidence in the existing systems and rules used to control corporate executives, with more and better governance often offered as the solution to these problems. These collapses were shocking, but in the two remaining sections of this chapter we want to shift the focus away from exceptional cases of dishonesty by a few executives and their professional advisers. Instead we wish to highlight the paradoxical result of governance for shareholders which sanctioned the general enrichment of giant-firm CEOs in the UK and USA who hugely increased their pay in the twenty years after 1980.

This section opens this argument by contextualizing corporate governance in two ways. First, corporate governance is situated as a control technology which represents the latest installment of and variation on the liberal government project of writing a constitution for the market. Second, the narrative of corporate governance is then described and its promise about value creation for shareholders related to its theoretical and empirical foundations. In the final section of this chapter we then consider the evidence on CEO pay increases, as part of a process that we term 'value skimming'.

In liberal democracies, governments must write a kind of constitution for the market. The promise of each successive control technology is that it can create a form of capitalism that combines the economic dynamism of profit-seeking competitive behaviour with a modicum of social responsibility which prevents the abuse of power and thereby makes the whole system democratically acceptable. From this point of view, proceduralized corporate governance in the UK, as introduced after the Cadbury Report in 1992 plays a similar role to Keynesianism and Beveridgean social insurance in the post-war settlement. Since Reagan and Thatcher broke up the post-war settlement, the aim has been to evict government from the economy by minimizing state ownership of infrastructure and state control of institutions such as labour market and social welfare, while de facto substituting governance, that is, frameworks and procedures of regulation in the public interest which limit and direct the processes of competition and profit-seeking. If corporate governance has its origins in established market economies such as the UK, it has also been identified as an important element of the development process for countries seeking to build private-sector capacity, capital markets and related institutions, as the OECD and the World Bank now emphasize through principles (OECD 1999) and initiatives such as the Global Corporate Governance Forum (<http://www.gcgf.org/ifcext/cgf.nsf>).

In the advanced market economies, corporate governance for giant firms (along with re-regulation of privatized utilities and financial services) is a key technology charged with reconciling economic dynamism and social responsibility. Many believe, as Alan Greenspan (2002) has argued, that large US corporations are CEO dominated and subject only to occasional capital-market intervention through change of management or company take-over. If the giant corporation is a kind of constitutional monarchy, corporate governance from the early 1990s aims to countervail this concentration of power by putting procedures in place that positively motivate and negatively police and discipline incumbent corporate managers so that they serve the interests of shareholders/owners. From a market constitution point of view, this immediately represents a significant shift in focus because the beneficiaries of policy are no longer the workers and citizens of the Keynes and Beveridge era but the shareholders of the corporate-governance era. Interestingly, earlier social-democratic thinking by authors such as Tawney (1921) disparaged 'coupon clipper' rentiers who represented wealth without function. Now 'shareholders are us' even though empirically, as we have demonstrated elsewhere (Froud, Johal et al. 2002) only those in the upper half of the income distribution in the USA and UK have significant long-term savings in the stock market.

All governance technologies arguably share some general characteristics, such as a preference for the procedural over the substantive. This generally displaces the old radical question about 'who runs the show' with a new one about 'how the show is run', because governance suggests that the question about who is in charge is irrelevant as long as we have procedural safeguards in place. But governance also develops on specific domains within the frame of local narratives about problems and solutions. This was certainly the case with corporate governance which was created by the discovery or invention of a problem–solution couple after the early 1990s in the UK and USA. The stereotyped problem was one of agency, which focused on whether corporate managers act in the interests of shareholders, and derived from the work of (mainly US) finance academics in the late 1970s and early 1980s. Its corollary was a well-understood solution in the form of a standard package of measures initially proposed in various reports by British establishment businessmen after the 1992 Cadbury Report.

The agency theory of the firm was initially formulated by academics such as Jensen and Meckling (1976) and Fama (1980) who developed the idea of the maximizing individual and the firm as a set of contracts. If they aimed to construct a general explanation of firm behaviour with interesting implications, their legacy was a much narrower agency model of top management pay, which authors such as Eisenhardt (1989) then popularized at the end of the 1980s. Their founding argument was usefully intelligible and open to empirical test and analytic deconstruction. With shareholder as principal and manager as agent, in a world of imperfect information and incomplete contracts, agency costs could and should be controlled by writing an outcome-based contract for management pay.

A second distinct contribution came from the reports of British establishment businessmen (Cadbury 1992, Greenbury 1995 and Hampel 1998) who chaired committees on corporate governance, representing the interests of investment institutions and big business whose aim was self-regulation through voluntary codes. Such codes responded politically to British corporate scandals of the late 1980s such as Maxwell, Polly Peck or Bank of Credit and Commerce International (BCCI) and to public criticism of 'fat cat' pay settlements in the newly privatized British utilities (Greenbury 1995: 20, 52). They echoed the finance academics in their insistence that governance was about ensuring managers acted in the shareholder interest while the British committees also added new themes about the importance of what Hampel (1998) called 'partnership' between giant firms and their big institutional investors.

The British committees were significant because they defined a standard package of measures that promised to motivate and police incumbent corporate managers in the interests of shareholders. Through these measures, consolidated as a voluntary *Combined Code* of good practice for UK corporations, Cadbury and his successors turned Anglo-American corporate governance into an intelligible problem–solution couple where good practice would include several key features:

- Positive motivation was supplied via appropriate performance-related management pay which would both retain and motivate. The reports explicitly recognized that many existing performance targets and stock-option schemes were too soft and did not do this.

- Negative policing of CEO or top-management misconduct with more general oversight of strategy was strengthened by changes in the composition of the board and proceduralization. Thus, Cadbury in the UK initiated the separation of chairman and CEO positions (still often combined in the USA) and also put a new emphasis on the role of independent non-executive directors. Proceduralization was represented via remuneration and audit committees, with the latter for Hampel to consist entirely of non-executives.
- A proactive capital market was recommended so that active institutional investors outside the firm would dialogue with and, if necessary, vote against management, subject, of course, to the backstop discipline of a market in corporate control.

In the 1990s, the US agency problem definition fused with the British solution to create an agency narrative of corporate governance. This narrative was not compelling because it was theoretically rigorous or empirically supported. Rather, its narrative power came from its capacity to create an intelligible world through strong, simple assumptions about what was wrong and what the appropriate solutions might be. In terms of problem definition, corporate governance asserts the centrality of a shareholder/manager agency problem. On the solutions, it assumes:

(a) the problem of executive reward can be solved by appropriate incentives, including share options which turn managers into owners;
(b) that changing the composition and procedures of the board can establish control over CEOs;
(c) the capital market is an external agent of discipline;
(d) government is an independent sponsor of frameworks and codes of practice, and also an enforcer of the public interest.

These assumptions (especially in the case of executive reward) have been dramatically challenged by events since spring 2000 when there were spectacular cases of US corporate collapse where control mechanisms failed and necessary actor identities were absent. Consider, for example, the case of Enron where special-purpose entities (SPEs) were used to hide losses from derivatives trading and enrich Enron managers. As we have argued elsewhere (Froud et al. 2004), Enron was a special case where the underlying problem was the conduct of an unrestrained power elite in sunbelt Texas. Nevertheless, in these circumstances, every governance mechanism failed when Enron used money to suborn and influence the judgement of its auditors, audit committee and public regulators.

- The auditor was Arthur Andersen whose $50 million per annum web of business relations on external audit, internal audit and consultancy made Enron a valued customer who could not be offended (Froud et al. 2004: 905). The SPEs could hardly be queried by Andersen because it had received nearly $7 million for advising on the setting up of LJM, Chewco and Raptor. Andersen's Houston partners convinced themselves that the off-balance-sheet vehicles were aggressive accounting, though, as Enron's whistleblower recognized, none would stand scrutiny 'in the bright light of day'.

- The audit committee was a six-strong assembly of the great and good from all over the world who never asked difficult questions because they had been incorporated (Froud et al. 2004: 905). One was on a consultancy contract, two others benefited from Enron donations to their universities and collectively they owned Enron shares worth $7.5 million at the peak.
- Regulators became part of Enron's network. The Federal Commodity Futures Trading Commission in 1993 allowed exemption of energy derivatives from government oversight, the commission's chair resigned five days later and shortly afterwards took a job in a Texas university which received Enron donations and subsequently moved onto the Enron audit committee (Froud et al. 2004: 905).

The policy response so far has taken the form of 'more governance' proposals for heavy-duty 2000s' versions of the standard 1990s' measures. In the UK, Higgs (2003) made proposals to increase the number of non-executives from non-standard backgrounds; while in the USA the Sarbanes Oxley Act in 2002 let the major interests (such as the accounting firms) off lightly, but threatened jail for individual CEOs and CFOs who signed off false accounts. The working assumption of 2000s' policy-makers is that orthodox corporate governance could work with better execution and implementation. Thus, in a post-Enron speech on corporate governance, Alan Greenspan (2002) criticized the wrong kind of stock options, which had 'perverse effects', but then maintained that the right kind of options 'in principle . . . can be highly effective in aligning corporate officers' incentives with those of shareholders'.

Perhaps this is the kind of thing that central bankers have to say, but the rest of us should recognize more fundamental problems. The corporate-governance narrative was theoretically weak because it rested on a simplistic single-factor account of management pay and motivation, and, furthermore, it was empirically implausible because it rested on a very weak evidence base.

The academic finance community has for some time recognized that broader multi-factor, context-sensitive accounts of pay are required (see, for example, Jensen and Murphy 1990 or Core et al. 2003). In this context, the recent work of Bebchuk et al. (2002) and Bebchuk and Fried (2004) is important in that it accepts that directors could not be relied upon to restrain 'rent-seeking' senior managers. However, even if we include some work based on contingency theory such as Barkema and Gomez-Mejia (1998), finance academics generally have failed to engage with existing multi-factor accounts of management action by non-economists. This failure to engage is most obvious in their caricature of the classic 1932 Berle and Means text, which does not so much problematize the separation of ownership and control as envisage a new kind of stakeholder firm whose technocratic managers would not serve shareholders but, 'balance a variety of claims by various groups in the community' (Berle and Means 1932: 312). Equally striking is the finance literature's neglect of 1950s to 1970s debates by political scientists and sociologists such as Mills (1956) and Nichols (1969) who were generally hostile to what Nichols called the 'one factor theory of economic behaviour' (1969: 150).

The general defence of orthodox finance is that the simplifying assumptions of economic theory may be crude but they do predict behaviour and can explain the stylized facts. In our view, this pragmatic justification may work elsewhere, but it cannot be used to save the agency model of pay. The key issue here is simple: if agency theory were a good basic simplification that explained key relations, the world should have discovered the practical benefits and we would expect top-management pay to vary with performance. The evidence, however, suggests a different story.

By the beginning of the 1990s, the early promoters of agency theory, Jensen and Murphy (1990), had run the tests on US corporate data and already concluded that the observed pattern of variation in CEO pay did not fit the incentive-based pay for performance predictions of the agency model. Subsequent research has broadly confirmed this negative result, so that a recent literature review by Core et al. (2003) concludes that 'empirical researchers have had difficulty documenting a robust relationship between incentives and performance' and adds, 'there is no consensus on the performance consequences of managerial equity ownership' (2003: 35). The irony is that agency theory was always theoretically crude and already empirically challenged before it enjoyed its huge popularity with academics keen to find a theoretical framework in which to analyse governance.

## VALUE SKIMMING AND TOP MANAGEMENT

The argument and evidence in this section aims to highlight a discrepancy between promise and outcome, prospect and retrospect in the decade of the 1990s. In prospect, the decade of the 1990s was ostensibly about managers acting to create shareholder value; in retrospect the 1990s was also about (maybe more about) managers enriching themselves. To establish this discrepancy we need to analyse and relate two variables: (a) the increases in management pay from the 1980s onwards and (b) the increases in shareholder value attributable to management effort. This section offers the first part of this two-variable analysis by demonstrating that, after 1980, US and UK CEOs of giant companies received handsome pay increases that relate strongly to company size but only tenuously to company performance so that we would use the term 'value skimming' to understand the process by which CEOs are enriched. In the next chapter of our introduction we shift to consider financialization and there present further evidence on corporate performance in the S&P 500 and FTSE 100 that demonstrates mediocre value creation.

The argument begins by making the point that over the past twenty years, US and UK CEOs have received sustained, cumulating real pay increases that other employees have not. If this point is often not made up-front in the literature on executive pay, that is because the cross-section and time-series differences in UK and US giant-firm CEO pay over the past twenty years are complex, and this complexity allows various commentators to focus on differences and similarities. The differences between the USA and the UK are certainly interesting because the USA was and is much more tolerant of mega-pay for giant-firm CEOs. Mega-pay has traditionally been achieved in the USA through the payment of various elements that supplement salary which, in the 1990s, typically took the form of stock options. Thus, when Conyon and Murphy (2000) compared CEO pay on both sides of the Atlantic, they contrasted the US 'prince' and the UK 'pauper', and thereby drew attention to the point that, as Exhibit 3.5 shows, for most of the past twenty years, US CEOs of giant companies have earned in dollar terms some five or six times what their British counterparts earned in pounds. As Exhibit 3.6 shows, cashed options accounted for more than two-thirds of US CEO pay in giant firms in the early 2000s. Disclosure of options in the UK is much more recent, thus making it difficult to compare this component of salary; however, analysis by Conyon and Murphy (2000) based on 1997 data (the first year covered by new disclosure requirements in the UK) suggests that share-option grants account for only 10 per cent of pay for CEOs in large UK firms, compared with nearly 50 per cent in large US firms. This suggests that national differences do matter and the transatlantic comparisons are striking, though Conyon's choice of the term 'pauper' does seem curious when the UK CEO was by the end of this twenty-year period, as Exhibit 3.5 shows, typically earning more than £1 million a year.

However, despite such differences in the overall levels of pay, there are striking similarities in terms of the trajectory of large, sustained pay increases for CEOs in the UK and USA. According to *Business Week*'s annual executive compensation survey, the average CEO pay in 2002 prices at America's 365 largest corporations (including exercised options) was $14 million in 2000, compared with $2.8 million in 1990 and $1.4 million in 1980 (*Business Week*, 16 April 2001). In the UK (and elsewhere in Europe) the CEO real-pay trajectory has been one of catching up with the US CEO, whose generous increases nevertheless keep him or her ahead. In the UK FTSE 100, the 'highest paid director', who was usually the CEO, earned in 2002 prices just over £200,000 in 1980 which, as Exhibit 3.5, shows had increased to more than £1.3 million by 2002.

Significant annual increases in pay were, in the US case, fuelled by the bull market which made stock options painless for the company that did not have to charge them

*Exhibit 3.5 A comparison of CEO and worker pay in the USA and UK (all values are in real 2002 prices)*

| | *Chief Executive Officer pay* | *Employee pay* | *Ratio between Chief Executive and employee pay* |
|---|---|---|---|
| **US** | | | |
| ***Business Week* 350 companies** | | | |
| | $ | $ | Ratio |
| 1980 | 1,392,857 | 27,946 | 50 |
| 1990 | 2,814,084 | 25,599 | 109 |
| 2000 | 14,010,695 | 26,705 | 525 |
| 2002 | 7,400,000 | 26,354 | 281 |
| **UK** | | | |
| **FTSE 100 constituents** | | | |
| | £ | £ | Ratio |
| 2002 | 1,130,000 | 26,737 | 42 |
| **UK** | | | |
| **FTSE 100 survivors** | | | |
| 1978–9 | 207,643 | 23,093 | 9 |
| 2002–3 | 1,363,718 | 25,474 | 54 |

*Source*: Erturk, I., Froud, J., Johal, S. and Williams, K. 'Pay for corporate performance or pay as social division. Rethinking the problem of top management pay in giant corporations' 2005 *Competition and Change*, vol. 9, no. 1, pp. 49–74

*Notes*: For the FTSE 100, constituents are those 100 companies that make up the index in the year in question (the largest 100 firms by market capitalization). Survivors are those companies that have been in the FTSE 100 continuously since it was introduced in 1984. The 1978–9 data refers to the highest-paid director rather than the chief executive. US compensation includes salary, bonus, cash options and other benefits. UK compensation includes salary plus bonus but excludes the value of options. The Monks data series is produced for historic comparison purposes and information on the value of options has only recently become available for UK companies

against profit and an attractive form of remuneration for executives who in any case did not have to exercise them if they considered the share prices as priced too low. As Exhibit 3.5 shows, average real CEO pay in the USA declined sharply after 2000, because the stock-market crash in 2000 wiped value from the stock options widely used in large companies. Yet, as Exhibit 3.7 shows, on average these reverses only knocked off the gains of the later 1990s so that by 2002, average CEO pay in the USA has fallen back to the level of 1997, around $7.4 million. At this point, it is also worth noting that *average* CEO pay becomes rather misleading after 2000 in the USA. In a 2003 survey, a one-third year-on-year decline in average CEO pay reflected the restraint of the top half-dozen CEOs who had earned more than $100 million in the previous year, while the median pay for all 365 giant-firm CEOs actually *rose* year on year by 5.9 per cent to $3.7 million (*Business Week*, 21 April 2003).

*Exhibit 3.6 Levels and composition of CEO pay in the USA and UK*

**US: S&P companies, 2001–2**

| | *Total compensation* | *Of which* | | |
|---|---|---|---|---|
| | | *Base salary* | *(All) bonuses* | *Cashed options* |
| | $mill. | % | % | % |
| S&P 500 | 7.990 | 11.5 | 17.3 | 71.2 |
| S&P 400 (Midcap) | 3.493 | 17.6 | 20.7 | 61.7 |
| S&P 600 (Smallcap) | 1.809 | 26.1 | 19.0 | 54.9 |

**UK: listed companies, 2001–2**

| | *Total pay* | *Of which* | |
|---|---|---|---|
| | | *Basic pay* | *Bonus* |
| | £ | % | % |
| Small company (turnover up to £5 million) | 62,250 | 93.2 | 6.8 |
| Medium company (turnover £5 million to £50 million) | 94,997 | 86.3 | 13.7 |
| Large company (turnover £50 million to £500 million) | 129,000 | 89.1 | 10.9 |
| FTSE 100 (turnover range £403 million to £119 billion) | 1,249,000 | 74.5 | 25.5 |

*Source*: Erturk, I., Froud, J., Johal, S. and Williams, K. 'Pay for corporate performance or pay as social division. Rethinking the problem of top management pay in giant corporations' 2005 *Competition and Change*, vol. 9, no. 1, pp. 49–74

*Note*: The UK data provided by Croner Reward and Monks Partnership does not include the value of stock options

If rates of real increase were damped in the USA, that was not so in the UK where FTSE 100 CEO total pay rose by 23 per cent in 2002. If UK CEOs have been frustrated in having to wait to enjoy the benefits of stock options on any significant basis (let alone at the levels of their US counterparts), they have been rewarded in other ways after the end of the bull market so that cash bonuses now account for nearly 60 per cent on top of basic pay (*Guardian*, 31 July 2003). Shareholders inevitably protested after 2001 as UK managers pocketed large cash increases at a time when share prices and profits fell. These events were dramatized by front-page headlines about shareholder revolts at large companies such as Abbey National, Barclays, GSK, Reuters and Shell, where remuneration committee proposals for top-executive pay were resisted.

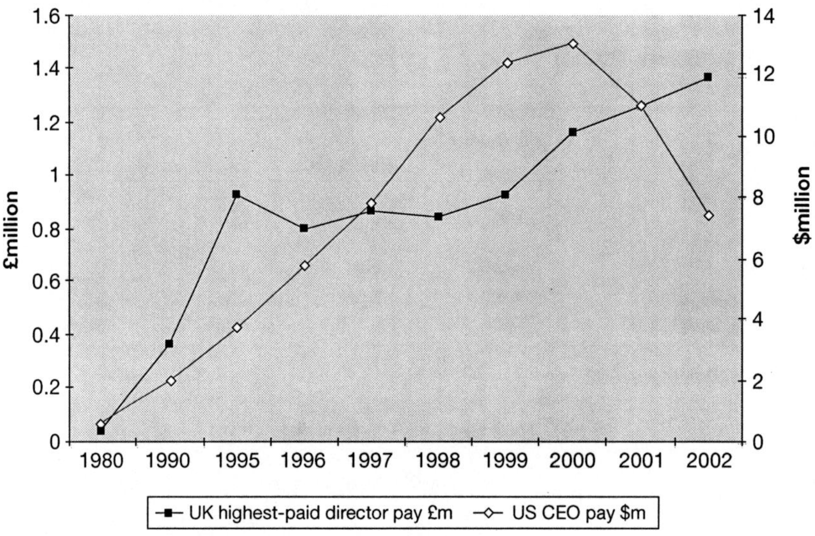


*Exhibit 3.7 Trends in executive pay, UK and USA*

*Source*: Datastream (UK data), Sklar et al. (2002) (US data)

The real-pay increases obtained by CEOs were shared by a few divisional heads and the chief finance officer (CFO) so that, as Exhibit 3.8 shows, in UK giant companies finance directors typically get half what the CEO is paid. However, the increases enjoyed by the CEO and other key senior managers are not shared by the majority of other employees inside the giant firm. The overall effect has been a dramatic increase in top-to-bottom inequality within the giant firm. Exhibit 3.5 illustrates this point by presenting comparative data on the US pay of production workers in manufacturing, construction workers and non-supervisory workers in services. Taken together, these are the rank and file who account for four-fifths of US non-farm employment. The real pay for this huge group of ordinary workers declines fractionally over twenty years to $26,000 so that the top-to-bottom multipicand against giant-firm CEOs increases from fifty to 525 times at the peak and 281 times in 2002. As for the UK, the comparable ratio starts at a very much more modest level with giant-company CEOs earning less than ten times the pay of workers in FTSE 100 survivor companies in 1980. Yet the contrast between flat real pay for ordinary workers and large sustained real increases for CEOs in the UK (as in the USA) opens up the differential to fifty times by 2002, by which time the British have normalized the relativities that prevailed in the USA twenty years previously.

Equally interesting, other senior executives with serious management responsibilities have not shared in the good fortune of giant-company CEOs. In the UK, senior politicians including the prime minister, senior civil servants including the permanent secretary or head of the Department of Health and senior armed-forces officers including all

**Exhibit 3.8** *Quintile breakdown of total pay of FTSE 100 company senior executives 2001–2 (companies ranked by turnover)*

| | *Quintile group* | | | | | *Average* | *Ratio Q%:Q1 (top to bottom)* |
|---|---|---|---|---|---|---|---|
| | Q1<br>£ | Q2<br>£ | Q3<br>£ | Q4<br>£ | Q5<br>£ | £ | Ratio |
| Turnover (£m) | 1,029 | 2,475 | 4,236 | 7,760 | 29,690 | 9,119 | 30:1 |
| Chief Executive | 933,000 | 1,061,000 | 947,000 | 1,008,000 | 1,678,000 | 1,130,000 | 1.8:1 |
| Finance Director | 464,000 | 516,000 | 514,000 | 587,000 | 821,000 | 583,000 | 1.8:1 |
| Divisional Director | 459,000 | 437,000 | 487,000 | 560,000 | 915,000 | 579,000 | 2:1 |

*Source*: Erturk, I., Froud, J., Johal, S. and Williams, K. 'Pay for corporate performance or pay as social division. Rethinking the problem of top management pay in giant corporations' 2005 *Competition and Change*, vol. 9, no. 1, pp. 49–74

*Note*: Bonus is calculated as a percentage of base salary

our generals, earn less than £200,000 per annum. The Permanent Secretary of the Department of Health, who arguably has the most difficult management job in the UK, earned just under £170,000 in January 2003 (*Guardian Society* web site, accessed 13 April 2004). And, as Exhibit 3.6 shows, the position is similar in smaller British companies where a CEO is doing well to be earning £150,000 plus car and expenses. In the UK, senior-management employees in the public and private sectors continue to earn moderate sums that are not much larger than what their direct predecessors earned twenty years ago, while their counterparts in giant firms have managed fivefold real-pay increases over the past twenty years.

At this point we could echo Marvin Gaye and ask, what's going on? The answer depends on how we conceive the process and its facilitators. Where mainstream strategist and business analysts would describe the CEO behaviour as 'rent-seeking', we would prefer to conceptualize it as value skimming. Furthermore, while empirical work has identified company size as an important influence on CEO pay, we would prefer a more complex account of enabling conditions which combine variably to produce the same result of pay increases year after year. This analysis is in itself interesting because it increases our understanding of how present-day capitalism operates. In particular, we can consider how giant-firm CEOs are able to look after themselves financially in a world where they do not determine their own pay.

Most mainstream economists and finance academics would use the term 'rent-seeking' to describe giant-firm CEO behaviour. We are disinclined to use the rent-seeking descriptor because this implies the search for some kind of surplus over and above a fair market rate. This is hardly a sensible way of constructing the CEO pay problem because, as Khurana (2002) has argued with some force, there is no market in CEOs, who are mostly recruited internally or on a network basis. Likewise, the idea of a market rate takes us towards a general economic law of value which relates price to marginal utility or some other general principle. This again is hardly sensible given Cutler's (1978) classic essay which disputed the possibility of any such law of value more than twenty years ago.

In our view, it is better to think about CEO pay as value skimming, which represents the quiet, unnoticed enrichment of the few and stands in contrast to the difficult process of value creation (for the many) which dominates the rhetoric of shareholder value and VBM. Value creation through strategies of cost reduction, business-portfolio change and suchlike usually requires considerable management exertion and offers uncertain returns to effort, with such returns divided between many claimants, including the workforce and all the shareholders whose individual benefits will be small. By way of contrast, value skimming requires only an elite structural position where one or a few senior figures can take advantage of ownership rights, deals or operations close to a large income stream. This then allows a small number of individuals to take out large sums, classically in the form of a few cents on every dollar of cost or revenue stream, so that the many other stakeholders indirectly suffer small individual losses.

In two classic cases, this is the modus operandi of private-equity principals or investment bankers. In a leveraged buy-out or private-equity transaction, most of the funding will be borrowed as debt which caps the capital repayment to bond holders so that those who hold a small tranche of the capital in the form of equity can make large gains on their equity stake from a modest increase in the total realized value of the business at the point of resale. Or in the case of large hostile take-overs worth several billion and involving bid premia of, say, 30 per cent over the pre-bid market price, a few investment bankers or other professional advisers can charge either side multimillion dollar fees without anybody noticing. In our view, CEO pay increases represent a third classic instance of value skimming of a slightly different kind because there is not one transaction event that allows skimming at a particular moment in time for the few who provide services or equity. But multibillion turnover in giant firms does create the opportunity for few top executives to draw mega-pay without greatly reducing the wages of other employees or the distribution of profit to shareholders. The leverage for wealth creation through value skimming is greatest at the moment of ownership change in financial deal-making, but in the aggregate, the largest ongoing opportunities for high incomes through value skimming probably arise from the continuing operations of giant corporations.

This argument takes us to the point where we introduce the idea of enabling conditions. The empirical tests by finance academics on the determinants of CEO pay have turned up two main results. First, as already noted in the previous section, finance testers have found that the relation between pay and performance is weak. Second, and more positively, they have found that the relation between pay and company size is strong because CEOs in larger companies claim larger salaries. As Conyon and Murphy observe, 'the best documented empirical finding in the executive compensation literature is the consistency of the relation between CEO pay and company size' (2000: 651). A recent meta-analysis of previous studies of CEO pay confirmed a weak link with performance but a strong link with firm size: Tosi et al. (2000: 301) conclude that firm size accounts for more than 40 per cent of the variance in total CEO pay, while firm performance accounts for less than 5 per cent of the variance.

This empirical association is important but arguably also unimaginative because pay can be related to other single variables: for example, the US public-interest group, United for a Fair Economy (UFE), has demonstrated an interesting cross-section relation whereby CEOs claim higher salaries in socially irresponsible giant companies. In 2002, UFE reported that CEO pay in twenty-three companies under investigation for accounting irregularities was 70 per cent more than the average for the 360 companies included in the *Business Week* annual survey of CEO pay. In 2003 they reported that in the twenty-four companies with the most subsidiaries in offshore tax havens, CEO pay was 67 per cent higher, just as it was higher in the companies announcing most lay-offs (Anderson et al. 2003). If this relation is not entirely unexpected, we would caution against attaching too much importance to any one variable (be it size, social irresponsibility or whatever) because the intellectual task is to understand how CEO pay rises are enabled by several heterogeneous variables.

To begin with, CEO pay rises from the early 1990s onwards were obtained in a specific institutional context. The irony here was that the procedures of good governance, which were designed to restrain CEO pay and to discourage unjustified increases, probably had the perverse effect of ratcheting up the going rate. In both the UK and USA, good governance in the 1990s promoted increased pay disclosure, determination of pay by remuneration committees and the involvement of consultants to provide unbiased comparative information as a basis for committee decision. If the aim was to curb pay increases unjustified by performance as Greenbury (1995) recognized, the result was often an institutionalized acceleration of pay increases. Disclosure resulted in the publication of more and more information, often without making it easier for outsiders to understand the terms and conditions of bonus schemes and suchlike. Simultaneously, the presentation of peer-group comparisons by consultancy firms undermined the ability of remuneration committees to resist comparability claims for CEOs which gave them the going rate, or even brought them into the top quartile and encouraged leap-frogging behaviour which served to increase the mean and median (see Ezzamel and Watson 1998, Bender 2003 on the UK). Our older readers will remember that in the 1970s comparability increases for unionized manual workers were widely criticized because their (non-proven) consequence was price inflation. After the 1980s, such comparability increases have been abolished for workers and institutionalized for bosses who often escape criticism even though the (certain) consequence is increasing inequality.

Within this institutional frame, the CEO pay increases depend on structural enablers, just as earlier pay increases for unionized workers depended on full employment and the ability of employers to pass on cost increases. In our view, the three key enablers are: first, a company's membership of the FTSE 100 or S&P 500 as a kind of club whose CEO members get a going rate; second, high sales turnover of at least £500 million or more which allows top management to claim a few million in pay without obviously hurting workers or shareholders; and third, healthy profitability as the outward and visible sign of management effort.

In distinguishing three enablers, we are unpacking the many things that the empiricist testers jumble together as firm size. Normally, all three enablers are aligned together because a high turnover provides the basis for a large lump of profit, and long-term profit is the usual precondition for the market capitalization that ensures continued membership of the FTSE 100 or S&P 500. The position is altogether more interesting if only two of three enabling conditions are met. If a FTSE 100 company such as the airline British Airways (BA) operates in a cyclical business and posts a loss in one year, its CEO would still expect to receive the FTSE 100 going rate; but if the BA CEO retires to run a start-up discount airline, it is simply not possible to pay FTSE 100 CEO wage levels from modest sales revenue without eroding profits and alienating shareholders. The timeframe is also relevant here: short-term declines in profitability often irk shareholders who then take a new interest in governance and pay, while sustained unprofitability in the medium and long term usually results in ejection from the FTSE 100 with subsequent downward pressure on CEO wages. These patterns of variation in enabling conditions can be seen more clearly from Exhibits 3.5, 3.6 and 3.8 which, in different ways, demonstrate the importance of high turnover and the influence of FTSE membership.

Exhibit 3.8 presents relevant evidence for the UK and show that the relation between CEO pay and company membership of the FTSE membership is much the same as in the case of footballers' pay and club membership of the UK's Premier League. Exhibit 3.8 classifies the FTSE 100 into quintile groups by turnover and shows that CEO pay does rise with company size, but by no means proportionately. In 2001–2, corporate turnover in Quintile 5 is nearly thirty times as large as the £1 billion turnover in Quintile 1 but CEO pay at under £1.7 million in Quintile 5 is less than twice as large as in Quintile 1. Thus, the going rate for the job of a CEO is currently at least £1 million a year regardless of company size within the FTSE 100. As previously mentioned, this also has a direct effect on the pay of finance and divisional directors who tend to earn around half the pay of their CEO. Thus, by entering the FTSE 100, a company effectively adopts a new set of pay norms for its elite personnel along with a rhetoric about the need to attract, retain and motivate talent (in an international market), although the measurement of CEO contribution is, of course, much more difficult than in the case of a goal-scoring striker. If Exhibit 3.8 is compared with Exhibit 3.6, it is also clear that non-FTSE 100 companies, just like non-Premier League football clubs in the UK, pay on a much lower scale. The CEO of a relatively large non-FTSE 100 company with several hundred million pounds of turnover may well be earning around £150,000 a year, or just one-tenth of the pay of his counterpart in a small FTSE 100 company. Exhibit 3.6 also shows that this falling away of CEO pay with company size is equally pronounced in the USA, suggesting that fat-cat pay is largely a FTSE 100 or S&P 500 phenomenon.

The basic impossibility of mega-pay for the CEO of a smaller company can be established by some back-of-envelope arithmetic. Consider the case of a medium-sized US company with a turnover of $200 million and a 5 per cent return on sales, which would generate $10 million of profit: in this case $5 million for the CEO and half that for his or her finance director and a divisional boss are obviously impossible because the cost of top pay would completely wipe out profit. At the opposite extreme, large US industrial and financial companies, such as Citibank, GE, IBM and Boeing have turnover of between $50 and $130 billion, so that CEO pay of $100 million or more will barely register on the shareholder radar as long as stock prices are going up. Even with generous pay for other senior executives, a top management pay bill of up to $500 million each year would only account for 2.5 per cent of net profit at a firm such as GE. Exhibit 3.9 presents more systematic evidence on CEO pay as a percentage of turnover and net income in the S&P 500 over the ten years from 1992. It shows that CEO pay (including bonus and exercised options) accounts for around 0.04 to 0.12 per cent of sales (turnover) and 0.56 to 3.25 per cent of net income (profit). In nine of the eleven years, CEO pay accounts for less than 0.10 per cent of turnover. And, although the trend is upwards for much of the 1990s, cyclical effects are also important so that the CEO pay as a proportion of net income is actually higher in 1992 than in 1999 and the really spectacular increase to over 3 per cent comes in 2001 and 2002 as profits turn down.

Within the frame of proceduralized governance, the enabling conditions ensured that US and UK giant-firm CEOs were winners in a process of value skimming. Many CEOs

*Exhibit 3.9 Average CEO pay compared with average sales and net income for S&P 500 companies, 1992–2002*

| CEO pay as a % of: | *1992* | *1993* | *1994* | *1995* | *1996* | *1997* | *1998* | *1999* | *2000* | *2001* | *2002* |
|---|---|---|---|---|---|---|---|---|---|---|---|
| Sales | 0.04 | 0.05 | 0.04 | 0.05 | 0.06 | 0.08 | 0.11 | 0.09 | 0.12 | 0.07 | 0.07 |
| Net income | 1.40 | 1.13 | 0.56 | 0.72 | 0.79 | 1.16 | 1.57 | 1.16 | 1.60 | 2.08 | 3.25 |

*Source*: Data extracted from Compustat ExecuComp

*Note*: Sales are the net annual sales as reported by the company and net income is the net income after extraordinary items and discontinued operations. CEO pay includes salary, bonus, other annual payments, total value of restricted stock granted, net value of stock options exercised, long-term incentive payouts and all other payments

of the 1990s defended their unprecedented pay rises by arguing they had made much more for their shareholders than they had ever taken out for themselves. Just before the collapse of the Tyco share price followed by his personal disgrace and indictment on criminal charges, Denis Kozlowski, Tyco's CEO, publicly defended his 1999 pay award by claiming 'while I gained $139 million (in stock options), I created $37 billion in wealth for our shareholders' (*Business Week*, 17 April 2000). The next chapter on financialization challenges this alibi by reviewing the evidence on giant-firm performance and management's contribution to value creation.

Chapter 4

# Financialization and corporate performance

This chapter develops an argument about whether and how financialization can serve as a social-scientific concept for thinking about the intrusion of the capital market and its effects on giant-firm strategy. In our view, this is possible provided we reject the political-economy approach to financialization and adopt a cultural-economy approach. The political-economy approach is to search for a set of generalizable relations (such as increased distribution to shareholders) which would structurally distinguish a financialized economy from (earlier) forms of capitalism, according to one or two key measures. Our cultural-economy approach instead argues that the rhetoric of shareholder value sets management on a utopian quest for growth and higher returns for capital which has variable and uncertain consequences. This argument is supported by long-run evidence on the FTSE 100 and S&P 500 which suggests that giant-firm management is often ineffectual in creating value through strategic interventions to improve the numbers. Given this discrepancy between promise and outcome, we envisage a financialized economy as one that runs on different narratives of achievement and assertions of identity and which has some trouble with the alignment of saying and doing.

This argument is developed by ranging across several literatures and by reviewing the evidence on value creation in giant US and UK firms. In the first section, the political-economy literature on financialization provides our point of departure. Authors such as Boyer and O'Sullivan in different ways try to find distinctive, durable and predictable consequences of financialization, such as asset-price bubbles or increased distribution to shareholders, which would then define and distinguish a new form of capitalism. In our view, such distinguishing consequences are very unlikely in so far as the driver of change is the mutable social rhetoric of shareholder value. This rhetoric adds a variety of (changing and contradictory) financial pressures on giant-firm managers, who then must accommodate them through different combinations of saying and doing within specific structural constraints. If social rhetoric is the driver, the new cultural-economy approach is immediately more interesting because it is sensitive to the constitutive powers of discourse. At the same time, we would caution against extending the overstated history-of-science arguments about how a discourse such as economics frames the economy. The point about management discourse and practice is that promising value is not the same as delivering value. Therefore we align more with the British cultural-economy approach, represented by MacKenzie's work on performativity in finance theory, which highlights the gap between saying and doing and the empirical possibilities of measuring verisimilitude.

Thus, we move from the idea of shareholder value as a rhetoric to explore the discrepancy between promise and outcome which forms the starting point for an empirical investigation in the second section of this chapter. Here we present evidence on long-run value creation by giant firms in the US S&P 500 and the UK FTSE 100, as well as on distributive shifts between capital and labour. From this evidence we develop an argument about management agency. In our view, US or UK giant-firm management can neither take the credit for the general increase in share prices during the 1990s, nor entirely avoid responsibility for mediocre ROCE in many firms or for modest aggregate sales growth in any group of giant firms over the same period. The third and final section of this chapter then explores and explains this discrepancy between promise and outcome by developing and illustrating the argument that giant-firm managers typically have access to many strategic moves but few levers that will transform the financial numbers. This argument marks a decisive break with classical strategy which generally assumes that management does have access to resources or positional levers which deliver results. In turn, this break provides the basis for the Chapter 5 analysis of management moves after financialization.

## POLITICAL AND CULTURAL ECONOMY

After mainstream economics took a technical turn towards what its internal critics call 'autism' (see, for example, Raveaud 2003), political and cultural economy have over the past thirty years flourished as intellectual alternatives that are capable of producing generalizations about capitalism and thus are able to engage a non-specialist audience. Liberal economic prescriptions dominate public policy in an age where all must support market allocation, low tax and small government. Yet mainstream economics has always had little to say about capitalism and that has created opportunities for political economy which theorizes social embeddedness, institutions and the role of collective social actors such as classes. The success of political economy can partly be attributed to its use of cartoon concepts like 'Fordism' or 'Rhenish capitalism' which package national and temporal differences just as they supposedly explain economic performance. Cultural economy, on the other hand, reflects more recent interests in the constitutive power of discourse arising especially from arguments about how the discourse of economics formats the economy.

We will discuss political and cultural economy in turn, beginning with the political economy literature on financialization which was produced in two phases. In a first phase, the US publications of the early 1990s by Useem (1993), Davis and Thompson (1994) and Fligstein (1990) responded to the leveraged buy out (LBO) and merger movement of the 1980s, often from a sociological or organizational perspective. In a second phase around 2000, political economists including Boyer (2000), Aglietta (2000) and O'Sullivan (2000) joined a transatlantic debate on the shareholder-value movement of the 1990s, with its explicit promotion of new objectives in Europe as well as in the USA. This literature was diverse because financialization could be accommodated as a new development within many existing problematics. Some of the resulting conjectures were bold and interesting, but the results of argument and debate were curiously indecisive because the political economists asserted but could not establish or prove that financialization existed as a set of empirical consequences for macro-economic dynamics or corporate-control regimes.

For a regulationist like Boyer (2000), financialization represented the macro-economic possibility of a new 'wealth-based growth regime' where the mass of the population were not only wage earners but also share owners. This was then the latest in a series of putative new growth regimes that could restore coherence and replace a faltering Fordism, which regulationists credit as the basis for thirty glorious years of prosperity up to the 1970s. Boyer's macro-model of the wealth-based growth regime highlights new problems about asset-price bubbles and also generates interesting paradoxes. In particular, it reverses the classic Keynesian suppositions about the benefits of high wages in sustaining aggregate demand in a wealth-based regime, where wage cuts increase share prices and thus have positive wealth effects. The problem is that these interesting predictions are derived from a highly simplified model which makes unrealistic assumptions. The immediate problem of Boyer's analysis is not the exclusion of commodity trade and capital flows, but the assumption that share ownership is widespread or universal. As we have demonstrated elsewhere (Froud, Haslam et al. 2001), in both the UK and the USA only households in the top half of the income distribution have significant share holdings, so that financialization in its current Anglo-Saxon form does not suspend the important link between the composition of employment and composition of demand (Froud et al. 1997).

For theorists of national forms of capitalism, financialization was inserted into another pre-existing problematic about bank versus market-based capitalisms. These concepts always mapped rather untidily onto national specificities when, for example, there were large differences about the inclusion of labour in the German and French forms of bank-based capitalism. Nevertheless, best-selling authors such as Hutton (1995) established a caricatured contrast between Anglo-American capitalism, whose forms of calculation were financialized and short-term, compared with Rhenish capitalism, where the forms of calculation were more productionist. Dore (2000) then inserted financialization into this pre-existing frame so that financialization became a mutation in the national form of Anglo-American capitalism, but with the possibility that it might spread into other national forms whose institutions had a limited capacity to frustrate change. This opened the way for subsequent debate about the extent of change in national models where the evidence of change was ambiguous. Morin (2000: 41) suggested that French network capitalism had changed considerably under the influence of US investors, who by 1997 owned 35 per cent of French shares. Yet change has until recently been much slower and the results ambiguous in the German case (Jürgens et al. 2000), while in Japan the basic institutional preconditions for change were absent (Morgan and Takahashi 2002).

From a different, more Chandlerian point of view, political economists also discussed the implications of shareholder value for corporate control and behaviour in giant firms. Thus, O'Sullivan (2000) hypothesized a historical transition in US corporate strategy after 1980 from 'retain and reinvest' to 'downsize and distribute' which defined a new era of financialization. According to O'Sullivan (2000: 186), the historical norm for giant US corporations had been, 'the retention of corporate revenues for reinvestment in plant, equipment and personnel', yet from the 1980s, the US giant-firm strategy changed to 'downsize and distribute' as increased competition and shareholder value produced a 'growing propensity of US corporations in the 1980s to downsize their workforces and to distribute corporate revenues to stockholders'.

O'Sullivan's book includes subtleties about the increasing remoteness of top executives who no longer understood the internal 'capabilities' necessary for innovation (O'Sullivan 2000: 209) and recognizes unevenness in different sectors such as cars and electronics, as well as the quasi-solution of investing in relatively narrow and concentrated skills bases (O'Sullivan 2000: 226). However, her basic proposition about the shift to downsize and distribute is open to empirical question. The increase in the proportion of post-tax income distributed from its long-term level of around 45 per cent is apparently modest on O'Sullivan's own evidence. The complication of share buy-backs is noted, but there is no discussion of the total distribution of dividends and interest to shareholders and bondholders in a US corporate sector which is substituting debt for equity, nor is there any discussion of their shares of cash rather than of profit (O'Sullivan 2000: 192–4). The evidence of downsizing (O'Sullivan 2000: 190–1) focuses on how the disemployment of blue and white collar workers was led by America's largest corporations in the 1980s and 1990s, but the book includes no aggregate figures on giant-company employment nor any figures on the balance between job destruction and creation by sector, even though one key chapter considers the 'new venture model' and Silicon Valley (O'Sullivan 2000: 226–30).

If this represents a particular problem about conjecture running ahead of evidence, O'Sullivan also faces general problems which are common to many different kinds of political economy writing on financialization. Put simply, the problem is that authors as diverse as Boyer and O' Sullivan share a mechanical, relational concept of the economy whose supposedly productive logic has been overlaid by finance to establish a new epoch. Within this frame, the aim of political economy is then to find definite effects in terms of process or outcomes (increased distribution, asset-price bubbles or whatever) which distinguish financialized capitalism from earlier forms of capitalism.

Though this is undoubtedly appealing, in our view, this approach rests on a fundamental misapprehension first, if (as we argued in the last chapter) the driver of shareholder value is a social rhetoric, second, if the nature and form of the demands are variable and, third, if the corporate response involves saying as well as doing. Under these conditions, financialization is not anchored in some behavioural fundamental of firms or households which has a status similar to that of the *General Theory*'s marginal propensity to consume of less than one (Keynes 1936). The implication is that, whether we face a new form of capitalism or not, we need to think about what is going on in a different kind of way. Thus, we have elsewhere argued that financialization inaugurates a form of 'coupon pool capitalism' where the capital market stands between households and firms who both invest in coupons or various classes of public and private security (Froud, Johal et al. 2002). This changes behaviour to create open dynamics and variable results distinguished by instability, reversibility and unpredictability. In contrast to these political-economy arguments, our diagram of monetary flows and effects under coupon-pool capitalism is not some kind of macro-model that specifies a coherent and self-supporting configuration that predicts outcomes; the diagram only provides a kind of check list for what needs to be investigated and analysed in each new national conjuncture.

While some issues can be explored and resolved through empirical investigation and calibration, the evidence will often be ambiguous so that it does not necessarily resolve all our problems. This is inevitable when available evidence is often organized in unhelpful or uninformative categories. Consider, for example, the striking increase in corporate holdings of financial assets in all the advanced countries, which in the US quadrupled in value from $1.5 billion in 1973 to more than $6 billion in real terms by 2000 as Exhibit 4.1 illustrates. The increasing relative and absolute importance of financial assets against tangible assets is immediately significant for political economy because it suggests that financialized capitalism has finally succeeded in realizing what Nitzan (1998) identifies as its long-term goal of redefining capital in pecuniary terms distinct from any physical embodiment in plant and equipment. Unfortunately, the empirics hardly justify such conclusions because 'corporate financial assets' is a kind of dustbin category in official statistics that includes everything that is not tangible fixed assets. The internal subdivisions within the category only increase the mystery because a large and growing proportion of corporate financial assets are classified as 'miscellaneous assets', a subcategory which in the USA now account for 70 per cent of all corporate financial assets. The category of corporate financial assets certainly includes goodwill arising from acquisitions, as well

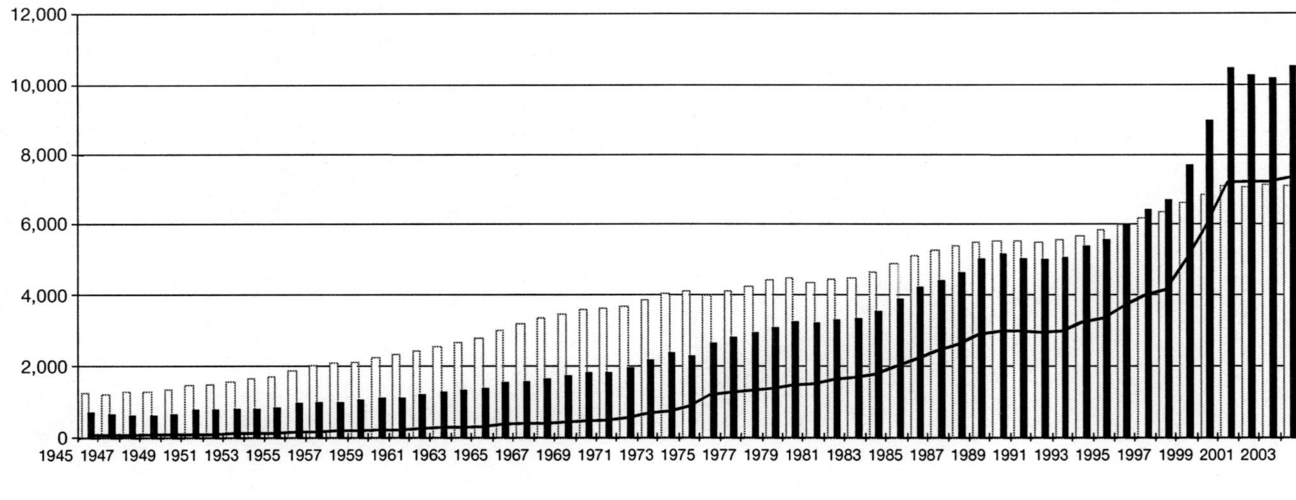


**Exhibit 4.1** *US corporate tangible and financial assets (in real 2003 values)*

*Source*: US Federal Reserve

*Notes*: Fixed assets include real estate, equipment, software and inventories, all valued at historic cost. Financial assets include cash, investments, trade receivables and the miscellaneous category listed separately as securities valued at market prices which increased hugely in the 1990s bull market. While such increases in the corporate financial asset base do reflect significant economy-wide developments, their short- and long-term significance for corporate behaviour and performance is unclear.

If political economy offers an established literature on financialization, cultural economy represents a new approach. The difference of cultural economy is best understood in terms of its relation to what DuGay and Pryke (2002: 11) term 'technical economics'. Political economy competes and overlaps with 'technical economics' through the work of academics such as Boyer who both do the algebra and develop concepts designed to challenge those of mainstream economics. By way of contrast, cultural economy eschews technical economics in favour of a kind of commentary on economics and politics whose antecedents are earlier French history of natural science and technology authors such as Latour and Callon, as well as Bourdieuvian sociology. The central assertion is that the logic of the economic world is not discovered by discourse but created by discourse because, 'economics in the broad sense of the term, performs, shapes and formats the economy, rather than observing how it functions' (Callon 1998: 2). Thus, 'the economy is embedded not in society but in economics' (Callon 1998: 30) or, more provocatively, 'capitalism is an invention of anti-capitalists' (Barry et al. 2002: 297). These quotes nicely illustrate the French intellectual taste for paradox and overstatement which, in our view, should not be treated with exaggerated respect.

In deflating such overstatement, it may be useful to distinguish between what might be called the holographic assumption and the interest in infelicity as two elements that coexist in variable combination in much cultural-economy analysis:

## Holography

Holography denotes the tendency of many cultural economists to propose generalities about the constitutive power of discourse which few could disagree with after the cultural turn. The holographic assumption has its main field of application in historical studies not in redoing economics or understanding the economy; and holography may not be relevant to redoing strategy or understanding the consequences of shareholder value.

The issues here have been focused by recent debates about the relation between economics and the economy. Here, Danny Miller (2002: 219) has introduced the term 'projection' when he argues in general terms that Michel Callon 'treats the economic model of the market as though it were core to actual economies rather than a projection of economists'. In our view, Miller's term 'projection' misses the point because the cultural-economy concept of the process is more like holography whereby a two-dimensional source provides a three-dimensional image with parallax and depth of field thanks to the properties of light and without any projector (Saxby 1994). If we substitute discourse for light, we then have DuGay and Pryke's position that economic objects are not observed but 'constituted through the discourses used to describe them and to act upon them' (DuGay and Pryke 2002: 2). Discourses are to be understood broadly as a material ensemble of language and techniques: 'Economic discourse here is not simply a matter of beliefs, values and symbols but rather a form of representational and technological (i.e. 'cultural') practice that constitutes the spaces within which economic action is formatted and framed' (DuGay and Pryke 2002: 2).

In response to such holographic generalities, we would make two points. First, if discourse is defined sufficiently broadly, the representational propositions must be uncontestably true and not necessarily trite because they open up a wide field of investigation. Second, the propositions in effect formalize the working assumptions of historiography, represented in the history of economic policy by authors such as Tomlinson (1981), who long ago recognized that policy objects were constituted not found. Any history of the macro-economy in the 1940s or 1950s would note that the calculation of an 'inflationary gap' presupposes some form of national-income accounting, while the management of that gap requires appropriate fiscal practices and instruments for demand management through credit controls and suchlike, as well as the authority of the *General Theory* as a canonical source that theorizes the new object. We make this point to establish that, before or after the cultural turn, the holographic assumption can open up interesting lines of analysis, and its main function is to move what was previously disparaged as 'sociology of knowledge' or 'history of thought' from a secondary, marginal status towards centre stage.

From this point of view, the difficult issue is about the relation of the newly promoted commentary discourse to the technical practice and substantive knowledge. It is immediately striking that, after making their holographic statement, DuGay and Pryke (2002: 11) assume that 'cultural economy' will coexist with 'technical economics' which is presumably equations, algebra and modelling for those who have concepts, techniques and influence on the world but lack sociological insight. These misgivings are reinforced if we consider the notorious paucity of Callon's evidence about how markets work or the poverty of the specific concepts used to understand the topography of the economy in recent cultural-economy surveys. Thus, Amin and Thrift (2004), in the introduction to their cultural-economy reader, locate their essays along the nodes of a 'value chain' without any recognition that this concept is highly problematic and (as we argue in the next chapter) may incorporate ideas of industry that are becoming obsolete after financialization: 'Cultural economy is in the process of re-figuring every aspect of the value chain, from production through to consumption. In this book, we look at the various cultural transubstantiations of the economic, by following this value chain in six steps' (Amin and Thrift 2004: xxi).

Insofar as the cultural-economy project runs on the holographic assumption, it must reinscribe the categories of mainstream economics with an added epistemological sophistication. The reinscription problem arises from the way in which cultural economy abandons alternative conceptual formulations within a discourse such as economics in favour of critical sociological insight about economics. If this is not a model for redoing economics, it is equally not a model for redoing strategy discourse or more specifically understanding the consequences of the shareholder-value rhetoric. And it is fortunate that we can draw on another aspect of cultural economy through its concern with infelicity that will immediately help us think through those consequences.

## Infelicity

Infelicity arises from the interest of some cultural economists in how things miscarry in the performative relation between saying and doing. The interest in infelicity opens up interesting possibilities of analysis in many fields where enactment miscarries and this kind of infelicity is highly relevant to redoing strategy discourse or understanding the consequences of shareholder value in terms of discrepancy between promise and outcome.

The concept of performativity goes back to Oxford linguistic philosophy's interest in statements that do more than describe facts in a positivistic way. Hence, J. L. Austin's focus on 'performative utterances' where, 'the issuing of the utterance is the performing of an action' as in rituals such as the naming of a vessel or the christening of a baby (Austin 1975: 6). These examples of social ritual allowed Bourdieu (1991: 73) to extricate enactment from language and assimilate it into sociology with his famous observation that 'the conditions of felicity are social'. But, more to the point, from Austin onwards the British have always had an interest in infelicities, which Austin originally classified as misfires, misexecutions and misinvocations. This tradition is continued through the recent work of MacKenzie (2004) and MacKenzie and Millo (2003) on the role of option-pricing theory in creating the financial derivatives market. This starts from the Callonesque assumption that economics performs the economy it describes but also crucially takes the imperfect and variable approximation between market prices and theoretical prediction as an empirical object of investigation.

MacKenzie's work on Austinian performativity in the options market represents a different kind of critical rationality because, instead of assuming or celebrating the holographic capacity of discourse, MacKenzie (2004: 306) examines 'the effect of the practical adoption of a theory or model on its verisimilitude'. Such verisimilitude can be empirically investigated in terms of market-price deviation from the theoretical prescription, and MacKenzie's empirics then show a very interesting two-stage pattern of more and less verisimilitude with approximation followed by renewed discrepancy. Hence, MacKenzie and Millo (2003) found that the initial adoption of models such as Black Scholes (now used extensively for option pricing) changed futures market prices towards greater compliance with the model in the 1976–87 period (MacKenzie and Millo 2003: 127), but after the 1987 stock market crash a new empirical discrepancy opened up because, 'the market has come to expect crashes' which are not in the model (MacKenzie and Millo 2003: 131). This is the kind of market behaviour anticipated by George Soros (2003) in a social world where human subjects and institutions are reflexive. The renewed discrepancy opens up several lines of conjecture for MacKenzie, including the possibility that, 'a theory can be counterperformative i.e. its widespread adoption can undermine the preconditions of its own empirical validity' (2004: 306).

Thus MacKenzie (2004: 328) suggests, 'Austinian performativity may be relatively rare' and the options market before 1987 represents an interesting special case, not some kind of prototype for wider social analysis.

How does this interest in infelicity help with our problem about the relation between shareholder value and some set of putative consequences termed financialization? Our answer is that, if a tightly specified technical model used by the financially literate is not realized in futures market prices, it is all the more unlikely that the rhetorical demand for shareholder value would be realized in any measurable improvement in corporate performance or some simple adjustment in distribution from labour to capital. This establishes the presupposition that we are probably looking for discrepancy between rhetorical promise and outcome, but the extent and form of any discrepancy needs to be empirically investigated and the next section turns to this task.

## GIANT-FIRM VALUE CREATION

Chapter 3 observed that top managers were awarded handsome pay increases in the twenty years after 1980. This section now examines what they delivered for other stakeholders, especially shareholders and workers, over the same period. The argument from evidence on S&P 500 and FTSE 100 firms highlights two key points which suggest continuity not change. First, top management's universal success at securing personal gains from value skimming far outruns its general ability to create value for shareholders in giant firms by raising ROCE or (organically) growing the firm. Second, this mediocre record on value creation is not generally coupled with ruthless redistribution whereby management downsizes the workforce to facilitate increased pay-out to shareholders. The empirics on the S&P 500 and the FTSE 100 therefore suggest a major discrepancy between the promise of shareholder value and the outcome that is delivered; and that observation, in turn, raises a series of very interesting questions about whether giant-firm CEOs are neither the action-man heroes of the business press nor the anti-labour villains of the Left, but just another ineffectual officer class.

The story of corporate performance and distribution is complex because the USA and UK offer two national stories with different variables and dynamics. The USA is the world's only superpower with a high-tech capability to match, and this economic base contrasts with that of the UK, which represents a subaltern capitalism on the edge of Europe where the expansion of services provides partial compensation for the halving of manufacturing employment over the past twenty-five years. Within each national story the S&P 500 and FTSE 100 provide us with a changing population of firms because new firms join the index each year while others leave. A firm may exit because its share price and market capitalization declines with (relative) failure. More commonly, a firm exits because acquisition or merger ends its existence as an independent entity, though its financial results may continue to be included in the index if the acquiring company is part of the group of giant firms that comprise the index. This is a major complication, given the frantic pace of merger and acquisition between public companies which, as our analysis shows, has removed more than half the members over twenty years. By 2003, only twenty-eight UK firms from the FTSE 100 of 1983 and only 185 firms from the S&P 500 of 1983 survived as independent entities and had been continuously part of their national indexes for twenty years. This complication is such that the exhibits on performance in this section present data on both constituents and survivors, showing two different populations of giant firms in each country. Constituents are the changing group of firms that are in the index in any one individual year, whilst survivors are that much smaller group of firms that survived independently over the twenty-year period and were continuously part of the index.

Whilst much basic information is available through standard databases such as Datastream in the UK and Compustat in the USA, this is not organized in a such a way as to easily allow production of long-run consistent data: for example, the time-series data on a specific group of firms, such as survivors, has to be derived a year at a time using manual lists of surviving, continuous membership companies to produce a supplementary dataset. The measures of value-creating performance are much more straightforward: the exhibits that follow present data on total shareholder return (divided into dividends and share-price appreciation), ROCE and growth in (real) sales and profit. If the measures are fairly obvious, most of the other choices need some explanation or justification.

- In the interests of clarity and intelligibility most of the value-creation measures are considered over a twenty-year period from 1983 to 2002. The start and finish years were approximately matched in cyclical terms as both represented weak years with low profitability in the business cycle. There is also a practical reason for choosing 1983, as this is the first year for which suitable UK data is available. The FTSE 100 index was officially formed on 1 January 1984 and so 1983 then becomes the start date where we summarize the performance of the 1984 list in the previous financial year. The year 2002 was chosen as the most recent year for which data was available and, only after the work was finished, did we fully realize the weak profitability of that year complicated twenty-year comparisons of profits and dividends, though not of sales and head-count employment.
- Again, in the interests of clarity and intelligibility, the exhibits usually present aggregate data on the group of giant firms. This effectively focuses attention on the performance of the average giant firm, which is sensible given the political economy search for general consequences and the claims about changes in US corporate-control regimes. The group performance also gives an indication of what the mainstream institutional investor with a broad portfolio of giant-firm

stocks can expect by way of returns. It is of course also necessary to consider the dispersion of performance between high and low performers and the causes of that dispersion. The issue of dispersion is covered in two ways: first, US and UK giant-firm ROCE is considered by quintile group in Exhibit 4.3; and second, the UK population of twenty-year survivors includes fewer than thirty companies, so we can also add Exhibit 4.9 with named UK survivors, allowing some comparison of the performance of individual companies.

- After we have summarized average performance and considered the distribution of high and low performers, it is of course still necessary to decide whether and how management should take the credit or the blame for a particular level of performance; and, as we shall see, that is not completely straightforward.

The measurement of changes in distribution, for instance between capital and labour, is much more complicated because of conceptual issues about how distribution is measured in numerator and denominator terms. This measurement issue is further complicated by limited evidence on numbers employed, pay and the national and regional location of employment for US companies where disclosure requirements in this area are limited.

- Dividend distribution to shareholders may provide a relevant measure in the UK case, but the focus on dividend distribution is inadequate in the USA where debt is being substituted for equity and shares are being brought back on a substantial scale. Thus Exhibits 4.6 and 4.7 consider these three distributions and relate them to cash or a very similar measure, earnings before interest, tax, depreciation and amortisation (EBITDA), which provides a clearer comparative long-term denominator in both the US and UK cases.
- For labour, there is a secondary problem about fragmentary evidence beyond the total head-count figures. For example, unlike in the UK, US public company accounts are not required to provide data on total labour costs. Thus, the calculation of value added and the trend of labour's share of internal costs are only possible in the UK case. In both the UK and the USA, giant-company reports and accounts do not provide a geographic breakdown of employment on a national (or sometimes even a regional) basis, so it is not possible to measure directly the shift to offshore low-wage production sites. However, in both national cases relevant evidence provides a sidelight on these issues. In the UK case, employment costs per employee (including all social charges) are available and these would probably show any substantial shift to low-wage employment. In the US case, the companies included in an official series on multinational company employment, inside and outside the USA, overlap significantly with the giant firms that comprise the S&P 500.

When all these caveats and complications have been registered, the evidence is complex, but our review suggests one simple conclusion that holds true for all groups of giant firms, whether we consider constituents or survivors or consider giant firms at the centre of capitalism in the USA against those in a subaltern economy such as the UK. The one conclusion is that, if we concentrate on giant-firm value creation that can plausibly be attributed to management, the US and UK record is disappointing and shows no signs of step-like improvements. This judgement can be supported by making four basic points about long-term value creation and distribution, using the measures described above: (1) the significance of share-price movements; (2) the stubbornness of ROCE; (3) modest growth; and (4) the complexity of redistribution.

## The significance of share-price movements

The dominant and volatile influence on giant-firm total shareholder return (TSR) after 1983 is (general) increases in share price and a rising P/E ratio. Yet giant-firm management cannot claim the credit because these price rises do not reflect purposive management action but external developments that generate windfall gains and losses for shareholders.

Overall, in this twenty-year period, general market trends in share prices during sustained bull and bear markets drive the outcome in total shareholder return in the USA and UK, with sectoral trends in the technology, media and telecoms sector also briefly important in the USA during the new-economy period from 1995 to 2000. Across all the groups over twenty years, share-price appreciation accounts for approximately 60–75 per cent of total shareholder return. As Exhibit 4.2 shows, over the whole period 1983 to 2002, 75 per cent of the annual return for S&P 500 constituents came from share-price increases and only 25 per cent from the earnings distributed as dividends. Over the same period, 63 per cent of the annual return on FTSE 100 constituents came from share-price increases and only 37 per cent from the earnings distributed as dividends. Putting this slightly differently, shareholders benefited from a near doubling of the P/E ratio in the bull market of the 1990s: the P/E ratio of S&P 500 constituents increased from an average of 14.4 in 1983–92 to 27.3 in 1993–2002 and the comparable P/Es for FTSE 100 constituents are 12.6 and 20.8.

This observation opens the way to fundamental questions about the assumptions underlying value-based management and the pay-for-performance problematic. These generally suppose the causal arrows should run one way from increased management effort and intelligent initiative through improved corporate performance and higher earnings to an increase in value through higher share price. But the arrows could be reversed. What if share prices generally have an independent life of their own driven by external variables? What if earnings rise (or fall) much more modestly than share prices, with giant-firm management assuming a dignified and rhetorical role as it generates a narrative of corporate purpose and achievement that ensures the firm participates in the windfall gains (or limits its windfall losses) in a shallow world of appearances? In deciding between these two views, the relevant and interesting issues are the strength of the external forces driving share prices and the success of giant-firm management in raising

**Exhibit 4.2** *The sources of shareholder gains in the UK and USA (based on real 2003 values)*

| | *Total shareholder returns* % | *Of which* *Share price* % | *Dividends* % | *P/E ratio (average during year)* |
|---|---|---|---|---|
| **FTSE 100 (constituents)** | | | | |
| 1983–92 | 17.6 | 72.8 | 27.2 | 12.6 |
| 1993–2002 | 10.8 | 57.2 | 42.8 | 20.8 |
| 1983–2002 | 22.2 | 63.4 | 36.6 | 17.6 |
| **FTSE 100 (survivors)** | | | | |
| 1983–1992 | 16.6 | 69.7 | 30.3 | 12.9 |
| 1993–2002 | 13.2 | 59.6 | 40.4 | 18.7 |
| 1983–2002 | 23.3 | 63.2 | 36.8 | 16.5 |
| **S&P 500 (constituents)** | | | | |
| 1983–92 | 14.3 | 65.4 | 34.6 | 14.3 |
| 1993–2002 | 18.2 | 78.8 | 21.2 | 27.3 |
| 1983–2002 | 23.0 | 74.6 | 25.4 | 22.1 |
| **S&P 500 (survivors)** | | | | |
| 1983–92 | 13.9 | 65.3 | 34.7 | 13.9 |
| 1993–2002 | 15.6 | 72.6 | 27.4 | 22.8 |
| 1983–2002 | 20.0 | 70.1 | 29.9 | 19.3 |

*Sources*: Datastream (UK data) and Compustat (US data)

*Notes*: 'Constituents' are the changing group of giant firms included in the FTSE 100 or S&P 500 each year, as newcomers enter and established firms exit when taken over or become too small to keep their membership. 'Survivors' are the subgroup of twenty-eight UK firms and 185 US firms that were in the FTSE 100 and S&P 500 in the early 1980s and have constantly remained in the relevant index over the twenty years of analysis

earnings. Our argument outlined below, which supports the shallow world presupposition, is that the exogenous forces were strong from the early 1990s and that giant-firm management struggles to raise earnings.

Through the 1990s, in both the UK and USA, share prices rose by 10–15 per cent per annum. This unprecedented price rise reflected the strength of external forces which included: first, the 'irrational exuberance' of investors emphasized by behavioural finance authors (Shiller 2000); second, declining rates of interest which orthodox finance would interpret as a decline in the discount rate applied to future earnings so that *ceteris paribus* security prices should increase; and third, institutionalized patterns of middle-class saving which, in the USA and UK, injected 10 per cent or more of GDP into the stock market for each year of the 1990s (Froud, Haslam et al. 2001: 78–9). We could debate the relative importance of these three developments and discuss whether they should be integrated into one explanation. But the more important point is that none of the three developments that boosted share prices during the 1990s had anything much to do with management agency, though they did in some cases help boost management reputation, encouraging the 1990s cult of the CEO.

## The stubbornness of ROCE

Giant-firm ROCE varies cyclically but shows no strong sustained upward trend in the UK or USA and, if we decompose the ratio, success in raising returns in the numerator is often counterbalanced by increases in the capital employed in the denominator. This negative result is a decisive piece of evidence because, if management works to deliver value, it could and should do so by raising returns through higher earnings and discipline on the capital base.

The second key indicator of the value created by a firm is ROCE. This does provide a relevant test of the effectiveness of management action because, during the 1990s, consultants selling VBM packages put much emphasis on delivering value by raising the target return to 10–12 per cent or more after tax. If that hurdle is the test of success, then giant-firm management conspicuously fails. Giant-firm ROCE moves cyclically but, in both the UK and the USA, there is no secular upward movement, only alternating movements down as well as up. This point emerges from the spot comparisons in Exhibit 4.3 for 1983 and 2002 where both years represent cyclically weak profitability but 2002 was undoubtedly more difficult. Under these circumstances, performance in 2002 was well below the 1983 spot and also below the long-run trend. In 2002, the FTSE 100 constituents' (post-tax) ROCE was 3.6 per cent, compared with the 1983–2002 average of 10.4 per cent; if we consider S&P 500 constituents, the 2002 post-tax ROCE is just 1.3 per cent, well below the 6.5 per cent 1983–2002 average.

The results in Exhibit 4.3 also suggest that the prospect of being taken over does concentrate the management mind: in the UK and USA from the 1990s onwards survivors (i.e. those firms that avoid closure, share-price collapse, take-over, buy-out, etc.) have rates of return that are usually above those of the constituents. This applies most clearly in the UK where the survivors of 2002 had a post-tax ROCE of 10 per cent against 3.6 per cent for the 2002 group of constituents. But too much weight should not be placed on the size of this gap because there are only twenty-eight firms in the FTSE 100 survivors' group and, as we argue later, the overall results of the group are influenced by the performance of a handful of giant firms such as Glaxo with track records of high growth and ROCE. There is one main difference between constituents and survivors in both the UK and USA which helps to explain better ROCE in survivor groups: the key difference is that the survivors' group has fewer corporate 'dogs' with negative ROCE of more than 5 per cent in the bottom quintile. Clearly, in the medium term, gross under-performers leave the FTSE 100 or S&P 500 through declining market capitalization or hostile take-over. These mechanisms tell us something about capital market rules and selections but they do not of course establish that survivors have superior management capability.

The quintile breakdown of ROCE performance in Exhibit 4.3 puts the high-return firms in Quintile 5, low-return firms in Quintile 1 and the rest in between. From this table we can see that strong returns of 20 per cent or more after tax are effectively confined to the top quintile in Quintile 5 whose ROCE in recent years has often been

**Exhibit 4.3** *ROCE in UK and US large companies, ranked by post-tax ROCE*

| | | *Average post-tax ROCE within each quintile group (with companies ranked by their ROCE from Q1 [lowest] to Q5 [highest] ROCE)* | | | | | *Average post-tax ROCE for the entire group of companies* |
|---|---|---|---|---|---|---|---|
| | | Q1 | Q2 | Q3 | Q4 | Q5 | % |
| **1983** | FTSE 100 constituents | 3.4 | 7.9 | 10.1 | 14.1 | 27.1 | 9.8 |
| | FTSE 100 survivors | 2.7 | 7.7 | 9.8 | 14.3 | 21.1 | 9.4 |
| | S&P 500 constituents | –3.3 | 5.5 | 7.7 | 10.9 | 16.6 | 7.8 |
| | S&P 500 survivors | 3.7 | 6.5 | 8.8 | 13.4 | 18.2 | 8.2 |
| **2002** | FTSE 100 constituents | –9.6 | 3.6 | 7.4 | 10.3 | 20.2 | 3.6 |
| | FTSE 100 survivors | –5.8 | 5.6 | 8.0 | 12.7 | 25.0 | 10.0 |
| | S&P 500 constituents | –34.4 | 1.7 | 5.8 | 9.1 | 20.4 | 1.3 |
| | S&P 500 survivors | –13.3 | 1.3 | 6.1 | 10.2 | 25.0 | 4.8 |

*Sources*: Datastream (UK data) and Compustat (US data)

*Notes*: 'Constituents' are the changing group of giant firms included in the FTSE 100 or S&P 500 each year, as newcomers enter and established firms exit when taken over or become too small to keep their membership. 'Survivors' are the subgroup of twenty-eight UK firms and 185 US firms that were in the FTSE 100 and S&P 500 in the early 1980s and have remained in the relevant index over the twenty years of analysis. The average ROCE figures for the FTSE in the final column excludes some financial companies as Datastream does not calculate a ROCE for financial companies

twice as high as that in Quintile 4, whether looking at the USA or UK, or survivors or constituents. Overall, ROCE performance remains unimpressive because the FTSE 100 and S&P 500 both contain a long tail of under-performing firms earning less than 6 per cent ROCE (and often very much less) in bad years. Again, as Exhibit 4.3 shows, more or less regardless of group or country, there is another sharp step down in ROCE from Quintile 2 to Quintile 1 whose ROCE will be negative in a bad year. In our view, the most striking result in Exhibit 4.3 is that the middle 60 per cent of giant firms turn in a fairly mediocre ROCE performance and that result holds whether we look at the USA or UK, or survivors or constituents.

From this point of view, it could be argued that the task of management is to engineer upward mobility in the ROCE quintiles. But corporate mobility between ROCE quintiles turns out to be like social mobility between major socio-economic groups: many individuals stay where they were while those who are mobile typically move short distances up or down. Thus, upward mobility from low to high ROCE groups is less common than standing still, and upward mobility is broadly balanced by downward mobility. Our research shows this when we rank survivors in quintiles by ROCE: in the UK, for example, 40 per cent of FTSE 100 survivors were in the same quintile group in 2002 as in 1983. Likewise the 26 per cent of companies that moved upwards by one or two groups were balanced by the 22 per cent that moved down by two or three groups. The story from quintile analysis is one about sustained mediocrity with as many short-range downward movements as upward movements. The S&P 500 and FTSE 100 are therefore not part of an imagined world where heroic managers produce 'turn-around' and step-like improvements in performance; they are part of an everyday world where, like other social actors, best efforts and activity often does not take them far from where they started.

The final point on ROCE is that it is ultimately an accounting ratio and, in the medium term, management influences outcomes as much by its control of the denominator/capital employed as by its attempts to boost the numerator/earnings. At an operating or divisional level, managers can improve results by increasing earnings or reducing capital employed through expedients such as leasing capital equipment, such as delivery trucks, which then appear on somebody else's balance sheet. At a corporate level, the questions are about the balance between debt and equity finance and how long-term debt and equity add up to create a total corporate capital base. If that capital base increases sharply, it reduces ROCE just as surely as a decline in earnings. So the responsibility of management is not simply to raise earnings but also to resist any increase in the capital base that is not justified by current or future earnings. In practice, this may be hard to do if acquisitions or development of new activities such as financial services are attractive because, for instance, they help reduce cyclicality of earnings or boost top-line growth, even if they also bring significant additional debt or other liabilities.

In giant firms in the USA since the 1980s there has been a substitution of debt for equity which partly reflects declining interest rates which made debt more appealing and also led to large capital-base increases. As Exhibit 4.4 shows, from 1983 to 2002, the

***Exhibit 4.4*** *Scale and composition of capital employed in (a) the S&P 500 and (b) FTSE 100, 1983–2002 (in real 2003 values)*

(a) S&P 500

| | *Equity* | *Debt* | *Total capital employed* | *Debt as a % of total capital employed* |
|---|---|---|---|---|
| | $m | $m | $m | % |
| 1983 | 1,736,091 | 809,972 | 2,546,063 | 31.8 |
| 1984 | 1,719,292 | 864,020 | 2,583,312 | 33.4 |
| 1985 | 1,701,120 | 914,189 | 2,615,309 | 35.0 |
| 1986 | 1,713,065 | 988,222 | 2,701,287 | 36.6 |
| 1987 | 1,732,322 | 1,004,738 | 2,737,060 | 36.7 |
| 1988 | 1,753,912 | 1,350,692 | 3,104,604 | 43.5 |
| 1989 | 1,769,266 | 1,417,407 | 3,186,674 | 44.5 |
| 1990 | 1,759,026 | 1,433,881 | 3,192,907 | 44.9 |
| 1991 | 1,758,474 | 1,462,627 | 3,221,100 | 45.4 |
| 1992 | 1,677,882 | 1,446,565 | 3,124,447 | 46.3 |
| 1993 | 1,702,238 | 1,526,110 | 3,228,348 | 47.3 |
| 1994 | 1,814,554 | 1,638,831 | 3,453,385 | 47.5 |
| 1995 | 1,993,633 | 1,734,826 | 3,728,459 | 46.5 |
| 1996 | 2,171,069 | 1,875,203 | 4,046,271 | 46.3 |
| 1997 | 2,283,418 | 2,068,697 | 4,352,115 | 47.5 |
| 1998 | 2,448,715 | 2,496,970 | 4,945,685 | 50.5 |
| 1999 | 2,720,110 | 2,908,005 | 5,628,115 | 51.7 |
| 2000 | 3,081,340 | 3,173,323 | 6,254,664 | 50.7 |
| 2001 | 3,235,938 | 3,630,768 | 6,866,706 | 52.9 |
| 2002 | 3,058,487 | 3,927,122 | 6,985,609 | 56.2 |
| Percentage change between 1983 and 2002 | 76.2 | 384.8 | 174.4 | |

*Source*: Compustat

(b) FTSE 100

| | *Equity* | *Debt* | *Total capital employed* | *Debt as a % of total capital employed* |
|---|---|---|---|---|
| | £m | £m | £m | % |
| 1983 | 182,277 | 36,104 | 218,380 | 16.5 |
| 1984 | 194,109 | 39,169 | 233,278 | 16.8 |
| 1985 | 198,330 | 49,319 | 247,649 | 19.9 |
| 1986 | 213,913 | 51,032 | 264,945 | 19.3 |
| 1987 | 232,492 | 46,159 | 278,651 | 16.6 |
| 1988 | 267,005 | 52,715 | 319,720 | 16.5 |
| 1989 | 284,838 | 61,020 | 345,859 | 17.6 |
| 1990 | 271,759 | 53,444 | 325,203 | 16.4 |
| 1991 | 267,729 | 57,846 | 325,575 | 17.8 |
| 1992 | 276,394 | 57,348 | 333,742 | 17.2 |
| 1993 | 293,496 | 72,133 | 365,629 | 19.7 |
| 1994 | 303,793 | 68,528 | 372,322 | 18.4 |

*Exhibit 4.4 continued*

| | | | | |
|---|---|---|---|---|
| 1995 | 315,068 | 73,292 | 388,360 | 18.9 |
| 1996 | 328,595 | 71,854 | 400,449 | 17.9 |
| 1997 | 338,591 | 74,310 | 412,901 | 18.0 |
| 1998 | 320,016 | 78,282 | 398,298 | 19.7 |
| 1999 | 375,227 | 96,732 | 471,959 | 20.5 |
| 2000 | 567,997 | 110,261 | 678,258 | 16.3 |
| 2001 | 573,791 | 132,720 | 706,511 | 18.8 |
| 2002 | 540,751 | 153,319 | 694,070 | 22.1 |
| Percentage change between 1983 and 2002 | 196.7 | 324.7 | 217.8 | 76.2 |

*Source*: Datastream

overall capital base of the S&P 500 increased by 174.4 per cent in real terms, much faster than the 5 per cent increase in constituent sales. Within this, total equity grew by 76.2 per cent and debt rose dramatically to finish 384.8 per cent greater by 2002. The overall result in the USA is that debt comprised 56 per cent of the long-term capital in 2002, compared with 32 per cent in 1983. Changes in the FTSE 100 have some similarities, with debt rising (325 per cent) faster than equity (197 per cent) to give an overall increase in the real value of the capital base of 218 per cent from 1983 to 2002, even though equity still accounted for 78 per cent of total capital employed by 2002, as Exhibit 4.4 shows. This nicely illustrates a series of contradictions within institutionalized finance: while the stock market was asking for higher returns and discipline on the capital base, investment banks were, as part of the merger and acquisition (M&A) process, making money by fitting up corporate America with an enlarged capital base. If giant-firm management claims it is managing ROCE, corporate managers cannot avoid some of the blame for acquiescing in this increase in the capital base that reinforced disappointing outcomes.

## Modest growth

If share-price performance is determined elsewhere and ROCE improvements are constrained, giant-firm management could appease shareholders by growing the firm and raising the rate of sales-growth. The complication of large differences in sales growth rates between individual firms needs to be recognized here, but in the aggregate, if we consider any large group of firms in the long term, real sales growth is modest and growth rates in giant-firm groups do little more than track GDP. This limits stock-market returns on any diversified portfolio of giant firms and begins to raise questions about the collective ability of giant-firm managements to capture increases in GDP (except by buying competitors).

If ratios such as return on capital cannot easily be improved, top-line growth is highly relevant because managers could seek to increase the lump of revenues and profit.

Delivering sales growth should be considerably easier in the USA and UK than in many continental European countries where hostile take-over is more difficult, so that acquisition can be used to buy in turnover and profits increases when organic growth falters. This in turn may also make it possible to improve shareholder returns through divestment to create value. As we will see below, the result is large differences in growth rates between individual giant firms. Yet, in the aggregate, if we consider the USA or UK, the positives and negatives cancel each other out and the real sales-growth record of any large group of giant firms is undistinguished, despite the opportunities for inorganic growth.

As Exhibit 4.9, discussed later in this case, shows in the UK case, the contrast between long-run individual firm growth rates is quite spectacular. At the top end, Glaxo increased its real sales more than nine times between 1978–9 and 2002; while a failing blue-chip like ICI or a struggling privatized utility like British Gas saw declines in real sales of the order of 50 per cent or more. There are exceptions, but it is notable that fast-growing companies with real sales increase of more than 100 per cent over almost twenty five years are typically acquisitive, while shrinking companies are divesting divisions. Under these circumstances, especially, if there is serial acquisition and divestment, it becomes very difficult to judge the competence of management at running an ongoing business because carriages are constantly being connected or disconnected from the train. The dispersion of growth rates also complicates any averaging because, if we consider growth rates of real sales and profit, we do not have a bell curve with most of the observations in the middle of the distribution. The group of twenty-one FTSE 100 survivors considered in Exhibit 4.9 has an aggregate real sales growth of 50 per cent between 1978–9 and 2002–3 but only five firms are in the middle of the distribution with individual real sales growth rates of 50 per cent plus or minus 25 per cent.

This no doubt helps to explain why there are puzzles in the aggregate evidence about different groups of firms summarized in Exhibit 4.5. Thus UK survivors grow real sales at 1.9 per cent per annum, which is less than constituents and broadly what we would expect if we consider the growth prospects of established firms like Marks & Spencer or BOC against those of newcomers like Vodafone who sell into rapidly expanding (often new) markets. But in the USA, the pattern is rather different with survivors growing at 3.7 per cent on average each year, significantly faster than constituents. Yet, through all this confusion and blur, two points stand out.

1 In three of the four giant-firm groups considered in Exhibit 4.5, the managers do not collectively manage to increase profits faster than sales. Indeed, in the S&P 500 survivors, the annual change between 1983 and 2002 is significantly lower with real annual growth of 3.7 per cent in sales and 2.5 per cent in profits. The FTSE 100 survivors are the exception because they rack up an impressive 5.7 per cent increase in pre-tax profit against 1.9 per cent in sales, but, as we have already noted, this is a small group of twenty-eight firms where one-third of the sales increase is accounted for by Glaxo alone.

***Exhibit 4.5*** *UK and US giant-firm performance between 1983 and 2002 (all financial values are based on 2003 prices)*

| | *% annual real change between 1983 and 2002* | | | | | |
|---|---|---|---|---|---|---|
| | *Sales* | *Pre-tax profit* | *Market value* | *Director's pay* | *Dividends (UK) Dividends and interest (US)* | *Headcount employment* |
| **FTSE 100 (constituents)** | 2.7 | 2.7 | 18.2 | 26.2 | 19.0 | 1.1 |
| **FTSE 100 (survivors)** | 1.9 | 5.7 | 17.5 | 28.5 | 16.8 | 0.8 |
| **S&P 500 (constituents)** | 2.5 | 1.5 | 13.3 | n/a | 5.6 | 1.2 |
| **S&P 500 (survivors)** | 3.7 | 2.5 | 11.2 | n/a | 4.3 | 1.5 |
| | *% total real change 1983 to 2002* | | | | | |
| | *Sales* | *Pre-tax profit* | *Market value* | *Director's pay* | *Dividends (UK) Dividends and interest (US)* | *Headcount employment* |
| **FTSE 100 (constituents)** | 53.4 | 53.7 | 365.7 | 523.5 | 380.0 | 22.4 |
| **FTSE 100 (survivors)** | 38.3 | 110.3 | 349.4 | 570.5 | 335.5 | 16.8 |
| **S&P 500 (constituents)** | 49.8 | 29.3 | 265.2 | n/a | 56.6 | 23.3 |
| **S&P 500 (survivors)** | 74.6 | 50.1 | 223.3 | n/a | 86.4 | 30.2 |

*Sources*: Erturk, I., Froud, J., Johal, S. and Williams, K. 'Pay for corporate performance or pay as social division. Rethinking the problem of top management pay in giant corporations' 2005 *Competition and Change*, vol. 9, no. 1, pp. 49–74

*Note*: Payments to capital in the S&P 500 includes interest as well as dividends given the growing significance of debt in corporate balance sheets (see Exhibit 4.4)

2 All four giant-firm groups considered in Exhibit 4.5 have modest annualized real sales growth rates over the period 1983–2002: the highest performing group, in terms of real sales increase, are the S&P 500 survivors who managed a twenty-year real sales growth rate of 3.7 per cent, while the rate is 2.7 per cent for the FTSE 100 constituents and 2.5 per cent for the S&P 500 constituents. In real terms, the constituents, the changing group of giant firms in the UK and USA, grows no faster than the economy as a whole and over twenty years does no more

> than increase real output by around 50 per cent. One possible explanation for such mediocre performance would be that the giant firms account for such a large percentage of GDP that the growth rates are bound to be similar. As our analysis of the giant firms in Chapter 1 shows, the aggregate sales revenue for the S&P 500 accounts for 36 per cent of total US corporate receipts in 2000, while the value added of the FTSE 100 is 36.5 per cent of that for the UK corporate sector as a whole. Thus while the constituents of the FTSE 100 and S&P 500 grow as if they are 'GDP companies', they account for fairly modest amounts of corporate output and also generate significant sales outside their national bases so that they are not fundamentally constrained by GDP growth.

At this point, we understand the perplexity of the animals who, at the end of Orwell's *Animal Farm*, looked through the window and found it increasingly difficult to tell the difference between pigs and men. We are accustomed to the idea that the managers of any large group of private-sector organizations will, in the long term, grow their organizations about as fast as GDP because, other things being equal, tax revenues give private-sector managers a lien on GDP increases. But, it now appears that, in the aggregate, giant-firm managers do no better in terms of sales growth (and profit) outcomes. That is seriously disappointing news for institutional investors with broad giant-firm portfolios because long-term value creation will be slow, and it starts to raise questions about the capability of giant-firm management. The jolting complications of merger and divestment no doubt take up their time and complicate appraisal of performance, but the modest long-term increase in real sales and profit must raise questions about how many of them have the ability to capture demand increases (without buying competitors) and turn that demand into profit. In all fairness, we need to consider the exceptional individual success as we shall do by taking Glaxo as one of our three historical cases, but we should not forget the modest, long-term, aggregate outcome of giant-firm management effort which raises a whole series of questions that can be partly answered by considering the evidence on redistribution to capital from labour.

## The complexity of redistribution

If real sales and profit growth rates are modest, then giant-firm management could redistribute between stakeholders in ways that increase the share available to capital. The record on redistribution to capital in the USA and UK does not confirm the pro-capital, anti-labour expectation at group level. In the absence of group-wide labour-shedding in the UK and USA or secular increase in pay-out rates in the USA, we have little evidence of the giant-firm ruthlessness that some academics and commentators would expect.

Insofar as shareholder value presses managers to deliver financial results under conditions where long-term value creation is difficult, we would logically expect management to opt for redistribution. Specifically, where management effort fails to deliver sustained rapid growth that increases the size of the cake, senior executives could decide to redistribute from labour and give capital a larger slice of the cake. This is what O'Sullivan (2000) argues did happen in US giant firms as they downsized the workforce and distributed cost savings to the capital market. The evidence reviewed later in this section suggests a more complex story: considered as a group, giant firms in the USA and UK are not ruthless labour shedders and, while distribution rates are high in cyclically difficult years, for the S&P 500 there is no evidence of a secular shift in distribution to capital, which we do find in the UK's FTSE 100 group. Overall, there is very limited evidence to support a view that in these giant-firms groups there is collective ruthless management behaviour that many critics would expect.

On pay-out ratios, it is important to distinguish between short-term pay-out ratios that rise in cyclically bad years and the secular trend which may be different. The pay-out ratio measures the percentage of net income distributed to shareholders, which is of interest because this is, to some extent, a discretionary matter (unlike interest payments which must be paid at a particular rate). The data in Exhibits 4.6 and 4.7 runs from the early 1980s to 2002 because it was the most recent year for which full data was available at the time this research was conducted. The ROCE figures in Exhibit 4.2 suggest that profits were weak in 2002 and (as in other years when profits were low) dividends are maintained out of reduced earnings, which leads mechanically to a higher pay-out ratio.

As Exhibits 4.6 and 4.7 show, while the 2002 payouts of 168.3 per cent and 141.3 per cent of net profit by S&P 500 and FTSE 100 constituents respectively are far larger than average pay-out rates over the whole period, they are part of a long-established cyclical pattern. For example, in the previous downturn in 1991, the FTSE 100 firms paid out two-thirds of net income, while the S&P 500 paid out almost three-quarters of their net income as dividends. Perhaps then, this data suggests that the relatively high pay-out figures for 2002 say more about the difficulties of balancing competing claims on profit over the cycle than a secular upward shift in distribution rates.

To get US secular trends into perspective, Exhibit 4.7 presents carefully considered data on S&P 500 constituents. Here we have added up the year by year totals of all three distributions (dividends plus interest plus share buy-backs): buy-backs are becoming increasingly important in US giant firms, and the substitution of debt for equity increases the absolute and relative significance of interest payments. For both the USA and UK, the most meaningful denominator for a measure of distributions is cash, or EBITDA, as a gross measure of surplus, because that removes several complications caused by changing behaviours, tax and accounting rules. On this basis, the time series in Exhibits 4.6 and 4.7 show quite an interesting difference between the USA and UK.

For the S&P 500, there is no secular upward shift in distribution rates. Exhibit 4.7 shows that dividend distribution rates remain fairly constant, with modest cyclical variation around the average of 14.7 per cent and no clear secular upwards long-term trend; if anything, since 2000, dividend pay-outs are slightly lower. If the other two forms of distribution to capital (interest and buy-backs) are added, the pay-out rates of

**Exhibit 4.6** *FTSE 100 annual constituents: a comparison of net income, dividends and retained earnings (in real 2003 prices)*

| | *Net profit* | *Dividends (ordinary)* | *Distribution rate (dividends as a proportion of net profit)* | *Dividends as a % of cash (EBITDA)* | *Retained earnings* | *Retention rate (retentions as a proportion of net profit)* |
|---|---|---|---|---|---|---|
| | £m | £m | % | % | £m | % |
| **1983** | 23,530 | 7,319 | 31.1 | 13.2 | 16,212 | 68.9 |
| **1984** | 25,798 | 8,360 | 32.4 | 12.8 | 17,438 | 67.6 |
| **1985** | 27,886 | 9,604 | 34.4 | 13.4 | 18,282 | 65.6 |
| **1986** | 29,893 | 11,413 | 38.2 | 15.8 | 18,479 | 61.8 |
| **1987** | 31,614 | 13,517 | 42.8 | 17.6 | 18,096 | 57.2 |
| **1988** | 41,953 | 15,947 | 38.0 | 17.1 | 26,006 | 62.0 |
| **1989** | 40,709 | 17,421 | 42.8 | 18.3 | 23,288 | 57.2 |
| **1990** | 36,856 | 18,034 | 48.9 | 19.9 | 18,823 | 51.1 |
| **1991** | 28,518 | 18,365 | 64.4 | 22.4 | 10,153 | 35.6 |
| **1992** | 29,686 | 18,455 | 62.2 | 22.8 | 11,231 | 37.8 |
| **1993** | 38,892 | 20,674 | 53.2 | 22.0 | 18,218 | 46.8 |
| **1994** | 46,074 | 22,738 | 49.4 | 22.1 | 23,336 | 50.6 |
| **1995** | 51,421 | 26,497 | 51.5 | 23.9 | 24,924 | 48.5 |
| **1996** | 57,642 | 28,772 | 49.9 | 24.2 | 28,870 | 50.1 |
| **1997** | 57,906 | 32,171 | 55.6 | 26.8 | 25,735 | 44.4 |
| **1998** | 53,678 | 44,968 | 83.8 | 38.6 | 8,710 | 16.2 |
| **1999** | 61,300 | 33,135 | 54.1 | 26.2 | 28,166 | 45.9 |
| **2000** | 61,102 | 34,773 | 56.9 | 26.5 | 26,329 | 43.1 |
| **2001** | 39,811 | 34,703 | 87.2 | 30.5 | 5,108 | 12.8 |
| **2002** | 24,851 | 35,122 | 141.3 | 34.6 | −10,271 | −41.3 |
| Average rates 1983–2002 | | | 55.9 | 23.5 | | 44.1 |

*Source*: Datastream

*Note*: EBITDA is earnings before interest, tax, depreciation and amortization, and is approximately equal to cash

36–9 per cent from 2000–2 EBITDA are broadly in line with the 1980–2002 average of 38.3 per cent. Of course, this stability is encouraged by the substitution of debt for equity because the shift to debt caps payments at the relevant interest rate.

In the UK, the story is interestingly different. If dividends are compared with cash there is a clear upwards shift in pay-outs from 13–20 per cent in the 1980s to 20–35 per cent in the 1990s and early 2000s. Pay-out rates at the bottom of the cycle have shifted from 31.1 per cent in 1983 to 64.4 per cent in 1991 and 141.3 per cent in 2002, implying some attempt by management to cover depressed share prices with (relatively) high distributions to shareholders. This apparent increase in distributions is of significance in its own right for those who wish to understand the dynamics of UK capitalism. But, from our comparative point of view, the key point is the difference between the UK and

*Exhibit 4.7 S&P 500 annual constituents: a comparison of interest, dividends, share buy-backs, cash, net income and retained earnings*

| | *Dividends as a % of net income* | *Dividends as a % of cash (EBITDA)* | *Interest plus dividends as a % of cash (EBITDA)* | *Interest, dividends and treasury share purchases as a % of cash (EBITDA)* | *Retained earnings as a % of cash (EBITDA)* |
|---|---|---|---|---|---|
| **1980** | 40.5 | 15.5 | 31.4 | 31.4 | 22.7 |
| **1981** | 42.2 | 16.2 | 35.2 | 34.0 | 22.2 |
| **1982** | 52.5 | 17.0 | 38.4 | 38.6 | 15.4 |
| **1983** | 48.4 | 16.2 | 34.7 | 34.9 | 17.3 |
| **1984** | 43.4 | 15.3 | 33.8 | 35.0 | 19.9 |
| **1985** | 52.8 | 15.6 | 35.2 | 37.6 | 13.9 |
| **1986** | 59.7 | 17.3 | 38.1 | 40.3 | 11.7 |
| **1987** | 54.6 | 17.4 | 37.4 | 41.7 | 14.5 |
| **1988** | 49.2 | 17.4 | 40.6 | 43.1 | 18.0 |
| **1989** | 48.9 | 15.5 | 42.3 | 43.2 | 16.2 |
| **1990** | 55.0 | 16.0 | 41.7 | 44.6 | 13.1 |
| **1991** | 72.7 | 17.1 | 44.0 | 44.2 | 6.4 |
| **1992** | 63.4 | 16.7 | 39.3 | 40.7 | 9.6 |
| **1993** | 56.0 | 15.8 | 35.5 | 36.4 | 12.4 |
| **1994** | 42.7 | 14.5 | 32.9 | 41.2 | 19.5 |
| **1995** | 45.2 | 14.1 | 32.6 | 35.5 | 17.1 |
| **1996** | 37.0 | 13.1 | 30.9 | 33.2 | 22.3 |
| **1997** | 37.6 | 12.6 | 31.0 | 29.1 | 21.0 |
| **1998** | 38.4 | 13.0 | 35.4 | 38.3 | 20.8 |
| **1999** | 54.9 | 19.3 | 40.7 | 45.6 | 15.9 |
| **2000** | 32.2 | 10.4 | 34.0 | 36.1 | 21.9 |
| **2001** | 72.4 | 11.1 | 36.7 | 38.5 | 4.2 |
| **2002** | 168.3 | 12.2 | 35.2 | 39.0 | –5.0 |
| Average rates | | | | | |
| 1980–2002 | 49.6 | 14.7 | 36.1 | 38.3 | 15.0 |

*Source*: Compustat

*Note*: EBITDA is earnings before interest, tax, depreciation and amortization, and is approximately equal to cash

USA, which supports our general argument that financialization does not imply one clear set of consequences: in this case, financialization in the USA and UK has led to quite different outcomes in terms of pay-out rates.

If pay-outs have diverged, there are some similarities between the two countries when we consider the workforce, where, at the FTSE 100 or S&P 500 group level, there is no clear evidence of downsizing. As Exhibit 4.5 shows over this whole twenty-year period, in the FTSE 100 constituents group the increase in employment head-count of 22 per cent is a little less than half the rate of increase of real sales or profit, which is not unsurprising given the expectation of routine productivity increases. Similarly, in the S&P 500 constituents group, employment increases by 23 per cent against a real sales increase of 50 per cent, which could hardly be characterized as ruthless downsizing in a group of companies where finance and high-tech companies with scope for labour-saving were becoming increasingly important.

Of course, some giant firms are restructuring at the expense of labour, and we explore this point in the next chapter. But the head-count evidence does not suggest that any group of giant firms in the USA or UK is dominated by such management behaviour. As Exhibit 4.8 shows in US and UK constituent groups, the total number employed in the giant-firm sector in 2002 is larger than in 1983. Even more striking, the same is true of the survivor groups of giant firms in both the USA and UK. S&P 500 survivors account for roughly half the employment in the constituent group, and the survivor group that employed a total of 9.3 million in 1980, employed 9.7 million in 2002; in the UK, the position is broadly similar because the FTSE 100 survivors employed 1.6 million in 1983 and 1.8 million in 2002.

The database sources do not disclose how much of this employment was in the US or UK home economy, but in the UK case it is possible to calculate cost per employee by dividing number of employees into total labour costs, and this shows that real labour costs have increased by one-third or more in the twenty years since 1983, which does not suggest either a large shift to part-time working or relocation to low-wage countries. If the real wage has gone up from £17,000 to £25,000 in the UK survivors' group, most of the exported jobs went to northern Europe and the USA, not Bangalore (source: Datastream). In the USA, limited disclosure on employment restricts our analysis, but there is helpful additional evidence in the form of an official series on multinational company employment which covers a group of firms that overlaps with the S&P 500. Whilst the match is not exact, the overlap would appear to be extensive given that in 2002 these multinational firms employed 31.6 million against 23.5 million in the S&P 500 constituents (Exhibit 4.8). The story here appears to be that US-based employment grew a little more slowly than non-US employment: total US multinational employment increased by 7.9 million or 33 per cent between 1982 and 2001 while US parent company employment (which excludes most of the non-US employment by multinationals) increased by 4.7 million or 25.4 per cent (*Survey of Current Business*, December 2002 (Bureau of Economic Affairs); *Statistical Abstract of the USA*, 2004/5).

The argument in this chapter so far has focused on groups of giant firms. If attention is refocused onto individual companies, the detail is often confusing, but the story generates greater interest and immediacy because it dramatizes the issue of undeserved pay increases. As Exhibit 4.5 shows, for the group of FTSE 100 constituents or survivors over twenty years, real CEO pay was increasing at more than 25 per cent per annum, well ahead of 17 per cent to 18 per cent increases in market value, and much faster than increases in sales or profits, which were below 3 per cent on average. Exhibit 4.9 presents comparable company-level data for a sample of eighteen companies for the period 1978 to 2002. Only one of these survivor companies (Glaxo, now GlaxoSmithKline) has long-run increases in profitability and sales that are commensurate with the dramatic increases in CEO pay. Elsewhere, none of the UK FTSE 100 survivors have growth trajectories or increases in profit that come anywhere near to the increases in CEO pay that have been

*Exhibit 4.8 Employment in S&P 500 and FTSE 100 listed companies*

| | *S&P 500* | | *FTSE 100* | |
|---|---|---|---|---|
| | Annual constituents No. | Survivors No. | Annual constituents No. | Survivors No. |
| **1980** | 19,388,408 | 9,318,030 | | |
| **1981** | 19,569,693 | 9,497,465 | | |
| **1982** | 18,876,060 | 9,076,767 | | |
| **1983** | 18,210,289 | 8,550,337 | 3,654,845 | 1,580,598 |
| **1984** | 19,385,742 | 9,018,987 | 3,859,160 | 1,703,299 |
| **1985** | 19,330,174 | 9,324,046 | 3,963,495 | 1,583,804 |
| **1986** | 19,062,409 | 9,457,550 | 4,295,543 | 1,622,054 |
| **1987** | 18,848,756 | 9,417,152 | 4,560,826 | 1,636,504 |
| **1988** | 18,839,658 | 9,478,320 | 4,728,038 | 1,695,111 |
| **1989** | 19,019,043 | 9,697,472 | 4,785,359 | 1,711,091 |
| **1990** | 19,119,566 | 9,770,311 | 4,818,542 | 1,708,722 |
| **1991** | 18,618,135 | 9,666,275 | 4,651,754 | 1,695,516 |
| **1992** | 18,415,144 | 9,406,760 | 4,073,463 | 1,614,634 |
| **1993** | 18,272,202 | 9,263,537 | 4,117,035 | 1,553,953 |
| **1994** | 18,080,854 | 9,105,904 | 3,917,649 | 1,523,766 |
| **1995** | 18,847,793 | 9,254,836 | 3,883,077 | 1,561,901 |
| **1996** | 19,274,825 | 9,279,953 | 3,874,714 | 1,603,016 |
| **1997** | 20,122,749 | 9,510,790 | 3,882,281 | 1,608,010 |
| **1998** | 21,762,062 | 9,817,251 | 4,312,894 | 1,718,833 |
| **1999** | 21,762,062 | 9,910,408 | 4,368,834 | 1,667,644 |
| **2000** | 22,207,295 | 9,907,942 | 4,012,280 | 1,793,656 |
| **2001** | 22,119,982 | 9,893,700 | 4,395,031 | 1,854,160 |
| **2002** | 22,258,468 | 9,748,709 | 4,474,089 | 1,845,523 |

*Source*: Compustat (US data) and Datastream (UK data)

granted. This is nicely ironic, when there has been much public criticism of the pay packages obtained by the high-profile UK CEOs of Vodafone and GlaxoSmithKline; though we leave it for the reader to decide whether the growth trajectories of these two companies reflect the unique contributions of their recent or current CEOs, Chris Gent or Jean-Pierre Garnier.

However, issues about CEO pay in individual companies should not distract us from the more important implications of the group performance analysis. This analysis is important because it suggests that giant-firm CEOs are neither the value-creating heroes of strategy texts and the business press, nor the pro-capital, anti-labour villains of the Left. Instead, the group analysis suggests that giant-firm CEOs might be just another averagely ineffectual officer class whose role is to manage events and avoid disaster but not to produce high performance or glorious victory. In this context, it is worth remembering that in both the USA and the UK, giant-firm CEOs are socially part of a long-established managerial class which is formed through distinctive national institutions. This is the point that Temin (1999) makes in a study of the US business elite,

**Exhibit 4.9** *Long-run performance of FTSE 100 companies*

| | *% Change between 1978/9 and 2002/3* | | | | *Highest paid director/CEO* | |
|---|---|---|---|---|---|---|
| | *Sales*<br>% | *Pre-tax profit*<br>% | *Net profit*<br>% | *Director/CEO pay*<br>% | *1978/9 (2002 prices)*<br>£ | *2002/3*<br>£ |
| AB Foods | –29.0 | 41.8 | 98.6 | 337.2 | 133,588 | 584,000 |
| Aviva | | –152.0 | –244.3 | 634.6 | 193,435 | 1,421,000 |
| BA | 22.8 | –60.9 | –75.6 | 494.1 | 93,080 | 553,000 |
| BAE | 136.5 | –368.3 | –729.7 | 288.5 | 110,687 | 430,000 |
| Barclays | | 124.9 | 145.7 | 684.4 | 234,439 | 1,839,000 |
| BAT | –58.4 | 27.9 | 37.8 | 248.3 | 300,927 | 1,048,000 |
| BG Group | –73.4 | 15.4 | 3.4 | 298.8 | 272,843 | 1,088,000 |
| BOC | –12.0 | 32.0 | 118.8 | 416.9 | 224,237 | 1,159,000 |
| Boots | 57.9 | 45.9 | 107.7 | 366.6 | 160,305 | 748,000 |
| BP | 115.3 | –11.6 | 303.6 | 637.7 | 403,832 | 2,979,000 |
| Cadbury Schweppes | 37.1 | 351.2 | 786.3 | 616.4 | 200,721 | 1,438,000 |
| Glaxo | 922.5 | 1,570.3 | 2,302.8 | 1,142.1 | 189,836 | 2,358,000 |

| | | | | | | |
|---|---|---|---|---|---|---|
| GUS | 36.3 | –22.3 | 6.6 | 1,092.0 | 100,668 | 1,200,000 |
| Hanson | 58.1 | 175.0 | 225.2 | 266.1 | 137,405 | 503,000 |
| ICI | –64.6 | –74.0 | –83.8 | 144.7 | 398,809 | 976,000 |
| Marks & Spencer | 70.0 | –25.3 | –37.5 | 1,098.5 | 171,710 | 2,058,000 |
| Pearson | 182.0 | –116.7 | –384.1 | 258.7 | 222,500 | 798,000 |
| Prudential | | 149.1 | 158.0 | 669.3 | 125,954 | 969,000 |
| Rexam | –47.1 | –111.4 | –191.4 | 433.7 | 211,187 | 1,127,000 |
| Sainsbury | 488.1 | 442.4 | 353.7 | 883.6 | 108,779 | 1,070,000 |
| Scottish & Newcastle | 177.0 | 157.0 | 81.3 | 633.4 | 83,588 | 613,000 |
| **Totals** | 50.0 | 28.6 | 116.9 | 512.0 | 4,078,530 | 24,959,000 |

*Sources*: Erturk, I., Froud, J., Johal, S. and Williams, K. 'Pay for corporate performance or pay as social division. Rethinking the problem of top management pay in giant corporations' 2005 *Competition and Change*, vol. 9, no. 1, pp.49–74

*Notes*: The sample of firms presented is taken from the group of FTSE 100 companies that were also operating in 1978/9. This group overlaps with the FTSE 100 survivors group but is not identical, as the FTSE 100 index was not established until 1984. In addition, not all survivor companies that were operating in 1978/9 are included. In 1978, British Airways, British Aerospace, British Gas and BP were all owned by the British state; in 2002/3, all were listed on the London Stock Exchange. The 1978 Director/CEO pay data refers to the highest-paid director. For 2002/3, Monks Partnership data is used: this includes benefits in kind and, therefore, may not be the same as the pay figure disclosed in the company accounts. In 2002/3 Hanson's CFO pay is used as the CEO position was vacant. Change in sales figures are not provided for financial services companies, e.g., Aviva (insurance) or Barclays (banking) as turnover does not have the same meaning as for a service or manufacturing company. Where companies are the product of single or multiple merger or acquisition, the data for 1978 is taken from one (usually the largest) of the component companies, whereas that in 2002/3 refers to the amalgamated entity. Thus, for the 1978/9 data, Commercial Union is used as the forerunner to Aviva (formed from CU, General Accident and Norwich Union); Bowater is used for Rexam; Glaxo is used for GSK. For such companies, some of the changes shown between 1978/9 and 2002/3 are the result of and reward for organic growth, while some of the difference between 1978/9 and 2002/3 reflects the management of and results from a larger merged entity: it is not possible to separate these effects out

which showed that in 1996 the CEOs of *Fortune 500* families were predominantly, 'male, white and mostly native born Protestants from good families', just as they were 100 years previously (1999: 189). The position is much the same in the UK where a recent study by Bauer and Bertin-Mourot (1999) demonstrated that 36 per cent of the top 200 CEOs in the UK had attended one of twenty elite public schools. Whatever the rhetoric about shareholder value, maybe the functional managerial performance of these very traditional social types is not so different from that of their gentlemanly precursors, even though today's CEOs are of course very much better paid for their trouble.

## MANY MOVES AND FEW LEVERS

The empirics in the previous section raise a series of broader questions. If capital market pressures for shareholder value produce a feeble group response in terms of higher ROCE or sales growth rates, these giant-firm results have to be understood in terms of external constraints as much as in terms of the internal characteristics of the leadership cadre. The fundamental question is what management can do and how should we understand the limits and constraints on management? An answer can be obtained by turning Porter and RBT upside-down to explain general mediocrity rather than exceptional success. The argument then is that the pursuit of (increased) value by giant-firm management is futile in the many competitive product markets where group behaviour by the firms ensure that the benefits are given away to consumers. Thus, giant-firm management makes many firm-level moves that ensure an organizational life of ceaseless activity and initiatives, but giant-firm management has few levers that act on the industry to deliver improved financial results for the individual firm. This viewpoint is explored and developed in this section through general argument, and a brief report of an earlier 'industry on firm' study of the US temporary-employment business.

A generation after it was first published, the Porter concept of 'generic strategies' (1980) can be reworked for the 2000s, not to explain how some firms can be positioned for competitive advantage but to argue why most firms produce mediocre financial results. If the mission of corporate management is cost recovery, there are three kinds of management moves that correspond to the different kinds of market, productive and financial interventions. The first is revenue recovery oriented to the product market; the second is cost reduction oriented to process improvement; and the third involves working on the financials directly (or 'financial engineering' as we call it) with the aim of impressing the capital market. If we consider these generic moves in turn and analyse the conditions under which such moves deliver leverage, then we will see why firm level financial results are so often disappointing.

## Revenue recovery

The leverage is positive here when there are small numbers of corporate players who deflect competition away from price. This is often achieved by establishing indirect competition in segments where only two or three firms have dominant positions. Using cars in the 1990s as an example, virtually all the cash and profit made by individual firms came from strong positions in relatively sheltered subsegments. For instance, during this period Ford and GM made 70 per cent or more of their auto profits from pick-ups and sport utilities where the American firms were dominant, while a similar share of Toyota and Honda's profits came from the Camry and the Accord, which together dominated the US sedan market. Elsewhere, Europe's most profitable auto brand is BMW which effectively shares premium sales with Mercedes and Audi in their European home markets. These successful, sheltered positions contrast favourably with the European 'D segment' where products such as the Ford Mondeo pitch on price against the competitive offerings of at least five European and three Japanese manufacturers, so that profits are elusive. The strategist concerned with business success would conclude that management should occupy or create a segment which the firm can dominate. This under-estimates the extent to which domination is often the result of interactive happenstance, such as the failure of Ford in the US sedan market of the 1990s which created the profit opportunities for Toyota and Honda. And it never confronts the more fundamental problem that all cannot succeed as some do. The leverage from revenue recovery strategies is generally limited in most activities because there is just too much direct competition based on price.

## Cost reduction

Effective cost reduction requires management that can identify the major controllable items of expenditure, typically internal labour and outside purchases. However, the problems arise when everybody can make the same move and then, under these conditions, cost reduction becomes just another endless race that often no firm can win. Large corporations must reorganize because they cannot afford to fall behind their competitors, but the net effect, as one cost-reducing programme succeeds another, is that the moves continuously lower the floor under competition in the industry. Benefits may arise from cost reduction for a single producer if others cannot replicate the cost reduction or if that one firm can execute cost-reduction strategies more effectively than the rest of the industry, as may be the case with Toyota in cars. Such cases would have to be explained by a sustainable set of distinctive competencies, but these will be rare if, as the popular business best-sellers suggest, everybody really can do lean production, business-process engineering and suchlike to an acceptable standard. This may be increasingly so if cost reduction involves accessing low-cost sites in Asia or eastern Europe and, in such cases, the burden of proof should surely be upon those who assert or assume a differential distribution of competences.

## Financial engineering

Financial engineering has most leverage in firms that are already successful, so that they are moving along a growth trajectory with a high share price and a good credit rating. This makes it cheap and easy to make acquisitions, to borrow money and to manoeuvre on tax and suchlike, with very few questions asked, as in the case of GE under Jack Welch in the 1980s and 1990s. Less successful firms have limited purchasing power and lower credit ratings and so transformational restructurings are often risky because the risks of over-paying, or simple bad timing can bring the dealmaker down. Thus, British GEC's transformation into Marconi after 1996 involved the sale of its defence interests to British Aerospace (now BAE Systems) followed by a disastrous move into telecoms where it bought second-rate companies at the peak of the market.

This brings us to the point where we explicitly part company with classical strategy because, as we noted in Chapter 1, 1990s' Prahalad and Hamel, like 1980s' Porter, believe that firms are capable of acting upon the industry to change its nature. Against this, our argument would be that this is very rarely the case because most firms most of the time cannot act on the industry through process or product to reposition or reinvent. In our analysis there are often limits to what individual firms can do. First, many business problems are too difficult for single firms to solve because they are rooted in the environment and external structural factors such as cyclicality, power relations with buyers and suppliers and forms of competition. Second, the problems that can be solved usually have fixes that can and will be imitated by other firms in competitive product markets. Incidentally, we would note that this explanation for low returns on capital is also strongly supported by the conditions prevailing in exceptional high-return sectors, such as pharmaceuticals or software. Here, most firms benefit from activity-based advantages such as immateriality, sector-wide barriers to entry and restraints on competition arising from licenses and patents whose value is increased by growing mass markets for the relevant products. 'Hard' variants of RBT emphasize firm-specific endowments (such as patents or airline landing slots) as much as management action, but the distribution of rates of return on capital suggests that few giant firms start with or maintain an endowment of resources that guarantee high corporate returns, while argument about divisional returns is, as we have argued, empirically indecisive and also practically irrelevant when nobody buys shares in divisions.

This fairly assertive argument is best developed through extended case studies which take an 'industry on firm' approach rather than the 'firm in industry' approach typical of most of the strategy literature. The three historical cases in Part II of this book, on Glaxo, Ford and GE, also broadly take a firm-in-industry approach so that they can demonstrate an alternative to classical strategy. But they do cover a range of industry issues and help to explain, for example, why pharma is an increasingly difficult activity and why car assemblers dream of reinvention. But we have elsewhere produced one extended industry-on-firm case study of US temporary-employment agencies, which illustrates the problems about the limits of single-firm action when moves can be imitated. Our brief report of that case study in the next few paragraphs is a vignette of the kind we have previously criticized, but it does report a longer case study (Froud, Johal et al. 2001) and also describes a collective failure that is most unlikely to turn into success over the next few years.

In all advanced countries, the temporary staffing business exists because government regulation allows the employment of some workers on a limited commitment basis. This appeals to some business clients who wish to avoid the social and financial obligations that accompany the hiring of full-time, contracted workers and remains true regardless of whether the temp firm (or the client) is the legal employer. In heavily regulated European countries, temporary staff are attractive because it is much more difficult to sack other workers. In the USA, temps are attractive because they both allow the volume of labour to be easily adjusted and they usually cost less in terms of social charges. Arguably, the organization of temping should be the industry of industries in the early twenty-first century because in a neo-liberal or regulated economy temp agencies can play a huge economic and social role in recommodifying labour in flexible forms that assist corporate cost reduction. But in the USA, double-digit sales growth for most of the 1990s and ROCE of 15 per cent or more for major corporate agencies, as illustrated in Exhibit 4.10, did not convince the stock market of this benefit. The agency business has a history of cyclicality and an industry that sells employers flexibility is *ipso facto* exposed to sales declines in any downturn when employers will want to reduce flexible employment.

Though government regulation of one sort or another creates a business opportunity for temp agencies, it does not create comfortable positions for public corporations as

***Exhibit 4.10*** *Temporary employment agencies performance indicators*

| | *Manpower (1995–2000)* % | *Kelly (1991–2000)* % | | *Adecco (1996–2001)* % | |
|---|---|---|---|---|---|
| US market share 1999 | 4.2 | 3.4 | | 3.1 | |
| Annual growth rate of revenues | 11–28 | −2–+23<br>14–23 | (1991–2000)<br>(1995–2000) | 21–79 | |
| Gross margin (mark-up) | 15–19 | 16–22<br>16–21 | (1991–2000)<br>(1995–2000) | 17–19 | (1997–2001) |
| ROS | 1.5–3.9 | 3–4<br>3.2–4 | (1991–2000)<br>(1995–2000) | −0.2–+0.7 | (1997–2001) |
| ROCE | 16–41 | 13–27<br>22–7 | (1991–2000)<br>(1995–2000) | 1.3–3.3 | (1998–2001) |

*Source*: Annual report and accounts

*Notes*: Revenues are for the company, not the brand and hence exclude sales by franchisees (but include fees paid by franchisees). Adecco was formed in 1996 from the merger of Adia and Ecco. ROS and ROCE are calculated using operating profit

temp agencies in the USA. The fundamental problems are in the industry structure and the product market. In the US market, the large US public companies such as Manpower and Kelly have low market shares and compete with a further sixty other domestic companies, and also with one large European-owned competitor, Addeco, which has been buying US market share by accepting low margins. As Exhibit 4.10 shows, in the 1990s Addeco's margins are well below the traditional industry norm of 3–4 per cent on sales. Quite unusually, all the corporate firms also compete with thousands of private companies because most temping agencies operate in a commodified product market where barriers to entry are low and capital requirements are small. Moreover, the operations of existing corporate and non-corporate employment agencies create a large potential pool of new entrants with management experience of how to run a temporary-staffing business. It is also an attractive business for private individuals or small companies who can scale up with borrowed money in growth years and retreat in difficult years. One of the few exceptions that escape such pressures is Robert Half International, which has built itself a profitable niche position in the specialist business of supplying accounting temps where it is the dominant player.

The cost-recovery problems in this industry are generally beyond the control of individual corporations and their senior managers. The major firms have made heroic attempts at reinvention through innovations such as 'vendor on premises' where the temp agency takes responsibility for more than just delivering labour in a bus and may become involved in staff supervision, delivering HR functions and so on. But, when all firms can imitate the prime movers, such 'value-adding' moves just add cost and build customer expectations of service. It is a classic case of a whole industry stuck in an impossible position, where a single firm cannot act to change the activity characteristics of too much competition and too little power. The temp-agency industry is one where standards and margins are set by shopfront operators who compete with giant temp firms much more directly than they do in other areas of retail such as groceries. This, of course, means that the industry's problems have a public-policy dimension because any solution of the margin problems of the corporates requires a re-regulation of labour-market intermediation whereby government disadvantages the small players. Rather than face these issues directly, many industry figures prefer to discuss the industry's broken business model and this in itself is an interesting development.

As Michael Lewis (2001) noted, the term 'business model' passed from Silicon Valley parlance into general usage some time in the mid-1990s, and it was used very loosely to denote old and broken, or new and optimistic plans for recovering costs incurred from product or capital market. We would add that the term business model is seldom used in activities where cost recovery is unproblematic. As our Ford case suggests, the term 'business model' is used obsessively in businesses with chronic cost-recovery problems, and the term itself is therefore part of a broader process of reconceptualization and restructuring under pressure for financial results which we consider in the fifth and final chapter of this introduction.

Chapter 5

# New interventions

## Sector matrix, restructuring, narrative and numbers

The first part of this book argues, and the historical cases subsequently explore, how growing pressure from the capital market has redefined company strategy and changed the work of management. It also argues that this process is embedded within product-market constraints in a world which does not automatically take giant-firm CEOs at their own estimation. The general strategic problem for giant firms is delivering the financial numbers combined with a narrative of strategic intent which 'keep it going' and this chapter presents some basic concepts for thinking through the distinctive interventions of giant-firm senior managers after financialization. As we have already argued, our premise is that we need to introduce new and different concepts to reconceptualize the interventions of management and to explore the discrepancies between promise and outcome. Without such new concepts we will end up simply reinscribing what management says and strategy discourse endorses.

When this point has been made, it must also be said that we represent an intellectual tradition that combines conceptual minimalism with empirical resourcefulness. This is signalled by the organization of our book: new concepts of intervention get some 15,000 words in this fifth and final chapter, which serves as prelude to three historical case studies that together account for 75,000 words. If this is less like formalized social science and more like free-form historiography, it is nevertheless a methodical historiography with a definite problematic. Our concern is with the long-run trajectory and reputation of giant firms because short-run sections can be misleading. Our concern is with corporate and industry narrative because that matters to investors and the capital market in ways that discourse analysis of terms or construction does not pin down. Our concern is with numbers because they are crucial to any *ex-post* evaluation of management promises about what the company will do and achieve next year; though, as we have already indicated, we expect infelicity. We do not share the preoccupation of other researchers with generalizable relations or consequences as disclosed by systematic empiricist techniques.

Hence the need for some new, light-touch concepts of management intervention that inform but do not overwhelm our understanding of management after financialization. The first section of this chapter breaks with the established ideas of chain and industry so as to analyse sector-matrix moves which classically involve adding finance or selling services. It does this while recognizing that matrix moves are important in some sectors, less relevant in others and absent in many. Thus, while sector matrix helps explain why some managers make particular strategic moves under certain circumstances, it does not signify a new epoch for large corporations, nor is it any kind of meta-explanation of corporate behaviour or organization. The second section of this chapter considers serial restructuring in giant firms which elevates breach of implicit stakeholder contract into a guiding principle of management. The task here is to explain the usually disappointing results for capital and the uneven results for labour within an accounting frame about the composition of costs and set in the broader frame of ongoing problems about value creation by management action in giant companies. These problems encourage private equity and the (only partial) eclipse of the giant public company.

The third section of this chapter takes up our concern with narrative and its (interestingly limited) constitutive capacity against financial numbers, which represent obdurate externals such as product-market constraints. This section serves to introduce the narrative and numbers approach which then frames our three historical case studies. After financialization, giant-company CEOs now need a story of purpose and achievement for fund managers, analysts and other commentators, and ideally a story backed by performative initiatives (for quality, cost reduction or whatever) which establish that management is doing as well as saying. But, elaboration of a narrative is only part of the challenge for senior management: the practical problem is to generate the financial numbers to corroborate the story which, in the case of discrepancy, is usually reshaped and jointly authored outside the company by analysts and business journalists. This argument uses examples from our three historical case on Glaxo, Ford and GE which explore the different ways in which company and industry narrative and numbers interplay. The historical cases develop the analysis of the first four chapters of this book but they are not mechanically constructed to illustrate some proposition about sector-matrix moves or any one privileged relation between narrative and numbers.

## SECTOR MATRIX

Our Chapter 4 argument about infelicity and the performative established that the gap between saying and doing was a key issue for all those wanting to understand financialization. The concepts outlined in this chapter now develop the idea of multiple discrepancies, and this section is about one such discrepancy which arises in this case because it is still possible to have the (management) thing without the (business-school) word. Thus, this section discusses a new kind of management intervention which thus far has no corresponding concept. The conditions under which conceptualization lags behind intervention are themselves interesting, and classically the lag occurs when an already-established concept creates a taken-for-granted world across several discourses, as in this case where strategy and political economy share an a priori about chain and industry. Against this we propose a new concept of 'sector matrix' which enlarges the field of the visible for business analysis to include a new kind of management intervention, which we illustrate by considering cars and motoring. At the same time, we would emphasize that sector-matrix moves do not represent a generalizable, new recipe for success. Indeed, the financial results of recent sector-matrix moves have been mixed or disappointing.

The chain concept can be traced across a variety of academic discourses, and this point can be illustrated by briefly considering Porter's (1985) strategy, plus Gereffi's and Korzeniewicz's (1994) and Gereffi's (1996) political economy. The idea of the 'value chain' was introduced in 1985 by Porter as a 'basic tool for diagnosing competitive advantage and finding ways to create and sustain it' (Porter 1985: 26). The concern was with the business unit that would implement a generic strategy by identifying a series of activities or functions and deciding which activity could serve as the basis for low cost or differentiation. The list of sources of advantage included operations, marketing and service, as well as indirect support activities such as purchasing in the 'value chain'. Nearly a decade later, Gereffi's and Korzeniewicz's (1994) political-economy concept of 'global commodity chains' (GCCs) was used to analyse different spatial issues around globalization. The concern here was with Nike, Wal-Mart and their Chinese factories in a world of uneven distribution of wealth and power which was enforced by governance within producer- or buyer-dominated chains.

At different levels of analysis, before and after globalization, Porter (1985), Gereffi and Korzeniewicz (1994) and Gereffi (1996) share the same a priori. Value chain or supply chain both assume a linear, input–output concept of production framed as nodes in a chain where the money moves back as the input moves forward. The chain concept of production goes along with the idea of the firm in the industry defined, as in orthodox applied economics, as a group of firms using common technologies to make products that compete in the final product market. As we observed in Chapter 2, orthodox strategy in the Porter (1985) or Prahalad and Hamel (1990) form has a firm-in-industry problem definition about how the firm in the industry can find 'sustainable advantage' by acting on 'the industry' to change its nature and to create a defensible product-market position. So Porter's generic strategies are about, 'how a firm can actually create and sustain a competitive advantage in its industry' (Porter 1985: 3), while for Prahalad and Hamel (1990: 21) a firm builds competences so as to 'control the destiny of its industry'. Gereffi (1996) rather confusingly talks about 'industrial sectors', but these are only industries that have escaped national boundaries in a globalizing world where the 'global organization of production links manufacturers, input suppliers, traders, bankers, designers and retailers'. Thus, for Gereffi, an industry is something like 'automobiles, aircraft or computers' or the structures around the GCCs in, 'apparel, footwear or toys', where industries are differentiated 'in terms of technology, competitive structures, and labour intensity' (Gereffi 1996: 434).

Our conclusion is that the supply-chain–industry concept recurs inside and outside strategy discourse and has survived many shifts and turns within discourse. It brings with it a set of assumptions:

1 It starts from supply and describes the organization of production and distribution from raw materials to retailer and after sales service, whether national or global.
2 It envisages the processes that bring a commodity to the final product market where the commodity is often a manufacture, sometimes a service, but usually stand alone.
3 It presupposes a productionist firm which seeks advantage from process or product market or, in Gereffi's case, from supply-chain management where the dominant position may be held by a retailer or designer without factories.
4 It envisages competition as a process that takes place within an industry of firms using similar technologies to produce competing products.

This framework of assumptions constitutes an a priori that can be illustrated by considering the case of the cars business where chain–industry thinking has united authors (such as Womack et al. 1990 and Boyer and Freyssenet 1999) who disagree about almost everything else. The shared-chain concept is summarized in Exhibit 5.1, where the main emphasis is on strong vertical chain links culminating in horizontal competition between substitutable, finished products. This concept also operates as a kind of problematic which limits the field of the visible to supply side issues about the organization of (new-car) production so that the taxonomic classification of different chains becomes important, and academic prestige accrues to those who can distinguish between five types of chain organization where previously there were three (see, for instance, Meijboom 1999, which notes the lack of academic discussion of international supply chains). And yet, as giant car-assembly company executives increasingly realized in the 1990s, this chain concept produces a very peculiar map of the activity in which their companies are engaged.

The difficulty is that that the chain–industry concept constructs a field of the visible that ignores relevant demand considerations and much of the money-making opportunity. On the demand side, in the case of a durable product such as cars, the second-hand business is important to new-car assemblers because there has been demand substitution between

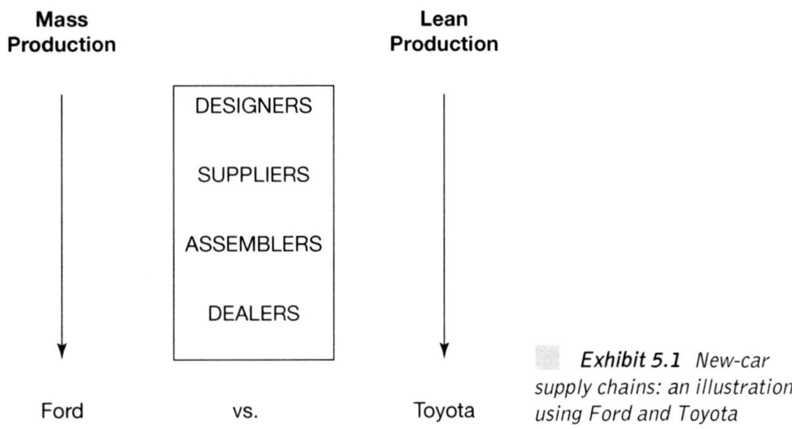


**Exhibit 5.1** *New-car supply chains: an illustration using Ford and Toyota*

new and used cars at least since second-hand Chevrolets undermined new sales of the Model T in the mid-1920s; and, with increasing over-production in 1990s Europe and North America, there is now supply interaction between new and nearly new cars which have been pre-registered or sold into daily rental fleets. Furthermore, the sale of new and used cars taken together usually accounts for less than half the total consumption spend in this area because car use depends on a bundle of complementary goods and services including finance, petrol, service, spare parts, tax and insurance. Exhibit 5.2 presents summary data on US expenditure patterns on private automobile transport over the past twenty years. If we ignore the complication about leasing payments which are included under maintenance, car purchase (with interest costs) accounts for 46–8 per cent of the total spend on motoring, with the balance accounted for by consumables. Through the 1990s, car-company managers (well ahead of the academics) gradually realized that their business was motoring not cars. The leader of the pack was Jacques Nasser whose services strategy is analysed in our Ford case, but he was echoed by others like Berndt Pischetsrieder, the CEO of Volkswagen (VW) who interestingly used the old chain language to describe new opportunities when he observed that with car making, 'you only get 8 or 12 per cent of the value chain' (*Financial Times*, 11 June 2004).

Academics faced much the same difficulty about old concepts by the late 1990s as they tried to think through the new moves. Thus, in a *Harvard Business Review* article titled, 'Go downstream', Wise and Baumgartner mixed the metaphor of the chain with the usual claims about recipes for success: 'if most manufacturers have floundered [in the 1990s], a few have prospered . . . [and] they've all taken a similar route to success: they've gone downstream towards the customer' (Wise and Baumgartner 1999: 133). Our own approach (Froud et al. 1998) was both more radical in terms of conceptualization and more cautious about the universal benefits of any such move. In particular, the evidence and argument we present below suggests that 'sector-matrix' moves are not a panacea for business problems inside or outside manufacturing.

***Exhibit 5.2*** *Breakdown of US private motoring expenditure*

| | | Breakdown of expenditure % | | | | | | | |
|---|---|---|---|---|---|---|---|---|---|
| | *Total real expenditure on motoring $ billion (in real 2003 prices)* | *New and used cars* | *Other motor vehicles (including light trucks)* | *Tyres, exhausts, etc.* | *Repairs, maintenance, leases and rentals* | *Fuel and oil* | *Insurance* | *Interest payments* | *Registration fees, permits and tolls* |
| **1980** | 663.4 | 24.1 | 4.0 | 6.9 | 13.2 | 33.5 | 3.6 | 13.2 | 1.5 |
| **1985** | 729.4 | 32.1 | 9.6 | 6.5 | 16.3 | 26.2 | 2.7 | 4.9 | 1.6 |
| **1990** | 714.4 | 29.2 | 11.3 | 6.5 | 18.4 | 23.3 | 3.9 | 5.6 | 1.8 |
| **1995** | 748.1 | 27.4 | 12.9 | 6.6 | 19.7 | 20.1 | 5.3 | 6.1 | 1.8 |
| **2000** | 865.7 | 25.4 | 15.6 | 5.7 | 21.7 | 20.3 | 3.8 | 6.0 | 1.6 |
| **2001** | 868.6 | 24.0 | 17.8 | 5.5 | 21.7 | 19.4 | 3.8 | 6.1 | 1.6 |

*Source*: Annual Abstract of the US, 2003

The concept of the sector matrix emerges from the context of financialization. Stock-market pressure for corporate financial results made the concept of chain and industry increasingly obsolete because managers who could not easily satisfy growing capital-market demands were pressed into new ways of thinking about their business. On the supply side, the old way of thinking was all about product or technology specific to (or transferable between) markets inside or outside a home industry. An alternative way of thinking is about the firm as a unit that consolidates financial surplus from diverse sources of profit inside and outside an activity matrix. On the demand side, the old issue was winning the nameplate competition between substitutable end products (for example, Ford vs. GM vs. Toyota). The new issue is about capturing expenditure on a function as it percolates downwards from firms and households onto complementary and substitutable products and services.

From this point of view, the sector matrix is a form of opportunist and divergent thinking on the part of corporate management, encouraged by financialization and starting from a completely different set of assumptions to the supply-chain–industry concept:

1 Household and corporate demand for related products and services is the starting point.
2 The boundary of the matrix is defined by the particular function, for example, motoring, mobility, health care, etc. (though the boundary might shift over time in response to regulatory, economic or social change that encourages, mandates or prevents certain kinds of consumption, e.g. recycling).
3 It presupposes a financialized firm that is constantly looking to lever more profit (or to defend its position within existing matrix activities).
4 Competition is not confined to the group of firms producing similar products; it is extended to all the other firms that aspire to positions in the matrix.

The concept of sector matrix is illustrated using a motoring matrix, summarized in Exhibit 5.3. This diagram considerably expands the field of the visible because it highlights the new–used-car relation as well as the general importance of non-manufacturing activities. The matrix allows us to redefine the competition between car companies: this is not a contest between manufacturing systems that Japanese lean or world-class manufacturing will win, as Womack et al. (1990) claimed. Nor is it simply a contest between social settlements so that the Europeans and Americans must lose because of their high wages and social costs, as argued at the end of our *Cars* book (Williams et al. 1994). The cars business is a contest to see whether and how these logics around assembly can be modified by the consolidation of non-manufacturing activity. In the case of Ford, as we shall see later, manufacturing in the left upper corner of the matrix is financially unrewarding because, in the mature, saturated markets of North America and Europe, the volume car assemblers have collectively undermined their own cost recovery and productive reorganization is part of the problem when everybody can do it and there are not enough upmarket sales or growing niches to cover these problems.

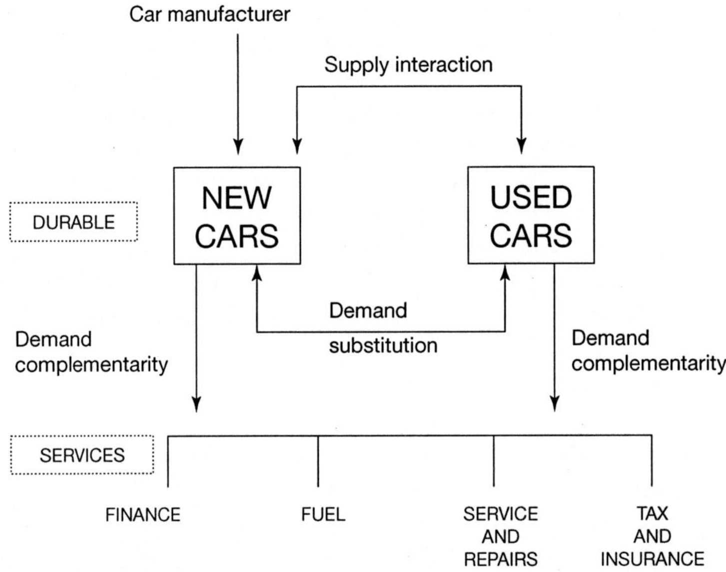


*Exhibit 5.3 Motoring sector matrix*

*Source*: Froud, J., Haslam, C., Johal, S. and Williams, K. 'Breaking the chains? A sector matrix for motoring', 1998 *Competition and Change*, vol. 3, no. 3, pp. 293–334, by permission of Maney Publishing <http://www.maney.co.uk>

This kind of grid can be drawn for any complex product that requires supporting infrastructure and is consumed along with ancillary services. It would, for example, be possible to construct a health-care matrix with primary and secondary health care in the choice boxes (corresponding to new and used cars). Ancillary support services could include pharmacy, ethical drug manufacture, laboratories and equipment supply, all ranged on the bottom row. The sector-matrix concept cannot be mechanically applied to health care (or any other sector), however, because of complexities about embedding, low definition and locked demand. Thus, motoring is embedded in a well-defined mobility matrix, where all motorists must buy a combination of services to keep a car (legally) on the road. In contrast, remedial health care is embedded in a less well-defined health matrix which notionally also includes preventive fitness via gyms and sports clubs. A further complication is that most remedial health-care purchases are made for (but not directly by) individual consumers.

Thus, at one level, the motoring matrix is a special case that lends itself to a neat diagram in a way that is less satisfactory in other areas of demand. However, the value of the general approach is that it does highlight the possibility of matrix moves that allow companies to gain sales and profits from activities that are functionally related to existing operations. Where the firm already has access to (business and domestic) customers, it can hope to gain a greater share of functional expenditures. In many cases, the sector-matrix moves start and stop with the high margin/low price adjunct to the higher price good or service that generates the primary transaction and the retail footfall. For example, insurance warranties on electrical goods sold by Circuit City in the USA or Dixons in the UK generate considerable profits but are really nothing more than the shoe polish that goes with the shoes or the sandwiches and bottled water sold by every petrol filling station. In other cases, sector-matrix analysis allows a focus on more complex corporate moves, for example, a consultancy company into running outsourced back-office functions.

While there is considerable scope, therefore, to extend the concept to firms outside the motoring sector, two important qualifications need to be registered about sector matrix and its limits. First, the concept does what it was originally intended to do intellectually by providing an explanation of how and why the cars industry has ceased to exist in ways that open up a new research agenda about motoring. Hence academics like Laplane and Sarti (2002) have subsequently analysed the role and financial contribution of credit subsidiaries for auto companies in Brazil, whilst Jullien (2002) explored the way in which a regressive redistribution of wealth occurs when the profits from car parts are used to subsidise the purchase price of new cars in France. But this analytical break should not be constructed as an indicator of a more general (future) transformation in either the practice or study of corporate management because many industries will not be reworked as sectors.

Indeed, it is possible to think of many industries that are difficult to transform by sector-matrix moves. The chain concept does work well for the kinds of commodity and designer products that Gereffi and Korzeniewicz (1994) discuss – after all, a pair of sports shoes does not need maintenance or insurance. As already noted, in other cases, there are complex infrastructure and support-service requirements around activities such as health care, but much of the demand is inaccessible to matrix moves by corporations because the institutional structures around private insurance or state medicine lock up consumer demand. In an ideal world each major pharma company would like to control distribution in at least one therapeutic area, through tied clinics that only prescribe that company's in-patent drugs. Likewise, success with one sector-matrix move does not establish any kind of precedent or prediction about the ability to execute further profitable moves. Ford and GM have large, long-established and lucrative captive-finance businesses which, as we shall see in Ford's case, have generated 40 per cent of the profits of the past twenty years, but car rental services through Ford's ownership stake in Hertz have never made a sustained contribution to profits.

The second general qualification is that firms that deliberately make major sector-matrix moves for profit are often disappointed. It should not be assumed that financially pressured firms that make matrix moves in motoring or in other sectors will always or usually obtain the desired improvement in financial performance. There are reasons to suppose that the outcomes of matrix moves are often mixed and sometimes disappointing. Our historical cases on Ford and GE clearly show this because adding credit subsidiaries buys extra cash and profit at the expense of secondary complications such as a lower return on capital employed. Furthermore, as we have argued elsewhere, the major development in the European cars business of the 1990s was a shift by the volume assemblers into car finance (Froud, Haslam et al. 2002), but this did not transform the profitability of European volume car assemblers even though it was originally represented by Bernd Pischetsrieder as the 'precondition for a successful car business' that could raise return on sales from 3–4 per cent to 6–7 per cent (*Financial Times*, 12 September 2001). Some four years later Pischetsrieder, as VW CEO, had come to terms with the impossibility of building or buying services businesses large enough to fundamentally transform the financials and concluded it was 'crazy' to imagine that VW could buy Shell or Allianz. Thus, the matrix diagram does not necessarily depict an operable strategy for competitive advantage even though it is possible to find examples where a sector-matrix approach to corporate development has been successfully employed.

One of the more interesting illustrations is GE where Jack Welch developed his own version of the sector matrix under his 'Services' initiative. Quite unusually, GE was also occupying large and profitable matrix positions in several sectors, made possible, of course, because it is (despite the company's denials) a conglomerate. For example, GE has a strong position in the aviation sector. Aviation is a little more complex than motoring because the delivery of the ultimate product, air travel, requires the presence of a range of suppliers (e.g. aircraft manufacture) and intermediaries (e.g. travel agents). However, as with motoring, aviation involves (owned or leased) durables plus a variety of services, all provided within a regulated institutional framework. GE secures a strong position in the aviation matrix not only as one of the world's largest aero-engine manufacturers, but also as one of the largest providers of aero-engine maintenance services. Added to this, GE Capital Aviation Services is the largest aircraft-leasing company in the world, which owns 1,300 airplanes and has $33 billion of loans and leases to the airline industry. Furthermore, since the twilight of TWA and Pan Am, GE has also had a lucrative side business in providing working capital for failing airlines (*Wall Street Journal Europe*, 1–3 April 2005). The exceptional success of GE makes it a worthy object of historical case study and incidentally rather undermines all those Porteresque business case studies which represent the airline industry as a contest between point-to-point low-cost carriers and hub-and-spoke flag carriers. Maybe the important point is that GE can make money in at least four different ways out of a sector where most airline carriers are losing money. However, if (as is often the case when discussing this company) GE's success in executing a matrix strategy is an exception, this helps explain why so many other firms have turned to restructuring their businesses to find growth and better or more stable returns.

## 'RESTRUCTURING'

Any consideration of restructuring takes us further into the issues around saying and doing and the multiple discrepancies around both. If one of the problems about sector matrix has been the absence of any generally accepted word for the thing, the problem about restructuring is the overpowering presence of the 1990s' word. 'Restructuring' tautologically includes much of what management does beyond routine operations when it promises to create shareholder value, though it should be noted from the outset that much of what is done does not deliver the hoped-for outcomes. Thus restructuring is the site of another major discrepancy between saying and doing because the *ex-ante* objective is defending or increasing the returns for shareholders, but the *ex-post* outcome for capital is often disappointing, despite labour-cost-reduction strategies.

This discrepancy is of some practical importance because, as the empirics show, M&A in the form of public companies buying other public companies is a major activity for giant firms in the USA and UK. There is also an interesting new development in the form of private equity which takes medium-sized public companies or giant-firm divisions private before selling them on after a few years. Both kinds of restructuring merit closer analysis which focuses on two issues: first, how and why is labour-cost reduction the object of management intervention in restructuring and what are the consequences for the workforce? And second, why is it practically so difficult to raise the return on capital? If the outcomes of restructuring will often continue to disappoint, serial defensive restructuring still remains an attractive option for giant firms, partly because it buys time and partly because it confuses like-for-like comparisons of ongoing business performance.

Since the 1890s, M&A (through public companies buying other public companies) has been a feature of corporate Britain and America, classically in the form of waves of take-over activity when stock-market prices are rising and facilitating acquisition without cash payment. Since the early 1990s, the neologism 'restructuring' has been used to bracket this kind of merger with new kinds of transfer of corporate assets and changes of ownership. Thus, in the later 1980s, the USA had leveraged buy-outs (LBOs), as firms such as Kohlberg, Kravis & Roberts sold junk bonds to raise the funds to buy public companies and take them private, most spectacularly in the case of the $25 billion RJR Nabisco deal (Baker and Smith 1998, Sudarsanam 1995: 243–60). This development did not survive a minor economic downturn but, from the mid-1990s, debt finance had a second coming in the USA and UK as management teams borrowed to fund management buy-outs and management buy-ins, which were often targeted on a division, not the whole public company. By the early 2000s, the debt-financed purchase of public companies was being organized by new actors: private equity funds. In popular usage, restructuring also includes financial engineering through share buy-backs and substitution of debt for equity within an independent public company where ownership does not change hands. It is also used in company reports or news bulletins to encapsulate all the 'right-sizing' operating adjustments in ongoing public companies via factory closures, down-sizing or out-sourcing.

The heterogeneity of these interventions means that they cannot be summed into one straightforward measure. But the relevant evidence below shows that both M&A and private equity are important activities in the UK and USA, where both take place against a background of brisk operating adjustments whenever the economy turns down. For example, in a survey of more than 600 firms in the last UK recession after 1989, Geroski and Gregg (1994) found that the most popular 'major form of restructuring chosen by UK firms' was plant closure, with 50 per cent of the firms in the sample closing one or more plants and a further 35 per cent of firms selling at least part of their operations.

Takeovers involving merger or acquisition between two public companies are a huge activity in both the UK and USA partly because both countries have institutionalized the hostile take-over whereby a 'raider' can usually buy another company without management consent by offering institutional fund managers 20–30 per cent over last week's close as an inducement to sell their shares. Exhibits 5.4 and 5.5 provide data on the scale and significance of M&A in the UK and USA respectively. In both economies, M&A is clearly a cyclical activity; given that many acquisitions are made using the acquiring company's equity as the currency, M&A is less attractive in years when share prices are depressed. Activity does not entirely vanish however, because a low share price for the target company makes it much cheaper to buy for an acquirer with cash or moderately valued shares. In the UK, the cyclical range is from £17 billion in 1992 to £307 billion in 2000 (in real 2003 prices). Similarly in the USA the range covers cyclical lows of less than $100 billion in 1980, 1982–3 and 1991–2, to cyclical highs of $217 billion in 1989 and $2,947 billion in 1999 (in real 2003 prices). Exhibit 5.5 also shows that the number of deals in the USA varies considerably from around 1,000 per year, to over 7,000 in the peak year of 2000.

The cumulative value of M&A activity is huge: £1,200 billion in the UK from 1987 to 2003 and $14,929 billion in the USA from 1980 to 2003. It should be noted that the UK data prior to 1995 excludes financial companies, which means that the total figures understates the level of M&A in the UK corporate sector. In the USA, where a longer data series is available, there is quite a large difference in the scale of activity in the 1980s, compared with the 1990–2003 period, in terms of number and value of deals. In a peak year like 1999 or 2000, the value of deals exceeds the total value of M&A in the 1980s. While the data on M&A is impressive in its own right, it is helpful to provide some benchmark, and Exhibits 5.4 and 5.5 compare M&A expenditures with gross fixed capital formation in the UK and a similar indicator, capital investment, in the USA. Over the periods considered, M&A is equivalent to 77 per cent of corporate investment in the UK (despite the exclusion of financial companies from 1987 to 1994) and, in the peak of 1999–2000, M&A far exceeds gross fixed capital formation. A similar pattern emerges

***Exhibit 5.4*** *The significance of expenditure on M&A in the UK, 1980–2003 (in real 2003 prices)*

| | *M&A expenditure by UK private corporations* | *Of which, in the UK* | *Of which, overseas* | *UK private corporations gross fixed capital formation (GFCF)* | *M&A as a % of GFCF* |
|---|---|---|---|---|---|
| | £ million | £ million | £ million | £ million | |
| **1980** | | 4,002 | | 50,355 | |
| **1981** | | 2,774 | | 45,905 | |
| **1982** | | 4,925 | | 46,418 | |
| **1983** | | 5,003 | | 46,338 | |
| **1984** | | 11,125 | | 54,246 | |
| **1985** | | 13,583 | | 63,721 | |
| **1986** | | 28,478 | | 62,232 | |
| **1987** | 50,898 | 29,437 | 21,461 | 71,882 | 70.8 |
| **1988** | 68,103 | 38,751 | 29,353 | 83,637 | 81.4 |
| **1989** | 78,495 | 42,889 | 35,605 | 92,306 | 85.0 |
| **1990** | 30,589 | 11,972 | 18,617 | 91,058 | 33.6 |
| **1991** | 27,311 | 14,162 | 13,149 | 79,183 | 34.5 |
| **1992** | 17,284 | 7,776 | 9,508 | 71,226 | 24.3 |
| **1993** | 20,968 | 9,099 | 11,869 | 70,765 | 29.6 |
| **1994** | 29,450 | 10,391 | 19,059 | 70,215 | 41.9 |
| **1995** | 54,171 | 39,625 | 14,546 | 85,127 | 63.6 |
| **1996** | 52,370 | 36,491 | 15,879 | 94,151 | 55.6 |
| **1997** | 52,967 | 30,889 | 22,078 | 100,004 | 53.0 |
| **1998** | 94,023 | 32,875 | 61,148 | 112,266 | 83.8 |
| **1999** | 150,533 | 28,673 | 121,860 | 111,577 | 134.9 |
| **2000** | 306,947 | 113,870 | 193,077 | 114,109 | 269.0 |
| **2001** | 73,695 | 30,322 | 43,373 | 109,941 | 67.0 |
| **2002** | 53,366 | 25,968 | 27,398 | 106,967 | 49.9 |
| **2003** | 39,435 | 18,679 | 20,756 | 100,987 | 39.0 |
| Total 1987–2003 | 1,200,606 | 521,870 | 678,735 | 1,565,400 | 76.7 |

*Source*: Financial Statistics, ONS, various years

*Notes*: Prior to 1995, the data in this table refers to non-financial private corporations; from 1995, the data includes financial companies, (partly) explaining the large jump in M&A expenditure from 1994 to 1995

in the USA where over the whole period 1980–2003, M&A is equivalent to 65 per cent of capital investment, with the 1997–2000 period showing M&A in excess of investment. The comparison is interesting because it suggests that UK or US corporations are almost as likely to buy new activity and growth as they are to build their own, and in an era of financialization, this provides a new (corporate) level twist on the old make-or-buy (component) decision that management-accounting students have traditionally been taught.

**Exhibit 5.5** *The significance of US restructuring: M&A, divestments and LBOs (in real 2003 prices)*

| | *M&A* | | *Total private fixed capital investment* | *M&A as % of capital investment* | *Divestments* | | *LBOs* | |
|---|---|---|---|---|---|---|---|---|
| | No. | $ billion | $ billion | % | No. | Value $billion | No. | Value $billion |
| **1980** | 1,445 | 62 | 810 | 7.6 | 104 | 11 | 11 | 1 |
| **1981** | 1,753 | 113 | 851 | 13.3 | 476 | 21 | 100 | 8 |
| **1982** | 1,572 | 93 | 813 | 11.5 | 562 | 16 | 164 | 7 |
| **1983** | 1,499 | 65 | 771 | 8.4 | 661 | 24 | 231 | 8 |
| **1984** | 1,336 | 165 | 867 | 19.0 | 801 | 79 | 106 | 27 |
| **1985** | 785 | 141 | 900 | 15.6 | 780 | 87 | 154 | 28 |
| **1986** | 1,174 | 154 | 872 | 17.7 | 1,090 | 142 | 233 | 78 |
| **1987** | 1,267 | 130 | 848 | 15.4 | 1,004 | 126 | 208 | 66 |
| **1988** | 1,405 | 172 | 877 | 19.7 | 1,274 | 180 | 291 | 86 |
| **1989** | 1,845 | 217 | 902 | 24.1 | 1,615 | 141 | 292 | 112 |
| **1990** | 2,155 | 137 | 877 | 15.6 | 1,907 | 128 | 177 | 25 |
| **1991** | 1,516 | 98 | 809 | 12.2 | 1,759 | 83 | 171 | 10 |
| **1992** | 1,705 | 80 | 803 | 9.9 | 1,598 | 75 | 199 | 9 |
| **1993** | 1,108 | 262 | 849 | 30.8 | 1,993 | 272 | 621 | 2 |
| **1994** | 2,205 | 345 | 908 | 37.9 | 2,005 | 294 | 173 | 13 |
| **1995** | 2,548 | 613 | 979 | 62.6 | 2,227 | 441 | 206 | 29 |
| **1996** | 3,047 | 849 | 1,028 | 82.6 | 2,423 | 375 | 169 | 20 |
| **1997** | 5,383 | 1,113 | 1,112 | 100.1 | 3,189 | 707 | 198 | 28 |
| **1998** | 6,092 | 2,144 | 1,189 | 180.3 | 3,304 | 627 | 238 | 31 |
| **1999** | 6,071 | 2,947 | 1,253 | 235.1 | 3,184 | 749 | 344 | 64 |
| **2000** | 7,196 | 2,632 | 1,317 | 199.8 | 3,497 | 954 | 476 | 92 |
| **2001** | 4,568 | 1,023 | 1,223 | 83.6 | 2,816 | 669 | 329 | 62 |
| **2002** | 4,098 | 643 | 1,087 | 59.1 | 2,631 | 483 | 303 | 85 |
| **2003** | 4,287 | 731 | 1,095 | 66.8 | 3,090 | 501 | 366 | 86 |
| Total 1980–2003 | 66,060 | 14,929 | 23,042 | 64.8 | 43,990 | 7,187 | 5,760 | 977 |
| Total 1980–1989 | 14,081 | 1,313 | 8,512 | 15.4 | 8,367 | 828 | 1,790 | 420 |
| Total 1990–2003 | 51,979 | 13,616 | 14,530 | 93.7 | 35,623 | 6,359 | 3,970 | 557 |

*Source*: Statistical Abstract of the USA, various years; Bureau of Economic Analysis, Department of Commerce

*Notes*: Only transactions valued at $5 million or above are included in the restructuring data which includes restructuring activities by US firms in the USA and overseas. The investment data includes expenditure on new facilities, expansion and replacement, including structures, equipment and software, by business in the USA (but excludes expenditure on land and mineral rights). Thus, expenditure by US firms overseas and by foreign firms in the USA is excluded

If M&A is a significant activity, Exhibit 5.5 reminds us there must also be large-scale divestment, which creates the opportunity for acquirers to add business activities and to generate inorganic growth. Since 1980 in the USA, there have been 8,367 divestments, against 14,081 mergers or acquisitions. Again, there is a striking difference between the 1980s and the 1990s: more than three-quarters of the number of divestments and 88 per cent of their value over the whole 1980–2003 period have taken place since 1990. As a point of interest, the distribution of LBOs is quite different, with intensive activity in the 1986–9 period, followed by a quiet spell and gradual build-up to a new peak in 2000 of $92 billion, slightly lower than the $112 billion of deals recorded in 1989.

In comparison with M&A, it is more difficult to analyse private equity because it includes different kinds of investment from early stage through expansion to management buy-out/buy-in (MBO/MBI). In addition, the best source of data on private equity in the UK is the British Venture Capital Association (BVCA) whose data often only covers its members, while in the US the data is focused on venture capital, rather than private equity more broadly defined. However, Exhibit 5.6 provides a useful breakdown of UK private equity by type of investment since the mid-1980s, showing that, in most years, MBO/MBI accounts for more than half of total private-equity spend. Over the whole period, BVCA members invested £52.7 billion (in real 2003 prices) into private equity from early stage to exit, with some cyclicality around peaks in activity in 1988–9 and 1999–2000. The fall back from the last peak year in 2000 has, however, been fairly modest at around one-third, unlike the pattern observed with M&A in Exhibit 5.4, where more than two-thirds of the peak level activity vanishes by 2002. While spot year comparisons need to be used carefully in an activity that is cyclical, private equity is increasing in significance, with 2001–2 representing a doubling in real value since 1990 and a sevenfold increase since the mid-1980s. For the USA, Exhibit 5.7 shows that venture capital grew from $5.2 billion to $113.2 billion in just seven years between 1994 and 2000, before marked reductions in both 2001 and 2002 as part of the hangover after the new economy.

Exhibit 5.6 understates private equity in the UK because it covers only BVCA members. However, the BVCA also publishes data on sources of private-equity funds in the UK, showing that, for instance, in 2002 £3,586 million and £4,468 million were raised from UK and overseas investors respectively and providing a total value of just over £8 billion, roughly twice that shown in Exhibit 5.6. Overall, however, UK private equity is fairly modest in scale compared with M&A, and in particular the extent of early stage (or venture capital) is only around £300–700 million per annum since 1998. Even MBO/MBI, the largest component of private equity in the UK, is only a fraction of the value of M&A; though, interestingly, at a global level, Morgan Stanley (2005) estimate that MBOs are equivalent to 15–20 per cent of M&A. In the USA, Exhibit 5.7 shows that venture capital is equivalent to less than 5 per cent of M&A investment, even at the 2000 peak. However, in six of the nine years from 2002, venture capital is at least 60 per cent of LBO investment, which perhaps provides a more useful benchmark of its significance.

**Exhibit 5.6** *UK private equity investment (in real 2003 prices)*

| | *Total* | *Early stage* | | *Expansion* | | *Management buy-out /buy-in (MBO/MBI)* | |
|---|---|---|---|---|---|---|---|
| | £ million | £ million | % of total | £ million | % of total | £ million | % of total |
| **1984** | 285 | 77 | 27.1 | 148 | 52.1 | 59 | 20.7 |
| **1985** | 531 | 96 | 18.1 | 230 | 43.3 | 205 | 38.6 |
| **1986** | 711 | 159 | 22.4 | 230 | 32.3 | 322 | 45.3 |
| **1987** | 1,662 | 214 | 12.8 | 536 | 32.2 | 913 | 54.9 |
| **1988** | 2,202 | 221 | 10.0 | 738 | 33.5 | 1,244 | 56.5 |
| **1989** | 2,235 | 338 | 15.1 | 532 | 23.8 | 1,365 | 61.1 |
| **1990** | 1,590 | 184 | 11.6 | 569 | 35.8 | 837 | 52.6 |
| **1991** | 1,342 | 79 | 5.9 | 525 | 39.1 | 738 | 55.0 |
| **1992** | 1,637 | 107 | 6.6 | 474 | 28.9 | 1,056 | 64.5 |
| **1993** | 1,586 | 89 | 5.6 | 506 | 31.9 | 991 | 62.5 |
| **1994** | 2,096 | 96 | 4.6 | 603 | 28.8 | 1,398 | 66.7 |
| **1995** | 2,601 | 103 | 4.0 | 602 | 23.1 | 1,896 | 72.9 |
| **1996** | 3,331 | 155 | 4.7 | 703 | 21.1 | 2,473 | 74.2 |
| **1997** | 3,530 | 183 | 5.2 | 1,044 | 29.6 | 2,303 | 65.2 |
| **1998** | 4,203 | 321 | 7.6 | 915 | 21.8 | 2,967 | 70.6 |
| **1999** | 6,761 | 380 | 5.6 | 1,267 | 18.7 | 5,114 | 75.6 |
| **2000** | 6,785 | 749 | 11.0 | 2,260 | 33.3 | 3,777 | 55.7 |
| **2001** | 4,970 | 408 | 8.2 | 1,711 | 34.4 | 2,851 | 57.4 |
| **2002** | 4,610 | 304 | 6.6 | 1,414 | 30.7 | 2,893 | 62.7 |
| Total 1984–2002 | 52,669 | 4,262 | 8.1 | 15,007 | 28.5 | 33,400 | 63.4 |

*Source*: Report on Investment Activity, BVCA (British Venture Capital Association)

*Notes*: The data in this table refers to BVCA members. From 1984–6, investment by 3i (one of the UK's largest private equity companies) is not included

**Exhibit 5.7** *The scale and significance of US venture capital investment*

| | *Venture capital $ million (in real 2003 prices)* | *Venture capital investment as a % of* | |
|---|---|---|---|
| | | *M&A* | *LBO* |
| **1994** | 5,178 | 1.5 | 39.3 |
| **1995** | 9,854 | 1.6 | 34.0 |
| **1996** | 13,519 | 1.6 | 66.2 |
| **1997** | 17,110 | 1.5 | 62.1 |
| **1998** | 24,115 | 1.1 | 79.1 |
| **1999** | 60,357 | 2.0 | 94.1 |
| **2000** | 113,202 | 4.3 | 123.1 |
| **2001** | 42,639 | 4.2 | 68.4 |
| **2002** | 22,055 | 3.4 | 26.0 |

*Source*: PricewaterhouseCoopers/Venture Economics/NVCA MoneyTree Survey, Statistical Abstract of the USA, various years

If dwarfed by M&A, private equity is still important for two reasons. First, a substantial part of the UK and US workforces now work for private equity: BVCA (2004: 4) claimed that in the UK in 2003–4 private-equity-backed companies employed 2.7 million, a number equal to 18 per cent of private sector employees. The big private-equity players such as Blackstone have stakes in thirty-five to forty firms with a total of 300,000 employees and turnover funds of more than $450 billion, which equals that of a Top 20 Fortune 500 company (*The Economist*, 20 November 2004). If LBOs were sold as the answer to conglomerate merger, private equity is creating new giant conglomerates.

Despite the very wide range of corporate actions included in 'restructuring', from venture capital to downsizing, some believe the term is useful because it ties together diverse management interventions through their 'renewed emphasis upon the maximisation of shareholder wealth' (Wright et al. 1990). Against this, critics from economic sociology and other disciplines complain that the term introduces tautology and circularity into the definition because, 'whatever a corporation does under pressure is restructuring' (Usui and Colignon 1996: 571). From our point of view, restructuring is not a concept but a social rhetoric that is appropriated by academic critics and defenders in different ways as breach of stakeholder contract or discipline for profligate managers. The academic verdict on M&A by economists has long been overwhelmingly negative, but the newer forms of debt-financed restructuring have been greeted very positively by finance professors.

Traditionally, studies of take-overs undertaken by economists have used returns to capital as a measure of success, classically by comparing profits, distributions and share prices in the two independent companies before merger and in the one entity after merger. In both the USA and the UK, the overall verdict is overwhelmingly negative. The title and contents of Meeks's (1977) book *A Disappointing Marriage* epitomizes all those classic studies which show that the profits of the combined companies after merger are often lower than before merger, so that the main beneficiaries are the shareholders in the acquired company who, in hostile take-overs, are persuaded to sell by the offer of a bid premium. Against this background, in response to the LBO boom in the late 1980s, economists focused on the mechanisms underlying successful M&A. In an important article, Shliefer and Summers (1988) accepted that some US corporate raiders of the 1980s did make money for shareholders but then argued that these gains represented private benefits arising from redistribution from labour and other stakeholders to capital (not social gains). From this point of view, successful restructuring is about breach of implicit contract with workforce and suppliers because take-over raiders are able to treat such stakeholders (especially labour) more meanly.

By way of contrast, the newer forms of restructuring were welcomed by finance researchers such as Michael Jensen (see, for instance, Jensen 1989) as a fundamentally, rational and beneficial process within the market for corporate control. Through take-overs, buy-outs and buy-ins, new management teams could bid to use assets 'more productively' and realize a higher rate of return than incumbent management, which in turn benefits shareholders who can retain their stakes or sell out. More generally, through restructuring and the threat of restructuring, the capital market could control the tendency of some incumbent managers to invest in unprofitable projects and maintain organizational inefficiencies (Morin and Jarrell 2000: 346). This was seen by other authors such as Wurgler (2000) to have benign social effects because it meant a more efficient allocation of capital at the national level. The association of the newer forms of restructuring with debt was seen as a positive development (Baker and Smith 1998) because debt 'makes managers get up in the morning' and controls the propensity of some incumbent managers to hoard or misinvest free cash which indebted managements must pay out (Gressle 1990). This essentially micro-level argument is extended to the aggregate, society-wide level where the market for corporate control is socially beneficial because it reallocates assets away from misinvesting managers to those who invest for returns, while restructuring plus share buy-backs return cash and decision-making to individual investors who make rational calculations (Kensinger and Martin 1992). The social results are more or less entirely positive, because the only identified losers are top managers who have behaved dysfunctionally (Jensen 1998).

Thus, the newer forms of restructuring may be breach of stakeholder contract or discipline for misinvesting managers. In either case, the empirical evidence on returns to capital and shareholders are immediately puzzling because the accumulating evidence shows that the newer forms of restructuring are, by the classic measures, no more successful than the old forms of restructuring and do not generally deliver the high returns that one would expect from breach of contract or the disciplining of profligate managers. Towards the end of a two-year bear market in 2002, it was possible to show that private equity (thanks to a sustained fall in share prices) had outperformed the S&P 500 or FTSE 100 index. For instance, a 2003 report by PriceWaterhouseCoopers for the BVCA found that the ten-year return on private-equity funds was 14.2 per cent against 6.1 per cent for the FTSE 100 and that UK private equity 'significantly outperformed Total UK Pension Fund Assets over three, five and ten-year periods' (PriceWaterhouse-Coopers 2003: 1). But these kinds of results are not confirmed by independent researchers over longer periods. Kaplan and Schoar (2003) concluded that, from 1980 to 2001 the average private-equity buy-out fund slightly underperformed the S&P 500. Some deals and funds do achieve high rates of return but many do not. This pattern of high returns on certain investments is familiar from the new economy where only some digital technology start-ups and IPOs came good quite spectacularly. The average investor may then find the net effect is an increase in risk and, if private equity is more illiquid and riskier than S&P 500 index shares, in terms of orthodox finance theory, the investor should of course require a higher return.

Many in the business community believe that successful restructuring is about breach of stakeholder contract and, if problems are unsolved, changes of ownership will empower nastier management. In the spring of 2005, GM's CEO Rick Waggoner politely indicated that his company wanted to renegotiate the costly health-care package of GM workers and retirees with the United Auto Workers (UAW) union. A Bernstein analyst then observed that 'the UAW can either deal with Rick . . . now or Gordon Gekko later' (*Bernstein*, 12 April 2005). Yet at the same time, the disappointing outcomes of old and new restructuring raise all kinds of questions about how and why management's reach exceeds its grasp, even when Gordon Gekko is in charge. The disappointment has often been explained within social science by invoking management incapacity or organizational conflict as a single general cause of merger success or failure. Thus, managerial theories of the firm highlighted the motives of management hubris and empire-building, while organizational-behaviour theorists emphasized post-merger operating problems about integration and cultural differences. We accept that vanity can be a motive for mergers where cultural differences and organizational resistance then lead to wasted meetings and postponed decisions, but we do not think that such considerations provide a general explanation of why some restructuring delivers financially and much does not.

Our historical cases suggest that we should try to understand more about the process and context of restructuring in ways that takes us away from stereotypes of good/bad (or nice/nasty) management as well as the issues about 'implementation'. From this point of view, the cases in this book offer an interesting sample of variable condition–outcome relations: first, we have the exceptional (overall) success of acquisition at GE where restructuring is used deliberately to reinforce the capacity of a specific business model to meet stock-market expectations; second, we have average results at Glaxo, where horizontal merger is used to defend profitability and buy time for a business model under threat; third, we have the 'no response' case of Ford where long-standing problems about mediocre profitability and cyclicality had not, by 2005, induced restructuring in the form of down-sizing.

The contrast between GE and Glaxo is particularly interesting. As our historical case demonstrates, GE buys and sells a stream of smaller companies in the same way that mutual funds buy and sell shares. Hence, in its 2000 report, GE reported more than 100 acquisitions for the fourth year running. The secret of GE's success is that, as we argue in the case, these acquisitions are made in a very focused way that reduces the likelihood of mistakes in acquisition or integration. The modus operandi of GE was to buy sales and profits growth through acquisitions in financial services, where spreads were semi-automatically improved when newly acquired businesses borrowed using the triple-A credit rating guaranteed by GE's slow-growing blue-chip industrial business. By way of contrast, Glaxo turned to defensive merger with a large competitor in an attempt to defend a business model and pay-out norms that could not be sustained in the absence of new blockbuster drugs. The lever was cost reduction through sacking so that, within two years of the 1995 merger with Wellcome, a number equal to two-thirds of Wellcome's pre-merger staff had lost their jobs (GlaxoWellcome Annual Report and Accounts). As we argue in our case, Glaxo thereby avoided profits collapse and bought a little time but still needed to do another major acquisition within a few years to 'keep it going'. The *absence* of restructuring is equally interesting in the case of Ford which, like many other FTSE 100 and S&P 500 companies, has not so far pursued down-sizing and wholesale sackings. Of course, a company like Ford is a social as much as an economic institution thanks to the ownership stake of the Ford family and the power of the UAW. Nevertheless, there is also a suspicion that restructuring is a last resort for Ford because the results of giant-firm restructuring are generally disappointing for capital.

The causes of disappointment can be understood if we analyse the mechanics of redistribution from labour to capital. Here, simple accounting analysis of the composition of costs and operating ratios can be used to clarify two issues: first, how and why downsizing and labour-cost reduction are immediately attractive; second, why the benefits for capital are so often disappointing. Exhibit 5.8 presents data on composition of costs and operating ratios for a sample of large British firms engaged in the diverse activities of pharmaceuticals, manufacturing, grocery-retailing and water utilities. Most obviously, the table shows that what Ricardo called the 'fund for the employment of labour' is usually substantial and offers large absolute savings. Labour is vulnerable in restructuring because labour is often the largest component of cost; if outside purchases are modest and suppliers cannot be squeezed further, then labour is often the only controllable item. Thus, in three of the four activities analysed in Exhibit 5.8, labour accounts for half or more of internal costs, the exception being water where the rain falls freely and liquid pumps easily once the necessary infrastructure has been constructed.

If the absolute size of the wage fund provides the motivation for downsizing or otherwise reducing labour costs, the outcome of such moves is complicated: profit is a residual, and its size depends on internal ratios that move slowly because they are governed by activity business model and competitive interaction. Furthermore, because profit is often compared with other variables such as capital employed in the form of ratios such as ROCE or return on sales (ROS), such measures of profitability can also be significantly affected by changes in the balance sheet (e.g. through issuing new debt) as well as by turnover and costs in the profit-and-loss account (or income statement). It is not easy to take several million dollars of labour cost out, but it turns out to be even more difficult to move from a 3 to 7 per cent return on sales, or from 10 to 14 per cent ROCE.

Exhibit 5.8 shows that cash (or EBITDA) is the residual available after suppliers and the internal workforce have been paid; if the external purchase/sales ratio or labour's share of internal costs ratio cannot be reduced, it is very difficult to generate more cash from a pound of turnover. As long as the business model does not change radically and competitive pressures (or regulators) act on prices, each activity has a distinct and slow-changing profile in terms of the two key ratios of external purchases and labour's share of internal costs, so that individual firms will struggle to beat the ratios. In retail, suppliers claim just over 80p of every £1 of customers' spend and the workforce typically claims another 10p so that, in ratio terms, it is difficult to generate more than 10p in the pound as cash surplus. The ratios tend to stay the same in this kind of competitive business because innovations including breach of stakeholder contract will be quickly copied and any cost savings are fairly quickly given away to the consumer, not pocketed by the producer. In operating terms, the attractive cash-generating activities are those such as ethical pharmaceuticals or water, which both combine a low purchase/sales ratio and

**Exhibit 5.8** *Activity ratios for four UK sectors: five-year averages, 1994–8*

| *Sector* | *External purchases as a % of sales revenues* | *Labour costs share of internal costs* | *Cash generated per £ of sales* | *Profit generated per £ of sales* | *Capital employed per £ of sales* | *ROCE* | *ROE* |
|---|---|---|---|---|---|---|---|
| | % | % | pence | pence | £ | % | % |
| Pharmaceuticals | 48.7 | 46.8 | 27.3 | 15.6 | 0.73 | 34.4 | 54.6 |
| Manufacturing | 62.1 | 64.7 | 13.3 | 8.9 | 0.66 | 20.9 | 27.3 |
| Grocery retail | 82.3 | 56.9 | 7.6 | 3.83 | 0.35 | 16.0 | 15.3 |
| Water utilities | 38.4 | 33.2 | 41.1 | 22.77 | 3.05 | 9.0 | 14.3 |

*Sources*: Datastream/ICV

*Notes*: Companies used are: pharmaceuticals = SmithKline Beecham, Zeneca, GlaxoWellcome; manufacturing = GEC, Smiths Industries, Associated British Foods, Siebe; Grocery retail = Tesco, Asda, Morrison, Iceland, Safeway, Sainsbury, Somerfield; Water utilities = Severn Trent, Anglian, Hyder, South Staff, Yorkshire. External purchases are not disclosed but can be derived by subtracting value added from sales revenue, where value added is calculated as operating profit plus depreciation plus total labour costs including social charges. Cash is calculated as operating profit plus depreciation. For calculating ROCE and ROE profit is taken as after tax, but adding back net interest charges (and including associate businesses). Capital employed is share capital and reserves plus long term debt

a low labour share. However, good cash generation from each pound of revenue only turns into a high ROCE when, as in pharmaceuticals (but not in water), the capital employed is modest.

The tyranny of operating ratios in competitive activities is such that management can change almost everything without ever shifting the basic operating ratios governing cash generation. Thus, British supermarkets have reformatted their sales several times since the 1960s as they first moved into larger self-service stores and then in the 1980s to superstores on edge-of-town sites, before returning in the 2000s to the town centre with convenience stores. They have also changed their offer, with more emphasis over twenty years on added-value items such as ready meals and in-store bakeries, just as, more recently, they have made a deliberate move into higher margin, cheap clothes and electrical goods combined with extra lines such as CDs, magazines and cosmetics.

But through all this, the basic supermarket operating ratios have stayed remarkably the same with 80p for suppliers and 10p for the internal workforce, leaving 10p of cash. The limits set by the operating ratios are such that business analysts often have a strong interest in marginal sales because the extra sales after fixed costs have been absorbed are an important driver of profitability. Hence, the obsessive interest of stock-market analysts in the trend of like-for-like sales in retail stores or the interest in car stocks and factory utilization in auto assembly, because the important difference between heavy losses and 7 per cent on sales is driven by marginal volume increases, just as performance is very quickly undermined by a modest erosion of market share. As Williams et al. (1994) argued, a car-assembly plant typically has a break-even around 70 per cent utilization: sales above that point are highly profitable because the extra car sells at full price but costs only one component set plus a little direct assembly labour. Unfortunately, increases in like-for-like grocery sales or the high utilization that comes from a best-selling car model often represent good fortune, which is powerfully influenced by the happenstance of competitive interaction and cannot therefore be made into the central objective of strategy.

The question in this case is why does management still do restructuring? The answer is that they do it because it keeps things going and buys time for firms who are under pressure from the capital market, just as it also usefully confuses things by making like-for-like comparisons very difficult when the corporate vehicle changes shape all the time. Glaxo's acquisition of Wellcome in 1995 and its merger with SmithKlineBeecham in 2000 suggest that defensive restructuring can become a drug where the more you do, the more you have to do to get the result. This greatly increases risk as we can see by considering the cautionary case of British GEC whose defensive restructuring through high-velocity corporate dealing and large-scale disemployment ends in disaster. GEC was created as a British national champion through merger in the late 1960s. The giant firm then retreated from consumer products and contested markets into heavy electricals, telecoms and defence electronics, where it was sharply managed for financial results. In an extended case study, Williams et al. (1983) established that GEC's basic problem was no growth in its core industrial business which had been run for margins, so that real profit increased by just 12 per cent over ten years from 1988 to 1998, roughly in line with value added or net output at the economy level.

To keep the stock market happy and to defend its independent existence, after the late 1980s GEC went for large-scale, high-speed restructuring as businesses were acquired and divested, along with very rapid run-down of employment in the combine as a whole. The annual reports between 1988 and 1998 disclose seventy-nine major restructuring events involving acquisitions, sell-offs, joint ventures and suchlike, which radically changed the shape of the company (Froud et al. 2000b). Most notably, in the early 1990s around one-third of turnover was backed into joint ventures such as GEC-Alsthom and Thomson Marconi Sonar, with the defensive aim of avoiding take-over and break-up of GEC. As Exhibit 5.9 shows, company-wide employment was more than halved from 157,000 in 1988 to 72,000 in 1998 and, in the remaining wholly owned parts of GEC, employment fell by 63 per cent over the same period. However, despite labour-shedding and the high-velocity dealing, the business was untransformed in operating terms. Labour as a share of internal costs remained at about 67 per cent until 1998 when it fell to 59 per cent as a further 8,000 jobs were lost. Part of the problem was a rising external-purchase-to-sales ratio which has increased fairly steadily from 53 to 72 per cent, presumably because sacked workers came back as contract labour. Hence, the need for more restructuring which involved selling the defence businesses to BAE, renaming the company Marconi and buying second-rate telecoms businesses at the top of the market, which brought the firm to ruin.

Thus the increasing popularity of private equity needs to be set in the context of modest returns to capital from restructuring and the risk of high-velocity restructuring.

***Exhibit 5.9*** *Employment in GEC, 1988–98*

| | *Employment in wholly owned operations* | | *Employment in joint ventures and associations* | | *Total employment* |
|---|---|---|---|---|---|
| | *Number* | *% of total* | *Number* | *% of total* | |
| **1988** | 118,458 | 75.3 | 38,804 | 24.7 | 157,262 |
| **1989** | 102,657 | 70.8 | 42,372 | 29.2 | 145,029 |
| **1990** | 74,653 | 69.5 | 32,782 | 30.5 | 107,435 |
| **1991** | 84,880 | 71.6 | 33,649 | 28.4 | 118,529 |
| **1992** | 75,430 | 71.8 | 29,565 | 28.2 | 104,995 |
| **1993** | 64,899 | 69.6 | 28,329 | 30.4 | 93,228 |
| **1994** | 59,062 | 68.6 | 27,059 | 31.4 | 86,121 |
| **1995** | 56,381 | 68.5 | 25,870 | 31.5 | 82,251 |
| **1996** | 57,142 | 68.9 | 25,825 | 31.1 | 82,967 |
| **1997** | 52,294 | 65.5 | 27,552 | 34.5 | 79,846 |
| **1998** | 44,323 | 61.6 | 27,640 | 38.4 | 71,963 |

*Source*: Froud, J., Haslam, C., Johal, S. and Williams, K. 'Restructuring for shareholder value and its implications for labour', *Cambridge Journal of Economics* 2000, vol. 24, no. 6, pp. 771–97, by permission of Cambridge Political Economy Society

If value creation through restructuring is problematic, the modus operandi of private equity becomes more intelligible. The current modus operandi is described in a recent Morgan Stanley report: the purchasers of the division or public company will fund two-thirds of the purchase price by selling bonds and then apply the cash flow to paying down the debt before (hopefully) selling the company on at a profit within five years (Morgan Stanley 2005). This has two benefits for those who provide equity: first, the returns to bond holders are effectively capped by fixed-interest payments and debt is also paid down so that the gains are concentrated in the hands of those (relatively few) who provide equity and thus enjoy leveraged returns. The aim is to sell surplus assets immediately and to sell the whole business on within five years after giving the business a 'haircut' so that any operating gains are augmented by a dealing profit. For all its prestige, the private-equity business model is almost exactly like used-car trading where capital is borrowed from the bank, the car-auction purchase is always cosmetically cleaned up though not mechanically fixed up, and the aim is a dealing profit over and above the cost of the borrowed money.

## NARRATIVE AND NUMBERS

As the previous sections have argued, financialization creates problems for corporate managers that complex moves such as 'restructuring' and 'sector matrix' cannot easily resolve. This takes us to narrative and numbers because giant-firm strategy is not only about moves and results in the product market, it is also about delivering a narrative of strategic purpose that is sometimes corroborated by financial results. These numbers are of obsessional interest because investors after financialization have an instrumental approach and (though calculations vary) most need cash and earnings to distribute to shareholders and to support the share price. Against this background, we propose a new method of analysis that involves playing narrative and numbers against each other to explore corroboration and discrepancy between the two registers of narrative and numbers.

The premise is that, whilst discourse may be constitutive in certain situations, at company level the financial numbers are not a simple function of the CEO's narrative (except in cases of fraud). Equally the relation between numbers and narrative is complicated because the numbers are a complex resource, not unproblematic evidence, and firm narrative often meshes with a broader industry narrative or an economic grand narrative. Various actors such as business journalists and stock-market analysts can endorse, modify or challenge company narratives or conventional understandings of an industry in a world where narratives are not controlled by the corporate CEO or any one group of actors. The framing of targets, the definition of results as good news or bad news and the criteria of success and failure are a kind of collective endeavour of an unstable kind. Our three historical cases illustrate and develop this approach to corporate strategy and demonstrate that it is very different from positivistic hypothesis-testing because the numbers are an awkwardly independent point of reference and object of construction in a world of contesting narratives. The crucial difference from positivism is that corroboration (like discrepancy) is not the end point but the start for our exploration which opens up new critical perspectives on firms such as GE.

The approach is revisionist in two ways. First, it takes us further away from the idea of the capital market as an external source of discipline in an agency-theory sense because, through key actors such as analysts and fund managers, the capital market is a kind of co-author of many firm and industry narratives. This challenges much mainstream finance and economics which views the economy as a collection of separate and distinct markets and believes the world runs on ascertainable, predictable general relations between numbers. It also challenges behavioural finance which refers the unpredictable and variable results of market operations to individual or group psychology. By way of contrast, our approach focuses on the narrative or discursive element which is (within explorable limits) constitutive. Second, the approach breaks new ground because, as Paulos (1998: 8) observes, 'the gap between stories and statistics' is a synecdoche for the broader division between literary and scientific culture. In social sciences, this division is being reworked because the soft social sciences have taken a cultural turn to recognize discourse and social construction, whereas mainstream economics and finance have taken a technical turn towards extracting general relations from large datasets. Each side now assumes the judgemental right to apply its apparatus to the other's corpus, so that studies of the rhetoric of economics are balanced by the application of content analysis techniques to discourse.

There is a huge literature on narrative in social-sciences literatures and a large enough literature on business and narrative, but regrettably much of it does not suit our immediate task. The most trenchant work has been produced by academics criticizing the Harvard type of business case which tells a story about management imposing itself on product market or organization to earn its just reward. Thus, Boje (2001: 8) criticizes a, 'one voiced and homogeneous way of narrating where the omniscient narrator hides behind every line', while Collins (2003) observes that these stories are like Readers' Digest abridged tales of real-life courage. We would agree that Harvard-type cases are inherently fragile and naïve because they over-simplify success and add assumptions about identity and causality that are challenged by subsequent events. This view of the standard case study enters into our judgement on classical strategy and our determination to do something different, but it does not immediately provide the tools for analysing something like the narratives about companies, as told by CEOs and challenged by journalists and analysts.

British research on 'corporate communications' clearly establishes that such story-telling activity has become more important. Thus, Pye (2001) interviewed senior FTSE 100 managers in the late 1980s and again in the late 1990s, where she found that the CEOs of 1989 spent 10 per cent of their time 'talking to the City' whereas the CEOs of 1998–2000 spent 20–5 per cent of their time on such activity. Pye also noted 'much greater consistency in the language executives use to account for their corporate actions, with almost all routinely using phrases such as strategic focus, shareholder value and corporate governance to frame their explanations' (2001: 193). But this issue of language is rather disappointingly not taken up in more substantial studies of corporate communications by authors such as Holland (1997), who quite conspicuously does not use terms such as discourse and narrative. Instead, Holland presents a dignified public relations concept of effective communication as the handmaiden of 'good management' in thirty-three large listed UK companies. Thus, in a first phase, 'each company held an extensive debate at board level to identify and clarify strategy and the main message to be communicated' (Holland 1997: vii); and then, 'the central task of corporate communications was to ensure that these decisions were well understood by the market' on the comfortable assumption that 'good management' not communications creates value (Holland 1997: 16).

The larger questions about the content of corporate communications have been taken up by systematic empiricist researchers in the USA and UK using tools such as content and linguistic analysis and empirical correlations. Much of the work has focused on company report and accounts, using the narrative front sections of reports to explore both the content and language of the messages prepared for shareholders. Some work focuses on particular issues such as the representation of gender, environmental disclosures or reporting good and bad news. The research then takes the form of either cross-sectional analysis of samples of firms or time-series analysis of a particular firm or group of firms over time. As with other kinds of technicist research, the availability of techniques and source materials is in itself enough to produce a burgeoning literature and specialist journals. The typical research study then becomes technical in itself and for itself, as with Thomas's (1997) analysis of transitivity and thematic structures at clause level in letters to stockholders from a failing machine-tool company. The efforts to find results with significance for non-specialists are often questionable, as when Kohut and Segars (1992) found that word count, number of sentences and content analysis in letters to stockholders may be predictors of future performance of a Fortune 500 company.

If we are interested in defining narrative and how it works, we have to turn to organization-studies analysts such as Gabriel (2000) and Boje (2001) who treat narrative as part of the internal life of the organization on the assumption that multiple polysemic (local, internal and intimate) narratives help us to understand the plural, fragmented nature of organizations and the difficulty of organizational change. Their research elaborates the everyday experience of organizational life where, for example, responsible individuals or support functions are often scapegoated by telling tales about how they have (once again) messed up. This process of identifying actors, competences and motives is highly relevant to the internal implementation of shareholder value and other performative initiatives which try to drive new priorities down the giant firm. But, it is not so relevant to understanding the converging (if not monologic) external, distant and impersonal narratives about companies (re)produced by stock-market analysts and journalists after briefings by CEOs and investor-relations departments.

Nevertheless, the organization-studies literature is a resource of concepts (and disagreements) that can be used to define narrative. Generically, narratives are ordering or constructive devices which work by packaging and borrowing identifications about character, imputing motive, adding causal assumptions and so forth. Sometimes, but not always, narratives do this by arranging these elements along a time-line to give a plot with a chronology so that some narratives can be distinguished by formal structure as well as by object or what they are about. Boje (2001) distinguishes between story fragments which he calls 'ante narratives' and more formally structured and coherent narratives. In the absence of formal structure, generic identifications or tropes become very important, especially *motive* on whether events are accidental or incidental; *causal connections* around actions; *responsibility*, which distributes blame and credit; *unity* such that a group comes to be defined as such; *fixed qualities* such that heroes are heroic and villains are villainous.

The relevance of some of these concepts to our case material is high, provided we define narrative broadly and do not insist on formal structure and chronology. For example, our Glaxo case shows that the debate about the social purpose and rationale of the pharmaceutical industry is a battle of the tropes when pharma is either virtuous research-led life-saving or vicious marketing-led profiteering. Both sides agree on the central importance of patents, but the industry spokespersons identify patents as the guarantee of reinvestment in fundamental research, while the industry's critics identify patents as the basis for holding society to ransom. Interestingly, despite the cultural turn, academics have been slow to develop this kind of narrative analysis, so that the most perceptive epitome of company narratives (as received by City fund managers) is an untheorised account produced by a practitioner, or more exactly a retired British investment banker.

Tony Golding's account (2001: 162–74) of 'what fund managers want' focuses on invariant key themes which recur in almost every City analysis. These themes include the prospects going forward for earnings and growth plus the 'quality of management' and the CEO, which will often be discussed in terms of delivery and shareholder friendliness. Other topics for general discussion include the business-model plan for cost recovery and any bold management moves, with much attention given to M&A (Golding 2001: 168). The analysis of individual companies is here filtered through the preferences of the market which generally rates pure plays and keeping it simple, though these preferences are apparently suspended for those companies such as GE that break the rules but reliably deliver financial results. As Golding notes, the market ideally also wants a 'story in a box' about something like 'recovery' whose outcomes define corporate reputation and management competence as well as the character of the stock as boring or exciting, growth or income, cyclical or stable (2001: 165–6).

The subtext of Golding's analysis is that every giant company needs a story for the City or Wall Street audience and some companies have more compelling and credible stories. In our case studies, we build on this perception to construct a more complex kind of analysis which focuses on multiple narratives as well as the performative in relation to the financial numbers. Thus, company narratives exist in a context that often includes industry narratives and grand narratives of macro-economic trajectory so that our analysis needs to distinguish different micro-, meso- and macro-narratives whose interrelation can involve contest and challenge as much as support and confirmation. It is also important to note that management involves doing as well as saying, so any discussion of the narrative needs to be cross-referenced to the performative in a world which, of course, does not solely consist of stories. Furthermore, the identifications and assumptions about the relation between financial numbers and management effort can be explored and challenged in cases of corporate success and failure where there is scope for independent analysis of the numbers.

It may be best to begin by considering the distinctive characteristics of company narratives by corporate CEOs or stock-market analysts which are primarily intended for fund managers with power to buy or sell shares. How is a narrative about, say, GE under Jack Welch different from a television soap opera where each episode of the soap will typically include sections from several different long-running narratives about a subset of characters facing melodramatic dilemmas? If it is quite difficult to distinguish between soap opera and the Harvard case study, the company narratives produced by CEOs and analysts are different mainly because they are pitched to a market audience of investors who have diverse preferences about income or capital gains but share a common instrumental orientation towards pecuniary return. While soap-opera audiences can be engaged by a stolen kiss or a wild punch thrown in the closing moments of an episode, the market audience is enchanted only by a story that is confirmed as a money making opportunity after cross-check against the financial numbers. This instrumental preoccupation powerfully influences the form of the company narrative which ideally takes a before-and-after form: *ex ante*, the firm and its management strategy is represented by the corporate CEO as purposive action for financial results, which is then *ex post* vindicated by the achievement of positive financial numbers on earnings which are celebrated by management, analysts and business press.

One of our historical case companies, GE, is included in this book because it has been generally understood in these stereotyped terms as a brilliant success. Through narrative and performative initiative about leadership and organization, GE management has gained the opportunity to take the credit for 'delivery' of sustained profits increase. Thus, just after Welch had retired, *Fortune* (19 February 2002) bracketed GE's long unbroken record of earnings increase with 'straight talking celebrity CEO (and) its vaunted culture of entrepreneurship and achievement'. In such cases of exceptional success, circulation then involves repetition without dissent, so that the company-originated narrative is taken up fairly uncritically in the commentary of business journalists and stock-market analysts and thereby gains a life (semi-)independent of the company before it becomes exemplar and icon for business-school authors such as Tichy whose 'recipes for success' books on GE appear on the management shelves of airport bookshops (see, for example, Tichy and Sherman 1993, Tichy and Cardwell 2002). But the sustained success of GE represents a special case, and the more usual condition of giant firms is represented by our two other historical cases, where Ford has ongoing problems about management credibility and GlaxoSmithKline has a diminished status as a fallen star.

In these two other cases, the circulation of company narratives generally involves challenge and critique of companies in a Micawberish predicament where the balance between income and expenditure discloses not enough profit or sales growth. In exceptional circumstances, as at the end of the new-economy period, in an under-performing old company such as Ford, Jacques Nasser as CEO could give interviews about new business models and then the media simply broadcast his promises about Ford becoming a service company. More usually, analysts and journalists criticize and evaluate promises, outcomes and outcomes against promises. Thus, Nasser's successor Bill Ford faced initial scepticism about his 'back to basics' plan for profitable car assembly (*Financial Times*, 4 December 2001, 12 January 2002), and by 2005 these same critics were noting that the profit contribution from European premium brands was well below target (*Financial Times*, 1 March 2005). Financial under-performance always empowers a company's external critics whose ranks include ambitious young graduates and embittered old hacks in journalism and research. Thus, all GlaxoSmithKline's plans and excuses after disappointing results in early 2004 were dismissed in one cynical paragraph by Lex in the *Financial Times* (13 February 2004) who observed the company had nothing in the new-drug pipeline that would make any difference in the next couple of years.

If company stories have multiple authors, there is a strong tendency towards convergence onto one narrative line about corporate problems, performance and prospects. This herding is encouraged by the way in which all the outside commentators on giant firms such as Ford or GlaxoSmithKline now have electronic access to the same press and analyst reports. E-mail circulation lists and the databases such as Investext (which retrieves analyst reports) have changed the nature of research and democratized access so that analysts reports are now read widely by many, including journalists, who are not clients or research subscribers. Ideas about corporate trajectory and management responsibility often materialize in the more substantial analyst reports and are then consolidated by repetition in the business print media whose stories work much like gossip in small communities. The exigencies of daily journalism mean that the same factoids and identifications are endlessly repeated in new stories, after a brief scan of what others have written in recent stories. This was classically the case in the journalistic line about how Shell's restatement of its reserves in 2004 undid its reputation for stodgy honesty. Within seventy-two hours of the shock announcement, the *Wall Street Journal Europe* (12 January 2004) had focused the reputational issue: 'the oil company might have had a reputation for being overly conservative, yet at least it was solid'. And this formula was subsequently taken up right across the media (see, for example, *Business Week*, 23 February 2004).

The corporate narrative is often, but not invariably, set in the context of an industry narrative. As we have already noted in an earlier section of this chapter, the concept of industry is problematic in so far as financialization encourages corporate management to think outside this box and to consider sector-matrix moves. But the financial-services conglomerates and the media hold to the idea of an industry-related space of production activity and final product market competition. This makes benchmark comparisons between companies such as Ford and GM or GlaxoSmithKline and Merck much easier, provided the analyst dodges the hard questions about whether two companies represent well-matched similarity or well-understood difference. As our case histories show, developments such as the growth of the finance businesses inside Ford and GE make companies more opaque and complicate activity so that comparisons become very difficult. But the industry frame will survive because it is an economizing device for journalists and analysts. They can become industry specialists who reuse their contextual information about product market trends and suchlike whenever they write another news story or report on an individual company. The result is a kind of community of those who 'follow' an industry and a company where many of the key actors are outside the company but are networked by briefings such as pharma company research days and PR jollies such as new car launches.

Company narratives usually have short and sometimes powerful lives as they are often discarded after three to five years; whereas many industry narratives have long but contested lives so that a forty-year life span is possible. Thus, the argument about the social purpose of the pharma industry can be traced back to the USA in the late 1950s, when Estes Kefauver produced his definitive critique of the industry (see Case study 1). The negative publicity of the 1990s focused new issues such as the price of AIDS drugs to sub-Saharan Africa which only revived the old criticisms in a different context. In other industries, old narratives get worn out and discredited under pressure of circumstances, values and interests, while new narratives are invented and disseminated. This is most obviously so in car assembly, as considered in our Ford case, where the representation of the industry has changed considerably over the past twenty years. In the initial response to Japanese competition, the problem of US competitiveness was constructed within a lean vs. mass production opposition, so that the problem became a deficiency of manufacturing technique. European researchers in the mid-1990s then pioneered the idea that the competition between Japan and America was a contest between social settlements. This argument about the costs of pensions and health care at Ford and GM had entered the mainstream of media commentary by the mid-2000s, by which time consultants and journalists were pressing new, failed business-model explanations for assembler under-performance.

It is of course possible to have a firm without an industry, as in the case of the conglomerate GE which cannot be easily fitted into an industry, though it jealously guards its status as an 'industrial' company because that deflects critical attention and helps defend its triple-A credit rating. If the industry narrative represents an optional kind of context, so does the overarching grand narrative which is relevant in some, but not all, company cases. Such economic grand narratives are typically tied to a specific time and place where they explain opportunity and constraint. So it was in the case of the 1970s British labour problem, which was always over-rated but served as a prism for (mis)understanding the drivers of manufacturing decline (Williams et al. 1983). This then provided a kind of meta-rationale both for Thatcher's anti-union politics and for the market's preference for bank and retail shares because the British were (apparently) bad at manufacturing. In a more positive way and over a much shorter period from the mid-1990s, the US new economy narrative about digital technologies, unglued supply chains and the falling costs of information was another hugely influential meta-narrative. For management and investors, the new-economy narrative provided a kind of heuristic about how technological paradigm change had undermined the old business models of incumbent giant firms now threatened by the emergence of agile start-ups, whose share price should reflect their potential share of huge new product markets, not next year's earnings (Feng et al. 2001).

The distinction between company, industry and grand narratives must then lead to questions about how it all fits together. The relation between the different narratives is not one of harmony as in a musical composition, whereby each narrative becomes a part or a melody assigned to a particular voice, and counterpoint then becomes one melody overlaid onto another. The end result is quite unlike a Bach cantata constructed according to strict rules of composition. In the absence of a composer and agreed rules, different voices sing from different hymn sheets and some voices are louder and more strident than others. Narrative is never a function or product of a social position, but some voices are louder because of the actor's structural position so that the new CEO or the star analyst can help to make or break a story. But the idea of narrative as voice is also fundamentally misleading because it encourages a very limited concept of performance as vocalization not enactment.

When management is about doing as well as saying, it is necessary to extend the concept of performance to include management initiatives that 'show' that strategy is being enacted. These are now a characteristic part of giant company management, which includes enactment as well as telling stories because stories can always be disparaged as what the British call 'spin', i.e. presentational gloss of the kind familiar from PR releases or legal pleas in mitigation. As our case explains, GE under Jack Welch was redefined by a succession of initiatives about No. 1 or 2, Six Sigma, boundarylessness and e-business, which all had action correlates starting with the divestment of businesses that could not be No. 1 or 2 (except in the GE finance business where the rule was quite sensibly deemed irrelevant). In the late 1990s, Ford under Jacques Nasser announced the strategy of becoming a services company and enacted that strategy by buying Kwik-Fit a British tyre, exhaust and battery fast-fit chain (as well as moving further into car assembly through the purchase of Land Rover and Volvo).

The idea of the performative has already been introduced in our Chapter 4 discussion on the promise and outcome of shareholder value. The recognition of this element in our case studies adds another powerful complication if we discuss the performative on the infelicity assumption that performance often miscarries and we live in a world of discrepancy and disappointment. The power arises from the materiality of initiatives which demonstrate that the giant company's management is walking the walk as well as talking the talk, because everybody knows that this kind of commitment does change things. Thus GE was materially different after the divestments of the early 1980s: between 1981 and 1984 some 20 per cent (some 117 business units) of the 1981 $21 billion asset base was divested (Tichy and Sherman 1993: 102). The complication arises because initiatives also symbolically enact strategy in ways that then complicate cause/effect attribution, in so far as management is also making other moves of different and contradictory kinds. GE was also symbolically different after each successive initiative, while senior management carried on unannounced with building a finance business that delivered the sales growth and earnings. The implication of our case histories is that Welch understood this powerful complication but Nasser did not and fell into a *post hoc ergo propter hoc* fallacy, as do many uncritical outside commentators on strategy.

If we then ask how the different elements of the narrative and performative all fit together, the answer seems to be in unstable, unique configurations very different from those envisaged in traditional political economy with its 'box and arrow' approach, centred on stable configurations with durable, mechanical links from institutions to conduct and performance in models of capitalism. Indeed, the narrative and performative add mediating and constructive complications which prevent any such relations working. As we explained in Chapter 3 of this introduction, one big problem about shareholder value is 'What do shareholders want?'. From the analysis in this chapter, we would add the point that a second big problem about shareholder value is 'Now you see it, now you don't'.

Our case studies suggest that the speed of representational change around the individual firm varies directly with the transparency and predictability of firm and industry. GlaxoSmithKline could be described as a single-activity firm operating in an ethical pharma industry that is relatively predictable for two reasons. First, because of the visibility of its future products in the research and development (R&D) pipeline, that will bring in new revenue, and second, because of the fixed patent length of its current products, that will result in a decline in revenue once the patent expires. By way of contrast, GE is an opaque firm with multiple activities, while Ford's activity mix is simple though car assembly is an unpredictable, mature and cyclical assembly business. These conditions encourage the (re)invention of narrative, bold appropriations and the dissolution of shared understandings about the drivers of profitability. Thus GE is the Zelig of corporate America, which reinvents itself by offering down-sizing in the 1980s, the learning organization and e-business for the 1990s and good governance for the 2000s. On Ford, various stock-market analysts seize on different individual predictors, such as vehicle stocks or interest rates. They do so in the absence of a shared understanding of how the variables fit together in a general business model such as that of the ethical pharma industry which adds marketing so as to sell imitative blockbusters.

If all this means the end of corporate capitalism as political economy used to know it, cultural economy needs to find new ways of critically interrogating management narratives and performance, and our argument is that the financial numbers become important at this point. In the discussion so far, we have observed that financial numbers matter because investors have instrumental orientations, but we have not analysed how numbers relate to narrative. The relation between numbers and narrative can be clarified in two steps. First, we can observe the way in which narrative is often understood, through the opposition of fact and fiction, fact and value, so that a narrative is something which is 'made up'. Second, we will consider the question of whether numbers are in any sense facts so that we can understand more clearly whether and how financial numbers can serve as a check on narrative invention and as a test of narrative promise. This does no more than vindicate the common sense of Golding's City fund managers who take it for granted that numbers are a check on the tendency of self serving actors to make it up as they go along. But we would note that cultural turn academics start from different assumptions about social construction and the best way to challenge such academic assumptions and vindicate common sense is by some old-style Oxford philosophy which aims to clarify concepts. In the spirit of C. E. M. Joad's catchphrase interjection on the wireless *Brains Trust* programme, 'it all depends what you mean by —'.

The opposition between fact and fiction (or fact and value) structures much recent discussion of narrative by academics and non-academics. The house intellectuals employed by leading advertising agencies have recently bought into the idea of narrative exactly because they believe that stories can be made up and now wish to communicate this good news to discouraged advertisers who might otherwise close their account or spend less. Thus Myra Stark of Saatchi & Saatchi claims 'the business community is increasingly turning to stories' to differentiate brands and then explains the attraction of stories to brand managers by summarizing Yann Martel's novel, *The Life of Pi*, whose theme is 'you can choose your story' (Stark 2003). Stark's pitch includes the claim that stories engage the emotions and can therefore shift product more effectively than 'rational economic appeals to consumers . . . in terms of reasons to believe, attributes and benefits' (2003: 2). Within organizational studies, academic researchers such as Boje (2001) take up these assumptions about emotional engagement through their recycling of the old positivistic opposition between fact and value. Thus Gabriel distinguishes between organizational stories and more sober, narrative, 'factual or descriptive accounts of events that aspire to objectivity rather than emotional effect' (Gabriel 2000: 5). Within this old-fashioned positivistic frame, an organizational story represents something entirely different from an 'objective account' such as, for example, a witness statement taken by the police in connection with a criminal investigation.

In these usages, narrative means fiction and emotional appeal which escapes the mundane constraints of fact. The function of advertising (old and new) is to promote this escape as with the Mercedes car adverts which continue to emphasize product engineering and quality despite, or because of, the unreliability of the Mercedes product and dissatisfaction with the dealer network. According to the J. D. Power 2005 Customer Satisfaction Index, the Mercedes E Class ranks ninety-fifth out of 124 models and Mercedes as a manufacturer rates 'below average' (*What Car*, 14 April 2005). Journalists and analysts routinely work in the same way as we have done in the sentence above. They treat giant-company narratives as forward-looking promises that can be checked against the backward-looking financial numbers so that, even if giant-company management chooses its narrative, outsiders can check the financial results. These assumptions can be seen every day in the business press, as for example, in the following story, which was more or less randomly chosen from the *Financial Times* on the day this paragraph was drafted. The story covers the 2004 results of Matalan, a minor British discount retailer which struggles to compete with Tesco and Wal-Mart. It is interesting because the story shows a journalist and two analysts treating disappointing numbers for the year ending February 2005 as a practical check on the further elaboration of any fiction about recovery at Matalan:

> Matalan's fragile recovery appears to have stalled, with the discount retailer's underlying sales falling nearly 9 per cent at the start of the new financial year, triggering a round of hefty downgrades by analysts . . . The concern remains that the company cannot return to its peak of 2002–03. One analyst said: 'the issues are pretty structural and it's very difficult to see them getting back to their former levels of profit. There are no signs of this ever being a growth business again'. Another said: 'Over the course of last year, the recovery was pretty unconvincing – it failed to make up for all the like-for-like losses and margins are still down'.
>
> (*Financial Times*, 5 May 2005)

If we wish to understand how and why journalists and analysts can in this way put their trust in numbers, it is useful to begin by distinguishing two different meanings of the word 'fact'. According to the *Concise Oxford English Dictionary*, 'fact' means in one sense a 'thing certainly known to have occurred or be true, a datum of experience' and, in a second sense, 'fact' means a 'thing assumed as a basis for inference'. The first 'primary datum' meaning comes out of discredited philosophy. Empiricism after Hume and positivism up to Popper believed that knowledge represented so many propositions that could, one way or another, be tested against neutral, unproblematic observations, and this obsolete epistemology formed the basis for a now-discredited attempt to rationalize natural scientific practice in these terms and to force social science into a frame of scientism. The second 'basis for inference' meaning is much more interesting because it comes with less epistemological baggage and certainly does not presuppose any kind of empiricism or positivism. The only precondition for inference is that the facts should be independent of, and not generated by, the narrative. The financial markets, civil society and the state all rest on this founding assumption because civil and criminal courts require inference by juries, regardless of whether the jury contains one or several culturally turned professors. In our view, the financial numbers are not facts in the 'datum of experience' sense but they are near enough facts in the 'basis for inference' sense. And that justifies the common-sense approach of journalists and analysts who use the numbers as a check on fictional company and industry narratives.

Thus, we would concede that financial numbers are socio-technically constructed in ways that often allow several different narratives to find empirical support. Financial numbers are presented within a framework of company law and accounting regulation, which specifies the reporting statements that must be produced and the rules about treatment of specific items. Thus the giant corporation must produce a profit and loss (or income) statement (as well as cash-flow and balance sheet) according to definite rules about, for example, the basis for valuing assets or whether stock options could or should be expensed. These pro-forma standard financial measures generate a complex set of numbers, which are not themselves a narrative but a resource which narratives draw on as users select and put numbers together to tell a story. The numbers do not speak for themselves and can be can be rearranged into various patterns so that several different firm or industry stories of success or failure can find some support in a complex set of numbers that includes indicators of strength and of weakness.

But this conclusion does not justify complete relativism and the supposition that any narrative can be justified by selective citing of numbers. The first constraint is established by the existence of a general market consensus on which financial numbers matter and form the basis for judgements of success and failure. If corporate management could choose its own numerical indicators of success for each new report, few companies would fail. But, in the world as it is, analysts and journalists usually agree on the primary shareholder relevant financial numbers such as share price, earnings and sales revenue so that they hold companies to these criteria. These financial numbers are contextualized with non-financials incorporating industry-specific, relevant product market information such as product market growth or market share, plus sectoral drivers and special measures such as average revenue per user in mobile companies, reserve replacement in integrated oil, and like-for-like sales in retail. The second constraint is established by the time slip between the orientation of forward-looking company narratives, which are about plans and purpose, and backward-looking financial reports, which are about results and delivery. If the audience for company reports was amnesiac, many more companies would succeed. But, in the world as it is, analysts and journalists who follow the company will remember or look up what management promised and highlight any shortfall in outcomes.

If this year's accounting numbers are not a function of last year's corporate narrative of purpose and achievement, then commentators will note relations of discrepancy and corroboration which then become a key object for our historical case study. But the independent status of the numbers does need some justification. The debate about creative accounting was initiated in the UK by the publication of Terry Smith's book *Accounting for Growth* in 1992 and these concerns were dramatized by the crisis after 2000 about false accounting in the USA at WorldCom and Enron. We will consider both of these issues in turn, beginning with creative accounting.

From Smith onwards, the books on creative accounting take a standard form which perhaps exaggerates the scope for such practices. Thus, the recent US text by Mulford and Comiskey (2002) includes chapters that each cover a separate dodge such as extended amortization or recognizing premature income, with supporting examples of quoted companies that have recently used these dodges to mislead investors. This creates a powerful cumulative impression that creative accounting is everywhere and can be used at will to mislead investors. Sober reflection suggests the scope for creative accounting is rather more limited. First, some numbers are harder to fix than others so that, for example, cash is much harder to manipulate than earnings. Second, many dodges, such as premature recognition of income do increase earnings but only by improving this year's results at the expense of later accounting periods. We would not deny that there is always some scope for finding extra earnings through such expedients as extending depreciation periods, and rapid expansion through take-over increases the scope for this kind of creativity because it usually puts large amounts of goodwill onto the balance sheet subject to US rules which allow its amortization over forty years (Mulford and Comiskey 2002). But, more generally, if creative accounting is so powerful, why are the financial results of most giant firms so mediocre? The feeble profitability of Ford and the declining organic growth of GlaxoSmithKline suggest there are limits on creative accounting in such blue-chip giant companies where product market weakness cannot easily be covered by creative accounting.

The Enron and WorldCom scandals about false accounting did however raise new fears about false accounting that have only been partly allayed by the provisions of the Sarbanes Oxley Act under which CEOs and CFOs can expect jail for signing off false accounts. How could a subset of giant US companies grossly manipulate their financial numbers to get the results they wanted within a system where governance, accounting rules and audit allowed illegal opportunism? Our article on Enron (Froud et al. 2004) focused on the underlying political problem about a well-connected, self-serving corporate elite whose dominant local position in a sunbelt community removed restraints on conduct, just as their national connections exempted them from regulation. In narrower accounting terms, the fraud was possible because Enron and WorldCom operated in special-case circumstances in which false accounting becomes possible; this line of argument is mostly reassuring because circumstances are different in most giant companies most of the time. In WorldCom, the special condition was headlong 1990s' M&A which had left the market rather unusually without any benchmark for the company's investment requirements. Thus, WorldCom management committed one-off egregious fraud and escaped detection when it improved profit by booking around $3.8 billion of line-maintenance and call-termination charges as investment (which could then be written off over time, rather than recognized as expenditure in the current year). The Enron case illustrates a rather different special condition because here, as part of the new-economy bubble, investors ignored clear warning signs in the published accounts;

thus the share price held up as the Enron management used special-purpose entities over several years to hide debt and operating losses. The (false) published numbers flattered Enron's performance, but should have been cause for concern because the company had a return on capital of less than 5 per cent and suffered complete earnings collapse in 1997 rising from problems on just one North Sea gas contract (Froud et al. 2004). In our view, neither WorldCom nor Enron justify the supposition that giant-company management can manipulate financial results at will.

If the numbers are independent of the narrative, promises can be checked against outcomes in a way that opens new complexities. The desired relation is that the numbers should be consistent with the firm's narrative so that management can claim to deliver what it promises and a company confirms its reputation. Disappointing numbers have feedback implications for the credibility of the narrative and underlying assumptions about management quality and firm reputation. Surprisingly, good numbers are equally problematic because they raise questions about whether management knows what it does or whether analysts understand the company. Discrepancy and corroboration between narrative and numbers are both objects of research and the starting points for historical case exploration.

Discrepancy takes two forms as either simple or complex. Simple, massive discrepancy practically means a general-interest story that is big enough to lead the front pages of business newspapers and business supplements, often because it raises questions of corporate reputation and management credibility. Such stories are usually, but not always, about underperformance on the earnings front. Complex stories do not make the front page of the business press and involve more intricate and varied discrepancies because the news involves a mix of good and bad which is partly included in the story and partly supplied by the critical reader. Thus in spring 2005, Ford announced a 38 per cent fall in quarterly earnings. The *Wall Street Journal Europe* reported on an inside page that these results were better than those of GM because Ford was cash and profit generative. The paper also reported that the European premium brands in Ford's Premier Automotive Group (PAG) had done no more than break even, but did not dwell on the negative point that all 2002 recovery-plan targets, including those for profit contribution from PAG, had been dropped. The story equally did not dwell on other positives such as the $23 billion in cash which Ford held. The brevity of most newspaper reports and the complexity of such results discourage complex analysis.

Corroboration is as interesting as discrepancy because corroboration is not the end of the matter, but just another starting point for an investigation. Apparent corroboration often vindicates a narrative whose causal identifications may be fundamentally awry. This is easiest to see in the case of grand narrative about the new economy. Between 1995 and 2000, the rise in share prices and the IPO boom were taken to confirm discursive prophecy about the new economy and digital transformation whose new rules (and the impending transformation of everything) would make old metrics irrelevant. Under these conditions, the absence of profit or sales was no obstacle to an IPO or a temporarily high share price. As we have argued, the work of levitation was actually being achieved by a flood of money as venture capital funded start-ups and ordinary investors and funds piled into IPOs: for example, between 1990 and 2000, $205 billion went into venture capital in the USA, while IPOs attracted some $195 billion in just three and a half years from 1997 (Feng et al. 2001: 496–7). The same problems about unsustainable causal identifications arise in the case of GE, whose record of earnings increase over the twenty years when Jack Welch was CEO is usually claimed as evidence of good management in the form of Welch's leadership and the various organizational initiatives that he launched. Our case argues from the numbers that an undisclosed business model which involved acquisitions in financial services was the driver of earnings increases, so that Welch's initiatives explained, ornamented and legitimated the increasing profits.

# References for Part I


Aglietta, M. (2000) 'Shareholder value and corporate governance: some tricky questions', *Economy and Society,* 29 (1): 146–59.

Althusser, L. (1969) *For Marx,* Harmondsworth: Penguin.

Amable, B. (2003) *The Diversity of Modern Capitalism,* Oxford: Oxford University Press.

Ameels, A., W. Bruggeman and G. Scheipers (2001) 'Value based management control processes to create value through integration: a literature review', Vlerick Leuven Gent Management School mimeo. Online. Available HTTP: <http://www.valuebased management.net/articles_ameels_valuebased_full.pdf> (accessed 21 March 2005).

Amin, A. and N. Thrift (2004) *The Blackwell Cultural Economy Reader,* Oxford: Blackwell.

Anderson, S., J. Cavanagh, C. Hartman and S. Klinger (2003) *Executive Excess 2003: CEOs Win, Workers and Taxpayers Lose,* Boston, Mass.: Institute for Policy Studies & United for a Fair Economy.

Ansoff, H. I. (1965) *Strategic Management,* New York: McGraw Hill.

Arthur Andersen (1997) *Shareholder Value Added,* London: Arthur Andersen.

Austin, J. L. (1975) *How to Do Things with Words,* 2nd edn, Oxford: Clarendon Press.

Bachelard, G. (1940) *La Philosophie de non: essai d'une philosophie de nouvel esprit scientifique,* trans. G. C. Waterstone, Paris: Presse Universitaires de France; reprinted in 1969, New York: Orion Press.

Baden-Fuller, C. and J. Stopford (1993) *Rejuvenating the Mature Business,* London: Routledge.

Baker, G. P. and G. D. Smith (1998) *The New Financial Capitalists: Kohlberg Kravis Roberts and the Creation of Corporate Value,* Cambridge: Cambridge University Press.

Barkema, H. G. and L. R. Gomez-Mejia, (1998) 'Managerial compensation and firm performance: a general research framework', *Academy of Management Journal,* 41 (2): 135–46.

Barney, J. (1986) 'Strategic factor markets: expectations, luck and business strategy', *Management Science,* 32 (10) (October): 1231–41.

Barry, A., D. Slater and M. Callon (2002) 'Technology, politics and the market: an interview with Michel Callon', *Economy and Society,* 31 (1): 285–306.

Bartlett, C. and S. Ghoshal (1995) *Transnational Management: Text, Cases, and Readings in Cross-Border Management,* 2nd edn, Boston, Mass.: Irwin/McGraw Hill.

—— (1998) *Managing Across Borders: The Transnational Solution,* London: Random House.

Bauer, M. and B. Bertin-Mourot (1999) 'National models for making and legitimating elites: a comparative analysis of the 200 top executives in France, Germany and Great Britain', *European Societies* 1 (1): 9–31.

Bebchuk, L. and J. Fried (2004) *Pay without Performance: The Unfulfilled Promise of Executive Compensation*, Cambridge, Mass.: Harvard University Press.

Bebchuk, L. A., J. M. Fried and D. I. Walker (2002) 'Managerial power and rent extraction in the design of executive compensation', *University of Chicago Law Review*, 69 (3): 751–847.

Bender, R. (2003) 'How executive directors' remuneration is determined in two FTSE 350 utilities', *Corporate Governance*, 11 (3): 206–17.

Berle, A. A. and G. C. Means (1932) *The Modern Corporation and Private Property*, New York: Harcourt Brace.

Bernstein Research Call (2005) *GM Retiree Healthcare Could Provide Lever to Unlock Restructuring in 2005*, 12 April 2005.

Boje, D. (2001) *Narrative Methods for Organizational and Communications Research*, London: Sage.

Boston Consulting Group (BCG) (1996a) *Meeting the Value Challenge*, Shareholder Value Management Booklet 1, Boston, Mass.: BCG.

—— (1996b) *Shareholder Value Metrics*, Shareholder Value Management Booklet 2, Boston, Mass.: BCG.

Bourdieu, P. (1991) *Language and Symbolic Power*, Cambridge: Polity/Basil Blackwell.

Boyer, R. (2000) 'Is a finance-led growth regime a viable alternative to Fordism? A preliminary analysis', *Economy and Society*, 29 (1): 111–45.

Boyer, R. and M. Freyssenet (1999) *The World that Changed the Machine*, Synthesis of GERPISA Research Programs 1993–1999, Evry: GERPISA.

Brenner, R. (2001) 'The world economy at the turn of the millennium', *Review of International Political Economy*, 8 (1): 6–44.

British Venture Capital Association (BVCA) (2004) *The Economic Impact of Private Equity*, London: BVCA.

Cadbury, A. (1992) *Report of the Committee on the Financial Aspects of Corporate Governance*, London: Gee.

Callon, M. (1998) *The Laws of the Markets*, Oxford: Blackwell.

Callon, M., J. Law and A. Rip (eds) (1986) *Mapping the Dynamics of Science and Technology: Sociology of Science in the Real World*, Basingstoke: Macmillan.

Canguilhem, G. (1966) *Le Normal et le pathologique*, Paris: Presses Universitaires de France.

Castells, M. (1996) *The Rise of the Network Society*, Oxford: Blackwell.

Chandler, A. (1962) *Strategy and Structure: Chapters in the History of the Industrial Enterprise*, Cambridge, Mass.: MIT.

—— *The Visible Hand: The Managerial Revolution in American Business*, Cambridge, Mass.: Harvard University Press.

Channon, D. (1973) *The Strategy and Structure of British Enterprise*, London: Macmillan.

Cioffi, J. (2000) 'Governing globalization? The state, law and structural change in corporate governance', *Journal of Law and Society*, 27 (4): 572–600.

Collins, D. (2003) *Riders on the Storm: A Sideways Look at a Celebrated Tale of Corporate Transformation*, University of Essex Working Paper, WP 03/08, October 2003.

Collins, J. and J. Porras (1994) *Built to Last: Successful Habits of Visionary Companies*, New York: Harper Collins.

Collis, D. and C. Montgomery (1995) 'Competing on resources: how do you create and sustain a profitable strategy?' *Harvard Business Review*, 73 (4) (July/August): 118–28.

Company Law Review Steering Group (1999) *Modern Company Law for a Competitive Economy: The Strategic Framework*, London: Department of Trade and Industry, HMSO, February 1999.

Conyon, M. J. and K. J. Murphy (2000) 'The prince and the pauper? CEO pay in the United States and United Kingdom', *The Economic Journal*, 110 (November): 640–71.

Core, J. E., W. R. Guay and D. F. Larcker (2003) 'Executive equity compensation and incentives: a survey', *FRBNY Economic Policy Review* (April): 27–50.

Cutler, A. J. (1978) 'Problems of a general theory of capitalist calculation', in A. J. Cutler, B. Hindess, P. Hirst and A. Hussain (eds) *Marx's Capital and Capitalism Today*, Vol. II, London: Routledge & Kegan Paul, pp. 128–62.

Davis, G. and S. Thompson (1994) 'A social movement perspective on corporate control', *Administrative Science Quarterly*, 37: 605–33.

de Witt, B. and R. Meyer (1998) *Strategy: Process, Content, Context: An International Perspective*, London: International Thompson Business.

Dore, R. (2000) *Stock Market Capitalism: Welfare Capitalism: Japan and Germany versus the Anglo-Saxons*, Oxford: Oxford University Press.

Drucker, P. (1955) *The Practice of Management*, London: Heinemann.

DuGay, P. and M. Pryke (eds) (2002) *Cultural Economy: Cultural Analysis and Commercial Life*, London: Sage.

Dupuy, C. and Y. Lung (2002) 'Institutional investors and the car industry geographic: focalization and industrial strategies', *Competition and Change*, 6 (1): 43–60.

Eisenhardt, K. M. (1989) 'Agency theory: an assessment and review', *The Academy of Management Review*, 14 (1): 57–74.

Erturk, I., J. Froud, S. Johal and K. Williams (2005) 'Pay for corporate performance or pay as social division: rethinking the problem of top management pay in giant corporations', *Competition and Change*, 9 (1): 49–74.

Evans, E. and T. Wurster (1997) 'Strategy and the new economics of information', *Harvard Business Review*, 75 (5) (September/October): 71–82.

Ezzamel, M. and R. Watson (1998) 'Market comparison earnings and the bidding-up of executive cash compensation: evidence from the United Kingdom', *Academy of Management Journal*, 41 (2): 221–31.

Faccio, M. and L. H. P. Lang (2002) 'The ultimate ownership of western European corporations', *Journal of Financial Economics*, 65 (3): 365–95.

Fama, E. F. (1980) 'Agency problems and the theory of the firm', *The Journal of Political Economy*, 88 (2): 288–302.

Feng, H., J. Froud, C. Haslam, S. Johal and K. Williams (2001) 'A new business model? The capital market and the new economy', *Economy and Society*, 30(4): 467–503.

Fligstein, N. (1990) *The Transformation of Corporate Control*, Cambridge, Mass.: Harvard University Press.

—— (2001) *The Architecture of Markets: An Economic Sociology of Twenty-First Century Capitalist Societies*, Princeton, NJ: Princeton University Press.

Foucault, M. (1975) *I, Pierre Rivière, Having Slaughtered My Mother, My Sister, and My Brother: A Case of Parricide in the 19th Century*, New York: Pantheon.

Froud, J., C. Haslam, S. Johal and K. Williams (1997) 'From social settlement to household lottery', *Economy and Society*, 26 (3): 340–72.

—— (1998) 'Breaking the chains: a sector matrix for motoring', *Competition and Change*, 3 (3): 293–334.

—— (2000a) 'Shareholder value and financialisation: consultancy promises, management moves', *Economy and Society*, 29 (1): 80–120.

—— (2000b) 'Restructuring for shareholder value and its implications for labour', *Cambridge Journal of Economics*, 24 (6): 771–97.

—— (2001) 'Accumulation under conditions of inequality', *Review of International Political Economy*, 8 (1): 66–95.

—— (2002) 'Cars after financialisation: a case study in financial under-performance, constraints and consequences', *Competition and Change*, 7 (1): 13–41.

Froud, J., S. Johal, V. Papazian and K. Williams (2004) 'The temptation of Houston: a case study of financialisation', *Critical Perspectives on Accounting*, 15: 885–909.

Froud, J., S. Johal and K. Williams (2001) 'The US staffing industry: the business model and the paradoxes of extension', paper presented at the 2001 SASE conference, Amsterdam.

—— (2002) 'Financialisation and the coupon pool', *Capital and Class*, 78 (autumn): 119–51.

Gabriel, Y. (2000) *Storytelling in Organisations: Facts, Fictions and Fantasies*, Oxford: Oxford University Press.

Gereffi, G. (1996) 'Global commodity chains: new forms of coordination and control among nations and firms in international industries', *Competition and Change*, 1(4): 427–39.

Gereffi, G. and M. Korzeniewicz (1994) *Commodity Chains and Global Capitalism*, London: Praeger.

Geroski, P. and P. Gregg (1994) 'Corporate restructuring in the UK during recession', *Business Strategy Review*, 5 (2) (summer): 1–19.

Glassman, J. (2001) *America's Reciprocal Stock Portfolio: How US Investors Invest in Foreign Companies that Invest in the US*, New York/Washington, DC: Citibank/OFII. Online. Available HTTP: <http://www.ofii.org/facts_figures/Stock_Study.pdf> (accessed 11 April 2005).

Goergen, M., M. C. Manjon and L. Renneboog (2005) 'Corporate governance in Germany', in K. Keasey, S. Thompson and M. Wright (eds) *Corporate Governance: Accountability, Enterprise and International Comparisons*, Chichester: John Wiley & Sons.

Golding, T. (2001) *The City: Inside the Great Expectations Machine*, Harlow: Pearson Education.

Goold, M., A. Campbell and M. Alexander (1994) *Corporate-Level Strategy: Creating Value in the Multibusiness Company*, New York: John Wiley.

Greenbury, R. (1995) *Directors' Remuneration: Report by a Study Group Chaired by Sir Richard Greenbury*, London: Gee.

Greenspan, A. (2002) 'Corporate governance', lecture at the Stern School of Business, New York University, 26 March 2002. Online. Available HTTP: <http://www.federalreserve.gov/boarddocs/speeches/2002> (accessed 21 March 2005).

Gressle, E. M. (1990) 'Corporate restructuring: the theme of the 1980s', in B. de Caires (ed.), *Corporate Restructuring*, London: Euromoney Publications, pp. 45–64.

Grun, R. (2004) 'Corporate governance in Brazil: From a "neo-liberal zealot" issue to a "practical consultant" business', conference paper given at SASE conference, 8–11 July 2004, Washington, DC.

Hamel, G. (2000) *Leading the Revolution*, Boston, Mass.: Harvard Business School Press.

Hamel, G. and C. K. Prahalad (1993) 'Strategy as stretch and leverage', *Harvard Business Review*, 71 (2) (March/April): 75–85.

—— (1994) *Competing for the Future*, Boston, Mass.: Harvard Business School Press.

Hampel, R. (1998) *Committee on Corporate Governance: Final Report*, London: Gee.

Haspeslagh, P., T. Noda and F. Boulos (2001) 'It's not just about the numbers', *Harvard Business Review*, 79 (7) (July/August): 64–73.

Hawawini, G., V. Subramanian and P. Verdin (2003) 'Is performance driven by industry- or firm-specific factors? A new look at the evidence', *Strategic Management Journal*, 24 (1): 1–16.

Hayes, R. H., and W. J. Abernathy (1980) 'Managing our way to industrial decline', *Harvard Business Review*, 58 (4): 67–77.

Henderson, B., N. Jegadeesh and M. Weisback (2003) *World Markets for Raising New Capital*, The National Bureau For Economic Research, Cambridge, Mass. Online. Available HTTP: <http://papers.nber.org/papers/w10225.pdf> (accessed 23 March 2005).

Higgs, D. (2003) *Review of the Role and Effectiveness of Non-Executive Directors*, London: Department of Trade and Industry. Online. Available HTTP: <http://www.dti.gov.uk/cld/non_exec_review/pdfs/higgsreport.pdf> (accessed 21 March 2005).

Hirst, P. and G. Thompson (1996) *Globalization in Question: The International Economy and the Possibilities of Governance*, Cambridge: Polity.

Holland, J. B, (1997) 'Corporate communications to institutional shareholders', *ICAS Research Report*, Edinburgh, November.

HOLT Value Associates (undated) *Providing Insights into Corporate Performance and Valuation: Introducing HOLT's Cash Flow Performance/Valuation Framework*, Chicago, Ill.: HOLT Value Associates.

Hutton, W. (1995) *The State We're In*, London: Cape.

Jensen, M. C. (1989) 'Active investors, LBOs and the privatization of bankruptcy', *Journal of Applied Corporate Finance*, 2 (1): 35–44.

—— (1998) *Foundations of Organizational Strategy*, Cambridge, Mass.: Harvard University Press.

Jensen, M. C. and W. H. Meckling (1976) 'Theory of the firm: managerial behavior, agency costs and ownership structure', *Journal of Financial Economics*, 3 (4): 305–60.

Jensen, M. C. and K. J. Murphy (1990) 'Performance pay and top management incentives', *Journal of Political Economy*, 98 (2): 225–64.

Johnson, G., K. Scholes and R. Whittington (2005) *Exploring Corporate Strategy: Text and Cases*, Harlow: Pearson Education.

Jones, E. L. (1916) *The Administration of Industrial Enterprises, with Special Reference to Factory Practice*, New York: Longmans.

Jullien, B. (2002) 'Consumer vs. manufacturer or consumer vs. consumer: the implications of a usage analysis of automobile systems', *Competition and Change*, 6 (1): 113–25.

Jürgens, U., K. Naumann and J. Rupp (2000) 'Shareholder value in an adverse environment: the German case', *Economy & Society*, 29 (1): 54–80.

Kaplan, S. and A. Schoar (2003) 'Private equity returns: persistence and capital flows', Unpublished working paper, University of Chicago. Online. Available HTTP: <http://gsbwww.uchicago.edu/fac/steven.kaplan/research/pereturns.pdf> (accessed 27 March 2005).

Kay, J. (1993) *The Foundations of Corporate Success: How Business Strategies Add Value*, Oxford: Oxford University Press.

Kensinger, J. and J. Martin (1992) 'The quiet restructuring', in J. M. Stern. and D. H. Chew (eds) *The Revolution in Corporate Finance*, 2nd edn, Oxford: Blackwell, pp. 621–30.

Keynes, J. M. (1936) *The General Theory of Employment and Money*, London: Macmillan.

Khurana, R. (2002) *Searching for a Corporate Saviour: The Irrational Quest for Charismatic CEOs*, Princeton, NJ: Princeton University Press.

Kohut, G. and A. Segars (1992) 'The president's letter to stockholders: an examination of corporate communication strategy', *Journal of Business Communcation*, 29 (1): 7–21.

Lane, C. (1992) 'European business systems: Britain and Germany compared', in R. Whitley (ed.) *European Business Systems*, London: Sage, pp. 64–97.

Laplane, M. and F. Sarti (2002) 'Costs and paradoxes of market creation: evidence and argument from Brazil', *Competition and Change*, 6 (1): 127–41.

Latour, B. (1987) *Science in Action*, Cambridge, Mass.: Harvard University Press.

Latour, B. and S. Woolgar (1979) *Laboratory Life: The Construction of Scientific Facts*, Beverly Hills, Calif.: Sage.

Law, J. (2002) 'Economics as interface', in P. DuGay and M. Pryke (eds) *Cultural Economy: Cultural Analysis and Commercial Life*, London: Sage, pp. 21–38.

Lawrence, P. (1980) *Managers and Management in West Germany*, London: Croom Helm.

Lazonick, W. and M. O'Sullivan (2000) 'Maximising shareholder value: a new ideology for corporate governance', *Economy and Society*, 29 (1): 13–35.

LEK/Alcar (1997) *Shareholder Value Added*, Vols I and V, Boston, Mass.: LEK/Alcar Consulting Group.

Levitt, T. (1983) 'The globalization of markets', *Harvard Business Review*, 61 (3) (May/June): 92–103.

Lewis, M. (2001) *The New, New Thing: A Silicon Valley Story*, London: Penguin.

MacKenzie, D. (2004) 'The big, bad wolf and the rational market: portfolio insurance, the 1987 crash and the performativity of economics', *Economy and Society*, 33 (3): 303–34.

MacKenzie, D. and Y. Millo (2003) 'Constructing a market, performing theory: the historical sociology of a financial derivatives exchange', *American Journal of Sociology*, 109: 107–45.

McCloskey, D. (1986) *The Rhetoric of Economics*, Brighton: Wheatsheaf.

McGahan, A. and M. Porter (1997) 'How much does industry matter, really?' *Strategic Management Journal*, 18: 15–30.

Meeks, G. (1977) *A Disappointing Marriage: A Study of the Gains from Merger*, Cambridge: Cambridge University Press.

Meijboom, B. (1999) 'Production-to-order and international operations: a case study in the clothing industry', *International Journal of Operations and Production Management*, 19 (5/6): 602–19.

Milano, G. and M. Schwartz (1998) 'Need to delegate profitability? EVA™ will show you how', *Sunday Times*, 27 September 1998: 11.

Miller, D. (2002) 'Turning Callon the right way up', *Economy and Society*, 31 (1): 218–33.

Mills, C. W. (1956) *The Power Elite*, New York: Oxford University Press.

Mintzberg, H. (1973) *The Nature of Managerial Work*, New York: Harper & Row.

Montgomery, C. (1994) 'Corporate diversification', *Journal of Economic Perspectives*, 8: 163–78.

Morgan Stanley (2005) *Euroletter: Barbarian Buyout Calculations*, 11 April 2005.

Morgan, G. and Y. Takahashi (2002) '*Shareholder value in the Japanese context*', *Competition and Change*, 6 (1): 169–92.

Morin, F. (2000) 'A transformation in the French model of shareholding and management', *Economy and Society*, 29 (1): 36–53.

Morin, R. and S. Jarrell (2000) *Driving Shareholder Value: Value-Building Techniques for Creating Shareholder Value*, New York: McGraw-Hill Professional.

Mulford, C. and E. Comiskey (2002) *The Financial Numbers Game: Detecting Creative Accounting Practice*, New York: John Wiley & Sons.

Myers, R. (1996) 'Metric Wars', *CFO Magazine* (October): 1–10.

Nichols, T. (1969) *Ownership, Control and Ideology*, London: Allen & Unwin.

Nitzan, J. (1998) 'Differential accumulation: towards a new political economy of capital', *Review of International Political Economy*, 5 (2): 169–216.

Organisation for Economic Co-operation and Development (OECD) (1999) *OECD: Principles of Corporate Governance*, Paris: OECD.

Orlean, A. (1999) *Le Pouvoir de la finance*, Paris: Éditions Odile Jacob.

O'Sullivan, M. (2000) *Contests for Corporate Control: Corporate Governance and Economic Performance in the United States and Germany*, Oxford: Oxford University Press.

Oxford English Dictionary (1989) *Oxford English Dictionary*, 2nd edn, Oxford: Clarendon Press.

Paulos, J. A. (1998) *Once upon a Number: The Hidden Mathematical Logic of Numbers*, London: Allen Lane.

Peters, T. J. and Waterman, R. H. (1982) *In Search of Excellence*, New York: Harper & Row.

Porter, M. E. (1980) *Competitive Strategy: Techniques for Analysing Industries and Competitors*, London: Collier MacMillan.

—— (1983) *Cases in Competitive Strategy*, New York: Free Press.

—— (1985) *Competitive Advantage: Creating and Sustaining Superior Performance*, New York: Free Press.

—— (1990) *The Competitive Advantage Of Nations*, New York: Free Press.

Prahalad, C. K. and G. Hamel (1990) 'The core competencies of the corporation', *Harvard Business Review*, 68 (3) (May/June): 79–92.

PriceWaterhouseCoopers (PWC) (in association with the BVCA and Westport Private Equity Ltd) (2003) *BVCA Performance Measurement Survey 2003 (Summary Report)*, London: PWC.

Pye, A. (2001) 'Corporate boards, investors and their relationships: accounts of accountability and corporate governing in action', *Corporate Governance: An International Review*, 9 (3): 186–95.

Quinn, J. (1978) 'Strategic change: logical incrementalism', *Sloan Management Review*, (fall): 71–92.

Rappaport, A. (1998) *Creating Shareholder Value*, 2nd edn, New York: Free Press.

Raveaud, G. (2003) 'Revolutionising French economics', Interview with Gilles Raveaud by Richard McIntyre, *Challenge*, 46 (6) (November/December): 5–25.

Ross, I. (1998) 'The 1997 Stern Stewart performance 1000', *Journal of Applied Corporate Finance* (winter): 116–25.

Rumelt, R. (1991) 'How much does industry matter?' *Strategic Management Journal*, 12 (3): 167–85.

Sarbanes-Oxley Act (2002) *The Sarbanes-Oxley Act*. Online. Available HTTP: <http://news.findlaw.com/hdocs/docs/gwbush/sarbanesoxley072302.pdf> (accessed 12 March 2005).

Savage, M., A. Warde and F. Divine (2004) *Capital Assets and Resources: Some Critical Issues*, mimeo, University of Manchester.

Saxby, G. (1994) *Practical Holography*, London: Prentice Hall.

Schmalensee, R. (1985) 'Do markets differ much?' *The American Economic Review*, 75 (3): 341–51.

Segal-Horn, S. (2004) *The Strategy Reader*, Oxford: Blackwell.

Shiller, R. (2000) *Irrational Exuberance*, Princeton, NJ: Princeton University Press.

Shliefer, A. and L. H. Summers (1988) 'Breach of trust in hostile takeovers', in A. J. Auerbach (ed.) *Corporate Takeovers: Causes and Consequences*, Chicago, Ill.: Chicago University Press/NBER, pp. 33–56.

Sklar, S., L. Mykyta and S. Wefald (2002) *Raise the Floor: Wages and Policies that Work for All of Us*, Cambridge, Mass.: South End Press.

Smith, T. (1992) *Accounting for Growth*, London: Century Business.

Soros, G. (2003) *The Alchemy of Finance*, 2nd edn, Hoboken, NJ: John Wiley & Sons.

Spanos, Y., G. Zaralis and S. Lioukas (2004) 'Strategy and industry effects on profitability', *Strategic Management Journal*, 25: 139–65.

Spender, S. (1973) 'The landscape near an aerodrome', in P. Larkin (ed.) *Oxford Book of Twentieth Century English Verse*, Oxford: Oxford University Press.

Stark, M. (2003) *'Storytelling', 2003: Ideas from Trends*, New York: Saatchi & Saatchi. Online. Available http: <http://www.saatchikevin.com/workingit/myra_stark_2003 ideasandtrends2.html> (accessed 26 April 2005).

Stern, J. and D. Chew (1998) *The Revolution in Corporate Finance*, 3rd edn, Oxford: Blackwell.

Stern, J., G. Stewart III and D. Chew Jr. (1998) 'The EVA financial management system', in J. Stern and D. Chew (eds) *The Revolution in Corporate Finance*, 3rd edn, Oxford: Blackwell, pp. 474–88.

Sudarsanam, P. S. (1995) *The Essence of Mergers and Acquisitions*, London: Prentice Hall.

Tawney, R. H. (1921) *The Acquisitive Society*, London: Bell.

Temin, P. (1999) 'The stability of the American business elite', *Industrial and Corporate Change*, 8 (June): 189–210.

Thomas, J. (1997) 'Discourse in the marketplace: the making meaning of annual reports', *Journal of Business Communication*, 34: 47–66.

Tichy, N. M. and N. Cardwell (2002) *The Cycle of Leadership: How Great Leaders Teach Their Companies to Win*, New York: Harper Business.

Tichy, N. M. and S. Sherman (1993) *Control Your Destiny or Someone Else Will*, New York: Harper Business; reprinted (2001) New York: Harper Collins.

Tomlinson, J. (1981) *Problems of British Economic Policy 1870–1945*, London: Methuen.

Tosi, H. L., S. Werner, J. P. Katz and L. R. Gomez-Mejia (2000) 'How much does performance matter? A meta-analysis of CEO pay studies', *Journal of Management*, 26 (2): 301–39.

Useem, M. (1993) *Executive Defense: Shareholder Power and Corporate Reorganization*, Cambridge, Mass.: Harvard University Press.

Usui, C. and R. Colignon (1996) 'Corporate restructuring: converging world pattern or societally specific embeddedness?' *Sociological Quarterly*, 4: 351–78.

Watson, M. (1999) 'Rethinking capital mobility, re-regulating financial markets', *New Political Economy*, 4 (1): 55–75.

Whittington, R. (1993) *What Is Strategy – and Does It Matter?* London: International Thompson.

Williams, G. A. (1985) *When Was Wales?* London: Black Raven.

Williams, K., C. Haslam, S. Johal and J. Williams (1994) *Cars: Analysis, History, Cases*, Providence, RI: Berghahn Books.

Williams, K., J. Williams and D. Thomas (1983) *Why Are the British Bad at Manufacturing?* London: Routledge & Kegan Paul.
Wise, R. and P. Baumgartner (1999) 'Go downstream: the new profit imperative in manufacturing', *Harvard Business Review* (September/October): 133–41.
Womack, J. P., D. T. Jones and D. Roos (1990) *The Machine that Changed the World*, New York: Rawson Associates.
Wright, M., B. Chiplin, S. Thompson and K. Robbie (1990) 'Management buyouts, trade unions and employee ownership', *Industrial Relations Journal*, 21: 136–46.
Wurgler, J. (2000) 'Financial markets and the allocation of capital', *Journal of Financial Economics*, 58 (1): 187–214.

Part II

# Cases

Case 1

# GlaxoSmithKline

Keeping it going?

## INTRODUCTION

In John Kay's 1990s bestseller, *Foundations of Corporate Success*, Glaxo was confidently identified as 'the most successful European company of the 1980s' using the then fashionable measure of excess profits, which Kay termed 'added value' (1993: 30). Glaxo was then the leading firm in the British pharmaceutical industry which the journalist and commentator Will Hutton described as 'a beacon of UK excellence in an industrial landscape otherwise depressingly bare of success' (*Guardian*, 8 March 1995). A decade and two mergers later in 2002–3, the high-profile public issue was how an under-performing GlaxoSmithKline (GSK) could possibly justify a pay deal which offered $18 million per annum to its chief executive. The now global pharmaceuticals industry had meanwhile suffered major reputational damage after pricing and drug-safety scandals, so that one of its conferences featured advice from a tobacco company executive 'on how an industry can improve its tarnished public image' (*The Economist*, 27 November 2004).

Strategy discourse is sometimes surprised and embarrassed by the discovery that (unexamined) corporate success has turned into (under-explained) under-performance as in the case of GSK. But classical strategy lacks the intellectual resources to do anything except regularly change the examples as individual companies lapse into failure, while confidently identifying the general basis for long-term corporate success through positioning, core competences and suchlike. Each company vignette is used to tell a simple story about the rights and wrongs of business choices, so that strategy deals in parables where the moral of the story is dependent on simple one-dimensional characterization and just desserts in the world of James 4:17 where sin is knowing the right thing to do and not doing it. Against this, our case tries to do something rather different because we believe that analysis of the transition from corporate success to under-performance adds depth and perspective. Thus, the case deconstructs Glaxo's earlier trajectory up to the mid-1990s which was one of upward mobility and financial achievement in a growth industry, before analysing Glaxo's subsequent slow-motion struggle after 1994 to keep things going by merger over a decade of increasing problems for the industry.

Any attempt at understanding this more difficult period from the late 1990s brings us quickly to the limits of orthodox strategy discourse, particularly RBT explanations, which immediately seems the most appropriate because such accounts would highlight patents and marketing as the basis of corporate success (and failure). While patents and marketing are relevant in pharma, RBT provides an inadequate explanation in so far as it fails to give proper weight to the narrative element and focuses unduly on intra-company resources when the industry and its environment are equally important. The first section begins by analysing the broader context in terms of the industry frame. The key issue here is the pharma industry's recurrent (and latterly rather unsuccessful) struggle with its critics. The struggle takes the form of a contest between two accounts of the activity: the industry's vision is of good pharma as a research-driven, innovative activity whereas its critics charge that bad pharma is about marketing-driven profiteering. The outcome of this struggle over reputation is crucial because it influences the regulatory environment in which the industry operates and the collective possibilities of cost recovery.

Within this broad social framing of the industry and its reputation, stock-market analysts, consultants and journalists understand the performance and prospects of individual companies in narrower terms. The second section analyses stock-market understandings of the pharma-company business model, where marketing is applied to create blockbusters, so the key questions are about patent expiry and new product coming through the pipeline. Under these conditions, the stock market has traditionally assumed that the pharma industry offers high visibility and predictability of future revenue. This differentiates it from other industries such as auto assembly, where predictability is necessarily limited when new models so often represent another throw of the dice.

The second half of the case study develops an analysis of the Glaxo company set within an industry frame about contested social accounts and narrow market understandings. The third section analyses Glaxo as the upwardly mobile, *arriviste* of the 1980s, on a brilliant trajectory of organic growth driven by focused marketing which made Zantac then the world's best-selling drug. With patent expiry imminent, the question from the early 1990s was how to keep things going for the stock market, and Glaxo's answer was defensive, cost-reducing horizontal merger. The third section shows how the Wellcome take-over of 1994 both bought time and encouraged market expectations of further success that could not easily be met in the subsequent much larger merger with SmithKline Beecham.

If the numbers increasingly disappoint, Glaxo has responded by putting more emphasis on a forward-looking public narrative about company achievement, which is intended for stock-market and media consumption. The fourth section shows how this narrative covers both process and product, as Glaxo makes promises about the reorganization of research for higher productivity and about the new drugs in the later stages of the pipeline. Of course, public promises without corroborating numbers do not convince everybody. Hence, as the fifth section demonstrates, the CEO pay of Jean-Pierre Garnier became an issue against a background of increasing uncertainty about Glaxo's performance in a pharma industry whose insecurities consultants now exploit with a flood of reports about reinvention and new business models.

The Glaxo company provides the basis for our first case because Glaxo as a company in the pharma industry is rather simpler and easier to understand than Ford in automotive assembly or the conglomerate GE. Unlike GE, Glaxo has all its turnover in one activity (pharmaceuticals) and the pharma-company business model about the global marketing of blockbusters to maximize revenue is easier to understand than the business model of the average car assembler which cross-subsidises between different segments and markets and combines assembly with variable amounts of parts manufacture and car finance. Furthermore, GSK is not reliant on a finance subsidiary in the same way that both GE and Ford are. However GSK does fit the developing argument about financialization, not least because of the expectations of its shareholders and the interest of the business press and analysts in a company with a large market capitalization that has, in the 2000s, failed to maintain both the growth and excitement that it delivered in the 1990s. Overall, GSK's strategy is one of keeping things going (by merger) for the stock market, in a world where multiple and contested narratives are as important as the financial numbers.

If the Glaxo company is relatively simple to understand, the case is not straightforward, because it illustrates the complexity of the strategic space around the corporation. As in many other late-capitalist companies with technology products, market-based cost recovery is only possible within an appropriate regulatory framework which depends on governmental regulation at national and international level. While the nature of that framework, especially in the USA, can be crudely influenced by corporate donations and lobbying, the nature and bounds of regulation also depend on the reputation of the industry. When reputation is lost, current events in pharma show that predictability is greatly reduced and the industry can no longer keep things going in the same way. This has already led to a revaluation of companies like Merck and Pfizer whose shares were once growth stocks with starry P/E ratios but which now figure as underperformers whose attraction is yield and current earnings.

## INDUSTRY FRAME: PHARMA'S CONTESTED REPUTATION

The major global pharmaceutical firms operate within an industry frame which is unusual because the major issues here are reputational ones about whether, in the terms of the established cliché, the industry exists for people or profits. In the first part of this section we present basic data that shows how patents allow large pharmaceutical companies to generate high profits. This analysis is fairly uncontentious for the industry's defenders and critics whose divisions are illustrated by their different answers to the question about whether the industry's high profits are the necessary precondition for continuing industry investment in fundamental scientific innovation.

There are two contesting representations of the pharma industry that imbue it with different moral value: on the industry's own account, good pharma is R&D led and recycles profits to sustain innovation that offers the social benefit of improved health and welfare; radical critics allege that bad pharma is marketing driven and makes large profits by exploiting the sick (and those who pay their health-care bills). One of the most interesting aspects of this contest is that much the same arguments are reworked by both sides (with regular updating of the supporting facts) over forty years. But the balance between positive and negative representations shifts over time and the reputation of the industry oscillates, with the 2000s (like the late 1950s and early 1960s) representing historic lows.

The accumulating criticisms of big pharma since the later 1990s by ourselves (Froud et al. 1998) and others fundamentally do no more than reinscribe or reinvent the critique produced by the radical US senator Estes Kefauver, whose Senate hearings from 1957 to 1963 criticized the industry for profiteering in unsafe drugs. But by the mid-2000s (like the 1960s), such criticisms have now gained social credence in ways that leave the industry once again with a tarnished public reputation. The intervening twenty years from the mid-1970s to the mid-1990s were much kinder to an industry that was much more in charge of its own publicity. These issues about reputation and image are important because they potentially have feedback effects on the regulatory regimes that determine the collective possibilities of making money from the industry.

### Pharma patents and the 'licence to print money'

One of the pioneers of commercial television in the UK and then-chairman of Scottish Television (STV), Roy Thomson famously described a radio- or television-station franchise as like 'having a licence to print money' (Sendall 1982: 120). Much the same point could be made about patents in the ethical pharmaceutical business. More exactly, the licence to print money comes out of a combination of three conditions: enforceable patent rights, price-insensitive purchasers and a sympathetic regulatory environment whereby the rules of the game have allowed high returns to be generated.

The pharmaceutical industry includes several kinds of company making different categories of drugs, as well as vaccines and other related health-care products. From a capital-market point of view, the most interesting are *ethical* pharmaceuticals, which are recently developed drugs, in patent, marketed under a brand name and available usually only on prescription. Ethical drugs should be distinguished from *generics*, which are patent-expired substitutes available on a prescription basis and made by various firms to one standard formula. Last, there are over-the-counter (OTC) products, which are branded medicines available without prescription at pharmacy counters, supermarkets and other places.

Patented ethicals are important because they command premium prices: generics represented 51 per cent of all US prescriptions in 2002 but captured just 17 per cent of the total value of the US drug market (UBS Warburg 2003: 6). In the absence of patent protection, generic prices are determined by competition and reflect costs of production so that generic substitutes are usually between 10 per cent and 70 per cent cheaper than their ethical counterparts (Reuters Business Insight 1998: 19). As such, the average margin for generics is considerably lower than for ethicals: in 1997 the top eight generic manufacturers managed an average net-income margin of 4.1 per cent compared with 19 per cent for the top eight ethical manufacturers (calculated from Reuters Business Insight 1998: 28, 196). Some of the giant pharma companies have diversified health-care businesses including OTC and health-care products but generally cede generic production to cost-conscious smaller manufacturing firms. The classic pattern is that the larger part of turnover, and an even larger share of profit, in giant pharma companies is in ethicals. As Exhibit C1.1 demonstrates, in 2002 almost all pharma giants generated over 80 per cent of their turnover from ethical pharmaceuticals. The exceptions include Merck, which at that time generated three-fifths of its revenue but only one-twentieth of its net income from the pharmacy benefit management service Medco Health, while Johnson & Johnson and Novartis both had extensive OTC interests.

Ethical pharmaceuticals are attractive not only because they offer high margins but also because historically they have offered strong year-on-year growth, so that a successful ethical company in the 1980s or 1990s could easily rack up double-digit growth of sales revenue. This growth came without any of the problems about cyclicality that afflict many consumer and producer goods or many of the risks attached to rapid and unpredictable change that afflict most technology companies. As we noted in this book's introduction, any large group of giant companies tends to grow at about the trend rate

*Exhibit C1.1 Ethical sales as a percentage of total sales for major pharmaceutical companies, 2002*

| | *Total sales revenue* $m | *Total ethical sales* $m | *Ethical sales as a % of total* |
|---|---|---|---|
| Pfizer | 32,373 | 28,288 | 87.4 |
| GSK | 31,819 | 27,003 | 84.9 |
| Merck | 51,790 | 21,631 | 41.8 |
| AstraZeneca | 17,841 | 17,343 | 97.2 |
| J&J | 36,298 | 17,151 | 47.3 |
| BMS | 18,106 | 14,700 | 81.2 |
| Novartis | 23,151 | 13,493 | 58.3 |
| Pharmacia | 13,993 | 12,037 | 86.0 |
| Wyeth | 14,584 | 11,733 | 80.5 |
| Lilly | 11,077 | 10,384 | 93.7 |

*Source*: Reuters Business Insight (2003a: 104), company accounts and SEC filings

*Note*: The apparent low significance of ethical drugs for Merck in 2002, compared with the other companies in the table, is due to the large sales generated by Medco Health, a pharmacy benefit management service which generated $30,159 in 2002. This business was owned by Merck in 2002 but has since been spun off. The BMS figure used is the 2002 figure restated from the 2003 accounts. The table excludes Roche/Genentech and Aventis due to non-standardization of total ethical sales

of GDP growth in advanced countries; and much of the manufacturing sector across the USA and Europe faltered after the mid-1970s as GDP growth slowed. But the long boom continued globally for two decades longer in ethical pharmaceuticals, as investors bought into a group of companies that grew at least twice as fast as GDP in most advanced countries, which provide the largest market for ethicals. Here, the high-income capitalist countries in western Europe, North America and Japan still account for more than 90 per cent of world consumption (Keynote 2002: 18).

The licence to print money rested on three interrelated conditions that jointly facilitated cost recovery by all ethical pharmaceutical companies. The conditions are: first, intellectual property rights in the form of time-limited patents; second, the existence of price-insensitive corporate and social purchasers; and, third, a regulatory environment that allows high returns to be made by companies. This schema of three conditions provides us with a first indication of complexity because together they indicate how pharma operates in an environment where market competition is channelled and constrained by institutions and regulations.

Intellectual property rights are generally important because they allow the exclusion of competitors and protect prices and margins from erosion. In pharma, the key rights are time-limited patents which are generally taken out at the earliest pre-clinical stage in the development of a drug and last (without possibility of renewal) for twenty years from the point at which the patent is filed (Keynote 2002: 45). However, this twenty-year period includes pre-clinical development with usually over a year of laboratory tests, followed by clinical trials, which can take around six years (though sometimes longer) and the process of obtaining approval once Phase III trials are completed.

Together this implies that the patent life for drugs after they have been launched has been typically around eleven to twelve years (Strongin 2002: 3). The Hatch–Waxman Act of 1984 allowed an extension of a further five years to this time, but in all cases the Food and Drug Administration (FDA) limits the total patentable life of a drug to fourteen years from the point of approval, including any extensions that might be granted (Center for Drug Evaluation and Research 2005). Over the patented period, pharmaceuticals firms can capture significant shares of particular therapeutic areas, which may also allow them to develop further products within these segments.

Property rights are of considerable importance when a substantial and enduring market for the product exists. This is certainly true of patents on ethical drugs where property rights are valuable because various forms of socialized medicine across western Europe, North America and Japan have created a mass market in medication paid for through social insurance in western Europe and corporate welfare or private insurance elsewhere. In almost all cases, the state one way or another subvents demand. Even in the USA where private health care is the dominant mode of funding, public-sector spending still accounted for 43 per cent of total national health-care expenditure in 2002, largely due to the high costs of the Medicare and Medicaid programmes (Deutsche Bank 2003a: 5).

Traditionally, both public- and private-sector purchasers have been relatively insensitive to the prices of prescription drugs in systems that pass cost on to a separate funding body. The structural separation of consumer (patient) from prescriber (doctor) and paymaster (usually the state or insurance firm) has generally reduced price sensitivity in a world of approved drug lists (Holman 1988: 3). This is all the more important when the cost of drugs has accounted for a relatively small proportion of very large budgets for private-sector purchasers such as US health-care providers or public-sector purchasers like the NHS in the UK. In both cases, labour and other costs are far larger items of expense so that drug costs have only fairly recently been closely scrutinized. As Exhibit C1.2 shows, pharmaceuticals and other medical non-durable items together accounted for only 10–20 per cent of all health-care expenditure between 1991 and 2000 in different advanced countries, and their share is actually lowest in the USA, presumably because the US system is even less successful at controlling other costs such as surgeons fees or the hotel costs of hospital stays.

Of course, drug-cost control has moved up the political agenda in recent years, especially in Europe and Japan. Thus, the National Institute for Clinical Excellence (NICE) was established in the UK in 1999 to consider, *inter alia*, the cost-effectiveness of medical treatments, including pharmaceuticals (NICE 2005). One of the objectives of NICE was to reduce what had become known as 'postcode prescribing' whereby doctors in different areas took varying attitudes to prescribing certain (usually relatively high-cost) treatments. Glaxo's flu drug, Relenza, was the first case that NICE considered, and its decision that the high cost of the product was not justified by its benefits (and hence that it should not be prescribed under the NHS) sent a clear warning to the drug companies (*Financial Times*, 1 October 1999).

*Exhibit C1.2 Total expenditure on pharmaceuticals and other medical non-durables as a percentage of total health expenditure, 1991–2000*

| | France % | Germany % | Italy % | Japan % | Spain % | UK % | USA % |
|---|---|---|---|---|---|---|---|
| **1991** | 17.1 | | 20.4 | 22.9 | 18.1 | 13.8 | 9.1 |
| **1992** | 17.0 | 14.7 | 20.4 | 22.0 | 18.3 | 14.2 | 8.8 |
| **1993** | 17.4 | 13.1 | 19.9 | 22.3 | 17.9 | 14.8 | 8.6 |
| **1994** | 17.3 | 12.8 | 19.9 | 21.1 | 17.8 | 15.1 | 8.6 |
| **1995** | 17.5 | 1.5 | 20.9 | 21.5 | 17.7 | 15.3 | 8.9 |
| **1996** | 17.5 | 12.6 | 21.1 | 21.3 | 18.2 | 15.6 | 9.2 |
| **1997** | 17.9 | 12.7 | 21.3 | 20.0 | 19.0 | 15.9 | 9.7 |
| **1998** | 18.5 | 13.2 | 21.8 | 17 | | | 10.3 |
| **1999** | 19.2 | 13.5 | 22.2 | 16.4 | | | 11.3 |
| **2000** | 20.1 | 13.6 | 22.6 | | | | 12.0 |

*Source*: OECD Health Data 2002, 4th edn, in Seget (2003: 27)

But, on the long view, the more important point is that efforts to control drug prices in the key US market have been conspicuously unsuccessful. Exhibit C1.3 shows that nominal prices for ethical drugs in the USA were more or less flat for over forty years from the mid-1930s to the late 1970s and during that period faithfully follow the consumer price index (CPI) for all items. However, the 1980s shows the rapid growth in prescription drugs prices (the vast majority of which are accounted for in value terms by ethical drugs) compared with the CPI for all items and non-prescription drugs. In 1990, the average cost per prescription for brand-name medications (i.e. ethical drugs) was $27.16, and by 2000 it had nearly tripled to $65.29 (Emanuel 2003). According to Balance et al. (1992: 29) price rises were the industry's response to broader problem of slow-down in new medical discoveries and stagnant demand in some therapeutic areas. This would appear to be supported by findings from Credit Suisse (2004: 12), who found that increases in retail pharmaceutical prices, either from direct price increases or benefits from therapeutic upgrades, have comprised 50 per cent of annual sales growth on average from 1984 to 2003 and 32 per cent from 1994 to 2003.

The third key condition has been the (favourable) regulatory framework which reflects a close relation between corporate pharma and supportive government. The main UK industry association, the ABPI (Association of British Pharmaceutical Industries) has its head office in Whitehall, while the US organization PhRMA (Pharmaceutical Research and Manufacturers of America), has its offices on 15th Street NW in Washington, DC, a short walk from the main political hub of the USA.

This close relationship has led to the creation of pricing regulations across most of western Europe, North America and Japan, which historically have been very favourable to the supplying industry of giant pharma firms. In the USA there are regulations with respect to safety and efficacy, but no direct price controls and a liberal approach to patents which results in drug prices that are up to 70 per cent higher in the USA than the UK

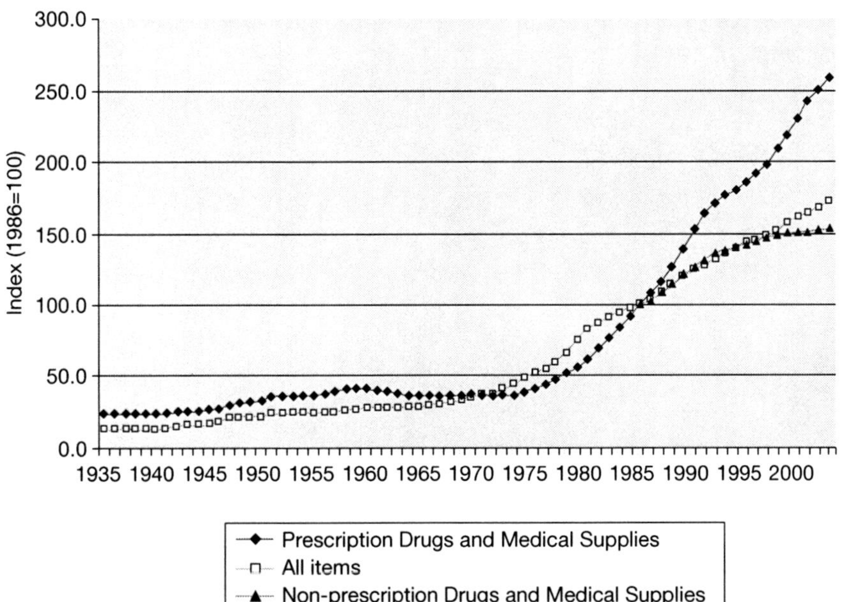


***Exhibit C1.3*** *Consumer price index of prescription drugs, non-prescription drugs and all items, 1935–2004*

*Source*: Bureau of Labour Statistics, Consumer Price Index Statistics

*Note*: Figures are not seasonally adjusted; figures are for US city average; 1986 is used as the base year

(McIntyre 1999: 151–2, 156). In the UK, the Pharmaceutical Price Regulation Scheme (PPRS) regulates ROCE rather than price, to ensure pharmaceuticals companies are guaranteed a minimum rate of return, which through most of the 1970s and 1980s was a very healthy 30 per cent (Froud et al. 1998), though this has been reduced over time and was set at 21 per cent in the 1999 and 2005 schemes (Department of Health 1999, 2004). In Japan, the situation is somewhat different with some price-setting by the Government based on either a classificatory or cost-based pricing scheme, with pharma firms reimbursed by national health insurance. However, even under this arrangement, pharmaceutical companies have prospered through the exploitation of a favourable regulatory system that offers a reimbursement price set up to one-third higher than the price charged to the doctor or medical institution (McIntyre 1999: 165).

## Contesting representations: 'researchers in white coats' or 'reps in cars'?

The basic facts about cost recovery as described above cannot be disputed; this is an industry that operates in a regulated space where competition is limited in a way that licenses high margins. The contest is then about the social value of this activity, which has for forty years been polarized around two competing representations of the pharma business: good pharma is represented in a positive way as a virtuously innovative activity by researchers in white coats who benefit society, while bad pharma is represented in a negative way as an insidious form of profiteering that uses intensive marketing by sales representatives, which also raises prices and, at times, foists potentially unsafe products onto consumers. The positive representation of good pharma was originally articulated by the pharma trade associations and developed by individual companies but has also been endorsed by many academics and politicians who are generally willing to embrace anything that could be described as knowledge-based. The negative representation of bad pharma originates with Senator Estes Kefauver in the late 1950s, who formulated a kind of intellectual charge sheet using arguments that have subsequently at various times been both marginalized and reintroduced into the mainstream. This section first outlines the industry's own positive justification for patents and high profits before introducing the critical perspective.

The industry's own argument differs slightly depending on audience. Publicly, the industry argues that patents are the necessary and appropriate means to encourage the large outlays on R&D that bring new drugs to market and thereby benefit patients. Without patents, R&D levels would be lower because companies would be much less certain about their ability to turn scientifically successful research into a revenue stream. These arguments have been reiterated by trade organizations like the ABPI in the UK and PhRMA in the USA, which have played a key role in presenting the pharmaceutical industry as one that is driven by research that finds better *medicines*.

Here, for example, is Alan Holmer (2002), the President of the PhRMA, rehearsing a familiar argument:

> weakening intellectual property would constrain progress in treating and curing disease . . . Copying most pharmaceuticals costs a small fraction of the amount invested in the research and development of that medicine. Without patents, competitors who have not invested in research could easily undercut the price charged by the company that did make the investment. No company could afford to invest hundreds of millions of dollars per drug in research on such terms.

The ABPI (2003: 2–3) took a very similar position when it argued that:

> An effective patent system . . . is essential to provide the necessary incentive to invest in R&D so as to deliver new innovative medicines to patients . . . Crucially any reform of the patent system should not erode the protection for medicines and thus dilute the incentive for pharmaceutical R&D. Otherwise, it would have a negative impact on the industry and on the provision of healthcare to patients.

However, pharmaceutical companies are also profit-oriented businesses with shareholders, and so this narrative changes when addressing the business community. Here companies, rather than trade organizations, extend the patents/R&D couplet to include profits, which might seem less acceptable in a public debate. The company-level articulation of this position was demonstrated by Merck which (until the recent Vioxx scandal) was widely considered to be the most ethical and science-based of all the big pharma companies. At an acceptance speech given at the Harvard Business School Alumni Awards, Raymond Gilmartin, the current CEO, resurrected the motto originated by George Merck, the founder's son, in the 1950s when the contested representations were first formulated in their modern form. George Merck famously claimed that 'medicine is for the people, not for the profits' and then went on immediately to add, 'if we remember that, the profits will follow' (Merck 2003). On this bold view, the pharma company's fundamental aim is to deliver improved health benefits and the circle is then squared (and critics are forestalled) by arguing that profits will follow so there is no inherent conflict between the two objectives.

In recent years, all the major pharma companies have publicly endorsed versions of the patents/social-benefits/private profits syllogism and Exhibit C1.4 illustrates how the big pharma companies associate innovation with quality of life in their mission statements, presenting intellectual property rights as the precondition of innovation.

Such statements by trade associations and companies create an image of good pharma as a research-driven activity where the continued employment of researchers in white coats depends on the company's patent lawyers who sagely understand the fundamental truth that profit in pharma is simply deferred investment in research. Other classes of employee, such as marketing executives and sales reps, barely figure at all in the positively imagined company which acquires a heroic quality – so much so that Alan Holmer, then President of the PhRMA, likened pharmaceutical companies to the firemen of 9/11 in their selfless struggle to serve the people (cited in Hawthorne 2003: 10).

This framing of good pharma has dominated public debate and convinced regulators, politicians and media commentators for most of the past thirty years. In the central decades of this period, from the mid-1970s to the late 1990s, many believed the industry's own publicity, and critics of the pharma industry found it difficult but not impossible to get an audience. In this period in the UK, for example, only one of three vociferously critical books (Heller 1977, Braithwaite 1984 and Chetley 1990) was published by a mainstream, large UK publishing house. But, both before and after this central period, critics of the industry mounted a better-received attack and ideas of bad pharma challenged the dominant representation to the extent that the industry lost control of its

**Exhibit C1.4** *Mission statements and defence of patents by major pharma companies*

| *Company* | *Mission statement* | *Defence of patents* |
|---|---|---|
| **Pfizer** | 'We dedicate ourselves to humanity's quest for longer, healthier, happier lives through innovation in pharmaceutical, consumer, and animal health products' | 'where inadequate therapies exist, patents provide the incentives to invest in the search for new medicines . . . Without patent protection it is unlikely that patients would receive many new medicines' (Pfizer 2000: 3) |
| GSK | 'our quest is to improve the quality of human life by enabling more people to do more, feel better and live longer' | 'we support intellectual property protection because it stimulates and fundamentally underpins the continued R&D of new and better medicines, including those for diseases prevalent in the developing world' (GSK 2002: 11) |
| Merck | 'to provide society with superior products and services by developing innovations and solutions that improve the quality of life and satisfy customer needs, and to provide employees with meaningful work and advancement opportunities, and investors with a superior rate of return' | 'To be successful, the pharmaceutical industry must help create an environment that encourages and rewards risk taking . . . Strong patent laws allow companies to generate the profits required to finance future R&D while providing investors with a competitive return on their capital' (Merck 1998: 6) |
| **AstraZeneca** | 'The people of AstraZeneca are dedicated to:<br>Discovering, developing and delivering innovative pharmaceutical solutions<br>Enriching the lives of patients, families, communities and other stake-holders<br>Creating a challenging and rewarding work environment for everyone' | 'The international protection of intellectual property rights underpins future investment by the pharmaceutical industry in the research and development of new medicines and, like other pharmaceutical companies, we will continue to work to uphold our intellectual property rights where appropriate' (AstraZeneca 2003) |
| **Johnson & Johnson** | Reject a mission statement and instead have a 'credo' which begins: 'We believe our first responsibility is to the doctors, nurses and patients, to mothers and fathers and all others who use our products and services' | N/a |

*Source*: All mission statements were taken from either mission statement links on the company web site or the captions that appear below company logos on company web sites. The defence of patents were taken from different publications also available on each company web site

own representation. In the early 2000s in the USA, mainstream publishers produced a slew of critical books (see, for example, Abramson 2004, Angell 2004, Goozner 2004, Hawthorne 2003 and Robinson 2001). The next part of this section focuses on these two critical periods: the first, in the late 1950s and early 1960s after the Kefauver hearings; the second, from the mid-1990s to the present time.

### *Kefauver's analysis and the political response*

The original and definitive indictment of bad pharma was put together by Estes Kefauver, a radical Democrat and Chairman of the Senate's Anti-Trust and Monopoly Subcommittee between 1957 and 1963, whose remit was to examine the effects of a lack of competition on an industry-by-industry basis. Against the backdrop of public concern about the pharmaceutical industry, Kefauver's committee began an investigation into the uncompetitive practices of the industry and into the efficacy and safety of the drugs the companies produced (Gorman 1971: 304, 341). Led by Kefauver, the investigative hearings and supporting research indicted the industry on three counts:

1 Patents sustained predatory prices and unreasonable margins that were much higher than in most other kinds of manufacturing. The immediate issue was drug prices and in particular why ethical drugs in the USA were much more expensive than those in mainland Europe and other parts of the world (Kefauver 1965: 55). Kefauver claimed that this could not be explained by higher costs of research or higher labour costs where labour costs per unit of net output were actually lower in the USA than in Europe (Kefauver 1965: 56). Instead, he charged that pharmaceutical companies were profiteering from the patent system and set prices so as to achieve handsome returns on investment. Evidence presented included statistics that showed the pharma industry averaged a return on investment (ROI) of 20 per cent compared with 10 per cent for all of manufacturing between 1957 and 1962 (Kefauver 1965: 61). As for individual companies, thirteen of the USA's fifty most profitable companies in 1958 were pharmaceutical companies based on net profit after taxes and return on invested capital. All of the top three at this time were pharmaceuticals companies (Kefauver 1965: 61).
2 Costs and prices were wastefully increased by large expenditures in marketing. Kefauver charged the industry with 'excessive advertising' as salesmen (or detail men as they are known) placed considerable pressure on physicians to prescribe new drugs. It was shown that, while R&D expenditure accounted for 6 per cent of total receipts, 25 per cent of receipts were attributable to sales and marketing (Kefauver 1965: 68), reinforcing the claim that, 'if new discoveries do not materialize from the corporation's laboratories, they are artificially created by the advertisers art' (Kefauver 1965: 72). Moreover, Kefauver argued that the dominance of marketing had created what we would now call an industry culture whose competitive dynamic militated against the time-consuming clinical tests and

encouraged the premature release of drugs, which could threaten the health of consumers (Kefauver 1965: 72).

3 Many industry products were ineffective (and some were unsafe) because the industry's regulatory institutions lacked the necessary independence. Kefauver noted that the industry charged high prices for new compounds that were often no more effective than established drugs already on the market. He criticized the industry's preoccupation with patentable, non-fundamental innovation and what we would now call 'me-too drugs', with minor molecular changes and performance similar to that of other patented drugs. Such drugs were routinely approved by weak regulatory institutions and an unhealthily close relation between the pharmaceuticals firms and the government departments responsible for vetting new drugs. For example, he found that a number of key officials in the FDA, the body responsible for the approval of new medical drugs, were paid by drug companies for a variety of 'promotional' purposes (Kefauver 1965: 352–3).

It is striking that all subsequent criticism of bad pharma reworks or reinvents these criticisms. They retain much of their original force because Kefauver's problem definition was more influential than his solutions, which involved patent reform and tougher regulation. The solution of patenting the process not the product was offered to prevent the proliferation of me-too drugs and to encourage price competition once a different process had been discovered (Kefauver 1965: 56–7). More generally, it was argued that the time-limited seventeen-year patent protection for ethical drugs should be scrapped and replaced by a system that cancelled new drug patents after three years if the patentee refused to license all 'qualified applicants' at a specific maximum royalty of up to 8 per cent of sales (Kefauver 1965: 44). Kefauver also pushed for a stronger FDA, not only with powers to grant patents only to those goods that could prove efficacy as well as safety, but also with the powers to remove drugs from the market where efficacy is unproven. The historians' verdict is that, following extensive lobbying by the pharmaceutical industry, the Kennedy Administration produced a very watered down version of these reform proposals in a Bill that that Kefauver himself denounced as 'the weakest possible' (Harris 1964: 166). The Bill abandoned not only Kefauver's pricing provisions, but also most of the safety and efficacy recommendations too (Gorman 1971: 335).

Events then intruded after the scandal about Thalidomide, which was not on the general prescription list in the USA but which had disastrous consequences in Europe when prescribed to control nausea in pregnancy. Some of Kefauver's original safety and efficacy proposals were then rehabilitated and incorporated into legislation in the Kefauver–Harris Amendments of 1962. Interestingly, this modest change had a significant effect on the number of new chemical entities (NCEs) (i.e. the number of new therapeutic molecular compounds never before used or tested on humans) and other drugs entering the market and on the number of existing drugs in circulation. Exhibit C1.5 shows that the number of patentable NCEs and other drugs per year dropped significantly from 1962 onwards so that the industry introduced on average three times

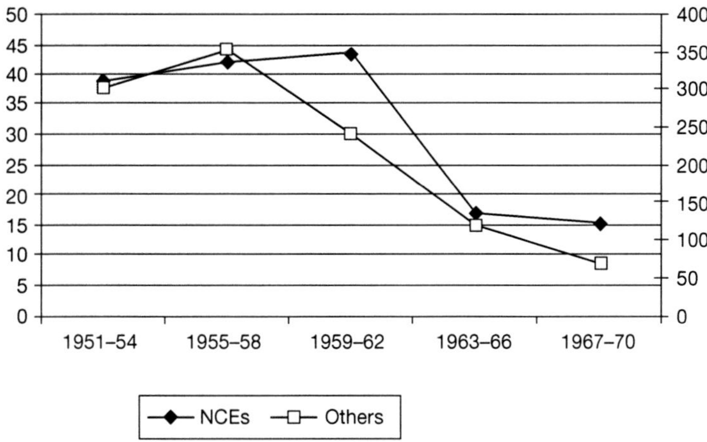


***Exhibit C1.5*** *Number of NCEs and 'other' drugs patented per year, 1951–70*

*Source*: Paul de Haen International Inc. (various years)

as many new drugs before the enactment of the law as after. Additionally, the law was applied retrospectively to drugs already on the market, leading to the additional withdrawal of 1,925 of the estimated 4,000 drugs in circulation (Warden 1992: 11).

The dramatic results of half-hearted pharma reform were a wake-up call to an industry which, in the mid-1960s, faced real political threats to cost recovery in its richest national market under Presidents Kennedy and Johnson. Paradoxically, the Democratic social conscience also created opportunities for the industry to rework its relation with government and to find new markets. The key measure here was the belated introduction in 1965 of a modicum of socialized medicine for the old and poor: Medicare promised comprehensive health care at an affordable cost for all older adults while Medicaid offered to pay medical bills for those on low incomes. The medium-term consequence of post-Kefauver reform plus Medicare was a new relation whereby the US Government became an active partner in the practice of medicine (Schnee 1978: 13). In the absence of any system for funding political parties or controlling electoral expenditure, that relation opened the way for intensive lobbying and political contributions that would increasingly align government and industry interests on the industry's own terms. For example, in the 1999–2000 election cycle alone, the pharma industry made campaign contributions topping $23.4 million as well as funnelling hundreds of millions of dollars to front groups and lobbyists and reportedly spending more than $40 million on 'issue-ads' (*Washington Post*, 11 February 2001). Drawing on lobby disclosure reports filed with the Secretary of the Senate and Clerk of the House, Public Citizen, a non-profit organization, found that pharmaceutical-industry expenditure on lobbying grew from $67 million in 1998 to almost $109 million in 2003 (Public Citizen 2004: 44).

It is thus unsurprising, given the pharmaceutical industry's political importance and the apparent general acceptance of the good pharma narrative, that the Drug Price

Competition and Patent Term Restoration Act (or Hatch–Waxman Act) was presented as a pro-generic manufacturer's Bill but in reality carried enough concessions in the detail to ensure that pharmaceutical profits were not badly damaged. Prior to the Hatch–Waxman Act, manufacturers who wanted to market generic copies of ethical drugs had to wait for the original patents to expire before beginning a lengthy application and approval process and proving efficacy and safety by repeating many of the clinical tests already undertaken on the ethical equivalent. Under Hatch–Waxman, generic manufacturers were allowed to seek FDA approval to market the generic drug before the expiration of the ethical drug using an Abbreviated New Drug Application (ANDA) which meant that manufacturers only had to demonstrate bio-availability (i.e. the amount of active ingredient in the blood over a period of time has to come within plus-or-minus 20 per cent of that which is observed when the innovator's drug is ingested) rather than repeat the same tests as the innovator drug (Mossinghoff 1999: 190). The aim of this legislation was to introduce price competition quickly into the market once a drug's patent had expired and thus save the state and the consumer money on expensive ethicals.

Yet the review that led to the Hatch–Waxman Act began under the Carter Administration as an attempt to compensate large pharmaceutical companies for the patent time lost whilst drugs were under regulatory review (Mossinghoff 1999: 188), and the Reagan Administration sought to remedy this problem to 'balance' the negative effects of generic competition on the large pharma companies. The Hatch–Waxman Act therefore also formally established a five-year data-exclusivity period and a total market-exclusivity time of fourteen years for new molecular entities. It also established that if a generic manufacturer claimed a patent was invalid or not infringed, then the patent owner had forty-five days to file an infringement action which automatically ensured another thirty months of exclusivity before an ANDA could be approved and generic competition could begin (Mossinghoff 1999: 190). Therefore, the industry was relatively protected from the effects of generic competition and managed the voracious competition from the generic companies by raising ethical prices during the patented period, as Exhibit C1.3 illustrates.

On market access, the Reagan Administration actively sought to open up international markets for US pharmaceutical companies, most notably through the 1985 market-oriented sector selected (MOSS) talks, which aimed to increase US access to the lucrative Japanese market. This priority was perhaps unsurprising when Edward Pratt, CEO of Pfizer Inc., was also a member of President Reagan's business advisory committee on international trade (Sherer 2000: 2248).

After the 1979 victories of Reagan and Thatcher in the USA and the UK, old social-democratic assumptions about regulation were turned upside down in the name of enterprise and without any recognition of the probability of unintended consequences. Thus, in the UK, the Thatcher Government reduced the Department of Health's regulatory requirements for the approval of clinical trials in a bid to boost efficiency in the sector in the early 1980s (Abraham 2000). Given that none of the problems analysed by

Kefauver had been solved it was highly probable that issues about drug safety would return to haunt legislators. As we have argued elsewhere, the emergent political ideology in the UK and USA was neo-liberalism with responsibility, where the electorate were promised a combination of market dynamism with social responsibility ensured by corporate governance and other kinds of re-regulation in financial services and privatized utilities (Erturk et al. 2004). From this point of view, scandals about drug safety and corporate social responsibility were a political crisis waiting to happen, even though Kefauver was more or less forgotten.

### *Back to the future: criticism of the industry in the 1990s and 2000s*

Nevertheless, the industry's lurch into crisis in a few short years after the late 1990s is really quite remarkable. When the authors of this case study published an updated statement of the bad pharma case (Froud et al. 1998), their academic article was seen by its few readers as a provocative, revisionist attack on an industry with a shining reputation. But within five years new stories about the old Kefauver problems of predatory pricing and unsafe drugs were on the front pages of the *Financial Times* and *Wall Street Journal* (e.g. *Financial Times*, 6 January 2005, 3 June 2004 and *Wall Street Journal*, 25 January 2005, 1 October 2004). These issues had a much higher profile in general business-press coverage of the pharma industry than the Ford Explorer roll-over problem had in coverage of Ford. The proportionality was not related to numbers killed or exposure to litigation, because the Explorer was in these terms very bad news when media reports alleged 600 had been killed in rollover accidents (see Case Study 2). The business press was obsessively interested in accumulating criticisms of bad pharma because everybody understood that (via reputation and regulatory change) these criticisms threatened pharma profitability in a way that overturned sport utilities did not in the auto sector. For example, large investors such as Legal & General, Schroder and Jupiter have warned that big pharma might find its corporate reputation shredded and profitability eroded if it failed to responsibly address health crises in poor countries (*Financial Times*, 24 March 2003).

The original issue at the heart of revived criticism of pharma was the unresolved contradiction between the high prices of ethical dugs and the low incomes of most of the rest of the world. Some low-income countries have ignored patents and produced copies of in patent ethical drugs for local consumption: for example, in Brazil, the Government licensed local production of in-patent anti-retroviral drugs, as well as importing generics from India, where patents have not until recently been recognized. Where patents have been respected by low-income countries, however, patients and funding bodies have been expected to pay the same prices as high-income countries, and this became the basis for the South African Government's 1997 Medicines Act, which was an attempt to provide a legal framework for producing lower-cost drugs. The law did not immediately come into effect because, in March 2001, thirty-nine of the world's largest pharma companies took the South African Government to court, with the public support of the Clinton Administration in the USA (Oxfam 2001a).

The legal dispute lasted two years and became the focus for newspapers and pressure groups in the late 1990s which focused on the needs of the 25 per cent of South Africans of working age who were HIV positive and who could not afford high-priced patented medicines (*Guardian*, 24 October 2001). Thus Kefauver's arguments were revisited and reworked in a new international context whereby the victims of pharmaceutical greed were not US citizens paying over the odds for drugs but poor Africans dying because they could not afford medication. Newspapers used human-interest articles and compelling photographs to mount a fierce critique of the prices pharma charged for drugs that might extend or save the lives of the poor (see, for example, *Observer*, 3 August 2003, *Guardian*, 22 February 2001). Such stories were supported with campaigns by organizations such as Medicins Sans Frontières (MSF) and Oxfam: the MSF newsletter condemned the high prices of Roche's AIDS drug Viracept (Medicins Sans Frontières 2002) while Oxfam's 'Cut The Cost' campaign highlighted the high costs of AIDS drugs and other medicines to sub-Saharan Africa (Oxfam 2001b).

The AIDS crisis in Africa changed the terms of public debate about pharma so that Stephen Lewis, the UN Special Envoy on AIDS, claimed 'the intellectual property debate is rendering human rights subsidiary to human greed' (quoted in the *Observer*, 3 August 2003). Pharma and Africa had been coupled to establish an image of corporate irresponsibility which overpowers discussion about practicalities such as the inadequacy of health-care infrastructure in some of the poorer countries. It was entirely appropriate that the questionable role of global pharma in Africa was the theme for a popular British novelist, John Le Carré (2001), who sets his thrillers against political backgrounds. If Le Carré dealt with imagined corporate social irresponsibility in a far-away country, drug safety was much more explosively damaging to reputation when it became an issue inside the USA in 2004.

Events in 2003–4 vindicate Kefauver against all those senators and lobbyists who accused him of exaggeration. Now one major pharma company, GSK, has been damaged by allegations of failing to disclose relevant but adverse clinical-trial data for a major product, while another company, Merck, has been forced to withdraw a hugely successful blockbuster under suspicion of its safety, as accumulating problems raise fundamental questions about the integrity of the drug-approval process more generally.

GSK's problem was the allegation that it had concealed data about the side effects of its anti-depressant Paxil (also known as Seroxat) on children and adolescents. An ABC *Primetime Live!* news programme alleged internal company documents showed that Glaxo knew the drug was ineffective in treating such cases (see ABC 2004 for the full allegations). In unprecedented legal action, New York State Attorney Eliot Spitzer charged that GSK had concealed side effects from doctors by publishing only one of five clinical studies (*Business Week*, 3 June 2004). GSK settled the Spitzer law suit for $2.5 million without admission of wrongdoing and on FDA instructions added a side-effects warning about suicide risk. Although the financial consequences of the case were fairly limited, standard industry practices were called into question. GSK has reacted by posting more information about its clinical trials on the Internet via its Clinical Trial Register (GSK 2004b), a move that has been followed by the world's major pharmaceutical associations.

Merck's withdrawal of Vioxx was more damaging to the company. Vioxx was a blockbuster anti-arthritis drug which, according to observational studies, has potentially serious side effects in the form of substantially increased risk of heart attacks and sudden cardiac death (*Financial Times*, 7 January 2005). Again, there were claims that senior management in the firm knew about the risks of Vioxx and failed to disclose the relevant information. This case showed how, although blockbuster drugs could be the making of a global pharma company, they could also wreak substantial damage or even be its undoing. Through withdrawal Merck directly lost $2.5 billion in annual sales and exposed itself to the threat of multi million-dollar lawsuits from patients and relatives. One month after the withdrawal Merck's share price was still down 40 per cent (*Financial Times*, 9 November 2004).

The next company in the dock was Pfizer, which spooked the market by toughing it out and refusing to withdraw Celebrex, another anti-arthritis drug with similarities to Vioxx, when it has already been censured by US regulators for misleading safety and efficacy claims in its consumer ads (*Financial Times*, 13 January 2005). The accumulating evidence suggests a systemic problem about how company financial interests colour safety and efficacy judgements and about thoroughly ineffectual regulation of drugs, especially after initial approval. These issues were focused by David Graham, a whistle-blowing FDA scientist called to testify before the US Senate's finance committee which was investigating Merck's withdrawal of Vioxx. Graham claimed the FDA was too close to the industry and that, as a consequence of flawed approval processes, it 'seriously undervalues, disregards and disrespects drug safety' while over-valuing the benefits of drugs (*The Economist*, 27 November 2004).

In December 2004, the White House Chief of Staff opined the FDA was doing a 'spectacular job' and 'should continue to do the job they do' (*Washington Post*, 21 December 2004). However, more bad news came for the industry when it was reported that controversial US documentary-maker Michael Moore had chosen health care as the subject of his next documentary. The PhRMA Director of Communications then showed he had learnt something but forgotten nothing: 'We have an image problem – not only with Michael Moore but with the general public . . . We're criticized on the Hill and in the press – put in the category of the tobacco industry even though we save lives' (*Detroit News*, 22 December 2004). Amidst all this criticism the FDA has proposed a new safety board, whilst even conservatives, such as Iowa's Republican senator Chuck Grassley, have called for more rigorous regulation through a new office of drug safety separate from the FDA (*Time*, 28 February 2005).

# THE PHARMA BUSINESS MODEL AND THE DRUGS PIPELINE

The focus now shifts away from contested representations of good or bad pharma and towards narrower issues about the pharma business model and how companies recover their costs, which involves analysis of corporate cost-recovery strategies and capital-market understandings of those strategies. These market understandings exist in a relation of constructive overlap with the companies' business practices on drug production and marketing, described in the opening pages of this section. And they are understood at firm level through the key analyst concept of the drugs pipeline.

Business models are, of course, dynamic and develop in response to changing industry conditions. It has been argued, for example, that in the 1940s and 1950s cost recovery in pharma was achievable through rapid scientific (mainly biochemical) advances which brought many new and socially useful drugs such as antibiotics to market (Bogner and Thomas 1996: 54). However, with the onset of tighter regulation following Kefauver and a more general slowdown in biochemical discovery, the pharmaceutical industry has developed a different business model that encompasses several interrelated practices. First, the objective is volume sales of blockbuster drugs as a basis for cost recovery; second, the means is productive conservatism and aggressive marketing to build such blockbuster sales.

Pharma-company strategy also includes a company narrative. Pharma companies have traditionally traded at starry P/E ratios, and any loss in confidence by the capital market can undermine the share price. At the centre of the business narrative about the pharma industry is the idea of the pipeline. This has become the subject of extensive corporate disclosure and explanation because it promises to give outsiders an insight into the future portfolio. The pipeline makes the future visible and revenues predictable in so far as drugs move slowly through the development phases towards the market and, for drugs that are in the market, patent-expiry dates are also public knowledge. While patent-expiry dates are apparently fixed, there is considerable uncertainty about other aspects of the business model.

## The pursuit of blockbuster sales

More than twenty years ago, Piore and Sabel (1984) announced a general tendency towards flexible specialization and manufacture of short runs of differentiated products. Nobody told the pharma companies, who constructed a growth industry around repeat sales of 'blockbuster drugs' which are defined technically as ethical drugs that generate annual sales of at least a billion dollars.

Blockbusters are important to the large pharmaceutical firms because they account for a significant (and growing) proportion of the total spend on drugs, thus increasing the incentive to own the relatively few drugs that capture a larger slice of total prescriptions in a particular therapeutic segment. The top-fifty selling drugs in the USA accounted for 44 per cent of total outpatient retail drug sales in 2001 while the remaining 9,482 drugs accounted for the other 56 per cent available for sale (NIHCM 2002a: 6). Moreover, pharmaceutical firms can charge more for blockbusters than they can for other drugs – in 2001 the average price of a prescription for one of the top fifty drugs was $71.56 compared with just $40.11 for the others, with those blockbusters with the largest market share in their therapeutic areas being the most expensive (NIHCM 2002a: 8). Evidence on the pharmaceutical industry shows that blockbuster drugs have become more important over the past twenty years. In 1990 there were just seven blockbusters but, by 2002, this figure was sixty-five (Deutsche Bank 2003b: 11). Furthermore, the top-ten best-selling drugs accounted for 5 per cent of industry revenues in 1985, while in 2002 this figure was 12 per cent (Deutsche Bank 2003b: 27).

Blockbusters are not accidental products, they are deliberately created by pharma firms who are now consequently more reliant on blockbusters than they have ever been historically (Reuters Business Insight 2004: 25). At the same time, the focus on blockbusters also reflects an adaptation to what the individual pharma company encounters as two environmental fixities: first, the segmentation of the market into discrete therapeutic areas and second, the marked slowdown in biochemical advance. Of course, therapeutic areas are partly the constructs of companies who use them as a way of classifying the drugs in their portfolio, but they also exist in a very real sense as ineluctable market constraints. Although companies attempt to patent drugs for as wide a range of patients and conditions as they can, no one drug has the healing properties to make it suitable to treat a broad spectrum of illnesses and conditions. The pharmaceuticals market is thus segmented into a number of small, fragmented and discrete therapeutic areas which companies aim to dominate.

The pharma industry is one of contrasts in terms of industrial structure and market segmentation. The supplying industry is unusual by late-capitalist standards because it remains relatively fragmented despite a whole series of M&A in the 1990s and 2000s: as Exhibit C1.6 shows, in 2003 only one company, Pfizer, had a market share of more than 10 per cent and only two (Pfizer and GSK) had shares of more than 5 per cent. But, as explained above, companies compete in a segmented market with discrete therapeutic areas within which small numbers of individual drugs have high shares: as Exhibit C1.7 indicates, the largest companies achieve market shares of more than 15 per cent in at least three therapeutic areas. The therapeutic areas are effectively separate product markets because there are few drugs that can be used to treat problems in more than one therapeutic area. This creates the opportunity to secure a large proportion of the revenue in particular therapeutic segments by convincing physicians that a particular drug is the most effective. Once achieved, market share is buttressed by patents which insulates successful drugs from competition for a substantial period.

***Exhibit C1.6*** *Market share of the ten largest pharmaceutical companies, 2003*

| *Ranking* | *Corporation* | *Market Share (%)* |
|---|---|---|
| 1 | Pfizer | 10.1 |
| 2 | GlaxoSmithKline | 6.6 |
| 3 | Merck & Co | 4.8 |
| 4 | Johnson & Johnson | 4.8 |
| 5 | Novartis | 4.3 |
| 6 | AstraZeneca | 4.1 |
| 7 | Aventis | 3.7 |
| 8 | Bristol Myers Squibb | 3.4 |
| 9 | Roche | 3.3 |
| 10 | Abbot | 2.8 |

*Source*: ABPI (2005)

Strategies of dominating particular therapeutic segments become all the more attractive under conditions of limited scientific advances and hence fewer new products. And this has been the case in pharma over the past few decades. In 1955 the total number of new products approved by the FDA was 403 compared with just seventy-eight in 2002 (Schnee and Calgarcan 1978: 94 and FDA/Centre for Drug Evaluation and Research statistics). The industry can make good the deficit of innovation by increasing the price of those drugs that are in the market (see Exhibit C1.3), which may partially compensate for the relative lack of new product, but it does also make the pharma companies more reliant on a small number of high therapeutic-share blockbuster drugs. Exhibit C1.8 illustrates this point: for some smaller pharmaceuticals companies such as Biogen, TAP and Forest, one or two blockbusters can account for 70 per cent to 90 per cent of company revenues for as long as the patent lasts. This also suggests that because fewer new patented products are in circulation it becomes easier to dominate one therapeutic segment with just one drug.

However, this makes the individual company desperately vulnerable to patent expiry. As Eli Lilly shows, patent expiry can be a big problem for medium-sized companies: once the Prozac patent ran out, there were severe falls in unit price and thus revenues and stock price, as generic competitor products become available while the Lilly company did not have another blockbuster that could maintain growth. The largest drug companies have a significant portfolio advantage here. Those like Pfizer, Merck and GSK are also heavily dependent on blockbusters to generate sales revenue but are less vulnerable because they have a portfolio of blockbuster drugs across therapeutic areas, which spreads risk and limits exposure to early patent challenges on one drug. As Exhibit C1.8 shows, Pfizer's eight blockbusters together contributed 79 per cent of company sales in 2002, while GSK's eight blockbusters generated a more modest 53 per cent of sales.

**Exhibit C1.7** *Share of key pharmaceutical products by therapeutic segment (2002)*

| | *Cardio* | *CNS* | *Anti-infectives* | *Respiratory* | *Metabolism* | *Gastro-intestinal* | *Oncology* | *Hormones* | *Muscular* | *Other* |
|---|---|---|---|---|---|---|---|---|---|---|
| AstraZeneca | XX<br>Crestor | X<br>Seroquel | | XX<br>Pulmicort | | XXX<br>Nexium | XXX<br>Zoladex | | | |
| Aventis | X<br>Lovenex | | X<br>Several | XX<br>Allegra | | | XX<br>Taxotere | X<br>Lantus | | |
| Bristol Myers Squibb | XX<br>Pravachol | | XX<br>Zerit | | | | XX<br>Various | | | |
| Eli Lilly | | XXX<br>Zyprexa | | | X<br>Evista | | X<br>Gemzar | XXX<br>Insulin | | |
| GSK | | XX<br>Paxil | XXX<br>Trizivir | XXX<br>Advair | X<br>Avandia | X<br>Zantac | | | | XXX<br>Vaccines |
| Merck | XXX<br>Zocor | | X<br>Crixivan | XX<br>Singulair | XX<br>Fosamax | | | | XXX<br>Vioxx | XXX<br>Vaccines |
| Novartis | X<br>Diovan | X<br>Clozaril | | | | XX | Zometa | X | XXX<br>Voltaren | Neoral |
| Roche | | | XXX<br>Rocephin | | X<br>Xenical | | XXX<br>Rituxan | | | X<br>Cellcept |
| Pfizer | XXX<br>Lipitor | XXX<br>Zoloft | XXX<br>Zithromax | X<br>Zyrtec | | | X<br>Camptosar | XX<br>Genotropin | XXX<br>Celebrex | X<br>Viagra |
| Schering-Plough | | | XX<br>PEG-Intron | XX<br>Clarinet | | | | | | |
| Sanofi Synthelabo | XX<br>Plavix | X<br>Ambien | | | | | | | | |
| Tak | X<br>Blopress | | | | X<br>Actos | XX<br>Prevacid | X<br>Lupron | | | |
| Wyeth | | X<br>Effexor | | | | X<br>Protonix | | XXX<br>Premarin | X<br>Enbrel | XX<br>Vaccines |

Key: XXX = 15+% market share, XX = 5–15% market share, X = good presence

*Source*: Deutsche Bank (2003b: 23)

*Exhibit C1.8 Contribution of blockbusters to total ethical sales, 2002*

| *Company* | *Blockbuster sales* $ million | *Total ethical sales* $ million | *Blockbusters as % of total sales* | *Number of blockbusters* |
|---|---|---|---|---|
| Biogen | 1,034 | 1,148 | 90 | 1 |
| TAP | 3,600 | 4,037 | 89 | 1 |
| Pfizer | 22,291 | 28,288 | 79 | 8 |
| Forest | 1,423 | 2,022 | 70 | 1 |
| Merck & Co | 14,670 | 21,631 | 68 | 5 |
| Aingen | 3,187 | 4,991 | 64 | 2 |
| J&J | 9,754 | 17,151 | 57 | 5 |
| GSK | 14,240 | 27,003 | 53 | 8 |
| Schering Plough | 4,538 | 8,745 | 52 | 2 |
| Novo Nordisk | 1,881 | 3,810 | 49 | 1 |
| Lilly | 4,692 | 10,384 | 45 | 2 |
| AstraZeneca | 7,746 | 17,343 | 45 | 3 |
| Wyeth | 5,022 | 11,733 | 43 | 3 |
| Aventis | 5,463 | 15,104 | 36 | 3 |
| Bayer | 1,588 | 5,352 | 30 | 1 |
| Sanofi-Synthelabo | 2,590 | 8,705 | 30 | 2 |
| BMS | 4,156 | 14,700 | 28 | 2 |
| Novartis | 3,810 | 13,493 | 28 | 3 |
| Pharmacia | 3,050 | 12,037 | 25 | 1 |
| Abbott | 1,102 | 8,451 | 13 | 1 |
| **Total** | 115,837 | 236,129 | 49 | 55 |

*Source*: Reuters Business Insight (2003a: 104)

*Note*: excludes Roche/Genentech due to non-standardization of total ethical sales and Purdue Pharma (privately owned); blockbusters are defined as ethical drugs that generate at least $1 billion of sales in one year

## Productive conservatism and aggressive marketing

If the aim of the giant pharma companies has been blockbuster-driven growth, how is this to be achieved? Blockbusters do not simply happen, they have to be created through a combination of scientific and marketing efforts. The discussion of means and instruments takes us back to the industry-framing about good and bad pharma. Are sales enhanced through investment in R&D which generates innovative products from fundamental advances as the industry claims? Or, are sales driven by marketing of imitative products which result from slower scientific advance as suggested by the industry's critics? This section's examination of the evidence supports the second, more critical, view of pharma as an industry characterized by modest innovation and aggressive marketing.

The good-pharma frame couples R&D expenditures with 'new medicines', but many patented drugs are 'me-too' variants of existing products and do not represent significant discoveries. Some of the most successful drugs of the 1990s and 2000s are simple variants with slight molecular alterations which allow a new patent: in Glaxo's case, Zantac was a variant on the original anti-ulcerant, Tagamet, from SmithKline just as Paxil/ Seroxat was a variant on Eli Lilly's Prozac. More systematic evidence confirms this impression. The US FDA has a grading system for new drugs awaiting patent approval. Of the 1,035 new drugs approved by the FDA between 1989 and 2000, two-thirds used active ingredients already on the market (Harrison 2003: 14). It was also found that just 153 of the 1,035 new drugs approved were 'Priority' rated NMEs (which indicates significant medical improvement). The rest were deemed to be 'Standard' rated, i.e. of little or no medical improvement (NIHCM 2002b: 3).

If relatively few significant medical improvements emerge from the R&D effort in pharmaceuticals companies, this may be because research is only a very small part of the R&D process: laboratory research by scientists in white coats typically accounts for less than 10 per cent of total R&D expenditure with development taking the form of product testing focusing on efficacy, dosage, safety and side effects in clinical trials accounting for the rest (Financial Times Management Report 1995: 32). Dosage and side effects are inherent major problems of the blockbuster model. The ultimate business objective is to find a universal remedy within each therapeutic class, i.e. a drug that could be prescribed to every patient who presents with high blood pressure, depression or whatever. But that is complicated by considerable variation in the response of individual subjects and the presence of other medical conditions.

If the good-pharma frame emphasizes research not development, it also glosses over the practice of marketing, which is central in the bad-pharma frame. Marketing is again inevitably costly because, in the absence of fundamental innovation, many ethicals are high-price drugs that are competing with older but cheaper generic alternatives which do much the same job. The data on the level of marketing expenditure is striking in two ways. First, giant pharma company accounts disclose that sales and marketing expenditure is typically two to three times higher than expenditure on R&D: as Exhibit C1.9 shows, typically companies spend 13–15 per cent of sales revenues on R&D while sales and marketing absorbs at least 30 per cent of sales. Second, as Exhibit C1.10 shows, many pharma companies spend as much or more of revenue on sales marketing as do companies, such as Coca-Cola, Nestlé or Proctor & Gamble, that sell branded goods to consumers.

The huge pharma expenditure on marketing is not generally visible to the ordinary citizen because pharma marketing has always been focused on the doctor prescriber, rather than the patient or the general public. Many countries, like the UK, retain regulations which prevent direct marketing of ethicals through television adverts and suchlike. Even in the USA, where direct-to-consumer (DTC) advertising is allowed, DTC marketing spend accounts for just 1.5 per cent of US pharmaceutical sales (PhRMA 2003: 14). Physicians are ideal targets for focused marketing because they are an identifiable,

**Exhibit C1.9** *Comparison of expenditure on sales and marketing with research and development in 2000*

| | *Spend on sales and marketing as a % of sales revenues* | *Spend on research and development as a % of sales revenues* |
|---|---|---|
| Pfizer | 39 | 15 |
| Schering Plough | 37 | 13 |
| GSK | 37 | 13 |
| AstraZeneca | 36 | 17 |
| Roche | 30 | 13 |
| Aventis | 32 | 15 |
| Novartis | 31 | 13 |
| Eli Lilly | 28 | 19 |
| Bristol Myers Squibb | 21 | 12 |

*Source*: Company Annual Report and Accounts, various years

**Exhibit C1.10** *The significance of sales and marketing costs for selected non-pharma companies in 2000*

| *Company* | *Spend on sales and marketing as a % of sales revenues* |
|---|---|
| Coca-Cola | 36 |
| Nestle s.a. | 32 |
| Panasonic | 27 |
| Proctor & Gamble | 26 |
| Sony | 24 |
| Microsoft | 18 |
| IBM | 17 |

*Source*: Company Annual Report and Accounts, various years

relatively small group (Harrell 1978: 70) with discretion about how to spend significant drug budgets. The industry employs a huge and growing sales force to influence the doctor's choice: Reuters estimate that the sales force of the largest pharmaceutical companies in the USA doubled between 1996 and 2001, with an estimated 100,000 sales reps presently servicing the US market alone (Reuters Business Insight 2003b: 116, 118).

It is estimated that in the USA, roughly 75 per cent of the sales and marketing budget of pharmaceutical companies goes on 'detailing', where a sales representative meets a doctor face to face, with roughly 70 per cent of physicians admitting that they would consider changing their prescription habits in response to detailing messages (Reuters Business Insight 2004: 33). If detailing is an attempt to educate physicians, it has also traditionally involved giving away free samples, small trinkets, meals and even all-expenses-paid trips to resorts (Madhaven et al. 1997: 207). This has sometimes led to allegations of malpractice, as in the case of AstraZeneca, which paid $355 million in criminal fines and out-of-court settlements following an investigation of their marketing of Zoladex, a prostrate cancer treatment. The Department of Justice alleged that AstraZeneca had given away free samples of the treatment 'knowing and expecting' that some doctors would seek reimbursement for the treatments from Medicare and Medicaid, while doctors were paid 'illegal remuneration' including travel and entertainment (*Financial Times*, 21 June 2003).

Even if detailing is an effective way of communicating, it is expensive and adds to the cost of every prescription paid for by the taxpayer or the patient. One campaign group estimates that in 2000 pharmaceutical companies' detailing expenditure amounted to a colossal $12.7 billion when the cost of free samples is included (CALPIRG 2004: 3).

The balance between R&D and marketing reflects the difficulty of fundamental biochemical advance which would create new treatment possibilities for diseases such as Alzheimer's and arthritis. But it also reflects the appropriation of research and marketing activity characteristics inside a capitalist business model. The two key activities in the business have very different characteristics: research is characterized by unpredictable timing, informality, modest expenditure and unpredictable results, while marketing is characterized by predictable timing, formality, huge expenditure and planned results (Chiesa 1996). Under pressure for financial results, giant capitalist enterprises find marketing much more congenially predictable and financially rewarding.

From a productive perspective, the industry estimates that there is only a one in 5,000 chance of any compound eventually getting approved by the FDA (PhRMA 2003: 6) and that the average development cost for each approved drug is approximately $800 million, with such costs recovered in only 30 per cent of cases (PhRMA 2003: 5). The cost of drug development is almost certainly exaggerated in such industry estimates; a public-interest group, Public Citizen (2001: 4) put the figure closer to $110 million. But the development costs are still significant enough for Big Pharma to pursue a two-pronged strategy of productive conservatism that reduces exposure to risk. First, companies develop and secure patents on me-too variants of already-successful drugs, as previously discussed; second, they attempt to manage the product life cycle so as to extend the patent life of a drug beyond the usual twenty years allowed by the FDA. A classic tactic here is to change the delivery method: thus, Bayer's Cipro was originally only available as an oral tablet, but was later developed as an intravenous formulation so that it maintained a strong revenue stream for a sixteen-year period, which contrasts favourably with the industry average of around six to ten years per drug (Reuters Business Insight 2003a: 53). The cost savings are spectacular when the $10–50 million cost of clinical trials for reformulations and line extensions is compared with the $800 million figure mentioned previously (Reuters Business Insight 2004: 22).

In stark contrast to the conservatism of Big Pharma's R&D effort, marketing is aggressively focused on the continuous promotion and regular relaunching of 'improved' product. Ideas are turned into saleable product over a development lead time of ten to fifteen years (Deutsche Bank 2003b: 13). And any policy of targeting R&D resources on what are currently the largest (cardiovascular and central nervous system (CNS)) or fastest-growing therapeutic areas (oncology) may prove misguided when these can change dramatically over that development period. By way of contrast, marketing is about nimble decisions to exploit therapeutic areas with volume potential once drugs clear the development stages or competitors' drugs lose patent. The pharmaceutical business model therefore is about positioning, but it is about positioning from a marketing perspective where quick, focused strategic moves can make or break a drug. Marketing moves can establish a strong sales base in areas with volume potential in several ways: by pushing a new drug, rejuvenating an old one or relaunching old drugs for new applications.

When new drugs clear the approval system, they must be established as quickly as possible to crowd out competitors. This is because the growth rate and market share gained in the first year after launch has a great influence on the sales that can subsequently be achieved (Reuters Business Insight 2003a: 43). However, marketing can also be used to extend the revenue stream despite equal or even weaker trial performance. AstraZeneca's aggressive marketing of Nexium as a successor to out-of-patent Losec led many physicians to change over to the new drug even though trials suggested Nexium performed no better and was perhaps even less efficacious than Losec (Reuters Business Insight 2003a: 50–2). Furthermore, the most successful drugs are not necessarily the new ones that have just emerged from Phase III trials. Blockbuster sales in the two largest therapeutic segments, cardiovascular and CNS, have been driven by Pfizer's Lipitor, Lilly's Zyprexa and Wyeth's Effexor (Reuters Business Insight 2004: 24) which are all established drugs that had been given a marketing push.

Timing is critical in pharma. This is particularly so if a major competing product comes off patent, where the vigorous marketing of either an old or new drug presents an opportunity to 'make' a new blockbuster. The successful pharmaceutical company is therefore one that can maintain a portfolio of drugs in areas of volume sales, and these are not (or at least not only) created and sustained by developing novel drugs with superior medical-trial results, but by applying marketing to new or existing drugs at critical times. This is supported by Reuters Business Insight's (2004) finding that pharmaceutical revenues are directly proportional to investment in sales and marketing, so that the more a company spends, the more it will recoup in terms of sales revenues.

The significance of marketing is also underlined by the growing importance of Phase IV trials. Phase IV trials are those that take place after the FDA, European Medicines Evaluation Agency (EMEA) or Ministry of Health and Welfare (MHW) Japan have given approval for the drug to be manufactured, distributed and marketed. The function of Phase IV trials are in theory to further monitor and assess drug safety once a product enters the open market. However, increasingly they are also used to gather further performance results from head-to-head studies, which can then be exploited by their marketing departments in an attempt to expand the remit of the drug to treat new ailments or to further differentiate the product from those of its competitors (Reuters Business Insight 2003a: 38, 40). Under conditions where fewer NCEs are passed by the FDA, pharmaceutical companies have to leverage maximum value from their existing products and provide whatever support they can for their marketing team. In each of these cases, the profitability of the drug in question does not depend on its overall record on safety or efficacy but on how sales and marketing exploit this information in a reactive way to secure positions in therapeutic areas with volume potential. Hence, it is not surprising that the compound annual growth rate of pharmaceutical spending on Phase IV trials increased from 17 per cent between 1985 and 1995 to 23 per cent between 1995 and 2000. This rate of growth is higher than that for Phase I–III trials where the comparable growth rates have been 14 per cent and 16 per cent over the same periods (Reuters Business Insight 2003b: 121).

## The analysts' view: visibility and predictability?

The pharma business model can be described from public interest and academic texts. What analysts offer is a stock-market appropriation of that business model with a distinctive extra emphasis on key indicators such as patent expiry and the development pipeline, which have direct implications for revenue and profit at the individual company level. Thus blockbusters for analysts have much the same significance as stars for Hollywood producers because the bankable star or product is a key indicator of present (and future) success. Until recently, blockbuster-driven sales growth has remained a largely unquestioned strategy in stock-market commentary with blockbusters presented as the only viable way of meeting shareholders' high growth expectations (Reuters Business Insight 2003a: 10).

One of the central dilemmas of the stock market is that the price of shares should notionally reflect the discounted present value of future earnings, but in most activities it is difficult to predict the future trend of earnings with any certainty because of product market competition, as for example in cars, where much depends on the relative success and failure of new and yet-to-be-launched models. From the analyst's point of view, pharma is different because the future stream of earnings is much more predictable under three special-case revenue conditions which derive from the property rights that limit competition: first, analysts know the unexpired patent life for the key products of the business; second, future earnings are closely related to the current portfolio of drugs; and third, the pipeline of new product is disclosed and discussed at length by the giant pharma companies. Some have proposed alternative measures for assessing the prospects of giant pharma companies, so that Brietzman et al. (2002) suggest a patent-based analysis, but the three orthodox indicators continue to dominate analyst understandings of the business.

In this section, we will briefly describe how the revenue conditions operate, noting that they increasingly do so in ways that complicate an already-stressed traditional business model. But the revenue conditions remain important for analysts because they should make the earnings prospects of pharma companies much more transparent and visible. The language used in analysts' reports explicitly refers to pipeline and patents as the principal generator of 'news flow' (CIBC 2003: 1, Bear Stearns 2003a: 1) while the visual language used in many reports is equally striking when, for example, Morgan Stanley (2002: 2) discusses the pipeline in terms of 'long-term revenue growth visibility'. It is also quite clear that pharma-company managements release news about pipeline developments, through briefings and annual R&D days, in ways that make the companies and their analysts joint-authors of a narrative. This emerges clearly in many reports as when Lehman Brothers (2004: 1) claim 'management reiteration of EPS guidance . . . (and) positive comments on pipeline visibility . . . has encouraged the market'.

Patent expiry is relevant in the pharma business because the expiry dates of major drug patents are public knowledge, and it is nearly certain that revenue will fall away precipitously as soon as the patent expires and generics become available. Generic versions of ethical drugs are exact molecular copies and hence, in principle, equally effective but, as previously mentioned, typically retail at a discount of between 10 per cent and 70 per cent (Reuters Business Insight 1998: 19) so that an ethical drug that comes to the end of its patent term will usually lose two-thirds of its revenues within three years. For example, three months after Naprosene went off patent, Syntax, its manufacturer, lost 75 per cent of its market to the generic product (Mossinghoff 1999: 191) or, more famously, Lilly's anti-depressant Prozac lost 73 per cent of its share of new prescriptions to generic copies in the first two weeks of going off patent (Tuttle et al. 2004: 89). The complication is that ethical drugs are typically covered by a variety of different patents and there is scope for attack and defence so that expiry dates are increasingly less certain than they appear. We have already noted that pharma companies are extending drug patents by, for example, changing delivery systems, and we could now add the point that the growing number of incrementally modified drugs provides a high return on investment because they use active ingredients with a proven track record of safety and efficacy, thus reducing both risk and costs (NIHCM 2002b: 4). Generic manufacturers also increasingly use legal challenges through the courts to break patent protection, such as Indian generic company Ranbaxy's audacious attempt to overturn Pfizer's patent on Lipitor (*Wall Street Journal*, 11 January 2005). The front pages of analysts' reports on pharma companies often discuss the implications of recent patent defences against generic manufacturers which might indicate a shortened patent life. Hence, in the past three years, various analyst reports on Pfizer have headlined at least three patent challenges: Lipitor (Smith Barney Citigroup 2004), Neurontin (Salomon Smith Barney 2003) and Norvasc (Credit Suisse 2002).

The loss of patents on old ethical drugs matters in so far as the company does not have new drugs coming through the pipeline and onto the product market. The stock market is therefore intensely interested in the new-product pipeline and in the number of promising products in the later stages of development. Analysts and companies stereotype the development process in terms of a series of phases which follow on from discovery with average duration from Phase I to market currently around eight years.

Phase I tests are conducted on a sample of healthy trialists; Phase II tests are on a small number of patients at various dosages; while Phase III tests the drug on a large number of patients at multiple sites (Hara 2003: 21). For analysts, the pipeline is of as much interest as the patent status and expected term of those products that have been approved.

More exactly, it is the later stages of the pipeline that matter because the failure rate is high as drugs move from one phase to the next. Thus, for example, ABN AMRO (2002: 7) includes only Phase III and marketed drugs in its discounted-cash-flow valuations of companies within the sector. Phase I and II drugs are completely omitted from forecasts because proof of concept or efficacy data is rarely generated until late Phase II trials. More generally, the fact that 60 per cent of all drugs entering Phase II trials will not make it to Phase III (Deutsche Bank 2003b: 34) justifies brokers' sceptical handling of Phase II pipeline products as there is little guarantee that these will eventually reach the market. Thanks to regular and detailed disclosures by the large companies, the products in the later stages of the pipeline are well understood by analysts.

Here again, complications prevent certainty and predictability. In the later stages of development, the key issue for analysts is which drugs are likely to gain approval (and for what treatments) and how quickly approval can be gained. There is uncertainty about both timing and outcomes when drugs can fail at the later stages of development. The rejection of late-stage drugs can have a dramatic effect on revenues and, by implication, future strategy. AstraZeneca sacked 10 per cent of its US workforce to save costs after the regulators rejected Exanta, a blood-thinning drug, and a study showed that its cancer treatment drug Iressa failed to help cancer patients live longer (*New York Times*, 7 January 2005).

All this discussion of individual company prospects takes place against a background where the pharma trade associations and others admit the business model is increasingly stressed by industry-wide developments. The stock market can of course adapt to all this because the market is both about the pursuit of perfection and the adaptation to radical imperfection. If analysts had sufficient understanding of the key indicators, and the indicators operated with clear-cut force, then the market could treat pharma shares as promissory notes. As the complications intrude in the form of events such as late stage failure or premature patent loss, they create trading opportunities related to what is not in the price, and trading pharma shares becomes just like trading auto shares without the cyclicality. Adaptation may be more difficult for the pharma companies whose property rights and research productivity traditionally justified a high P/E ratio. For the companies, it is increasingly a struggle to keep things going.

## GLAXO: KEEPING IT GOING

Glaxo since the early 1980s is a brilliant story of upward corporate mobility. In earlier decades it had been a minor national player like many others in Europe, and the company only entered the US pharmaceuticals market in 1978 (GSK 2004a). Thanks first to organic growth and subsequently to merger, between 1981 and 2002 Glaxo then rose from the twentieth- to the second-largest pharmaceutical company in the world by sales (Deutsche Bank 2003b: 18). In the absence of any kind of indigenous British technology sector, this trajectory ensured that Glaxo became an important constituent of the FTSE 100. On a market capitalization basis, by 2002 GlaxoSmithKline was one of the three largest companies in the UK and, together with BP Amoco and Vodafone, accounted for some 25 per cent of the aggregate market valuation of the FTSE 100 (Randles 2002: 344).

Glaxo is also a suitable case for analysis because, as many observers understand, its success has never rested on fundamental innovation. Lynn's (1991) book internalized the good-pharma–bad-pharma opposition through his contrast of innovative Merck and marketing-led Glaxo. More recently, Deutsche Bank (2003b) agrees in a less moralistic way when it recognizes Glaxo's competence in marketing as the company's key corporate asset. Furthermore, the means to growth in successive periods make Glaxo emblematic of the broader industry. From the early 1980s onwards, Glaxo's organic growth was driven by Zantac, the biggest blockbuster the industry had ever seen. Whereas in a second phase, Glaxo shifted to M&A with the 1995 acquisition of Wellcome and the 2000 merger with SmithKlineBeecham (SKB), which were both classic exercises in defensive horizontal merger.

This section considers in turn these two successive phases of Glaxo's growth. In the first phase, the marketing of Zantac brought a brilliant financial success where the stock market was the main beneficiary; and in the second phase, defensive merger aimed to keep things going for the stock market through two major deals within six years. None of this is intended to disparage the company: Glaxo's success has been built on its early and complete recognition of the conditions of success (in first marketing and then cost-cutting) in an industry where others were more complacent or arrogant. Glaxo's first acquisition Wellcome was sometimes described as the only university with a stock market quotation. Glaxo could certainly not be disparaged in these terms and indeed has reversed the relation in so far as Richard Sykes, its CEO from 1993 and Non-Executive Chairman from 2000 retired to become Rector of Imperial College and to found a new role in bringing his expertise to university reorganization.

## Zantac or up, up and away (1982–94)

Glaxo is quite unlike the average FTSE 100 company which, as we have seen in the introduction to this book, grows about as fast as GDP. As *Exhibit C1.11* shows: between 1980 and 1994, nominal sales increased 815 per cent while nominal operating profits increased 2,656 per cent, albeit both from low bases (see also Tables C1.1 and C1.2 in the appendix, pp. 210, 211). Glaxo had several successful products including the asthma drug Ventolin, which in 1981 was the world's most prescribed medicine in terms of number of prescriptions (Glaxo Annual Report and Accounts 1981: 7). But the spectacular growth of revenue and profit was driven by one successful blockbuster, Zantac, an anti-ulcerant launched in 1982 in Europe and 1983 in the USA and aimed primarily at patients with duodenal and gastric ulcers. Zantac became the best-selling drug in history (Wright 1996) and the first pharmaceutical product to achieve sales of £1 billion (Glaxo Annual Report and Accounts 1988: 4).

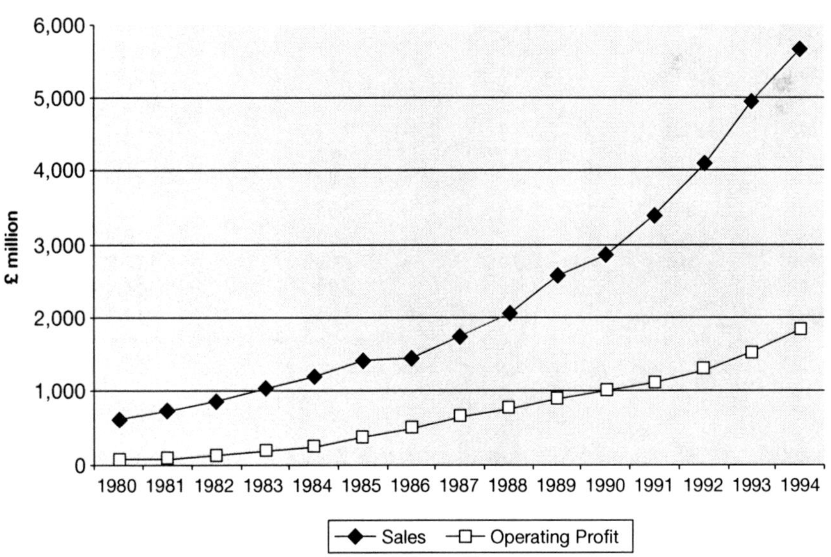


***Exhibit C1.11*** *Glaxo sales and operating profit, 1980–94 (nominal data)*

*Source*: Company Annual Report and Accounts, various years

Exhibit C.12 clearly shows Zantac's contribution. In terms of revenues, Zantac contributed half of overall sales at the peak in 1989, and this one drug accounted for more than 30 per cent of overall sales in each of the eleven years between 1985 and 1995 (see also appendix, Table C1.13, p. 222). Zantac produced strong and consistent growth

**Exhibit C1.12** *Zantac's share of total sales at Glaxo, Glaxo Wellcome and GlaxoSmithKline, 1980–2002*

| | *Zantac sales* | *Zantac sales as a % of overall company sales* | *Zantac sales as a % of therapeutic segment (anti-ulcerant/metabolic and gastro-intestinal)* | *Annual change in Zantac's sales* |
|---|---|---|---|---|
| | £ million | % | % | % |
| **1980** | 0 | n.a. | n.a. | n.a. |
| **1981** | 0 | n.a. | n.a. | n.a. |
| **1982** | 37 | 4.3 | 100.0 | n.a. |
| **1983** | 97 | 9.4 | 100.0 | 162.2 |
| **1984** | 248 | 20.7 | 100.0 | 155.7 |
| **1985** | 432 | 30.6 | 100.0 | 74.2 |
| **1986** | 606 | 42.4 | 100.0 | 40.3 |
| **1987** | 829 | 47.6 | 100.0 | 36.8 |
| **1988** | 989 | 48.0 | 100.0 | 19.3 |
| **1989** | 1,291 | 50.2 | 100.0 | 30.5 |
| **1990** | 1,401 | 49.1 | 100.0 | 8.5 |
| **1991** | 1,606 | 47.3 | 100.0 | 14.6 |
| **1992** | 1,807 | 44.1 | 100.0 | 12.5 |
| **1993** | 2,172 | 44.1 | 100.0 | 20.2 |
| **1994** | 2,442 | 43.2 | 100.0 | 12.4 |
| **1995** | 2,255 | 32.2 | 100.0 | −7.7 |
| **1996** | 1,931 | 23.2 | 99.2 | −14.4 |
| **1997** | 1,375 | 17.2 | 99.6 | −28.8 |
| **1998** | 757 | 9.5 | 99.5 | −44.9 |
| **1999** | 640 | 7.5 | 98.9 | −15.5 |
| **2000** | 575 | 3.2 | 46.7 | −10.2 |
| **2001** | 505 | 2.5 | 34.1 | −12.2 |
| **2002** | 382 | 1.8 | 26.7 | −24.4 |
| **2003** | 328 | 1.5 | 23.0 | −14.1 |

*Source*: Company Annual Report and Accounts, various years

through the 1980s and mid-1990s, with double-digit sales growth in every year between 1983 and patent expiry in 1997, with the one exception of 1990. This growth trajectory was possible because Zantac had succeeded in capturing the segment: by 1993, Zantac had secured 38 per cent of the total worldwide anti-ulcerant therapeutic segment, having gained well over 50 per cent of the H2-receptor blocker market in the USA four years previously (Wright 1996: 29). (An H2-receptor blocker is an antihistamine that reduces stomach-acid secretion and helps heal peptic ulcers.) Table C1.13 (p. 222) also shows that Zantac was the one and only Glaxo product within its therapeutic area (anti-ulcerant, metabolic and gastro-intestinal) until the merger with SmithKlineBeecham in 2000.

Zantac's exceptional sales contrasts with its relatively ordinary medical performance. Zantac was a me-too copy of Smith Kline's pioneering anti-ulcerant, Tagamet. Zantac sold at a 15–20 per cent premium and offered twice-a-day dosing over Tagamet's schedule of four to five times a day (Wright 1996: 25). But Zantac was virtually identical to Tagamet in terms of molecular structure, and trials showed few significant medicinal advantages (Lynn 1991: 203). This anecdotal evidence is further supported by Wright's well-documented study of Zantac, which argues that the difference was marketing, playing off the insecurities of doctors and patients. According to Wright (1996: 26, 28, 29), Glaxo's emphasis on 'educating' primary physicians as well as 'educating' patients suffering from heart-burn managed to generate an estimated extra 500,000 visits to the doctor and a boom in mail-order purchases. Lynn (1991: 203–4) argues that Glaxo's marketing of Zantac was managed cleverly:

> Questioning Tagamet's safety was a neat line of attack. It could not be proved that Zantac was better: it had not been used widely enough yet for its side-effect profile to emerge. But by the same logic it could not be disproved. This is the kind of information which, in the hands of skilled marketing professionals, can be twisted into a decisive advantage [because] . . . Doctors are generally cautious people, particularly in the United States where the threat of being sued for negligence makes them fearful.

As a Glaxo marketing employee observed, 'the best way of making more money at Glaxo was to spend more money on Zantac' (Lynn 1991: 206). The industry had always spent on marketing drugs but, according to Lynn (1991: 206), the marketing techniques applied to Zantac established a new marketing model within the industry, whereby considerable amounts were spent on promoting the drug over its whole lifespan rather than to just in its first few years on the market. The aim was also to build a global company rather than license production to competitors. In the late 1970s Glaxo was effectively UK-based: the purchase of Meyer Laboratories Inc. in 1978 only gave the company a US R&D base (GSK 2004a), and in the first half of the 1980s, more than two-thirds of Glaxo's sales revenues were from Europe, Africa and the Middle East (see appendix, Table C1.3, p. 212). To get Zantac into the huge and lucrative US market, Glaxo mounted a textbook two-stage operation. In the first phase between 1983 and 1989, Glaxo forged a co-promotion strategy with French pharma firm Hoffman La Roche who had an under-utilized US sales force (Wright 1996: 25). In the second phase from 1990 to 1994, Glaxo rapidly consolidated the success of Zantac by building its own marketing workforce in the USA to sell what was by then an established product.

The aggressive application of marketing to a single me-too drug gave Glaxo enviable financial results as it moved along a brilliant trajectory of growth. Between 1988 and 1994, Glaxo had a very healthy (pre-tax) return on sales of 30–40 per cent and an outstanding pre-tax ROCE generally exceeded 25 per cent, as Exhibit C1.13 shows (see also appendix, Table C1.11, p. 220), with a balance sheet where less than 10 per cent of the long-term capital was provided from debt (appendix, Table C1.6). These favourable ratios were achievable because Glaxo's business was based entirely on ethical drugs. In operating terms, Glaxo also enjoyed favourable ratios: external purchases accounted for less than 40 per cent of sales revenue and the labour share of internal cost was well under

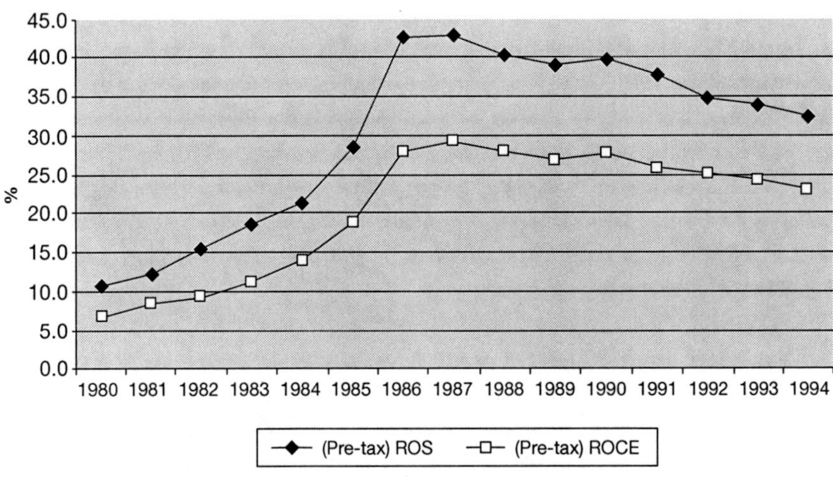


*Exhibit C1.13 Glaxo rates of return, 1980–94*

*Source*: Company Annual Report and Accounts, various years

40 per cent, resulting in cash generation of more than 30 pence per pound of sales revenues, roughly twice as much as SmithKlineBeecham or Zeneca, which combined ethicals with other activities (see appendix, Table C1.12, p. 221).

Glaxo offered the stock market a combination of high rates of return and spectacular growth (with none of the usual disadvantages of cyclicality or risky exposure to fast moving technology) and the market found that quite irresistible. The predictable result of the high rates of return and low gearing was a massive growth in market capitalization for Glaxo from £379 million in 1980 to £16.6 billion in 1994, or in real terms (using 2003 prices) a twentyfold increase from just over £1 billion in 1980 to £20.8 billion by 1994, largely due to a rise in year-end share price from £2.24 in 1980 to a peak of £16.60 in 1987 as investors chased this growth stock (see appendix, Table C1.10, p. 219).

As a globalizing pharma company, Glaxo's record on employment creation sets it apart from other UK organic growth success stories such as the retailer, Tesco, where sales growth directly feeds an expanding domestic employment base. In the first phase of US marketing using Hoffman La Roche employees, total employment in Glaxo actually fell between 1980 and 1986, from 29,187 to 24,728. After 1987, company employment begins to increase, but as Table C1.8 in the appendix (p. 217) shows, most of the growth in employment up to the mid-1990s (after which the relevant data is no longer disclosed) is outside the UK because marketing employment is usually close to the customer. Marketing employment was always dominant in the Glaxo workforce: as a result, in 1991 there were 2.5 marketing employees for every person engaged in R&D, and by 1994 this ratio had risen to 2.9 (Exhibit C1.14). The internal workforce did benefit from a relaxed approach to pay rises and wage levels as real annual labour costs per employee rose from £13,964 in 1980 to £34,624 (in 2003 real prices) by 1994 (Table C1.9, 2003 prices, see p. 218), but with no overall increase in labour's share of internal costs (see Table C1.12, appendix, p. 221).

If we turn to look at distributions to shareholders, they were rather differently treated because they did claim an increasing share of the growing cake. As Exhibit C1.15 shows, the amount Glaxo distributed to shareholders as dividends grew over the period of

**Exhibit C1.14** *Glaxo: breakdown of employment by geographic region and activity, 1990–4*

| | | *% share by region* | | *% share by function* | | |
|---|---|---|---|---|---|---|
| | *Total number employed* | *UK* | *Overseas* | *Manufacturing* | *R&D* | *Sales and marketing* |
| **1990** | 31,327 | 39 | 61 | | | |
| **1991** | 35,640 | 35 | 65 | 37 | 18 | 45 |
| **1992** | 37,083 | 32 | 68 | 35 | 18 | 47 |
| **1993** | 40,024 | 30 | 70 | 34 | 18 | 48 |
| **1994** | 47,189 | 25 | 75 | 37 | 16 | 47 |

*Source*: Company Annual Report and Accounts, various years

*Note*: Employment by geographical area is unavailable after 1996 and employment by activity is unavailable before 1991. See also appendix, Table C1.8 for full series

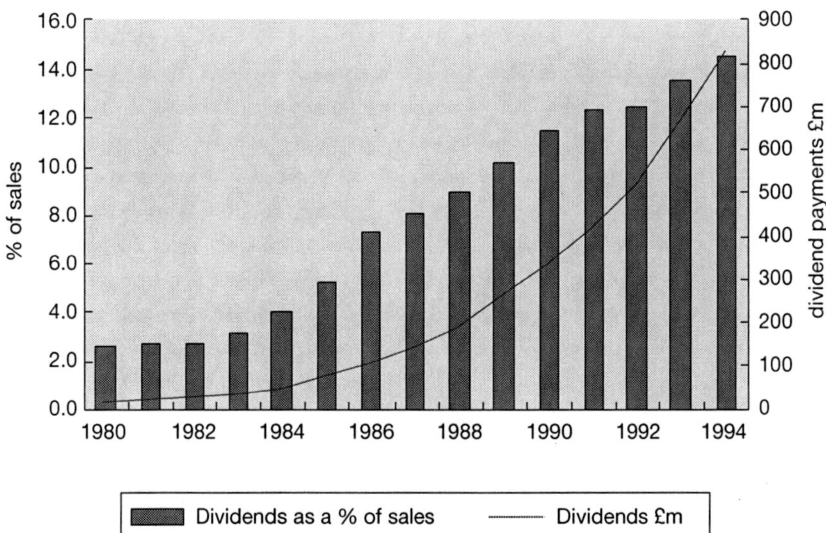


**Exhibit C1.15** *Glaxo: dividend payouts, 1980–94*

*Source*: Company Annual Report and Accounts, various years

*Note*: See Table C1.5 in the appendix for full data

organic growth. Glaxo's dividend payments, which were equivalent to less than 10 per cent of sales revenues in the 1980s, grew to reach 15 per cent by 1994. By pharma standards, this was certainly a high level of distribution because the comparable rates for SKB and Zeneca were around 6 per cent in 1994. Although total dividends rose fairly smoothly, as Exhibit C1.15 shows, as a percentage of net (i.e. post-tax) profit, there was a marked step up from a range of around 26–40 per cent in the 1980s to a level of at least 60 per cent after 1994. With generous distributions to shareholders, however, Glaxo made a rod for its own back because it created expectations of dividends, especially as distribution rates were raised in the 1989–94 period with patent expiry on Zantac due in 1997 and effective competition beginning in 1990 with the launch of Astra's Losec, which rapidly began to eat into Zantac's therapeutic market share.

The overwhelming question by the early 1990s was: how would Glaxo keep things going after Zantac? That question was more urgent because Glaxo's best-selling anti-asthma drugs Becotide and Ventolin were also close to expiry and possible replacements – such as Zofran, Immigran and Serevent – seemed incapable of filling the sales gap (*Financial Times*, 9 September 1994). By the early 1990s, it was already fairly clear that the answer to that question would not be supplied by the efforts of internal R&D. Glaxo's R&D expenditure as a percentage of sales revenue was just 6.1 per cent in 1982 when Zantac was launched, and it was the success of this 'me-too' drug that enabled Glaxo to invest a greater proportion of its sales revenues in R&D while also delivering higher profits and dividends: by 1994, the R&D spend had increased tenfold in real terms and the R&D spend reached 15.2 per cent of sales revenues (Exhibit C1.16).

Yet despite this increase in R&D expenditure, no new blockbuster drug emerged that could feasibly replace the losses that would accrue after Zantac's patent expired. Moreover, while the growth of Glaxo's R&D spend was impressive, throughout most of the 1980s Glaxo's R&D expenditure was well behind the industry norm of 13.5 per cent of sales (Taggart 1993: 260). Although Glaxo significantly increased its expenditure on R&D as the company expanded, reaching levels of 14 per cent of sales revenues in the early 1990s, by the early 2000s it was again falling behind others in the industry. In 2003, GSK's R&D as a percentage of sales was 12.9 per cent, compared with 17.2 per cent for Astra Zeneca, 17.9 per cent for Aventis, 16.7 per cent for Pfizer and 15.6 per cent for Roche (*Wall Street Journal*, 24 March 2003). Lehman Brothers also estimated in 2003 that the current value of GSK's expected R&D investment over the following twenty-five years was equivalent to 39 per cent of its current sales compared with 67 per cent for the average European pharma company and 100 per cent for the average US company (*Wall Street Journal*, 24 March 2003).

Did the preference for distribution compromise the capacity for productive innovation? In many ways, it could be argued that Glaxo's more limited spend on R&D was an intelligent response to the realization that its own competences were based on marketing and that the generic business model did not offer clear productivity gains from growing R&D any faster than the business as a whole. However, it did suggest that growth would have to be sustained through some means other than simply new drug development.

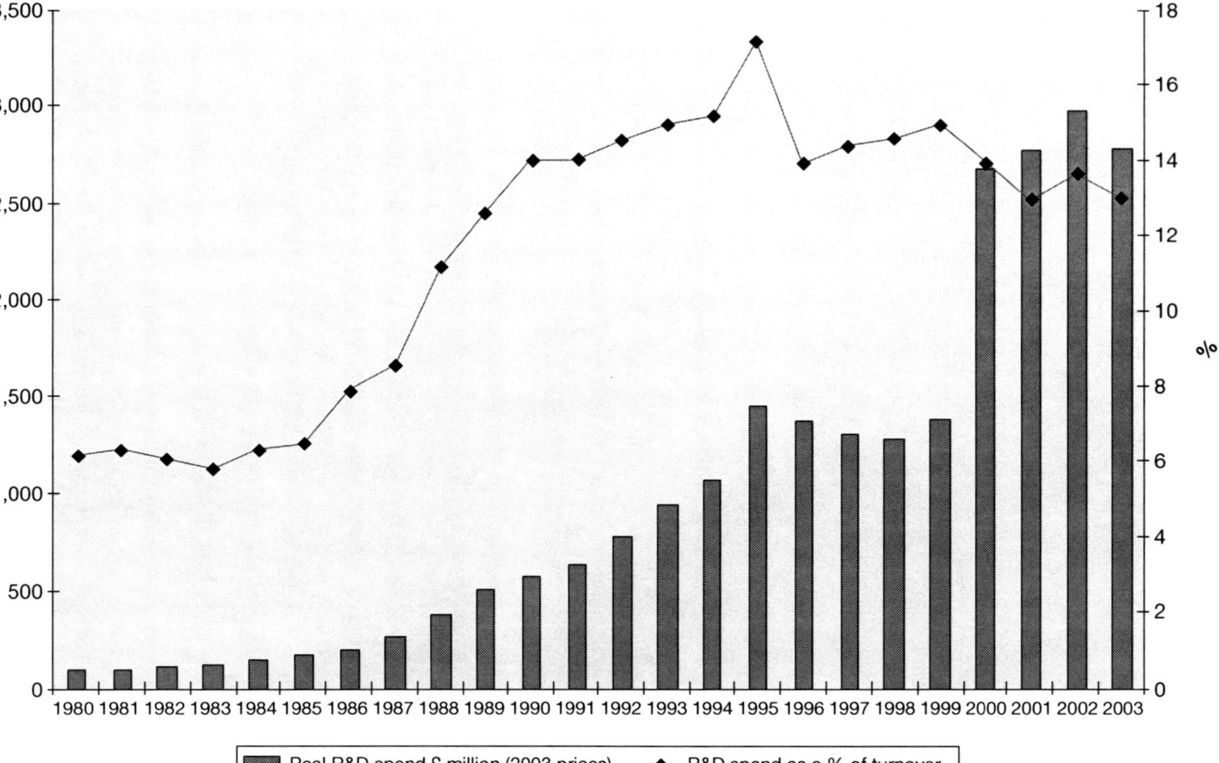


**Exhibit C1.16** *Glaxo, Glaxo Wellcome, GlaxoSmithKline: the scale and significance of R&D expenditure, 1980–2003 (in real 2003 prices)*

*Source*: Company Annual Report and Accounts, various years

*Note*: R&D expenditure includes capital expenditure and labour costs

## M&A to keep the numbers going (1995–2002)

One of the few general laws (or behavioural regularities) of corporate capitalism is that, when cost recovery falters, firms turn to defensive horizontal merger which offers cost reduction and improved positioning. The point will be most familiar to older British readers who remember 1960s' amalgamations such as British GEC or British Leyland Motor Corporation/British Leyland (BLMC/BL) in faltering industries of electrical engineering or autos. If the quasi-corporate framework around British business has since been dismantled, the recent history of pharma shows that the defensive response remains important, or has become even more so, because after financialization the desideratum is not profit but enough profit and growth to keep the share price going. And, in Glaxo's case, M&A was logically inevitable because organic growth would never keep things going when the Zantac patent expired.

The results of defensive merger are very variable. Such acquisitions can produce sustained advantage, as they did in integrated oil for BP where Lord Browne had the fundamental good sense to buy other oil companies and their reserves in the decade of the 1990s when oil (and oil companies) were cheap and product-market competitors such as Shell were too slow to see the necessity for acquisitions. And, from this point of view, Glaxo deserves some credit as a first mover that was prepared to do mergers that establishment pharma companies such as Merck and Pfizer would not consider at all (in the case of Merck) or only much later (in the case of Pfizer). Glaxo's problem was that its first deal, the acquisition of Wellcome in 1995, bought time but did not solve any of its fundamental problems about a business model that required more new product than the pipeline could generate. This left Glaxo almost immediately searching for a second, bigger deal and SKB has been publicly targeted by 1998. But this turned out to be much more problematic, both before and after the second deal was completed in 2000.

### *Glaxo Wellcome: the unsolved problem*

The 1995 purchase of Wellcome was a well-executed bolt-on acquisition of a smaller firm. The purchase was straightforward and the financial consequences in terms of capital structure and balance sheet were entirely manageable in such a cash-generative business. The £9.3 billion purchase of Wellcome was made with £6.3 billion of cash (of which around 20 per cent was funded by debt) and the rest paid in shares. This deal was attractive to the Wellcome Trust, which owned 40 per cent of Wellcome, because this not only provided the funds to allow it to become the largest endowed medical charity in the world, but also gave it a stake in the new company of somewhere between 4 and 5 per cent (Ogilvie 1998: 634). For Glaxo, the increase in debt to help finance the deal was not a major issue. Prior to the acquisition, Glaxo had a remarkably strong balance sheet, characteristic of a highly cash generative company whose growth to date had been financed from internal sources: in 1994 the long-term debt to shareholder equity ratio was 1:17 (appendix, Table C1.6, p. 215), so that the addition of around £1.2 billion of debt introduced a net interest payment equivalent to around 2 per cent of sales (or 10 per cent of operating profit) that could quite easily be met in a high-margin business (appendix, Table C1.5, p. 214).

In operating terms, the acquisition of Wellcome allowed growth to be maintained or, more exactly, prevented a collapse of sales revenue because Glaxo was able to consolidate revenue from the two companies and gained opportunities to rationalize operations and to cut costs, allowing margins to be maintained or even improved. In terms of sales growth, the acquisition of Wellcome was well timed in preventing a collapse in sales. Wellcome's sales of £2.3 billion in 1994 were an attractive bolt-on to Glaxo's £5.7 billion, so that by 1996, the new company had £8.3 billion of sales. Given that Zantac's sales revenue fell from £2.44 billion at the peak in 1994 to £1.93 billion by 1996, as Exhibit C1.12 shows (with Zantac eventually losing 84 per cent of its 1994 total peak sales value by 2003, by which time it was making only a modest contribution to the company of £328 million) the stabilization of Glaxo's nominal sales growth is perhaps an achievement.

However, in real terms, there was no growth after 1996, and it is interesting to observe that a real 20 per cent increase in sales in 1995, following the acquisition of Wellcome was not much more than the organic growth achieved at the peak in 1992 (16 per cent) or 1993 (18 per cent) (see appendix, Table C1.2, p. 211). Wellcome was not large or dynamic enough in terms of product to cover the loss of Zantac sales when the patent finally expired in 1997. Thus, in 1996, one year after the merger and before patent expiry, Zantac still provided around 50 per cent of Glaxo Wellcome's profits (*The Economist*, 26 April 1997). After patent expiry in July 1997, the Glaxo Wellcome results for 1997 showed the first drop in nominal sales in over seventeen years and the combined companies' share of the pharma market fell from 6.2 per cent in 1995 to 5.2 per cent in 1997 (*The Economist*, 22 January 2000). But the bolting-on of Wellcome created opportunities for cost-cutting that cushioned the jolting shock to profit ratios and allowed the pre-tax return on sales (pre-tax profit margin) to be held at around 33 per cent (23 per cent post-tax), which was as good at the immediate period before Wellcome's acquisition, though weaker than in the late 1980s when a pre-tax return on sales of more than 40 per cent was achieved (see appendix, Table C1.11, p. 220). The cost-cutting was achieved through more or less immediate redundancy: 7,105 jobs were cut between the acquisition and the accounting year end in 1995 as 11.6 per cent of the combined Glaxo Wellcome workforce were selected out. Just under 50 per cent of this job rationalization were in marketing and administration, because one sales force could handle the two ranges of drugs, but there were also significant cut-backs in R&D (1,953 jobs) and in manufacturing (1,683 jobs). As well as headcount reductions, Glaxo managed to contain the overall salary bill with real labour costs per employee falling from £41,164 in 1996 to £36,202 by 1999 (in 2003 prices).

From Glaxo's perspective, the acquisition was a success because adding Wellcome's sales helped avoid the revenue and profit collapse that would have accompanied Zantac's expiry. However, it was clear that buying Wellcome was an interim solution with only short-term savings and, according to *The Economist* (22 January 2000), no long-term growth. It was unlikely that bolt-on acquisition and defensive restructuring would keep the stock market happy for long because they did not resolve the fundamental problem about the pipeline and, after 1997, Glaxo Wellcome had no more internal levers to pull that could improve operating ratios. Between 1995 and 1999, Glaxo Wellcome launched just two new blockbusters (Heracleous and Murray 2001: 436) and suffered notable setbacks with the withdrawal of Lotronex, Raxar and Romozin (Bosanquet and Atun 2001: 74). Despite the failure to solve Glaxo's problem of a weak pipeline, there was no overall boost to R&D effort. After the acquisition of Wellcome, R&D investment was cut as both a percentage of sales revenue and in real terms, signalling that research was not to be at the centre of the new company. As Exhibit C1.16 shows, in 1995 Glaxo Wellcome committed £1,456 million to R&D (2003 prices), which represented 17.1 per cent of total sales revenue. The R&D budget, in real terms, was then cut successively in 1996, 1997 and 1998, only to grow slightly in 1999 as the top line improved. Despite this minor improvement, by 1999 the £1,391 million spent on R&D was still lower in real terms than the peak in 1995, and R&D as a percentage of sales was also lower at 14.9 per cent.

Despite these signs of strain and the near certainty of future under-performance, shares in the new Glaxo Wellcome company rose sharply from 1995 to 1999 so that market value grew from £21 billion in 1995 to just under £77 billion in 1999. This was, of course, in the middle of the bull market but, as Exhibit C1.17 shows, between 1995 and 1998 the Glaxo Welcome share price (corrected for stock splits) significantly outran the FTSE 100 index. This substantial rise in share price is only intelligible on the assumption that the market believed that the Wellcome acquisition represented not so much an event as a formula that Glaxo management could subsequently repeat. This point was proved in 1998 when a second merger with SKB was mooted. This merger then fell through due to boardroom disagreements about how top jobs would be shared between Glaxo Wellcome and SKB senior management (*The Economist*, 28 February 1998) and the share prices of both companies then dropped sharply with Glaxo Wellcome shares falling by £2.47 to £16.57 and SKB shares dropping 83p to £7.24, so that collectively the two companies wiped out 60 points from the FTSE 100 index (*Financial Times*, 25 February 1998).

### *GlaxoSmithKline: more of the same?*

The aggravation over whether Jan Leschly of SKB or Richard Sykes of Glaxo Wellcome was to become CEO in 1998 should have given everybody pause for thought. So too should the merger mania of the pharma business by late 2000 when Glaxo Wellcome manoeuvred to prevent the merger of SKB with American Home Products (AHP), who

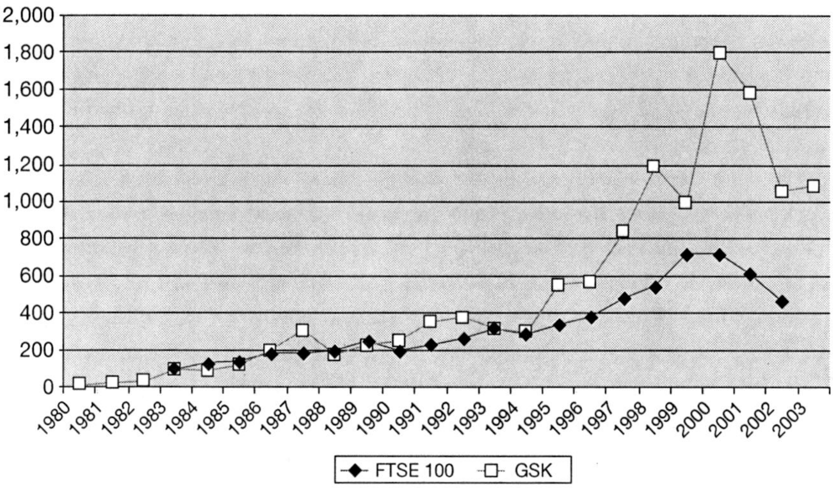


*Exhibit C1.17 Index of GlaxoSmithKline share price against the index of FTSE 100 market value (1983=100)*

*Source*: Datastream and GSK report and accounts

*Note*: GSK share price is corrected for stock splits so that the graph shows the value of one share in Glaxo bought in 1980 and held throughout the period

had previously been in merger talks with Warner Lambert (WL) before WL eventually decided it preferred to hook up with Pfizer (*Financial Times*, 8 February 2000). In 1995, Glaxo had been ahead of the game when it picked up Wellcome; by 2000 Glaxo was just another pressured player in a major round of industry consolidation. The Glaxo Wellcome/SKB merger had been subject to two further embarrassing postponements in August and September of 2000 (*Financial Times*, 13 December 2000) before it was finally completed in December 2000. The merger made GSK the largest pharmaceutical company in the world at that time, with a market value exceeding £110 billion, as well as the second largest firm on the UK stock market behind Vodafone and on par with BP. The dispute about who was to become CEO was solved by recruiting Leschly's deputy, Jean-Pierre Garnier, but a range of other problems were quite unresolved: as the purchase consideration was less favourable to Glaxo, the scope for immediate labour cost-cutting was more limited and the pipeline remained inadequate.

The purchase consideration was notably less favourable because the deal with SKB was not a take-over but a merger achieved through a £115 billion all-share deal that more than doubled the amount of capital in the business from £4.9 billion in 1999 to £11.6 billion in 2000 (Table C1.7, appendix, p. 216). In return, Glaxo got a bolt-on that more or less doubled its size. In 2000, the first full year of the new company, GSK's sales were £18.1 billion, an increase of 113 per cent over Glaxo Wellcome's £8.5 billion in 1999, the year before the merger, and comparing favourably with the £16.9 billion 1999 combined sales of GW and SKB (see Table C1.1, appendix, p. 210). The impact on operating profit was, however, rather less encouraging with an increase of 79 per cent from 1999 to 2001 and a rise of rather less than 10 per cent compared with the combined operating profits of GW and SKB in 1999, as Exhibit C1.18 shows. This meant that the operating margin (return on sales) fell significantly to 2001, before rising in 2003 back to the level that Glaxo Wellcome enjoyed in 1999.

The immediate impact on profit was limited because there was much less scope for redundancy at the point of merger so that labour-cost reduction in GSK has been a more gradual process than that following the acquisition of Wellcome. This was partly because the SKB workforce had been pruned pre-merger: in 1998–9 SKB sacked 12,300 workers from their total workforce of 59,500 (SKB Company accounts 1999), leaving much less scope for rationalization after the merger (see also *Financial Times*, 22 January 2001). As Exhibit C1.19 shows, between 2000 and 2002 GSK reduced headcount by just 3,702, representing around 3.5 per cent of the 108,201 workforce at the point of merger (see also appendix, Table C1.8, p. 217). A more aggressive cost-cutting strategy was adopted in 2002–3 as GSK reduced its closed manufacturing plants from 102 to seventy-two, reducing the manufacturing workforce by 7.7 per cent between 2001 and 2003, as well as rationalizing its use of advertising agencies (from 100 to just two), which cut $3 billion out of operating expenses and boosted GSK's margins (*Forbes*, 8 November 2003).

The merger allowed GSK to take advantage of its size in two ways that were helpful in business-model terms: first, the merger allowed a more focused deployment of the sales force, especially in the USA; and second, it helped cover risk by broadening the firm's range of products and therapeutic areas. After the merger, GSK had a total of 43,000 sales representatives, including 8,000 in the USA, which gave it the largest US sales force in the industry, as Exhibit C1.20 shows. The addition of the SKB sales force allowed more effective targeting of the relatively small number of high prescribing physicians in the USA who write most of the prescriptions that generate high margins in a world where governments in Europe and Japan have sought to contain their drug budgets. The merger immediately brought an increase in sales of 114 per cent in the large and lucrative US market, compared with 52 per cent in Europe and the Middle East and 61 per cent in Asia Pacific.

The merger also allowed Glaxo to extend its portfolio of blockbuster products and spread the risk from generic challenges, product withdrawals and other setbacks. By 2003, GSK had eight blockbusters in a variety of segments, including one in the lucrative CNS segment, and two drugs with at least a 15 per cent segment share (Deutsche Bank 2003b: 23). But adding SKB did not improve a relatively weak pipeline because SKB was just another unproductive drug company that had created just one blockbuster drug since 1995 (Heracleous and Murray 2001: 436). Maybe Glaxo needed that broader portfolio because GSK also experienced increased problems about the limits on patent protection. By 2001, 22 per cent of GSK's sales were exposed to generic competition including their then best-selling drug, Augmentin (*Forbes*, 11 August 2003) and, significantly, there have been a series of high-profile patent challenges to Paxil and Wellbutrin, which in 2003 accounted for 15 per cent of sales (CIBC 2003: 2).

**Exhibit C1.18** *Glaxo Wellcome/GSK sales and profitability, 1999–2003*

| | *Sales* £m | *Operating profit* £m | *Operating profit margin* % |
|---|---|---|---|
| Glaxo Wellcome 1999 | 8,490 | 2,625 | 30.9 |
| Glaxo Wellcome plus SmithKline Beecham 1999 | 16,871 | 4,338 | 25.7 |
| GSK 2000 | 18,079 | 4,455 | 24.6 |
| GSK 2001 | 20,489 | 4,697 | 22.9 |
| GSK 2002 | 21,212 | 5,662 | 26.7 |
| GSK 2003 | 21,441 | 6,525 | 30.4 |

*Source*: Company Annual Report and Accounts, various years

**Exhibit C1.19** *Glaxo Wellcome and GSK employment and split by activity, 1999–2003*

| | | *Share of employment by function %* | | |
|---|---|---|---|---|
| | *Total employment* | *Manufacturing* | *R&D* | *Selling, general and admin* |
| **1999** | 60,726 | 35.6 | 16.2 | 48.2 |
| **2000** | 108,201 | 33.4 | 15.4 | 51.2 |
| **2001** | 107,899 | 34.4 | 14.0 | 51.6 |
| **2002** | 104,499 | 34.0 | 14.0 | 52.0 |
| **2003** | 103,166 | 33.2 | 14.3 | 52.5 |

*Source*: Company Annual Report and Accounts, various years

*Note*: See Table C1.8 in the appendix for full series

**Exhibit C1.20** *The US sales force of leading pharma companies, 2000*

| Company | US sales force |
|---|---|
| GSK | 8,000 |
| Pfizer | 7,500 |
| Pharmacia | 7,000 |
| Johnson & Johnson | 5,000 |
| Merck & Co | 5,000 |
| AstraZeneca | 4,800 |
| Schering-Plough | 4,500 |
| Aventis | 4,200 |
| Bristol Myers Squibb | 4,000 |

*Source*: Company Annual Report and Accounts, various years

This second merger with SKB had been greeted with initial cynicism in the business press, where some anticipated difficulties in merging two such large corporations (*The Economist*, 25 November 2000) and others could not see how the merger could immediately alter the numbers due to the long development cycles required to get a drug to market and the limited research projects they each had underway (Ansell 2000). And, after the event, the inherent transparency of the activity meant that it was difficult for GSK to present the merger as a solution to its pipeline problems. In financial terms, the results were at best mixed: the combination of the increasing capital in the business, which was partly the consequence of SKB having £1.2 billion worth of minority interest on its balance sheet pre-merger and the only modest increases in profit meant that the ROCE has failed to recover the level that Glaxo Wellcome delivered in the 1996–9 period. As Exhibit C1.21 shows, GSK's performance is very far from being spoilt, but the pre-tax ROCE of 43 per cent to 53 per cent is much lower than the 58–100 per cent range produced in 1995–9 shown in Exhibit C1.13 (see also Table C1.11, appendix, p. 220).

Certainly, the fall in share price from £18.63 at the end of 2000 to £12.80 at the end of 2002 (see appendix, Table C1.10, p. 219), (even allowing for the effects of the tech stock crash in 2001 and its repercussions), suggests that investors were not convinced that adding SKB resolved the product-market problems. Moreover, Exhibit C1.17 shows that, after 2000, the GSK share price falls much faster than the FTSE 100 index as a whole. Although there was no collapse in operating performance after the SKB merger, and ROS and ROCE were still at high levels, investors appear to have formed a much

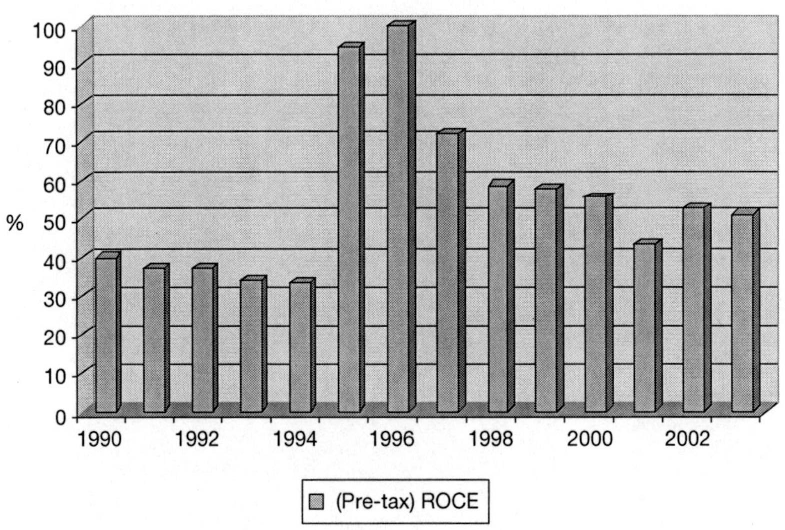


***Exhibit C1.21*** *Glaxo and Glaxo Wellcome ROCE*

*Source*: Company Annual Report and Accounts, various years

more negative view of the company's prospects so that the P/E ratio had fallen from a peak of 40 in 1998, to 17 in 2003 (appendix, Table C1.10, p. 219). GSK has meanwhile continued to increase its dividend payouts so that, with the falling share price, GSK increasingly looks like an income, not a growth stock. Exhibit C1.22 presents the P/E ratio and the dividend yield of GSK over the period since 1980. This historical perspective shows that, after the peak at the end of the 1990s, the P/E ratio had returned to the more typical (though still respectable) range of 12 to 20 times, with the dividend yield returned to the pre-Wellcome level. However, according to Morgan Stanley, the high dividend yield of around 3.5 per cent in 2003 kept stock prices buoyant and allayed investor fears during late 2002 (Morgan Stanley 2003: 3), though this implies it is the handsome payouts rather than the underlying strength of the pipeline that has been securing investor support.

## COMPANY NARRATIVE: MAKING PROMISES

Through the sale and purchase of pharma shares, the stock market is reclassifying the pharma companies in front of our eyes. As organic growth is unsustainable from the internal pipeline and the market is cautious about endorsing more defensive mergers, the pharma company becomes an income not a growth stock: after the recent falls in share price, in early February 2005, Merck and AstraZeneca's shares are valued at $28.46 and $39.21 respectively, compared with closing prices of $48.07 and $49 on the same day one year earlier (2 February 2004). And in the stock market's broader scheme of things, pharma companies could be filed under mature industries next to utilities, which offer much the same combination of limited organic growth and good earnings subject to uncertainty about future regulatory regimes.

The pharma companies and their analysts are not, however, quite ready to embrace that identification through a discourse of maturity even if the industry's previous success creates expectations that can become a burden and should be revised downwards. The current paradox is that the difficulty of keeping the numbers going at GSK has made the company narrative and promises about the future even more important, because these promises become the main support for the idea that management is in control and the company is moving forward on a trajectory of purpose and achievement. And, of course, the promises have to be made within the orthodox framework about patent expiry and the pipeline, which may not make the future predictable but certainly do make GSK's promises open to scrutiny and challenge by analysts and business-press specialists.

At this point, we move from paradox to irony. As we have argued, Glaxo has historically been a marketing-led company. But all its forward-looking promises are

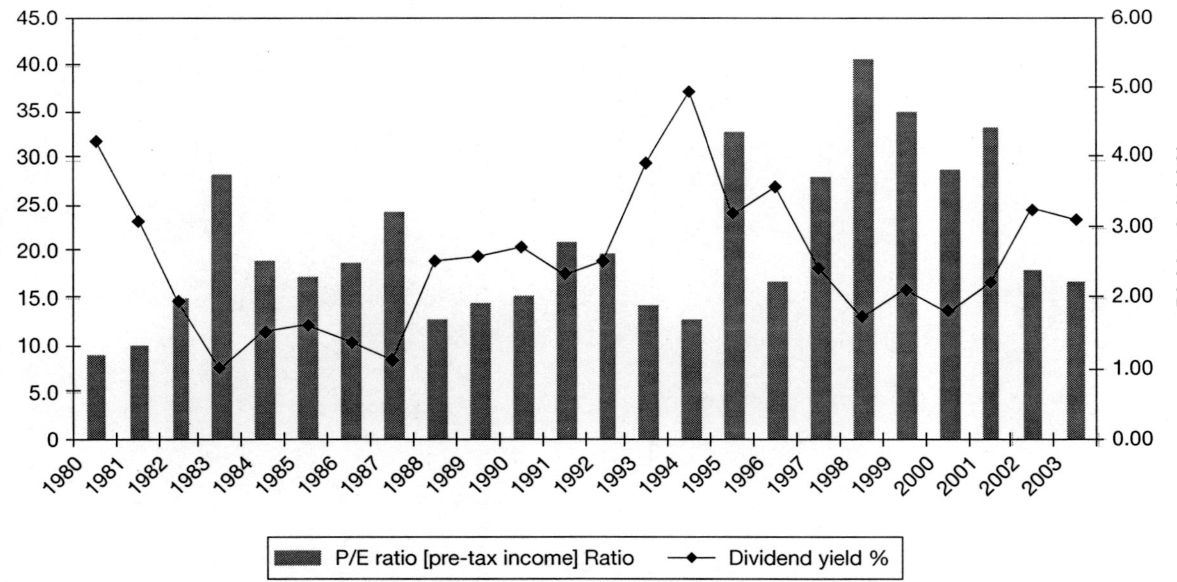


***Exhibit C1.22*** *Glaxo, Glaxo Wellcome and GSK P/E ratio and dividend yield, 1980–2003*

*Source*: Company Annual Report and Accounts, various years

now about what research can deliver. This section analyses the current GSK narrative in two parts: first, it considers GSK's repeated promises about how the reorganization of research can improve research productivity and cost effectiveness and secure revenue streams in the long term; second, it analyses GSK's claims about products emerging from the pipeline that will cover patent expiry in the medium term. The analysis of pipeline claims usefully allows us to consider issues about the reception of the narrative and the extent of scepticism by analysts and the business press.

## The (re)organization of drug development

If the industry's problem is the low productivity and high cost of R&D, Glaxo's narrative response has been to make a series of claims about how it is reorganizing the early stages of drug research in ways that will deliver more new products at lower cost. On the long view, these claims all appear to be rather flimsy because each new and revolutionary approach to R&D is pushed for a short period of time before being dropped from the company's public discourse. The inconsistency of successive large claims does the management no favours.

For example, towards the end of the 1990s, GSK was talking up the possibilities of combinatorial chemistry. According to the then CEO, this introduced a mixture of computer software, chemistry, molecular biology and automated technology to overcome the lottery of new drug discovery (Ingram 1999: 217). It was designed specifically to reduce the number of failed projects and to select scientifically the potentially lucrative new compounds. However, discussion of combinatorial chemistry was dropped immediately before and during the merger with SKB when genomics 2000 became the new *elixir vitae*. This was seen again as a move away from 'blue skies research and towards a more "rational drug design"' (J.-P. Garnier quoted in Heracleous and Murray 2001: 431), which would build 'a platform for finding new targets based upon a fundamental understanding of disease mechanisms and for generating a new class of medicines' (Milmo 2000).

Immediately after the merger with SKB, GSK reorganized its R&D departments to emulate small bio-technology firms by creating seven Centres for Excellence in Drug Discovery (CEDDs), each focusing on a separate therapeutic area (*Forbes*, 11 August 2003). CEO Garnier proclaimed that this reorganization would make them 'kings of science' (cited in *Business Week*, 30 July 2001) while also allowing GSK to externalize more of the R&D function. More significantly, Garnier also instructed Yamada, GSK's head of R&D, to fold the licensing division into R&D, so that in-licensing deals could be struck with bio-techs, universities and other pharma companies (*Forbes*, 11 August 2003).

The irony of this reorganization was not lost on the more astute financial commentators: 'no sooner had GSK completed its gargantuan merger than it started breaking itself up into little pieces. It seemed odd that, after arguing vehemently for consolidation, its management should be hell bent on keeping things small' (*Financial Times*, 3 April 2001).

## The pipeline, R&D days and their reception

Most of Glaxo's narrative is not about the reorganization of drug research but about products in the development pipeline that will cover any short- and medium-term problem about patent expiry. On the pipeline issue, Glaxo's corporate public relations, in documents such as the annual report, offers an upbeat overview, though analysis shows that there is a fairly obvious bias towards optimism. Analysts and business journalists are more closely concerned with exactly what's in the pipeline, and the response to Glaxo's R&D day in December 2003 illustrates the range of responses and shows how the usually kindly analysts are increasingly sceptical about GSK's prospects.

The annual reports of Glaxo Wellcome and GSK are, of course, upbeat about what is in the pipeline, though closer analysis suggests that this impression is sustained by emphasizing the scale of expenditure and the number of drugs in early stage development without admitting there is relatively little in Phase III. For example, in Glaxo Wellcome's 1999 annual report, the joint statement by the Chairman and CEO claimed that 'a deliberate decision (was made) to increase our sales and marketing expenditure in the US and Europe to prepare for the excellent range of new medicines in our pipeline' (1999: 3), implying that new products were close. By 2000 it turned out these new medicines were in fact at a fairly early stage: 'in 2000 we invested £2.5bn in R&D. That, and our previous investment in key technologies . . . have yielded a formidable early stage pipeline of promising compounds' (GSK Annual Report and Accounts 2000: 3). By 2001, little had changed: 'we currently have one of the strongest early-stage pipelines in the industry with 118 projects in clinical development, including 56 new chemical entities, 21 new vaccines and 41 line extensions' (GSK Annual Report and Accounts 2001: 3). The 2002 accounts also emphasized the 'promising early stage pipeline' (GSK Annual Report and Accounts 2002: 3), while the 2003 R&D day for investors talked up the number of what it interestingly classed as Phase II/III drugs (GSK 2003). In reality, most of the Phase II/III drugs were in fact in Phase II: out of the eighty-two NCEs in development, roughly 90 per cent were in Phase I or Phase II, leaving Garnier's promises of being the fastest growing pharma company between 2006 and 2008 highly doubtful (Deutsche Bank 2004: 13).

The Deutsche Bank response shows how expert observers such as analysts are not easily deceived by generalized claims in pharma, because they have the expertise and knowledge to deconstruct them by cross-reference to previous company accounts of the pipeline. Nevertheless, analysts in pharma and other sectors are generally kind to the companies they cover. For example, within a month of the SKB merger, Goldman Sachs raised GSK to a *market outperform* recommendation, arguing that GSK's mid-stage pipeline had been underestimated and that recently launched products would generate significant earnings growth in the first three years of merger (*Financial Times*, 22 January 2001). Interestingly, the independent business press, such as the *Financial Times* and *The Economist*, has a much more distant relation to the companies and is consistently more sceptical about Glaxo's pipeline promises.

The range of analyst and media responses can be illustrated by considering reports of GSK's R&D day on 3 December 2003. This was an important occasion because it was the first for Glaxo since 2000 in an industry where R&D days for analysts and journalists are normally an annual event. Clearly, GSK had problems because analyst opinion split three ways between the reassured, the indifferent and the disappointed.

Some analysts, were reassured by the company's presentation: 'we are upgrading shares of GSK to sector performer from sector underperformer. This is based on improved pipeline visibility and low earnings expectations' (CIBC 2004: 1); and 'GSK's R&D day was significantly better than we had feared. The company unveiled a well stocked mid-term pipeline' (Bear Stearns 2003b: 1). Others were indifferent: '[The R&D day] . . . turned out to be a somewhat mixed affair, with news of a further sizeable uplift in the number of pipeline candidates more than counter-balanced by delays for certain projects and generally distant submission timelines for the majority of compounds' (Deutsche Bank 2004: 3); and Garnier and Yamada are 'doing and saying the right things in terms of running the business . . . but in R&D there is an element of both brains and luck and at this early stage it is difficult to ascertain which of the more interesting Phase II drugs will make it to market and, equally important, when' (Prudential Equity 2003: 2).

Others were disappointed: 'all in all, a fairly disappointing day . . . Whilst our expectations were not very high, we were expecting some details on the pipeline . . . [in particular] progress of some of the phase II pipeline into phase III' (UBS 2003: 2); and 'The company's presentation did not leave us with any positive impression that GSK will be able to manage the decline of Paxil and Wellbutrin sales in the US . . . The question that arises is whether GSK's valuation could end up worse than its current level?' (Credit Lyonnais Securities 2004a: 4).

The business press has been sceptical about Glaxo for some time before and after the SKB merger because there is so little in the later stages of the pipeline. Here, for example, is *The Economist* (25 November 2000) on Glaxo Wellcome immediately prior to the GSK merger:

> They have retooled its R&D, investing heavily in new discovery technologies, reaching out to biotechnology firms through acquisitions and alliances, and realigning the new firm's research and marketing units. But drug making is a slow business, and it will

be at least another five years before these new initiatives bear fruit in terms of lucrative new drugs.

Thus, the *Financial Times*'s front-page story about GSK's 2003 R&D day responded coolly to the event and observed that many of the projects were still at too early a stage to guarantee near-term prosperity:

> Despite the upbeat comments, investors remained uncertain about the group's long-term prospects and the shares, which had risen in anticipation, fell 1.4 per cent to £13.11. While analysts welcomed the size of the pipeline, adding that several products had considerable sales potential, they said that many of the projects were still at too early a stage to inspire considerable confidence.
>
> (*Financial Times*, 4 December 2003)

The *Financial Times* has also on several occasions noted that generally few drugs move from Phase I to final market and specifically GSK has had a lower success rate than the industry norm for drugs moving from Phase II and III to the final market (*Financial Times*, 1 December 2003, 4 December 2004). The evidence here is not clear-cut but obviously, in so far as investors base their decisions on late-stage products, companies have a short-term incentive to 'push' drugs into the later stages regardless of the long-term impact this may have on failure rates.

The net result is that the incumbent management at Glaxo Wellcome and then at GSK has suffered a loss of credibility that can be illustrated in various ways. The market appreciates GSK's management focus on cost-cutting and margin-improvement which delivers the numbers in the short run. For example, Morgan Stanley acclaimed GSK's solid Quintile 1 2004 results which, despite 'lighter' than anticipated sales, managed better than expected profits due to *reduced* R&D and sales, general and administration costs (Morgan Stanley 2004b: 1). But, as Morgan Stanley recognize, this is not a recipe for longer term growth (2004a: 1). And, the market does not trust the management to make another big move. Given scepticism about the results of the SKB merger, further M&A might not be well received (SG Cowen 2004: 6). This can be clearly seen in the negative market response and share-price drop following rumours of mergers with both Bristol-Myers Squibb BMS (*Financial Times*, 1 June 2002) and Sanofi/Aventis (Credit Lyonnais Securities 2004b). Ultimately, the verdict is that GSK has become a (relatively) cheap income stock which should carry a health warning: 'trading at 13.5 times our 2005 EPS estimate, GSK is the cheapest major drug stock. However, in recent times cheapness has been more indicative of the possibility that the forecasts are wrong. In most cases, the market has been correct and profit warnings have followed' (Morgan Stanley 2004a: 1).

After GSK has gone ex-growth, management has so far won the struggle to keep the numbers going in ratio terms and to deliver earnings but it has lost the struggle to sustain a narrative that can offer credible promises about an exciting future. And that is reflected in the public discussion of new issues such as top management pay and reinvention of the business model.

## BETWEEN THE FUTURE AND THE PAST: UNRESOLVED ISSUES

It is generally impossible and unwise to try to predict corporate futures, so in the final section of this case study we discuss some key unresolved issues that are pertinent to understanding GSK's current position and the difficulties of delivering convincing narratives and numbers. The loss of management reputation in the GSK company and the damage to the pharma-industry business model change the whole terms of debate around the company in its industry and have brought new issues into focus. The first of these issues is the public-interest issue of top-management pay where the remuneration package of CEO Jean-Pierre Garnier became an issue in 2002–3. While this was an interesting test case for UK corporate governance, in our view the company's confrontation with its shareholders was largely driven by short-term concerns about GSK's financial performance. This same concern about the performance of GSK and other pharma companies is manifest in the second issue which arises from media and consultancy concern with the broken business model of ethical pharma companies such as GSK and the consensus that ethical pharma needs a new business model.

GSK came under sustained attack from shareholder groups after the company told investors in November 2002 about a plan to enhance the remuneration package of Jean-Pierre Garnier to a level that was estimated to be worth around $18 million per annum (*Financial Times*, 10 February 2003). The company argued that such levels of pay were necessary to recruit and retain exceptional staff in a global industry where US levels of pay have been far higher than those prevailing in the UK. Despite making such arguments, GSK withdrew the plan but then ran into further trouble with shareholders in May 2003 at the annual general meeting when a revised pay package was criticized. In particular, shareholder groups objected to the severance provision that would have ensured a generous 'golden parachute' for Garnier whereby resignation or sacking would result in a pay off of $23.7 million in bonus, salary and GSK stock, as well as pension enhancements (*New York Times*, 20 May 2003).

The trouble-making investors took advantage of new laws in the UK that only came into effect in 2002 (Directors' Remuneration Report Regulations [SI 2002/1986] and the Companies [Summary Financial Statement] Amendments Regulations [SI 2002/1780]). This allows shareholders to vote on their company's proposed remuneration package as well as obliging enhanced disclosure of the level and conditions of executive remuneration. Such votes are advisory rather than binding, but criticisms from shareholders, both prior to and during the AGM, have received considerable attention in the press. GSK had little alternative but to make further concessions and, as a result, Garnier's contract was reduced from two years to one (in line with UK corporate governance best practice) and the company also tightened the performance targets that trigger share-option grants (*Financial Times*, 16 December 2003, 27 March 2004).

If all this made good corporate theatre, the furore reflected all the confusions of the broader pay-for-performance debate. One of the underlying problems was that GSK was adopting US practices on pay and contract length in a company that was still nominally British. As we have noted in Chapter 3 of the introduction to this book, the CEOs of giant US companies get six or seven times the million-pound going rate for British CEOs, and the one-year contract that limits compensation is British good practice but not common in the USA. The *Financial Times* identified GSK as part of a new elite of British companies, like Vodafone and Prudential, who were attempting to breach UK top-management pay norms and establish American pay rates (*Financial Times*, 19 November 2002). In Glaxo's case, there was some justification for high pay because, as the introduction showed, Glaxo is just about the only FTSE 100 company which over the past twenty years has offered shareholders a return equal to the growth of management pay.

But the point is not so much that the criticism of Garnier's pay was fair or unfair but that its vehemence reflected deep unease about the performance of GSK. This then spilled over onto the issue of Garnier's pay because GSK's practices were provocatively American. The unfairness was perhaps that incumbent company management was being blamed for industry-wide problems that no management could fix. And this demonstrates the practical difficulties about corporate governance which is ostensibly about universal rules but which is actually context-specific and expectations-dependent. Most importantly, in our view, if GSK had been delivering, Garnier would have got away with it. As GSK was not delivering, the question, as the *Financial Times* (19 November 2002) put it, was whether Garnier was really worth it: 'what investors really need to do is ask themselves whether the man is worth his cornucopia. He has not exactly impressed the city . . . If Mr Garnier walks, perhaps that will be no bad thing.'

If the criticism of Garnier and Glaxo is depersonalized, the unresolved issue is currently framed as one about the industry's need for a new business model. Many commentators share the general view that the business model of 'Big Pharma' needs reinvention, but there is no consensus as to what a new business model would look like nor indeed about whether there will be one or several such models. *Business Week* (29 November 2004), for instance, argues that 'Big Pharma is far too focused on looking for the next best-seller', which leads to a conservative drug-development approach and urges a more creative, less risk-averse strategy. As part of this, there are calls for a shift to 'personalized medicine', where treatments are targeted more specifically on individual patients (*Business Week*, 18 October 2004).

These ideas of reinvention are, predictably, exciting stimuli for consultancy firms and other organizations, which hope to win business by offering visions of the pharma future.

- Accenture outlines its vision of the 'bioeconomy' which 'augurs a shift from medicine created for large populations to focus on the individual patient and the evolution of a patient-centric model of health care' (Baker 2001: 69).
- Datamonitor's new business model has a different starting point, the failure of large scale M&A to solve the underlying problem of the industry's 'deepening productivity crisis' (Coe 2002: 1). Here 'networked pharma' is introduced as a solution to the problem identified by Datamonitor's quite detailed analysis. There are no scale economies from expenditure on sales and marketing and that 'R&D investment is directly proportional to pipeline productivity'; hence getting bigger does not help bolster deteriorating margins. The networked-growth model allows growth 'by downsizing' (Coe 2002: 5) so that companies 'keep in house only the intellectual capital that is critical to its competitive advantage and outsources the rest in the form of temporary and long term, domestic and international strategic alliances with peers and vendors' (Coe 2002: 5).
- Mercer's (2003) response to the end of the 'blockbuster model' is to encourage business-design analysis that does not presuppose any one new model.
- For Arthur D. Little (2003: 1 and 4), the 'unravelling of the value chain' and a shift in power from big pharma to smaller specialists, such as bio-tech firms, leads to two successful new business models: 'activity specialists' that concentrate on one part of the value chain (e.g. drug development, clinical research or production) and 'market specialists' who are integrated through the value chain but who focus on specific 'lucrative markets, such as vaccines, HIV, hormones or dermatology'.

The accumulating problem is that there are so many different (and untried) new business models partly because it is much easier to write a 10,000-word report or give a good presentation than it is to reconfigure the fundamentals of a giant company while ensuring that it meets the next quarter's earnings target. Thus GSK, like other giant pharma companies, has only toyed with new business models in an experimental way. The company remains vertically integrated because R&D expenditure has not been cut back and there have not been wholesale redundancies in the labs. But Glaxo, like other giant companies, has a growing interest in supplementing in-house developed drugs with bought-in product. Under in-licensing deals, Glaxo sales representatives market a competitor's drug for a cut of the profits (*Business Week*, 30 July 2001). Over twenty such deals struck were struck in two years after the 2000 merger with SKB (ABN: Amro 2002: 41). A typical deal would involve licensing a drug for around $50 million with the aim of eventually earning royalties of up to 10–12 per cent on upwards of $1 billion sales, and such deals are seen as an important contributor to GSK's new product flow (*Business Week*, 30 July 2001).

This development is interesting because vertical disintegration and a retreat onto marketing represents an admission of failure which raises a whole series of further questions about whether a vertically disintegrated model would be viable for giant pharma companies. The viability of a disintegrated business would partly depend on the balance of power between giant marketing companies and smaller research-based organizations that can probably play off the big firms. More fundamentally, like everything else in pharma, it brings us back to the arguments about good pharma and bad pharma rehearsed at the Kefauver's hearings (discussed in the first section of this case study) and, interestingly, this official debate has been renewed in a 120-page report by the UK House of Commons Health Committee published in April 2005 as this case study went to press. What is the justification for the patents that protect the high prices and handsome margins that still survive in the 2000s after market growth has faltered? If giant ethical companies were to reinvent themselves as marketing organizations, they could not so easily invoke the 'good pharma' argument and argue that their high profits represent deferred investment in drug R&D. This demonstrates the point that now (as in the 1950s) the future of pharma depends on the framing of social benefits and the choice of private business model, on narrative as much as numbers.

## REFERENCES

ABC (2004) 'Drug maker withheld Paxil study data'. Online. Available HTTP: <http://abcnews.go.com/Health/story?id=311956&page=1> (accessed 20 January 2005).

ABN AMRO (2002) *Playing the Numbers Game*, 27 May.

ABPI (2003) *Keeping Science Open: The Effects of Intellectual Property Policy on the Conduct of Science*, June 2003: 2–3. Online. Available HTTP: <http://www.abpi.org.uk/information/word_documents/royal%20_society_%20abpi_03.doc> (accessed 19 January 2005).

—— (2005) *Facts and Statistics from the Pharmaceutical Industry*. Online. Available HTTP: <http://www.abpi.org.uk/statistics/section.asp?sect=1#4> (accessed 2 February 2005).

Abraham, J. (2000) 'A licence to print money?' *Health Matters*, 43 (winter) 2000/1. Online. Available HTTP: <http://www.healthmatters.org.uk/stories/abraham.html> (accessed 20 January 2005).

Abramson, J. (2004) *Overdosed America: The Broken Promise of American Medicine*, New York: Harper Collins.

Angell, M. (2004) *The Truth about Drug Companies: How They Deceive Us and What to Do about It*, New York: Random House.

Ansell, J. (2000) 'The billion dollar pyramid' *Pharmaceutical Executive*, 20(8): 64–74, Eugene, Oreg.: Advanstar Communications Inc.

AstraZeneca (2003) *Access to Medicines*. Online. Available HTTP: <http://www.astrazeneca.com/article/11122.aspx> (accessed 14 May 2004).

Baker, A. (2001) 'Report from the new frontier', *Outlook 2001*, 2, Accenture. Online. Available HTTP: <http://www.accenture.com/xd/xd.asp?it=enweb&xd=ideas%5Coutlook%5C7.2001%5Cfrontier.xml> (accessed 15 January 2005).

Balance, R., J. Pogany and H. Foster (1992) *The Worlds Pharmaceutical Industries*, Aldershot: Edward Elgar.

Bear Stearns (2003a) *GSK: The GSK Pipeline – Our Initial Analysis*, 5 December 2003.

—— (2003b) *GSK: GSK's Mega-Brands*, 5 December 2003.

Bogner, W. and H. Thomas (1996) *Drug to Market: Creating Value and Advantage in the Pharmaceutical Industry*, New York: Pergamon.

Bosanquet, N. and R. Atun (2001) '1998–2001 in the pharma industry: from deep river to white water rapids', *European Business Journal*, 13 (2): 74–83.

Braithwaite, J. (1984) *Corporate Crime in the Pharmaceutical Industry*, London: Routledge & Kegan Paul.

Breitzman, A., P. Thomas and M. Cheney (2002) 'Technological powerhouse or diluted competence: techniques for assessing mergers via patent analysis', *R&D Management*, 32 (1): 1–10.

California Public Interest CALPIRG (2004) *Tis always the Season for Giving: A White Paper on the Practice and Problems of Pharmaceutical Detailing*, September 2004, Sacramento, Calif.: CALPIRG.

Center for Drug Evaluation and Research (2005) *The Patent Term Restoration Programme*. Online. Available HTTP: <http://www.fda.gov/cder/about/smallbiz/patent_term.htm> (accessed 19 January 2005).

Chetley, A. (1990) *A Healthy Business? World Health and the Pharmaceutical Business*, London: Zed.

Chiesa, V. (1996) 'Separating research from development: evidence from the pharmaceutical industry', *European Management Journal*, 14: 638–47.

CIBC (2003) *Glaxo SmithKline: Revised: R&D Pipeline Unveiled – Lots of Potential but still a Ways Away*, 7 December 2003, New York: CIBC World Markets Corp.

—— (2004) *GSK: Upgrading to Sector Performer – Earnings Bottoming Out; Pipeline to Take Over*, 18 February 2004, New York: CIBC World Markets Corp.

Coe, J. (2002) 'Networked pharma: innovative strategies to overcome margin deterioration', *Datamonitor*, June 2002. Online. Available HTTP: <http://www.contractpharma.com/June021.htm> (accessed 19 January 2005).

Credit Lyonnais Securities (2004a) *GSK: Could It Be Worse?* 20 February 2004.

—— (2004b) *GSK: 2003 Preview/GSK-Aventis*? 28 January 2004.

Credit Suisse (2002) *Pfizer: Norvasc Patent Challenge Update*, 22 September 2002.

—— (2004) *US Major Pharmaceuticals: Assumed Coverage – Fundamentals Remain Unchanged*, 13 December 2004.

Deutsche Bank (2003a) *Dissecting the US Pharmaceutical Market*, 11 April 2003.

—— (2003b) *Pharmaceuticals for Beginners: A Guide to the Pharmaceutical Industry*, Deutsche Bank AG, 12 March 2002.

—— (2004) *GSK: The Year Ahead*, 5 February 2004.

Department of Health (DoH) (1999) *The Pharmaceutical Price Regulation Scheme*, London: Department of Health.

—— (2004) *Summary of the Pharmaceutical Price Regulation Scheme 2005*, London: Department of Health.

Emanuel, R. (2003) 'Congressman Rahm Emanuel Seeks to Reduce Prescription Drug Costs through Market Reforms, Co-Sponsors Bills to Foster Competition and Lower Prices', 20 June 2003, House of Representatives Press Release. Online. Available HTTP: <http://www.house.gov/apps/list/press/il05_emanuel/pr_030620.html> (accessed 2 February 2005).

Erturk, I., J. Froud, S. Johal and K. Williams (2004) 'Corporate governance and disappointment', *Review of International Political Economy*, 11 (4): 677–713.

Financial Times Management Report (1995) *Global Pharmaceuticals: Winning Strategies in the Major Manufacturing Markets*, Vol. I, London: Financial Times.

Froud, J., C. Haslam, S. Johal, K. Williams and R. Willis (1998) 'British pharmaceuticals: a cautionary tale', *Economy and Society*, 27 (4): 554–84.

Goozner, M. (2004) *The $800 Million Pill: The Truth behind the Cost of New Drugs*, Berkeley, Calif.: University of California Press.

Gorman, J. (1971) *Estes Kefauver: A Biography*, New York: Oxford University Press.

GSK (2002) *Facing the Challenge: One Year On*. Online. Available HTTP: <http://www.gsk.com/community/downloads/facing_the_challenge_one_year_on.pdf> (accessed 14 May 2004).

—— (2003) 'Press Report: GSK Unveils Abroad R&D Pipeline of Innovative Science and Class-Leading Compounds', 3 December 2003.

—— (2004a) 'Company website, corporate history'. Online. Available HTTP: <http://www.gsk.com/about/background.htm> (accessed 19 January 2005).

—— (2004b) 'GlaxoSmithKline announces major advance in on-line access to clinical trial information', press release, 18 June 2004. Online. Available HTTP: <http://science.gsk.com/news-frame.htm> (accessed 15 January 2005).

Hara, T. (2003) *Innovation in the Pharmaceutical Industry*, Cheltenham: Edward Elgar.

Harrell, G. (1978) 'Pharmaceutical marketing' in C. Lindsay (ed.) *The Pharmaceutical Industry*, New York: Wiley Medical Publications.

Harris, R. (1964) *The Real Voice*, New York: Macmillan.

Harrison, A. (2003) *Getting the Right Medicines? Putting Public Interests at the Heart of Health Related Research*, London: Kings Fund.

Hawthorne, F. (2003) *The Merck Druggernaught: The Inside Story of a Pharmaceutical Giant*, Hoboken, NJ: Wiley.

Heller, T. (1977) *Poor Health, Rich Profits*, Nottingham: Russell Press.

Heracleous, L. and J. Murray (2001) 'The urge to merge in the pharmaceutical industry', *European Management Journal*, 19 (4): 430–7.

Holman, G. (1988) *The Pharmaceutical Industry and the NHS: A Presentation to the Manchester Statistical Society, 18 October 1988*, Manchester: Manchester Statistical Society.

Holmer, A. (2002) 'The case for innovation: the role of intellectual property protection', November 2002, The Economist's Second Annual Pharmaceuticals Roundtable. Online. Available HTTP: <http://www.phrma.org/publications/publications/20.11.2002.629.cfm> (accessed 19 January 2005).

House of Commons Health Committee (2005) 'The Influence of the Pharmaceutical Industry', Fourth Report of Session 2004–05, (HC 42–1), 5 April 2005, London: The Stationery Office.

Ingram, R. (1999) 'The pharmaceutical industry: creating health instead of treating disease', *New York*, 15 January, 65 (7): 213–19.

Kay, J. (1993) *Foundations of Corporate Success*, Oxford: Oxford University Press.

Kefauver, E. (1965) *In A Few Hands*, Harmondsworth: Penguin.

Keynote (2002) *UK Pharmaceutical Industry*, London: Keynote.

Le Carré, J. (2001) *The Constant Gardener*, London: Hodder & Stoughton.

Lehman Brothers (2004) *Glaxo Smithkline: Stronger Dollar the Driver of EPS Hike*, 30 April 2004.

Little, A. D. (2003) *Unravelling the Pharmaceutical Industry*. Online. Available HTTP:

<http://www.adl.com/insights/studies/pdf/emerging_business_models_pharma.pdf> (accessed 19 January 2005).

Lynn, M. (1991) *Merck vs Glaxo: The Billion Dollar Battle*, London: Mandarin.

Madhaven, S., M. Amonkar, D. Elliot, K. Burke and P. Gore (1997) 'The gift relationship between pharmaceutical companies and physicians: an exploratory survey of physicians', *Journal of Clinical Pharmacy and Therapeutics*, 2290: 207–15.

McIntyre, A. (1999) *Key Issues in the Pharmaceutical Industry*, Chichester: John Wiley & Sons.

Médicins Sans Frontières (2002) 'AIDS patients in poor countries pay higher prices for Roche's drugs than people in Switzerland'. Online. Available HTTP: <http://www.msf.org/content/page.cfm?articleid=013E49F3-B70A-4C07-881E3E214A97FFAD> (accessed 19 January 2005).

Mercer (2003) 'Beyond the blockbuster: finding the next profit zone in pharmaceuticals through business design thinking', *Executive Briefing: Pharma Trends 1*. Mercer Management Consulting.

Merck (1998) *Merck Annual Review 1998*. Online. Available HTTP: <http://www.merck.com/overview/98ar/p6.htm> (accessed 14 May 2004).

—— (2003) *The Strength of People at Merck: Filling Unmet Medical Needs Through Science*. Online. Available HTTP: <http://www.merck.com/about/feature_story/10282002_harvard_award.html> (accessed 19 January 2005).

Milmo, S. (2000) 'SKB and Glaxo merger creates a powerhouse', *Chemical Market Reporter*, 257 (4): 1.

Moore, J. (1998) *Generic Pharmaceutical Outlook 1998–2008*, London: Datamonitor.

Morgan Stanley (2002) 'GlaxoSmithkline: delivering on promises', 25 April 2002.

Morgan Stanley (2003) 'Beneath currency impact lurks surprising strength', 13 February 2003.

—— (2004a) 'GSK: cheapest drug stock: or is the multiple telling a story?' 15 April 2004.

—— (2004b) 'GSK: solid first quarter results: R&D news expected in H2', 29 April 2004.

Mossinghoff, G. (1999) 'Overview of the Hatch–Waxman Act and its impact on the drug development process', *Food and Drug Law Journal*, 54 (2): 187–94.

National Institute for Clinical Excellence (NICE) (2005) 'About NICE'. Online. Available HTTP: <http://www.nice.org.uk/page.aspx?o=aboutnice> (accessed 4 April 2005).

National Institute for Healthcare Management (NIHCM) (2002a) *Prescription Drug Expenditures in 2001: Another Year of Escalating Costs, National Institute for Health Care Management*, March 2002, Washington, DC: NIHCM.

—— (2002b) *Changing Patterns of Pharmaceutical Innovation*, May 2002, Washington, DC: NIHCM.

Ogilvie, B (1998) 'Working with the Wellcome Trust', *Medical Journal of Australia*, 169: 634–9.

Oxfam (2001a) *South Africa vs the Drug Giants*. Online. Available HTTP: <http://www.oxfam.org.uk/what_we_do/issues/health/drugcomp_sa.htm> (accessed 19 January 2005).

—— (2001b) *Implausible Denial: Why the Drug Giants Arguments on Patents Don't Stack Up*. Online. Available HTTP: <http://www.oxfam.org.uk/what_we_do/issues/health/implausible_denial.htm> (accessed 19 January 2005).

Pfizer (2000) *Pfizer Journal: Intellectual Property Protection*. Online. Available HTTP: <http://www.thepfizerjournal.com/PDFs/TPJ13.pdf> (accessed 14 May 2004).

PhRMA (2003) *Pharmaceutical Industry Profile 2003: New Medicines, New Hope*, Washington, DC: PhRMA.

Piore, M. J. and Sabel, C. F. (1984) *The Second Industrial Divide: Possibilities for Prosperity*, Oxford: Basic Books.

Prudential Equity Group (2003) 'GSK: pipeline filling – still a bit early; difficult to quantify what's real vs. what's not', 5 December 2003.

Public Citizen (2001) *Rx R&D Myths: The Case against the Drug Industry's R&D Scare Card*, Washington, DC: Public Citizen.

—— (2004) *The Medicade Drug War*, Washington, DC: Public Citizen. Online. Available HTTP: <http://www.citizen.org/documents/Medicare_Drug_War_Appendices_AB.pdf> (accessed 19 January 2005).

Randles, S. (2002) 'Complex systems applied? The merger that made Glaxo Smithkline', *Technology Analysis and Strategic Management*, 14 (3): 331–54.

Reuters Business Insight (1998) *Generic Pharmaceutical Outlook 1998–2008*, London: Datamonitor.

—— (2003a) *The Blockbuster Drug Outlook until 2007: Identifying, Creating and Maintaining the Pharmaceutical Industry's Growth Drivers*, London: Datamonitor.

—— (2003b) *The Pharmaceutical Market Outlook Until 2010: Essential Analysis of Key Drivers of Change*, London: Datamonitor.

—— (2004) *Healthcare Future Growth Strategies: Drivers of Sustainable Development in Biotech, Specialist and Major Pharma Sectors*, London: Datamonitor.

Robinson, J. (2001) *Prescription Games: Life, Death and Money inside the Global Pharmaceutical Industry*, New York: Simon & Schuster.

Salomon Smith Barney (2003) *Pfizer: Neurontin Patent Challenge*, 12 January 2003.

Schnee, J. (1978) 'Government control of therapeutic drugs: intent, impact and issues', in C. Lindsay (ed.) *The Pharmaceutical Industry*, New York: John Wiley & Sons, pp. 9–14.

Schnee, J. and Caglarcan, E. (1978) 'The changing pharmaceutical research and development environment', in C. Lindsay (ed.) *The Pharmaceutical Industry*, New York: John Wiley & Sons, pp. 91–104.

Seget, S. (2003) *Pharmaceutical Pricing Strategies: Optimising Returns through R&D and Marketing*, London: Datamonitor.

Sendall, B. (1982) *Independent Television in Britain: Volume 1. Origin and Foundation, 1946–62*, London: Macmillan.

Sendall, B. (1982) *Independent Television in Britain*, Vol. I, *Origin and Foundation, 1946–62*, London: Macmillan.

SG Cowen (2004) *GSK: Don't Wait for the Second Wind*, 16 February 2004.

Sherer, F. (2000) 'The pharmaceutical industry and world intellectual property standards', *Vanderbilt Law Review*, 53 (6): 2248–57.

Smith Barney Citigroup (2004) *The Lipitor Chronicles*, Days 1–9, December.

Strongin, R. (2002) 'Hatch Waxman, generics and patents: balancing prescription drug innovation, competition and affordability', National Health Policy Forum Background Paper. Online. Available HTTP: <http://www.nhpf.org/pdfs_bp/BP_HatchWaxman_6–02.pdf> (accessed 19 January 2005).

Taggart, J. (1993) *The World Pharmaceutical Industry*, London: Routledge.

Tuttle, E., A. Parece and A. Hector (2004) 'Your patent is about to expire: what now?' *Pharmaceutical Executive* (November), 24 (11): 88–94.

UBS (2003) 'GSK: more development needed', 4 December 2003.

UBS Warburg (2003) 'Specialty pharmaceuticals: industry outlook – generic drugs: fertile landscape', 30 May 2003.
Warden, C. (1992) 'The prescription for high drug prices', *Consumers Research*, 75 (12): 10–15.
Wright, R. (1996) 'How Zantac became the best-selling drug in history', *Journal of Healthcare Marketing* (winter), 16 (4): 24–30.

## APPENDIX

**Table C1.1** *Glaxo, Glaxo Wellcome and GlaxoSmithKline: sales and profits, 1980–2003 (nominal data)*

| | *Sales* | *% change in sales year on year* | *Operating profit* | *% change in operating profit year on year* | *Net profit* | *% change in net profit year on year* |
|---|---|---|---|---|---|---|
| | £ million | % | £ million | % | £ million | % |
| **1980** | 618 | | 66 | | 42 | |
| **1981** | 710 | 14.9 | 87 | 31.8 | 61 | 44.9 |
| **1982** | 866 | 21.9 | 126 | 45.8 | 80 | 32.8 |
| **1983** | 1,028 | 18.7 | 178 | 41.2 | 115 | 43.5 |
| **1984** | 1,200 | 16.8 | 235 | 32.0 | 169 | 46.2 |
| **1985** | 1,412 | 17.7 | 361 | 53.6 | 267 | 58.1 |
| **1986** | 1,429 | 1.2 | 499 | 38.1 | 400 | 50.0 |
| **1987** | 1,741 | 21.9 | 665 | 33.2 | 510 | 27.5 |
| **1988** | 2,059 | 18.3 | 764 | 14.9 | 578 | 13.3 |
| **1989** | 2,570 | 24.8 | 876 | 14.7 | 688 | 19.0 |
| **1990** | 2,854 | 11.1 | 998 | 13.9 | 793 | 15.3 |
| **1991** | 3,397 | 19.0 | 1,104 | 10.6 | 881 | 11.1 |
| **1992** | 4,096 | 20.6 | 1,287 | 16.6 | 1,033 | 17.3 |
| **1993** | 4,930 | 20.4 | 1,525 | 18.5 | 1,207 | 16.8 |
| **1994** | 5,656 | 14.7 | 1,819 | 19.3 | 1,303 | 8.0 |
| **1995** | 6,993 | 23.6 | 1,588 | –12.7 | 972 | –25.4 |
| **1996** | 8,341 | 19.3 | 3,132 | 97.2 | 1,997 | 105.5 |
| **1997** | 7,980 | –4.3 | 2,822 | –9.9 | 1,850 | –7.4 |
| **1998** | 7,983 | 0.0 | 2,683 | –4.9 | 1,836 | –0.8 |
| **1999** | 8,490 | 6.4 | 2,625 | –2.2 | 1,811 | –1.4 |
| **2000** | 18,079 | 112.9 | 4,455 | 69.7 | 4,154 | 129.4 |
| **2001** | 20,489 | 13.3 | 4,697 | 5.4 | 3,190 | –23.2 |
| **2002** | 21,212 | 3.5 | 5,662 | 20.5 | 4,045 | 26.8 |
| **2003** | 21,441 | 1.1 | 6,525 | 15.2 | 4,484 | 10.9 |
| **1994** | | | | | | |
| Glaxo | 5,656 | | 1,819 | | 1,303 | |
| Wellcome | 2,276 | | 911 | | 404 | |
| Total G+W | 7,932 | | 2,730 | | 1,707 | |
| **1999** | | | | | | |
| GW | 8,490 | | 2,625 | | 1,811 | |
| SKB | 8,381 | | 1,713 | | 1,053 | |
| Total GW+SKB | 16,871 | | 4,338 | | 2,864 | |

*Source*: Glaxo, Glaxo Wellcome, GlaxoSmithKline Annual Report and Accounts, various years

**Table C1.2** *Glaxo, Glaxo Wellcome and GlaxoSmithKline: real sales and profits, 1980–2003 (in real 2003 prices)*

| | *Real sales* | *% change in sales year on year* | *Real operating profit* | *% change in operating profit, year on year* | *Real net profit* | *% change in net profit, year on year* |
|---|---|---|---|---|---|---|
| | £ million | % | £ million | % | £ million | % |
| **1980** | 1,677 | | 178 | | 113 | |
| **1981** | 1,723 | 2.7 | 210 | 17.7 | 147 | 29.5 |
| **1982** | 1,933 | 12.2 | 282 | 34.3 | 180 | 22.3 |
| **1983** | 2,193 | 13.5 | 380 | 35.0 | 246 | 37.2 |
| **1984** | 2,439 | 11.2 | 478 | 25.8 | 343 | 39.2 |
| **1985** | 2,705 | 10.9 | 692 | 44.8 | 511 | 49.0 |
| **1986** | 2,647 | –2.1 | 925 | 33.6 | 741 | 45.1 |
| **1987** | 3,099 | 17.1 | 1,184 | 28.0 | 908 | 22.4 |
| **1988** | 3,493 | 12.7 | 1,296 | 9.5 | 981 | 8.0 |
| **1989** | 4,045 | 15.8 | 1,379 | 6.4 | 1,083 | 10.4 |
| **1990** | 4,102 | 1.4 | 1,434 | 4.0 | 1,140 | 5.3 |
| **1991** | 4,611 | 12.4 | 1,498 | 4.5 | 1,196 | 4.9 |
| **1992** | 5,361 | 16.3 | 1,685 | 12.4 | 1,352 | 13.1 |
| **1993** | 6,351 | 18.5 | 1,965 | 16.6 | 1,555 | 15.0 |
| **1994** | 7,109 | 11.9 | 2,286 | 16.4 | 1,638 | 5.3 |
| **1995** | 8,500 | 19.6 | 1,930 | –15.6 | 1,181 | –27.9 |
| **1996** | 9,901 | 16.5 | 3,718 | 92.6 | 2,370 | 100.6 |
| **1997** | 9,188 | –7.2 | 3,249 | –12.6 | 2,130 | –10.1 |
| **1998** | 8,889 | –3.3 | 2,987 | –8.1 | 2,044 | –4.0 |
| **1999** | 9,304 | 4.7 | 2,877 | –3.7 | 1,985 | –2.9 |
| **2000** | 19,255 | 106.9 | 4,745 | 64.9 | 4,424 | 122.9 |
| **2001** | 21,428 | 11.3 | 4,912 | 3.5 | 3,336 | –24.6 |
| **2002** | 21,827 | 1.9 | 5,826 | 18.6 | 4,162 | 24.8 |
| **2003** | 21,441 | –1.8 | 6,525 | 12.0 | 4,484 | 7.7 |
| **1994** | | | | | | |
| Glaxo | 7,109 | | 2,286 | | 1,638 | |
| Wellcome | 2,861 | | 1,145 | | 507 | |
| Total G+W | 9,969 | | 3,431 | | 2,145 | |
| **1999** | | | | | | |
| GW | 9,304 | | 2,877 | | 1,985 | |
| SKB | 9,185 | | 1,877 | | 1,154 | |
| Total GW+SKB | 18,489 | | 4,754 | | 3,139 | |

*Source*: Glaxo, Glaxo Wellcome, GlaxoSmithKline Annual Report and Accounts, various years

**Table C1.3** *Glaxo, Glaxo Wellcome and GlaxoSmithKline: geographical breakdown of sales revenue, 1980–2003 (nominal data)*

| | *Total sales* | *Geographic breakdown of sales* | | | | *% share of sales* | | | |
|---|---|---|---|---|---|---|---|---|---|
| | | *North America* | *Europe, Africa and the Middle East* | *Asia Pacific* | *Other* | *North America* | *Europe, Africa and the Middle East* | *Asia Pacific* | *Other* |
| | £ million | £ million | £ million | £ million | £ million | % | % | % | % |
| **1980** | 618 | 52 | 457 | 110 | 0 | 8.4 | 73.9 | 17.8 | 0.0 |
| **1981** | 710 | 65 | 502 | 143 | 0 | 9.2 | 70.7 | 20.1 | 0.0 |
| **1982** | 866 | 81 | 593 | 192 | 0 | 9.3 | 68.5 | 22.2 | 0.0 |
| **1983** | 1,028 | 97 | 732 | 199 | 0 | 9.4 | 71.2 | 19.4 | 0.0 |
| **1984** | 1,200 | 193 | 861 | 113 | 33 | 16.0 | 71.8 | 9.4 | 2.8 |
| **1985** | 1,412 | 333 | 904 | 144 | 31 | 23.6 | 64.0 | 10.2 | 2.2 |
| **1986** | 1,429 | 468 | 768 | 137 | 56 | 32.8 | 53.7 | 9.6 | 3.9 |
| **1987** | 1,741 | 662 | 880 | 154 | 45 | 38.0 | 50.5 | 8.8 | 2.6 |
| **1988** | 2,059 | 831 | 1,010 | 187 | 31 | 40.4 | 49.1 | 9.1 | 1.5 |
| **1989** | 2,570 | 1,081 | 1,140 | 229 | 120 | 42.1 | 44.4 | 8.9 | 4.7 |
| **1990** | 2,854 | 1,233 | 1,348 | 222 | 51 | 43.2 | 47.2 | 7.8 | 1.8 |
| **1991** | 3,397 | 1,359 | 1,560 | 383 | 95 | 40.0 | 45.9 | 11.3 | 2.8 |
| **1992** | 4,096 | 1,715 | 1,826 | 434 | 121 | 41.9 | 44.6 | 10.6 | 3.0 |
| **1993** | 4,930 | 2,132 | 2,086 | 529 | 183 | 43.2 | 42.3 | 10.7 | 3.7 |
| **1994** | 5,656 | 2,459 | 2,100 | 610 | 487 | 43.5 | 37.1 | 10.8 | 8.6 |
| **1995** | 7,973 | 3,495 | 2,936 | 1,110 | 432 | 43.8 | 36.8 | 13.9 | 5.4 |
| **1996** | 8,341 | 3,683 | 3,087 | 1,244 | 327 | 44.2 | 37.0 | 14.9 | 3.9 |
| **1997** | 7,980 | 3,589 | 2,849 | 1,162 | 380 | 45.0 | 35.7 | 14.6 | 4.8 |
| **1998** | 7,983 | 3,565 | 2,968 | 1,034 | 416 | 44.7 | 37.2 | 13.0 | 5.2 |
| **1999** | 8,490 | 3,776 | 3,142 | 1,170 | 402 | 44.5 | 37.0 | 13.8 | 4.7 |
| **2000** | 18,079 | 8,087 | 4,779 | 1,881 | 3,332 | 44.7 | 26.4 | 10.4 | 18.4 |
| **2001** | 20,489 | 9,455 | 5,100 | 1,860 | 4,074 | 46.1 | 24.9 | 9.1 | 19.9 |
| **2002** | 21,212 | 10,224 | 5,276 | 1,889 | 3,823 | 48.2 | 24.9 | 8.9 | 18.0 |
| **2003** | 21,441 | 9,884 | 5,807 | 1,893 | 3,857 | 46.1 | 27.1 | 8.8 | 18.0 |

*Source*: Glaxo, Glaxo Wellcome, GlaxoSmithKline Annual Report and Accounts, various years

*Notes*: North American 1980 sales includes sales to Central and South America. Alongside Pharma sales, Glaxo produces Farley Rusks, Ostermilks and Complan. (p.8) European 1984 and 1985 sales includes Middle East. 'Other' category includes consumer health-care sales and are significant from 2000 onwards

**Table C1.4** *Glaxo, Glaxo Wellcome and GlaxoSmithKline: cost structure, 1980–2003 (nominal data)*

| | *Sales* | *Labour costs* | *R&D* | *Depreciation* | *Net interest payments* | *Dividends* | *Retained profit* |
|---|---|---|---|---|---|---|---|
| | £ million | £ million | £ million | £ million | £ million | £ million | £ million |
| **1980** | 618 | 150 | 38 | 18 | –3 | 16 | 26 |
| **1981** | 710 | 174 | 45 | 19 | –3 | 19 | 42 |
| **1982** | 866 | 207 | 53 | 24 | 1 | 24 | 56 |
| **1983** | 1,028 | 224 | 60 | 30 | –4 | 33 | 83 |
| **1984** | 1,200 | 254 | 76 | 33 | 7 | 48 | 121 |
| **1985** | 1,412 | 296 | 92 | 39 | 14 | 74 | 193 |
| **1986** | 1,429 | 316 | 113 | 42 | 95 | 104 | 297 |
| **1987** | 1,741 | 358 | 149 | 55 | 51 | 141 | 369 |
| **1988** | 2,059 | 425 | 230 | 73 | 68 | 185 | 396 |
| **1989** | 2,570 | 537 | 323 | 93 | 130 | 260 | 426 |
| **1990** | 2,854 | 645 | 399 | 117 | 142 | 329 | 464 |
| **1991** | 3,397 | 811 | 475 | 151 | 179 | 420 | 461 |
| **1992** | 4,096 | 944 | 595 | 191 | 140 | 512 | 521 |
| **1993** | 4,930 | 1,187 | 739 | 225 | 150 | 667 | 540 |
| **1994** | 5,656 | 1,300 | 858 | 282 | 21 | 823 | 480 |
| **1995** | 6,993 | 1,710 | 1,198 | 355 | –58 | 1,020 | –48 |
| **1996** | 8,341 | 1,866 | 1,161 | 410 | –187 | 1,202 | 795 |
| **1997** | 7,980 | 1,827 | 1,148 | 373 | –123 | 1,249 | 601 |
| **1998** | 7,983 | 1,808 | 1,163 | 358 | –91 | 1,300 | 536 |
| **1999** | 8,490 | 2,042 | 1,269 | 360 | –92 | 1,341 | 470 |
| **2000** | 18,079 | 4,487 | 2,526 | 735 | –182 | 2,097 | 2,057 |
| **2001** | 20,489 | 4,686 | 2,651 | 761 | –69 | 2,356 | 703 |
| **2002** | 21,212 | 4,940 | 2,900 | 764 | –141 | 2,346 | 1,569 |
| **2003** | 21,441 | 5,058 | 2,791 | 773 | –132 | 2,374 | 2,110 |
| **1994** | | | | | | | |
| Glaxo | 5,656 | 1,300 | 543 | 282 | 21 | 823 | 480 |
| Wellcome | 2,276 | 513 | 159 | 95 | –58 | 203 | 200 |
| Total G+W | 7,932 | 1,813 | 702 | 377 | –37 | 1,026 | 680 |
| **1999** | | | | | | | |
| GW | 8,490 | 2,042 | | 360 | –92 | 1,341 | 470 |
| SKB | 8,381 | 2,031 | | 295 | 118 | 664 | 389 |
| Total GW+SKB | 16,871 | 4,073 | | 655 | 26 | 2,005 | 859 |

*Source*: Glaxo, Glaxo Wellcome, GlaxoSmithKline Annual Report and Accounts, various years

*Note*: Under net interest payable, a positive payment implies net interest payments; a negative figure indicates net interest received

**Table C1.5** *Glaxo, Glaxo Wellcome and GlaxoSmithKline: significance of cost items, 1980–2003, as a % of sales revenues*

| | *Labour costs* | *R&D* | *Depreciation* | *Net interest* | *Dividends* | *Retained profit* |
|---|---|---|---|---|---|---|
| **1980** | 24.3 | 6.1 | 2.9 | 0.5 | 2.6 | 4.2 |
| **1981** | 24.5 | 6.3 | 2.6 | 0.4 | 2.7 | 5.8 |
| **1982** | 23.9 | 6.1 | 2.8 | −0.1 | 2.8 | 6.5 |
| **1983** | 21.8 | 5.8 | 2.9 | 0.4 | 3.2 | 8.0 |
| **1984** | 21.2 | 6.3 | 2.7 | −0.6 | 4.0 | 10.1 |
| **1985** | 21.0 | 6.5 | 2.8 | −1.0 | 5.2 | 13.6 |
| **1986** | 22.1 | 8.0 | 3.0 | −6.6 | 7.3 | 20.8 |
| **1987** | 20.6 | 10.9 | 3.2 | −2.9 | 8.1 | 21.2 |
| **1988** | 20.6 | 11.2 | 3.5 | −3.3 | 9.0 | 19.2 |
| **1989** | 20.9 | 12.6 | 3.6 | −5.1 | 10.1 | 16.6 |
| **1990** | 22.6 | 14.0 | 4.1 | −5.0 | 11.5 | 16.3 |
| **1991** | 23.9 | 14.0 | 4.4 | −5.3 | 12.4 | 13.6 |
| **1992** | 23.0 | 14.5 | 4.7 | −3.4 | 12.5 | 12.7 |
| **1993** | 24.1 | 15.0 | 4.6 | −3.0 | 13.5 | 11.0 |
| **1994** | 23.0 | 15.2 | 5.0 | −0.4 | 14.6 | 8.5 |
| **1995** | 24.5 | 17.1 | 5.1 | 0.8 | 14.6 | −0.7 |
| **1996** | 22.4 | 13.9 | 4.9 | 2.2 | 14.4 | 9.5 |
| **1997** | 22.9 | 14.4 | 4.7 | 1.5 | 15.7 | 7.5 |
| **1998** | 22.6 | 14.6 | 4.5 | 1.1 | 16.3 | 6.7 |
| **1999** | 24.1 | 14.9 | 4.2 | 1.1 | 15.8 | 5.5 |
| **2000** | 24.8 | 14.0 | 4.1 | 1.0 | 11.6 | 11.4 |
| **2001** | 22.9 | 12.9 | 3.7 | 0.3 | 11.5 | 3.4 |
| **2002** | 23.3 | 13.7 | 3.6 | 0.7 | 11.1 | 7.4 |
| **2003** | 23.6 | 13.0 | 3.6 | 0.6 | 11.1 | 9.8 |

*Source*: Glaxo, Glaxo Wellcome, GlaxoSmithKline Annual Report and Accounts, various years

*Note*: Under net interest payable, a positive payment implies net interest payments; a negative figure indicates net interest received

**Table C1.6** *Glaxo, Glaxo Wellcome and GlaxoSmithKline: capital structure, 1980–2003 (nominal data)*

| | *Shareholder equity* | *Long-term debt* | *Other capital (e.g. minority interests)* | *Total capital employed* | *All other debt* | *Gearing (long-term debt as % of capital employed)* |
|---|---|---|---|---|---|---|
| | £ million | £ million | £ million | £ million | £ million | % |
| **1980** | 338 | 44 | 17 | 399 | 211 | 11.0 |
| **1981** | 382 | 44 | 16 | 442 | 244 | 9.9 |
| **1982** | 428 | 37 | 6 | 471 | 322 | 7.9 |
| **1983** | 542 | 50 | 4 | 597 | 329 | 8.4 |
| **1984** | 676 | 53 | 8 | 736 | 409 | 7.1 |
| **1985** | 852 | 75 | 9 | 937 | 434 | 8.0 |
| **1986** | 1,090 | 59 | 10 | 1,159 | 559 | 5.1 |
| **1987** | 1,450 | 107 | 14 | 1,571 | 711 | 6.8 |
| **1988** | 1,784 | 114 | 19 | 1,917 | 869 | 5.9 |
| **1989** | 2,291 | 192 | 22 | 2,505 | 863 | 7.7 |
| **1990** | 2,732 | 89 | 32 | 2,853 | 1,335 | 3.1 |
| **1991** | 3,208 | 78 | 164 | 3,450 | 2,027 | 2.3 |
| **1992** | 3,572 | 177 | 67 | 3,816 | 1,568 | 4.6 |
| **1993** | 4,546 | 243 | 111 | 4,900 | 2,200 | 5.0 |
| **1994** | 5,043 | 298 | 123 | 5,464 | 2,130 | 5.5 |
| **1995** | 91 | 1,466 | 130 | 1,687 | 5,466 | 86.9 |
| **1996** | 1,225 | 1,699 | 42 | 2,966 | 4,154 | 57.3 |
| **1997** | 1,843 | 1,841 | 47 | 3,731 | 3,886 | 49.3 |
| **1998** | 2,702 | 1,804 | 66 | 4,572 | 4,145 | 39.5 |
| **1999** | 3,142 | 1,260 | 51 | 4,453 | 5,263 | 28.3 |
| **2000** | 7,711 | 1,894 | 1,244 | 10,849 | 9,084 | 17.5 |
| **2001** | 7,517 | 2,108 | 862 | 10,487 | 9,430 | 20.1 |
| **2002** | 6,581 | 3,092 | 807 | 10,480 | 8,808 | 29.5 |
| **2003** | 7,720 | 3,883 | 745 | 12,348 | 8,597 | 31.4 |

*Source*: Glaxo, Glaxo Wellcome, GlaxoSmithKline Annual Report and Accounts, various years

**Table C1.7** *Glaxo, Glaxo Wellcome and GlaxoSmithKline: capital structure, 1980–2003 (in real 2003 prices)*

| | *Shareholder equity* | *Long-term debt* | *Other capital (e.g. minority interests)* | *Total capital employed* | *All other debt* | *Gearing (long-term debt as % of capital employed)* |
|---|---|---|---|---|---|---|
| | £ million | £ million | £ million | £ million | £ million | % |
| **1980** | 918 | 119 | 45 | 1,082 | 572 | 11.0 |
| **1981** | 926 | 106 | 39 | 1,071 | 592 | 9.9 |
| **1982** | 955 | 83 | 14 | 1,052 | 719 | 7.9 |
| **1983** | 1,157 | 108 | 9 | 1,274 | 701 | 8.4 |
| **1984** | 1,373 | 107 | 16 | 1,496 | 832 | 7.1 |
| **1985** | 1,632 | 144 | 18 | 1,795 | 830 | 8.0 |
| **1986** | 2,019 | 110 | 19 | 2,148 | 1,036 | 5.1 |
| **1987** | 2,581 | 190 | 25 | 2,796 | 1,265 | 6.8 |
| **1988** | 3,027 | 193 | 32 | 3,253 | 1,474 | 5.9 |
| **1989** | 3,606 | 302 | 35 | 3,943 | 1,358 | 7.7 |
| **1990** | 3,927 | 128 | 46 | 4,101 | 1,919 | 3.1 |
| **1991** | 4,354 | 106 | 223 | 4,683 | 2,751 | 2.3 |
| **1992** | 4,675 | 232 | 88 | 4,995 | 2,052 | 4.6 |
| **1993** | 5,856 | 313 | 143 | 6,312 | 2,834 | 5.0 |
| **1994** | 6,338 | 375 | 155 | 6,867 | 2,677 | 5.5 |
| **1995** | 111 | 1,782 | 158 | 2,051 | 6,644 | 86.9 |
| **1996** | 1,454 | 2,017 | 50 | 3,521 | 4,931 | 57.3 |
| **1997** | 2,122 | 2,120 | 54 | 4,296 | 4,474 | 49.3 |
| **1998** | 3,009 | 2,009 | 73 | 5,091 | 4,615 | 39.5 |
| **1999** | 3,443 | 1,381 | 56 | 4,880 | 5,768 | 28.3 |
| **2000** | 8,213 | 2,017 | 1,325 | 11,555 | 9,675 | 17.5 |
| **2001** | 7,861 | 2,205 | 901 | 10,967 | 9,862 | 20.1 |
| **2002** | 6,772 | 3,182 | 830 | 10,784 | 9,063 | 29.5 |
| **2003** | 7,720 | 3,883 | 745 | 12,348 | 8,597 | 31.4 |

*Source*: Glaxo, Glaxo Wellcome, GlaxoSmithKline Annual Report and Accounts, various years

**Table C1.8** *Glaxo, Glaxo Wellcome and GlaxoSmithKline: employment, 1980–2003*

| | *Total employment* | *Geographic breakdown of employment* | | | | *Functional breakdown of employment* | | | | | |
|---|---|---|---|---|---|---|---|---|---|---|---|
| | | *UK* | | *Overseas* | | *Manufacturing* | | *R&D* | | *Selling, general and admin* | |
| | No. | No. | % | No. | % | No. | % | No. | % | No. | % |
| **1980** | 29,187 | 14,816 | 50.8 | 14,371 | 49.2 | | | | | | |
| **1981** | 28,218 | 13,725 | 48.6 | 14,493 | 51.4 | | | | | | |
| **1982** | 28,106 | 13,188 | 46.9 | 14,918 | 53.1 | | | | | | |
| **1983** | 27,768 | 13,605 | 49.0 | 14,163 | 51.0 | | | | | | |
| **1984** | 25,053 | 13,685 | 54.6 | 11,368 | 45.4 | | | | | | |
| **1985** | 25,634 | 13,463 | 52.5 | 12,171 | 47.5 | | | | | | |
| **1986** | 24,728 | 11,815 | 47.8 | 12,913 | 52.2 | | | | | | |
| **1987** | 24,954 | 10,867 | 43.5 | 14,087 | 56.5 | | | | | | |
| **1988** | 26,423 | 11,035 | 41.8 | 15,388 | 58.2 | | | | | | |
| **1989** | 28,710 | 11,444 | 39.9 | 17,266 | 60.1 | | | | | | |
| **1990** | 31,327 | 12,291 | 39.2 | 19,036 | 60.8 | | | | | | |
| **1991** | 35,640 | 12,422 | 34.9 | 23,218 | 65.1 | 13,358 | 37.5 | 6,389 | 17.9 | 15,893 | 44.6 |
| **1992** | 37,083 | 11,968 | 32.3 | 25,115 | 67.7 | 12,905 | 34.8 | 6,643 | 17.9 | 17,535 | 47.3 |
| **1993** | 40,024 | 12,149 | 30.4 | 27,875 | 69.6 | 13,515 | 33.8 | 7,133 | 17.8 | 19,376 | 48.4 |
| **1994** | 47,189 | 12,000 | 25.4 | 35,189 | 74.6 | 17,688 | 37.5 | 7,476 | 15.8 | 22,025 | 46.7 |
| **1995** | 54,359 | 13,967 | 25.7 | 40,392 | 74.3 | 19,122 | 35.2 | 9,047 | 16.6 | 26,190 | 48.2 |
| **1996** | 53,808 | 13,000 | 24.2 | 40,808 | 75.8 | 19,629 | 36.5 | 8,822 | 16.4 | 25,357 | 47.1 |
| **1997** | 53,068 | | | | | 18,519 | 34.9 | 8,808 | 16.6 | 25,741 | 48.5 |
| **1998** | 55,273 | | | | | 18,824 | 34.1 | 9,269 | 16.8 | 27,180 | 49.2 |
| **1999** | 60,726 | | | | | 21,596 | 35.6 | 9,836 | 16.2 | 29,294 | 48.2 |
| **2000** | 108,201 | | | | | 36,177 | 33.4 | 16,659 | 15.4 | 55,365 | 51.2 |
| **2001** | 107,899 | | | | | 37,154 | 34.4 | 15,090 | 14.0 | 55,655 | 51.6 |
| **2002** | 104,499 | | | | | 35,503 | 34.0 | 14,624 | 14.0 | 54,372 | 52.0 |
| **2003** | 103,166 | | | | | 34,265 | 33.2 | 14,773 | 14.3 | 54,128 | 52.5 |

*Source*: Glaxo, Glaxo Wellcome, GlaxoSmithKline Annual Report and Accounts, various years

Table C1.9 *Glaxo, Glaxo Wellcome and GlaxoSmithKline: employee analysis, 1980–2003 (in real 2003 prices)*

| | *Real sales per employee* | | *Real value added per employee* | | *Real compensation per employee* | |
|---|---|---|---|---|---|---|
| | £ | % change, year on year | £ | % change, year on year | £ | % change, year on year |
| **1980** | 57,457 | | 21,517 | | 13,964 | |
| **1981** | 61,045 | 6.2 | 23,778 | 10.5 | 14,950 | 7.1 |
| **1982** | 68,772 | 12.7 | 29,049 | 22.2 | 16,429 | 9.9 |
| **1983** | 78,975 | 14.8 | 33,927 | 16.8 | 17,186 | 4.6 |
| **1984** | 97,353 | 23.3 | 44,664 | 31.6 | 20,641 | 20.1 |
| **1985** | 105,535 | 8.4 | 56,224 | 25.9 | 22,144 | 7.3 |
| **1986** | 107,056 | 1.4 | 79,730 | 41.8 | 23,647 | 6.8 |
| **1987** | 124,176 | 16.0 | 86,302 | 8.2 | 25,534 | 8.0 |
| **1988** | 132,214 | 6.5 | 89,769 | 4.0 | 27,290 | 6.9 |
| **1989** | 140,891 | 6.6 | 96,815 | 7.8 | 29,439 | 7.9 |
| **1990** | 130,950 | −7.1 | 93,785 | −3.1 | 29,594 | 0.5 |
| **1991** | 129,369 | −1.2 | 92,314 | −1.6 | 30,886 | 4.4 |
| **1992** | 144,571 | 11.8 | 95,369 | 3.3 | 33,319 | 7.9 |
| **1993** | 158,682 | 9.8 | 104,189 | 9.2 | 38,206 | 14.7 |
| **1994** | 150,642 | −5.1 | 91,701 | −12.0 | 34,624 | −9.4 |
| **1995** | 156,376 | 3.8 | 80,469 | −12.2 | 38,237 | 10.4 |
| **1996** | 184,004 | 17.7 | 111,470 | 38.5 | 41,164 | 7.7 |
| **1997** | 173,128 | −5.9 | 103,335 | −7.3 | 39,637 | −3.7 |
| **1998** | 160,817 | −7.1 | 95,608 | −7.5 | 36,422 | −8.1 |
| **1999** | 153,221 | −4.7 | 88,160 | −7.8 | 36,852 | 1.2 |
| **2000** | 177,956 | 16.1 | 108,955 | 23.6 | 44,167 | 19.8 |
| **2001** | 198,590 | 11.6 | 95,908 | −12.0 | 45,419 | 2.8 |
| **2002** | 208,874 | 5.2 | 108,996 | 13.6 | 48,644 | 7.1 |
| **2003** | 207,830 | −0.5 | 116,589 | 7.0 | 49,028 | 0.8 |

*Source*: Glaxo, Glaxo Wellcome, GlaxoSmithKline Annual Report and Accounts, various years

*Note*: Value added is sales revenues less external purchases. It is equivalent to operating profit plus depreciation plus labour costs (and this is usually how it is calculated given that external purchases are not normally separately disclosed in company accounts)

*Table C1.10* Glaxo, Glaxo Wellcome and GlaxoSmithKline: capital market performance, 1980–2003

| | (Nominal) Share price | (Nominal) Share price corrected for share splits | (Nominal) Market value | Market value (real 2003 prices) | P/E ratio (post-tax) | Dividends per share (real 2003 prices) |
|---|---|---|---|---|---|---|
| | £ | £ | £ million | £ million | Ratio | £ |
| **1980** | 2.24 | 2.24 | 379 | 1,028 | 9.1 | 0.26 |
| **1981** | 3.62 | 3.62 | 613 | 1,486 | 10.1 | 0.27 |
| **1982** | 7.04 | 7.04 | 1,210 | 2,702 | 15.0 | 0.31 |
| **1983** | 9.00 | 18.00 | 3,294 | 7,029 | 28.5 | 0.19 |
| **1984** | 8.65 | 17.30 | 3,184 | 6,473 | 18.9 | 0.26 |
| **1985** | 12.32 | 24.64 | 4,559 | 8,735 | 17.1 | 0.38 |
| **1986** | 10.13 | 40.52 | 7,498 | 13,892 | 18.7 | 0.26 |
| **1987** | 16.60 | 66.39 | 12,287 | 21,869 | 24.1 | 0.34 |
| **1988** | 9.91 | 39.63 | 7,335 | 12,445 | 12.7 | 0.42 |
| **1989** | 13.61 | 54.44 | 10,138 | 15,956 | 14.7 | 0.55 |
| **1990** | 8.17 | 65.39 | 12,213 | 17,554 | 15.4 | 0.32 |
| **1991** | 12.20 | 97.56 | 18,289 | 24,823 | 20.8 | 0.38 |
| **1992** | 6.79 | 108.63 | 20,438 | 26,750 | 19.8 | 0.22 |
| **1993** | 5.63 | 90.07 | 17,065 | 21,983 | 14.1 | 0.28 |
| **1994** | 5.44 | 87.03 | 16,587 | 20,847 | 12.7 | 0.34 |
| **1995** | 9.14 | 146.22 | 32,025 | 38,927 | 32.9 | 0.35 |
| **1996** | 9.47 | 151.53 | 33,578 | 39,858 | 16.8 | 0.40 |
| **1997** | 14.39 | 230.28 | 51,451 | 59,237 | 27.8 | 0.40 |
| **1998** | 20.66 | 330.54 | 74,903 | 83,402 | 40.8 | 0.40 |
| **1999** | 17.50 | 280.00 | 63,714 | 69,826 | 35.2 | 0.40 |
| **2000** | 18.63 | 298.08 | 118,910 | 126,644 | 28.6 | 0.36 |
| **2001** | 17.21 | 275.38 | 106,245 | 111,113 | 33.3 | 0.40 |
| **2002** | 11.95 | 191.27 | 72,016 | 74,105 | 17.8 | 0.40 |
| **2003** | 12.80 | 204.80 | 76,153 | 76,153 | 17.0 | 0.39 |

*Source*: Glaxo, Glaxo Wellcome, GlaxoSmithKline Annual Report and Accounts, various years

*Table C1.11 Glaxo, Glaxo Wellcome and GlaxoSmithKline: key rate of return ratios, 1980–2003*

| | (Pre-tax) ROS | (Net) ROS | (Pre-tax) ROCE | (Post-tax) ROCE | Return on equity |
|---|---|---|---|---|---|
| | % | % | % | % | % |
| 1980 | 10.7 | 6.8 | 16.6 | 10.5 | 12.4 |
| 1981 | 12.3 | 8.5 | 19.8 | 13.7 | 15.9 |
| 1982 | 15.4 | 9.3 | 28.4 | 17.1 | 18.8 |
| 1983 | 18.7 | 11.2 | 32.2 | 19.3 | 21.3 |
| 1984 | 21.3 | 14.1 | 34.8 | 22.9 | 25.0 |
| 1985 | 28.5 | 18.9 | 43.0 | 28.5 | 31.3 |
| 1986 | 42.8 | 28.0 | 52.8 | 34.5 | 36.7 |
| 1987 | 42.8 | 29.3 | 47.5 | 32.5 | 35.2 |
| 1988 | 40.4 | 28.1 | 43.4 | 30.2 | 32.4 |
| 1989 | 39.1 | 26.8 | 40.2 | 27.5 | 30.0 |
| 1990 | 39.9 | 27.8 | 40.0 | 27.8 | 29.0 |
| 1991 | 37.8 | 25.9 | 37.2 | 25.5 | 27.5 |
| 1992 | 34.8 | 25.2 | 37.4 | 27.1 | 28.9 |
| 1993 | 34.0 | 24.5 | 34.2 | 24.6 | 26.6 |
| 1994 | 32.5 | 23.0 | 33.7 | 23.8 | 25.8 |
| 1995 | 22.8 | 13.9 | 94.3 | 57.6 | 1068.1 |
| 1996 | 35.5 | 23.9 | 99.9 | 67.3 | 163.0 |
| 1997 | 33.7 | 23.2 | 72.0 | 49.6 | 100.4 |
| 1998 | 33.5 | 23.0 | 58.4 | 40.2 | 67.9 |
| 1999 | 30.3 | 21.3 | 57.8 | 40.7 | 57.6 |
| 2000 | 33.3 | 23.0 | 55.6 | 38.3 | 53.9 |
| 2001 | 22.0 | 15.6 | 43.1 | 30.4 | 42.4 |
| 2002 | 26.0 | 19.1 | 52.5 | 38.6 | 61.5 |
| 2003 | 29.5 | 20.9 | 51.3 | 36.3 | 58.1 |

*Source*: Glaxo, Glaxo Wellcome, GlaxoSmithKline Annual Report and Accounts, various years

**Table C1.12** *Glaxo, Glaxo Wellcome and GlaxoSmithKline: operating analysis, 1980–2003*

| | *External purchases as a % of sales* | *Internal costs (value added) as a % of sales* | *Labour costs as a % of internal costs* | *Depreciation as a % of internal costs* | *Cashflow compared with internal costs (value added)* |
|---|---|---|---|---|---|
| | % | % | % | % | % |
| **1980** | 62.6 | 37.4 | 64.9 | 7.6 | 35.1 |
| **1981** | 61.0 | 39.0 | 62.9 | 6.7 | 37.1 |
| **1982** | 57.8 | 42.2 | 56.6 | 6.6 | 43.4 |
| **1983** | 57.0 | 43.0 | 50.7 | 6.8 | 49.3 |
| **1984** | 54.1 | 45.9 | 46.2 | 6.0 | 53.8 |
| **1985** | 46.7 | 53.3 | 39.4 | 5.2 | 60.6 |
| **1986** | 25.5 | 74.5 | 29.7 | 4.0 | 70.3 |
| **1987** | 30.5 | 69.5 | 29.6 | 4.5 | 70.4 |
| **1988** | 32.1 | 67.9 | 30.4 | 5.2 | 69.6 |
| **1989** | 31.3 | 68.7 | 30.4 | 5.3 | 69.6 |
| **1990** | 28.4 | 71.6 | 31.6 | 5.7 | 68.4 |
| **1991** | 28.6 | 71.4 | 33.5 | 6.2 | 66.5 |
| **1992** | 34.0 | 66.0 | 34.9 | 7.1 | 65.1 |
| **1993** | 34.3 | 65.7 | 36.7 | 7.0 | 63.3 |
| **1994** | 39.1 | 60.9 | 37.8 | 8.2 | 62.2 |
| **1995** | 48.5 | 51.5 | 47.5 | 9.9 | 52.5 |
| **1996** | 39.4 | 60.6 | 36.9 | 8.1 | 63.1 |
| **1997** | 40.3 | 59.7 | 38.4 | 7.8 | 61.6 |
| **1998** | 40.5 | 59.5 | 38.1 | 7.5 | 61.9 |
| **1999** | 42.5 | 57.5 | 41.8 | 7.4 | 58.2 |
| **2000** | 38.8 | 61.2 | 40.5 | 6.6 | 59.5 |
| **2001** | 51.7 | 48.3 | 47.4 | 7.7 | 52.6 |
| **2002** | 47.8 | 52.2 | 44.6 | 6.9 | 55.4 |
| **2003** | 43.9 | 56.1 | 42.1 | 6.4 | 57.9 |

*Source*: Glaxo, Glaxo Wellcome, GlaxoSmithKline Annual Report and Accounts, various years

*Note*: Value added is sales revenues less external purchases. It is equivalent to operating profit plus depreciation plus labour costs (and this is usually how it is calculated given that external purchases are not normally separately disclosed in company accounts)

**Table C1.13** *Glaxo, Glaxo Wellcome and GlaxoSmithKline: pharmaceutical sales by therapeutic area (in nominal £ million)*

| | | *Sales split by therapeutic area* | | | | | | |
|---|---|---|---|---|---|---|---|---|
| | *Total sales* | *Anti-ulcerant/metabolic and gastro-intestinal* | *of which Zantac* | *Respiratory* | *Systemic antibiotics/ bacterial infections* | *Cardio-vascular and urogenital* | *Dermatologicals* | *Anti-emesis/oncology* |
| | £m | £m | £m | £m | £m | £m | £m | £m |
| **1980** | 618 | | | 84 | 64 | 5 | 52 | |
| **1981** | 710 | | | 115 | 80 | 10 | 61 | |
| **1982** | 866 | 37 | 37 | 148 | 91 | 12 | 67 | |
| **1983** | 1,028 | 97 | 97 | 179 | 94 | 22 | 66 | |
| **1984** | 1,200 | 248 | 248 | 217 | 95 | 19 | 70 | |
| **1985** | 1,412 | 432 | 432 | 255 | 112 | 33 | 74 | |
| **1986** | 1,429 | 606 | 606 | 287 | 181 | 36 | 77 | |
| **1987** | 1,741 | 829 | 829 | 362 | 226 | 46 | 86 | |
| **1988** | 2,059 | 989 | 989 | 457 | 299 | 48 | 96 | |
| **1989** | 2,570 | 1,291 | 1,291 | 585 | 396 | 46 | 101 | |
| **1990** | 2,854 | 1,401 | 1,401 | 682 | 481 | 44 | 105 | |
| **1991** | 3,397 | 1,606 | 1,606 | 775 | 608 | 43 | 128 | 78 |
| **1992** | 4,096 | 1,807 | 1,807 | 964 | 681 | 63 | 145 | 259 |
| **1993** | 4,930 | 2,172 | 2,172 | 1,087 | 827 | 67 | 168 | 365 |
| **1994** | 5,656 | 2,442 | 2,442 | 1,229 | 872 | 75 | 183 | 404 |
| **1995** | 6,993 | 2,255 | 2,255 | 1,603 | 963 | 187 | 205 | 451 |
| **1996** | 8,341 | 1,946 | 1,931 | 1,757 | 939 | 221 | 240 | 434 |
| **1997** | 7,980 | 1,380 | 1,375 | 1,828 | 862 | 228 | 236 | 460 |
| **1998** | 7,983 | 761 | 757 | 2,193 | 836 | 260 | 243 | 480 |
| **1999** | 8,490 | 647 | 640 | 2,461 | 836 | 253 | 254 | 521 |
| **2000** | 18,079 | 1,232 | 575 | 2,789 | 2,472 | 463 | 249 | 710 |
| **2001** | 20,489 | 1,480 | 505 | 3,537 | 2,604 | 591 | | 838 |
| **2002** | 21,212 | 1,429 | 382 | 3,987 | 2,210 | 655 | | 977 |
| **2003** | 21,441 | 1,426 | 328 | 4,417 | 1,815 | 752 | | 1,001 |

*Source*: Annual report and accounts, various years
*Note*: In 1980, phama total sales includes sales from the foods division

*Sales split by therapeutic area*

| *Anti-migraine/ CNS disorders* | *Anti-viral infections* | *Anaesthesia* | *Arthritis* | *Vaccines* | *Other pharma* | **Total PHARMA sales** | *Zantac: % year-on-year change in sales* | *Zantac as % of therapeutic area* |
|---|---|---|---|---|---|---|---|---|
| £m | £m | £m | £m | £m | £m | £m | % | % |
| | | | | | 126 | 331 | | |
| | | | | | 148 | 414 | | |
| | | | | | 149 | 504 | | 100.0 |
| | | | | | 158 | 616 | 162.2 | 100.0 |
| | | | | | 130 | 779 | 155.7 | 100.0 |
| | | | | | 154 | 1,060 | 74.2 | 100.0 |
| | | | | | 174 | 1,361 | 40.3 | 100.0 |
| | | | | | 149 | 1,698 | 36.8 | 100.0 |
| | | | | | 138 | 2,027 | 19.3 | 100.0 |
| | | | | | 151 | 2,570 | 30.5 | 100.0 |
| | | | | | 141 | 2,854 | 8.5 | 100.0 |
| 2 | | | | | 157 | 3,397 | 14.6 | 100.0 |
| 43 | | | | | 134 | 4,096 | 12.5 | 100.0 |
| 116 | | | | | 128 | 4,930 | 20.2 | 100.0 |
| 243 | | | | | 208 | 5,656 | 12.4 | 100.0 |
| 501 | 1,099 | 117 | | | 388 | 7,769 | −7.7 | 100.0 |
| 724 | 1,360 | 112 | | | 608 | 8,341 | −14.4 | 99.2 |
| 949 | 1,422 | 96 | | | 519 | 7,980 | −28.8 | 99.6 |
| 1,231 | 1,348 | 96 | | | 535 | 7,983 | −44.9 | 99.5 |
| 1,316 | 1,635 | 97 | | | 470 | 8,490 | −15.5 | 98.9 |
| 3,279 | 1,899 | | 210 | 842 | 1,284 | 15,429 | −10.2 | 46.7 |
| 4,007 | 2,128 | | 156 | 948 | 916 | 17,205 | −12.2 | 34.1 |
| 4,511 | 2,299 | | 23 | 1,080 | 824 | 17,995 | −24.4 | 26.7 |
| 4,455 | 2,349 | | | 1,123 | 843 | 18,181 | −14.1 | 23.0 |

Case 2

# Ford

## Effort and reward

## INTRODUCTION

When Ford Motor Company celebrated its centenary in 2003, the company had a glorious legacy and an uncertain future. The legacy was that created by Ford's founder, Henry Ford, and the 15 million Model Ts his company produced from 1908 to 1926. His productive and innovative achievements were such that Fordism became the eponymous term by which social scientists understood and defined an industrial era of prosperity for thirty glorious years after 1945. Now Henry Ford's celebrated legacy foreshadows that of his grandson and current chief executive of the company, William Clay (Bill) Ford, whose 2002 announcement of a 'revitalization plan' was greeted sceptically by stock-market analysts who now regard the company and the US car industry as synonymous with financial underperformance and value destruction.

The legacy is such that the Ford Motor Company and the car industry as a whole continue to attract comment and analysis in a way that many other industries do not. In other industries, factory closures are local or regional news stories, whereas car-factory closures are always high-profile national news stories because they involve the loss of reasonably well-paid jobs and have a cumulative effect of symbolizing the decline of local and national prestige in manufacturing, as in the UK when Ford ended blue-oval car assembly at Ford Dagenham or Jaguar assembly at Brown's Lane. The emblematic status of the industry has also led to the publication of many academic books, initially mainly by social scientists soberly interested in issues such as workplace labour process. Since the early 1990s the field of publication has been ceded to business-school academics and consultants, above all Womack, Jones and Roos with their upbeat, best-selling book on lean production (1990).

In all this, there is an element of challenge and response which is given by T. S. Eliot's (1929) line about 'the pain of living and the drug of dreams'. The industry's dreary, persistent inability to deliver sizeable and consistent profits sustains and spurs the bright new literatures which explain the possibility of reinvention through good management and alternative business models. The first section of this case study, on the industry frame, takes forward the argument about narrative by examining how diverse visions of transformation popularize (changing) ideas of an industry-wide break with old production and business models. We also note the limits on the circulation of such visions which do not generally impress social-science critics who, in a downbeat way, emphasize complications and qualifications.

Visions of transformation fail to impress stock-market analysts for rather different reasons. The mundane problem for analysts is that auto-assembly companies operate in a cyclical, mature industry which encourages investors to adopt a rent-not-buy approach to assembler shares as they try to identify good or bad news not already in the individual company's share price so as to anticipate and hence benefit from future share-price changes. Interestingly, this has put car-company analysts in a different position from analysts of ethical pharmaceuticals industry who, until recently, operated with a shared understanding of the industry and its business model, where the pipeline supposedly made things predictable. As the second section argues, in the case of car-assembly companies, the analysts find themselves in the position of racing tipsters whose different predictions reflect underlying uncertainty about the relevant variables and their interaction.

Against this background, the present-day car-company CEO has a difficult task because each incoming company head has to justify his or her status (and salary) by promising to make a strategic difference, as well as to improve hitherto mediocre results without promising a transformation that most would find implausible. This highlights the importance of the CEO's new initiative where the narrative shades into performative, as analysed in the third section of the case study. Thus, Jacques Nasser from 1999 promised a services-led company while his successor Bill Ford promised in early 2002 to get back to basics. Differentiation in the form of reversal arises partly because such new strategies are often symbolically enacted not coherently implemented, as when Ford under Nasser not only bought services firms but also car companies like Volvo which took it further into car assembly.

With struggling companies in mature industries, the other driver of strategy reversal is the perceived failure of the previous strategy to deliver promised improvements. This takes us away from the just-desserts world of business-school and consultancy texts, where appropriate management effort always gets its reward and takes us back to Ecclesiastes 9:11, where 'the race is not to the swift nor yet riches to men of understanding'. The fourth section analyses the disproportion between management effort and financial results in a struggling company with profit problems in mature markets, and argues that Ford has managed large-scale innovation without much benefit for the bottom line. This section considers how Ford's design expertise contributed to the repackaging of the full-size American car as a pick-up or sport utility, and also how financial engineering, as the company's

10K filings to the Securities and Exchange Commission (SEC) show, took the company further into finance via leasing and securitization.

In all this, the message of Ford is that in many old industries there is no clear relation between effort and reward, so that solid management effort may deliver only meagre financial reward, which often also comes at the price of increased opacity, secondary problems and risk. In this respect, the case study of Ford offers a view that challenges the a priori of much orthodox management thinking which supposes there is or should be a positive and linear relation between intelligent effort and the reward of competitive advantage. In the case of Ford, the result is a highly financialized company that has not moved onto an upward trajectory but has only bought time so that it is now stuck between the future and the past in a new and different way. Hence the commitment to leasing provides a new source of income but also pushes up depreciation so that the company is still only marginally profitable. The fifth section finally notes that, despite all these unsolved problems, Ford has not engaged in large-scale labour-shedding. Like other giant companies who abjure large-scale acquisition and divestment, Ford is an economically unrewarded but innovative social institution of a remarkably stable kind. As such, Ford is quite different from the Manichean (good or bad) imaginary corporations of social-science and business-school texts and represents an unplanned but real achievement with a precarious future.

## INDUSTRY FRAME: VISIONS OF TRANSFORMATION

The idea of a break that heralds a new era is central to business-school and consultancy texts from the 1980s onwards, which use the notion of 'before and after' as a useful dramatic device. In everything from government to car assembly, such texts have announced breaks or new eras that rationalise the perceived failure of the past and open the prospect of future success through something completely new and different. Such texts tend to oversimplify both stages and the complexities around the articulation and enactment of the changes required to deliver anything like transformation. In our analysis, breaks are complex and not easily achieved, and the case study of Ford illustrates the difficulties both of explaining new 'strategies' to (often cynical) external commentators and of executing the plan to achieve at least some of the intended outcomes.

By the late 1980s, the Western auto industry certainly needed a break. The big three US car assemblers (the giant firms of Ford, GM and Chrysler) had suffered an entirely unexpected defeat in their home market at the hands of Japanese manufacturers who had taken 20 per cent of the US car market by delivering compact cars of superior quality at keen prices. Against this background Womack et al. (1990) mined the results of the assembler-funded International Motor Vehicle Program (IMVP) to produce a book that would both explain Japanese success and motivate the US and European fight back. The Japanese industry's success was attributed to 'lean production' or superior factory organization which the Americans and Europeans could and should adopt. The form of the imagined difference is significant because Womack et al. shared a common productionist frame with their 1990s' social-science critics who challenged lean production. Interestingly, this form then changes so that by 2003 the consultancy firm AT Kearney is promoting a new business model for the auto industry, which aims to restore profitability by accessing new revenue streams rather than by changing production techniques.

## Lean production or better in every way

The basic argument of *The Machine That Changed the World* is that mass-production modes of organization obstruct productivity improvements and may even create problems of industry overcapacity, business cyclicality and inflation more generally across many manufacturing industries (Womack et al. 1990: 250). This supply side problem definition is coupled with a supply side solution because, according to Womack et al., it is possible to 'do manufacturing better' through waste-reducing processes and techniques such as Just-In-Time, which reduce stocks, indirect workers and rework (1990: 79–80). The technical changes are connected to the development of 'industrial citizenship', a new social model which eschews conflict and realizes win–win outcomes for all stakeholders (1990: 103). These technical and social modes of organization are together labelled 'lean production', which combines the best of craft and mass production and offers low cost and flexibility (1990: 13).

The argument for lean- and against mass-production techniques is developed in a familiar way using forms of persuasion characteristic of best-selling business texts. Three key devices are used to buttress and drive the lean-production argument: first, the use of rhetorical binarism and the announcement of the 'one best way' new-paradigm solution which by its very nature precludes alternative futures; second, the highly selective use of packaged evidence which is used not as a source of development but simply to sidestep complexity and to corroborate the conceptual opposition; and third, the use of forward-looking promises about significant general improvements in performance that will come as soon as the new model is adopted.

The central device in Womack et al. (1990) is a binary opposition between (good) lean and (bad) mass production. In business and social-science literatures in the later 1980s and early 1990s, such epochal oppositions were characteristic of much discussion of mass production and its alternative (Kenney and Florida 1993, Piore and Sabel 1984, Toffler 1980, Tomaney 1994). In Womack et al. the opposition ensures that the 'one best way' for solving the problems of mass production is Japanese-originated lean, which is also claimed to be transferable so that its Western spread is both natural and inevitable: 'it was clear to us by the end of 1986 that Toyota had truly achieved a revolution in manufacturing, that old mass-production plants could not compete, and that the new best way – lean production – could be transplanted successfully to new environments' (1990: 84).

This framing of industry choice gained plausibility by the way it combined a strong conceptual opposition with a selective evidence base that reinforced the polar vision by removing messy complexities. Thus, 'box score' type exhibits illustrate the claimed 2:1 superiority of lean production, as in the now notorious table (shown in Exhibit C2.1) about three assembly plants (GM Framingham in the US, Toyota Takaoka in Japan and NUMMI Fremont, a Japanese transplant in the USA) which supports the argument that lean can reduce build hours while at the same time improving quality. The sleight of hand here includes a comparison between Japan's best and America's worst assembly plant as well as a framing of the problem which crops profit-determining variables such as wage costs from the field of the visible.

The inclusion of the NUMMI transplant in Exhibit C2.1 is a crucial corroboration of the Womack et al. claim that lean is not culture-specific but transferable and the related promise that all Western manufacturers could gain by adopting lean methods. In a way characteristic of business best-sellers, Womack et al. then make a series of extravagant predictions about the win–win gains that all assemblers can achieve from adopting lean. Hence, they argue that lean production could solve the chronic overcapacity caused by mass production (1990: 12), halve build hours in the West (1990: 81–3), 'eliminate [North America's] massive trade deficit in auto vehicles' and 'triple the productivity of the motor vehicle industry' in Europe (1990: 256) without apparently causing mass unemployment. This farrago of claims predictably impressed some readers but upset

**Exhibit C2.1** *General Motors Framingham versus Toyota Takaoka versus NUMMI Fremont 1987*

| | *GM Framingham* | *Toyota Takaoka* | *NUMMI Fremont* |
|---|---|---|---|
| Assembly hours per car | 31 | 16 | 19 |
| Assembly defects per 100 cars | 135 | 45 | 45 |
| Assembly space per car | 8.1 | 4.8 | 7.0 |
| Average holding of inventories of parts | 2 weeks | 2 hours | 2 days |

*Source*: IMVP World Assembly Plant Survey, reproduced in Womack et al. (1990: 83)

critical social scientists who could hardly be expected to believe that supply would create its own demand (Froud et al. 2002a: 3).

Interestingly, the critical intellectual response was led by European social scientists who rejected the idea of simple technical breaks and added social complications and qualifications. Thus Williams et al. supported continuism against the mass/lean break while Boyer and Freyssenet (1999) and Freyssenet et al. (1998) argued for more than one best way. Both European responses, in the traditions of classical political economy, set these complications in the social context of compromise and conflict between stakeholder groups.

Williams et al. (1994) produced a continuist history of repetitive flow manufacturing which saw no epochal break between the methods of Henry Ford and Toyota. On the supply side, their comparison between Toyota in the 1980s and 1990s and Ford Highland Park in the 1900s and 1910s demonstrates basic continuity in terms of productive organization for material flow. The Japanese add refinements, but Henry Ford's company and Toyota cannot be used as prototypes for different types of production. Equally, much emphasis is put on external demand conditions of flow because all car assembly is a struggle of productive flow against market restriction (Willliams et al. 1994: 133); furthermore, it was argued that these external conditions were exceptionally favourable for the Japanese as they were for Henry Ford.

Freyssenet (1998: 45) rejects Womack et al.'s central claim by arguing, 'there is no "one best way". There was none in the past, and there is none today. In all likelihood, there will be none in the future'. But Freyssenet et al. (1998) and Boyer and Freyssenet (1999) equally oppose the continuism of Williams et al., and argue their case for more complexity by introducing the quasi-regulationist concept of 'industrial models' that adapt to different national demand configurations and local stakeholder compromises. Hence, contrary to Williams et al., Freyssenet argues that Toyota, Honda and VW represent not variants on one set of flow principles but three different industrial models. The different companies follow unique profit strategies and so construct productive organization and employment relations that best suit their own socio-economic context (Freyssenet 1998: 45). Thus, whilst lean might be appropriate for the Japanese context, it may not be elsewhere and therefore cannot be generalized as the solution for Western manufacturing (Boyer and Freyssenet 1999: 6).

Despite such manifest differences about continuity and discontinuity, there are important elements of similarity in the Boyer and Freyssenet and Williams et al. positions. Both sets of authors aim to understand factory production and assembly through financial analysis of operations. Williams et al. (1994) introduced wage cost information that shows a large Japanese wage advantage up to the point of yen appreciation after the Plaza Accord in 1985; their book also pioneered the use of break-even analysis which shows how improved flow removes labour and highlights the issue of how labour's share of internal cost varies with cyclicality. These break-even measures were then used by Freyssenet (1998) to identify firms with viable industrial models. Such financial analysis was confined to the analysis of auto operations. It was only later, at the end of the 1990s, that Williams et al. incorporated discussion of balance-sheet considerations and the significance of non-assembly businesses such as finance into their analysis (see Froud et al. 1998, 2000 and 2002b).

Both sets of authors also put much more emphasis on the social. Boyer and Freyssenet (1999) are explicitly concerned with the implications of national income distribution for product strategy and with how stakeholder compromises create the basis for viable companies. The two key issues are how the enterprise profit strategy relates to the national income strategy and growth mode. Hence Boyer and Freyssenet discuss whether the social actors in the firm have achieved an appropriate 'enterprise government compromise' (Boyer and Freyssenet 1999: 6). Williams et al. are equally interested in social aspects and the last chapter of their book refers differences in wage costs to differences in national social settlements that determine working hours and welfare costs. For the British authors, competition is ultimately a matter of social standards not economic efficiency and large sections of the Western manufacturing workforce stand to lose their jobs in the wake of low-wage competition from East Asian producers (Williams et al. 1994: 244–5).

The social scientists' critique of lean does, however, have a limited audience of mainly academic researchers, subsequently organized into an alternative researchers' network, Groupe d'Études et de Recherches Permanent sur l'Industrie et les Salriés de l'Automobile (Permanent Group for the Study of the Automobile Industry and its Employees, GERPISA). Complicated stories and empirical detail from GERPISA researchers are less immediate and accessible than Womack et al.'s high concept and simple message format. This gave *The Machine That Changed the World* its broad appeal and made it an enduring business best-seller so that Womack et al. is one of only three texts over ten years old in Amazon's Top 25 recommended management publications in 2004. The book's key concept of 'lean production' was widely appropriated through how-to guides (Dailey 2003, Henderson et al. 1999, Thompson 1997) and in more academic texts (Lamming 1993, Maxton and Wormald 1995), while Womack and Jones (1996) subsequently implied that lean could be applied to any activity including retail and services.

The commercial success of the notion of lean also owes much to the way in which it fitted the internal motivational politics of managers in giant companies. Senior managers bought into the concept because it not only provided a packaged problem definition but it also suggested management had a solution. This sometimes stretched good faith, as in one large European car firm that distributed large quantities of the Womack et al. book to its employees and middle managers who were encouraged to believe in 2:1 Japanese superiority in productivity. However, after a presentation by some of the authors of this book, the company's own researchers agreed the deficit was more like '50–70 per cent depending on the year or the measure' (rather than the implied 200 per cent). More generally, Stewart (1996) identified lean production as one element in a broader project that pushes a 'one best way' Japanization agenda for British management and that underestimates cultural and institutional factors restricting transferability.

The inevitable consequence of such usage was a loss of meaning so that lean production finally came to denote productivity gaps that had, of course, existed long before lean came along. Thus, in 2001, Patricia Hewitt, then Secretary of State for Trade and Industry, announced a new 'best-practice' initiative following a report by the Engineering Employers' Federation suggesting that the slow take-up of 'lean manufacturing' practices had left UK productivity lagging behind the US by 25–40 per cent (*Financial Times*, 3 December 2001). Time and hindsight also added confusions through the 1990s. The importance of the Japanese exemplar faded when the Japanese economy turned down at the end of the Hesei boom in the early 1990s and when, more specifically, Japanese car manufacturers did not continue to make major and rapid market-share gains in Europe or the USA over the decade of the 1990s. Nor could Japan be cast as the cause of misfortune when, despite this respite, Western car assemblers remained mired in problems about cyclicality and weak profitability. This, of course, immediately suggests a complicated relationship between effort and reward where it is difficult enough to understand the underlying problems of the business leave alone find and implement epochal change.

## Moving on to a new business model?

The epochal argument has moved on in at least two ways in the decade since Womack et al. was published and debated. First, some of the younger researchers associated with IMVP tried to develop the concept of lean beyond the factory and to move it further along the supply chain; thus Holweg and Pil (2004) have argued that 'build to order' is the new solution necessary after the original lean revolution failed because it was not complete. Second, some of the management consultants have begun to think in more radical terms of a different kind of revolution that would change not factory techniques but the business model and do so in ways that improve not physical productivity but financial performance.

Holweg and Pil, in their 2004 book *The Second Century*, belatedly introduce demand-side factors as they redress the supply side focus of Womack et al. They claim that 'competitive advantage ultimately stems from customer responsiveness' (Holweg and Pil 2004: 4) and argue that lean was always about 'pull' factors or producing a car when needed, not just about waste reduction (2004: 6). The new villain of the piece is the forecast-based model of manufacture which seldom produces the right mix of product (2004: 85) so manufacturers must induce customers to buy their vehicles through discounts and attractive finance packages (2004: 88). The solution is the new economic model of 'build-to-order' which can reconnect the consumer and the value chain, thus improving service and reducing the need to finance inventory as sales become more profitable for assembler and dealer (Holweg and Pil 2004: 100–1).

The familiar rhetorical devices are then used by Holweg and Pil. (Bad) demand forecasting is contrasted with (good) build-to-order as manufacturers have a clear choice: 'either a) sell as many cars as can be sold with the liberal use of incentives and stock holding or b) sell fewer cars at higher price by meeting customers' needs' (Holweg and Pil 2004: 81). The empirical supporting evidence is fragmentary and selective as figures from a variety of sources are used to suggest build-to-order would generate large potential savings, estimated by Goldman Sachs to be $1,200 per vehicle (2004: 85). All this has limited persuasive value because Holweg and Pil provide no example of brilliant company success that can confidently be attributed to the new techniques; in the world of build-to-order there is nothing that corresponds to Toyota's Takaoka factory in the world of lean; and this in turn means Holweg and Pil are much more exposed to critical objections about, for example, their neglect of the second-hand market.

The Holweg and Pil book is of interest mainly to those who are interested in why most business-school books are not best-sellers and why it is so difficult to repeat Womack et al.'s success by writing what Orwell (1968) might have called 'a good bad book'. In the larger scheme of things, what is on the airport bookstand also probably now matters rather less. From the later 1990s, the notion of a break with the past and the possibility of a different future is now often envisioned not in academic books but in consultants' reports, and these circulate in rather different ways.

A good example here would be the AT Kearney Indego project, led by the (then) Vice-President of the Kearney automotive practice, Steve Young, along with the former President of Ford Europe, Martin Leach. They start from the financial problem that 'shareholder returns for auto companies lag behind other industries' and set out to address the question: 'If you could invent the automotive industry without the existing constraints, what would it look like?' (AT Kearney 2004a: 25–6). The answer was 'Indego, the hypothetical company . . . that could provide you with an enhanced mobility service more economically than you could imagine, and yet make more money than any other car manufacturer' (AT Kearney 2004a: 25). Their full report is intended both for the car companies and those outside the industry: this latter group, in fact, are seen as having the advantage in taking the Indego concept forward because new entrants do not have the massive 'cost baggage (such as retiree health costs)' of the incumbents (AT Kearney 2004a: 26). A press campaign of placed stories and interviews was used to market the report and to stoke corporate interest in new business models, not simply for the auto sector, but apparently for 'just about any other well-established industry' (AT Kearney 2004a: 30). (See, for example, *The Economist*, 4 September 2004, *Automative News Europe*, 19 April 2004, *Financial Times*, 20 April 2004, *Telegraph*, 25 April 2004.)

The Indego concept is interesting, not so much because of its impact on the industry, but because the AT Kearney report and the related press coverage shows how Womack et al. are already passé. The Womack et al. 1980s' vision of productive transformation in the interests of all stakeholders has now become the Kearney early 2000s' vision of a new business model in the interests of corporate shareholders. Womack et al. addressed an earlier concern with Japanese manufacturing success and explained how Western companies might emulate the underlying organizational models and arrest decline in the interests of all stakeholders. The resulting public-interest issue of lean production attracted a diverse audience including business-school lecturers, government officials, managers and journalists. It also prompted strong criticism and resistance from unionists including the UAW's eight-week strike at two of GM's Flint, Michigan plants where just-in-time, lean-production techniques were introduced (Babson 2001).

However, work intensification on the Japanese model in Western factories is no longer a high-profile issue partly because the export of Western service and manufacturing jobs to China and India is seen as inevitable. Indego is a project for a 'next generation' car company because it adjusts to these new assumptions. It explicitly moves away from a focus on 'selling cars' (AT Kearney 2004b: 3) and also envisages the outsourcing of manufacturing to low-wage countries with small-scale 'flat-pack' final assembly close to the high-income market (*The Economist*, 4 September 2004, *Financial Times*, 20 April 2004). Womack et al.'s preoccupation with comparative physical productivity in assembly becomes more or less irrelevant. Indeed, according to the *Financial Times*, Indego-type 'production would actually be slightly more expensive than the big factories' (20 April 2004), and there is more emphasis on non-manufacturing issues such as lack of IT and the patchily linked design and distribution processes (*Autocar*, 20 July 2004). Indego's promoters, however, assert that 'this "next generation car company" generates a return on sales of around 22 per cent, compared with an industry average of around 6 per cent' (AT Kearney 2004a: 27), which can be achieved, not by selling cars, but by providing 'an all-inclusive package of premium product and services on an ongoing leasing basis for a daily fee of between US$7 and US$16' (AT Kearney 2004a: 27).

This alternative view of the product as a bundle of mobility goods and services is at the heart of Young and Leach's 'new business model', a term that corresponds to Womack's 'lean factory'. '[Car] companies would offer an enhanced mobility service including all existing auto-related services such as finance, insurance and maintenance, with cars leased over an eight-year period (to several customers in succession) before being scrapped' (AT Kearney 2004a: 28). This mobility package would also include a range of exciting new options including high-tech services such as paying for petrol via mobile phone or the ability to download music direct through Indego to signify and augment the sense of novelty (*Autocar*, 20 June 2004). The contrast between old and new business model was taken up in the press. For example, *Automotive News Europe* on 19 April 2004 cited both authors of the concept: 'The financial performance of the auto industry is constrained by the current business model' (Stephen Young); and 'By taking a ground-up view, it has enabled us to achieve a business model that could achieve substantially better returns than are achieved in the volume business today and at relatively low levels of scale' (Martin Leach).

However, while such claims were dutifully repeated, the Indego story was generally reported without the proselytizing enthusiasm that accompanied the earlier hyping of lean production. Perhaps this was because AT Kearney's vision of the break is too radical in its implications for most assemblers and the existing industry. The idea makes for an interesting feature in a business magazine or newspaper but, as a blueprint for transformation, it threatens the existence of the average car assembler. Significantly, AT Kearney's immediate aim is to sell the new business model not to car companies but to a bank/retail financial-services conglomerate or to a credit house such as GE Capital which could supply start-up funding for an operation that could possibly displace giant assemblers from part of the new car market. At the end of 2004, AT Kearney report that Stephen Leach 'recently left . . . to focus on making the Indego concept a reality' (2004a: 31) without apparently joining a car company. While a long way from realization, Indego-type ideas are simply more bad news for the assemblers who stand to lose now from any business-model revolution as they had earlier hoped to win from lean production.

The new ideas once again cast the assemblers in the role of under-achievers, even though the alternative business model with superior returns remains hypothetical. It is perhaps because the major car-assembly firms already have such intractable problems that stock-market analysts downplay the possibilities of transformation and focus instead on developing a more grounded understanding of company performance within the context of continuous and inescapable demand and supply side constraints, as the next section explains.

## ANALYSTS ON CAR COMPANIES: HOW TO BEAT THE MARKET

Most car-company analysts are unconvinced by business-school and consultancy visions of transformation because, as UBS (2004) observes, the car industry is one that perennially lacks 'big picture catalysts' such as consolidation through merger, so that the industry is more likely to reproduce old patterns than transform itself in one great leap forward. From this point of view, car-company analysts also face special difficulties that are different from those facing pharma-company analysts, who until recently believed they had a clear understanding of the industry, company business models and the pipeline that made future developments predictable. The problem for car-company analysts is that they do not have a clear list of variables and mechanical relations determining company prospects and thus this group of analysts finds itself in the position of horse-racing tipsters.

It may be useful to begin by recapitulating our analysis of the pharmaceutical industry where, until recently, analysts and investors believed in a transparency and predictability that allowed them to see well into the future. All companies could potentially benefit from an overall market for ethical (i.e. patented prescription only) drugs whose value increased year on year in high-income countries. Market access and prospects for individual companies depended on pipeline and patent expiry considerations which are public knowledge, with changes (for example, expiry of patent on a blockbuster product) often visible from some way off. Most companies with product could manage effective marketing which targeted a small number of high-prescribing doctors. From an analyst perspective this meant that companies, not the industry, were the most appropriate focus of analysis and much of what happened was fairly predictable.

By way of contrast, analysts have long recognized that car assemblers in their industry represent a different set of problems that reflect uncertainties that limit transparency and predictability. Arguably, picking car stocks is rather like picking winners in horse-racing. Here, the list of relevant variables in the next race is uncertain and probably include horse's condition, suitability of ground and distance and the jockey on the day; this futurology intersects with past 'form' which, in the narrow sense, focuses on how the horse was placed last time at the distance and going. All this interacts with the flow of money from other punters which will determine the odds that make a bet worthwhile. In this situation, the racing tipsters can do no more than review a series of relevant variables that in combination could affect the final result and make a guesstimate prediction about the outcome. The prediction of one tipster often disagrees with that of another tipster who weighs variables and combinations differently, and the tipsters do not always agree with the punters, whose failure to demonstrate collective wisdom is evidenced by the fact that favourites win only about one horse race in three.

In analysts' discussions of the cars business, the contextual information (corresponding to form in horse-racing) is supplied by product-market analysis which is essential given the mature, cyclical and competitive nature of the car market. Analysts accept that cyclical variation in the overall demand for cars in the major national markets is central to determining auto-assembler profitability; market segmentation is another important aspect of demand because, in most markets, only a few segments of limited and indirect competition generate reasonable profits. The international company is therefore viewed as a complex structure of (imperfectly understood) cross-subsidies with different elements such as specific segments or national markets contributing variable amounts of profit over the cycle; additional special considerations, such as pension-fund deficits or health-care costs, will intrude as further local complications at specific points.

On this basis, the practical issue arising is how should investor strategy and the analysts' buy–hold–sell recommendations relate to assemblers operating in an industry where individual firm performance is not predictable and collectively assemblers perform poorly. At company level, the car firms are destroyers of value in so far as their average ROCE is low and declining over the past thirty years (Froud et al. 2002b: 19–23). Such assemblers are unlikely to create long-term value through sustained share-price increases in so far as increases in market demand are mainly cyclical not secular. Given these secular and cyclical problems about value creation, the investor's aim must be to find companies whose shares offer opportunities for value-taking before the market once again turns up or down. Such opportunities can be found by reviewing physical and financial evidence on company performance and management guidance so as to identify relevant information which is apparently not already in the price. This approach licenses a fairly aggressive attitude to share-trading by investors who eschew 'buy to hold' and instead pursue 'rent not buy' investor strategies.

To illustrate the analyst's approach, we draw on a range of reports on European and US companies and specifically on the classic work of Gary Lapidus, currently of Goldman Sachs (and previously of Bernstein Research), who originally developed the analysis of Ford and GM as structures of cross-subsidy. Lapidus was identified as the top US auto and auto-parts analyst of 2003 by Bloomberg (Peltz 2004), and he is consistently ranked amongst the top three auto analysts in *The Institutional Investor*. Along with Morgan Stanley's Stephen Girsky, Lapidus represents the most authoritative and influential US analyst voice within the sector. In Europe, no analyst has quite the same established prestige, but Stephen Cheetham of Sanford C. Bernstein can be considered one of Europe's leading analysts.

## Product market cyclicality and the company as a structure of cross-subsidies

For most analysts, product-market analysis is the fundamental behind every recommendation. In mature markets with limited secular growth and strong cyclicality, variation in overall demand is an important driver of earnings; the individual company's segment profile and its portfolio of national markets are also significant because analysts recognize that giant companies such as Ford and GM are complex structures of cross-subsidy.

Any review of US car sales since the late 1970s shows limited secular growth in overall demand and strong cyclicality. Cars are big-ticket items for most households whose purchase can be deferred in times of economic recession, with a subsequent surge of purchases in the upturn (Lapidus and Mohsenian 1998: 22). This results in a cyclical demand pattern, as can be seen from the US sales volume data in Exhibit C2.2 which, taking the cars and light trucks market as a whole, shows clear cyclical sales peaks in 1973, 1978, 1986 and 2000, and troughs in 1982 and 1991. US and European assembler earnings have historically closely follow the demand cycle because, with a strongly unionized workforce, labour is effectively a fixed cost that must be spread over fewer units whenever sales fall. In any downturn, revenues fall faster than costs, which reduces profit in a way that often moves assembly operations from profit into loss (Exhibit C2.3). Lapidus and Mohsenian's (1998: 28) analysis of the 'Big Three' US auto assemblers' (Ford, Chrysler and GM) long-term performance suggests an interesting relationship between operating profit and US auto demand as illustrated in Exhibit C2.3. This shows Ford's automotive-division profit between 1980 and 2003 compared with the US market and suggests that variation in profit is much more pronounced than the cyclicality of demand that is such an important driver.

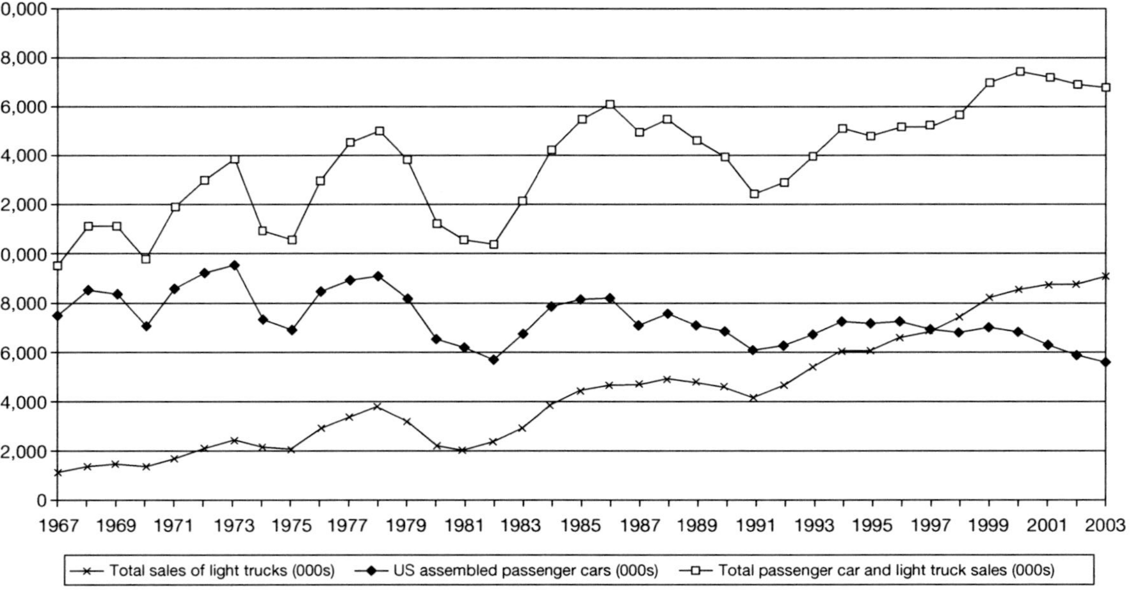


***Exhibit C2.2*** *US auto market sales split by passenger cars and light trucks (000s), 1967–2003*

*Source*: US Bureau of Economic Analysis

*Note*: Data on vehicle sales has not been seasonally adjusted

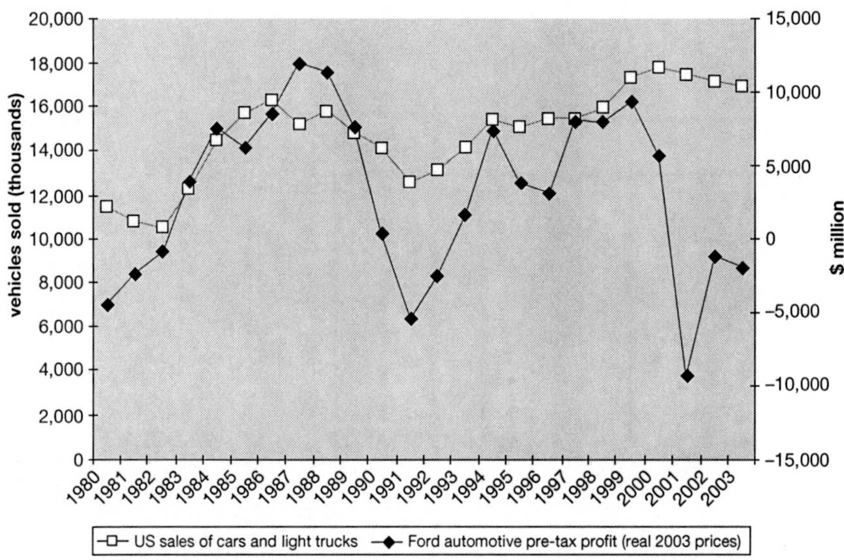


**Exhibit C2.3** *US car and light truck market compared with Ford automotive pre-tax profit, 1980–2003*

*Source*: US Bureau of Economic Analysis; Company Annual Report and Accounts, various years

These relations are so important that most analysts believe that any stock recommendation should start from where the industry is in its cycle (see, for example, UBS 2004: 5). While Womack et al. or AT Kearney dream of a different future after the break, analysts assume and argue that cyclicality is a permanent feature of consumer demand for cars in the mature high-income markets of Europe and America. Indeed, Lapidus gives several reasons why cyclicality is likely to persist or even get worse. First, there is little future growth in the huge but mature North American market where there are already 2.3 vehicles for every multi-person household, 1.0 vehicle for every person old enough to drive and 1.1 vehicles per licensed driver (Lapidus 1997: 17). Second, technological advance has produced more durable vehicles and has extended useful vehicle life, which allows longer ownership terms and creates a growing fleet of second-hand vehicles that can substitute for new cars. In 1970, the average vehicle had been on the road for 5.8 years and only 32 per cent of vehicles were older than seven years; whereas by 1997 the average vehicle was 8.2 years old and 55 per cent were over seven years old (Lapidus 1997: 18).

Because demand cyclicality is crucial in the auto industry, analysts devote a significant portion of their reports to analysing industry trends but without reaching any fixed conclusion about turning points and implications. As analysts framed it in the 1990s, the key imponderable then was the difficulty of predicting the exact point at which 'pent-up' consumer demand had been released or exhausted and hence determining when the 1990s' upswing would stall and the market would turn down. Even the most prestigious analysts get turning points wrong, as Lapidus did in 1997 (1997: 15) when he argued that North American trend demand had stalled and pent-up demand was already exhausted although, in the event, US unit sales continued to grow right up until 2001. Uncertainty about the existence of pent-up demand continues to figure in a range of more recent reports (see, for instance, Samsung Securities 2003, Deutsche Bank 2003a, UBS 2004).

Analysts have often tried to reduce uncertainty about future demand by identifying one leading indicator which predicts trends in demand. Thus, National Bank Financial (2004) use consumer confidence/sentiment indicators to predict demand; Deutsche Bank (2004a) focuses on the importance of personal disposable income and interest rates; while Prudential (1999b) examined interest rates and the relation between auto and total industry production. Just like the horse-racing tipsters, every analyst has his or her technical system but this is of limited help given that the future may not be like the past. Thus, for many analysts, as for tipsters, past results are observed and understood but predictions must rely as much on informed guesswork and instinct as on sophisticated models or systems.

Whilst overall demand is important for analysts, cyclical variation in volume is not the only key variable because company presence in different segments, the portfolio of national markets and the contribution of car finance also drive earnings. Disaggregated analysis of performance in different markets is then informative because different activities generate diverse levels of profit and make various contributions over a cycle; a financially robust assembler would then have a portfolio of markets and should be able to find strength elsewhere when it hits problems in one market. For analysts, such considerations have become increasingly important in the past decade because few assemblers are robust. Increased segmentation and intensifying competition in mass-market segments together ensure that many assemblers now effectively operate via precarious cross-subsidy with a few more profitable segments supporting many weakly profitable and loss-making areas. Thus, assembler earnings not only track overall volume but also reflect changes in the profitability of product mix (Lapidus and Mohsenian 1998: 1), which analysts routinely describe as 'positive or negative', 'good or bad', 'rich or poor'.

From this point of view, analysts tend to bracket groups of companies that fit together in terms of their segment portfolios, though this is complicated when, as in the case of Volkswagen AG or DaimlerChrysler, the company often includes several brands with different market portfolios and segment profiles But, there are some clear-cut cases, principally Toyota and Honda who both depend on profits from sedan/saloon sales in the USA or Ford, GM and Chrysler who depend on profits from pick-ups and sport utilities. In classic 1990s' work on the US assemblers (Ford, GM and then Chrysler), Lapidus (1997) and Lapidus and Mohsenian (1998) highlighted the role of segment profits from light trucks and pioneered a cross-subsidy analysis of the Big Three (including then independent Chrysler) and then of the two giant US assemblers (Ford and GM). Analysts now recognize that both these two US giants have operated three forms of cross-subsidy: first, in segment terms, cars have been subsidized by trucks; second, in national market terms Europe has been subsidized by the USA; and, third, in divisional terms, autos have been subsidized by finance.

Table C2.1 (in the appendix to this case, p. 285) shows that the US auto market may be overall mature, slow-growing and cyclical but it also divides into two major segments (cars and light trucks) with very different growth trajectories. Light trucks (mainly full-size pick-ups and sport utilities) have increased their share of the value of all US auto sales in every year since 1990, accounting for more than half of total value in every year since 1996, and light trucks outsold cars on volume in 2000. The US car market has been flat with sales of just over 8 million in every year since 1991 because this is a pure replacement market (Lapidus and Mohsenian 1998: 11 and 14). Excess competition and price competition via incentives explains the lack of any rise in real price per car since 1990, as illustrated in Exhibit C2.4 and Table C2.2 (p. 286). Light trucks on the other hand have experienced secular growth, with demand outstripping supply. This, plus the reinvention of the truck as a more fashionable product, reduced the need for financial incentives to push new truck sales and so average prices have increased. At the same time, the longer product life cycles and cheaper development costs per unit tend to increase margins on trucks, enhancing their attractiveness to car companies.

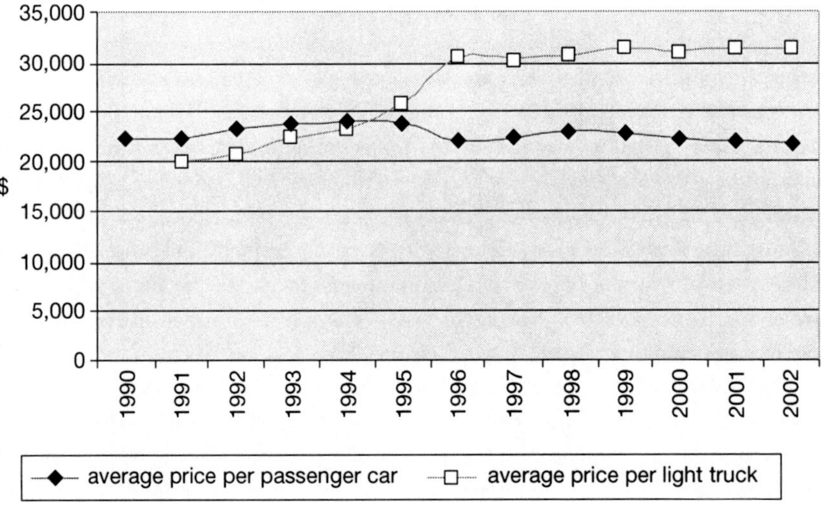


***Exhibit C2.4*** *Average vehicle prices in the US market, 1990–2002 (in real 2003 prices)*

*Sources*: BEA, interactive tables, Annual Abstract of Statistics of the United States, AutoExec (May 2004) and National Accounts of OECD Countries, 1990–2002

*Notes*: Passenger cars include station wagons. Light trucks are those up to 14,000 pounds gross vehicle weight, including mini-vans and SUVs. Prior to the 2003 Benchmark Revision, light trucks were up to 10,000 pounds. Sales figures include US sales of vehicles assembled in the USA, Canada, and Mexico. The prices are those received by the dealer (not the assembler) and are net of any incentives or other discounts. Average prices are weighted on the basis of each model in the category

If the US Big Three were struggling also-rans against the Japanese in cars, the US firms completely dominated the expanding category of full-size trucks so that, from the early 1990s, the 'flood of light truck profits [cover] the losses in highly unprofitable passenger car lines' (Lapidus and Mohsenian 1998: 8, 10). According to Lapidus's estimates, in 1997, the Big Three made $22,258 million operating profit on trucks compared with an operating loss of $10,374 million on cars, with small cars alone losing $5,323 million (1997: 10). More recent reports on the sector suggest that little has changed so that trucks remain a crucial source of profit and cross-subsidy. For example, despite an overall negative assessment, Deutsche Bank (2003b) report positively on the consumer trends in light trucks, whilst Bear Stearns (2000: 14) emphasize the importance of trucks to Ford's North American performance.

The portfolio of national and regional markets is also important in both the Ford and GM cases, with Europe a source of weakness for both firms. GM has historically made better margins on European cars than US cars, but its Opel/Vauxhall subsidiary is now loss-making while Ford's blue-oval European operations have made no money since the early 1990s and have long been dependent on cross-subsidy. Most analysts believe the European market is more difficult than the US market. Lapidus (1997: 36) argues that this is largely because Europe is a market of 'unmatched competitive intensity' due in part to stronger price competition from indigenous and often politically protected assemblers, as well as the presence of a strongly unionized labour force that limits efforts to improve margins via cost-cutting. The inclusion of Europe in the Ford and GM portfolio is thus seen as a source of weakness and potential (if not need) for cross-subsidy. Thus, a recent broker report downgraded US auto assemblers to 'underweight' arguing that, 'the European market will continue to be a challenge for both Ford and GM, despite the introduction of several new products, as this market has become increasingly competitive – particularly in the C-segment (Ford Focus, Opel Astra to name two)' (Bear Stearns 2004).

Analysts recognize a third element of cross-subsidy from auto finance and other non-core activities to autos and total earnings. Analysts generally discuss finance with less informed conviction and enthusiasm than production, and this suggests that analysts are, like most car-company managers, preoccupied with a petrol head agenda about product and process; and, more generally, as our GE case shows, industrial company and sector analysts are fazed by the complications of finance activity. Discussion of finance is indeed a relatively new development in analyst reports on Ford. When Ford had negative operating income at group level in 1991–2, our review of major reports by analysts showed that they either ignored Ford Credit or mentioned it in passing in one or two lines without discussing its overall contribution to the bottom line. This survey covered broker reports over ten pages for Deutsche Bank, Dean Witter Reynolds, Smith Barney Citigroup, Prudential Equity, Paine Webber Inc. & Kidder, Peabody & Co. Inc. between 1991 and 1992, available via the Investext database. Although Ford Credit was mentioned in a few of these reports, it was only usually given one or two lines and not discussed within the context of cross-sbsidizing he auto segment or its overall contribution to group profits. In the early 2000s, substantial twenty-five page-plus reports by Lehman Brothers (2000) or Bear Stearns (2000), still look solely at production and ignore car-company finance arms. Others, such as Morgan Stanley (2002) have latterly analysed auto production and finance independently, dedicating a separate report to GM and Ford's finance subsidiary so that Bank One, Americredit, Citigroup and other finance houses can be used as comparators.

To be fair, analysts find it much harder to understand the relationship between auto assembly and finance divisions than to compare stand-alone US and European geographic divisions. The current state of knowledge is summarized in Lapidus's reports of the later 1990s, when finance contributed 54 per cent of Ford's and 28 per cent of GM's net income in 1996. For Lapidus (1997: 77) the earnings of auto assemblers can only be understood after analysis of the contribution of credit subsidiaries. The margins on credit activities are both higher and more stable so that revenues from credit act as an important cushion against the cyclicality of assembly (see also Credit Suisse 2004c). However, this benefit comes at a cost because market share in credit is bought by increasingly aggressive loan policies that result in lower credit quality, higher credit losses and declining returns on assets (Lapidus 1997: 78). Finance also leaves companies more exposed to new risks on interest rates and credit ratings that affect the cost of borrowing. The growing substitution of leasing for instalment loans makes things worse because, *inter alia*, auto companies are now exposed to falling residuals in the second-hand market (Lapidus 1997: 81).

## Investor strategies and beating the (capital) market

The question of investor strategy was historically not an issue for the analysts of a cash-generative growth industry such as pharmaceuticals, because those investors who wished to make money could do so by buying and holding shares in quality companies with good late pipelines and limited exposure to patent expiry. This only works as long as such companies can be found. But in car assembly, analysts must start from the opposite supposition because most assemblers do not offer sustained earnings growth and solid margins that justify buying to hold. Thus, auto analysts have to face the question of how investors can hope to make money from the rather discouraging fundamentals about declining, precarious and fluctuating profits determined by intense competition and market cyclicality.

Earnings cannot justify holding auto shares long term, when cyclicality makes earnings slim and precarious and when analysts calculate that ROCE in the whole auto sector has been declining over the past twenty-five years: Ford and GM had post-tax returns on capital employed of just 3–4 per cent between 1989 and 2000 and both companies resisted any pressures to raise pay out ratios because they wished to conserve cash reserves

(Froud et al. 2002b: Tables 5 and 6, appendix). Auto stocks usually trade at a P/E discount to the Dow Jones Industrial Average (Fahey 2003) and, in terms of share-price appreciation, few Western car companies do better than the relevant national index of giant companies and many do worse for quite long periods of time; as Exhibit C2.5 shows, in the long run from the late 1980s to 1998, Ford shares just about track the index and GM shares do a little worse in the 1990s. But, importantly, these long-run graphs also understate the significant short-term movement in the shares of Ford and other auto companies, and this creates an opportunity to beat the capital market. Thus UBS concluded a report on Ford and GM with the following summary:

> We believe the share's volatility, combined with severely limited secular growth potential, stand to make the stocks poor long-run investments . . . but also reasonably attractive trading vehicles . . . Obviously beta is a significant driver of short-term returns, but sector-specific factors like volume trends and company performance can create separate timing opportunities.
>
> (UBS 2004: 4)

Analysts understand the cyclical timing opportunities in a stereotyped way within an industry frame where demand upswing translates directly into early cycle booms in auto stock prices followed by lacklustre performance. Thus, Lapidus (1997: 86) shows that during the early cycle boom of recovery from the trough of the 1991–2 recession up to 1994, Chrysler shares rose 740 per cent, Ford rose 160 per cent and GM rose 80 per cent relative to the market. In the next three-year phase of consolidation, as demand plateaus at higher levels of demand between 1994 and 1997, Chrysler shares slid 75 per cent, Ford slid 45 per cent and GM slid 85 per cent relative to the market as shareholders sold up to avoid being left holding the stock in the downturn. This 'early cyclical' analysis does not so much provide solutions as create new problems for several reasons: first, as we have already noted, analysts and others find it very difficult to call the crucial turning points in market demand because nobody has an adequate model of market demand; second, if investor strategies were geared to early cyclical recovery, analysts and their reports would only be required for one or two years every decade.

This explains the professional interest of auto-industry analysts in more active trading strategies geared to events and information that is not yet in the price but is (this week) being divulged to all those who read the analyst report. Here again, the analogy with horse-racing tipsters is illuminating. Picking stocks to beat the capital market is just like getting good odds on an unfancied horse and investors in auto stocks must be able to spot the winner before other investors catch on and ensure that the general expectation of future performance is in the price. In autos, this often translates into 'buy company failure and sell company success'. Thus, in autumn 2004, a Bernstein Research Call rated troubled VW as 'outperform' with upside potential in the belief that the bad news was all in the price; whereas one week later (2004a), Bernstein's verdict on Renault was

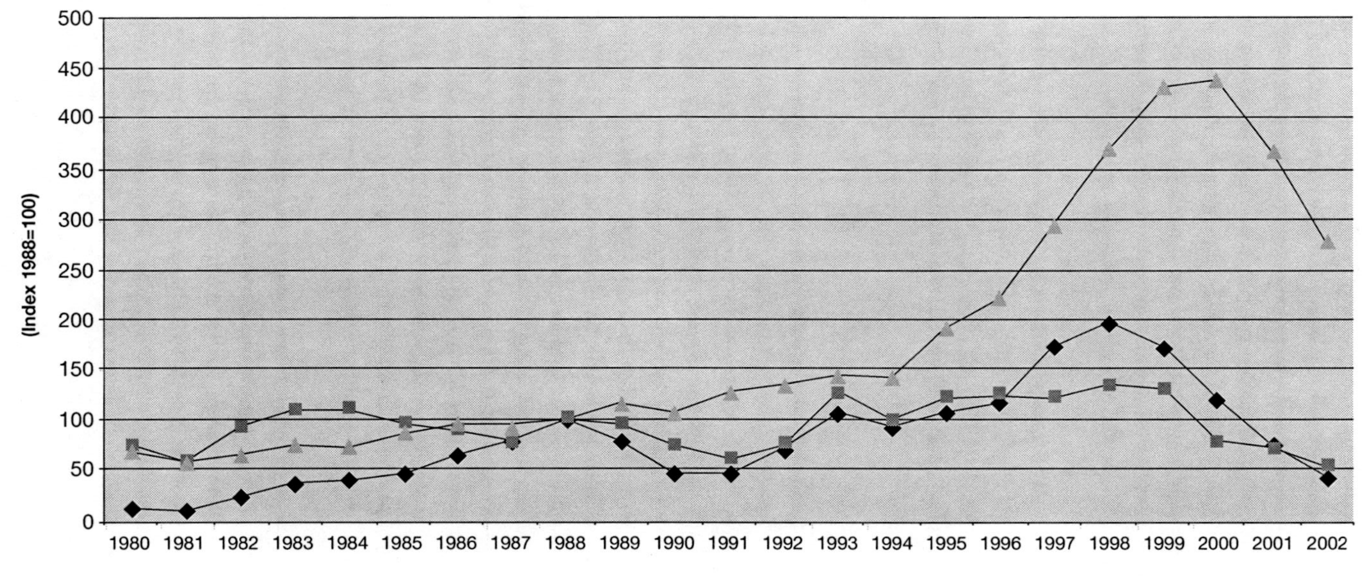


***Exhibit C2.5*** *Ford and GM market value compared with the S&P 500, 1980–2002*

*Source*: Compustat

*Notes*: The series for Ford, GM and the S&P 500 are indexed using 1988=100. All market values are based on share prices at the year end

'underperform' because the good news is already in the price so that there is little room for further improvement:

> With both earnings and stock price depressed, VW has many of the characteristics of a good automotive investment. It is cheap, ugly and unloved – yet its fundamentals are adequate and better 2005 earnings are likely to be driven by new product launches in North America. We reiterate our outperform rating.
>
> (Bernstein Research Call 2004a)

> Should investors in Renault hold on for yet more good news or look to take profits? The key issue in our view is Renault's core operating margin, which is now equal to historic peaks: further upside requires belief in structural change resulting in durably superior profitability . . . the probability of the company reinventing the European car industry seems low . . . We rate Renault underperform.
>
> (Bernstein Research Call 2004b)

For auto-industry investors, timing is the key, and auto-industry analysts do not have to fear unemployment and redundancy because the industry is usually somewhere around the mid-point of the cycle and institutional investors are therefore generally in need of more analyst reports to clarify the timing issues and to identify the company share to buy (which is about as much of a sure thing as the tipster's prediction for the winner of tomorrow's 2.30 p.m. jump race at Aintree). As analysts CJ Lawrence (1994) explained in the mid-1990s, 'because we are currently at the midpoint of the cycle, stock selection is critical . . . [because] auto shares do not necessarily peak at the same time nor do they always plateau prior to the cycle peak'.

The search for variables that are not in the price focuses on a number of stereotyped key indicators and relations that recur in various reports on different companies. In a recent report on US autos, Deutsche Bank (2004a) highlight three key relations:

1. Volume produced by the assembler versus actual demand: are car assemblers such as Ford and GM over- or under-producing for the current market?
2. Pricing versus inventories: if over-producing, do assemblers need to discount further to push product?
3. Product mix versus 'externals' : how do variables (such as interest or exchange rates) outside the control of management impact on the controllable?

Within this frame, Deutsche Bank in 2004, for example, focuses on externals in relation to Ford and GM's credit business because 'the risk that interest rates move higher in 2004 presents a significant risk to . . . earning power as interest expense or cost of funds is their largest expense' (2004a: 14).

The new model pipeline is a perennial in analysts' reports, with some expectation that manufacturers should changeover 16–20 per cent of volume per year (Prudential 1999a:

4). The argument here is complicated by uncertainty as to how new models will sell, but many analysts believe their role is to identify 'sweetpoints' when popular models are updated, thus reinvigorating demand. Hence, a recent report that reported positively on BMW: 'we are fast approaching the critical changeover on the 3-Series, the majority of group sales in past model generations and even now 40 per cent of a much diversified group production. This 2Q05E renewal will propel BMW to a best-ever product age of just 1½ years' (Citigroup Smith Barney 2004: 3).

Much of this consists of analyst commentary on the stylized facts in a world where upcoming launch dates are nowadays public knowledge and are listed in enthusiast magazines. But such reports are also part of a two-handed game played by analysts and companies who can pitch and spin in a way that influences recommendations. Thus UBS notes that dividend increases are used by management to signal that the company is now on a recovery trajectory: 'automakers dividend prospects are one of the best catalysts for share price performance . . . A particularly strong buy signal is generated by the first dividend increase for the cycle' (2004: 5). Equally, investors are reassured when companies such as Ford or GM maintain dividends through a downturn when profits evaporate, because this signals the company's belief in the temporary nature of the difficulties.

Within the US and UK system of reporting, quarterly reports provide useful information on current progress, and management guidance is also important as a source of information about new models and initiatives and the relation between market demand, inventories, production schedules and discounts. In reporting all this, companies are typically very cautious and understated because their basic principle is *no surprises*. When uncertainty is high, the unexpected can unsettle investors even when it represents good news, if analysts are either suspicious of or simply confused about the drivers and levels of performance (Golding 2001: 174–6).

Much management guidance is therefore vaguely reassuring but frustratingly inexplicit so that analysts put much effort into working out its Delphic meaning. Thus, a recent Credit Suisse report on GM explained,

> the run rate for the first 6 months of the year is about 16.5 million [units] . . . the second half will have to 'pick up the pace' to quote GM's Paul Ballew. We would interpret that comment as foreshadowing a rise in incentive levels, which would be consistent with the pattern over the past couple of years.
>
> (2004b: 2)

Similarly a 2004 analyst meeting at Ford left the Credit Suisse analyst looking for 'guidance on the guidance' (Credit Suisse 2004a: 1), while Deutsche Bank read the meeting as a game of double bluff:

> There was no news out of the Ford analyst meeting in Detroit yesterday. We thought that management's tone was relatively cautious . . . We believe management's

> cautiousness reflects their concern about Street expectations possibly getting ahead of reality . . . While we believe that Ford has left a significant cushion in its guidance . . . we are maintaining our estimates and our sell recommendation.
>
> (2004b: 1)

Against this background, when all the numbers have been crunched and the guidance has been pondered, instinct and intuition rather than analysis are crucial for most auto analysts (just as they are for most tipsters). Here, for example, is the doyen of European analysts reflecting on how Renault's margins over the past few years owe much to the success of one model, the Scenic Midi MPV introduced in 1997:

> the Scenic is undoubtedly a good product . . . but in our view its hard to make a case for the product's going on forever. In other words the bull case has no more analytical grounding than the bear case, and given the money is on the table today in the shape of a record stock price, we would be inclined to take it and run. This is the key element in our 'sell' recommendation.
>
> (Bernstein 2004b)

Overall, because the relationship between effort and reward is uncertain, analysts cannot be sure that a particular move at a specific point in time will deliver useful benefits for the company in terms of sales, margins or whatever. And, of course, this in turn implies that corporate managements in car firms can never be sure just how analysts and other commentators will respond to their narratives, actions and results.

## CEOS, STRATEGIZED DIFFERENCE AND ENACTMENT

If academic and consultancy visions of transformation do not engage analysts more mundanely preoccupied with what's in the price, the CEOs of companies such as Ford produce a kind of third-way narrative that represents a neither/nor response to these alternatives. The inauguration of a new CEO is in itself an important event in an S&P 500 or FTSE 100 company, given the status of the CEO as the constitutional monarch of the giant company whose reign is likely to last for more than five years. In struggling companies such as Ford, the incoming CEO must promise to make a strategized difference and improve hitherto-mediocre results without offering a transformation that media and analysts would find implausible. The result is often a vague prospectus that reflects the conventional wisdom of the age both because that is safe and because, practically, there is no time for developing detailed plans or testing alternatives.

This section considers the prospectuses produced by two successive Ford CEOs: from 1999 to 2001 the CEO was Jacques Nasser, who promised to make a difference by adding consumer services; whereas his successor Bill Ford promised to get back to basics with a prospectus about product and process. Such visions are interesting because they are quasi-performative as much as narrative, that is, they are partly about what the new CEO does as well as what he says through media interviews. If the new CEO must make some moves that are coherent with the announced strategy, the Ford case suggests that the moves often represent symbolic enactment rather than what strategy texts call 'implementation' because the company makes other moves that are not obviously coherent with the new strategy. Unfairness is another recurrent element because the new CEOs vision of difference is often not generous about the achievements of the previous CEO as well as being disingenuous about the persistence of long-run constraints.

Thus, we should begin by noting that Ford's CEO for most of the 1990s was Alex Trotman under whom the company prospered so that it was seen by most analysts as a better company than GM. Ford recovered from the early 1990s downturn, rode the light truck boom and maintained its position in services through Ford Credit and Hertz car rentals so that the company was able to build substantial cash reserves in anticipation of another downturn. Trotman apparently also understood strategized management. His Ford 2000 programme was about redesigning process and product so that the company could save costs globally by platform-sharing and switching production between sites with common manufacturing systems (*Financial Times*, 16 November 1998). When Trotman retired at the end of 1998, Ford was somewhere near a cyclical peak and Wall Street was generally pleased with Ford's financial results (*Financial Times*, 16 November 1998).

## Jacques Nasser and Ford as 'consumer services company'

Trotman's successor Jacques Nasser was (as is usually the case in giant companies) an internal candidate who had joined Ford in 1968 and who had claimed his promotion on the strength of his contribution to the outgoing CEO's programmes; his nickname 'Jacques the Knife' was earned when implementing the Ford 2000 cost-cutting strategy (*Financial Times*, 12 September 1998). Nasser was represented in the business press as a cars and operations man who had done well previously in product development with his input into the European success of the Ford Ka. But, once installed as CEO, Nasser developed a vision of a new strategy for Ford that would position it as a consumer company (not merely a car assembler). While Nasser never blamed Trotman, the implication was that the company now needed to change direction quite radically; Nasser's ideas about reinvention incidentally fitted very well with the later stages of the new economy and the rhetoric about unglued value chains.

Nasser's new strategy never became a programme with a name (like Trotman's Ford 2000 or Bill Ford's Revitalization Plan) and it was never summarized in one Ford document. Instead, his prospectus existed in a rather postmodern way as an assemblage of elements that could be added to and rearranged in a loose and unsystematic discourse. Nasser himself presented this as a virtue: 'You start with a vision to be the world's leading consumer company for automotive services and products . . . I'm not a believer in telling people [exactly] what to do. If you start giving people a cookbook, you start to get very narrow solutions' (Nasser, interviewed in *Business Week*, 11 October 1999).

The forms of dissemination allowed repetition and rearrangement of elements because the strategy was articulated externally in a long series of media interviews that Nasser and his associates gave to the business press and articulated internally through e-mails to employees that also explained the why and the how of the new strategy. The 100,000 Ford employees with office e-mail got a weekly e-mail, 'let's chat about the business', from Nasser (Wetlaufer 1999: 87) and all 350,000 employees worldwide were offered a home PC and Internet access for $5 a month (Ford Annual Report 1999: 3).

The Nasser strategy was always about several (different but not necessarily contradictory) things, including financial literacy and e-commerce. When Nasser summarized his approach for the *Harvard Business Review*, he claimed that Ford 'can't build the company if it holds on to a mind set that doesn't respond swiftly to consumer needs and pay attention to the capital markets' (Wetlaufer 1999: 80). Nasser certainly aimed to build financial literacy in a productionist organization as he encouraged workers to, 'think more like shareholders and develop a consumer headset' (*Financial Times*, 9 August 1999). Over time, new themes were added. Thus, in a later interview, Nasser announced that the development of e-commerce at Ford promised to achieve, 'nothing short of reinventing the auto industry' (*Business Week*, 28 February 2000) and in the 1999 Annual Accounts, the Annual Report quotes Chair Bill Ford announcing that 'the internet will be the moving assembly line of the 21st century' (Ford Annual Report and Accounts 1999: 24).

But the element that attracted the media attention was Nasser's new vision of what we would term a sector-matrix strategy (Froud et al. 1998). Ford was to become a consumer company (not merely a car maker) and it would do this by moving (beyond manufacturing) into services so that the company would become, 'horizontally integrated with the lifeline of the consumer' and where the benefits from marketing would establish 'a long term relationship with the consumer' (*Sunday Times*, 19 September 1999). As Wolfgang Reitzle, the head of its luxury cars division, explained, 'we do not see ourselves as a car company only but the leading consumer company for providing automotive products and services like Ford Credit or Kwik-Fit. And you will see ever more of that in the future' (*Financial Times*, 9 August 1999).

In press interviews, Nasser did not address the issue of how this would transform performance and (quite typically) his prospectus was generally reported, rather than challenged by the journalists in the business press (see, for instance, the *Business Week* story on 11 October 1999). Some analysts and academic commentators were immediately sceptical about whether the strategy would deliver. John Lawson, Head of Automotive Industry Research at Salomon Smith Barney in London explained that he had 'reservations about this strategy' (*Financial Times*, 9 August 1999); the *Financial Times* of 15 November 1999 mentions in passing (unnamed) 'analysts' who were not convinced. Academics such as Froud et al. (2000) explored and questioned the extent to which a services-led strategy could transform the business. By 1999 Ford was assembling more than 7 million autos a year worldwide, had already built a large and profitable adjunct auto-credit business and the overall financial results were mediocre. From this starting point, a sector-matrix transformation of Ford's financial results depended on an unfeasible combination of the unthinkable and the unaffordable: the large-scale divestment or closure of low-return car operations (such as Ford of Europe) remained unthinkable, while Ford could not afford to pay in cash or shares for the large-scale acquisition of profitable service businesses on the scale necessary to counterweight an auto business that assembled 7 million autos a year.

Nasser discursively avoided such awkward issues about the unthinkable and the unaffordable in two ways: first, a corporate move from manufacturing into services was rationalized by asserting that margins in services were higher; second, the strategy of moving into services was symbolically enacted by a few key moves. Nasser did not publicly set out targets on how much rebalancing between manufacturing and services was required nor any scenarios on how much these segments would contribute to the top and bottom line in future years. The move into services was rationalized by arguing that volume manufacturers generally achieved no more than a weak 2 per cent return on sales, whereas a quality service business such as Kwik-Fit in the UK could putatively make 12.5 per cent on sales (*Financial Times*, 13 April 1999). This kind of quasi-justification, which conspicuously ignores ROCE and balance-sheet considerations is commonly used by CEOs of car assemblers eager to diversify out of their unattractive core business. For example, only a few years later Berndt Pischetsrieder at VW was arguing for a push into credit, with the €2.13 billion purchase of Leaseplan, a car-leasing specialist from the Dutch bank, ING, and the possibility of other moves to reshape VW into what he described as a 'global mobility group' that captures more of the supply chain (*Financial Times*, 11 June 2004).

At the same time, Nasser's new strategy was symbolically enacted by moves that suggested a limited commitment to vertically integrated manufacturing and more outsourcing as well as a purposive move into services. Ford announced an experiment in outsourcing assembly at its Brazilian Bahia plant, a story that led to front-page speculation in the *Financial Times* (4 August 1999) about the end of Ford as a car maker.

This was apparently corroborated in 2000 when Visteon, Ford's wholly owned parts operation, was spun off by distributing stock to Ford shareholders. Meanwhile, Ford cooperated with GM and others to set up Covisint, a web-based auto exchange for parts procurement so that it could buy from the cheapest source (and hopefully in due course spin off the business with a lucrative initial public offering).

Ford was at the same time making moves into services. Ford expanded the reach of its credit business (for example, buying Mazda credit), consolidated its success with the introduction of Personal Contract Purchase or leasing for private customers in Europe and developed insurance joint ventures. Ford was also buying into distribution of Ford cars via dealership joint ventures in the UK and 'auto collection' in the USA, as well as developing the Internet for on-line retailing. The company also moved into after-sales service of other brands, such as through the $1.6 billion acquisition of Kwik-Fit in 1999, the UK's leading independent 'fast-fit' chain which retailed tyres, exhausts and batteries for all makes (Ford 1999a). When Kwik-Fit was bought, Ford announced the aim was to use the chain to expand its business in Europe, where it already had outlets in seven countries (*Financial Times*, 13 April 1999).

The much-publicized moves from manufacturing into services were about enactment not implementation. The spin-off of Visteon parts symbolically created a separate share certificate. But the operating businesses and balance sheets of Visteon and Ford remained effectively linked in ways that meant that Ford had much the same responsibilities as in the case of a wholly owned, consolidated subsidiary, except that there was little upside for Ford which had renounced any claim on the profits from Visteon's productivity gains or new contracts with third parties. Though Visteon moved quickly to find new customers, Ford remained the main source of Visteon's contracts, supplying 80 per cent of revenues in 2002 and 76 per cent in 2003 (Ford Annual Report and Accounts 2003: 20). Equally significantly, the terms of the original deal included the crucial guarantee that Visteon's 20,000 UAW members keep the same terms and conditions that they had previously enjoyed as Ford employees and that Ford would also take back these employees if Visteon ran into financial difficulties (*Wall Street Journal*, 14 October 1999, *Business Week*, 21 April 2003: 68). All this implied that Visteon was likely to be a high-cost producer of components and Ford would cover the consequences. The financial cost of ongoing links between Ford and Visteon were later illustrated in late 2003 when Ford agreed to take on $1.65 billion of Visteon's estimated $3 billion post-retirement health-care and life-insurance benefit liabilities (*Wall Street Journal*, 23 December 2003); this prevented financial crisis at the parts maker but contributed to Ford's loss of $793 million in the fourth quarter of 2003 (*Wall Street Journal*, 23 January 2004).

Ford did make some moves, such as the Kwik-Fit purchase, which were coherent with Nasser's services-focused narrative. But these were countervailed by other moves that took the company further into car assembly, through the support and acquisition of a stable of European premium brands. This had started with the $2.5 billion purchase of the Jaguar brand in 1989, which was in need of new processes and a product range. Nasser continued the policy of supporting investment at Jaguar, even though the brand continued to lose money: taking together the original purchase, the subsequent investment (which was at least as large) and the continued losses, *Forbes* (3 January 2000) estimated that Jaguar had cost Ford some $6 billion by 2000. Undeterred by the ongoing problems at Jaguar, Ford under Nasser spent another $10 billion on buying two sub-premium European brands: Ford completed the purchase of Volvo cars for $6.5 billion in March 1999 (*Financial Times*, 9 March 1999) and signed an agreement with BMW for the purchase of Land Rover for €3 billion ($2.8bn) only a year later in March 2000 (*Financial Times*, 18 March 2000).

Ford's new strategy was endlessly rehearsed by Nasser and his senior managers in interviews and motor-show presentations so that even the business press began to dub it a 'mantra' (*Financial Times*, 15 November 1999). As we have noted, the new strategy was symbolically enacted not systematically implemented and the overall result was contradiction and incoherence that more or less guaranteed financial disappointment. Nevertheless, Jacques Nasser talked up the ambition of the new strategy through which Ford suggested it could meet the expectations of every stakeholder including the shareholders: 'Ford wants to become the "and" company that delivers the highest quality products AND the best customer satisfaction AND the best shareholder returns' (Ford 1999b); and 'our goal is to be in the top quartile of S&P 500 companies for shareholder returns over time' (Ford Annual Report and Accounts 1999: 6).

Nasser was sacked on 30 October 2001 with a generous settlement that ensured his silence and prevented his immediate defection to another car firm. Interestingly, it was not the gap between promise and outcome that was his immediate undoing because Nasser had only been in the job for eighteen months and his strategy was no more than a year old. Most of the intended outcomes in his prospectus were still well in the future and the promises of 1999 and 2000 were already history that could be rewritten as and when a revised version of the CEO prospectus was prepared. By mid-2001 Nasser's urgent problem was not strategy but events that would make his reign a brief interlude not a historical period.

The company-specific event was the crisis about roll-over accidents involving the Ford Explorer sport utility vehicle killing or injuring its occupants; the larger home-market event was the 11 September 2001 attacks which generally undermined US consumer confidence and more specifically weakened domestic car and light truck sales so that Ford was forced into offering rebates and incentives which reduced margins. Most of this was bad luck. Certainly, 9/11 and its consequences could not have been foreseen by any corporate strategist or planner, while the problems about Explorer chassis design and tyre quality these had their origins in the Trotman era. But events at Ford through 2001 did create a damaging impression of a company in crisis whose management was responding ineffectually, and that impression was legitimated by Ford's profits collapse, dividend cut and credit down-rating. In an interview reported only a few days before he was sacked in late October 2001, Nasser complained 'what's happening is that people are confusing current events with strategic intent' (*Financial Times*, 24 October 2001) without ever recognizing that such confusion is the norm.

Rollover accidents involving the best-selling Ford Explorer sport utility led to around 600 deaths according to John Lampe, the then Executive Vice-President of Bridgestone (*Financial Times*, 13 September 2000). As the flood of litigation began, there were Congressional inquiries into what Ford knew before it acted, which in turn led to public recrimination between Ford and its tyre supplier (Bridgestone Firestone). Each blamed the other for design and manufacturing faults. In August 2000 Firestone accepted partial responsibility and recalled 6.5 million defective tyres. But the accidents did not stop and, in May 2001, Ford decided to spend $3 billion to recall the remaining 13.5 million Firestone tyres (*Financial Times*, 24 May 2001). This pushed Ford into loss in the second quarter and led to the first dividend cut for a decade (*Financial Times*, 31 October 2001).

Second, after the 9/11 terrorist attacks, GM (which had a relatively strong product line and favourable cost position against Ford) decided to keep the car market going and to increase the pressure on Ford by offering generous incentives, including zero finance, for purchasers of new vehicles (*Financial Times*, 19 December 2001). Ford was forced to follow suit at considerable cost so that in the third quarter it registered an increased loss (*New York Times*, 18 October 2001). The bond and share markets reacted negatively to more bad news: both Moody's and Standard & Poor's downgraded Ford Motor Credit during 2001 (Ford Motor Credit 10K) which made it more expensive for Ford Motor Credit to borrow, while between April and September 2001 Ford's share price was more or less halved to $16 and then halved again by mid-October 2001 to $7.15 (*New York Times*, 30 September 2001, 10 October 2001).

Under pressure of events, it became clear that Nasser had not cultivated enough friends in the Ford family who, as major voting stockholders, could use the financial numbers as an excuse for getting rid of their CEO. This makes the point that managing relationships with influential large stockholders can be quite as important as generating narrative or confirming numbers in strategy after financialization.

The A and B share system with differential voting rights had been designed to give the Ford family a continuing voice in the firm's affairs that was out of all proportion to their share of the equity: although Ford family members held only around 5.8 per cent of the equity in 2001, they controlled some 40 per cent of the voting stock and three seats on a board with fourteen members (*Business Week*, 23 December 2003). While many founding families lose effective power through feud and division in the second and third generation, the Ford family is organized to act collectively: the thirteen members of the fourth generation apparently hold biannual meetings to discuss issues and to try to ensure that their shares are effectively voted as a block (Sherrin 2000). For most of the company's 100-year history, the public company has also been headed by a family member. From the mid-1990s the family had, according to Sherrin's interviews with Ford family members, 'began plotting' to find a suitable family member to head the company after Alex Trotman (then CEO and Chairman) retired. After some disagreement with Trotman about the succession, a compromise was reached whereby the career manager Jacques Nasser became CEO and the family's candidate William Clay (Bill) Ford became Chairman, splitting the two roles in a way that is (still) quite unusual in the USA.

At the same time, Nasser had also made enemies amongst other Ford stakeholder groups, including employees, suppliers and dealers who disliked his toughness and cost-cutting strategies and could express their discontent to the Ford family who have grandee status for other stakeholders. It was for example, widely seen as a mistake to press ahead with a GE-style management-appraisal scheme that threatened established, white middle-aged staffers because two successive C grades in appraisal put them at risk of demotion or termination (*Wall Street Journal*, 2 November 2001). If the family started with a prejudice against Nasser, he blundered by alienating other stakeholders as events and bad luck made all this into a fatal mistake. Nasser did not win enough time to get a financial judgement on his management of the firm for shareholder value because he failed an early political test about mobilizing and retaining the support of influential stakeholders.

## Bill Ford and 'the best cars and trucks'

A two-class system of voting and non-voting shares gave the Ford family board members the leverage to sack Jacques Nasser and to install William Clay (Bill) Ford as CEO. Bill Ford was a family member with limited senior operating experience who played up his lineage by claiming the very day after Nasser's resignation that his own blood was 'Blue Oval-blue' (*Financial Times*, 31 October 2001). This was worth something in Detroit where the second Henry Ford had rescued the failing Ford Company after 1945. Like Henry the second, Bill Ford had limited operating experience and unlike Henry the Second, he became CEO in a much more difficult product market with the business press and the capital market hoping for 'turnaround'. Of course, such expectations can seldom be met in under-performing old companies without fortuitous favourable developments in the product market or transformative acquisitions and divestments, which would usually require adding or subtracting at least 30 per cent of turnover. Without either form of assistance, Bill Ford was always going to struggle and had to hope that his 'revitalization plan' that (in an ostentatious reversal of Jacques Nasser's services strategy) took the company back to basics could at least stop the flow of bad news stories.

In a series of interviews and speeches, Bill Ford and his new lieutenants, such as Nick Scheele, immediately embarked on differentiation through strategy reversal. By implication, the incoming CEO blamed Ford's troubles on Nasser's consumer-services strategy which could be reversed so that Ford would once again become a builder of the best cars and trucks (*Financial Times*, 4 December 2001): 'We pursued strategies that were either poorly conceived or poorly timed. We strayed from what got us to the top of the mountain and it cost us dearly' (Bill Ford, cited in the *Financial Times*, 12 January 2002); and 'This business is about one thing and one thing only: great products . . . [It is] a fundamental truth of our industry. The company with the best cars and trucks wins' (Bill Ford and Nick Scheele, cited in the *Financial Times*, 4 December 2001).

This line was convenient for Bill Ford, unfair to Jacques Nasser and, of course, highly rhetorical. When was the golden age in which Ford had been at the top of the mountain? And how could product-led recovery resolve the endemic problems of cyclicality, overcapacity and price competition that Nasser aimed to sidestep through a service-led strategy?

If Jacques Nasser had an easy time with the media and succeeded in avoiding all the difficult questions about his strategy, the event-led crisis ensured that Bill Ford would have a hard time and could not for long continue extemporizing in interviews. Thus, the Bill Ford prospectus turned into a plan and a crucial presentation on 11 January 2002 when the new CEO and his team explained in detail how their 'revitalization plan' would not only improve Ford's performance but 'turn things around' over the next five years (Ford 2002a). The plan reflected on what had gone wrong and provided a 'back to basics' outline of how the turnaround was to be achieved (Ford 2002b). This plan was inherently problematic because the plan was not a quick fix that offered immediate results. Instead, the Bill Ford plan combined cost reduction and increased investment in ways that immediately confused both capital market and employees and promised distant results. At the same time, the plan made promises about improved financial performance that were not very plausible and that would become hostages to fortune.

Cost reduction would come through plant closure of old blue-oval Ford assembly plants. The revitalization plan offered 35,000 redundancies and five plant closures over three years: this amounted to a 10 per cent cut in the global workforce and a capacity reduction of around 1 million units. In terms of new product development, the revitalization plan also involved substantial higher investment in autos. Ford's capital expenditure of $7 billion a year was to be increased as the company planned to spend $20 billion over five years on new product and plant flexibility (*Business Week*, 19 January 2002). At the forefront of this strategy was the so called Premier Automotive Group (PAG) which was a legacy of Nasser. This division combined Jaguar, Land Rover, Volvo and Lincoln marques and would now give Ford an opportunity to rationalize mechanicals and to sell the same basic platforms with different upmarket body and trim. Crucially, the revitalization plan accepted that blue-oval profitability would not be transformed and promised that PAG would contribute one third of Ford's $7 billion pre-tax profit goal by 2006 (Deutsche Bank 2004c: 2).

This left Ford with a new kind of credibility problem, because nobody outside senior management believed that the sub-premium brands collected together as PAG could deliver profit on this scale: the market was being asked to believe that a rag-bag collection of BMW's struggling competitors could turn in a BMW-style financial performance. The specific promise on the numbers was both Bill Ford's mistake, because it would raise questions in future years about his achievement, and also his hostage, which he had to offer in early 2002 to reassure the market about his purpose. If Nasser's strategy was quite different because he avoided specifics, it is also worth noting that there were strong elements of similarity between Jacques Nasser's thesis and Bill Ford's antithesis in so far as both were about prospectuses that could only be symbolically enacted. If Nasser's fundamental problem was the unfeasible scale of the necessary shift from manufacturing to services, Bill Ford's was the extreme difficulty of labour-shedding.

Prior to the public presentation of the plan in January 2002, Ford's immediate difficulty was a five-year contract with the USA automobile workers' union, the UAW, which prevented plant closures in the US until after September 2003 so that Ford's restructuring was unlikely to take out enough costs to please Wall Street. The UAW was not prepared to give ground and had demonstrated its industrial muscle by fighting long and bitter strikes at Caterpillar through the 1990s and by giving GM a bloody nose in a shorter subsequent strike in Michigan. Against this background, the 35,000 figure for redundancies in the 'revitalization plan' was obtained by including 18,000 redundancies from January 2001 that had already been announced and then by adding further redundancies through to 2004 that had yet to be negotiated. As the US media noted, the 35,000 total was thus ambiguous and overstated the likely impact of the revitalization plan (*Wall Street Journal*, 14 January 2002). As for the 17,000 new redundancies, the first assembly plant closure was scheduled for 2003 in Ontario, Canada. The first US assembly plant (Edison, New Jersey) could not close until 2004, when the then current agreement with the UAW (which effectively prevents plant closure) had expired.

Against a background of media and analyst comment about spin and presentation in the revitalization plan, it was hardly surprising that Bill Ford chose to distance the company symbolically from the consumer-services strategy of Nasser by ostentatiously selling off some service businesses, including Hertz and Kwik-Fit. Most interesting was the sale of Kwik-Fit in 2002. Ford had spent $1.6 billion on buying the chain of exhaust and maintenance outlets, but only three years later claimed that the $505 million sale proceeds represented 'the present market value of the business' (Ford statement, cited in the *Financial Times*, 13 August 2004). The seemingly rapid decline in Kwik-Fit's value could be explained by a combination of factors, including simply paying too much for a business that lent symbolic meaning to Nasser's bold new service strategy. Ford also had to rebate the sale price because the discovery of apparent 'accounting irregularities' at Kwik-Fit helped the private equity acquirer, CVC Capital Partners, to obtain 'a lower price and more preferential terms' (*Financial Times*, 22 July 2002).

If Kwik-Fit illustrates the general problem of delivering the old CEO's prospectus, the involvement of Bill Ford as the new CEO adds another layer of irony to the explicit reversal of strategy. The early 2002 announcement of the 'revitalization plan' was a deliberate attempt to differentiate old and new strategies, old and new CEOs after an interlude that ended badly with Nasser's sacking (and before any clear success could be demonstrated). However, Bill Ford's own position as author of the new production strategy is nicely ironic because, when Nasser was CEO, Bill Ford as Chair of Ford Motor Company was a public advocate of the old sector-matrix services strategy. Thus, in an interview with Martha Sherrin, which appeared in a *New York Times Magazine* article in November 2000, Bill Ford enthusiastically expands on what was then the company narrative: 'Rather than sell vehicles, Ford might rent them by the hour, or even the mile, and provide servicing, insurance, even the fuel. "We're not in the car business, or the truck business," he says. "We're committed to the personal-mobility business" ' (Sherrin 2000). Similarly, in an interview with *Business Week* in 1999, Bill Ford states that 'the board has "never said no to Jac because, frankly, we've bought into the strategy"' (*Business Week*, 11 October 1999).

The implication is that strategy after financialization is partly about knowing when to change one's line and then arguing the opposite case with conviction and no embarrassment. This irony is not captured in discussions of the learning company and means that corporate strategy can be intellectually much more like sectarian Marxist politics of the 1960s than most would suppose; the question of whether or not services are the answer for a struggling car company has echoes of earlier disputes about whether Cuba or Yugoslavia represented socialist models. If Bill Ford finds himself in the position of a commentator who has changed his position, that is partly because (regardless of the CEO and the strategy) the relationship between effort and reward is so uncertain in a company such as Ford. The next section outlines two areas (trucks and credit) where Ford has innovated over the past twenty years, but it also demonstrates the difficulty of turning innovation into financial success in the context of product-market competition and cyclicality and capital-market contingencies.

## TRUCKS AND CREDIT: INNOVATION AND FINANCIAL RESULTS

This section explores the way in which Ford was kept afloat in the 1990s through a variety of innovations whose overall results were disappointing. It is also partly about detaching the idea of innovation from its current associations in classic strategy which regresses 'doing things differently' in two ways. Porter (1985) explicitly refers the reader from innovation to technological change which, within the field of economics, invokes production functions and doing things better via the product market. Prahalad and Hamel (1990) implicitly relate innovation (again in terms of new product) to internal competence which, in an organizational behaviour field, invokes organizational learning and experience.

This section argues that this set of associations in classic strategy mistakes the part for the whole and, specifically in the case of Ford, ignores the role of financial innovation, which is distinct in terms of its character and objectives. Financial innovation is unlike most product-market innovation because it is often ongoing and trajectory-forming, not episodic and reversible, and also because existing competences and experience have a much more limited role than in the case of incremental innovation in most product markets. In terms of objectives, the distinctive functions of innovation after financialization also need to be recognized: in a financialized economy with competitive product markets, corporate innovation is unlikely to be a process involving building better product to delight consumers (and thereby benefit society); instead innovation (productive and financial) is a way of finding cash and profit that gets the company through the year.

On this basis, we would then question the assumption that the innovative sectors are those based around the new technology industries such as pharmaceuticals, biotechnology, digital technologies and telecoms, with supposedly fast-moving process and product-market change. Specifically, it could be argued that, on close inspection, a company such as Glaxo is less innovative than its narrative about research might imply. On the other hand, Ford is considerably more innovative than it appears on the basis of its mediocre financial results: the move into light trucks shows as much or more initiative as any pharma company in developing another me-too product; while the Ford Motor Credit business required continuous innovation to maintain its key contribution in covering weakness in product-market performance and to deal with the complications caused by occasional credit downgrading. Strategy literatures that begin with the result and then, *ex-post*, rationalize success and failure within a frame of reference about positioning or competences, miss all this productive and financial effort. In Ford, the profits from trucks and credit were applied defensively within the structure of internal cross-subsidies so that the company was simply running hard to stand still.

The analysis of Ford's financial innovation also provides a basis for comparisons with GE, our third case, which is, from this point of view, another industrial company that added finance. In these cases the addition of finance put the two firms on different trajectories as cash and profits from finance provided a good deal of the basis for GE's brilliant success, whereas they did no more than cover weakness elsewhere at Ford. Many of the differences can be attributed not to execution but to the difference of starting point. GE started with a diverse set of quality industrial businesses and a triple-A credit rating that allowed it to build a portfolio of finance businesses where it could decide freely what activities to enter and leave; Ford's decisions were often reactive and determined by circumstances such as credit downrating.

## Product innovation and light trucks

To begin with product innovation: as a rule of thumb, any volume auto assembler must now do one of two things if it wants to make decent margins from auto product. The first objective in market terms is to find a sheltered segment where the profits are divided between two or three dominant players, because margins are almost always destroyed in autos when five or more players compete aggressively for volume. The second overlapping objective in product terms is to innovate and introduce upmarket or differently packaged product, as Chrysler did with mini-vans in the 1980s, because the first mover can realize higher profits up to the point when the competition catches up. Light trucks (pick-ups and sport utility vehicles [SUVs]) in the 1990s represented the simultaneous realization of both advantages which, for nearly a decade, released Ford and GM from the consequences of always higher social costs and often lower productivity than their Japanese competitors.

The light truck represented a repackaging of the full-size American car which is now a curiosity that survives only as a taxi and police car. But the crude, low-cost, mechanical componentry in the form of V8 engines, drive lines and suspension, plus factory processes such as body-over-frame construction could be carried over into truck product lines. Crucially, Ford, GM and Chrysler had such componentry and techniques, whereas the Japanese did not. Thus, in the absence of Japanese and European competition in trucks, GM, Chrysler and Ford collectively shared the spoils, and margins were not competed away. By 1994, US assemblers had a combined share of 83 per cent of the truck market, and this share did not fall below 80 per cent until 1999 (Ford 10K, various years), which explains why in 1997 Ford were able to make $10.3 million operating profits from trucks, while losing $3.2 million on cars (Lapidus and Mohsenian 1998: 27). Even by 2003, Honda and Toyota collectively had captured less than 15 per cent of the US truck market.

The runaway success of light truck sales surprised everyone, because the big four-wheel-drive SUV and the pick-up, like many other vehicles in specific cultural contexts, tapped into expressions of personal identity (Miller 2001, Gartman 2004) and a decade of low gas prices in a way that could not have been easily predicted. But Ford designers did have an intuitive understanding of American taste that has eluded European and Japanese designers, who find it difficult to understand the historical American attachment to extra-large cars that are big on the outside, small on the inside and deliver not much more than 12–15 miles per gallon. Within this overall configuration, Ford product, such as the (annually face-lifted and refined) F150 pick-up was a very well-judged offering in the 1990s, and Ford reaped the benefits: in 1995, Ford had almost 32 per cent of the whole US light truck market. Exhibit C2.6 shows that in 2003, Ford had more than a third of the full-size pick-up market and more than 20 per cent of the US market in compacts, SUVs and full-size vans. The only segment in which Ford has very few sales is heavy trucks, having sold its Freightliner business in 1997. The light truck segments provided really dynamic growth (which in turn loaded Ford's US factories) because SUV unit sales grew 230 per cent and pick-up sales by 49 per cent between 1987 and 2003. As a result, as Exhibit C2.7 shows, Ford has sold more trucks than cars in the US every year since 1994 (see also Table C2.1 in the appendix, p. 285).

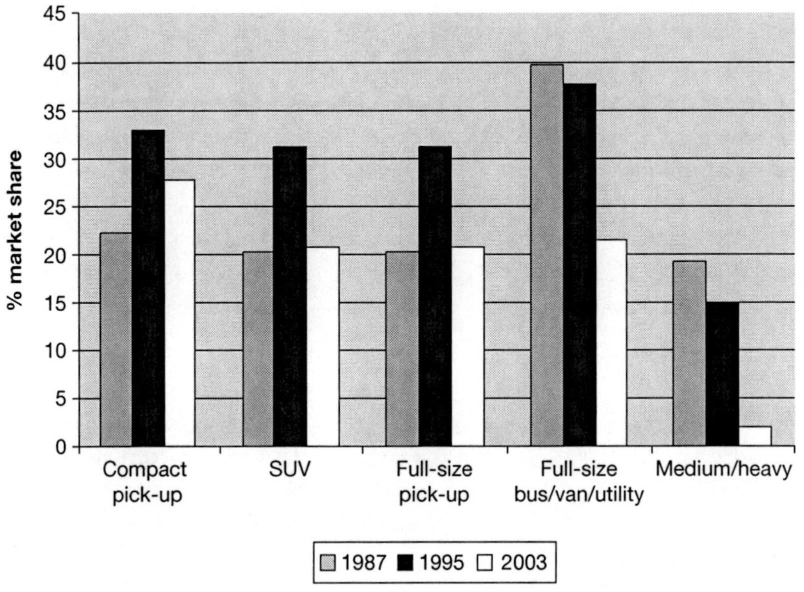


***Exhibit C2.6*** *Ford's market share in the US truck market sub-segments*

*Source*: Ford 10K, various years

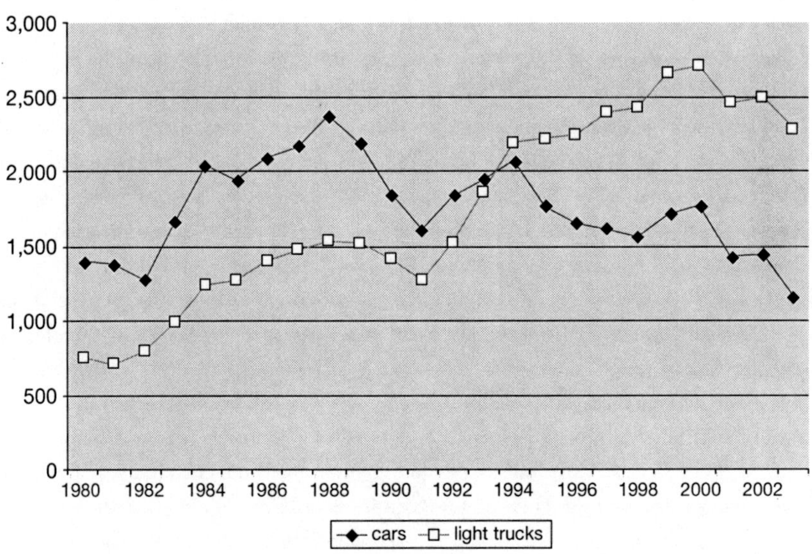


***Exhibit C2.7*** *Ford: US sales of passenger cars and light trucks, 1980–2003*

*Source*: Ford 10K, various years

In some ways, light trucks were Ford's automotive equivalent of the pharma blockbuster: a massively successful segment-dominating revenue earner which bought ten years of profits (thanks, in this case, not to patent protection but to competitors' delays in producing imitative product, which requires design-and-development lead time). While the discount war captured the headlines after 9/11, the more threatening long-term development was the advance of the Japanese assemblers into the full-size light truck categories with practice products such as the Nissan Titan and Toyota Tundra pick-ups or the Nissan Armada and Toyota Sequoia SUVs. By the 2000s, the sheltered competition in trucks started to come to an end so that Ford's share of the US truck market has fallen from a high of 31.9 per cent in 1995 to 24.7 per cent in 2003, with non-US assemblers growing from 16.9 per cent of the market to 27.4 per cent over the same period (Ford 10K filings, various years). More critically, Ford is losing its share of the lucrative SUV subsegment in which it previously had a dominant position, with a fall from 34.5 per cent of the US market in 1994 to 20.7 per cent in 2003. The entrance of Japanese and European assemblers into the SUV and light truck market has predictably eroded volume and margins (McAlinden 2005) and, when in April 2005 Ford cut its 2005 earnings outlook by around $900 million (and retreated from its much-proclaimed 2006 pre-tax earnings goal of $7 billion), S&P 500 credit analyst Scott Sprinzen highlighted falling SUV sales as the most important cause of falling sales (*Wall Street Journal*, 11 April 2005).

If Ford's 1990s' success with trucks did little for shareholders, that was because the profits of trucks were being applied to cover weakness elsewhere in a company where every other major product area was losing market share, losing money or both. The problems in Europe with Ford-badged European cars and with the premium brands such as Jaguar as well as the problems with US sedans are well worth analysing. They nicely illustrate both the difficulties of strategic decision and action in difficult markets and the unpredictable nature of the effort–reward relationship that often leads to a small gap between success and failure. They also incidentally show fundamental continuities in product-market strategy which connect the Trotman, Nasser and Bill Ford eras, even as the CEOs were busily differentiating themselves.

If light trucks were the innovation that came good for Ford, Europe was an unsolved problem that illustrated not only the intensity of competition, which analysts always lament, but also the limits of the 'success through better product' philosophy that Bill Ford and many other car managers usually endorse. In Europe, Ford made two attempts at product-led recovery, first through designing better Ford-badged cars and second through building the PAG brands of Jaguar, Land Rover and Volvo.

The product-led recovery policy for Ford-badged European product was inaugurated in 1993 with the launch of the original Mondeo and continued triumphantly with the launch of the first Ford Focus in 1998. This VW Golf-challenging hatchback was, throughout its six-year life, best in class for style, packaging and driving quality. The enthusiast magazines raved and the residuals showed that the second-hand market recognized the merits of the Focus. But the Mondeo was not good enough to stem the decline in sales of mass-market mid-size saloons as customers defected to prestige German marques. While the new Focus models had to be deeply discounted because in the UK, its main market, the car was not perceived as good enough to escape the stigma of the Ford brand and its overwhelming association with an earlier generation of sales reps. The design-icon status of the original Focus also created problems about what Ford would do for its next act and, significantly, the Mark II Focus in 2004 was widely dismissed as a car that represented no major advance over its predecessor.

Ford's European operations registered sales that were rising only very slowly in unit terms (Exhibit C2.8), so that despite some growth in sales revenue between 1998 and 1999 Ford's European profits sank from $193 million to $28 million (*Financial Times*, 3 February 2000). With Europe barely breaking even for Ford, the main issue by the end of the 1990s became the adjustment of capacity downwards to what the company could sell. In 1999 Ford operations in Europe assembled 1.65 million cars and claimed excess capacity of 600,000 cars (*BBC News* 2000). In May 2000 the company announced a cost-cutting programme to save $1 billion through measures including the end of car assembly at Dagenham (*Detroit News*, 12 May 2000).

More disturbing was the failure of Ford's European Plan B which was to buy neglected premium and sub-premium brands, save expense by sharing componentry, sort product and process and then bank the profits from rapidly increasing sales. The strategy was inaugurated by the purchase of Jaguar in 1989 for $2.5 billion and then continued with the purchase of Volvo cars for $6.45 billion and Land Rover from BMW for $2.8 billion in 1999. The strategy was not a complete failure because it half-worked at Volvo, which

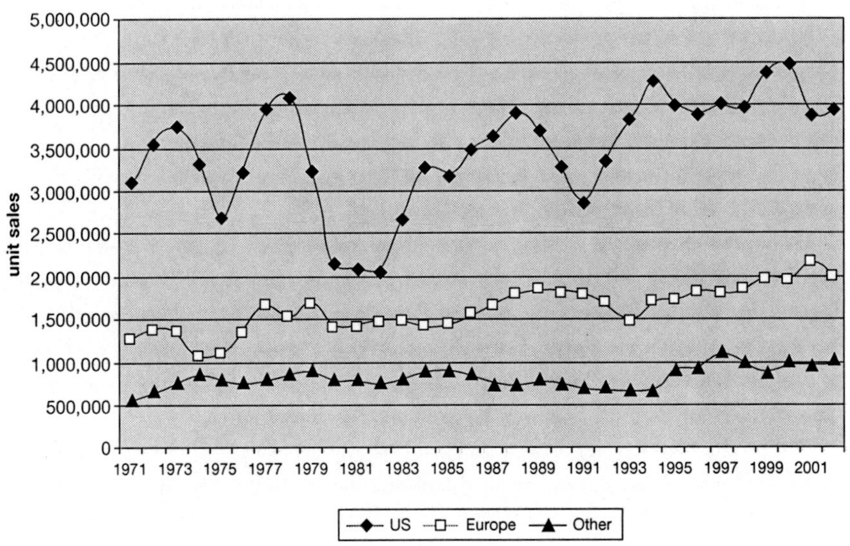


***Exhibit C2.8*** *Ford's vehicle sales by geographical region, 1971–2002*

*Source*: Ford Annual Report and Accounts, various years

had a track record of making money in brisk markets and was able to contribute more than $600 million in profit each year from 2001 to 2003 (*Detroit News*, 17 April 2004).

But Jaguar and Land Rover both represented intractable problems because they were pitched directly against the German premium brands of Audi, BMW and Mercedes who had protected their position by proliferating estate, coupé and convertible model variants with diesel and petrol engines. By 2004, Jaguar had completely reequipped English factories and a new three-car range including one estate and a couple of diesels all with acceptable product quality. But Jaguar sales were stuck around 125,000 cars a year (*Financial Times*, 18 September 2004) which was well below full capacity utilization and, with half of the sales in the USA, there were also complications from the weak dollar (*Financial Times*, 22 July 2004). In September 2004, Ford announced the closure of assembly at Jaguar Brown's Lane, after the chronically loss-making PAG had racked up losses of $362 million in the second quarter of 2004, leaving Ford a long way away from its (re)stated target of one-third of profit from PAG by 2007. The *Detroit News* quoted a Merrill Lynch analyst who blamed 'poor execution' and reported that 'analysts are asking whether Ford's European luxury strategy will ever pay off' (*Detroit News*, 20 September 2004).

If the failure in Europe was an unsurprising result of pitting Ford's (old and new) brands against much better resourced BMW and Mercedes, the outcome in US sedans was much less inevitable. Ford never had much of a grip on the small-car market in the USA, but it did have a position in mid-size sedans where it enjoyed intermittent sales success against the Toyota Camry and Honda Accord, depending on product-development cycles. The decade of the 1990s began well and ended badly for Ford. The original Ford Taurus/Mercury Sable introduced in 1986 was America's best-selling sedan in at least five successive years in the early 1990s and arguably Ford's most successful sedan model since the Model A. Sales volumes of half a million a year from two assembly plants would have ensured its significant contribution to company profits. But the 1992 face-lift was half-hearted and the 1996 replacement was overpriced and curiously styled (*Ward's Auto World*, October 1995) so that by 1997 the Taurus had slipped to third place behind the Camry and the Accord (DiPietro, undated).

As Exhibit C2.9 shows, Ford's weak performance in US passenger cars in the later 1990s is above all attributable to the declining sales of its mid size sedans. The Ford company, which sold 1 million mid-size sedans in 1992 and 1993 could sell no more than 358,000 by 2003 (Ford 10K filings, various years) when Ford's market share of just 15.4 per cent of the US car market as a whole (excluding trucks) was the lowest in its history. Having overtaken Ford to become the second-largest car assembler by vehicle sales in 2004 (AFX Europe 2005), Toyota was close to gaining the Number 3 slot in the US market from Chrysler in January 2005 (*The Economist*, 29 January 2005). Significantly, the volume figures understate the extent of the problem because, in the US (as in Europe), Ford kept its factories ticking over by making distress sales into the fleet market. By 2003, 67.1 per cent of Ford's US passenger cars were sold to fleet buyers compared with just 34 per cent of trucks (Ford 10K filing 2003), which goes some way

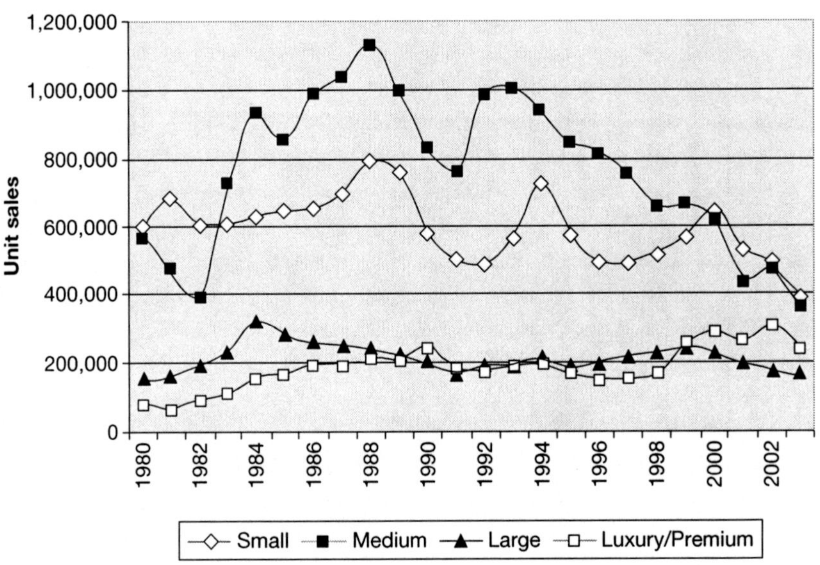


***Exhibit C2.9*** *Ford's sales of passenger cars in the US by segment, 1980–2003*

*Source*: Ford 10K various years

to explaining why Ford made a loss of $3.2 million on their car segment in that year. Companies such as daily rental firms, who buy directly in bulk from the assemblers, always bargain large discounts on otherwise unsaleable volume output.

Arnold Weinstock, the long-standing Chief Executive of GEC, did know something about wringing returns from manufacturing, and his view was that manufacturing management was like playing a fruit machine because the difficult thing was to get all three fruits lined up so that the jackpot cash came pouring out. Realistically, Ford was not playing a three-lemon game because its European business was never going to come good against adroit defensive moves by premium German brands. But, in the early 1990s after trucks had come up, Ford did have some hope of a more modest prize if US sedans could be nudged in the right way. At one level, the outcome was then determined by happenstance and misfortune such as poor product development on the 1996 Taurus sedan, plus events such as 9/11 and the Explorer roll-over crisis discussed in the third section. At another level, Ford's failure is systematic and perhaps inevitable because, like many giant old companies competing in difficult markets, its hopes depend on infeasibly faultless decisions and execution across a broad range of product-market segments. As long as such perfection was unattainable, supplementary earnings from finance were crucial.

## Financial innovation and Ford Credit

At this point we can turn to the role and contribution of Ford finance which, as we noted, is a significant part of the consolidated company but one that has not been considered in detail by most analysts. Our analysis is based on close study of the 10K filings to the SEC over the past twenty years for Ford Motor Credit which accounts for the overwhelming proportion of Ford's finance operations. The Ford Motor Credit Company was founded as far back as 1959 as a wholly owned subsidiary; financial services were consolidated in Ford's company accounts from 1988, which symbolically and actually reflected the growing importance of the credit business (Datamonitor 2004: 6). The 10K statements for Ford Credit are an invaluable and essential source because it is not possible to reconstruct the story of Ford finance from the parent Ford's consolidated report and accounts. Understanding such technical sources is crucial if we are to develop an understanding of strategy that is more than a descriptive restatement of what management says.

Any analysis of Ford's finance operations should start from the observation that Ford was adding finance to an industrial company and running a credit operation from a position of weakness determined by its low return, cyclical auto business. This makes a neat contrast with GE which, as we shall see in the next case study, was adding finance from a position of strength determined by its quality portfolio of industrial businesses. In Ford's case, the two businesses are practically inseparable because Ford assembly could not survive in its present form without support from Ford Credit, while Ford Credit has limited capacity to stand alone without a parent that puts business its way. In effect, Ford is no longer an industrial company: Ford Credit has transformed the balance sheet, as much as it has made a crucial contribution to the generation of cash and profit, as Exhibit C2.10 illustrates for 2000.

One of the key differences between Ford and GE's development of financial services activities is in terms of the credit ratings that determine the cost and possibility of borrowing to finance the credit business. Because the credit subsidiary is always rated broadly in line with its industrial parent, GE Capital benefits from the way in which parent GE has always held a triple-A rating by S&P. This means that GE can compete on terms of equality or superiority with major banks that also have good credit ratings. By way of contrast, Ford Credit suffers from the way in which its parent, Ford Motor Company, has much weaker ratings and is exposed to risk of credit downrating every time the car market turns down. According to the 10K filings, Ford Credit held a double-A from S&P briefly from 1986 to 1989 and has usually been rated at single A, but Ford Credit has also had periods of triple-B ratings in 1982–3 and 2001–3 with the 2003 rating of triple-B just one step above junk. Exhibit C2.11 shows the rating of Moody's and S&P for Ford Motor Credit's long-term debt and short-term commercial paper,

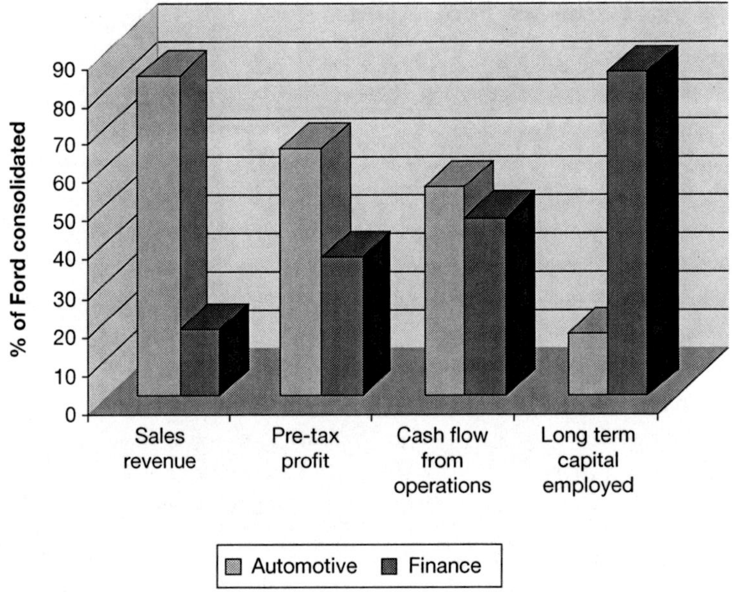


*Exhibit C2.10 Contribution of automotive and finance activities to Ford in 2000*

*Source*: Ford Annual Report and Accounts, various years

illustrating the cyclicality of the ratings as well as some suggesting a secular decline in ratings.

The practical effects are considerable when finance subsidiaries are not deposit-taking banks and must borrow what they lend. First, low and uncertain credit ratings have limited Ford's capacity to move beyond captive auto finance and to build a diversified finance business. In the second half of the 1980s, after the 1985 acquisition of the savings and loan firm First Nationwide, Ford moved into real estate, mortgages, credit cards and suchlike. The major move here was the acquisition of The Associates, a consumer finance company that specialized in sub-prime lending, for $3.4 billion in 1989, when coincidentally Ford Credit also lost the double-A rating it briefly held in the late 1980s. The question of how then to compete with better rated competitors was never solved. The practical answer was to sell The Associates after the bull-market euphoria in the capital market allowed a paper profit, but before cyclical difficulties in the auto product market produced a downrating crisis. The one-off gain on floating 20 per cent of The Associates in 1996 was $650 million and, with nice timing, the spin-off of the remaining 80 per cent in 1998 produced a one-time (non-cash) gain of approximately $16 billion (Ford Annual Report and Accounts, 1998).

The second major effect is a consequence of occasional downrating when the captive finance subsidiary is massively exposed to increased costs of borrowing and exclusion from specific markets. After a credit downrating, rapid distress-induced shifts in sources of funding are required which may avoid a cash-flow crisis but do increase risk on the

***Exhibit C2.11*** *Ford Motor Credit ratings by Moody's and Standard & Poor's*

| | *Long-term senior debt* | | *Commercial paper* | |
|---|---|---|---|---|
| | *Moody's* | *S&P* | *Moody's* | *S&P* |
| **1981** | A | A | Prime-1 | A-1 |
| **1982** | Baa | BBB+ | Prime-2 | A-2 |
| **1983** | A3 | BBB+ | Prime-2 | A-2 |
| **1984** | A1 | A- | Prime-1 | A-1 |
| **1985** | A1 | A | Prime-1 | A-1 |
| **1986** | A1 | AA- | Prime-1 | A-1+ |
| **1987** | Aa2 | AA- | Prime-1 | A-1+ |
| **1988** | Aa2 | AA | Prime-1 | A-1+ |
| **1989** | Aa2 | AA | Prime-1 | A-1+ |
| **1990** | A2 | A | Prime-1 | A-1 |
| **1991** | A1 | A | Prime-1 | A-1 |
| **1992** | A2 | A | Prime-1 | A-1+ |
| **1993** | A2 | A | Prime-1 | A-1 |
| **1994** | A1 | A+ | Prime-1 | A-1 |
| **1995** | A | A+ | Prime-1 | A-1 |
| **1996** | AI | A+ | Prime-1 | A-1 |
| **1997** | A1 | A | Prime-1 | A-1 |
| **1998** | A1 | A | Prime-1 | A-1 |
| **1999** | A1 | A+ | Prime-1 | A-1 |
| **2000** | A2 | A | Prime-1 | A-1 |
| **2001** | A3 | BBB+ | Prime-2 | A-2 |
| **2002** | Baa1 | BBB | Prime-2 | A-2 |
| **2003** | Baa1 | BBB- | Prime-2 | A-3 |

*Source*: Ford Motor Credit 10K, various years

*Note*: The credit ratings for Ford Motor Credit are closely related to the financial conditions and outlook of Ford. Where Ford discloses separate credit ratings for Ford and Ford Credit, these are identical for long-term debt. Short-term ratings apply mostly to Ford Credit as Ford Automotive relies on (a modest amount of) long-term borrowing only

downturn. Ford has not yet seen its long-term rating downgraded to junk, a catastrophe which forced Chrysler out of credit and ensured there was nothing then to do but sell the assembly business (Froud et al. 2002b: 29–30). But Ford Credit has faced two separate crises in the early 1980s and early 2000s (see Exhibit C2.11), when downrating of its short-term commercial paper effectively locked it out of this important market, which had hitherto met one-third to one-half of its borrowing requirements.

In the early 1980s, Ford responded by selling receivables (i.e. the amounts owed to Ford from customers who have taken out finance packages and thus contracted to make future payments on instalment plans) to banks and suchlike because its retail customers were a rather better credit risk than Ford: from 1981 to 1983 Ford in each year sold $1.3 billion to $1.4 billion of receivables. In the early 2000s new techniques of securitization using bankruptcy-remote special-purpose entities were available and used on a massive scale, so that securitization removes $19.5 billion of receivables from the balance sheet in 2000, rising to $41 billion in 2002. The 10K filings indicate that the scale of Ford Motor

Credit's receivables pledged to special-purpose entities rose from the equivalent of 6.8 per cent of total receivables still on the company's balance sheet in 1999 to 28.7 per cent in 2002, before falling back to 14.6 per cent in 2003 as Table C2.3 in the appendix shows (p. 287). The immediate benefit of such securitization is that, by taking assets (i.e. amounts receivable) off its balance sheet, Ford reduces its requirement for capital to finance its assets and associated interest payments. Table C2.6 (appendix, p. 290) shows that short term borrowing fell from $60.6 billion in 1998 to $16.6 billion in 2002 (partly as a result of securitization as well as through a shift into long-term debt). Securitizing receivables also brings a secondary benefit in the form of income, which can be recognized in the income statement at the point when these assets are sold, rather then needing to wait until customers make lease and loan payments, as is the case for those receivables that Ford retains on its balance sheet.

Any mention of special-purpose entities recalls Enron, another industrial company that pushed further into finance as the counter-party in derivatives transactions without the necessary superior credit rating (Froud et al. 2004). Of course, there is no evidence that Ford has, or had, Enron's problem about the absence of culture and controls to manage continuous financial innovation from a position of weakness. But the addition of finance does make Ford more opaque, and it is impossible for outsiders to judge the wisdom and consequences of Ford's new securitization deals from available published information. We know much less about how Ford is incentivizing purchasers of parcels of receivables than we know about its price rebates and discounts for retail customers. And it is also clear that on leases, where Ford sells the income stream, almost all the risk stays with Ford, as do liabilities associated with falling residual values on the leased vehicles.

The trajectory of Ford Motor Credit is one of continuous innovation driven by the absence of what the strategists term 'sustainable advantage'. If the common-sense question is 'Why should the parent company bother with this kind of risk?', the answer is, 'in the hope of financial benefits that would ease the problems of the auto business'. And we turn next to analysing the contribution of finance to the auto business.

Within strategy discourse from Chandler onwards, the standard way of thinking about diversification is in terms of the share of different activities in turnover. But this measure does not work very well for captive finance, where the assembled product is financed by a captive finance house. To avoid double-counting the turnover on each product, the turnover is usually credited to assembly and the captive finance 'turnover' or revenue is either income from credit agreements or the gap between lending and borrowing costs. On this basis, Ford's finance does not amount to much because total financial services have never accounted for more than 20 per cent of turnover in the consolidated accounts and auto finance alone probably never accounts for more than 15 per cent, as Exhibit C2.12 shows (see also Table C2.4 in the appendix, p. 288).

But the answer changes if we try to understand how assembly and finance fit together in Ford in business-model terms. Ford Motor Company needs auto finance as a non-cyclical adjunct source of profit and cash to buttress a weak and cyclical core auto business that would otherwise be threatened with forced restructuring in every downturn, and

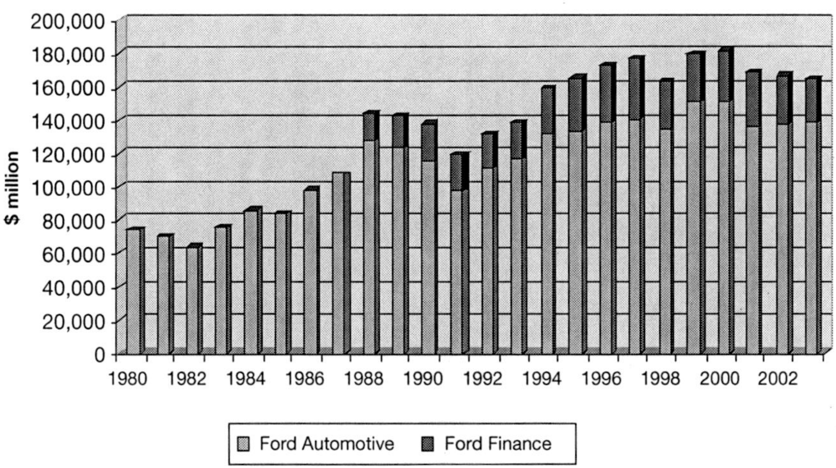


*Exhibit C2.12 Contribution of automotive and finance activities to Ford's sales revenues, 1980–2003 (in real 2003 prices)*

*Source*: Ford Annual Report and Accounts, various years

*Note*: Up to 1988, Ford's finance activities were not separately disclosed. Since 1988, the financial results of Financial Services have been separately disclosed (see full data in Table C2.4 in the appendix)

ideally these benefits should be delivered without generating secondary complications. Our argument is that Ford assembly and finance fit together so that the first requirement for profit and cash generation has been met over the past twenty years but at the expense of increasing secondary complications about ROCE and profit which together imply that Ford is now at the end of a trajectory.

The generic attraction of adding captive finance can be understood in input and output terms that explain why so many car assemblers and equipment manufacturers, from Boeing to Caterpillar, have moved into finance. From the viewpoint of the consolidated parent accounts (i.e. assembly plus finance), the finance business delivers to the giant assembler a large increment of profit and cash that is usually much less cyclical than the revenue from equipment sales (see Table C2.5 in appendix, p. 289); the profit initially comes easily because captive finance has a modest labour requirement and hence cost. Over the period considered in this case study, finance has made a very substantial contribution to Ford's overall profit, with the credit business accounting for $47 billion or about 50 per cent of total Ford profit since 1988, even after excluding the one-off gains of $16 billion from the sale of The Associates. In an otherwise precarious and cyclical business, this support is crucial because, as Exhibit C2.13 shows, in ten out of sixteen years after 1988, Ford's financial services generate more than half of total profit and, in bad periods such as 1991–2 or 2001–3, financial services accounts for all the profit in the consolidated company.

The costs of profit subvention are very different in terms of labour and capital inputs. Finance is typically sold by dealers so a large captive finance operation can run with a very

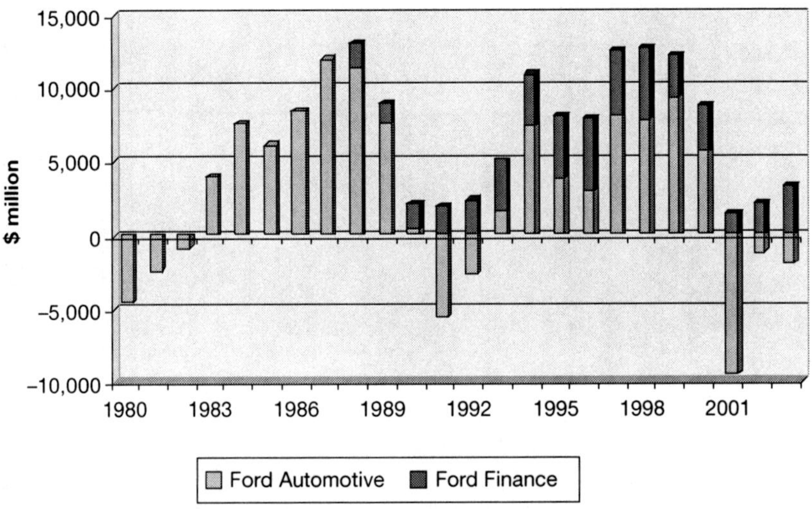


*Exhibit C2.13 Contribution of automotive and finance activities to Ford's pre-tax profits, 1980–2003 (in real 2003 prices)*

*Source*: Annual Report and Accounts, various years

*Notes*: Up to 1988 Ford's finance activities were not separately disclosed. Since 1988 the financial results of Ford Motor Credit have been separately disclosed. The data for 1988 excludes the $16 billion gains on sale from The Associates

small number of employees: the 10K filings show that Ford Motor Credit employed around 10,000 in the mid-1990s and no more than 21,000 in 2003. But captive finance requires a huge increase in capital in so far as the captive finance house is not a deposit-taking bank and has to borrow so as to finance a substantial part of the turnover from auto assembly. Thus Ford Motor Credit had $32 billion of short- and long-term borrowing in 1980, $75 billion by 1993 and $150 billion by 2003 (Exhibit C2.14 and Table C2.6, p. 290). The increase in capital requirement is a complication because it ensures finance may generate high rates of returns on its sales revenue as Exhibit C2.14 demonstrates, but produce low rates of ROCE. It should be noted that, in these kinds of finance activities operated by industrial companies, the most meaningful calculation of return on capital uses short- as well as long-term debt in the denominator (along with the equity), rather than the conventional measure which includes only long-term debt (i.e. that repayable after more than a year). Ford Motor Credit uses both short- and long-term debt to finance retail lending and, on that basis, as Exhibit C2.15 shows, Ford Motor Credit has never earned more than 4 per cent ROCE before tax (or 2 per cent after tax – see Table C2.7, appendix, p. 291).

Immediately, the low ROCE in finance is a complication rather than a roadblock threat to the expansion of captive finance. It has the obvious effect of pulling down the overall return on capital for the consolidated business, spoiling the relatively high ROCE on the car-assembly operations which benefit from a modest capital requirement, as Exhibit

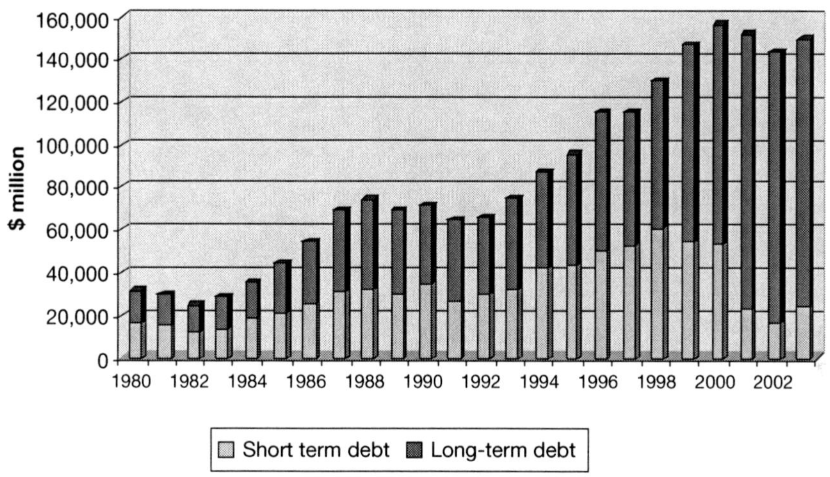


***Exhibit C2.14*** *Ford Motor Credit debt financing, 1980–2003 (in real 2003 prices)*

*Source*: Ford Motor Credit, 10K, various years

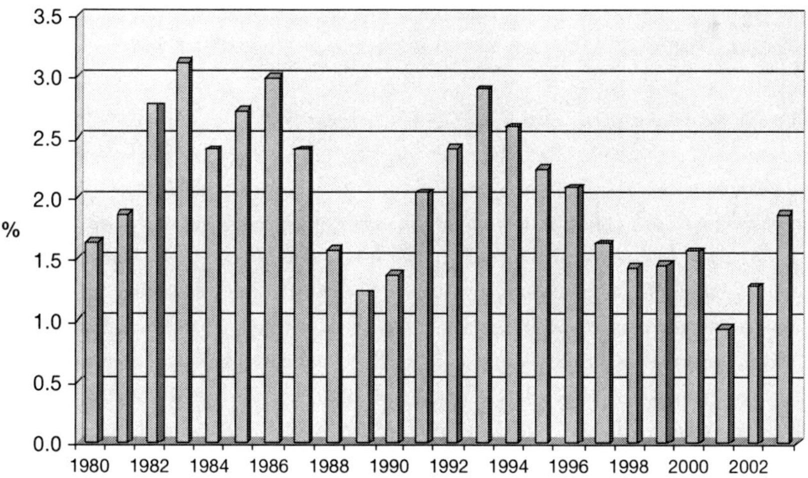


***Exhibit C2.15*** *Ford Motor Credit pre-tax ROCE, 1980–2003*

*Source*: Ford Motor Credit 10K, various years

C2.16 shows. This will be cause for concern to consultants and others promoting value-based management schemes but is less of an issue for the stock market which cares more for earnings and cash and is therefore grateful for the boost to profit from finance operations, regardless of balance-sheet consequences. But, in the medium term, finance puts an assembler such as Ford on a trajectory of increasing finance dependence and intensifying complications about generating profit.

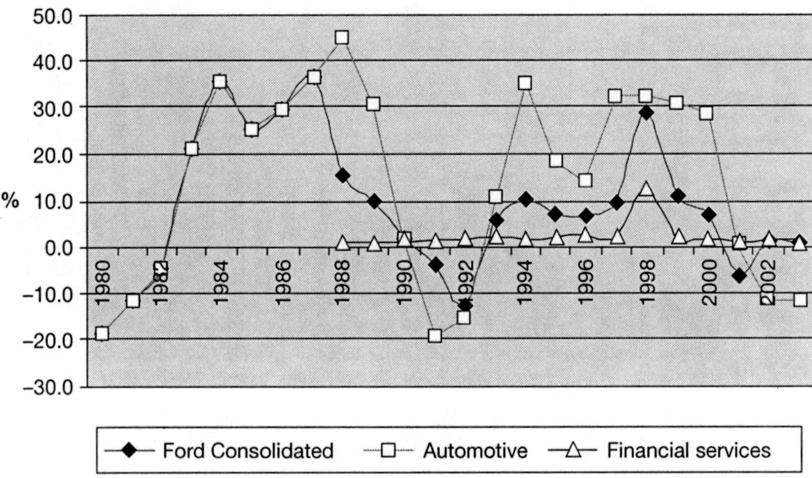


*Exhibit C2.16 Pre-tax ROCE for Ford consolidated and its divisions, 1980–2003*

*Source*: Ford Annual Report and Accounts, various years

*Notes*: Up to 1988 Ford's finance activities were not separately disclosed. Since 1988 the financial results of Ford Motor Credit have been separately disclosed. The data for 1998 includes the $16 billion gains on sale from The Associates. (See full data in Table C2.7 in the appendix.) The Ford Automative ROCE in 2001 is −102.3. In this exhibit the ROCE has been set at zero to avoid distorting the scale

In most kinds of captive finance, the tendency is for profit margins to decline under pressure of competition because there are few barriers to entry and dealers cannot be compelled to sell overpriced assembler packages. In the case of Ford Motor Credit, the pre-tax return on revenue (i.e. income as a proportion of revenues) was at or above 20 per cent in good years up to 1993 but it averages around 10 per cent since 1997, as shown in Exhibit C2.17. This declining rate of profitability meant that the only way to maintain a constant profit contribution from finance was by expanding the credit business: this shows up in the growth of Ford Motor Credit revenue which, in real terms (in 2003 prices) rose from $10.8 billion in 1993 to a peak of $26.5 billion in 2003 with vehicles financed increasing from 1.7 million in 1989 to 3.5 million in 1995 and 5.5 million in 2001 (Exhibit C2.18). The decline in the numbers of vehicles financed since 2001 reflects the attempt to move away from financing higher-risk private customers and lower-return fleet customers. Ford management were later explicit that this was part of a conscious strategy to focus on profits not sales. Hence the results in the first quarter of 2004, when Ford's market share in the US fell by 1.2 per cent and its sales revenue fell by 1.3 per cent, were presented as successes because they marked a move away from low-margin rental and fleet income (Forbes 2004).

Scaling up the credit business with declining margins on ever-increasing amounts of borrowed money made the old complication about inherently low ROCE on finance into a much bigger issue. As Exhibit C2.15 shows, ROCE in Ford Motor Credit more or less halved from the early 1990s to the early 2000s and after 1998 it varied between

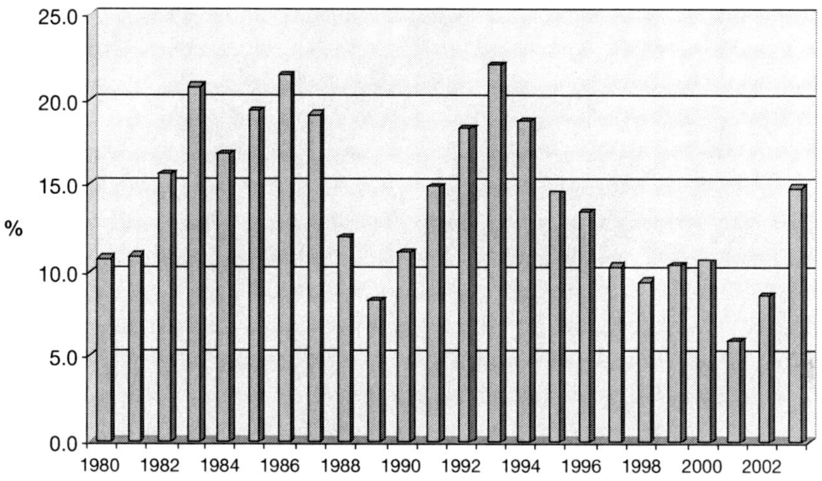


***Exhibit C2.17*** *Ford Motor Credit pre-tax return on revenue, 1980–2003*

*Source*: Ford Motor Credit 10K, various years

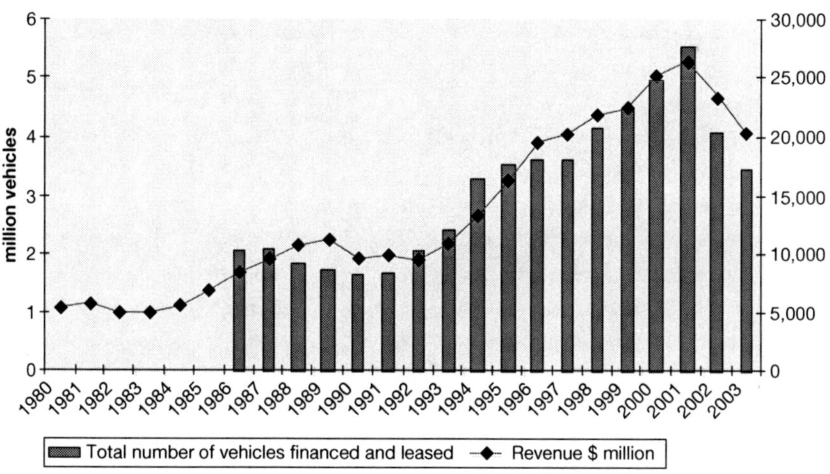


***Exhibit C2.18*** *Ford Motor Credit vehicle financing and revenues*

*Source*: Ford Motor Credit 10K, various years

1.1 and 2.2 per cent (using pre-tax ROCE) on borrowings of between $130 and $150 billion (Table C2.7, p. 291). This is not the kind of credit business that anybody would start up (nor one that Wall Street financiers would want to encourage), but finance could still make sense for Ford if it continued to generate profit for the parent company. However, delivering profit became more complicated because of the shift from old kinds of instalment plan to new kinds of leasing, putting Ford on a trajectory of increasing problems about finding profit, as explained below.

In the UK, Ford pioneered private-customer leasing in the form of Personal Contract Purchase, but in the USA, Ford's move into leasing was basically defensive. At US dealers, the price sticker on the car windscreen generally shows the monthly repayment not the list price, and leases allow the dealer to quote a lower monthly payment because the customer is not buying the whole car but only covering the depreciation over the term of the lease. This helps to make 'buying' a new car more attractive for customers whose limited budgets could not otherwise satisfy their aspirations. This new development in auto financing did not undermine traditional instalment plans, and Ford was able to increase instalment customers from 2.4 million in 1994 to 4.5 million in 2001 (Table C2.8, appendix, p. 292). But the 10K filings also show that at the same time Ford was building up a substantial new lease business after 1985 so that by 1994 Ford leased 852,000 vehicles, rising to 1.2 million vehicles in 2000.

The growth of the new leasing business had two implications for profit subvention. First, there is increased risk of profits collapse because the lease is written on an assumption about residuals at end of the term, with all the risk of lower realized residual values carried by Ford (not the customer, who carries residual value risk in a traditional instalment plan). This is a major practical consideration because the 10K filings disclose that 65–70 per cent of Ford-leased cars in the USA are returned to the dealer at the end of the term and two-thirds of those then go to auction and are sold at wholesale prices. The resulting risk of a significant hit on profits is quite frightening. For example, if Ford in one year writes 900,000 US car leases, 600,000 cars are returned at end of lease and the shortfall on residuals is a modest $1,000 per vehicle, then the hit against profit is of the order of $600 million. These consequences are not hypothetical because most US car-lease companies wrote over-optimistic residuals into their later 1990s leases and were losing serious money per car after 2000. A survey by the Consumer Banking Association of forty-one lenders and assembler finance companies shows they lost an average of $2,451 per vehicle in 2001, up from $2,342 in 2000 and double the loss of $1,200 in 1998 (*Detroit News*, 6 August 2002). As a consequence of overly optimistic assumptions about residual values, as well as an unusually high proportion of bad loans, Ford had to inject $700 million into Ford Motor Credit's balance sheet in 2001 and accept that Ford Motor Credit would contribute no profit in the fourth quarter (*Business Week*, 15 July 2002).

Second, there is also a problem about reduced profits every year. Under a leasing deal, Ford retains ownership of the vehicle and hence the depreciation charges on leased vehicles are carried by Ford as a routine charge against profit in the consolidated accounts. The rise of leasing is traceable most easily via the huge shift in the internal composition of costs within Ford Motor Credit. In this credit subsidiary, depreciation was 3 per cent or less of revenue up to 1986 and then rose to nearly 38 per cent by 1995. At the same time, pre-tax income was squeezed so that it accounted for around 10 per cent of revenues in the late 1990s and early 2000s, as against closer to 20 per cent earlier in the period (Table C2.9, appendix, p. 293). This has implications for Ford as a whole because this depreciation charge does not affect cash generation but does reduce consolidated profit.

Ford's post-2000 profits crisis is generally seen as a new kind of postmodern downturn combining high volumes with low profits, which are attributed by analysts and media to the incentives (i.e. price reductions) being used to keep the US market going. Exhibit C2.19 supports this argument and shows that Ford's revenue per vehicle in the USA has been more or less flat in the USA since 1997, which is hardly surprising given the scale of incentives: the *Wall Street Journal* (6 January 2004) reported that Ford's average rebate in 2003 was $2,752 per vehicle sold, almost double that of $1,654 in 2001. But just as significant is the problem about the composition of costs and the burden of depreciation, which ensures that Ford now finds it difficult to make a profit even when labour's share of internal costs is moderate. Exhibit C2.19 makes the point that, even in periods when average revenues per vehicle are flat (i.e. 1980–95 and 1997–2002), net income per vehicle is strongly cyclical. As Table C2.10 (p. 294) shows, in Ford's consolidated accounts, depreciation and amortization has risen from its 1980s' level of 10–15 per cent of internal costs (or value added) to a level of 25–30 per cent in recent years and higher just after 2000. This means that, in order to make a reasonable profit, labour costs must be contained at what are probably unsustainably low levels of around 50 per cent of internal costs. As Table C2.10 also demonstrates, such low-cost levels are achievable only in years like 1998 where vehicle sales are high enough to ensure good capacity utilization.

Ford's recent response has been to shrink the (lease) business in pursuit of higher profits. According to its 10K filings, in 2001, Ford financed 54 per cent of its US vehicle

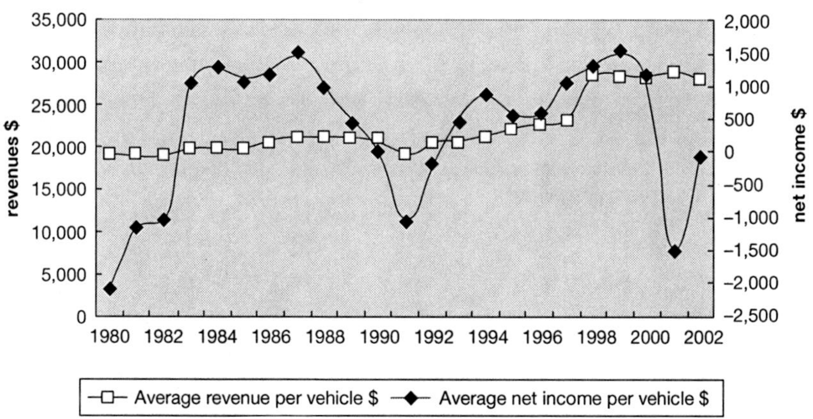


**Exhibit C2.19** *Ford Automotive: average real revenue and net income per vehicle sold in the USA, 1980–2002 (in real 2003 prices)*

*Source*: Ford Annual Report and Accounts, various years

*Note*: The graph shows a step-up in average revenue per vehicle in 1998. This is caused by a change in required disclosures (FAS 103 Disclosures about segments) which abandoned geographic disclosure as the primary method of segment analysis in favour of divisional breakdowns. Hence 1998 represents a break in the series. After 1998, US totals for Ford Automotive sales revenues now include finance revenues, where previously they were excluded. This change explains most of the apparent increase in average revenue per vehicle in 1998

sales, but by 2003 this had fallen sharply to 39 per cent because the company took a decision to write fewer leases on its North American output. From 2000 to 2003, the number of new Ford vehicles leased in the USA declined from 819,000 to 274,000; globally, the total number of vehicles under lease contracts issued by Ford declined from a high of 1.2 million vehicles worldwide in 2001 to less than 0.5 million in 2003 (Ford 10K filings, various years).

Ford has made its defensive move, but the question we would ask is whether it is at the end of trajectory of adding finance to help boost the profit of the parent. It is too soon to tell for sure whether the core auto-finance business has either become cyclical or, even worse, inherently unprofitable: certainly smart players with diverse portfolios (like GE Capital) had quit car-leasing by 2002 so that only those under pressure and financially less sophisticated (like VW) are getting further into car-leasing. The leasing element of the finance operation is risky because of the exposure to residuals and steadily depressive because of the depreciation burden that it adds. Ford will no doubt try to manage its way through these contradictions, balancing lease and instalment business and weighing size against risk, but Ford is at the end of a trajectory because, given the return on borrowed capital and the problems about depreciation, it cannot easily (and profitably) cover problems elsewhere by adding more finance.

At this point, it is also relevant to note that, because Ford innovated (through trucks and finance) and kept things going through the 1990s, it still carries the social obligations towards pensions and health care. In the work of Williams et al. (1994) these were identified as a major source of competitive disadvantage for the Big Three (Ford, GM and Chrysler) against the Japanese. And they remain sources of cost disadvantage because, as the US airline and steel industries show, only bankruptcy and restructuring releases the firm from its social obligations. A Dominion Bond Rating Service (DBRS) report of

***Exhibit C2.20*** *Pension fund and post-retirement benefit liabilities for the US Big Three auto assemblers*

*Pension fund liabilities*

| $ billion | *1996* | *1997* | *1998* | *1999* | *2000* | *2001* |
|---|---|---|---|---|---|---|
| GM | 2,755 | (1,290) | (1,956) | 7,193 | 1,735 | (9,061) |
| Ford | 4,456 | 6,632 | 5,587 | 9,285 | 6,548 | 596 |
| DaimlerChrysler | | 1,966 | 3,414 | 6,245 | 4,084 | (14) |

*Post-retirement benefit liabilities*

| $ billion | *1996* | *1997* | *1998* | *1999* | *2000* | *2001* |
|---|---|---|---|---|---|---|
| GM | 43,190 | 38,388 | 33,503 | 34,166 | 34,306 | 34,515 |
| Ford | 15,950 | 16,047 | 15,134 | 16,338 | 15,169 | 16,681 |
| DaimlerChrysler | | 8,818 | 7,020 | 7,756 | 8,636 | 9,442 |

*Source*: Dominion Bond Rating Service 2002

Note: For pension-fund liabilities, ( ) denotes unfunded liabilities. Most of the post-retirement benefit liabilities are unfunded

2002 showed that Ford had managed its pension liabilities fairly prudently, as Exhibit C2.20 shows, so that the collapse of the bull market did not produce a large deficit as it did in GM. But, just like GM and Chrysler, Ford had a large problem about unfunded liabilities, which DBRS (2003: 2) estimate to be around $16 billion for pensions and $27 billion in post-retirement health care benefits at the end of 2002, mainly arising from health-care costs of its former employees charged to the giant firm in the absence of socialized medicine. Such liabilities are directly important because they represent a substantial obligation to make future cash payments which, in the absence of a marked and sustained stock-market boom, must come from operations (Keller 2003). As GM has found out, such liabilities can also weaken credit ratings and hence push up the cost of capital, as well as damaging investor confidence still further.

## FORD AFTER FORDISM

The development of Ford since the early 1980s illustrates the theme that management is about many moves and few levers. We can begin here by discarding the academic and consultant notions of breaks and reinvention which are irrelevant because they do not yield enough leverage on costs unless and until Ford breaches its implicit social contract with stakeholders symbolized by the explicit agreement with the UAW. Against this background, Ford did move purposively, and through the 1990s did deliver substantial innovations that were recognized in trucks and largely not understood in finance. These innovations in trucks and finance yielded enough cash and profit to defend the status quo, which meant low profits in most other activities. Thus, Ford is running to stand still because most of the company-wide indicators of overall financial results and stakeholder benefits are stubbornly untransformed. This section begins by demonstrating these points before turning to consider the future of Ford after Fordism.

Taking the simplest profit measure of return on sales, Ford is untransformed because, like other assemblers, it has to generate large (or, more precisely, ever larger) amounts of revenue to realize small and declining amounts of profit in the cyclically better years. Thus, as Exhibit C2.21 shows, there is a secular increase in units sold and sales revenue while profits are effectively flat between 1980 and 2003. Thus, net margin (i.e. net income or profit expressed as a percentage of revenues) peaks at around 5–6 per cent in 1984–8, but the overall average margin between 1980 and 2002 is a meagre 2.49 per cent and the recent average is just 0.79 per cent between 1999 and 2003 (Table C2.11, appendix, p. 295). Problems about the consequences of demand cyclicality appear to get worse not better with a close relation between units sold, sales revenue and net income in the downturns around 1980–2 and 1990–3, which push the company into losses with

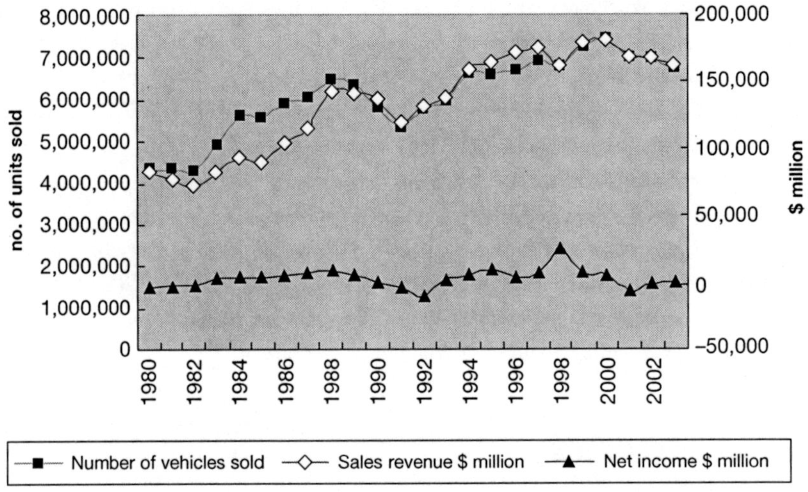


*Exhibit C2.21 Ford operating performance: sales and profit (income), 1980–2003 (in real 2003 prices)*

*Source*: Ford Annual Report and Accounts, various years

*Note*: The 1998 net income total is inflated by the spin-off of the Associates

negative net income that returns in 2001–2 with only a relatively small downturn in unit sales, as Exhibit C2.21 shows (see also Table C2.11, p. 295).

These dispiriting fundamentals translate into modest real gains for any shareholder who holds long term for value. Quite strikingly, after the collapse of the share price between 2000 and 2002, there is little long-term gain through share-price appreciation: Exhibit C2.22 shows how the share price rose fairly steadily through the 1990s but fell very sharply after 1999 so that by 2003 it is no higher in real terms than in the mid-1980s. The P/E ratio is generally around 5 or less in the 1980s and 10 or less in the 1990s. However, Exhibit C2.23 clearly shows the (increasing) cyclicality of this indicator. The weakness of the share price means capital gains account for less than 10 per cent of the total shareholder return on Ford stock between 1980 and 2003: $60 invested in a common share in 1980 would in 2003 only be worth $108 in real terms, which is well under the average gain of the S&P 500 (Table C2.12, appendix, p. 296). If dividends account for 90 per cent of total shareholder return between 1980 and 2003, these payouts of course depend on the feeble and cyclical stream of profits. Ford cut its total dividend payout from $2,941 million in 2000 to $733 million in 2003, the lowest amount paid in real terms since 1983 (Table C2.10, p. 294). And nearly half the total dividend comes in the form of a one-off gain on the sale of The Associates. Yet Ford, like other auto stocks, presents trading opportunities for tipsters and punters who call the turns, so that any shareholder who bought in the 1991 trough and sold at the 1999 peak would make handsome rewards.

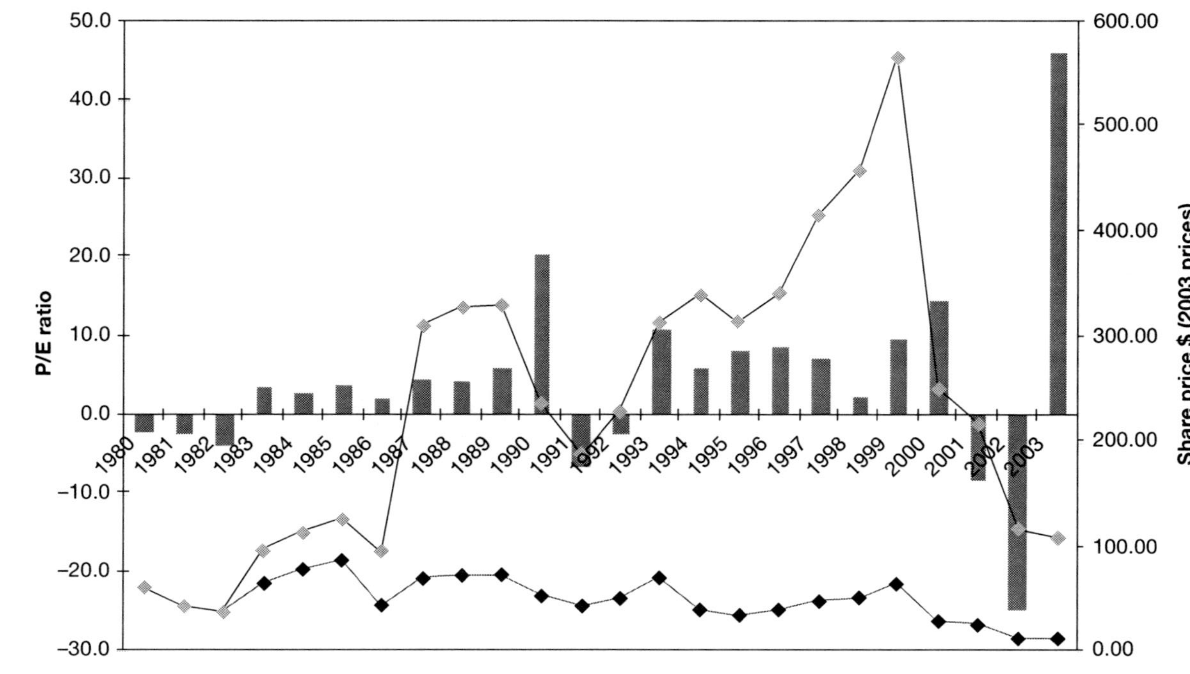


***Exhibit C2.22*** *Ford Motor Company share price and P/E ratio, 1980–2003 (share prices in real 2003 prices)*

*Source*: Ford Annual Report and Accounts, various years

*Note*: Share price is adjusted for stock splits. The P/E ratio is calculated using net income

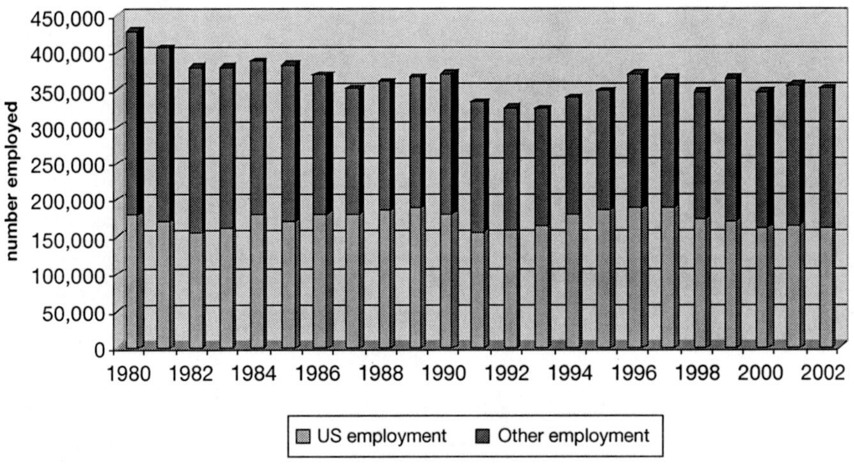


*Exhibit C2.23 Ford Motor Company employment, 1980–2002*

*Source*: Ford Annual Report and Accounts, various years

*Note*: The 2003 accounts do not disclose the geographical breakdown of employment. See notes to Table C2.13

If shareholder gains have been mixed and partly dependent on the timing of transactions, the experience of Ford's employees has been more marked by stability and continuity; acquisition and divestment in the finance division has a limited effect on employment, while in auto assembly the pattern was acquisition without divestment and only modest downsizing. As Exhibit C2.23 shows, long-term employment is more or less flat with some very modest cyclical declines when the product market turns down: the company that employed 379,000 in the cyclical trough year of 1982 employed 350,000 some twenty years later in 2002, another poor year. Ford avoided European downsizing for most of the decade of the 1990s and maintains almost half of its total employment in the USA (Table C2.13, appendix, p. 298) where (as elsewhere) it is a high-wage employer. Real average labour costs per global employee have fallen since the mid-1990s but currently average just under $70,000, which is ahead of early 1980s' pay levels in real terms. Significantly, this is also considerably better than the average employee pay in a *Business Week 350* firm in 2002 of $26,354, where real labour costs per employee have not increased if we compare this recent figure with the average for the same index in 1980 of $27,946 and 1990 of $26,705 (both in real 2002 prices) (Erturk et al. 2005: Table 1).

The three continuities are: weak and cyclical profitability, poor performance for shareholders and the maintenance of a high-wage employment base. Politically, these continuities can be constructed in various ways: from the Right, this could be criticized as a case of vicious labour inflexibility, while the Left could applaud a virtuous defence of the social settlement. Intellectually, the story is more complex and interesting, and it tells us something about Ford after Fordism which was always a fairly uninformative stereotype.

The containment of pressures for shareholder value and the maintenance of employment at Ford usefully indicates the limits of generalization about Fordist periods and regimes. While the dissolution of established social settlements was sponsored by the national governments of Reagan and Thatcher after 1979, the enforcement of change was decided by local struggles within industries and firms under conditions of confusion. The US air-traffic controllers or British coal miners may have been defeated but, in other industries, organized labour could locally maintain its position and use collective bargaining to capture a good deal of the gains from innovation by resourceful management. Ford's wages per employee are, in real terms, now $10,000 ahead of the wages paid in the early 1980s trough, and that represents a gain of several billion dollars for Ford's internal workforce.

As for the character of the Fordist enterprise, in classic work on Ford and the Model T more than a decade ago we argued that mass production was a caricature and Ford's productive inflexibility was a myth because Highland Park was a high-flow factor (Williams et al. 1992). We would now add the point that Henry Ford had sound grasp of financial engineering in so far as he, for example, persuaded his suppliers to provide his working capital by selling assembled Model T cars before he paid his suppliers for the parts. From this revisionist point of view, the classic Ford enterprise deployed its productive and financial expertise for the social purpose of sustaining high-wage employment symbolized by the $5 day. In the intervening ninety years, inflation has turned this into the $70,000 year but the basic orientation survives for the time being thanks to trucks and credit, which cannot sustain everything else for much longer.

## REFERENCES

AFX Europe (Focus) (2005) 'Toyota plans assault on last bastion of US automakers' profitability', report, 12 January 2005.

AT Kearney (2004a) 'Thinking beyond 4,000 pounds of metal', *Executive Agenda*, 7 (4): 25–32.

—— (2004b) 'Auto company of the future won't sell cars', *Alumni Matters*, 1 (1) winter 2004: 3.

Babson, S. (2001) 'The 1998 Flint–GM strike: bellwether of continental integration and lean production', paper presented to the 7th GERPISA Colloquialism, *Internationalization: Confrontation of Firms, Trajectories and Automobile Areas*, Paris 18–20 June. Online. Available HTTP: <http://www.univ.evry.fr/Pages/Html/laboratoires/ancien-gerpisa/actes/30/30-8.pdf>.

BBC News (2000) '2000: Ford quits Dagenham after 70 years'. Online. Available HTTP: <http://news.bbc.co.uk/onthisday/hi/dates/stories/may/12/newsid_2512000/2512645.stm> (accessed 14 January 2005).

Bear Stearns (2000) *Ford Motor Company: Just Getting Started*, 9 November 2000.

—— (2004) *Too Many Headwinds: Autos Moved To Underweight*, 4 October 2004.

Bernstein Research Call (2004a) *VW: Where Does the Earnings Rebound Come From?* 7 September 2004.

—— (2004b) *Renault: Product Mix and the Margin Outlook*, 13 September 2004.

Boyer, R. and M. Freyssenet (1999) 'The world that changed the machine', Synthesis of GERPISA Research Programs 1993–9, Evry: GERPISA.

Citigroup Smith Barney (2004) *Model Behaviour: Ups and Downs of the Product Cycle*, 3 September 2004.

CJ Lawrence (1994) *Auto Update: Is the US Auto Cycle Over?* 27 May 1994.

Credit Suisse (2004a) *Auto Sales Hit the Brakes: SAAR Drops to 15.4M*, 2 July 2004.

—— (2004b) *Ford: Looking For Guidance on the Guidance*, 20 May 2004.

—— (2004c) *Strong First Half Begets Weak Second Half*, 21 July 2004.

Daily, K. (2003) *The Lean Manufacturing Pocket Handbook*, Grand Blanc, Mich.: DW Publishing.

Datamonitor (2004) *Ford Motor Credit Company*, July 2004.

Deutsche Bank (2003a) *Autos and Auto Parts: Cautious on Auto Demand and Pricing Outlook in 2004*, 3 December 2003.

—— (2003b) *June Sales Not As Good As They Appear*, 1 July 2003.

—— (2004a) *Autos and Auto Parts: US Autos, A Triple Threat*, 20 February 2004.

—— (2004b) *Ford Motor Company: Ford on the Fence*, 20 May 2004.

—— (2004c) *Auto Weekly: That Was the Week That Was*, 24 September 2004.

DiPietro, J. (undated) 'A Ford Taurus/ Mercury Sable history'. Online. Available HTTP: <http://www.edmunds.com/reviews/generations/articles/46007/article.html> (accessed 2 February 2005).

Dominion Bond Rating Service (DBRS) (2002) *The Global Auto Study* (Appendix B. Captive Finance Companies in the Auto Area), 14 November 2002, Toronto: DBRS Ltd. Online. Available HTTP: <http://www.dbrs.com/web/sentry?COMP=2900&DocId=115624> (accessed 5 January 2005).

—— (2003) 'Ford Motor Company', 9 May 2003, Toronto: DBRS Ltd. Online. Available HTTP: <http://www.dbrs.com/web/sentry?COMP=2900&DocId=122841> (accessed 5 January 2005).

Eliot, T. S. (1929) 'Animula', in *Ariel Poems*, No. 23. London: Faber & Faber.

Erturk, I., J. Froud, S. Johal and K. Williams (2005) 'Pay for corporate performance or pay as social division: re-thinking the problem of top management pay in giant corporations', *Competition and Change*, 9 (1): 49–74.

Fahey, J. (2003) 'Taking stock in auto stocks'. Online. Available HTTP: <http://www.forbes.com/2003/04/07/cz_jf_0407feat.html> (accessed 7 April 2004).

Forbes (2004) 'UPDATE 3-Ford has robust 1st quarter, boosts profit forecast', 21 April 2004. Online. Available HTTP: <http://www.forbes.com/newswire/2004/04/21/rtr1340386.html> (accessed 11 February 2005).

Ford (1999a) 'Ford reaches agreement to buy Kwik-Fit', Press Release, 12 April 1999.

—— (1999b) 'Ford posts record 2nd Q operating earnings of $2.5 billion', 14 July 1999.

—— (2002a) 'Ford Motor Company announces revitalization plan', Press Release, 11 January 2002.

—— (2002b) 'Ford corporate revitalization plan', presentation to analysts, 11 January 2002. Online. Available HTTP: <http://media.ford.com/events/Images/revitalize_large/COLOR_slides.pdf> (accessed 1 October 2004).

Freyssenet, M. (1998) 'Intersecting trajectories and model changes', in M. Freyssenet, et al. (eds) *One Best Way? Trajectories and Industrial Models of the Worlds Automotive Producers*, Oxford: Oxford University Press, pp. 8–48.

Freyssenet, M., A. Mair, K. Shimizu and G. Volpato (1998) *One Best Way? Trajectories and Industrial Models of the Worlds Automotive Producers*, Oxford: Oxford University Press.

Froud, J., C. Haslam, S. Johal and K. Williams (1998) 'Breaking the chains? A sector matrix for motoring', *Competition and Change*, 3: 293–334.

—— (2002b) 'Cars after financialisation: a case study in financial underperformance, constraint and consequences', *Competition and Change*, 6 (1) 13–41.

—— (2000) 'Ford's new policy: a business analysis of financialisation', mimeo, University of Manchester, School of Accounting and Finance.

Froud, J., S. Johal and K. Williams (2002a) 'New agendas for auto research: financialisation, motoring and present day capitalism', *Competition and Change*, 6 (1): 1–11.

Froud, J., S. Johal, V. Papazien and K. Williams (2004) 'The temptation of Houston: a case study of financialisation', *Critical Perspectives on Accounting*, 15 (6–7): 885–909.

Gartman, D. (2004) 'Three ages of the automobile: the cultural logic of the car', *Theory, Culture and Society*, 21 (4–5): 169–95.

Golding, T. (2001) *The City: Inside the Great Expectations Machine*, London: Prentice Hall.

Henderson, B., J. Larco and S. Martin (1999) *Lean Transformation: How to Change Your Business into a Lean Enterprise*, Richmond, Va.: Oaklea Press.

Holweg, M. and F. Pil (2004) *The Second Century: Reconnecting the Consumer and Value Chain Through Build-To-Order*, Cambridge, Mass.: MIT Press.

Keller, M. (2003) 'Why aren't investors buying the auto stocks?', Automotive Industries, January 2003. Online. Available HTTP: <http://www.ai-online.com/issues/article_detail.asp?id=39 (accessed 20 March 2005).

Kenney, M. and R. Florida (1993) *Beyond Mass Production: The Japanese System and its Transfer to the US*, Oxford: Oxford University Press.

Lamming, R. (1993) *Beyond Partnership: Strategies for Innovation and Lean Supply*, London: Prentice Hall.

Lapidus, G. (1997) 'The big three autos: fixing the business, still looking to get paid', *Bearnstein Research*, 16 June 1997.

Lapidus, G. and D. Mohsenian (1998) 'Peak auto warnings – it's peak not volume', *Bearnstein Research*, 21 May 1998.

Lehman Brothers (2000) 'North America continues to drive profit', 3 February 2000.

Manheim, *The Used Car Market Report*, various years.

Maxton, G. and J. Wormald (1995) *Driving Over a Cliff? Business Lessons from the World's Car Industry*, Workingham: Addison-Wesley.

McAlinden, S. (2005) 'Understanding the economics of the auto industry', Paper given at FACS conference 'What drives Detroit? Reporting on the economic crisis and technology changes of the auto industry', 8 January, Detroit, Michigan.

Miller, D. (2001) 'Driven societies', in D. Miller (ed.) *Car Cultures*, Oxford: Berg, pp. 1–33.

Morgan Stanley (2002) 'Finance specialty: auto finance channel check: signs of sanity', 25 January 2002.

National Bank Financial (2004) 'August US vehicle sales of 16.5m SAAR weak, inventories lead to lower Q4 production schedule', 1 September 2004.

Orwell, G. (1968) *The Collected Essays, Journalism and Letters of George Orwell*, edited by Sonia Orwell and Ian Angus, London: Secker & Warburg.

Peltz, M. (2004) 'Analysts: the power of positive thinking', Bloomberg Markets, June 2004. Online. Available HTTP: <http://www.bloomberg.com/media/markets/analysts.pdf> (accessed 20 December 2004).

Piore, M. and C. Sabel (1984) *The Second Industrial Divide*, New York: Basic Books.

Porter, M. (1985) *Competitive Advantage: Creating and Sustaining Superior Performance*, New York: Free Press.

Prahalad, C. K. and G. Hamel (1990) 'The core competence of the corporation', *Harvard Business Review*, 68 (May–June): 79–91.

Prudential (1999a) 'Auto manufacturers: prospects look good for demand and valuation', 9 November 1999.

Prudential (1999b) 'Ford Motor: Company Report', 16 November 1999, pp. 3–4.

Samsung Securities (2003) 'Auto industry: auto demand never dies, it just gets pent up', 8 October 2003.

Sherrin, M. (2000) 'The Buddha of Detroit', *New York Times Magazine*, 26 November, p. 112.

Stewart, P. (ed.) (1996) *Beyond Japanese Management: The End of Modern Times*, London: Frank Cass.

Thompson, J. (1997) *Lean Production: How to Use the Highly Effective Japanese Concept of Kaizen to Improve your Efficiency*, Toronto, Ont. : Productive.

Toffler, A. (1980) *Third Wave*, London: Collins.

Tomaney, J. (1994) 'A new paradigm of work organisation and technology' in A. Amin (ed.) *Post-Fordism: A Reader*, Oxford: Blackwell.

UBS (2004) 'Ford and GM: initiating with neutral 2 ratings', 14 May 2004.

Welch, J. (2001) *Jack*, London: Headline.

Wetlaufer, S. (1999) 'Driving change: an interview with Ford Motor Company's Jacques Nasser', *Harvard Business Review*, March–April: 77–88.

Williams, K., C. Haslam, S. Johal and J. Williams (1994) *Cars: Analysis, History, Cases*, Providence, RI: Berghahn Books.

Williams, K., Haslam, C. and Williams, J. (1992) 'Ford versus "Fordism": the beginning of mass production?', *Work, Employment and Society*, 6 (4): 517–55.

Womack, J. P. and D. T. Jones (1996) *Lean Thinking*, New York: Simon & Schuster. Reprinted 2003 by New York: Free Press.

Womack, J. P., D. T. Jones and D. Roos (1990) *The Machine That Changed the World*, New York: Rawson Associates.

## APPENDIX

**Table C2.1** *Ford sales of passenger cars and light trucks in the US market, 1980–2003*

| | *Ford passenger car sales in the US (thousands)* | | | | | *Ford truck sales in the US (thousands)* | | | | | |
|---|---|---|---|---|---|---|---|---|---|---|---|
| | *Small* | *Medium* | *Large* | *Luxury/ premium* | *Total passenger car sales* | *Compact pick-up* | *SUV* | *Full-size pick-up* | *Full-size bus/van/ utility* | *Medium/ heavy* | *Total truck sales* |
| **1980** | 599,498 | 561,767 | 156,512 | 79,654 | 1,397,431 | | | | | | 753,195 |
| **1981** | 682,891 | 476,500 | 163,451 | 62,333 | 1,385,174 | | | | | | 716,648 |
| **1982** | 600,955 | 390,049 | 191,848 | 87,666 | 1,270,519 | | | | | | 803,484 |
| **1983** | 605,205 | 727,249 | 230,714 | 108,669 | 1,671,837 | | | | | | 993,874 |
| **1984** | 628,635 | 937,833 | 323,532 | 157,671 | 2,047,671 | | | | | | 1,238,928 |
| **1985** | 647,536 | 851,713 | 278,071 | 163,342 | 1,940,662 | | | | | | 1,260,123 |
| **1986** | 651,140 | 990,319 | 259,619 | 192,620 | 2,093,698 | | | | | | 1,404,002 |
| **1987** | 697,033 | 1,037,949 | 247,544 | 188,915 | 2,171,442 | 311,022 | 285,844 | 561,321 | 268,072 | 54,799 | 1,481,059 |
| **1988** | 793,840 | 1,131,341 | 237,677 | 213,909 | 2,376,766 | 302,022 | 312,808 | 590,175 | 274,285 | 61,637 | 1,540,928 |
| **1989** | 758,661 | 996,973 | 220,821 | 209,889 | 2,186,344 | 297,038 | 310,747 | 592,553 | 265,049 | 57,884 | 1,523,272 |
| **1990** | 576,313 | 830,187 | 207,547 | 239,049 | 1,853,095 | 281,579 | 359,795 | 523,339 | 211,895 | 45,508 | 1,422,116 |
| **1991** | 501,063 | 759,625 | 162,203 | 183,081 | 1,605,972 | 233,181 | 397,038 | 451,237 | 147,471 | 31,511 | 1,260,439 |
| **1992** | 489,772 | 983,226 | 193,331 | 174,919 | 1,841,248 | 258,408 | 509,216 | 510,736 | 199,126 | 42,561 | 1,520,049 |
| **1993** | 561,669 | 1,002,422 | 193,074 | 193,074 | 1,950,238 | 354,509 | 770,917 | 465,176 | 198,825 | 86,283 | 1,875,711 |
| **1994** | 726,950 | 940,881 | 213,931 | 195,238 | 2,077,000 | 406,815 | 888,396 | 578,337 | 217,701 | 107,751 | 2,199,000 |
| **1995** | 571,343 | 843,771 | 185,403 | 166,484 | 1,767,000 | 334,109 | 839,448 | 747,568 | 246,405 | 58,469 | 2,226,000 |
| **1996** | 494,218 | 815,091 | 195,474 | 151,216 | 1,656,000 | 300,969 | 813,430 | 813,430 | 268,432 | 44,739 | 2,241,000 |
| **1997** | 488,043 | 753,200 | 215,200 | 157,557 | 1,614,000 | 318,886 | 782,721 | 799,286 | 455,552 | 45,555 | 2,402,000 |
| **1998** | 515,751 | 657,484 | 224,411 | 165,355 | 1,563,000 | 337,811 | 727,902 | 856,592 | 486,609 | 16,086 | 2,425,000 |
| **1999** | 569,377 | 662,164 | 240,403 | 253,056 | 1,725,000 | 378,071 | 796,650 | 940,677 | 531,100 | 13,503 | 2,660,000 |
| **2000** | 641,833 | 615,274 | 225,748 | 292,145 | 1,775,000 | 357,544 | 864,442 | 945,908 | 529,528 | 13,578 | 2,711,000 |
| **2001** | 528,941 | 433,808 | 197,877 | 266,373 | 1,427,000 | 272,234 | 915,339 | 903,502 | 359,034 | 7,891 | 2,458,000 |
| **2002** | 496,585 | 472,749 | 174,798 | 309,869 | 1,454,000 | 243,795 | 998,773 | 884,740 | 357,828 | 7,864 | 2,493,000 |
| **2003** | 391,898 | 357,521 | 165,010 | 240,639 | 1,155,067 | 206,262 | 945,368 | 835,361 | 288,767 | 6,875 | 2,282,633 |

*Source*: Ford 10K, various years

*Note*: The faster rate of decline in the medium car segment compared against the general trend is due to a withdrawal of product, e.g. Ford Thunderbird and Contour and the Mercury Mystique. By 2001 Ford made lower fleet sales of the Ford Taurus which accounts for most of the decline in the segment. In 2003, Ford discontinued production of the Lincoln Continental, which accounts for the decline in the premium segment. Ford trucks sold to Freightliner in 1997

*Table C2.2* *US vehicle sales in volume and value terms, 1990–2002 (in real 2002 prices)*

| | *Unit sales* | | | *Average price per passenger car* | *Average price per light truck* | *Consumer sales* | |
|---|---|---|---|---|---|---|---|
| | *Total retail sales of passenger cars* | *Total retail sales of light trucks* | *Total retail sales of passenger cars and light trucks* | | | *Passenger car share of consumer sales revenue* | *Light truck share of consumer sales revenue* |
| | 000s | 000s | 000s | $ | $ | % | % |
| **1990** | 9,300 | 4,560 | 13,860 | 22,435 | | | |
| **1991** | 8,175 | 4,134 | 12,309 | 22,510 | 20,095 | 68.9 | 31.1 |
| **1992** | 8,214 | 4,643 | 12,857 | 23,397 | 20,761 | 66.6 | 33.4 |
| **1993** | 8,518 | 5,365 | 13,883 | 23,684 | 22,414 | 62.7 | 37.3 |
| **1994** | 8,990 | 6,055 | 15,045 | 24,174 | 23,362 | 60.6 | 39.4 |
| **1995** | 8,636 | 6,081 | 14,718 | 23,871 | 25,897 | 56.7 | 43.3 |
| **1996** | 8,527 | 6,563 | 15,090 | 22,047 | 30,479 | 48.4 | 51.6 |
| **1997** | 8,273 | 6,842 | 15,114 | 22,417 | 30,326 | 47.2 | 52.8 |
| **1998** | 8,142 | 7,392 | 15,534 | 23,012 | 30,680 | 45.2 | 54.8 |
| **1999** | 8,697 | 8,183 | 16,879 | 22,851 | 31,464 | 43.6 | 56.4 |
| **2000** | 8,852 | 8,492 | 17,344 | 22,352 | 31,066 | 42.9 | 57.1 |
| **2001** | 8,422 | 8,696 | 17,118 | 22,100 | 31,394 | 40.5 | 59.5 |
| **2002** | 8,102 | 8,708 | 16,810 | 21,912 | 31,204 | 39.5 | 60.5 |

*Sources*: BEA, interactive tables, Annual Abstract of Statistics of the USA, AutoExec (May 2004) and National Accounts of OECD Countries, 1990–2002

*Notes*: Autos: all passenger cars, including station wagons. Light trucks: trucks up to 14,000 pounds gross vehicle weight, including mini-vans and SUVs. Prior to the 2003

*Table C2.3* *Ford Motor Credit receivables and securitization (in nominal values)*

| | *Net finance receivables* | *Of which* | | *Total receivables* | *Receivables securitized/sold* | | |
|---|---|---|---|---|---|---|---|
| | | *Retail* | *Wholesale* | | | *As % of net finance receivables* | *As % of total receivables* |
| | $ million | $ million | $ million | $ million | $ million | | |
| **1980** | 16,094 | 12,112 | 3,909 | 16,094 | 52 | 0.3 | 0.3 |
| **1981** | 17,069 | 13,699 | 3,821 | 17,069 | | | |
| **1982** | 15,312 | 12,302 | 3,610 | 15,312 | 1,389 | 9.1 | 9.1 |
| **1983** | 18,434 | 14,806 | 4,619 | 18,434 | 1,300 | 7.1 | 7.1 |
| **1984** | 23,110 | 18,742 | 6,082 | 23,110 | 737 | 3.2 | 3.2 |
| **1985** | 29,842 | 27,168 | 5,604 | 29,842 | 185 | 0.6 | 0.6 |
| **1986** | 38,061 | 33,954 | 6,824 | 43,401 | 0 | 0.0 | 0.0 |
| **1987** | 48,788 | 42,448 | 9,201 | 54,277 | 0 | 0.0 | 0.0 |
| **1988** | 53,327 | 44,494 | 10,027 | 57,357 | 0 | 0.0 | 0.0 |
| **1989** | 52,375 | 38,309 | 11,058 | 55,871 | 0 | 0.0 | 0.0 |
| **1990** | 55,192 | 38,877 | 12,722 | 58,149 | 0 | 0.0 | 0.0 |
| **1991** | 50,639 | 37,648 | 11,466 | 53,412 | 0 | 0.0 | 0.0 |
| **1992** | 54,257 | 43,348 | 10,057 | 56,520 | 0 | 0.0 | 0.0 |
| **1993** | 51,037 | 38,609 | 11,699 | 63,638 | 0 | 0.0 | 0.0 |
| **1994** | 56,791 | 40,567 | 15,253 | 76,785 | 3,105 | 5.5 | 4.0 |
| **1995** | 61,044 | 43,773 | 16,507 | 85,855 | 4,360 | 7.1 | 5.1 |
| **1996** | 80,848 | 53,099 | 22,706 | 112,617 | 4,669 | 5.8 | 4.1 |
| **1997** | 81,312 | 55,601 | 21,605 | 117,006 | 3,850 | 4.7 | 3.3 |
| **1998** | 95,942 | 67,733 | 22,650 | 131,765 | 7,908 | 8.2 | 6.0 |
| **1999** | 108,754 | 76,182 | 26,450 | 145,035 | 9,929 | 9.1 | 6.8 |
| **2000** | 122,738 | 80,797 | 34,122 | 164,882 | 19,544 | 15.9 | 11.9 |
| **2001** | 109,701 | 85,478 | 15,610 | 161,584 | 40,831 | 37.2 | 25.3 |
| **2002** | 94,636 | 70,837 | 16,571 | 143,885 | 41,289 | 43.6 | 28.7 |
| **2003** | 108,912 | 80,015 | 22,618 | 145,093 | 21,115 | 19.4 | 14.6 |

*Source*: Ford Motor Credit 10K, various years

*Note*: Total receivables include net finance receivables, plus net investments in leases. Securitized assets are not included in Ford Motor Credit's receivable as listed on Ford's balance sheet. The receivables in this table are those to which Ford has a legal claim. Those receivables that have been sold or securitized are those assets sold to special-purpose entities and not booked as Ford Motor Credit assets

*Table C2.4 The contribution of Ford automotive and Ford finance to sales revenue*

| | *Ford consolidated sales revenue* $million | *Ford automotive sales revenue* $million | *Ford finance sales revenue* $million | *Ford automotive contribution* % | *Ford finance contribution* % |
|---|---|---|---|---|---|
| **1980** | 82,841 | 74,392 | | 89.8 | |
| **1981** | 77,458 | 70,219 | | 90.7 | |
| **1982** | 71,029 | 64,232 | | 90.4 | |
| **1983** | 82,144 | 75,707 | | 92.2 | |
| **1984** | 92,775 | 85,948 | | 92.6 | |
| **1985** | 90,248 | 83,587 | | 92.6 | |
| **1986** | 105,250 | 97,790 | | 92.9 | |
| **1987** | 115,941 | 107,662 | | 92.9 | |
| **1988** | 143,858 | 127,898 | 15,954 | 88.9 | 11.1 |
| **1989** | 142,758 | 123,059 | 19,699 | 86.2 | 13.8 |
| **1990** | 137,563 | 115,296 | 22,266 | 83.8 | 16.2 |
| **1991** | 119,358 | 97,409 | 21,949 | 81.6 | 18.4 |
| **1992** | 131,431 | 110,790 | 20,640 | 84.3 | 15.7 |
| **1993** | 138,293 | 116,689 | 21,604 | 84.4 | 15.6 |
| **1994** | 159,528 | 133,070 | 26,458 | 83.4 | 16.6 |
| **1995** | 165,692 | 133,503 | 32,188 | 80.6 | 19.4 |
| **1996** | 172,592 | 138,579 | 34,013 | 80.3 | 19.7 |
| **1997** | 176,328 | 141,101 | 35,227 | 80.0 | 20.0 |
| **1998** | 163,146 | 134,527 | 28,619 | 82.5 | 17.5 |
| **1999** | 179,688 | 151,407 | 28,281 | 84.3 | 15.7 |
| **2000** | 181,803 | 150,979 | 30,824 | 83.0 | 17.0 |
| **2001** | 168,842 | 136,735 | 32,107 | 81.0 | 19.0 |
| **2002** | 166,163 | 137,382 | 28,781 | 82.7 | 17.3 |
| **2003** | 164,196 | 138,442 | 25,754 | 84.3 | 15.7 |

*Source*: Ford Annual Report and Accounts, various years

*Note*: In 1988 Ford consolidated the financial services segment

**Table C2.5** *The contribution of Ford automotive and Ford finance to pre-tax profit (in real 2003 prices)*

| | Ford consolidated pre-tax profit | Ford automotive pre-tax profit | Ford finance pre-tax profit | Ford automotive contribution | Ford finance contribution |
|---|---|---|---|---|---|
| | $million | $million | $million | % | % |
| **1980** | –4,424 | –4,424 | | | |
| **1981** | –2,305 | –2,305 | | | |
| **1982** | –778 | –778 | | | |
| **1983** | 4,003 | 4,003 | | 100.0 | |
| **1984** | 7,588 | 7,588 | | 100.0 | |
| **1985** | 6,208 | 6,208 | | 100.0 | |
| **1986** | 8,507 | 8,507 | | 100.0 | |
| **1987** | 11,943 | 11,943 | | 100.0 | |
| **1988** | 12,982 | 11,378 | 1,604 | 87.6 | 12.4 |
| **1989** | 8,953 | 7,655 | 1,298 | 85.5 | 14.5 |
| **1990** | 2,106 | 387 | 1,719 | 18.4 | 81.6 |
| **1991** | –3,497 | –5,477 | 1,980 | | 100.0 |
| **1992** | –9,693 | –2,562 | 2,395 | | 100.0 |
| **1993** | 5,101 | 1,645 | 3,456 | 32.3 | 67.7 |
| **1994** | 10,916 | 7,449 | 3,468 | 68.2 | 31.8 |
| **1995** | 8,101 | 3,825 | 4,276 | 47.2 | 52.8 |
| **1996** | 7,976 | 3,019 | 4,957 | 37.8 | 62.2 |
| **1997** | 12,555 | 8,129 | 4,427 | 64.7 | 35.3 |
| **1998** | 28,690 | 7,860 | 20,829 | 27.4 | 72.6 |
| **1999** | 12,188 | 9,337 | 2,851 | 76.6 | 23.4 |
| **2000** | 8,802 | 5,631 | 3,172 | 64.0 | 36.0 |
| **2001** | –7,884 | –9,394 | 1,509 | | 100.0 |
| **2002** | 974 | –1,181 | 2,155 | | 100.0 |
| **2003** | 1,370 | –1,957 | 3,327 | | 100.0 |

*Source*: Ford Annual Report and Accounts, various years

*Note*: In 1988 Ford consolidated the financial services segment. Consequently, segment totals may not equal consolidated total

**Table C2.6** *Ford Motor Credit structure of capital employed (in real 2003 prices – all data in $ million)*

| | Commercial paper | Other short-term borrowing (mainly banks) | Total short-term borrowing | Long-term debt | Long-term debt maturing within 12 months | Total long-term debt | Other long-term liabilities | Total debt (short- and long-term) | Stockholder equity | Total capital employed (debt and equity) |
|---|---|---|---|---|---|---|---|---|---|---|
| **1980** | 14,223 | 2,693 | 16,917 | 13,487 | 1,311 | 14,797 | 2,121 | 33,835 | 3,433 | 37,268 |
| **1981** | 11,799 | 3,520 | 15,319 | 13,300 | 1,627 | 14,927 | 2,358 | 32,604 | 3,281 | 35,885 |
| **1982** | 7,464 | 4,258 | 11,722 | 11,370 | 1,837 | 13,208 | 2,377 | 27,308 | 3,513 | 30,821 |
| **1983** | 10,790 | 3,246 | 14,035 | 12,945 | 1,910 | 14,856 | 2,901 | 31,792 | 3,516 | 35,309 |
| **1984** | 15,239 | 3,192 | 18,431 | 14,887 | 2,491 | 17,378 | 3,084 | 38,893 | 3,688 | 42,581 |
| **1985** | 19,085 | 1,813 | 20,898 | 19,634 | 3,941 | 23,575 | 5,065 | 49,539 | 4,009 | 53,548 |
| **1986** | 24,017 | 1,104 | 25,121 | 26,147 | 3,696 | 29,842 | 7,002 | 61,965 | 4,998 | 66,963 |
| **1987** | 27,771 | 3,342 | 31,113 | 33,030 | 5,377 | 38,407 | 7,502 | 77,023 | 5,902 | 82,925 |
| **1988** | 30,205 | 2,288 | 32,493 | 35,398 | 6,073 | 41,471 | 6,978 | 80,942 | 6,627 | 87,570 |
| **1989** | 26,989 | 3,197 | 30,187 | 32,136 | 6,902 | 39,038 | 5,754 | 74,979 | 6,583 | 81,562 |
| **1990** | 32,155 | 2,756 | 34,911 | 30,346 | 6,027 | 36,372 | 4,916 | 76,200 | 6,872 | 83,072 |
| **1991** | 24,394 | 2,474 | 26,868 | 30,815 | 7,256 | 38,071 | 5,585 | 70,524 | 6,341 | 76,865 |
| **1992** | 27,840 | 2,343 | 30,184 | 28,138 | 7,188 | 35,326 | 5,480 | 70,990 | 6,409 | 77,399 |
| **1993** | 31,229 | 1,276 | 32,505 | 32,471 | 10,045 | 42,516 | 6,315 | 81,336 | 7,359 | 88,695 |
| **1994** | 41,272 | 1,411 | 42,683 | 38,953 | 5,853 | 44,807 | 7,604 | 95,094 | 8,275 | 103,369 |
| **1995** | 42,261 | 1,840 | 44,102 | 43,543 | 8,007 | 51,550 | 9,480 | 105,131 | 9,127 | 114,257 |
| **1996** | 44,886 | 5,623 | 50,509 | 53,811 | 10,777 | 64,588 | 16,986 | 132,083 | 10,809 | 142,892 |
| **1997** | 46,894 | 6,142 | 53,036 | 51,586 | 10,987 | 62,573 | 13,273 | 128,882 | 11,116 | 139,997 |
| **1998** | 52,179 | 8,411 | 60,589 | 58,343 | 10,946 | 69,289 | 13,145 | 143,023 | 12,025 | 155,048 |
| **1999** | 47,617 | 7,483 | 55,100 | 70,006 | 21,990 | 91,996 | 13,964 | 161,061 | 12,075 | 173,136 |
| **2000** | 45,172 | 8,419 | 53,590 | 89,059 | 13,744 | 102,803 | 16,866 | 173,259 | 13,028 | 186,287 |
| **2001** | 16,284 | 7,333 | 23,617 | 106,452 | 22,117 | 128,569 | 15,304 | 167,491 | 12,458 | 179,949 |
| **2002** | 8,360 | 8,190 | 16,550 | 103,527 | 23,344 | 126,871 | 16,644 | 160,065 | 13,848 | 173,913 |
| **2003** | 6,095 | 18,602 | 24,697 | 95,474 | 29,534 | 125,008 | 16,650 | 166,355 | 12,474 | 178,829 |

*Source*: Ford Motor Credit 10K, various years

*Note*: Commercial paper in 2000's declines because of legislative rules but Ford use asset backed commercial paper which appears in bank finance

*Table C2.7 Ford Motor Credit performance*

| | *Pre-tax return on sales revenue* | *Net return on sales revenue* | *Pre-tax return on all capital employed* | *Net return on all capital employed* |
|---|---|---|---|---|
| | % | % | % | % |
| **1980** | 10.8 | 6.6 | 1.6 | 1.0 |
| **1981** | 10.9 | 6.5 | 1.9 | 1.1 |
| **1982** | 15.6 | 8.7 | 2.8 | 1.5 |
| **1983** | 20.8 | 11.1 | 3.1 | 1.7 |
| **1984** | 16.8 | 9.8 | 2.4 | 1.4 |
| **1985** | 19.3 | 11.0 | 2.7 | 1.6 |
| **1986** | 21.4 | 12.3 | 3.0 | 1.7 |
| **1987** | 19.1 | 11.6 | 2.4 | 1.5 |
| **1988** | 12.0 | 8.3 | 1.6 | 1.1 |
| **1989** | 8.3 | 5.9 | 1.2 | 0.9 |
| **1990** | 11.1 | 8.2 | 1.4 | 1.0 |
| **1991** | 14.9 | 10.4 | 2.0 | 1.4 |
| **1992** | 18.3 | 14.4 | 2.4 | 1.9 |
| **1993** | 22.0 | 14.0 | 2.9 | 1.8 |
| **1994** | 18.8 | 12.4 | 2.6 | 1.7 |
| **1995** | 14.6 | 10.4 | 2.2 | 1.6 |
| **1996** | 13.4 | 8.6 | 2.1 | 1.3 |
| **1997** | 10.3 | 5.9 | 1.6 | 0.9 |
| **1998** | 9.4 | 5.6 | 1.4 | 0.9 |
| **1999** | 10.3 | 6.2 | 1.5 | 0.9 |
| **2000** | 10.6 | 6.5 | 1.6 | 1.0 |
| **2001** | 5.9 | 3.3 | 1.0 | 0.5 |
| **2002** | 8.6 | 5.4 | 1.3 | 0.8 |
| **2003** | 14.8 | 8.9 | 1.9 | 1.1 |

*Source*: Ford Motor Credit 10K, various years

Table C2.8 *Ford Motor Credit operations*

| | Total number of vehicles financed by installment plans | Total number of vehicles under lease contracts | Total number of vehicles financed and leased | Revenue $million | Pre-tax income $million | Net income $million |
|---|---|---|---|---|---|---|
| 1980 | | | | 5,365 | 577 | 356 |
| 1981 | | | | 5,771 | 628 | 377 |
| 1982 | | | | 5,019 | 785 | 437 |
| 1983 | | | | 4,849 | 1,007 | 539 |
| 1984 | | | | 5,639 | 949 | 550 |
| 1985 | | | | 6,829 | 1,320 | 753 |
| 1986 | | | 2,061,000 | 8,345 | 1,789 | 1,026 |
| 1987 | | | 2,115,000 | 9,463 | 1,811 | 1,099 |
| 1988 | | | 1,867,000 | 10,611 | 1,271 | 878 |
| 1989 | | | 1,736,000 | 11,331 | 935 | 666 |
| 1990 | | | 1,667,000 | 9,661 | 1,075 | 793 |
| 1991 | | | 1,712,000 | 9,726 | 1,453 | 1,013 |
| 1992 | | | 2,049,000 | 9,487 | 1,737 | 1,364 |
| 1993 | | | 2,424,000 | 10,878 | 2,389 | 1,522 |
| 1994 | 2,432,000 | 852,000 | 3,284,000 | 13,192 | 2,483 | 1,631 |
| 1995 | 2,557,000 | 965,000 | 3,522,000 | 16,148 | 2,350 | 1,686 |
| 1996 | 2,436,000 | 1,160,000 | 3,596,000 | 19,573 | 2,630 | 1,692 |
| 1997 | 2,389,000 | 1,206,000 | 3,595,000 | 20,204 | 2,073 | 1,183 |
| 1998 | 3,030,000 | 1,138,000 | 4,168,000 | 21,806 | 2,047 | 1,225 |
| 1999 | 3,428,000 | 1,065,000 | 4,493,000 | 22,505 | 2,325 | 1,394 |
| 2000 | 3,777,000 | 1,228,000 | 5,005,000 | 25,235 | 2,667 | 1,643 |
| 2001 | 4,495,000 | 1,050,000 | 5,545,000 | 26,458 | 1,567 | 872 |
| 2002 | 3,322,000 | 775,000 | 4,097,000 | 23,475 | 2,013 | 1,261 |
| 2003 | 2,960,000 | 487,000 | 3,447,000 | 20,441 | 3,035 | 1,817 |

*Source*: Ford Motor Credit 10K, various years

*Note*: Data on numbers of vehicles financed and leased before 1994 refers only to the USA. After 1994, it includes vehicle financing worldwide

Table C2.9 *Cost structure of Ford Motor Credit, 1980–2003*

| | *Revenue* | *Major costs as a % of revenues* | | | |
|---|---|---|---|---|---|
| | $ million (in 2003 prices) | *Depreciation* % | *Interest expense* % | *Other expenses* % | *Pre-tax income as a % of revenues* |
| 1980 | 5,365 | | 67.6 | 21.7 | 10.8 |
| 1981 | 5,771 | | 71.6 | 17.6 | 10.9 |
| 1982 | 5,019 | | 64.4 | 20.0 | 15.6 |
| 1983 | 4,849 | | 57.3 | 22.0 | 20.8 |
| 1984 | 5,639 | 2.3 | 60.7 | 20.2 | 16.8 |
| 1985 | 6,829 | 2.8 | 55.1 | 22.8 | 19.3 |
| 1986 | 8,345 | 3.0 | 51.1 | 24.5 | 21.4 |
| 1987 | 9,463 | 3.5 | 52.0 | 25.4 | 19.1 |
| 1988 | 10,611 | 3.7 | 55.9 | 28.4 | 12.0 |
| 1989 | 11,331 | 4.2 | 60.8 | 26.8 | 8.3 |
| 1990 | 9,661 | 8.3 | 62.6 | 18.0 | 11.1 |
| 1991 | 9,726 | 14.3 | 52.7 | 18.0 | 14.9 |
| 1992 | 9,487 | 22.9 | 42.6 | 16.3 | 18.3 |
| 1993 | 10,878 | 31.3 | 34.2 | 12.5 | 22.0 |
| 1994 | 13,192 | 36.8 | 33.3 | 11.0 | 18.8 |
| 1995 | 16,148 | 37.7 | 37.1 | 10.6 | 14.6 |
| 1996 | 19,573 | 33.2 | 37.3 | 16.0 | 13.4 |
| 1997 | 20,204 | 35.2 | 37.1 | 17.5 | 10.3 |
| 1998 | 21,806 | 38.0 | 35.8 | 16.9 | 9.4 |
| 1999 | 22,505 | 37.2 | 35.3 | 17.2 | 10.3 |
| 2000 | 25,235 | 33.2 | 38.0 | 18.2 | 10.6 |
| 2001 | 26,458 | 34.8 | 35.2 | 24.1 | 5.9 |
| 2002 | 23,475 | 37.1 | 30.2 | 24.2 | 8.6 |
| 2003 | 20,441 | 34.3 | 28.5 | 22.3 | 14.8 |

*Source*: Ford Motor Credit 10K, various years

**Table C2.10** *Ford consolidated, major cost items, 1980–2003 (in real 2003 prices)*

| | *Labour costs* | *Significant cost items* | | | *Operating cost structure* | | |
|---|---|---|---|---|---|---|---|
| | | *Depreciation and amortization* | *Interest payments* | *Dividends* | *External purchases as a % of sales revenues* | *Labour costs as a % of internal costs* | *Depreciation and amortization as a % of internal costs* |
| | $ million | $ million | $ million | $ million | | | |
| **1980** | 27,738 | 4,399 | 966 | 699 | 61.2 | 100.1 | 15.9 |
| **1981** | 24,785 | 4,414 | 1,366 | 292 | 62.3 | 92.2 | 16.4 |
| **1982** | 22,420 | 4,112 | 1,422 | 0 | 62.5 | 87.1 | 16.0 |
| **1983** | 22,817 | 4,235 | 1,048 | 168 | 62.2 | 73.5 | 13.6 |
| **1984** | 24,041 | 4,089 | 950 | 784 | 61.5 | 67.3 | 11.4 |
| **1985** | 23,998 | 4,092 | 764 | 758 | 62.0 | 70.0 | 11.9 |
| **1986** | 26,197 | 4,967 | 810 | 992 | 62.3 | 66.0 | 12.5 |
| **1987** | 26,811 | 5,126 | 713 | 1,303 | 62.2 | 61.1 | 11.7 |
| **1988** | 28,178 | 5,901 | 9,551 | 1,733 | 67.3 | 59.9 | 12.5 |
| **1989** | 26,936 | 6,279 | 12,766 | 2,085 | 70.5 | 63.9 | 14.9 |
| **1990** | 26,643 | 6,874 | 13,486 | 1,957 | 74.1 | 74.8 | 19.3 |
| **1991** | 24,332 | 7,812 | 12,464 | 1,253 | 73.1 | 84.9 | 27.3 |
| **1992** | 26,020 | 8,867 | 10,391 | 1,282 | 73.5 | 74.9 | 25.5 |
| **1993** | 25,598 | 9,517 | 9,289 | 1,384 | 70.9 | 63.7 | 23.7 |
| **1994** | 28,438 | 11,596 | 9,618 | 1,497 | 68.1 | 55.8 | 22.8 |
| **1995** | 28,588 | 14,159 | 12,138 | 1,884 | 69.3 | 56.2 | 27.8 |
| **1996** | 30,161 | 15,019 | 12,210 | 2,114 | 69.2 | 56.7 | 28.3 |
| **1997** | 29,321 | 15,590 | 12,052 | 2,318 | 67.4 | 51.0 | 27.1 |
| **1998** | 29,068 | 16,187 | 10,015 | 30,050 | 54.7 | 39.3 | 21.9 |
| **1999** | 30,473 | 16,518 | 10,032 | 2,531 | 67.1 | 51.5 | 27.9 |
| **2000** | 27,424 | 16,427 | 11,655 | 2,941 | 71.0 | 52.1 | 31.2 |
| **2001** | 24,485 | 19,886 | 11,277 | 2,005 | 73.7 | 67.1 | 54.5 |
| **2002** | 24,396 | 15,470 | 9,018 | 759 | 75.4 | 59.7 | 37.9 |
| **2003** | | 14,263 | 7,690 | 733 | | | |

*Source*: Ford Motor Company 10K, various years

*Note*: The 1998 totals include the proceeds from the sale of The Associates. In 2003, Ford did not disclose labour costs

**Table C2.11** *Ford Motor Company operating performance (in real 2003 values)*

| | *Number of vehicles sold* | *Sales revenue* | *Pre-tax income* | *Net income* | *Pre-tax ROS* | *Net ROS* |
|---|---|---|---|---|---|---|
| | | $ million | $ million | $ million | % | % |
| **1980** | 4,328,450 | 82,841 | –4,424 | –3,447 | –5.3 | –4.2 |
| **1981** | 4,313,188 | 77,458 | –2,305 | –2,147 | –3.0 | –2.8 |
| **1982** | 4,267,587 | 71,029 | –778 | –1,254 | –1.1 | –1.8 |
| **1983** | 4,934,231 | 82,144 | 4,003 | 3,450 | 4.9 | 4.2 |
| **1984** | 5,584,851 | 92,775 | 7,588 | 5,150 | 8.2 | 5.6 |
| **1985** | 5,550,500 | 90,248 | 6,208 | 4,303 | 6.9 | 4.8 |
| **1986** | 5,915,745 | 105,250 | 8,507 | 5,515 | 8.1 | 5.2 |
| **1987** | 6,051,374 | 115,941 | 11,943 | 7,483 | 10.3 | 6.5 |
| **1988** | 6,440,672 | 143,858 | 12,982 | 8,247 | 9.0 | 5.7 |
| **1989** | 6,336,354 | 142,758 | 8,953 | 5,693 | 6.3 | 4.0 |
| **1990** | 5,804,819 | 137,563 | 2,106 | 1,212 | 1.5 | 0.9 |
| **1991** | 5,345,557 | 119,358 | –3,497 | –3,053 | –2.9 | –2.6 |
| **1992** | 5,764,374 | 131,431 | –9,693 | –10,186 | –7.4 | –7.7 |
| **1993** | 5,963,586 | 138,293 | 5,101 | 3,223 | 3.7 | 2.3 |
| **1994** | 6,639,000 | 159,528 | 10,916 | 6,593 | 6.8 | 4.1 |
| **1995** | 6,606,000 | 165,692 | 8,101 | 10,750 | 4.9 | 6.5 |
| **1996** | 6,653,000 | 172,592 | 7,976 | 5,220 | 4.6 | 3.0 |
| **1997** | 6,943,000 | 176,328 | 12,555 | 7,943 | 7.1 | 4.5 |
| **1998** | 6,823,000 | 163,146 | 28,690 | 24,933 | 17.6 | 15.3 |
| **1999** | 7,220,000 | 179,688 | 12,188 | 8,000 | 6.8 | 4.5 |
| **2000** | 7,424,000 | 181,803 | 8,802 | 5,783 | 4.8 | 3.2 |
| **2001** | 6,991,000 | 168,842 | –7,884 | –5,669 | –4.7 | –3.4 |
| **2002** | 6,973,000 | 166,163 | 974 | –1,002 | 0.6 | –0.6 |
| **2003** | 6,720,000 | 164,196 | 1,370 | 495 | 0.8 | 0.3 |

*Source*: Ford Annual Report and Accounts, various years

*Note*: Accounting changes in 1992 have the effect of increasing the losses stated by $6.9 billion. The profit stated in 1998 includes a gain on sales from The Associates of around $16 billion (this is an accounting adjustment, not a cash gain)

**Table C2.12** *Ford Motor Company capital market performance, 1980–2003 (in real 2003 values)*

| | *Ford Motor Company share price (adjusted for splits)* | *Market capitalization* | *P/E ratio* | *Dividends per share* | *Dividend yield (net)* | *Total annual return per share* | *Cumulative return per share* |
|---|---|---|---|---|---|---|---|
| | $ | $ million | | $ | $ | $ | $ |
| **1980** | 60.17 | 7,257 | −2.11 | 5.67 | 9.60 | | |
| **1981** | 42.28 | 5,098 | −2.37 | 2.42 | 5.20 | −15 | −15 |
| **1982** | 36.71 | 4,655 | −3.71 | 0.00 | 0.00 | −6 | −21 |
| **1983** | 96.32 | 11,751 | 3.41 | 1.38 | 1.43 | 61 | 40 |
| **1984** | 114.10 | 14,157 | 2.75 | 6.32 | 5.54 | 24 | 64 |
| **1985** | 127.29 | 15,793 | 3.67 | 6.11 | 4.80 | 19 | 83 |
| **1986** | 93.93 | 11,204 | 2.03 | 8.31 | 8.85 | −25 | 58 |
| **1987** | 154.52 | 34,854 | 4.66 | 5.78 | 3.74 | 66 | 125 |
| **1988** | 326.05 | 35,561 | 4.31 | 15.89 | 4.87 | 187 | 312 |
| **1989** | 327.40 | 34,399 | 6.04 | 19.84 | 6.06 | 21 | 333 |
| **1990** | 234.95 | 24,701 | 20.39 | 18.61 | 7.92 | −74 | 259 |
| **1991** | 185.94 | 19,969 | −6.54 | 11.67 | 6.28 | −37 | 222 |
| **1992** | 226.30 | 24,616 | −2.54 | 11.79 | 5.21 | 52 | 274 |
| **1993** | 312.89 | 34,696 | 10.77 | 12.48 | 3.99 | 99 | 373 |
| **1994** | 339.20 | 38,555 | 5.85 | 13.17 | 3.88 | 39 | 413 |
| **1995** | 313.31 | 40,382 | 8.08 | 14.61 | 4.66 | −11 | 402 |
| **1996** | 340.80 | 45,024 | 8.62 | 16.00 | 4.69 | 43 | 445 |
| **1997** | 414.49 | 55,403 | 5.98 | 17.35 | 4.18 | 91 | 536 |
| **1998** | 456.26 | 61,949 | 2.48 | 221.32 | 48.51 | 263 | 799 |
| **1999** | 567.68 | 77,078 | 9.64 | 18.64 | 3.28 | 130 | 929 |
| **2000** | 250.25 | 53,053 | 14.31 | 13.87 | 5.50 | −304 | 626 |
| **2001** | 215.76 | 45,740 | −8.07 | 9.46 | 4.38 | −25 | 601 |

| | | | | | | | |
|---|---|---|---|---|---|---|---|
| **2002** | 115.57 | 24,501 | −24.46 | 3.58 | 3.10 | −97 | 504 |
| **2003** | 107.60 | 22,810 | 46.08 | 3.46 | 3.21 | −5 | 499 |
| TOTAL/ cumulative return $ | 47.42 | | | 452.00 | | 499 | |
| Total % return from each share 1980–2003 | 9.49 | | | 90.50 | | 100 | |

*Source*: Ford Annual Report and Accounts, various years

*Notes*: Market Valuation uses the annual average of high and low share price. The cumulative return column refers to the sum of the returns from the current and previous years; e.g. if a shareholder had cashed shares in 1999, he or she would have gained $929 in share appreciation and dividends since 1980. If the shares were cashed in 2003, the return would have been $499. The table incorporates a correction for share splits. The P/E ratio calculated using net income

**Table C2.13** *Ford employment and labour costs, 1980–2003*

| | *US employment* | | *All other employment* | | *Total employment* | *Average labour cost per employee (real 2003 values)* |
|---|---|---|---|---|---|---|
| | No. | % of total | No. | % of total | No. | $ |
| **1980** | 179,917 | 42.2 | 246,818 | 57.8 | 426,735 | 64,999 |
| **1981** | 170,806 | 42.2 | 233,982 | 57.8 | 404,788 | 61,229 |
| **1982** | 155,901 | 41.1 | 223,328 | 58.9 | 379,229 | 59,119 |
| **1983** | 163,356 | 43.0 | 216,721 | 57.0 | 380,077 | 60,033 |
| **1984** | 178,758 | 46.2 | 208,159 | 53.8 | 386,917 | 62,133 |
| **1985** | 172,165 | 45.0 | 210,109 | 55.0 | 382,274 | 62,775 |
| **1986** | 181,476 | 49.1 | 187,838 | 50.9 | 369,314 | 70,933 |
| **1987** | 180,838 | 51.6 | 169,482 | 48.4 | 350,320 | 76,531 |
| **1988** | 185,540 | 51.7 | 173,399 | 48.3 | 358,939 | 78,50 |
| **1989** | 188,286 | 51.4 | 178,355 | 48.6 | 366,641 | 73,466 |
| **1990** | 180,940 | 48.9 | 189,443 | 51.1 | 370,383 | 71,934 |
| **1991** | 156,079 | 47.0 | 175,898 | 53.0 | 331,977 | 73,295 |
| **1992** | 158,377 | 48.7 | 166,956 | 51.3 | 325,333 | 79,981 |
| **1993** | 166,943 | 51.8 | 155,270 | 48.2 | 322,213 | 79,443 |
| **1994** | 180,460 | 53.4 | 157,318 | 46.6 | 337,778 | 84,191 |
| **1995** | 185,960 | 53.6 | 161,030 | 46.4 | 346,990 | 82,387 |
| **1996** | 189,718 | 51.0 | 181,984 | 49.0 | 371,702 | 81,142 |
| **1997** | 189,787 | 52.2 | 174,105 | 47.8 | 363,892 | 80,575 |
| **1998** | 173,899 | 50.4 | 171,276 | 49.6 | 345,175 | 84,212 |
| **1999** | 173,064 | 47.5 | 191,486 | 52.5 | 364,550 | 83,590 |
| **2000** | 163,236 | 47.2 | 182,755 | 52.8 | 345,991 | 79,261 |
| **2001** | 165,512 | 46.7 | 188,919 | 53.3 | 354,431 | 69,083 |
| **2002** | 161,868 | 46.2 | 188,453 | 53.8 | 350,321 | 69,639 |
| **2003** | | | | | 327,531 | |

*Source*: Ford Annual Report and Accounts, various years

Notes: Employment is measured as the average number of employees during the year. Unconsolidated employees are included so that Hertz employees are counted from 1994 and onwards. In 2003, Ford no longer provided geographical breakdowns for its financial service employees, hence the data on US and other employment ends in 2002. Information on labour costs was not disclosed in 2003. From 2003 Visteon employees are not included in Ford's total, accounting for the apparent fall in total employment of a little over 20,000 between 2002 and 2003. As the text explains, Ford retains some residual liability for its

Case 3

# General Electric

## The conditions of success

### INTRODUCTION

By the late 1990s, GE and its long-serving CEO Jack Welch were icons of business success whose lustre was not diminished by the new economy crash at the beginning of the decade. In 2002, GE came top of *Fortune*'s most admired companies list for the fifth year in a row (19 February 2002) and, at the beginning of this period, *Fortune* (22 November 1999) described Welch as 'the most widely admired and imitated CEO of his time'. In 2004, several years after his retirement, Jack Welch still commands a Top 3 position in the *Financial Times*'s list of most admired executives. It is easy to understand the basis for this hero worship. GE under Welch in the decades of the 1980s and 1990s was the only US giant firm from the glory days of the 1960s that could, despite increasingly difficult product markets, apparently meet the requirements of a more demanding capital market. *The Financial Times*'s report (20 January 2004) on the 'world's most respected companies' asked CEOs about the companies they most admired, and one CEO then commented that GE had 'survived the pitfalls of many blue chips, while others have fallen'. Against this background, GE and Welch must appear as a brilliant success.

Behind the iconic status of GE and Welch is a familiar long-established frame of reference which explains 'greatness' by cutting between the undisputed exceptional achievement and its socio-technical conditions, which are identified within a belief system and then elaborated in a hagiographic literature. This includes many books because in academe, as in journalism, length is the writer's homage to worldly importance. Thus, there are at least fifty books about GE and Welch (including almost inevitably an uninformative autobiography by Welch himself) which reflect on the conditions of GE's financial achievement in Welch's leadership and GE's organization and thus generically identify the conditions of achievement as the right kind of management. Although the identification starts with the well-known financial success, such books, however, are generally not interested in financial analysis of GE's operations and performance.

Before turning to GE, it may be helpful to note that this kind of cross-cutting reference between achievement and conditions was established long before the concept 'management' came into general use in the 1950s, and the identifications made through such reference are usually problematic. Thus, if we consider the original Henry Ford and Ford Motor Company in the early twentieth century, Henry's undisputed achievement was the motorization of America through a combination of cheap product and high wages, and the conditions of that achievement were generally located in the production techniques and factory lay-out that were definitively described in Arnold and Faurote's (1914) book describing the Highland Park Plant. The preoccupation with productive intervention was coherent with assumptions of the epoch, articulated in the textbooks of 'business administration' by authors like E. L. Jones (1916) who included layout in the syllabus. But our own revisionist work on how Henry Ford built the Model T shows that the established causal identifications were largely imagined: the moving assembly line was relatively unimportant at the time as a source of cost reduction, and Ford's high-flow proto-Japanese techniques have subsequently been caricatured as (inflexible) mass production (Williams et al. 1993).

The current doxic accounts of GE and Welch raise many of the same problems in a different register where the discursive a priori is supplied by the management of change (not business administration). GE and Welch's undisputed achievement is the nearly unbroken run of earnings increases which sustains the stock price and justifies a P/E ratio much higher than for other 'old economy' stocks. As *Fortune* (19 February 2002) enthused, 'quarter after quarter, year after year, GE's earnings come gushing in, usually at least 10 per cent higher than the year before, and almost invariably inline with analysts' estimates'. This achievement is both interestingly less socially transformative and apparently more technically difficult than anything that Henry Ford did. And the achievement is generally referred to its socio-technical conditions in the leadership of Welch as CEO and the internal culture and organization of GE. Thus *Fortune* (19 February 2002) noted GE's 'long history of training great managers, its straight talking celebrity CEO, its vaunted culture of entrepreneurship and achievement'. In so far as different media and academic authors only disagree about the relative contributions of leadership and organization, our case makes a revisionist argument that all these identifications are imagined and have misleading effects (just like so much earlier analysis of Ford's assembly line and mass production).

The case study that makes this revisionist argument is organized in a relatively straightforward way with two sections on narrative followed by another two on numbers. The first two sections explore existing identifications which relate GE's exceptional financial achievement to its conditions, and these two sections analyse in turn the industry frame and company narrative. As the first section argues, the industry frame is problematic because GE is by most standards a conglomerate that operates across many industries when conglomerates are out of fashion. GE avoids the stigma by putting up the narrative and performative defence that GE is not a conglomerate because the diverse operations of GE across unrelated product markets are unified by management initiatives such as 'Work Out' and 'Six Sigma'. When these initiatives are validated by their link with the unbroken record of financial achievement, we argue the result is that GE has become a (management) brand.

The second section turns to the company narrative which mainly originates with outsiders and does so in ways that illuminate how financialized economies proliferate much information but very little critical knowledge. This section shows that, while some analysts have raised criticism of GE's performance, they are generally incorporated into a community where media critics allege that 'unbelievers' are ostracized and marginalized. Business media coverage is more independent, which is evident in its questioning or (sometimes) negative treatment of GE in the early 1980s; subsequent analysis shows that Welch and GE move along a reputational S curve which flattens out in the early 2000s. Popular business books are then analysed in the remaining part of the second section where a comparison of several books by different authors brings out their stereotyped nature because they refer GE's success to either leadership or organization.

If GE is described in these many admiring narratives, our case then aims to deconstruct that achievement. For this purpose, the financial information from GE is an invaluable resource because basic information such as business-segment sales revenue, cannot be manipulated, and, moreover, forensic analysis discloses much about the how and why behind the headline results. The third and four sections demonstrate this point by analysing the numbers in the long twenty-year time frame which is particularly illuminating in this case because GE has changed its sources of revenue quite radically over two decades.

Thus, the third section uses basic divisional information which shows that GE over this period is a tale of two complementary businesses that combine to produce the miraculous financial achievement of the Welch years: GE's industrial business generates high ROCE with low sales growth, while a financial business, GE Capital, generates high sales growth and low ROCE. This view is immediately different because GE Capital barely figures in the management-school narratives of GE. The fourth section then takes the argument one step further by providing an in-depth analysis of what we call GE's (undisclosed) business model, whereby the industrial business is run for cash and bulked out with services that cover the hollowing out that would otherwise be inevitable. Meanwhile, the financial business is expanded up to the limit of the credit rating against a background of continuous large-scale acquisition and (to a lesser extent) divestment of business units. This (undisclosed) business model is in no sense a hidden one; all of the elements we identify are derived from GE's accounts or other relevant sources such as company statements. But there is little attempt by external commentators to go beyond the company's narrative of initiatives and achievement in a way that seeks to understand the business model, rather than the organization and its leader.

In contrast, our analysis is interesting in a number of ways. It provides an essential context within which the fifth section of this chapter analyses the moves of GE since 2001 under its new CEO, Jeff Immelt. Because GE is at the end of a finance-led growth trajectory, Immelt has turned to large industrial acquisitions, which are a much riskier way of buying growth and earnings. It also allows us to revalue Welch's achievement. GE under Welch was a brilliant success but the conditions of that success are very different from those that figure so prominently in GE's own performative frame, or in the many outsider narratives that unquestioningly accept the attribution of GE's exceptional success to outstanding management. If we assume the business model is the result of something other than inadvertence and serendipity, the Machiavellian virtue of Welch and his senior management team was to see that the narrative and performative moves were necessary but not sufficient. Sustained success also depended on pulling levers to obtain earnings from finance, an important part of a business model that was little discussed in public. While such insight and complexity is exceptional, issues about undisclosed business models do arise in other business cases and always have the effect of making corporate governance and investor decisions much more difficult.

While this sets GE's achievement in a different perspective, we would emphasize that this case is not an exercise in muck-raking that impugns GE's corporate integrity or its management's honesty. Our methods of analysis are completely different from those of O'Boyle (1998) in his highly critical book which establishes GE's bad character by focusing on negative incidents such as GE's responsibility for polluting the Hudson river with polychlorinated biphenyl (PCBs). Our revisionism is based on publicly available financial information, which gives an overview of the two businesses and GE's undisclosed business model. If our story is new and different, it is because considerable effort is required to analyse the information so as to generate a different story. The lesson of this case is that a shallow world prefers congenial narratives of management success, which falsely present GE as a model for others and a source of transferable lessons for success. That shallow preference needs to be challenged if we wish to understand what management can do in a world where it is very unlikely that GE's management techniques would lead to financial success in firms with different business models. GE demonstrates only that exceptional success depends on aligning a strong and appealing corporate narrative with a corroborating record of financial performance that deflects difficult questions.

## INDUSTRY FRAME: 'NOT A CONGLOMERATE'

The idea of industry frame may seem paradoxical in this case because GE has no strong industry affiliation. By any standard, GE in 1980 or 2000 was (and is) a conglomerate that sells into unrelated product markets. This section describes how this identity was a representational and practical problem for GE from the early 1980s because conglomerates were unfashionable and regarded with suspicion by the capital market so that their shares generally traded at a conglomerate discount and there was often pressure for divestment and spin-offs to increase value. GE under Welch dealt with the stigma of being a conglomerate in a way that was coherent with the rest of its management style. Thus, discursive attack was used as the best form of financial defence, which could enhance the GE share price and protect the combine from break-up. The conventional narrative defence was that the different GE businesses were, in one way or another, connected so that there was synergistic gain from combining the apparently unrelated businesses as a 'business engine'. The innovative performative defence was that the company was unified under Welch's leadership by a series of initiatives such as 'Work-Out' and 'Six Sigma', which were widely discussed in the media and business press before being imitated by other giant firms.

The huge success of these efforts, in their own terms, is indicated by the way in which GE now figures in *Business Week* lists, not as the world's most successful conglomerate but as one of the 'world's ten most valuable brands'. The *Business Week* 2004 list (9 August 2004) credits GE with a brand value of $44 billion, which makes it the fourth most valuable brand in the world behind Coca-Cola, Microsoft and IBM. As is usually the case, the calculation of brand values involves statistical hocus-pocus with adjustments for patents and 'customer convenience' subtracted from a total for abnormal profits after deducting cost of capital. But the interesting point is that eight of the other top ten brands are corporations, such as Coca-Cola or Disney, which have a limited span of goods and service products (for example, soft drinks) or have a range of goods and services that are related in the product market (for example, film production, distribution, theme parks, cable television and merchandising). The two exceptions in the *Business Week* list of brands are Marlboro and GE, with Marlboro having a product line that is much narrower than the parent corporation and GE being a conglomerate whose product lines are so diverse that, in 2004, it advertises under the meaningless slogan of 'imagination at work'. If brand unity is discernible in GE, it is because Welch created a management brand by insisting that unrelated products embody the common values of GE leadership and organization.

In any discussion, the starting point must be that GE's product range is bewilderingly diverse. GE's business units, for example, currently make or sell domestic refrigerators, jet aircraft engines, medical scanners, TV and film content and distribution, plus a huge variety of financial products such as leasing or insurance to corporate and domestic consumers, including many who have never bought any GE industrial product. In this respect, GE is completely different from GSK, which has all its activity in pharmaceuticals and most of its profit in ethical pharmaceutical blockbusters in a small range of therapeutic segments. Equally, GE is not much like Ford whose industry affiliation remains strong because Ford's assembly and manufacture is in autos, as is its captive finance house which mainly meets the needs of Ford dealers and customers.

Within a few years of becoming chief executive, Jack Welch began a process of restructuring the company which involved selling off or closing down some outlier activities: for example, Utah Mining was sold in 1982 and small appliances/GE Housewares was sold to Black & Decker in 1984. In this period under Welch's No. 1/No. 2 initiative (described below) the aim was to focus on a core of well-positioned, high-performing businesses. But it quickly became clear that this initiative did not prevent the acquisition of new businesses in unrelated activities, if they could be represented as quality businesses. Thus, GE in the first half of the 1980s moved into new activities such as broadcasting, with the purchase of RCA in 1986, and diversified its financial activities with purchase of Employers Reinsurance in 1984. The net result of Jack Welch's acquisitions and divestments was not a company with a narrower scope, but rather a differently put-together conglomerate.

Exhibit C3.1 presents a basic classification of GE's business activities in 2002 as disclosed by the company. Two main points stand out. First, in terms of generic categories, GE has large industrial and commercial businesses, each of which contribute well over $50 billion of turnover. Within each of these two main divisions, GE has a range of diverse activities, and the two largest activities (power systems and insurance) each separately accounts for no more than about 20 per cent of GE's total turnover. The second major point arises from the awesome size of GE whose aggregate turnover in 2002 was $131 billion. In a company of this size, many household-name GE business units would make medium-sized stand-alone businesses, but account for a very small part of the giant conglomerate's revenue or profits. Thus, NBC, which includes the US terrestrial TV network, accounted for no more than 5.5 per cent of turnover in 2002.

When Welch came into office in 1981, conglomerates had already gone out of fashion. Business analysts as diverse as Michael Jensen (1989) and George Soros (1987: 133–4) were concerned to distinguish the potential of the leveraged buy-outs (LBOs) and mergers of the 1980s from the earlier failed conglomerate merger boom of the 1960s, which Soros described as an 'ultimately self defeating process'. Investment-fund managers were sceptical on the grounds that conglomerates were not transparent and undermined the investor's ability to allocate capital between sectors. As a British investment banker explains, the market now prefers 'pure plays' to conglomerates:

> today's fund managers do not want corporate management to select their exposures for them. They want to be able to pick and choose between a range of quoted

> companies that have stripped themselves down to their core business and are, as a consequence, focused. They want simple and understandable investment propositions. Hence the pressure for the divestment of non-core operations, demergers, spin-offs, tracking stock, carve outs.
>
> (Golding 2001: 165)

This strong preference, which dated from the 1980s, was reinforced by the pursuit of shareholder value in the 1990s, when under the influence of authors such as Rappaport (1998) and consultants such as Stern Stewart (Stern et al. 1995), firms were encouraged to review under-performing assets and to unbundle or divest low-return activities.

All this was reflected in GE's share price up to the later 1990s. For a blue-chip conglomerate like GE, the benchmark is the overall P/E ratio of the S&P 500, which collectively is a kind of mega-conglomerate bundling many of the activities in GDP. The obvious target is for a conglomerate like GE to have a higher P/E ratio than the S&P 500 as a whole. But from the early 1980s into the late 1990s GE was trading at a level no better than, and in some years at a discount to, the S&P 500. Towards the end of this period, the *Wall Street Journal* (4 August 1994) stated that, although many admired

***Exhibit C3.1*** *GE sales revenues and profit in 2002, by reported business segments*

| *GE business segment* | *Sales revenues* $ million | *Earnings* $ million |
|---|---|---|
| ***GE Industrial*** | | |
| Aircraft engines | 11,141 | 2,060 |
| Consumer products | 8,456 | 495 |
| Industrial products and systems | 9,755 | 999 |
| Materials | 7,651 | 1,125 |
| NBC | 7,149 | 1,658 |
| Power systems | 22,926 | 6,255 |
| Technical products and services | 9,266 | 1,562 |
| **GE Capital Services** | | |
| Commercial finance | 16,040 | 3,185 |
| Consumer finance | 10,266 | 1,930 |
| Equipment management | 4,254 | 311 |
| Insurance | 23,296 | (509) |
| All other GE capital services | 4,331 | (291) |
| **GE Consolidated** | 131,698 | 14,118 |

*Source*: GE Annual Report, 2002: 16

*Notes*: Earnings are presented as operating profit for GE Industrial businesses (i.e. earnings before interest and other financial charges, income taxes and accounting changes) and as after tax earnings (before accounting changes) for GE Capital Services businesses, reflecting the importance of financing and taxation to the capital businesses. Note that GE Consolidated is not equal to the arithmetic sum of the GE Industrial and Capital Services businesses because of corporate items, such as the effect of pension and other benefit plans and restructuring costs, which are not allocated to a particular segment

Welch's management, some in the investor community viewed GE as 'a growing collection of disparate companies in which a domineering personality substitutes for business focus'.

If GE wanted to displace 'the "C" word' (Slater 1993: 198–201), the first most obvious resource was narrative, and Welch made the argument that, despite the apparent diversity, the different parts of GE did fit together in ways that added value. Conglomerate diversity has traditionally been defended with claims that the conglomerate's portfolio of business units can raise returns or at least reduce investor risk if the diverse activities in the business portfolio combine different patterns of cyclicality, growth and cash generation. Welch's early 1980s version of this argument was his so-called 'business engine' concept, whereby GE was described as a collection of businesses that make a strong whole, allowing participation in many markets and working together 'like pistons' so that slow-growing businesses, such as lighting, provide the cash fuel for the faster-growing parts, such as financial services (Tichy and Sherman 1993: 25). The engine metaphor was new and was then rather confusingly developed by adding the distinction between long- and short-cycle businesses. But all this does little more than restate the Boston Consulting Group 'product portfolio matrix' and the box diagram about stars, dogs and cash cows which may still figure in strategy textbooks but does not much influence market judgements.

Hence, the importance of adding a performative element around several company-wide initiatives that stemmed from a few 'big ideas' and that manifestly did reshape the company quite radically. This did represent a new style at GE which enacted Welch's claims that, 'I don't run GE, I lead GE' (Slater 1999: 31). He used a performative method to rationalize GE's existence to outsiders and employees alike and increasingly to identify a unifying organizational focus within the business portfolio. The initiatives came in two successive phases: the 'hard' restructuring initiatives of the 1980s which met with a mixed reception but did help the share price; and the 'soft' restructuring of the 1990s that framed Welch and GE as brilliant successes and turned GE into a brand.

The first and most controversial of Jack Welch's initiatives was set in motion in the early 1980s by his declared mission to 'become the most competitive enterprise in the world by being number one or number two in market share in every business we are in' (GE Annual Report 1984: 2). Where this target could not be met, management should 'fix, close or sell'. As Tichy and Sherman (1993: 72) note, at the end of his first year as CEO Welch explained he did not believe in a centralized strategy but he did believe in a 'central idea – a simple core concept that will guide General Electric in the eighties and govern our diverse plans and strategies'. Of course many organizations set themselves targets for upward mobility. But most such organizations do not then enact their ambition and disrupt organizational lives, as GE did in the 1980s, by dramatically restructuring its activity base and sacking a substantial part of the workforce. When Welch took over, GE employed 420,000 and, according to Tichy and Sherman (1993: 10), some 170,000 jobs were then lost through 'lay offs, attrition and other means' as part of a larger restructuring where 150,000 were transferred in through acquisitions and 135,000 jobs were transferred out via sale of businesses, with divestment between 1980 and 1984 accounting for 20 per cent of the 1980 asset base.

As is often the case with such management exercises, the No. 1 or 2 rule was not consistently used and could not be rigorously applied. As Welch (2001: 237) admitted in his autobiography, the rule was ignored at GE Capital where 'we didn't have to be No 1 or No 2', and in a 1999 interview he accepted GE managers' claims that industrial managers were playing redefinition games as 'everyone is defining their markets smaller so they can be number one or two' (Slater 1999: 180). The performative achievement also remains thoroughly ambiguous though not without admirers. In retrospect, for his admirers of the 1990s the No. 1 or No. 2 initiative reflected Welch's unsentimental prescience about a world that would become ever more (internationally) competitive so that still profitable businesses would struggle unless they had (or could move towards) market leadership. Reflecting on the 1980s in his 1990 'Letter to Share Owners', Welch wrote: 'we believed only businesses that were number-one or number-two in their markets could win in the increasingly global arena' (GE Annual Report 1990: 1).

At the same time, Welch's detractors suspected that GE was, like many other giant firms, in retreat and avoiding Japanese competition: maybe GE was not so different from a financially opportunist, low-tech conglomerate like Hanson whose house rule was not to compete in markets where it faced Japanese competition. The reception was thus understandably mixed. The business media (which will be considered in the next section) were initially negative as the new CEO lost his family name and acquired an unflattering epithet as 'Neutron Jack', in a phrase supposedly coined in 1982 by *Newsweek*, which implied ruthless downsizing that was surely more about cost-cutting management than about leadership. The market was more positive but also guarded: GE's P/E ratio did no more than track the S&P 500 as the market responded to restructuring associated with 10 per cent compound growth of earnings, and many wondered whether GE could do any more than cut costs.

In performative terms, by the late 1980s Welch needed another big idea and some new initiatives that would accentuate the positive and eliminate the negative. This was supplied by some fresh thinking about how the CEO, head office and corporate infrastructure could add value to GE's diverse operations. The arguments for defending a head office traditionally came out of Chandler's 1962 work on M-form and rested on a set of rational planning assumptions about how head office could allocate capital and add strategic vision. And such controls remained part of Welch's management practice, which involved tight management on allocation of capital and careful scrutiny of financial results (Tichy and Sherman 1993: 95). But the rhetoric was changed as Welch inflected the arguments for head office, so that they fitted with 1990s thinking about competence and the learning organization by emphasizing values, leadership and knowledge transfer across divisions. From this point of view, Welch's next big idea at the end of the 1980s was 'integrated diversity'. This allowed Welch to explain that GE was not a conglomerate because it demonstrated 'integrated diversity', 'A conglomerate is a group of businesses with no central theme. GE has a common set of values. We have Crotonville, where we teach leadership. We have a research lab that feeds all of our businesses. We have all the resources of a centralized company' (Welch, quoted in Slater 1993: 199).

> It is this elimination of boundaries between businesses and the transferring of ideas from one place in the company to another that is at the heart of what we call integrated diversity. It is this concept that we believe sets us apart from both single product companies and from conglomerates. . . . by sharing ideas, by finding multiple applications for technological advancements and by moving people across businesses to provide fresh perspectives and to develop broad-based experience. Integrated diversity gives us a Company that is considerably greater than the sum of its parts.
>
> (GE Annual Report 1990: 2)

In due course, this big idea segued into Welch's early 1990s' principle of 'boundarylessness' as 'the value that underlies GE's increasingly supple organizational style' (Tichy and Sherman 1993: 74). This principle emphasized informality and candour in a de-layered organization without 'organizational silos'. Though linguistically clumsy, boundarylessness was, according to Welch, the only way that GE would be able to achieve its productivity goals (GE Annual Report 1991: 2–3).

The 'Work-Out' initiative was a further development of GE's 'software' (GE Annual Report 1991: 1), introduced in 1989 as an enactment of GE values and a central element in the attempt to break through boundaries. It reflected frustration with the limited reach of the GE staff college at Crotonville, which could only involve a fraction of the workforce through traditional training methods (Welch 2001: 182). Under Work-Out, GE staff from all levels came together for sessions based on the idea of the town meeting, where employees were allowed to ask their managers awkward questions about why things were done in particular ways and to suggest improvements to processes that would save time and cash. The initiative was based on the principle of empowering the workforce, requiring middle managers to come out from their offices and making all employees responsible for GE's continued success. By 1992, more than 200,000 employees, some 85 per cent of GE's staff, had taken part in a Work-Out session (Welch 2001: 183) and the company considered this an important element in the kind of cultural change it was trying to work at GE, while also improving processes and reducing costs or expanding sales. According to Welch:

> my view of the 1990s is based on the liberation of the workplace, everybody a participant . . . In the new culture, the role of leader is to express a vision, get buy-in, and implement it. That calls for open, caring relations with every employee, and face-to-face communication. People who can't convincingly articulate a vision won't be successful. But those who can will become even more open – because success breeds self-confidence.
>
> (Tichy and Sherman 1993: 247)

This was reflected in the development of Work-Out through successive phases that put more emphasis on leaders as 'professional change agents'. Indeed, if Welch has been lauded as *the* business leader of the 1990s, his claim would be that he had created a whole culture of leadership within GE where leadership is likened to guerrilla warfare against bureaucracy and formality. This has benefited the company as a whole as well as nurturing executive talent for other corporations. 'With the reduction of "management" and the dismantling of bureaucracy, leaders have moved quickly to the front, creating a vision for each business and articulating their vision so clearly and compellingly that an entire organization can rally around it and turn it into reality' (GE Annual Report 1987: 4).

But the touchy, feely stuff was interestingly combined with the hard edge of performance requirements. Work-Out was accompanied by Welch's now-famous annual review of all GE managers, foreshadowed in the 1991 'Letter to Share Owners', which announced that it was necessary for managers to share GE 'values' as well as deliver on the targets (GE Annual Report 1991: 4–5). This annual review involved classifying managers into the ranks of A, B and C where the As got stock options and the Cs were encouraged to find new challenges outside GE. As Welch wrote in 1991, 'In the first half of the 1980s we restructured this Company and changed its physical make-up. That was the easy part. In the last several years, our challenge has been to change ourselves' (GE Annual Report 1991: 4) and performance review was a way to enforce this.

Interestingly, the next major new initiative from the mid-1990s was Six Sigma, which combined hard and soft management. Six Sigma was a set of generic statistical techniques that GE borrowed from AlliedSignal and Motorola. They were used to improve product and process quality and thereby to reduce costs and improve relations with customers. Again, GE explains this initiative as involving and rewarding the workforce at all levels: 'quality is the responsibility of every employee' (GE undated a: 2), while also delivering a bottom line impact as costs are lowered and customers are 'delighted'. According to the company: 'GE's success with Six Sigma has exceeded our most optimistic predictions. Across the Company, GE associates embrace Six Sigma's customer-focused, data-driven philosophy and apply it to everything we do' (GE undated a: 3). Various estimates have been given of the savings made through quality improvements, but the more important aspect of all this, according to Welch, is that it contributes to building GE as a 'learning organization' where 'everyone in GE gets up in the morning and comes to work every day trying to find a better way' (Collingwood and Coutu 2002: 94). If the earlier ruthless focus on cost-cutting never vanished from GE in the 1990s, the wrapper changed so that the initiatives were increasingly about vision and values.

The succession of initiatives ended in dot-com farce in a way that raised serious questions about what Welch was doing as CEO and what his initiatives contributed. At the height of the new-economy boom, Welch decided that 'the opportunities ebusiness creates for large companies like GE are unlimited' (Slater 2003: 131). He then launched an e-business initiative whereby divisions were obliged to set up a unit called 'DestroyYour Business.com', charged with reinventing the business model, just as senior colleagues were to be mentored by their juniors in using the net (*The Economist*, 16 September 1999,

*Forbes*, 24 July 2000). Interestingly, again this was inflected towards the hard stuff of saving internal costs and meeting external needs because Welch was very clear about the need to use digital technology to improve productivity and to make GE a global supplier of choice (GE Annual Report 1999: 6–7, Welch 2001: 341–5). Thus, medical systems could overtake Siemens if it used e-business internally to reduce product-development time by 25 per cent and inventory by 40 per cent (*Line 56 Magazine*, October 2001).

This e-commerce initiative must be considered in the context of the earlier initiatives from 'No. 1 or No. 2' onwards. Taken together, they suggest very strongly that Welch had excellent timing and a shrewd intuitive sense of how passing management fashion and new economic direction could be turned into a GE initiative. This then demonstrated the company's timely commitment to going forwards through management and incidentally gave Welch a Zelig-like ability to put himself into all the big historic pictures of late twentieth-century management. The e-business initiatives also demonstrated GE and Welch's luck because they were not reputationally damaged by DestroyYour Business.com. The business, media and political scripts in the years 1999 and 2000 were then full of performative folly, so that the majority afterwards had a vested interest in discounting whatever was said and done in that period as a kind of dalliance with e-business, an out-of-character madness in an otherwise exemplary life.

This was all the more appropriate because, by this stage, Welch had made himself into a star through touring, one-man performances and memory feats. Each year began with a January meeting for Welch and GE's top 500 operating managers at Boca Raton, Florida. 'Session C reviews' in April and May took Welch into the field to review the progress of GE's top 3,000 executives where he knew the top 1,000 by sight and name (*Business Week*, 8 June 1998). Through the year, there were monthly sessions at the GE training centre in Croton-on-Hudson, NY that might involve a four-hour unscripted session in 'the pit' for Jack and a group of GE executives completing a three-week development programme (*Business Week*, 8 June 1998). Here again there was development because by the 1990s, according to one of his former colleagues, Welch had replaced 'yelling and screaming for performance . . . [with] a much more motivational approach' (Larry Bossidy, cited in Tichy and Sherman 1993: 257). There was the same development in Jack's communication with outside audiences where, by the end of the 1990s, Welch's annual letter to shareholders had become an annual event. Increasingly, smaller amounts of the letter were taken up with outlining the financial performance of the year, which was generally presented in an understated and factual way, while most of the text was given over to explaining GE and the unifying philosophy that was driving it on to ever better results.

From Welch's explanation of the importance of learning and development (Welch 2001: 169–84), and the reception from commentators such as *Business Week*'s John Byrne (who later co-authored the Welch autobiography), casual readers might be excused for thinking that GE had become an educational institute, or even a centre for personal development. In his final letter to shareholders in the 2000 annual report and accounts, Welch summarizes his achievement:

> The most significant change in GE has been its transformation into a Learning Company. Our true 'core competency' today is not manufacturing or services, but the global recruiting and nurturing of the world's best people and the cultivation in them of an insatiable desire to learn, to stretch and to do things better every day.
>
> (GE Annual Report 2000: 2)

All this was a considerable achievement for Jack and GE who continuously reinvented themselves for twenty years. In an interview for the *Harvard Business Review* in 2002, Welch concludes by saying that he would like his gravestone to say 'People Jack' (rather than 'Neutron Jack' or some other epithet), because the single most important part of his job has been 'spend[ing] time with people' (Collingwood and Coutu 2002: 94). It is hard to think of any other company that managed, through performative initiatives and big ideas, to reincarnate as soft leadership-for-change in the 1990s after previously incarnating the hard, defensive management in the 1980s. But, as we saw in the case of Ford, other firms had their own initiatives, and the main difference is that the GE initiatives were increasingly identified as the conditions of GE's success and packaged as lessons or exemplary, transferable techniques that others could use. The intense interest in the initiatives was, of course, stimulated by outstanding financial results, as summarized in Exhibit C3.2. The 400-fold increase in sales and the much larger rises in profit and market value provide the context for the sustained fascination with the company by outside commentators. We take up this issue of outside reception in the next section on external commentary, especially media and popular business books.

*Exhibit C3.2* *GE's headline performance*

| | *1980* | *2000* | *Per cent (nominal) change 1980–2000* |
|---|---|---|---|
| Sales revenues $ million | 24,959 | 129,853 | 420 |
| Net income $ million | 1,514 | 12,735 | 741 |
| Market value $ million | 12,441 | 507,377 | 3,978 |

*Source*: GE Annual Report and Accounts, various years

## COMPANY NARRATIVE IN MEDIA AND BUSINESS BOOKS

This section turns from the company's own account to the reception of that account and the overlapping construction of a narrative by three groups of outsiders: analysts, journalists and the academics and consultants who write popular business books. The story here is complex because the main role in analysing and interpreting GE has been taken up by the business media and writers of business books, while analysts have generally played a more low-key role. The business media provide a kind of real-time commentary where judgements change over the 1980s and 1990s as Welch and GE move along a reputational S curve, while the popular business books from the early 1990s onwards offer a hagiography that builds the cult of Jack Welch as great CEO. The narrative reception and embroidery of GE's account by writers and journalists establishes GE as a management practice that can be encapsulated in key principles, actions and beliefs that, significantly for many commentators, can be learnt by others and transferred to different organizations.

The differences in these diverse literatures should not be suppressed. But it is also worth noting that there is a generic form to the argument that GE management saves. In management thought, as in cinema, the power is in the editing and the causal connection between GE's management techniques and superior performance is suggested by juxtaposition through a jump-cut from results to initiatives. The technique can be illustrated by choosing, more or less randomly, any competently written business book where GE figures as a major example. Consider, for example, the book on 'trajectory management' by Paul Strebel, a professor at the Swiss IMD management school. Strebel's first shot announces GE's undisputed achievement, which is 'two decades of high powered growth' (Strebel 2003: 163). In the second shot, Strebel identifies key initiatives (Globalization and Work-Out; Services and Boundarylessness; Six Sigma and A team; and e-Business) as 'trajectory drivers' that allowed the company to engineer upward shifts in 'product/market innovation' and 'value chain efficiency' (see Strebel 2003: 172–5 and especially Figure 10.2). Although Strebel explicitly does not believe in 'one best way', the juxtaposition suggests that others can get the results by applying the techniques. More explicitly, Ulrich et al. (2002) have made one of GE's initiatives the focus for a 300-page book, *The GE Work-Out*, whose subtitle 'How to implement GE's revolutionary method for busting bureaucracy and attacking organizational problems – fast' gives an instant guide to the purpose of the book and its potential relevance to other firms.

## The analysts

No giant company of GE's scale and scope could escape critical analysis of its actions and results. But an infatuation with Welch began to develop in the late 1980s and was sustained through to his retirement in 2001, so that the CEO and his company mainly got media hagiography. Journalists and writers of business books increasingly pushed a line on exemplary GE and inspirational Welch, often including how-to-do-it tips, so that these writers were selling the management brand in much the same way as style magazines sell a look. This case study focuses on the GE publishing industry in book and article form. The combination of sustained media interest with many book-length studies is almost unique to GE and Welch and so provides an interesting opportunity to consider a narrative of corporate purpose and achievement developed outside the company. The availability of this resource (as well as reasons of space) means that in this case study we do not give the same degree of attention to analysts as in our cases on GSK and Ford. However, the analysts do deserve a few paragraphs of comment because they are a potentially important part of the GE story: they are generally a low-key group of commentators who occasionally make important interjections whose impact seems muffled.

Discussion of the analysts' contribution to understanding GE must start from events since the new-economy crash in 2000. The failure of analysts to anticipate the Enron and WorldCom collapses and their earlier role in boosting new-economy companies have cast doubt over analysts' capacity to produce an independent critical commentary on the substance and sustainability of (apparent) corporate success (see, for example, Fuller and Jensen 2002). The problems are clearly greatest in the case of companies that are heavy users of investment banking services for acquisition, IPO or bond sales and that thereby generate fee income for the financial-services conglomerates that employ many of the analysts. The resulting conflicts of interest and double standards were dramatized by the conduct of star Internet stock analysts such as Henry Blodget whose published reports boosted a dot-com stock that he rubbished in private e-mails, or Mary Meeker who was alleged to have had conflicts of interest between equity research and investment banking (*Wall Street Journal*, 29 April 2003, 3 November 2003). GE was not of course an insubstantial dot com, but its continued acquisitions over twenty years must have generated fee income that set up substantial conflicts of interest and potentially inhibited criticism by many analysts. When Welch's successor, Immelt, turned to large-scale industrial acquisition, GE became in 2004 the largest single corporate source of fee income for the investment-banking industry when it paid $454 million to its financial advisers, according to Deallogic Research. This was reported in the *Financial Times* under the worldly headline 'GE tops the list for helping to boost bankers' bonuses' (24 January 2005).

If much analyst commentary on GE has been anodyne and descriptive, this cannot be attributed simply to conflicts of interest. Given the sustained combination of alluring headline performance numbers and the apparent difficulty in understanding such a large and diverse company from its published accounts, most commentators (including analysts) have tended to fairly uncritically recap the headline numbers and the company's explanation. The size and complexity of GE has been repeatedly invoked as a major problem itself because, as one analyst observed, 'it is an extremely difficult company to evaluate because there are so many moving parts' (cited in *Fortune*, 24 May 2001). Diversity certainly adds complications. GE is generally followed by industrial analysts because it is classed as an industrial, not a financial firm, given that its share of turnover from industrial divisions is (deliberately) kept above 50 per cent. Of the nineteen analysts listed on GE's web site in November 2004, all appear to have their major affiliation or experience in following industrial companies. Arguably, most industrial analysts will have limited ability to understand GE's capital services, whose financial products and markets are both bewilderingly various and often disconnected from those in the industrial businesses. As SEP's credit-rating analyst, E. Richard Schmidt, writes in his explanation of how S&P analyses GE Capital Corp., 'in the current environment of increasing disclosure in financial statements, many analysts who are more familiar with industrial companies do not fully understand what the expanded disclosure information means in terms of risk for a finance company' (S&P 2002: 2).

GE also allegedly works to incorporate its analysts into a small community around the company. In the web casts of analyst calls, CEO Immelt replies to each questioner by first name (see, for example, GE 2003). *The Economist* (2 May 2002) has argued that GE 'manages expectations about its earnings by managing its analysts', so that analyst forecasts are within a very narrow range, and all are within GE's own range. In all fairness, this kind of convergence is not unique to GE, but critics allege that GE goes further by giving preferential treatment to those who play a part in developing the corporate narrative. Again according to *The Economist*, GE 'continues to treat analysts, journalists and other outsiders as if they either belong to the family and are believers, or do not' (2 May 2002).

It is also interesting to note that GE is covered by relatively few analysts despite its huge market value. For instance, *Fortune* (24 May 2001) points out that only twenty-eight Wall Street analysts cover GE, compared with the forty-seven who follow Gillette (with one-thirteenth of GE's market capitalization). Arguably, none of those analysts has the independent status and reputation of an auto analyst such as Gary Lapidus in the USA and certainly they have not put together an independent critical narrative, as Lapidus did for Ford, by emphasising the cross-subsidy from trucks to cars that was not disclosed in the accounts. Various GE analysts have made shrewd critical points, as Jeanne Terrile of Merrill Lynch did when she calculated that 4 percentage points of GE's 9.9 per cent annual growth between 1985 and 2000 came from acquisitions (*Fortune*, 4 September 2001), but somehow or other anomalous findings are not turned into an independent critical narrative, nor are they taken up by other commentators in a sustained way. Such observations are neutralized by GE's reassuring performance and steady earnings growth that makes some analysts feel comfortable in treating GE as a 'trust-me' story with no further (critical) analysis required. Interestingly, GE has had on and off problems with non-believers from outside the analysts' community, most notably with Bill Gross of the Pacific Investment Management Company (PIMCO) fund management, who advised against buying GE commercial paper on grounds of risk because, he claimed, this was a financial company masquerading as an industrial company.

This line of criticism is an important cue for our analysis of the business model in the next major section on numbers.

## Business press

If analysts are too often inhibited, media journalists have a good deal of formal freedom, subject to the practical constraint of deadlines. Their urgency limits the scope for research and reflection and establishes a bias against understanding. This is reinforced by media specialization, which increases the demand for short items that fit formats such as business-news bulletins. Contrarian and dissident narratives need development time which everyday journalism does not provide. Hence, the strong tendency to herding in journalists' business-press stories about GE where new stories typically are pegged to a foreground event (for example, the latest GE results or a major acquisition) whose background is then filled in by a quick scan of clippings files and analysts' reports where collective judgement congeals and is supported by interviews with company insiders. The business journalists' judgement of corporate achievement and purpose changes over time, though usually rather more slowly than in political journalism. Under multi-party systems, where sceptical judgement can seldom be contained for long, most administrations move along a curve of rapidly declining reputation as experience of actions and outcomes accumulate so that all political careers end with unfulfilled promise or failure. The case of Welch and GE is interestingly rather different because here the CEO and his company move along a rising reputational S curve over a much longer time frame of some twenty years. Media hostility and scepticism about GE in the early 1980s gave way to admiration and a sharp rise in reputation through the later 1990s, which then levels off in the early 2000s.

The real-time commentary of business journalism is often fixed, rationalized and valued by a few labels or factoids that convey powerful images that can be used in two-and-a-half-minute stories. Through the early 1980s, the unease of media commentators was epitomized in the 'Neutron Jack' epithet that circulated through the pages of the business press. In 1984, *Fortune* had named Welch as 'America's toughest boss' on the basis of GE's plant closures and lay-offs, as well as the way in which Welch treated his management staff. The tone of business-press features on the GE company was usually questioning and sometimes hostile. Here, for example, as late as 1986, is an openly sceptical *Fortune* magazine:

> to the casual eye, much of what General Electric has been up to lately seems to epitomize the humbled circumstances of American business. For more than a century GE brought the world wondrous inventions, from light bulbs to electric dishwashers

> to CAT scanners, enhancing people's lives and creating jobs. By contrast GE's most visible moves in this decade appear grim and unimaginative. . . . [H]as this great enterprise been reduced to boosting profits by firing people and buying other businesses?
>
> (*Fortune*, 7 July 1986)

However, by the mid- to late 1980s, the doxa was changing as the media came to accept that Welch had wrought a transformation in GE and identified the need for change well before other companies and commentators. This discovery should be set in the larger context of increasing social acceptance of the Reagan/Thatcher programmes of neo-liberal framework reform, which of course required managers who ostentatiously did what was necessary to exploit new opportunities at the company level. Thus, while Welch was frequently criticized for large-scale downsizing in the early 1980s (sometimes at profitable plants and businesses), by the end of the 1980s other giant corporations had added down- or rightsizing to their armoury and this was no longer treated as exceptional. The reputational transformation was complete when, in 1991, Welch was named 'American Manager of the Year' by the National Management Association in an award that reinterpreted the lay-offs as a radical de-layering of the company (*Management Review*, October 1991). As for the GE company, from the late 1980s it began to get very positive reviews in the US and British business press. The reviews generally worked by antithesizing old GE as a supposedly slow, flabby bureaucratic company and new GE as a lean and agile competitor created by Welch: 'In less than seven years, John F. Welch Jr has transformed an overweight, somnolent General Electric Company into an agile and highly profitable corporate enterprise – a model for American industry in the Age of Japan', taking GE from 'smokestack' to 'fastmoving, high-tech behemoth' (*Business Month*, March 1988); and Jack Welch turned 'GE from a textbook case of massive, bureaucratically managed conglomerate into a new model of decentralised, liberated management' (*The Economist*, 7 January 1989). Through acts such as throwing away rulebooks and reducing HQ staff from 1,700 to 1,000, 'this change has been traumatic, requiring a mixture of ruthlessness and constant cajoling and speechmaking' (*The Economist*, 7 January 1989).

And, by this stage, it was possible to quote analysts and others whose judgements concurred and added authority to the revaluation: 'According to James Magin of L.F. Rothschild, Unterberg, Towbin: "when he took over, Wall Street considered GE a well-managed, successful, powerful company. Welch was one of the few people who recognized that this wasn't true. He's proved to be an absolutely terrific manager"' (*Financial World*, 15 April 1986).

Through the 1990s, the reputation of Welch and GE rose in much the same way as the company's share price and the doubts of the 1980s vanished into the rear-view mirror. The Harvard academic Christopher A. Bartlett was cited in *The Economist* (18 September 1999), noting that Welch's early years of brutal, cost-cutting had been balanced by 'revitalization' and that subsequent success was rooted in the 'movement of ideas and management talent around the group'. Through the 1990s, the media put more and more emphasis on the leadership techniques and organizational innovations of GE so that, as Welch was coming up to retirement, the issue was very much framed in terms of Welch's historical legacy and GE's contribution to US corporate management more generally. Thus, thirteen years after its 1980s' questioning of the downsizing of GE, *Fortune* was adopting a very deferential tone in its reflections on Welch's legacy of management techniques when it claimed that 'his real legacy is the tools and leaders he has helped to forge' (27 September 1999). A few weeks later it noted that 'in addition to his transformation of GE, he has made himself far and away the most influential manager of his generation. (Indeed his only competition would be Alfred P. Sloan.)' (*Fortune*, 22 November 1999). Thus, Welch as CEO had become a business-press icon, whose conduct and techniques have exemplary, transferable value.

All this was barely dented by Jack's messy divorce, which cast doubt on his motives but not on his achievements. The papers released during the course of reaching a divorce settlement showed that Jack Welch was just like other US top managers in that he cut himself a very good deal as CEO and in retirement, with free tickets to major international sporting events and large bills for the running of his New York apartment among the items disclosed (*Forbes*, 6 September 2002, *Wall Street Journal*, 27 November 2002). Following hostility in the business press, Welch voluntarily modified the deal to eliminate all the perks, except those associated with office support normally given to retired GE chairmen and vice-chairmen (*Forbes*, 16 September 2002). While Jack the Star was personally diminished by the public disclosure of his cupidity, nothing that came out during the divorce settlement had any implications for Jack the Manager who has remained a hero and on that basis continues in retirement to publish his management pensées.

## (Popular) business books and media

Through the media commentary of the 1990s, Welch became an A-list celebrity whose persona and achievement were all the more interesting because his background was working-class Irish and, on the law of averages, Welch should have become a police lieutenant or fire chief rather than a sharp doctoral student with a mild stutter who joined a blue-chip company and metamorphosed into the most admired CEO of a whole generation. As *The Economist* (18 September 1999) observed with a little condescension, 'the train conductor's son from Salem has become the Princess Diana of the business press, his every move recorded in a series of cover stories'. According to an interview published in the *Harvard Business Review*, in an era when business leaders moved much closer to 'the center of popular culture [.] No CEO exerted a more magnetic pull on the media than Jack Welch' (Collingwood and Coutu 2002: 88–90). The result was 'more than a dozen books at last count, innumerable mentions in the press and more than a half-dozen appearances on the covers of both *Fortune* and *Business Week*' (Collingwood and Coutu 2002: 90).

This section considers the books that take (or include) Welch and GE as their subject. It does so primarily by considering two best-selling books: *Control your Destiny* by Tichy and Sherman, originally published in 1993, and *Built to Last*, originally published by Collins and Porras in 1994 (and where we refer to the third edition, published in 2000). These books have been chosen for two reasons. First, both books are generally well presented and fluently argued from a reasonable evidence base so that they provide classic examples of how the devices and techniques of the popular business text can be used to wrap Welch and GE by plausibly associating achievement and conditions. Second, these two books usefully illustrate opposite choices within the one field about the conditions of that achievement: Tichy and Sherman put the main emphasis on Welch's leadership in his term of office as CEO, while Collins and Porras put the emphasis on the long-term excellence of the organization before and after Welch. While this interpretative difference about the lessons of Welch and GE is interesting, both texts illustrate an intellectual problem that is characteristic of popular business texts: just as in Womack et al. (1990) on the auto industry, these two books on GE cite confirming evidence in a way that does not stimulate discovery or reflection but vindicates a pre-existing position. Our discussion of these texts is rounded off by a broader survey of other books on Welch and a brief discussion of Robert Slater's *29 Leadership Secrets from Jack Welch* (2003), which is a good example of hagiography about the business leader.

The Tichy and Sherman and the Collins and Porras books are written by teams that combine a hybrid academic consultant with a collaborator who is a journalist or a full-time consultant. The hybrid academic–consultant has a CV that includes periods of (staff) employment in blue chips or major consultancies. They are unlikely to spend much time grading student essays and are more likely to be working on executive education as well as consulting outside the university. Consider, for example, the bookjacket biographies of Jerry Porras and Noel Tichy:

> Jerry J. Porras is the Fred H. Merrill Professor of Organizational Behaviour and Change at Stanford University Graduate School of Business. He is the author of *Stream Analysis* and the co-inventor of stream analysis software, used for organizational change diagnosis. He also directs Stanford's Executive Program in Organization Change. Previously he held positions at General Electric and Lockheed.
>
> Noel Tichy is an authority on organizational transformation. He is a professor at the University of Michigan School of Business and director of the school's Global Leadership Program. He has consulted to GE since 1982 and ran GE's Crotonville Training Centre for two years.
>
> (Tichy and Sherman 1993)

*Deformation professionelle* encourages such authors to meet the demand for a 'runaway national best-seller', where airport-bookstand sales are encouraged by endorsements from the *Harvard Business Review* and quotes by businessmen. The centrepiece (or final section) of the work is likely to be the packaged lessons of success which means that this is as much a product as it is a good read.

Thus, Tichy's and Sherman's book, written in the early 1990s, is, first, an explanation of Welch's management principles and actions within GE and, second, a 'Handbook for Revolutionaries' who wish to emulate the success by applying the Welch approach. The authors assert that 'the lessons we have drawn from General Electric's experiences apply to almost everyone' (1993: xxv), whether 'a small business, a ten person corporate department, or in a multi-billion enterprise'. The book ends with an eighty-page handbook for revolutionaries that offers examples, diagrams, checklists and questionnaires, which together provides a kind of generic workshop manual to allow any reader to do in his or her company what Jack did in GE. The emphasis on packaged lessons of success is even stronger in Collins and Porras (2000). These authors take GE and Westinghouse as one of eighteen pairs of companies where, in each case, the authors claim to have matched a 'visionary company' and a more mundane 'comparison company' with the aim of determining the organizational conditions of long-term excellence by a small elite of super companies (2000: 2–3). The book then substantially consists of series of chapters that draw on company experiences to distil general lessons. From this point of view they find the history of GE and Westinghouse instructive because Westinghouse invented AC technology, which GE subsequently adopted (over its own product), while GE instead 'invented GE' through institutions such as the GE Research Laboratory. The lesson is: 'if you see the ultimate creation as the company, not the execution of a specific idea or capitalizing on a timely market opportunity, then you can persist beyond any specific idea – good or bad – and move towards becoming an enduring institution' (Collins and Porras 2000: 29).

The nature and conditions of success are differently identified in the two books. For Tichy, the success of GE is attributed to Welch as the leading man in a 'three act drama' which presents the performative initiatives as a story about how reverses and struggle were turned into the resolution of permanent revolution. Act I ('the awakening') runs from 1981 to about 1986 with 'the fusty, bureaucratic company Welch had inherited no longer existing' (Tichy and Sherman 1993: 149). Act II focuses on building values and capacity amongst GE's senior managers and features Tichy's own involvement with GE from 1985 to 1987 as manager of Crotonville, where executives were trained to lead by sharing ideas and information and building the values of GE. Act III ('revolution as a way of life') after 1988 extends change to the lower and middle tiers of management and spreads boundarylessness.

Throughout, much emphasis is put on the idea of leadership, as opposed to management: 'managing doesn't interest Welch much. Leadership is what he values because that's what enhances his control over the organization' (Tichy and Sherman 1993: 195). Welch is credited throughout with a crucial role, for example, in Act II through 'transformational leadership' (2003: 159) and interpersonal skills (2003: 196). The twin notions of the visionary leader and the learning organization permeate Tichy's other books, where GE is used as a case study in leadership. For instance, Tichy and Cardwell (2002: 8) described GE as 'the world's largest teaching infrastructure', citing the claim from Jack Welch that 'I probably spend 40 per cent of my time leading the company, selecting, coaching, deciding who gets which jobs' (2002: 112).

By way of contrast, Collins and Porras simply take a much longer-term view of the case and attribute the success not to Jack but to the organization he inherited:

> Obsessing on Welch's leadership style diverts us from a central point. Welch grew up in GE; he was a product of GE as much as the other way around. Somehow GE the organization had the ability to attract, retain, develop, groom and select Welch the leader. GE prospered long before Welch and will probably prosper long after Welch. After all, Welch was not the first excellent CEO in GE's history and probably will not be the last.
>
> (Collins and Porras 2000: 34)

Thus, for Collins and Porras, Welch was not special in GE terms but the latest in 'a long heritage of managerial excellence atop GE' (2000: 171), and they claim that 'Welch's immediate predecessor, Reginald Jones, retired as 'the most admired business leader in America' (2000: 170).

If the conditions of success are differently identified in the two books, the Collins and Porras account is immediately much more interesting because it suggests the cult of Welch rests on a rewriting of history. But both teams of authors are alike in that neither is much interested in deconstructing the achievement of GE by focusing on empirics or in including any empirics that might challenge or complicate the authorial line. As in Strebel (2003) considered at the beginning of this section, in both books the relation of causality or justification is established by juxtaposing assertions about brilliant success with claims about its conditions.

Collins and Porras have some excuse for this because their object is eighteen pairs of companies and they present long-run comparative analysis, including a curve of Total Shareholder Return, which shows that the visionary companies outperformed the market from 1926 to 1990 (2000: 6–7). Apart from such generalities, they do include one interesting GE exhibit which ranks Welch against his predecessors: taking the first eight years of his term, these authors find that Welch did no better in financial terms than Jones in the eight years of his office (2000: 169–73). Using return on equity as the measure, Welch comes fifth out of seven, although, tellingly, if the measure is whether GE beats average stock-market returns, Welch does better than most of his predecessors, as Exhibit C3.3 shows.

This exhibit offers a measured assessment of the relative success of Welch's stewardship and also focuses attention on one key piece of evidence that vindicates Collins and Porras's focus on the organization rather than on the individual. Those who turn to Tichy

***Exhibit C3.3*** *Collins and Porras's performance rankings of chief executive eras at GE*

| *Rank* | *GE Chief Executive era* | Average annual pretax return on equity % |
|---|---|---|
| 1 | Wilson, 1940–49 | 46.7 |
| 2 | Cordiner, 1950–63 | 40.5 |
| 3 | Jones, 1973–80 | 29.7 |
| 4 | Borch, 1964–72 | 27.5 |
| 5 | Welch, 1981–90 | 26.3 |
| 6 | Coffin, 1915–21 | 14.5 |
| 7 | Swope/Young, 1922–39 | 12.6 |

| *Rank* | *Average stock relative to general market* | | *Rank* | *Average stock relative to Westinghouse* | |
|---|---|---|---|---|---|
| | *Annual return* | *Cumulative performance* | | *Annual return* | *Cumulative performance* |
| 1 | Swope/Young, 1922–39 | | 1 | Cordiner, 1950–63 | |
| 2 | Welch, 1981–90 | | 2 | Jones, 1973–80 | |
| 3 | Cordiner, 1950–63 | | 3 | Swope/Young, 1922–39 | |
| 4 | Borch, 1964–72 | | 4 | Wilson, 1940–49 | |
| 5 | Wilson, 1940–49 | | 5 | Welch, 1981–90 | |
| 6 | Jones, 1973–80 | | 6 | Borch, 1964–72 | |

*Source*: Collins and Porras, 2000: 308–9

*Note*: Return on equity database available back to 1915 (Coffin was in office from 1892). Stock-return database available back to January 1926

and Sherman in search of further information on performance in the Welch years will be disappointed. The main exhibits are six graphs and barcharts covering the 1981–92 period on two facing pages: on the one side we have 'the performance story' in three exhibits with GE total sales, productivity and stock price all increasing gratifyingly; on the other side is 'the human story' with head count and organizational layers both going down appropriately and the number of employees with stock options going up appropriately (Tichy and Sherman 1993: 6–7). This might be called the mixed-assortment approach to confirming evidence. Other evidence used in the book to illustrate Welch's positive results is very limited with, in some cases, opinion substituting for any more elaborate evaluation, as when it is claimed that: 'Work-Out has made believers of GE's top 1,000 or 2,000 executives. I've been inside scores of the world's best and biggest companies, and I can't think of another where intellectual freedom and like-mindedness co-exist to an equal degree' (Tichy and Sherman 1993: 258).

In many other books, the focus is on Welch and the titles of these books indicate the preoccupation with the man. See, for example, Stuart Crainer and Des Dearlove's *Business the Jack Welch Way: 10 Secrets of the World's Greatest Turnaround King*; Jeffrey A. Krames's *The Welch Way: 24 Lessons from the World's Greatest CEO* and *Jack Welch Lexicon of*

*Leadership*; Robert Heller's *Jack Welch: The Giant of Corporate Management who Created Billions for Investors*; Janet Lowe's *Jack Welch Speaks* and *Welch: A Business Icon*; Robert Slater's *29 Leadership Secrets from Jack Welch*, *The New GE* and *Jack Welch and the GE Way*; and James W. Robinson's *Jack Welch on Leadership: Executive Lessons of the Master CEO*. Such books are generally distinguished by their striking absence of interest in the GE organization and their claimed understanding of the mind of Welch. They are variably derivative and secondary, with Heller's book one of the most limited in terms of analytical content and Slater's three books amongst the best. But all these books fit into a problematic where the object is leadership and the result is hagiography of the leader as a kind of religious prophet or great political leader whose thoughts and epigrams must be extensively quoted in a context where Jack's analyses and actions are invariably correct.

The whole genre is epitomized by the interview with Welch in Slater's (2000) *The GE Way Fieldbook*. Welch responds to the sycophantic first question about brilliant success by invoking the initiatives: 'Q. The last year or two at GE have been so excellent. Every year GE gets better and better. How do you account for that? . . . A. . . . You have to take the initiatives and you have to understand they've all become broader and deeper' (Slater 2000: 171).

As for Welch's contribution, that is summed up in a series of extended quotes in Slater's shortest book, which presents the thoughts of chairman (and CEO) Jack. Thus Slater reprises Welch's distinction between (inspirational) leadership and (routine) management: 'Leaders . . . inspire people with clear visions of how things can be done better. Some managers, on the other hand, muddle things with pointless complexity and detail. They equate [managing] with sophistication with sounding smarter than anyone else' (Welch, quoted in Slater 2003: 17).

Simplicity in message or product design is crucial to the communication of that vision because as Welch says: 'whatever it is – we're going to be number one or number two, or fix/close/sell or boundarylessness – every idea you present must be something you could get across easily at a cocktail party with strangers' (Welch, quoted in Slater 2003: 66).

The status of visionary prophet/leader is conferred by reporting every Welch diagnosis as correct and every initiative as an appropriate response, as in the following quote from Welch's 2000 letter to shareholders: 'seeing reality for GE in the '80s meant a hard look at a century-old portfolio of business. Seeing reality today means accepting the fact that e-business is here, it's not coming, it's not the thing of the future, it's here' (Welch, quoted in Slater 2003: 10).

Jack Welch does not inhabit an everyday world of ambiguity, contradiction and unintended consequences, and the key giveaway in the hagiography is that there is never any irony in any of the descriptions of initiatives and their implementation. At times, the result is unintentionally comic, as in Slater's deadpan report of how Jack Welch encouraged reluctant managers to take Six Sigma training and enrol in a 'new warrior class' of 'green belts' and 'black belts' by sending a fax that announced that completion of such training was a prerequisite for future promotion: 'after Welch's fax, the number of applicants for Six Sigma training programs skyrocketed' (Slater 2003: 103). But laughter would be inappropriate for those who believe in the visionary leader who in hagiographic books and media coverage of the late 1990s was increasingly credited with superhuman insight. Here, for example, is Slater citing Welch's claim that he can see into the heart of managers: 'I can smell when someone running [a business] isn't doing it right' (2003: 16). Or again, here is *Business Week* quoting a GE middle manager on how Welch knows them, despite their relative insignificance in the huge organization: 'We're pebbles in an ocean, but he knows about us' (8 June 1998).

In many ways, the increasingly cultish tone of commentary on Jack Welch from the later 1990s is not so much a lapse from good taste as the logic of the management belief system given GE's twenty-year record of financial success, which ensures that many who might otherwise mock have stayed to pray. At which point, it is sensible to switch between registers, from narrative to numbers and to register some discrepancies that can provide a critical antidote.

## DECONSTRUCTING THE NUMBERS: A TALE OF TWO BUSINESSES

For critical researchers wishing to understand GE under Jack Welch, the financial numbers are a hugely neglected resource. This is partly because, as noted in our introduction, academics are increasingly divided into two camps. On the one side are economic fundamentalists whose positivistic use of numerical evidence is limited by their pointillist concept of capitalism, and on the other side there are the social constructionists who see numbers as just another social fabrication. Our own position is rather different. GE's numbers are of course produced within the socio-technical–legal conventions of generally accepted accounting practice (GAAP) but the corporate financial results are quite distinct from the narrative and performative because there is limited scope for creativity when it comes to key measures such as corporate cash or divisional sales. Although GE may work hard within the (sometimes flexible) framework of accounting rules and norms to present results in such a way as to support management objectives, GE's financial numbers are not a function of the narrative and performative assemblies that we have considered in previous sections. Thus, interesting insights and analysis can be generated in the GE case by cutting between the two registers of numbers and the narrative, especially when the time frame is lengthened so that analysis can focus on longer-term performance trends which are not the main concern of journalists or stock-market analysts.

As we have seen in the review of the literatures on GE, the books on Welch and GE do include long-run comparisons of ten- or twenty-year performance after 1981. But the dominant approach is to cite what in Tichy's case we called a mixed assortment of corroborating numbers in a before-and-after frame so that readers can appreciate the x-fold increase in share price or the y-fold increase in sales over the two decades when Welch was in charge. In such comparisons, statistics are being used in a rhetorical, decorative kind of way. There is, for example, usually no attempt to deflate output and profit indicators from nominal to real, though the 1980s and 1990 were decades of commodity price inflation, nor is there any discussion of whether the share-price increase reflected unsustained bull-market price rises rather than permanent management success in creating value. When comparisons are included, as with Slater's graph of GE returns vs. S&P returns (1999: 8), the claim 'GE consistently outperforms the market' manifestly does not fit the graph presented in the book, which suggests this claim does not apply to the decade of the 1980s.

There is nothing new about all this because corporate financial performance has often in the past been constructed (at least in the short term) by finding numbers whose increase confirms a stereotype of purpose and achievement that derives from narrative and performative sources. Fortunately, it is possible to deconstruct such numbers as we showed in our analysis of another GEC (General Electric Company) some twenty years ago (see also Chapter 5 of the introduction to this book). British GEC was, like GE in the 1970s, a manufacturing conglomerate that made everything from power-generating sets to consumer white goods and televisions. The defensive merger that created the new firm under Arnold Weinstock was regarded as an outstanding success. Our 1983 case revised that judgement by the simple expedient of applying a price index: although nominal sales increases were impressive, real sales had increased by just 13 per cent over the decade of the 1970s and there was no organic growth (Williams et al. 1983: 145). British GEC's industrial operations were being run for margins on exacting financial criteria that also encouraged risk aversion and defensive retreat. By the 1990s this revisionism had become the received wisdom, as Weinstock and his company were increasingly seen as clever but uncreative in a world that had discovered exciting new forms of management. In his autobiography, Welch himself dismisses Weinstock as the 'green eye shade accountant' (Welch 2001: 306).

Interestingly, Robert Heller's web site sets up a contrast between bad GEC under Weinstock and good GE under Welch. The quality of the oft-cited evidence on GE under Jack is such that this comparison only raises new questions about these two giant manufacturing conglomerates: does Welch's inspired leadership through performance produce hugely better results than Weinstock's financial control, which produced a profitable but shrinking manufacturing base? This question can only be answered in the 2000s by producing a much more sophisticated analysis, for several interrelated reasons. First, GE is more complex than British GEC. Second, our standard analysis now includes a much broader range of variables, including balance sheet as well as operating performance. And, third, the advance of financialization means that stock-market performance indicators now have a primary importance that they did not have in the early 1980s. This more sophisticated analysis is provided in two stages as this section of our case deconstructs the financial numbers on GE and the next section adds the necessary interpretation by providing an analysis of what can be termed, 'the undisclosed business model'.

The deconstruction of the financial numbers in this section does undoubtedly diminish the achievement of GE under Welch, but this deconstruction should be read in the context of the next section on the business model. Taken together, the third and fourth sections of this case study accept that GE's performance was a huge achievement, but a rather different one from that constructed by writers exclusively preoccupied with endless management moves and initiatives. What Welch did was to identify business-model levers (such as the growth of financial services) and to pull the levers hard while also generating narrative and performative framing that increases advantage by projecting purpose.

## Stock market performance: dividends and stock price

The analysis begins with returns to shareholders because these returns have a primary importance after financialization when they are the privileged measure of success. The two components of total shareholder return are dividend payouts and share price, and the immediate task is to consider the relative importance of each variable and the extent to which it reflected a durable contribution to value that made GE an attractive investment.

During the period that Welch was CEO of GE, as we noted in Chapter 4 of our introduction to this book, giant US firms were not generally increasing distributions to shareholders. And, in this context, GE's policy was to maintain its already generous payout rates. Since 1980, total dividends have generally remained at about 40–5 per cent of net income, with some cyclical variability; payout rates are usually higher in years with lower net income (Table C3.1 in appendix, p. 369). This pattern is fairly similar to (and, if anything, slightly lower on average than) what can be observed in the S&P 500 as a whole, where dividend payouts as a share of net income vary cyclically from about 35 per cent to 75 per cent and with an average of almost 50 per cent from 1980 to 2002. GE's dividends per share (allowing for share splits) rose from $0.13 in the early 1980s to around $0.75 (in 2003 prices), while dividend yield has fallen from around 5 per cent to around 2 per cent as the share price has risen. The importance of dividends is very variable and depends on the year and the investor's holding strategy. Exhibit C3.4 and Table C3.1 shows that dividends are an insignificant part of total return to shareholders in years of booming stock price (for example, 1996–2000) but they account for all or most of the gain in seven of the years between 1980 and 2003, including 2001 to 2003. In this sense, dividends matter as soon as stock prices cease to rise and GE's ability to

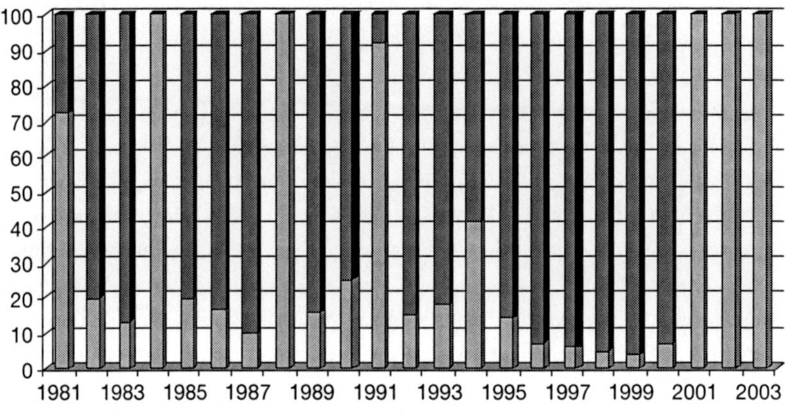


*Exhibit C3.4 Composition of GE's total shareholder return (% shares)*
*Source*: GE Annual Report and Accounts, various years

sustain generous pay-outs from increasing profits differentiates it from weaker manufacturers such as Ford.

For long-term shareholders, the major element in total shareholder return was the increase in GE's stock price, in line with other US giant firms. After adjusting for stock splits and using real 2003 prices, GE's share price rose from around $120 per share in 1980 to $2,600 at the peak in 2000, before falling back to a little under $1,300. In nominal terms, the 1980 base point was $54 per share, rising to $2,450 at the peak. This represents an increase of 974% in real terms (2,287 % in nominal terms) from 1980 to 2003, or a more impressive 2,084 % real increase from 1980 to 2000 (4,441% in nominal terms). This trend, illustrated in Exhibit C3.5, certainly appears to support the widely held view that Jack Welch was responsible for a huge increase in shareholder wealth, though clearly even the behemoth GE was not immune from general investor sentiment after 2000, when GE's share price fell by some 51% in real terms (47 % in nominal terms) over the three years to 2003. Thus, while all shareholders have enjoyed the dividends, the extent to which individuals have benefited from share price appreciation depends on the timing of purchase and sale. GE's stock performance in Exhibit C3.5 is clearly strong but it is also important to put this in the context of, first, the company's steady growth over two decades and, second, the larger group of US giant companies, to establish the extent to which it is exceptional.

Many commentaries on Welch and GE use market capitalization (rather than share price) as the measure of value creation for shareholders and Table C3.2 shows that GE's market capitalization did increase around twenty-one-fold, from $12 billion to $270

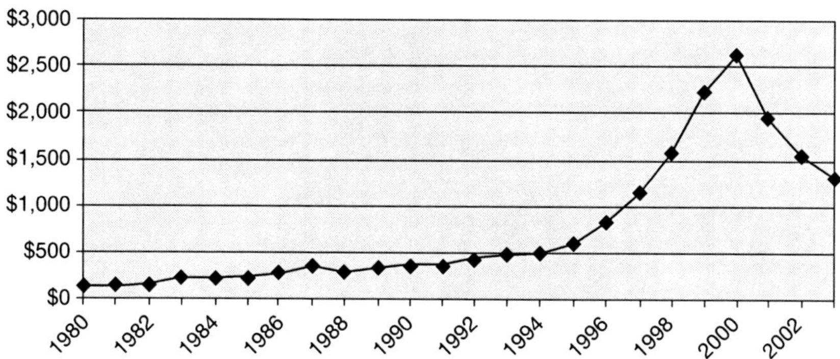


***Exhibit C3.5*** *GE stock price, 1980–2003 (using the average stock price during year and adjusted for stock splits, in real 2003 prices)*

*Source*: GE Annual Report and Accounts, various years

billion by 2003 (and to $500 billion at the 2000 peak). In interpreting this large increase, of course, it is important, first, to bear in mind that GE was expanding fast during this period and its market value is partly a reflection of size and thus future earnings potential of the firm, and, second, to consider whether GE's valuation was moving ahead of other giant firms in the USA. Exhibit C3.6 presents indices of market capitalization and net income to provide some perspective on the first of these points. This graph shows that it is after 1995 that there is a difference in trends so that GE's market valuation moves significantly ahead of its earnings performance. Of course, the latter part of the 1990s was characterized by a heady bull market in which stock process generally moved sharply upwards. In order to assess GE, therefore, we also need to compare the company against other giant US firms: did GE's market value race ahead of its peers, or are the trends in Exhibit C3.6 part of a more general corporate phenomenon?

Exhibits C3.7 and C3.8 provide some insight on this by comparing the market capitalization and P/E ratio of GE against the S&P 500 as a whole. As in Exhibit C3.6, there is a marked change in Exhibit C3.7 after 1995: up to 1995, GE's market value moves in an almost identical way to that of the S&P 500; after 1995, the GE's market value begins to rise faster than that for the S&P 500 as a whole, followed by a sharper decline after the peak in 2000. Similarly, in Exhibit 3.8, GE's P/E ratio rises from around 15 towards 40 at the 2000 peak, before falling back to less than 20. The answer to the question of whether an investment in Welch's portfolio of businesses is valued more highly than the S&P 500 as a whole is interesting: in P/E terms, GE does not consistently out-perform the S&P 500, as Exhibits C3.7 and C3.8 show. On these measures of performance, GE matches the S&P 500 during the 1980s, lagged during the first half of the 1990s in terms of P/E, before racing ahead in the period 1996–2000. After 2000, however, GE's P/E ratio is again lower than that for the S&P 500 as a whole, as a result of a stock price that has fallen more precipitously than those of many other companies.

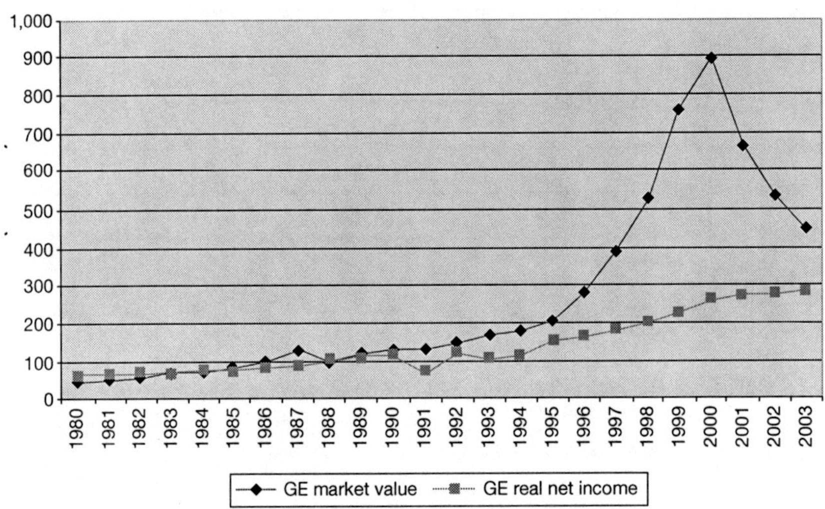


***Exhibit C3.6*** *A comparison of GE's market capitalization and net income, 1980–2003 (index: 1988=100)*

*Source*: GE Annual Report and Accounts, 10K, Annual Abstract of the US and NYSE web site

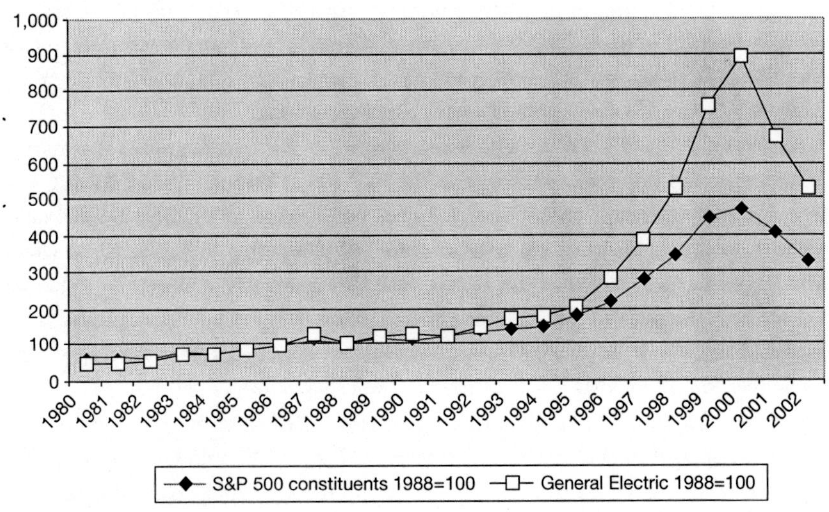


***Exhibit C3.7*** *GE market capitalization, compared with the S&P 500 (indexed at 1988=100)*

*Source*: GE Annual Report and Accounts and Compustat

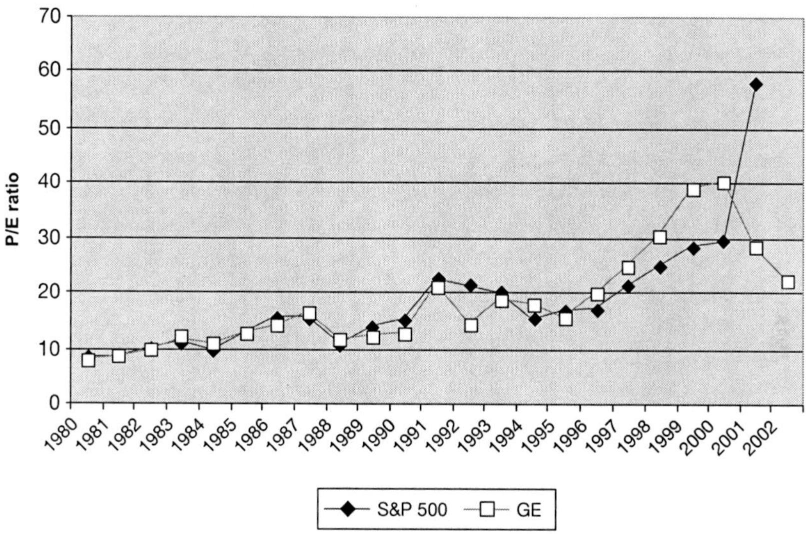


***Exhibit C3.8*** *GE P/E ratio, compared with the S&P 500*

*Source*: GE Annual Report and Accounts, SEC 10K, Compustat

*Note*: The S&P 500 P/E value for 2002 has been removed from this graph. In 2002 the overall P/E was 103: this is an outlier figure, distorted by write-downs at AOL Time Warner. The removal of this observation improves the scaling and readability of the graph. The full data is in appendix Table C3.2

The results of this brief examination of stock-market performance are insightful. The narrative and performative accounts of GE suggest twenty glorious years of management, an assertion usually supported with dubious before-and-after long-run statistical comparisons. A more detailed deconstruction of stock-market performance shows that in market terms, there were five glorious years from 1996 to 2000. In comparative terms, GE's dividend yield was no higher than the S&P 500 in most years and GE's P/E ratio more or less tracks the S&P 500 almost exactly up to 1997 when it starts to grow faster, with a large difference in growth rates from 1997 to 2000. This was clearly an achievement for a blue-chip conglomerate in the period of the 'new economy' when investors were buying into technology stocks under the influence of narratives of digital transformation. But it very definitely is not a sustained increase in shareholder value, because in most years the market's belief in Welch is clearly limited.

## Operating performance: sales growth and ROCE

Operating performance is not the same as stock-market performance but, by the 1990s, it has to be constructed through the gaze of the stock market and the promises of the academics and consultants selling shareholder value. Thus, it is not enough to increase sales and to have profits but, according to opportunity cost logic, the company must also have a rate of profit greater than the cost of capital if it is not to destroy value. In practice, this means more than 10–12 per cent after tax in the 1990s. If we exclude the new-economy period in the second half of the 1990s, the stars of the stock market with fancy P/E ratios were pharma firms such as Glaxo, which combined sustained double-digit rates of sales growth and of return on capital. The question about operations is, how far does GE fall short of this star status?

Many of the before-and-after comparisons cite GE's fivefold increase in sales revenues (turnover) from $25 billion to $129 billion between 1980 and 2000 (see Exhibit C3.2 and Tables C3.3 and C3.4, pp. 371–2). In considering sales growth, we can begin by converting nominal data into real values (by discounting to remove the effects of inflation). Table C3.5 (p. 374) presents sales in 2003 prices. Predictably, the rate of real sales growth is much less impressive than the nominal rate of growth. In real terms, GE sales rose from $59 billion to $134 billion over the twenty-three years from 1980, suggesting real growth over the period of 128 per cent, compared with 438 per cent in nominal terms. As we noted in the introduction to this book, any large group of giant companies tends to grow no faster than GDP. So GE's twenty-year compound growth rate of almost 4 per cent looks very respectable because it is nearly twice as fast as the long-run rate of GDP growth, though it should be noted that this headline rate of growth was achieved by a company that, as we shall see in the next section, was making large acquisitions that boosted growth. If GE was not a GDP company over this twenty-year period, there was always the suspicion that it might become one. This was explicit in the early 1980s and again by the early 2000s when problems of cyclicality hit several of the industrial businesses at the same time as unexpected downturns in areas such as insurance.

The story of sales growth gets much more interesting if we divide GE into its two main components in Exhibit C3.9: industrial and finance (GE Capital or GE Capital Services as it has also been known, GECS). It then becomes clear that almost all of the growth in sales originates in GECS and that therefore this is a tale of two businesses, one high growth and the other low or no growth. The result over twenty years is that GECS's share of turnover increases rapidly. There is also a sharp contrast in nominal growth rates, as Table C3.4 illustrates (p. 372). GE Consolidated has grown at an average of 8 per cent per annum with a small fall in nominal sales recorded in only four years since 1980 and with growth of more than 10 per cent achieved in nine years (Table C3.4). The financial-services side of the business has achieved double-digit growth in every year since 1980, with the exception of just three years when GECS lost sales. GECS's average annual growth of 23 per cent dwarfs that of the industrial side of the business, which grew at around 5.3 per cent (or 3.8 per cent in real terms) per annum. The result of differential

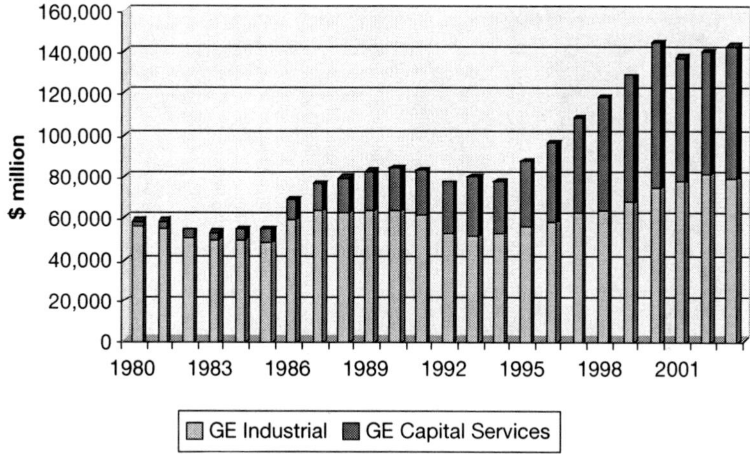


**Exhibit C3.9** *GE real sales revenue, 1980–2003, $ million (in real 2003 prices and showing the split by major division)*

*Source*: GE Annual Report and Accounts, various years

growth rates is that industrial becomes relatively less important as GECS becomes more important. In 1980 GE's industrial businesses contributed more than 95 per cent of total sales revenues and this remained above 90 per cent until 1988. From the late 1980s, however, GECS contributed an increasingly large part of corporate revenues until it accounted for almost half of all sales by 2000.

If the analysis is made in terms of real sales and the focus is narrowed onto industrial and the businesses within industrial, the results are even more striking because the no-growth status of industrial becomes all the more clearer. As Table C3.5 (p. 374) and Exhibit C3.10 show, from 1980 to 1998, in real terms, GE Industrial sales are flat but varying cyclically with successive economic cycles leading to peak-to-trough variation from $63 billion to $48 billion. By way of contrast, GECS has real growth of 1,825 per cent from 1980 to 2003 which lifts sales from $3 billion to $64 billion in 2003 prices (Table C3.5). Broadly, over this long period, GE Industrial follows the pattern of US manufacturing: Exhibit C3.11 compares GE Industrial with both US GDP and US manufacturing growth and shows that GE Industrial and US manufacturing follow almost exactly the same pattern of growth over twenty-two years, with a faster growth only apparent after 1998. Maintaining real growth in GE Industrial over this period is, at one level, an achievement, made possible by renewing the industrial businesses to remove those that fail to make sufficient contribution to growth.

In narrative and performative terms there is a huge difference between Jack Welch and Arnold Weinstock, but if we compare the real-sales growth of Weinstock's GEC industrial conglomerate in the 1970s with the Welch GE industrial business up to 1998, there does not seem to be much difference in terms of their consequences for long-term sales growth. As Table C3.5 shows, after 1998 there is a change in the trend because real

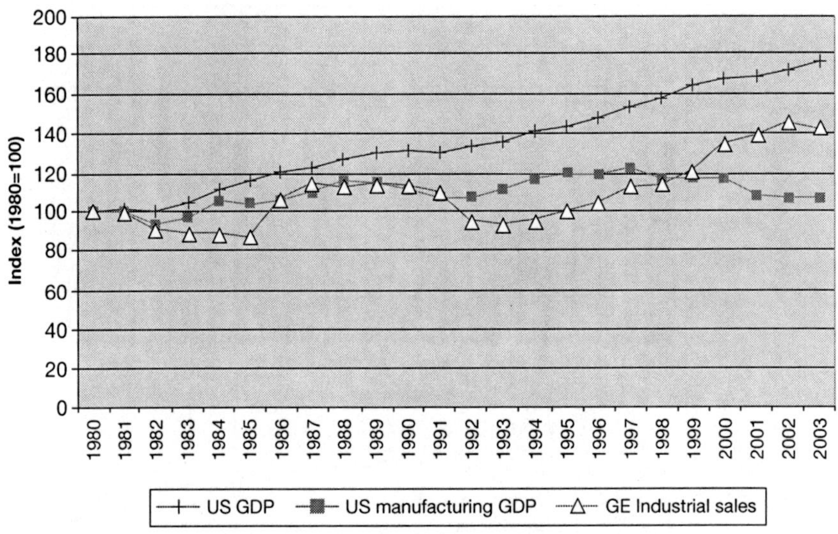


**Exhibit C3.10** *GE Industrial growth, compared with GDP and US manufacturing (all in real 2003 prices, indexed at 1980=100)*

*Source*: GE Annual Report and Accounts, various years and US Bureau of Economic Affairs

*Note*: GE Industrial sales in the late 1990s and early 2000s were boosted by is power systems business, see Exhibit C3.11

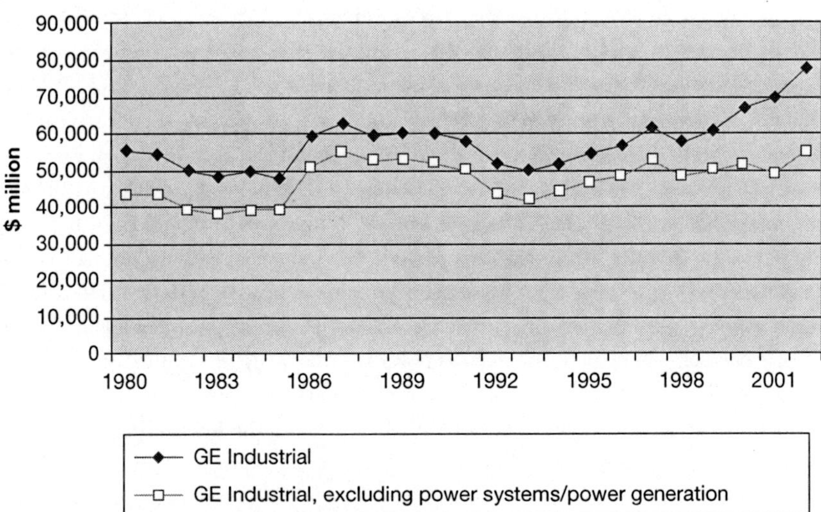


**Exhibit C3.11** *GE Industrial real sales, $ million (in real 2002 prices and showing the power systems/power generation segment)*

*Source*: GE Annual Report and Accounts, various years

sales in GE Industrial then move up by a step increase towards $80 billion at the peak in 2002 (Exhibit C3.11). This step increase is an undoubted achievement but does not indicate a break and a new trend to organic growth. As we argue below, the increase of industrial sales after 1998 is due to particular and non-sustainable circumstances; this becomes clearer by looking at GE Industrial sales by division.

Analysis of GE Industrial sales by division is, however, complicated by acquisition and divestment. Some divisions are relatively new with the broadcasting division, for example, created after the acquisition of NBC in 1986. Meanwhile, other divisions, such as natural resources, were discontinued after the sale of operations such as Utah mining acquired by Reg Jones towards the end of his term. Matters are further complicated by segment reclassifications in 1987 and 2002 (and again in 2003). The net result is that like-for-like comparisons are very difficult and, for this reason, some of our series in the statistical appendix end in 2002 and have not been updated to 2003. For earlier years, using information from change years when old and new classifications are presented, we have constructed a continuous, consistent series on the divisions presented in Table C3.6 (p. 375).

As might be expected, Table C3.6 shows that the industrial businesses have different patterns of cyclical and secular growth in real sales with no real growth in appliances, cyclical variation in aircraft-engine sales and fairly steady growth in broadcasting. But on the industrial side, GE's problem is that (despite acquisitions and initiatives), it has no one large industrial business that is growing fast enough to cover weakness elsewhere and to lift the real volume of industrial sales. And this is not changed by the recent rise in industrial sales, which reflects a temporary boom in power systems that is due to increased orders for gas turbines arising from the deregulation of energy markets in the USA. In a presentation to analysts in November 2002, GE describes the booming power systems sales as a 'bubble', implying inevitable decline after the peak effects have worked through (GE 2002b).

The business of power systems, which was cyclical between 1980 and 1999, had real sales running at around double the level of previous cyclical peaks by 2002 so that power systems provided $12 billion of GE Industrial's overall sales growth of $17 billion since 1999 (Table C3.6, appendix, p. 375). According to the company, the bubble generated 'proceeds' of an additional $7 billion of sales between 1996 and 2002 (GE 2002b). For the power systems and energy segment as a whole, GE expected that revenues would fall from $23 billion in 2002 to $19.7 billion in 2003 as sales of equipment decline. The 2003 accounts do confirm this and show that power systems generated sales of $18.5 billion in 2003. The projected reduction is so far modest because GE assumes it can increase revenues from power-generation services by winning contracts to operate and or maintain new generating sets. The effects of the 'bubble' have taken some time to work through GE's income statement and reach the bottom line because there are delays between ordering and delivery of such a large and complex product. But, the results were delivered at just the right time because they usefully cover declining real profits in several segments including appliances and materials. In terms of profit, power systems generated

$6.4 billion of GE Industrial's total operating income of $14 billion in 2002, which is some $4 billion more than power systems had generated in any year before 1999.

It is much more difficult to say anything sensible about the sources of the sustained real-sales increase in GECS because historically GE has disclosed limited consistent segmental data on GECS's financing and insurance operations. But from published information it is straightforward to compare the overall ROCE in GECS against that for industrial services and this comparison highlights a central paradox which Table C3.7 (p. 376) illustrates: the relatively declining industrial-services business has a high ROCE, while the fast-growing financial business has a very low ROCE so that the shift towards financial services leaves GE with an overall ROCE that is well below the target 10–12 per cent post-tax recommended in 1990s' shareholder-value texts and discussed in Chapter 3. It is not unusual for giant firms to combine high- and low-growth activities, nor is it unusual for giant firms to be changing the balance of their portfolio. But we would expect such firms to be moving into growing activities that were at least as profitable as the contracting activities. In a world where the issue is not profit but the rate of profit, there is perhaps little point in achieving sales growth at the expense of substantially lower ROCE. But this is exactly what GE did under Welch.

Table C3.7 in the appendix shows that GE Industrial is a set of businesses, which combined have a high and increasing ROCE. The Industrial ROCE (calculated using income before interest and tax) has grown from 25–28 per cent in the first half of the 1980s to 33–43 per cent since 1995. The improvement in GE Industrial ROCE calculated using post-tax income is less spectacular and amounts to only a 2 or 3 per cent rise with more pronounced cyclicality. But, in terms of post-tax return income, GE Industrial still achieves a ROCE of 16–19 per cent since the mid-1990s, with a return of 23 per cent achieved in 2002, which is handsome by any standard and hugely better than returns for the S&P 500 as a whole which were described in Chapter 4 of this book. GECS is a completely different story of low and (quite significantly) declining ROCE which falls from well over 20 per cent to less than 10 per cent, using income before interest and tax) or, using post-tax income as the numerator, from around 4 per cent to 2 per cent over twenty years. The ROCE performance of the company as a whole in Exhibit C3.12 is therefore determined by the growth of low ROCE finance activities at the expense of high ROCE industrial businesses, with the result that, as GECS has expanded, the consolidated company ROCE on post-tax income has more than halved from 11 per cent to a little under 5 per cent using net income.

Of course, it would not be appropriate to apply the same ROCE targets to a financial as to an industrial company. Financial companies have large amounts of borrowed capital on their balance sheets (whether from retail banking customers or from the money markets in the case of non-banks) and this will always depress the return on total capital. For this reason, a bank or other financial company might consider an alternative measure of capital efficiency such as the difference between the costs associated with borrowing and the gains made from charging those to whom these funds are then lent on. This change of standards also introduces a handicap element because a company that borrows

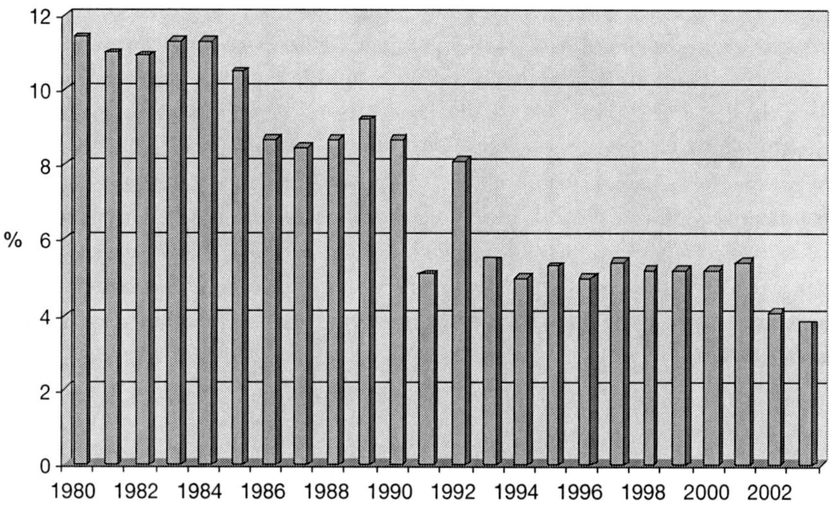


**Exhibit C3.12** *GE Consolidated (post-tax) ROCE*

*Source*: GE Annual Report and Accounts, various years

cheaply, courtesy of an triple-A or double-A credit rating, has some inherent advantages over corporations who have to pay more to borrow and who then lend on in competitive markets. On this argument it might be unfair to consider a ROCE measure for the whole of GE, given the growing weight of its finance business. But, in our view, ROCE is an appropriate measure because GE has continued to stress that it is a technology, manufacturing and services company (and definitely not a financial-services conglomerate). The logic of that identification is that ROCE does matter.

The increasingly meagre ROCE of GE as a whole in Exhibit C3.12 is extraordinarily interesting for several reasons. First, it exposes the simplicity and irrelevance of 1990s shareholder-value consultants and writers such as Rappaport (1998), whose value-management packages took abnormal profits or high ROCE as the key objective for corporate management after shareholder value. Such opportunity cost measures may be intellectually important but GE shows they can be practically irrelevant. As we have seen, GE's share performance is unremarkable and mostly tracks the S&P 500 index (with out-performance most obvious in the 1996–2000 period) which implies very clearly that the stock market is not vindictive about low ROCE, provided earnings are being delivered and everything else is going up. But, even more interestingly, the low ROCE of GE as a whole implies that Jack Welch presided over an increasingly massive destruction of value, which did not figure in the company narrative and was never engaged by the performative initiatives. In an earlier generation, giant firms such as ICI built industrial plants, expanded relatively unprofitably and paid the price in two ways: first, their main boards had to listen to presentations from young consultants whose slides showed the extent of their value destruction; second, when City opinion was against them and take-over threatened, such firms had to divest and unbundle activities such as chemicals and pharma in an attempt to create value for the market. Compare and contrast GE as it piled further into relatively unprofitable financial services. Here, the rest of the world had to read interviews with Welch and books by academic consultants which explain how he delivered results for everybody through performative initiatives. The GE conglomerate was not threatened by break-up but allowed to carry on making acquisitions. If the numbers are not a function of the narrative, it is true that the narrative can powerfully frame judgement of the numbers. If this helps to explain how Jack Welch succeeded in deflecting interest away from an understanding of the financials and onto the initiatives, the more interesting issue for the next section is, what was GE doing?

## GE'S UNDISCLOSED BUSINESS MODEL

The third and fourth sections of this case both use numbers for critical purposes. The previous section uses numbers descriptively to observe GE's portfolio choice, which was to combine a low-growth/high-ROCE industrial business with a high-growth/low-ROCE finance business in way that generated overall increases in sales and earnings but at the cost of spoilt ROCE. This fourth section shows how numbers can be used more analytically to explore the business model that explains the observed results. The term 'business model' probably originated in Silicon Valley and passed into general usage through the writings of authors such as Michael Lewis (1999) about the new economy. As we observed in the Ford and Glaxo cases, the term 'business model' is now widely used by consultants for analysing or recommending cost-recovery paradigm shifts and we have ourselves used it for critical purposes in an analysis of the way in which the new economy opened up the possibility of cost recovery from the capital market not the product market (Feng et al. 2001). Given that the term is used in different ways by various authors, it may be best to begin with a very brief discussion of business models which distinguishes between accidental and purposive business models and between explicit and undisclosed business models.

Generically, business models are about how firms recover their costs, including a surplus that represents the cost of capital. To that extent, all firms that survive for any length of time must have a business model, though this result could be either the consequence of accidental developments of purposive movement planned by management. Accident here includes changes of circumstance arising from unexpected product-market developments, changes in input cost or whatever; this would include a car company's unexpected success in a new market segment or an integrated oil company's windfall gains on the rising price of oil. Purpose includes actions such as deliberate labour-cost reduction or avoidance of major airport hubs in a start-up airline adopting a low-cost model. Explicit business models are models that are disclosed in the company's narrative of purpose and achievement and discussed by analysts. The pharma industry provides a good example where the business model of marketing blockbusters is well understood by all capital market and business-press analysts (though even here, companies play down the significance of me-too products). But it is also possible to have an implicit business model where major sources of profit and cash do not figure prominently in the company narrative and their implications are not understood outside the company. Thus, although everyone understands that a substantial part of Ford Motor's profits come from finance, few register the more arcane consequences such as the burden of depreciation arising from vehicle leasing.

Long-run analysis of the financial numbers is crucial in distinguishing between accidental and purposive business models, as between explicit and undisclosed business models. The fascination of GE is that such analysis shows very clearly that GE had a purposive business model whereby management is clearly pulling levers hard to get cost recovery. But the model is little discussed in so far as it does not fit the narrative and performative account of moves under Jack Welch. In the section below, we dissect the different elements of a business model which, taken together, were hugely effective in generating increases of sales and earnings, thus apparently validating the cult of performative management at GE. By *undisclosed* business model we do not mean that this model was ever hidden or concealed; that cannot be so in so far as this case study develops its account of GE's business model from publicly available accounting information. Rather, we use the term *undisclosed* to denote a business model that was not explicitly articulated by the company and its CEO who preferred to talk about other things and sometimes denied elements of the business model; just as outside analysts and commentators never brought the business model into focus so that it became an important element in the narratives explaining GE's success. On some issues, such as acquisition, our analysis of the business model makes points that overlap with the more sceptical analysts' discussion of GE; this overlap is identified in the discussion below. But, as we have already noted, the analysts have never had a high-profile role in shaping understanding of GE. As the first section of this case study explains, the media did question GE's achievement in the early 1980s or early 2000s. But, for most of the past twenty years, the media and business books have been in thrall to what Jack Welch (and, more recently, Jeff Immelt) tells us about leadership and organization at GE. This is certainly the easiest option for outside commentators: first, because, GE is a complicated company to understand and the financial accounts are highly aggregated; and, second, the sustained success of the company means that some commentators see the pressing issue as explaining GE's success, rather than understanding it. Our narrative instead shows how we can put together financial information to provide an analysis of GE's success.

Our analysis of the undisclosed business model is relatively straightforward and focuses on seven principles of GE's cost recovery under Welch:

1 run the industrial business for earnings;
2 add industrial services to cover hollowing out of the industrial base;
3 buy and sell companies through acquisition and divestment to achieve returns and growth objectives;
4 rely on large-scale acquisition to prevent like-for-like comparisons and to increase opacity and the power of narrative;
5 grow the financial-services business up to the limit of the company's credit rating;
6 accept the balance-sheet costs in terms of return on capital but focus on managing return on equity and cost of capital;
7 add financial engineering to smooth earnings and manage growth.

These seven corporate cost recovery principles are analysed in turn below and, in each case, the discussion of the numbers is prefaced by a brief discussion of how the issue is represented in GE's own discourse where the principles are never acknowledged and sometimes denied.

The existing literature on GE is full of transferable management precepts that could supposedly be applied to improve performance in other giant firms. It is worth insisting therefore that the business-model principles we outline are nothing of the sort because these seven principles only work in combination for GE. Other companies may combine industrial and financial businesses, as Ford does. But, with a cyclical core industrial business and without GE's triple-A rating, Ford's trajectory and results are completely different. Thus, the principle denotes an internal rule that cannot be questioned or broken without risk of consequences inside GE, but such principles cannot provide rules of conduct or guides for cost recovery in other companies. As Auden observed in his marvellous poem about W. B. Yeats, after his last afternoon as himself, the great man became his admirers when he died; just as Jack Welch became his admirers when he retired. But only the foolish admirer believes in the possibility of greatness by mimesis.

## Principle 1: run the industrial business for margins so that its profits cover the earnings requirement

Companies that explicitly run blue-chip businesses for margins, such as Weinstock's British GEC, seldom enjoy a very positive reputation because there is something inherently unconstructive about management by financial hurdle. For GE, the narrative and performative is used to deflect such criticism in so far as they suggest that brilliant numbers are not the objective of management but a result that drops out from initiatives. Equally interesting in GE from the mid-1980s onwards is the absence of a high-profile discourse of cost reduction. This is probably because cost reduction would sound too negative and also because it is difficult to understand the composition of costs across a diverse range of industrial businesses. In most of these businesses, the largest and most controllable internal cost would be labour, so productivity increase was used as coded GE management speak for cost reduction. Thus, the 'change acceleration process coaches workshops' at Crotonville started with an overview: 'CAP has proven to be a valuable tool that is helping GE businesses achieve measurable growth and productivity improvements' (Slater 2000: 162).

Against this rather blurred background, the numbers show very clearly that GE Industrial is an operation that has been run for higher earnings when management has found it difficult to wring increasing margins out of GE Capital. The argument on this point begins with the observation that profit margins on industrial businesses have increased to the point where they are higher than the margins on finance, which nevertheless retains a valuable role in generating cash. For GE as a whole, the ROS increased from around 6 per cent in the early 1980s to around 10 per cent by the early 2000s, with remarkably little cyclicality (Table C3.8, appendix, p. 377). ROS in GE Industrial grew fairly steadily from around 5–6 per cent to around 11–13 per cent, with some drop in 1991. For GECS, however, the ROS has been much more variable with some increase from 8 per cent in the early 1980s to 11–13 per cent by 1983–4, but this has since fallen back to around 6–9 per cent.

In terms of cash generation, again GE Industrial manages to extract more cash in the 1990s than in the 1980s, as Table C3.9 (p. 378) shows; but the rank order between industrial and financial businesses is interestingly different because, like Ford's captive finance business, GE Capital is more successful at generating cash than profits. In GE as a whole, operating cash flow expressed as a percentage of sales increases from around 10 per cent in the early 1980s to around 20 per cent by the end of the 1990s (Exhibit C3.13). In GE Industrial, the 1990s saw a greater extraction of operating cash, from around 10 per cent of sales to 15 per cent plus by the mid-1990s. Cash-flow generation in GECS has been more erratic but nonetheless generally larger in relation to its sales than in the industrial division (Table C3.9, appendix).

The cash from GE Capital was useful but the earnings from GE Industrial were crucial in helping to corroborate the company's narrative where one of the key confirming pieces of evidence was the unbroken twenty-year record of increases in quarterly earnings. In the company as whole, pre-tax income (profit) grew from $2.5 billion to $19.9 billion between 1980 and 2003, while net (post-tax) income grew from $1.5 billion to $15 billion (Table C3.10, appendix; Exhibit C3.14). This result depended on GE Industrial extracting higher earnings from flat sales (while GE Capital increased sales with flat margins) through most of the 1980s and 1990s. While GE Industrial's real sales remained largely flat over the period considered, as Exhibit C3.9 shows, real net income rose from around $1.5 billion in the early 1980s to $10 billion by 2002, falling back in 2003 (Table C3.12, appendix, p. 381). At the same time, GECS net income rose spectacularly from $0.2 billion to over $5 billion in 2000/1 and $7.4 billion in 2003. The size of GE

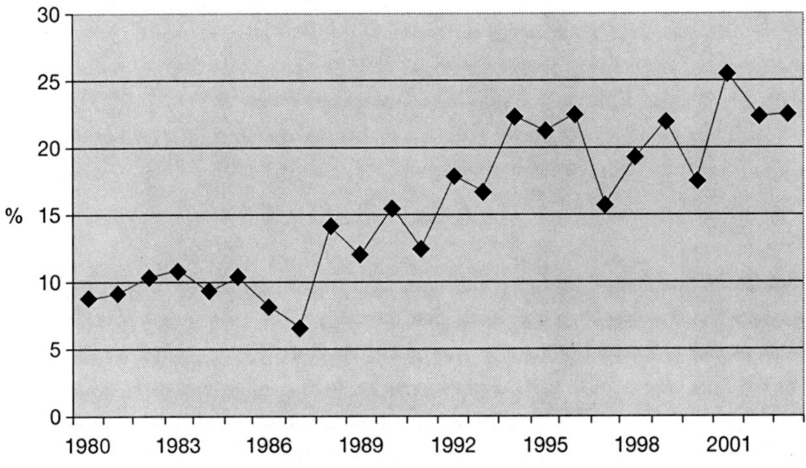


*Exhibit C3.13 GE cashflow from operations as a percentage of sales*

*Source*: GE Annual Report and Accounts, various years

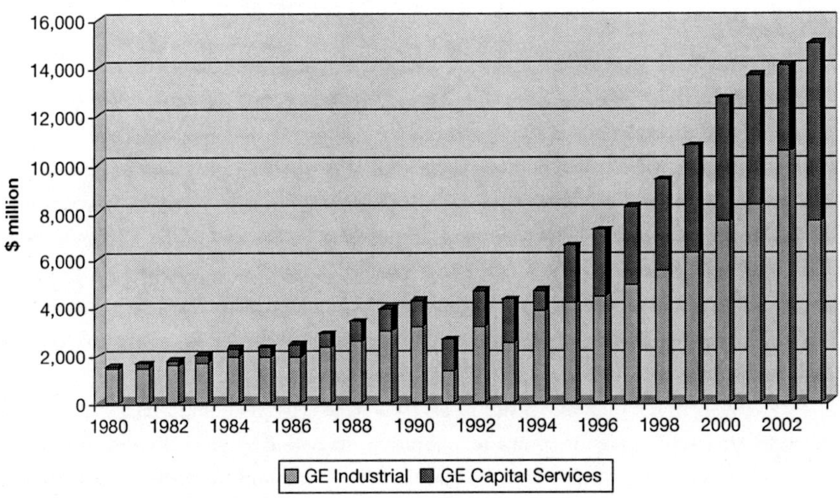


*Exhibit C3.14 GE real net income, $ million (in real 2003 prices and showing contribution of the major divisions)*

*Source*: GE Annual Report and Accounts, various years

Industrial and the improvement in margins were enough to raise GE's overall ROS through a process that was reaching its limits by the end of the 1990s. Attempts to maintain cost savings, and to extend these from GE Industrial into GECS, have been the impetus for the company's digitization initiative which was started under Welch and continued under Immelt. According to the 2001 Annual Report, cost savings of $1.9 billion were generated through 'e-Make' and 'e-Buy' (GE 2001 Annual Report: 3).

Looking back at the 1980s and 1990s, a sustained margin improvement of the kind observed at GE is unlikely to be delivered without explicit targeting of financial returns, rewards and punishments for business managers who deliver or default, and maybe acquisitions and divestments of businesses with the right and wrong characteristics. This is especially so, given the record of GE as a whole in two successive decades: as Table C3.4 shows, in the 1980s, sales and profits were rising at roughly similar rates, while in the 1990s, GE Consolidated managed to increase net income by 12.7 per cent on the back of a 6.9 per cent average increase in sales revenues (see also Exhibit C3.15). The implication is that GE's earnings success story, especially in the 1990s, is explained as much by focused cost control in GE Industrial as by growth in GE Capital. GE Industrial has contributed the greater share of income in every year although this share had fallen from over 90 per cent to around 60 per cent by the early 2000s with the growth of GE Capital. GE Industrial becomes proportionately more important in 2002 due to the boost received from booming sales in the power-generation business (as discussed above, p. 333). Overall, GE Industrial (nominal) net income grew in every year except 1985, 1991, 1993 and 2003, as Table C3.4 shows, and, in most years, growth was in excess of 10 per cent with some years showing much larger gains. On this point, the GE narrative aligns with outcomes, because the absence of strong cyclicality is almost certainly the joint result of a diverse portfolio of businesses with strong market positions.

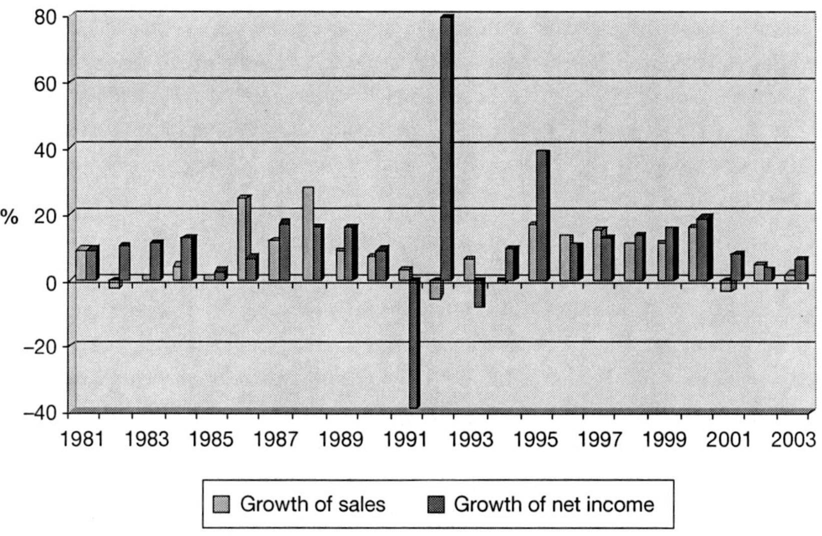


***Exhibit C3.15*** *GE annual growth in sales and net income (%)*

*Source*: GE Annual Report and Accounts, various years

Early in Welch's tenure, GE made a major miscalculation when it anticipated manufacturing growth and invested in 1980s factory automation: 'GE lost a mound of money after getting carried away by intoxicating – and wildly unrealistic – forecasts of the new factory automation industry and GE's place in it' (*Fortune*, 11 November 1985: 52). This mistake was not subsequently repeated on this scale (though there were problems about over-optimistic demand for railway locomotives and suchlike), because GE had learnt its lesson, which was to pursue increased margins from manufacturing and to pursue growth elsewhere from industrial services or finance.

## Principle 2: build industrial services to cover the inevitable hollowing out of ongoing manufacturing businesses

GE's commitment to services demonstrates the company's capacity to be first mover through sector-matrix strategies (see Chapter 5) before the term had been invented. The contrast with Ford under Jacques Nasser is interesting because in so many ways, including sector-matrix and management evaluation, Nasser was a follower who had read (and indeed hired) Noel Tichy and rather naively admired the other Jack (Tichy 1999: 82, *Detroit News*, 21 November 2001, *Business Week*, 25 June 2001). More to the point, the development of industrial services met a local need at GE Industrial. Here, the growth of services turnover could cover the otherwise inevitable hollowing out of ongoing manufacturing businesses through downsizing or divestment of those businesses that could not meet increasingly exacting return criteria. The contrast with GEC under the clever Arnold Weinstock is instructive because Weinstock could not combine margins and growth as Welch's GE did by acting so as to avoid the consequences of perceived hollowing-out of the industrial businesses. As with the substitution of productivity increase for cost reduction, GE also showed considerable narrative flair in the way it represented its commitment to services, where it elided financial and industrial services in a way that discouraged questions about either.

By far the largest element in GE's service offering is financial services which generally have no connection with GE industrial products (GE Capital is definitely not a captive finance operation like Ford Credit). But GE has traditionally constructed a narrative of GE as a technology-based company that puts the emphasis on industrial services as support for the primary industrial product which is a jet engine, a turbine or a medical scanner. Thus Welch argued, 'without products you are dead. . . . If I fail to introduce a new medical scanner, how many hospitals are likely to come and see me for new services?' (Welch, quoted in Slater 2003: 117). As for GE Capital, that does not just supply credit for the buyers of GE aircraft engines or Ford vans, but adds other services into a bundle. According to former GECS head, Gary Wendt:

> We try hard not to finance straight, basic stuff. Instead of just leasing a van, we'll bring it to you, give it new tires and drop it off in Portland. Sure we'll charge you a little more, [but] it's the push toward service – and we don't just mean being friendly.
>
> (*Forbes*, 21 April 1997)

Thus logistics management is provided alongside truck leasing, while aircraft leasing and flight training are packaged up with aero engines.

The development of services within GE Industrial was clearly an explicit objective in the 1990s, symbolically illustrated by the purchase of aero-engine maintenance businesses from British Airways and Varig. From the GE accounts, it is difficult but not impossible to measure the importance of services in the GE Industrial product mix and the contribution that services make to GE Industrial profitability. Exhibit C3.16 presents data on the share of services in GE Industrial sales for the period 1992–2002; this is consistent with the more limited internal information on the share of services in GE Industrial sales revenue that the company released to Slater (1999: 178). The company accounts show there was a major push into services after the early 1990s which raised the share of services in GE Industrial sales from 21 per cent in 1992 to 29 per cent by 2003. Some $7 billion of the 2003 $22.7 billion sales revenue from services is derived from NBC and related broadcasting activities, but this clearly leaves significant product-related services, worth some $15 billion. The data in Table C3.12 (p. 381) also shows that the service businesses in GE Industrial was consistently profitable, with gross margins never below 23 per cent and the long-run average margin on services broadly in line with that on products.

By any standards this was a success that by 2000 allowed GE to represent itself as a post-industrial company for whom customer not product was primary. GE's services used to be called 'after-market' but, according to Paolo Fresco when in charge of the

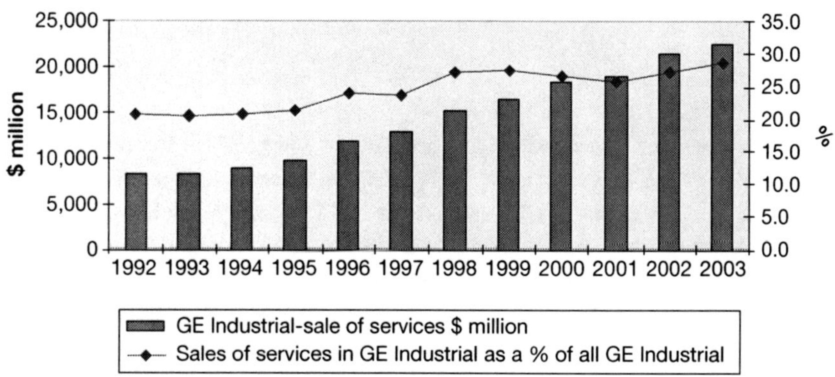


***Exhibit C3.16*** *The significance of sales revenues from services in GE Industrial, 1992–2003*

*Source*: GE Annual Report and Accounts, various years

services initiative, 'Now we think servicing the customer is our primary market' (cited in Slater 1999: 182), not least because of the limited potential for growth in manufactured items, compared with the opportunities to increase market share in related services. In its efforts to expand the size and significance of services within GE Industrial, the company started with the advantage of 'a huge installed base of industrial equipment' (Slater 1999: 179) particularly producer goods, where the norm is repair and overhaul over a long life. However, if this expansion of industrial services helped to bulk out GE Industrial, that did not solve the problem of finding growth, implying that several other levers had to be pulled at the same time.

## Principle 3: deal, so that large scale acquisition and divestment of businesses and companies assists with returns and growth objectives

To what extent was GE's cost recovery under Welch buttressed by selling low-margin industrial businesses and buying growth and profits through financial-services acquisitions? This question could not be openly discussed by an incumbent CEO because, if Welch or Immelt admitted GE's limited ability to generate organic growth, the market would immediately ask about where/when the next big deal was coming and whether a company of GE's size could do enough deals to maintain forward momentum. Thus, the company line has to be that it is not built on acquisitions. For example, Immelt in a 2002 interview claimed that

> when you look at how GE has been put together, you'll see that we are a long term player in every industry we're in. We've really invented most of these industries. We haven't acquired our way into specific businesses, except maybe for NBC; we've developed these businesses from the ground up.
>
> (*Money*, 1 September 2002)

In his autobiography, published after he had stepped down, Welch was notably more frank when he described GE Capital in the 1990s as 'an acquisition machine' (Welch 2001: 235) and disclosed that GE Capital under its CEO Gary Wendt had closed more than 400 deals involving over $200 billion in assets. The company's continuing prickliness about acquisitions is illustrated by the way that the listing of selected recent deals on the investor-information web site has recently been modified so that, while in 2004 deals were listed under the heading 'acquisitions', in 2005 they are listed as 'growth platforms'.

GE's deal-making is legendary yet it is difficult to obtain systematic information on the individual and total value of deals, let alone the effect on the company's financial results. Various estimates can be cited. The 2000 Annual Report states that 'the Company made over 100 acquisitions for the fourth consecutive year' (GE Annual

Report 2000: 1) but provides no systematic information on these. *Business Week* cites information from Thompson which estimates that some 534 companies were acquired in a six-year period, working out at 'more than seven per month' (*Business Week*, 14 October 2000). The *Financial Times* (12 December 2004) estimates that in 2004 GE paid for or committed to $42 billion of acquisitions, suggesting that Immelt has not turned his back on acquisition as often the quickest way to find growth in a giant company.

Despite limited disclosure of such deals in the published accounts, many analysts supposed that GE was acquisition-dependent and some alleged GE was in denial on the point. As we have already noted, Merrill Lynch analyst Jeanne Terrile estimated that 4 per cent points of GE's 9.9 per cent annual growth between 1985 and 2000 came from acquisitions (*Fortune*, 4 September 2001). Nicholas Heymann, of NatWest Securities, emphasized denial when he stated 'GE Capital's official lie is that 80 per cent of its growth will be internal and the rest from acquisition' (*Forbes*, 21 April 1997: 46). Heymann observes that GE Capital had bought its way into some of its growth markets. In 1993, for example, it had just one annuity product, distributed through banks, and $525 million in deposits. 'Last year, after 9 acquisitions, costing $6 billion, it has 14 major annuity products, 13 distribution channels and $5.2 billion in deposits. In 1996 alone, GE Capital made 44 acquisitions, costing $16 billion'. Immelt's moves suggest that his claim in the quote from *Money*, reprinted above, is hard to sustain as recent acquisitions have helped to position GE in new areas such as water, security and Hispanic media (*Wall Street Journal*, 2 December 2004). At the same time, Immelt, like Welch, has been unsentimental in disposing of businesses that don't contribute sufficiently to growth or profitability or which bring too much risk. Thus, in 2004, GE spun off a significant portion of its (slow-growing) insurance business in Genworth, raising $2.83 billion (*Business Week*, 20 May 2004).

On the basis of our own systematic analysis of the fragmentary information in the company accounts, we would agree with the analysts about acquisition dependence. The incomplete lists of GE's acquisitions in SEC filings and other sources are frustrating. They disclose much activity, with over 100 deals in some years of the 1990s, but many of these reported deals were small and did not involve significant additions such as NBC (or Honeywell, which was the one that got away at the end of Welch's term). Table C3.13 in the appendix, p. 382, provides summary information on acquisitions, as disclosed by the company in press releases and, though it only lists some of the largest acquisitions, it does give some indication of the scale and range of businesses that GE has bought in the early 2000s.

In general, however, the accounts provide exiguous information on the funding of acquisition and on the cash-flow consequences of acquisition and divestment. The one useable broad measure in the accounts is cash flow applied to acquisitions – this is not a perfect indicator because it is a net figure, after the cash in-flow from disposals has been offset, but it does nonetheless provide a useful guide to the scale of activity. Our data on cash flows in Exhibit C3.17 does suggest that the analysts like Terrile and Heymann were right: GE very much looks like it has been a serial acquirer on a grand scale. Over the

**Exhibit C3.17** *Cash flow on acquisitions, including the significance of acquisitions in GE Capital Services*

| | *Cash applied to acquisitions* $ million (2003 prices) | *Of which, % used for GE Capital Services acquisitions* |
|---|---|---|
| 1988 | 5,452 | 15.4 |
| 1989 | 2,762 | 59.2 |
| 1990 | 6,473 | 97.2 |
| 1991 | 5,096 | 75.2 |
| 1992 | 2,642 | 100.0 |
| 1993 | 2,663 | 100.0 |
| 1994 | 3,237 | 77.9 |
| 1995 | 6,816 | 95.8 |
| 1996 | 6,477 | 79.7 |
| 1997 | 6,020 | 72.8 |
| 1998 | 21,024 | 92.2 |
| 1999 | 12,882 | 86.3 |
| 2000 | 2,493 | 50.4 |
| 2001 | 12,921 | 88.4 |
| 2002 | 22,045 | 58.5 |
| 2003 | 14,407 | 73.1 |

*Source*: GE Annual Report and Accounts, various years

1988–2003 period, a total of $144 billion of cash (in 2003 prices) was applied to acquisitions and of this, the largest sum of $103 billion was for GE Capital acquisitions, with some $40.4 billion for industrial acquisitions. Table C3.14 in the appendix (p. 384) shows that the amount varies by year but that the spend on industrial acquisitions is fairly steady at around $1 billion to $2 billion per annum (except 2002 and 2003, when it is much larger), while the cash cost of acquisitions in GE Capital varies between $1 billion and $19 billion. If billions quickly become meaningless in any discussion of GE, the relative importance of the activity to the company can be measured by comparing the cash spent on acquisitions with that distributed as dividends. Cash dividends account for 26–38 per cent of net income, with the average from 1988 to 2002 some 30.2 per cent of net income. Cash applied to acquisitions, however, is equivalent to anything from 12 to 138 per cent of net income and the comparable 1988 to 2002 average is around 63 per cent. Over the period 1988–2003, total cash applied to acquisitions was $144 billion, compared with $80 billion (all in 2003 prices) distributed as dividends (GE Annual Report and Accounts, various years).

## Principle 4: use acquisition and divestment to increase opacity by making like-for-like comparisons more difficult

Opacity is important for a company such as GE because it increases the creative power of the narrative and performative elements in so far as they cannot easily be checked against a numbers-based understanding of corporate achievement. As we argued in the GSK case, no capitalist business is ever transparent to the point of complete predictability. But in pharmaceuticals it is certainly difficult to hide upcoming pipeline and patent problems at the end of a growth trajectory, while, in autos, there is nearly continuous real-time feedback on national market trends and company market shares which gives warning of cyclicality and allows judgement of current product offering. By way of contrast, the GE accounts at segment level provide very little basis for any kind of story in a company whose conglomerate activities also prevent outsiders from using one or two product-market measures as proxies for long-term success or current fortunes. On this point, we would argue that GE's senior management did not generally need to pursue opacity as an end in itself because GE benefited from the increased opacity created by serial acquisition and divestment under conditions of limited disclosure (even without changes in business-segment reporting) in a giant industrial company.

GE has developed considerable expertise in the serial-acquisition activities of finding businesses to buy, undertaking the due diligence, avoiding over-payment and then swiftly integrating its new activities into existing operations (Ashkenas et al. 1998). In a presentation to analysts in March 2002, the company explained that over forty acquisitions had been completed in the Global Consumer Finance division and that the process was 'becoming a science', involving significant work preacquisition, including 'making hard decisions early' and having 100-day plans in place to ensure rapid integration (GE 2002a). Nevertheless, acquisition sometimes results in expensive mistakes about the choice or management of acquired businesses. The Kidder Peabody fraud (*Business Week*, 22 August 1994, O'Boyle 1998: 332–56) and the Montgomery Ward bankruptcy (*Business Week*, 19 May 1997) were both expensive mistakes for GE which illustrate the point that a proficient serial acquirer cannot avoid local risk and specific costs. The valuable general offset is that serial acquisition increases opacity and makes it more likely that outsiders will focus on company-level, bottom-line, aggregate results and accept narrative and performative claims.

Opacity increases because acquisition and divestment with limited accounting disclosure makes long-run like-for-like comparisons very difficult so that it quickly becomes impossible to judge the achievement of continuing operations or the success of bolt-on acquisitions. GE has to be a 'trust me' story for believers because the published accounts make it difficult for outsiders to probe the sources of GE's growth or the capacity of GE managers either to run existing businesses or to implement acquisition. Several interrelated problems arise from GE's limited disclosure of acquisition and divestment and the limited information on business segments. As we have noted, the cash-flow statement after 1988 gives cash applied to acquisitions, but it does not separate the cash flow that results from divestments, nor is there any comprehensive, systematic disclosure of what is bought (or sold), when, for how much and how was it financed. The very large number of acquisitions, especially in GE Capital, aggravates these problems because deal flow in itself makes it difficult to isolate the effects of any particular single deal or group of deals. *Business Week* notes the difficulty in understanding the finance business: 'many [investors] also wonder how a huge collection of workaday finance businesses can continue to get double-digit earnings growth without an undue reliance on acquisitions. Most comparable rivals, such as Citigroup, sport rates of just 4%' (18 February 2002).

In terms of business-segment information, that is highly aggregated and fairly uninformative. As Exhibit C3.18 shows, up to the 2002 reorganization of the segments, many of the 1980 GE Industrial business segments still existed in recognizable form, but meaningful comparisons are difficult when the segments have changed in size and content. As for the sales turnover of GE Capital, in 1980 that was not disaggregated and, by 2002, the GE Capital turnover was organized into huge categories such as 'consumer services' with more than a third of finance turnover in the residual category of 'other'. The information disclosed on each segment is so fragmentary that many basic financial ratios cannot be calculated at this level. Even after Immelt's 2002 reorganization intended to improve transparency (GE Annual Report 2002: 6), GE still does not break down assets by business segment and, while there is now more information about changes in segmental revenues, there is no systematic breakdown of sales revenues into ongoing and acquired activities, as would be found in UK corporate accounts.

The limited and arguably inadequate disclosure through the 1980s and 1990s is explained partly by GE's huge size and its status as a non-financial company, which means that GE does not have to disclose events and information that smaller companies or banks would be obliged to do. To begin with, GE is a huge company with more than $130 billion of turnover in 2002 and several divisions large enough to become stand alone S&P 500 companies. In 2002, average sales revenue in S&P 500 companies was $6.2 billion so that almost all of the 2002 segments (and all but one of the new business segments identified in the note to Exhibit C3.18) are larger than this benchmark. Our analysis of the S&P 500 companies, reported in Part I of this book allows a fairly specific size comparison, presented in Exhibit C3.19. This exhibit shows that, in each of the years reported, all of the GE segments have sales revenues that would place them in the top half of the S&P 500, if ranked by sales revenues. For some segments (for example, financing or power systems) their sales revenue places them in the top 150 S&P 500 companies by sales revenues.

The sheer size of the company eases GE's disclosure burden because many events that would need to be disclosed by a GE division if it were a stand-alone company are less

**Exhibit C3.18** *Snapshots of GE's main business segments: sales revenues in $ million (in real 2002 prices)*

| ***GE Industrial business segments*** | *1980* | *2002* |
|---|---|---|
| Aircraft engines | 5,710 | 11,141 |
| Consumer products | 13,558 | |
| Major appliances/appliances | | 6,072 |
| Industrial products and systems | 9,439 | 12,139 |
| Natural resources | 2,990 | |
| Power systems and generation | 12,061 | 22,926 |
| Technical systems, products and services | 6,628 | 9,266 |
| Materials (including plastics) | 4,419 | 7,651 |
| Other | | 4,331 |
| ***GE Capital Services*** | *1988* | *2002* |
| Financing | 8,833 | 42,877 |
| Consumer services | | 22,583 |
| Equipment management | | 2,694 |
| Mid-market financing | | 9,943 |
| Specialized financing | | 1,773 |
| Insurance | 3,743 | 10,979 |
| Securities broking and dealing | 3,511 | |
| Other | 65 | 16,151 |

*Source*: GE Annual Report and Accounts, various years

*Note*: In 2003, GE reclassified its business segments into the following (2003 sales revenues shown in brackets): Advanced Materials ($7,078 million), Commercial Finance ($20,813 million), Consumer Finance ($12,845 million), Consumer and Industrial ($12,843 million), Energy ($19,082 million), Equipment and Other Services ($4,427 million), Health-care ($10,198 million), Infrastructure ($3,078 million), Insurance ($26,194 million), NBC Universal ($6,871 million), Transportation ($13,515 million)

**Exhibit C3.19** *GE segments compared with S&P 500 companies, by sales revenues (The number of S&P 500 constituent companies with sales revenues SMALLER than the GE business segment)*

| *GE business segment* | *1980* | *1990* | *2000* | *2002* |
|---|---|---|---|---|
| Aircraft engines | 300 | 376 | 347 | 347 |
| Major appliances and appliances | | 338 | 243 | 251 |
| Industrial products, systems and industrial | 392 | 372 | 354 | 358 |
| NBC and broadcasting | | 243 | 262 | 274 |
| Power systems and power generation | 428 | 341 | 381 | 430 |
| Technical systems and technical products and services | 333 | 308 | 293 | 323 |
| Services and materials, materials and plastics | 251 | 319 | 291 | 286 |
| Financing | | 404 | 480 | 472 |
| Insurance and specialty insurance | | 218 | 357 | 345 |

*Source*: GE Annual Report and Accounts, various years and Compustat

*Note*: The table should be read as follows: in 1980 there were 300 S&P 500 companies with sales revenues less than those in GE's aircraft-engines segment

significant at the level of GE Consolidated. One of the principles of US (like UK) GAAP is that companies should explain *material* changes, that is, those changes that are potentially large enough to influence outcomes in the consolidated accounts and therefore those that an investor should be aware of. There is no mechanical or agreed definition that could be used to constitute a formal percentage rule for when an event or item is deemed material. But it is easier to argue immateriality for most transactions for a $130-billion-turnover giant than for a $6-billion-turnover S&P 500 average company. Moreover, financial companies are subject to more onerous disclosure requirements than industrial companies because of fears about the consequences of bank failure. Despite its massive finance operations, GE is classified as an industrial company and thus avoids a whole series of disclosures that financial companies would be obliged to make. It is hard to avoid the conclusion that, while GE is inherently a more complex object than most other companies in the S&P 500, in relative terms it discloses less information partly because it benefits from the unintended consequences of disclosure rules that were framed with other, simpler and smaller companies in mind.

## Principle 5: grow the financial-services business, up to the limit of the company's credit rating

In Edgar Allen Poe's (1845) story 'The Purloined Letter', when the apartment was searched, the purloined letter could not be found because it had been hidden in the letter rack. GE Capital is hidden in much the same way inside the GE accounts exactly where it should be and, though disclosure is limited, any undergraduate accounting student could calculate (as we did in the third section of this case study) that real sales increased from $3 billion to $58 billion from 1980 to 2002 so that once-negligible financial services now account for nearly half of turnover. Wall Street did worry about the dependence on GE Capital, and Welch responded in 1999 by proposing a reclassification whereby GE had twenty top businesses of which ten were in GE Capital (Slater 2000: 261). More generally, the growth of financial services does not register as GE's central achievement in the Welch years because GE Capital does not fit the narrative and performative frame. As we have noted, the company prefers to talk about growing service business in a way that brackets financial and industrial services, while much of the performative element (like No. 1 or No. 2 in every business) simply doesn't apply in GE Capital. Furthermore, the connection between GE Industrial and GE Capital is limited unless we start from belief in the shared values of the GE management and occasional executive move between the two parts of the business. In this context, the general lack of interest in GE Capital in many management books on GE is symptomatic: if there is a discrepancy between what management says in its script of purpose and achievement and what the company does for growth and cost recovery, outsiders with a limited interest in the mechanics of cost recovery quickly become confused about cause and effect and prefer the narrative.

The story of GE Capital is a story of upward mobility, as GE has found growth of sales revenue by moving beyond captive finance into many other lines of financial business. GE has sold financial services since the 1930s, starting with domestic credit for refrigerators, a classic form of captive finance. Up to the late 1970s, GE was arguably not so different from other US corporates, such as GM or Westinghouse, with a financial-services division whose central activity was captive finance. However, through the 1980s and 1990s, GE Capital greatly expanded and increased its offering in everything from LBO finance to store cards. GE has stayed away from retail banking and, after its problems with Kidder Peabody, moved out of securities dealing. But, in general, its expansion has been as a general supplier of consumer and commercial financial services, while also developing niche areas, such as mortgage insurance. The company's expansion into financial services is neatly summarized by *Fortune*: 'GE Capital pours wealth into the corporate coffers by doing just about everything you can do with money except print it' (21 February 1994). Hence, GECS overtook General Motors Acceptance Corp. (GMAC) in terms of total assets in 1993 and was twice as large by 1997 (*Forbes*, 21 April 1997).

Some of the major milestones are listed below:

- **1960** The first move outside consumer finance, developing supplier credit for commercial and industrial borrowers with no connection with GE products and leading to the development of asset-based lending (*American Banker*, 18 October 1984).
- **1967** The start of airline leasing with USAir, subsequently leading to working capital loans for distressed airlines such as PanAm and Continental in the 1980s (*Air Transport World*, August 1984). By 2001, GECAS (GE Capital Aviation Services) managed $18 billion in assets (Welch 2001: 238).
- **1983** GE issues a private-label credit card for Apple Computer, the first time a card was issued for a specific manufacturer's product (*American Banker*, 12 July 1983). This was the first step to GE becoming the world's largest supplier and manager of private-label credit cards.
- **1980s** The development of a range of services including employers' insurance, explicitly to help offset cyclicality in the industrial businesses (*American Banker*, 8 July 1985). GE became established as a leader in the development of the LBO; GE 'is almost synonymous with the term leveraged buyout' according to an analyst quoted in *American Banker* (20 February 1986) and by the early 1990s GE had been involved with more than 100 LBOs.

- **Early 1990s** GE was one of the largest auto-finance companies through the 1980s and 1990s, and in the early 1990s it moved into sub-prime lending in autos for a short time.
- **1992** GE moved into mortgage insurance, after the US Federal Government withdrew support.

Much of the expansion into new lines of finance business was done by bolt-on acquisition accompanied by quiet exits from old lines of finance business. Welch's (2001) autobiography discloses that there were some 400 acquisitions by GE Capital in the 1990s and many of these were serial acquisitions designed to build specific lines of business. For example, GE spent $27 billion between 1986 and 1994 on acquisitions in store cards (*Fortune*, 21 February 1994). The whole process of internal expansion and acquisition was driven by high margins. In the late 1970s, for example, Welch claims that leveraged leases on aircraft 'could earn 30 per cent or better returns' (Welch 2001: 233). Because such finance businesses have few barriers to entry, the classic pattern is that returns fall with intensifying competition and the flip side of serial acquisition is serial exit as GE protects its margins on finance by quitting commodified areas. It is much easier to do this in finance by withdrawing capital than in manufacturing where employees, suppliers and dealers are all affected. According to Gary Wendt, then CEO of GE capital, 'the LBO business was like being on a treadmill. . . . The opportunities were so great at the inception, it was hard to get off' (*US News and World Report*, 29 April 1991), but GE then had to reduce its involvement as the profitability of such deals declined in the late 1980s.

GE Capital is therefore a changing portfolio of (temporarily) high-return finance businesses with a quite different set of profit possibilities than a captive-finance operation such as Ford Credit, which is effectively confined to auto finance. Serial acquisition was possible because there was a formulaic element to many of the finance businesses that GE entered or exited. In the case of store cards, for example, it was possible before acquisition to assess the quality of the receivables and the effectiveness of debt control, just as it was possible to measure the post-acquisition gains that could be made by using GE's triple-A credit rating and treasury expertise to borrow more cheaply than the average mid-western department-store operator. High-velocity acquisition was also attractive given the falling return on capital discussed in the second section, suggesting that movement into new markets and products (as well as expansion of the more profitable existing ones) was driven by the need to prevent overall GECS returns falling too quickly.

At the same time, entrance into and exit from so many different financial businesses requires judgement, skill and procedures that should not be underestimated. We know very little about how the acquisition and exit machine was operated but the Welch autobiography does include some clues. Much depended on the prospecting and deal-making abilities of a handful of individuals such as Gary Wendt at GE Capital; this may well be a special case where the divisional CEO was probably worth much more than he was paid. And this was backed up by scrutiny of acquisition proposals at monthly GE

Capital board meetings (Welch 2001: 231), where Welch almost certainly added more value than in his (higher-profile) monthly performances in the pit at Crotonville: 'potential deals are put through a monthly torture chamber. The meetings are hands-on, no-holds-barred discussions among some 20 GE insiders with more than 400 years of diverse business experience' (Welch 2001: 231). The discussion was based on a 'deal book', summary and a 'pitch' to the board which through the 1990s was accepting about four deals per month and considering more (Welch 2001: 244).

In all this, the GE Capital board was engaged in high-stakes risk management where misjudgements about a class of business would have undermined GE's financial record. By way of contrast, Westinghouse, GE's conglomerate rival, had its finance arm liquidated by the parent company after losing almost $1 billion in bad property loans in 1990 (*The Economist*, 30 April 1994). GE Capital's expertise in making acquisitions is acknowledged by S&P as one of the factors that supports its triple-A rating: 'GECC (GE Capital Corp.) tends to be a very savvy buyer, understanding the various business risks and pricing the acquisition appropriately' (S&P 2002: 2).

If the expansion of GE Capital rested on judgement and controls, it also reflected the structural advantage of the triple-A credit rating, which effectively made the financial business (as user of the credit rating) dependent on the industrial business (as credit-rating generator), and this in turn set limits on how much GE could expand without risking reclassification by credit-rating agencies. GE Industrial may be a low-growth business but it has high margins, is consistently profitable over the cycle and has funded almost all of the dividends that GE Consolidated has paid out, as well as providing the funds for acquisitions and repayment of debt. This solid industrial base is the basis for GE's triple-A credit rating, which allows GE Capital to borrow cheaply the large sums of money that it lends on to consumers and commercial customers. A good credit rating has traditionally lowered the cost of borrowing and has provided GE Capital with a competitive advantage over other (financial) companies that have to pay more to borrow. GE frequently boasts that it is one of only seven industrial companies in the USA to have an triple-A rating, and this provides a considerable cost advantage over rivals including banks such as Citigroup which enjoys only an double-A rating. Citigroup's rating is the highest of any US bank but implies an extra $400 million a year in interest on its long-term debt (*Business Week*, 8 April 2002). As the argument in our Ford case suggests, matters have been complicated by securitization which does not completely neutralize the cost and risk advantages of a high credit rating. From this point of view, GE has to contain growth of GE Capital revenues because, if more than 50 per cent of GE's revenues come from finance, GE would be reclassified as a financial company and the credit rating would probably be lowered in line with that for other finance houses. Thus by the late 1990s, with GE Capital accounting for 40 per cent of turnover, if GE wanted to maintain growth, it had to find ways of bulking out the industrial part of the business, and this partly explains the interest in large-scale industrial acquisitions such as those of Honeywell (which was blocked by EU regulators in 2001) and of Universal, which GE did acquire from Vivendi in 2004.

## Principle 6: add financial engineering to smooth earnings and improve results

Earnings management had not acquired its current negative connotations when the smooth upwards trend of GE quarterly profits and the management that always delivered were being celebrated in the 1980s and 1990s. Nevertheless, the company has always been defensive about its use of financial engineering to smooth earnings and find extra profits because, of course, the narrative of growth with the supporting numbers hardly fits with suspicions about cheap tricks and improvement of the numbers. The standard company response is that GE 'manages businesses, not earnings' (GE 2001 Annual Report: 3, *Fortune*, 4 March 2002 [quoting Welch]). Cynicism was also partly forestalled by folksy domestic-economy imagery: thus Jack Welch used to say 'We pay our bills quarterly' (*Money*, 1 September 2002) and he played with the idea of GE as a grocer's shop (*Business Week*, 8 June 1998). GE was not of course a grocer's shop but a highly financialized company run by financial sophisticates who had entirely legitimate opportunities to smooth earnings and find extra income from sources such as pension-contribution holidays.

In a large, complex and endlessly restructuring company such as GE, smoothed earnings could notionally be produced by off-setting gains and losses from operations and from restructuring. For example, this might include off-setting gains from the sale of an asset against non-operating costs (such as those that result from restructuring activities) in another part of the business. Given the limited amount of accounting disclosure, such arguments must be speculative and hypothetical, though many might think the perfect quarter-by-quarter earnings-growth record must raise suspicions. GE has been defensive about this: in the 2001 Annual Report, Immelt states that GE delivered over $17 billion of cash flow in 2001 – 'try "managing" your way to cash flow of that magnitude – year after year' (2001: 3). Immelt and his CFO Keith Sherin have also asserted that, even in a post-Enron era, 'they find it incomprehensible that anyone would want them to report 30% earnings growth one quarter and 3% the next if they can avoid it. "It just doesn't make any sense to us in managing a business" Sherin says' (*Fortune*, 4 March 2002).

On the use of pension-fund contributions to stoke earnings growth, the position is much more straightforward. During the 1990s bull market, GE, like other giant US companies, boosted its net income (entirely in accordance with US GAAP) by taking an extended break in its contributions to the corporate pension scheme, as the value of pension assets rose and the fund accumulated large surpluses. More unusually, for GE, this continued into the bear market as the company has continued to enjoy a contributions holiday up to and including 2002. This has a significant and beneficial effect on net income. Our data (extracted from the company accounts) in Exhibit C3.20 shows that net income was boosted by around 10 per cent or more in most years from 1988 to 2002 (see also Table C3.15, appendix, p. 354).

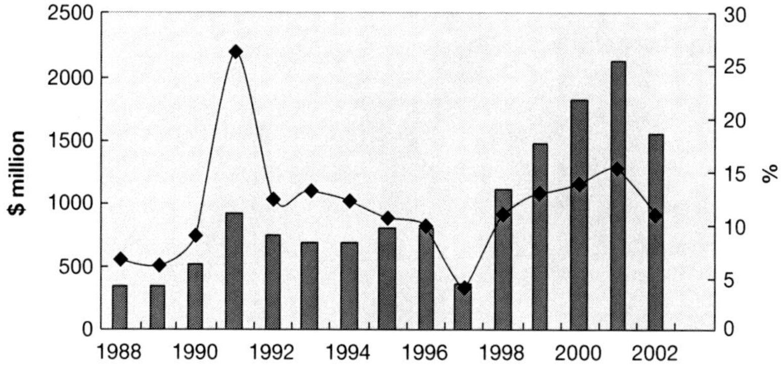


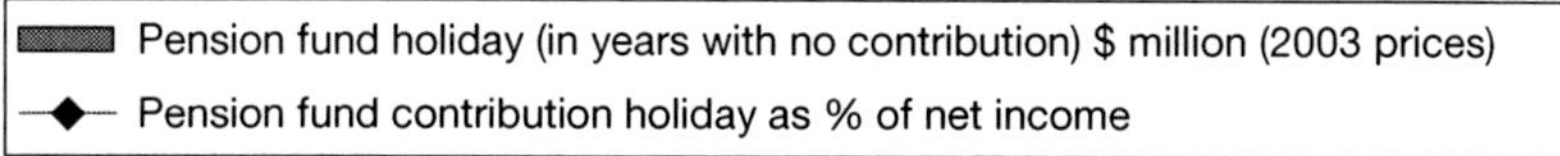


***Exhibit C3.20*** *GE: the value of pension-fund contribution holidays*

*Source*: GE Annual Report and Accounts, various years

Of course, since equity prices have slumped with the 2000 bear market, the accumulated pension surpluses have been steadily declining, as Table C3.15 shows. At the peak in 1999, the pension fund was in surplus of $26.6 billion, which had fallen to $4.5 billion by the end of 2002 due to lower contributions and much lower rates of return on pension-fund investments. This suggests that the pension-contribution holiday must now be fairly short lived and GE's net income will be some 10 per cent lower when the company begins to contribute again. Even making optimistic actuarial assumptions, it is hard to see how GE can avoid paying into its pension scheme unless equity values recover quickly and strongly.

Pensions provide one, significant example of how earnings can be affected by the way in which management treats certain items. S&P's analyst Robert Friedman reworked GE's profits more systematically over the period 1995–2001: when non-core items (such as gains on pension-fund assets) were removed, he found that annual growth was only 9.2 per cent (*The Economist*, 26 October 2002). Though many firms would be pleased with such an achievement, Friedman's figures suggest that GE failed to make the 'double-digit growth' for which the company had become so renowned.

## Principle 7: accept the balance-sheet cost and risk of expanding financial services

This is an issue where GE does not need a narrative because the balance sheet is nearly invisible in most public discussions of GE. Under the letter 'B' in their book's index, Tichy and Sherman include 'boundarylessness' and 'business engine' but not 'bonds' or 'balance sheets'. And as we have seen in our discussion of share price, Wall Street and the analysts know but do not apparently care about the low ROCE that is the result of a heavily capitalized balance sheet. But this is an issue for the company because cost recovery through finance had a balance-sheet cost and created new risks. Because GE does not have a retail banking operation it needs large amounts of debt finance to support its activities of consumer and commercial financing. Thus the decision to grow GECS has resulted in a transformation in GE's balance sheet as the company is now geared up for financial-services lending and requires sophisticated treasury operations to ensure that it borrows at the lowest possible cost to the company.

Capital productivity is something GE does not talk about because the push into finance has meant that capital employed has risen much faster than sales: as Table C3.16 (p. 386) shows, in the early 1980s, less than a dollar of capital was required per dollar of annual sales, whereas by the early 2000s, this now stands at more than four dollars of capital for each dollar of annual sales. The balance sheet has been quite radically restructured as a result of the expansion of the finance business, as Exhibit C3.21 and tables C3.17 and C3.18 (pp. 387–8) show. Most of the extra capital comes in the form of debt not equity: at the consolidated level, equity has fallen from around 45 per cent of long-term capital employed in 1980 to around 12 per cent by the late 1990s, as GE has become much more reliant on debt and other liabilities (Table C3.18, p. 388). Long-term and short-term liabilities have risen by 4,670 per cent and 1,290 per cent in real terms respectively, while shareholder equity has grown by a much more modest 260 per cent since 1980 (Table C3.18). Almost all of the liabilities are associated with GECS. GE Industrial liabilities have not risen far or fast during the 1980s and 1990s; because the industrial businesses were cash-generative there have not been large demands for borrowing to fund new investments. Short-term finance has always been important to GE, but as the GECS operations have grown, the finance side of the company had around $170 billion in short-term debt and other forms of finance at any one time by 2002. Table C3.18 shows that while GECS has a little more than half of all the equity, it has around 75 per cent of the short-term liabilities and more than 90 per cent of the total long-term liabilities.

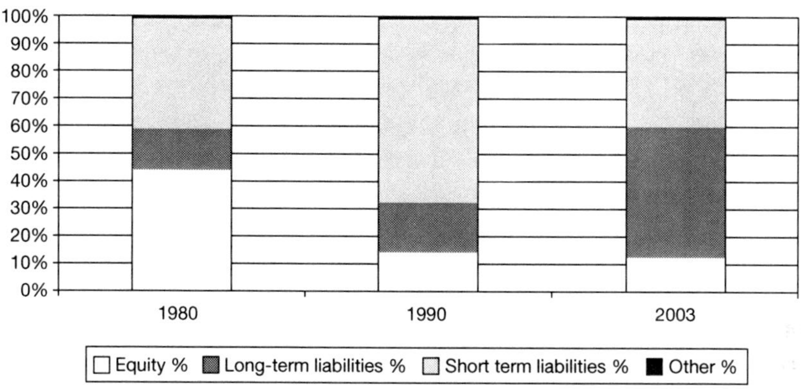


***Exhibit C3.21*** *The structure of GE's balance sheet: composition of capital employed (in real 2003 prices)*

*Source*: GE Annual Report and Accounts, various years

This restructuring of the balance sheet has been achieved through very large issues of debt: for example, in 1992, *Institutional Investor* estimated that GE issued $5–$7billion of commercial paper every day (October 1992). GE's vast appetite for debt (like its propensity to smooth earnings) earned it criticism in the early 2000s, most notably from Bill Gross of Pimco, one of the world's largest buyers of corporate debt. In March 2002, Gross announced that he would cease to buy GE's short-term debt, then valued at around $100 billion, because of concerns about the amount of commercial paper and the limited support for GE Capital in the form of bank lending. Typically, commercial paper is backed by equal amounts of bank lending but, according to Gross, 'GE Capital has been allowed to accumulate $50 billion of unbacked [commercial paper] because of the lack of market discipline' (quoted in CNN Money 2002b). In addition, Gross made a more general criticism of the company as over-reliant on acquisitions for growth, financed using cheap paper or GE's own highly rated stock. Overall, Gross stated that he was concerned that GE, which should be understood as a finance company, was exposed to risks that were poorly disclosed (*The Economist*, 2 May 2002). Coming in the wake of Enron, such criticisms from an influential market commentator unsteadied the market, leading to falls in the value of both GE's stock and its commercial paper and pushing up its financing costs (CNN Money 2002a). GE denied the accusations but also acted swiftly to reduce commercial paper from 42 per cent of total debt to 25–30 per cent, with an increase in bank lines from $33.5 billion to $50 billion (*Euroweek*, 22 March 2002, CNN Money 2002b, GE 2002c).

Within the constraints of its funding requirement, GE has no immediate problem and some room for manoeuvre about how it borrows but must accept longer-term risks. The stock market can be kept happy because only a small part of GE's capital is now in the form of equity, so ROCE may be poor but return on equity can be kept high. Thus GE Consolidated achieves a ROE of well over 20 per cent in most years since 1990, while the ROCE has struggled to get much above 5 per cent, despite GE Industrial's heroic performance of at least 12 per cent post-tax in most years and often closer to 16 per cent (Table C3.7). To what extent is this a problem? GE's debt and increase in gearing can be thought of as the inevitable outcome of running a large-scale finance business: industrial companies that wish to lend money to commercial or domestic customers must themselves first borrow the funds to allow the transaction to occur. The debt-heavy balance sheets at GE or Ford reflect activity characteristics rather than (necessarily) any sign of corporate weakness or a failed business model. But the scale of debt does leave the company exposed to significant potential risks arising from changes in interest rates and downgrading of GE's own credit rating, as well as to the kinds of criticisms made by Bill Gross in 2002.

Though there is no imminent threat of a credit downgrade in GE's case, the credit-rating agencies as much as the equity analysts require a clear, believable narrative that must now be focused on the strengths in GE's industrial division. For much of the 1990s, GE expanded finance (through numerous acquisitions) to cover the absence of growth in its profitable industrial businesses. By the end of the 1990s, as finance grew towards 50 per cent of sales, this bolt-on finance-based growth trajectory was nearing an end. Immelt's response has been to maintain the velocity of dealing but to focus more on large acquisitions for its industrial business, as well as sales of its insurance businesses to help rebalance the company, to reduce the requirement for debt and to help sustain the 2000s' narrative of GE as a technology-based company with a sound balance sheet and sustainable growth.

## IMMELT: A NEW CHAPTER

When Jeff Immelt took over as CEO in 2001 he faced several challenges. First, any CEO who replaces an icon of management success has to live up to the inevitable comparisons amidst sentimentality about historic achievements and fading memories of the great man's fallibility and foibles. Second, Welch had left the GE company in 2001 somewhere near the end of a growth trajectory driven by higher industrial margins and increasing finance sales, so that any successor would have to find new ways of sustaining the growth of sales and earnings. Third, after the Enron and WorldCom scandals about false accounting and failed governance, GE by 2002 had to face hostile questions about earnings management, disclosure and governance controls. The story so far is that Immelt as CEO has risen to these challenges, but the prospects for GE remain uncertain. Immelt has demonstrated his competence on the moves by putting together a narrative and performative response to a post-Enron America that is newly suspicious of giant firms. And the business media has been suitably impressed, so that those who were initially sceptical are now increasingly respectful. But GE's prospects remain uncertain because the new strategy of buying sales through industrial acquisitions (which was initiated under Welch) remains a risky and expensive way of finding leverage. If Immelt survives until retirement at age sixty-five, *Business Week* and *Fortune* may then be less kind to him than they were to Welch.

Integrity was something Welch did rather well. A series of scandals and crises did not tarnish the reputations of GE or its chief executive, who instead earned plaudits for dealing with the problems. The standard source on GE scandals is former *Wall Street Journal* journalist Thomas F. O'Boyle's (1998) critical book which constructs a kind of charge sheet by devoting one chapter to each major scandal or crisis. These include specific incidents, such as GE's pollution of the Hudson river with PCBs, fraud and inadequate internal in the case of the securities-trading business Kidder Peabody, charges of defrauding the US Government on military contracts, as well as unfair and uncompetitive business practices in the DeBeers case. All this is set against a background of more general criticisms about Welch's management style, his focus on financial results (rather than technology) with resulting downsizing and closure and the reverberative effects on corporate America as other companies have sought to emulate GE's success. O'Boyle's title *At Any Cost* gives us the radical allegation that GE is a company whose ruthless ambition creates problems for those involved in GE and society more broadly. The following from the prologue of O'Boyle's book gives a flavour of the argument about the wider impact of Welch and GE:

> [Welch] has been a proactive catalyst of change, anticipating events rather than reacting to them, and he ruthlessly excises the cancer that has killed many large institutions, including Westinghouse – complacency. At the same time, Welch is a person of glaring weaknesses. His way of doing business carries with it a heavy penalty, not necessarily for him or stockholders, but for the people who do his bidding and for the government and society which must often clean up his mess.
>
> (O'Boyle 1998: 12)

> Welch has defined the landscape in which dramatic change has occurred not only at GE but elsewhere in American business. As CEOs have sought to emulate his success, they have also adopted his tactics, and in this sense he is the father of a bare-knuckle approach to business that has won more and more believers. What mergers and acquisitions were to the 1980s, productivity – extracting more work out of every fewer people – has been to the 1990s. It is a manic quick-fix done at the behest of Wall Street in which businessmen have become desensitized to the damage they do to society.
>
> (O'Boyle 1998: 15–16)

While Welch was usually quick to acknowledge scandals and other problems once they had become public, his response was often that problems reflected local (cultural) failures which the CEO and head office then resolved in ways that demonstrate corporate integrity and personal honesty (while not accepting culpability at the corporate level). Thus, on the $350 million fraud about fictitious trades at Kidder Peabody, Welch (2001: 225) in his autobiography concluded that the Wall Street firm 'Kidder was as culturally distant from us as GE appeared to the Kidder employees'. In the same book Welch, as honest Jack, insisted that 'integrity' is a key part of 'what this CEO thing is all about': 'I never had two agendas, there was only one way – the straight way' (2001: 381).

This kind of self-confidence was no longer good enough when Immelt faced new challenges after the false accounting at Enron and WorldCom raised more general concerns about the reliability of reported earnings in giant corporations. This inevitably raised questions about GE's opaque accounting practices and, in a changed climate, the unbroken record of earnings increase was not so much achievement as cause for concern. The business-magazine headlines of early 2002 reflect a new paranoia about GE's record of sustained earnings growth with limited disclosure. *Fortune* (19 February 2002) summarized the new view by posing and answering a question: 'What's so great about GE? Plenty. But now that smoothly rising earnings are now suspect, our most admired company is too'. Limited disclosure quickly became an issue. *Business Week* (18 February 2002) asked quite directly 'GE: More disclosure please' and a couple of months later returned to raise larger issues about whether it could be kept going 'How does GE grow? Investors ask if it can keep delivering those famous double digits' (*Business Week*, 8 April 2002). *Fortune* (24 May 2001) was facetious: 'Accounting in Wonderland, Jeremy Khan goes down the rabbit hole with GE's books'. The problem was not that GE was any less solid, but the media were (finally) more sceptical. As *Business Week* observed in a cover story (29 April 2002), Welch's achievements were now part of an earlier age of credulity: 'when (Jack) . . . delivered double digit earnings growth quarter after quarter, everyone marvelled at the accomplishment rather than question how he did it'.

What Immelt did was to move purposively in narrative and performative terms so as to contain the reputational threat and to ensure that a phase of hostility and cynicism towards corporate America after Enron (coming at a time when GE's growth rates had faltered) did not lead to any long-term falling out with GE. He showed his grip on affairs by operating at several levels: Immelt played the old narrative defence but also in 2002 offered finely judged concessions on disclosure as well as taking the performative initiative through governance reform (GE Annual Report 2002: 5–6, 14–15). In response to criticisms about smoothing income, GE restated the standard GE defensive line about how 'GE manages businesses, not earnings', sometimes adding rather cryptic explanations such as: 'we offset our losses with our gains and vice versa. As we have gains, we do restructuring – we improve our other businesses to basically offset those gains' (*Money*, 1 September 2002). But Immelt recognized this was not enough and also offered the concession of increased disclosure in the company accounts alongside a reorganization of GE Capital into four separate business which, it was claimed, would give investors a clearer view of performance (GE Annual Report 2002: 6, *Wall Street Journal*, 19 April 2004), as well as making analysts' briefings and other such meetings available for all via web casts. The concessions aimed at increasing accounting disclosure were well judged from the company's point of view because two changes in segment classification in three years had the practical effect of making long-term like-for-like performance comparisons more difficult.

In performative terms, Immelt took the initiative to position GE as a company on the leading edge of good governance. Following the passing of the Sarbanes–Oxley legislation, GE produced its own nineteen-point principles of corporate governance (GE undated b) intended to allow the company not only to comply fully with all regulatory requirements but to 'try to satisfy the spirit, not just the letter, of the new corporate governance requirements and . . . to act promptly to implement changes in governance, and not wait for "formal" effective dates in the law' (GE undated c). In this way, GE set itself up as a company that was committed to good governance, for example introducing strict independence tests for directors and changing the membership of its board to ensure that a majority were independent. The retirement of two long-standing board members, Paolo Fresco and Scott McNealy served to underline governance as a new priority (GE Annual Report 2002: 42). Immelt's early emphasis on corporate governance has now broadened into 'values' (GE Annual Report 2002: 14, *Fortune*, 15 November 2004), which of course echoes Welch very strongly.

In narrative and performative terms, Immelt's early moves suggested he understood that side of the business. Immelt's more difficult task, however, was to find the levers that could sustain the trajectory of double-digit revenue and earnings expansion when, as already argued, Welch had taken GE to the limits of its old trajectory. When it came to levers, Immelt acted in a way that was entirely logical and immediately satisfied the markets and the business press. But, in our view, Immelt's actions leave unposed and unanswered questions about whether GE can keep it going in the longer term. As Exhibit C3.16 shows, the distinction between the industrial and services part of GE is not always clear-cut, with services contributing around a quarter of the revenues for GE Industrial. But, if we wish to understand business-model levers and leverage, it is best to start from a distinction between the industrial- and capital-services divisions of GE, not because it has any inherent significance but because it separates two bundles of businesses with different characteristics in terms of revenue growth, margins and implications for the credit rating. Immelt's strategy in relation to financial services and industrial may not represent a set of principles but it does represent a new direction.

## New direction 1: review the portfolio of financial holdings and sell as well as hold

The portfolio of financial businesses cannot grow much beyond its current 40 per cent share of GE without threatening the credit rating, and the natural tendency of margins in many established financial services businesses is to decline under pressure of competition. Hence, the importance of reviewing the portfolio and discarding unattractive financial businesses (which logically creates space for their replacement with financial or industrial businesses). For example, in 2004, GE began the process of spinning off its life- and mortgage-insurance businesses, Genworth Financial Inc., with sales of $9.8 billion and net income of $935 million in 2003. *Business Week* estimated that, when completed, this will release $3.34 billion, which could be applied to acquire faster-growing businesses as well as to improve the transparency of the balance sheet by removing the insurance business's need for significant amounts of debt (supported by GE), which provides the collateral for insurance but also lowers rates of return (*Business Week*, 31 May 2004).

## New direction 2: make major industrial acquisitions

The portfolio of industrial businesses offers limited growth in the longer term and industrial margins have already been raised to the point where it would be difficult to extract more. Hence, the attraction of buying more industrial turnover and earnings through acquisitions, which also incidentally help to create the space for a financial acquisition because any growth in the industrial part of the business allows GE Capital Services to expand in line. Welch had recognized as much with his attempt to buy Honeywell, a deal that was frustrated by EU competition policy. However, Immelt has subsequently acquired a number of large businesses, including Universal Studios from Vivendi and Amersham (see Table C3.13, appendix, p. 382) which bolster the non-finance part of the business, allowing Immelt to reposition GE more strongly as a technology company.

The dialectic of financial-portfolio review and industrial acquisition is a complex one whose outcome cannot be predicted. Immelt and GE almost certainly do not have any worked-out game plan but will move opportunistically on acquisitions, as and when opportunity arises, especially in sheltered areas such as media or defence contracting. But our verdict on the new directions has to be that it is going to be much more difficult for Immelt to keep things going with large industrial acquisitions than it was for Welch to keep things going with acquiring books of Thai auto loans or UK store-card credit in many small batches. Immelt is now much more dependent on luck and judgement as the odds on continued success deteriorate. On big industrial acquisitions, there are major risks about overpaying (particularly as other players such as Phillips and Siemens have overlapping approaches to expanding their health-care and other operations) and failing to execute in a way that delivers the required operating margins or sales growth. A couple of good big industrial acquisitions would buy some breathing space, particularly if Immelt could also find some financial services bolt-ons at reasonable P/E ratios but, given GE's scale, adding 5 to 10 per cent to revenues from acquisitions means having to buy in activities or companies with annual sales of around $7–$14 billion.

Most of this has not yet been registered by the media who, after some initial caution in his first few difficult years, have generally been impressed by Immelt's words and actions. The emphasis on transparency and governance plus the action on big acquisitions have kept media and markets satisfied. Immelt now promises a resumption of double-digit earnings increases and the industrial acquisitions have been rationalized by a new Immelt narrative about a technology-led GE which reconnects the company with its past as a company that fostered scientific advance through the GE Laboratory.

Immelt's first year was not easy, and 2001 marked a very decisive departure from the kinds of earnings announcements that had become the norm under Welch. In retrospect, the problems in 2001/2 with depressed stock markets, a faltering US economy and terrorist attacks allowed a rebasing of GE as a company which, like others, was not immune to disappointing results. In 2001, GE's revenues fell 3 per cent, while earnings rose 11 per cent and stock price fell 16 per cent (GE Annual Report 2001: 1); in 2002, revenues were up 5 per cent, earnings up 7 per cent and stock price down 39 per cent (GE Annual Report 2002: 5). While the incoming CEO could not be blamed for weak results in 2001 and 2002, he can, of course, take charge of the return to form and put his own mark upon GE's new era. At the end of 2003, Immelt started to talk about a return to double-digit earnings growth in 2005 (*Business Week*, 1 December 2003, 10 January 2005) and this has helped to encourage investors whose growing confidence led to a share-price recovery that has allowed some of the post-2000 slump to be regained. In the first quarter of 2005 (as this book went to press), Immelt was able to deliver his earnings triumph, with a 19 per cent increase in revenues producing a 25 per cent boost to earnings (GE 2005a: 1). Interestingly, the company was also sufficiently confident about its strong results to offer a breakdown of growth, revealing that just over half (i.e. 10 per cent) of the overall revenue gain was organic.

While it is too soon to tell whether GE is back on a sustained path of double-digit quarterly earnings growth, it is clear that Immelt has launched his first Welch-style major initiative on innovation. This has captured media interest just as Jack Welch's initiatives did, adding a creative performative theme to accompany Immelt's necessarily more sober governance agenda. According to *Business Week*, 'Immelt is obsessed with rebuilding a culture of innovation within GE' (26 April 2004) evidenced by investing in the company's research facilities. Welch's advertising slogan 'We Bring Good Things to Life' has been replaced with the new slogan 'Imagination at Work' and the implicit promise of the new slogan is being fleshed out. Immelt promotes 'Imagination Breakthroughs', where 'each project has the potential for at least $100 million of incremental growth' (GE 2005b, *Business Week*, 28 March 2005) as the means to (re)focus GE businesses on innovation. But the initiative also suggests that Immelt has studied Welch's performance and in this case has learnt some transferable knowledge about the need for a concept that can be applied on a company-wide basis, that will apparently transform culture and that, in due course, can take the credit for transformative change with a worthwhile bottom-line impact.

If it took several years for Welch to shake off his 'Neutron Jack' image and acquire more respectful coverage in the business press, Immelt has been accumulating respectful (and, later, more enthusiastic) coverage after less than two years in the job. By 2003, the *Financial Times* was representing Immelt as a kinder, gentler leader:

> Jack Welch did not often need to apologise as part of his management armoury. But since he took over in September 2001, Mr Immelt, by choice and by necessity, has styled himself as a different type of leader – more collegial, less autocratic – focused on growth rather than on acquisition strategy.
>
> (3 January 2003)

One year later, the *Financial Times* presented a rather stronger and more upbeat narrative of corporate purpose, explaining how 'at the heart of Mr Immelt's strategy lies a belief that science holds the key to reinvigorating GE's growth potential' (11 October 2004). And in this climate, GE and Immelt continued to win new and old 'most admired' awards. In early 2005 Immelt won a place in the *Business Week* gallery of best managers (10 January 2005) with a commendation which concluded with the observation that investors were now 'along for the ride'.

## (LIMITS OF) THE GE WAY

This case has offered revisionist argument and evidence that questions two widely believed assumptions or assertions about GE under Welch. The first assumption is that Jack Welch's initiatives explain GE's performance: this assumption originates with Welch himself who in his penultimate 1999 letter to shareholders argued 'this performance has been driven this decade by three big Company-wide growth initiatives: Globalization, Services and Six Sigma quality' (GE Annual Report 1999: 3–6). The second assumption is that GE under Welch offers transferable lessons which could improve performance in other giant companies: this is popularized in books by authors such as Slater whose dustjacket for the *GE Way Fieldbook* (1999) promises 'An action-oriented blueprint for managing like Jack Welch – and achieving Welch-like results in your organization'.

These assumptions have been challenged in our case by arguing that the initiatives were part of the narrative and performative moves that projected corporate purpose and achievement; while the levers of financial success were part of an (undisclosed) business model about running industrial businesses for higher margins and a credit rating that allowed expansion into financial services. This argument implies limited transferability. It would be possible for other companies to buy the workbooks and to copy some of the Welch initiatives, such as No. 1 or No. 2, Work-Out, digitization, etc. Such imitation might achieve positional advantage or cost reduction, but such initiatives in other companies would not produce the sustained growth of sales revenue and earnings that then becomes truly dynamic in terms of the responses from investors and others when it is coupled with a corporate narrative of purpose and achievement. Management of giant firms is more complicated than authors such as Slater make out or Welch would have us believe.

This conclusion forces us to rethink what we mean by corporate success and good management. Of course GE was a brilliant financial success, but not quite of the type and kind supposed in the prevailing culturalist accounts of management which, in our view, should always be cross-checked against the financial numbers in a different register. Of course, Jack Welch offered leadership of the highest calibre, but his was a Machiavellian virtue that rested on his understanding that narrative and performative excellence were necessary but not sufficient. In the absence of direct evidence about Welch's private calculations, we would infer his insight from the record of sales and margins in the industrial- and financial-services businesses which implies understanding of business model levers that are being purposively pulled to achieve results.

Maybe it is sensible to turn the doxic question round and to ask not 'How did Jack do it?', but 'Why can most other CEOs not do it?' In the terminology of Part I, most of the Welch era initiatives that preoccupy the popular business books were moves (e.g. programmes for reducing costs) not levers. These were important in so far as they helped generate narrative and performative purpose and incidentally deflected hard questions about the sources of growth and profit and the future trajectory. But the GE numbers were generated by pulling cost recovery levers which most managers do not have or cannot easily shift: for example, GE built financial services on a triple-A credit rating where Ford had to do the job on a single-A rating in the 1990s (see Exhibit C2.11 for details). Even the brightest and best of managers cannot escape structural constraint: in businesses such as lighting or domestic appliances, GE returns performances that are what we would expect in mature, competitive activities.

The only general lesson of Welch and GE is that high-level management in complex operations is an activity that is perhaps best understood through the classic Machiavellian categories of *virtu*, *fortuna* and *occasione*. The art of management here is to understand what is possible and necessary by holding the narrative and performative separate from the business model in internal calculation and then to bring them together by public association in media and market commentary. As for the CEO, he or she then becomes the actor who first follows the script and then learns to improvise a public rhetoric and performance while operating an undisclosed business model. This is why all these interviews with great managers about the 'secrets of management success' offer the reader so little because their well-chosen words for the *Harvard Business Review* spin the narrative as part of the performance without clarifying the relation between moves and levers.

As for the rest of us outside GE, the main result of Jack Welch as exemplar is twofold. First, specific companies, especially in the late 1990s at the height of the cult, implemented copies of what they imagined Jack did: thus, Welch was an influence on the sector-matrix strategy and the grading of managers in Ford under Jacques Nasser. Second, more generally, Welch's example has encouraged the motivational and evangelical tone that makes the modern organization into a place of obligatory enthusiasm for endless initiatives that often have very little connection with the levers of business performance. It was Jack

Welch who encouraged GE managers to carry around statements of GE values on laminated plastic cards:

> **'All of us . . . Always with unyielding integrity**
>
> - Are passionately focused on driving customer success
> - Live Six Sigma Quality. . . ensure that the customer is always its first beneficiary . . . and use it to accelerate growth
> - Insist on excellence and are intolerant of bureaucracy
> - Act in a boundaryless fashion. . . always search for and apply the best ideas regardless of their source
> - Prize global intellectual capital and the people that provide it. . . build diverse teams to maximize it
> - See change for the growth opportunities it brings. . . eg digitization
> - Create a clear, simple, customer centred vision. . . and continually renew and refresh its execution
> - Create an environment of 'stretch', excitement, informality and trust. . . reward improvements and celebrate results
> - Demonstrate. . . always with infectious enthusiasm for the customer. . . the **'4-Es' of GE leadership**: the personal **Energy** to welcome and deal with the speed of change. . . the ability to create an atmosphere that *Energizes* others. . . the Edge to make difficult decisions. . . and the ability to consistently **Execute**.'
>
> (Welch 2001: 190)

In private corporations and public-sector organizations, management has become something that draws on the language and emotions of sales conference and religious revival as we must all now, through passion and works, attain a higher state for love of the customer. For that, Jack Welch is partly responsible.

## REFERENCES

Arnold, H. L. and F. L. Faurote, (1914) *Ford Methods and the Ford Shops*, New York: The Engineering Magazine.

Ashkenas, R. N., L. J. DeMonaco and S. Francis (2000) 'Making the deal real: how GE Capital integrates acquisitions', *Harvard Business Review*, January–February 1998: 165–78.

Chandler, A. (1962) *Strategy and Structure: Chapters in the History of the Industrial Enterprise*, Cambridge, Mass.: MIT Press.

CNN Money (2002a) 'Funds stand by GE', 21 March 2002. Online. Available HTTP: <http://money.cnn.com/2002/03/21/pf/investing/q_ge/> (accessed 25 May 2004).

—— (2002b) 'GE drops on Gross comments', 21 March 2002. Online. Available HTTP: <http://money.cnn.com/2002/03/21/news/companies/ge/index.htm> (accessed 25 May 2004).

Collingwood, H. and D. L. Coutu (2002) 'Jack on Jack', *Harvard Business Review*, February 2002: 88–94.

Collins, J. C. and J. I. Porras (2000) *Built to Last: Successful Habits of Visionary Companies*, 3rd edn, London: Random House.

Crainer, S. and D. Dearlove (2002) *Business the Jack Welch Way: 10 Secrets of the World's Greatest Turnaround King*, New York: John Wiley & Sons.

Feng, H., J. Froud, C. Haslam, S. Johal and K. Williams (2001) 'A new business model? The capital market and the new economy', *Economy and Society*, 30 (4): 467–503.

Fuller, J. and M. C. Jensen (2002) 'Just say no to Wall Street', mimeo, Harvard, Mass.: Monitor Group.

General Electric (GE) (2002a) Investor meeting 'What makes GE different?' Online. Available HTTP: <http://www.ge.com/files/usa/en/company/investor/downloads/Analyst_Combi ned_Web_rev3-22.pdf> (accessed 18 March 2002).

—— (2002b) Presentation to analysts by John Rice, Chief Executive Officer of GE Power Systems. Online. Available HTTP: <http://www.ge.com/files/usa/en/company/investor/downloads/112102_RICE_Part2_a.pdf> (accessed 21 November 2002).

—— (2002c) 'GE responds to inquiries about debt funding strategy', GE Press Release 21 March 2002. Online. Available HTTP: <http://www.ge.com/pr/display.php?highlight=true&id=1142&keyword=> (accessed 25 May 2004).

—— (2003) General Electric Annual Business Meeting Update and Outlook, hosted by Jeffrey Immelt, 16 December 2003. Event transcript provided by CCBN Street Events, New York: Thomson Financial.

—— (2005a) 'GE delivers strong first quarter 2005 financial results'. Press Release 15 April 2005. Online. Available HTTP: <http://www.ge.com/files/usa/company/investor/downloads/webcast_04152005/press_release_04152005.pdf> (accessed 19 April 2005).

—— (2005b) 'Imagination breakthroughs'. Online. Available HTTP: <http://www.ge.com/en/product/imagination_break.html> (accessed 10 April 2005).

—— (undated a) 'What is Six Sigma? The roadmap to customer impact'. Online. Available HTTP: <http://www.ge.com/sixsigma/SixSigma.pdf> (accessed 12 March 2004).

—— (undated b) 'Governance principles'. Online. Available HTTP: <http://www.ge.com/en/spotlight/commitment/governance/governance_principles.htm> (accessed 18 April 2005).

—— (undated c) Letter from Jeff Immelt on Corporate Governance to employees, shareowners and customers. Online. Available HTTP: <http://www.ge.com/en/company/investor/corp_governance.htm> (accessed 18 April 2005).

Golding, T. (2001) *The City: Inside the Great Expectations Machine*, London: Financial Times/Prentice Hall.

Heller, R. (2001) *Jack Welch: The Giant of Corporate Management who Created Billions for Investors*, London: Dorling Kindersley.

Jensen, M. C. (1989) 'Active investors, LBOs and the privatization of bankruptcy', *Journal of Applied Corporate Finance*, 2 (1): 35–44.

Jones, E. L. (1916) *The Administration of Industrial Enterprises, with Special Reference to Factory Practice*, New York: Longmans.

Krames, J. A. (2001) *Jack Welch Lexicon of Leadership*, New York: McGraw Hill.

—— (2002) *The Welch Way: 24 Lessons from the World's Greatest CEO*, New York: McGraw Hill.

Lewis, M. (1999) *The New New Thing*, London: Hodder & Stoughton.

Lowe, J. (1998) *Jack Welch Speaks*, New York: John Wiley & Sons.

—— (2002) *Welch: A Business Icon*, New York: Wiley.

O'Boyle, T. F. (1998) *At Any Cost: Jack Welch, General Electric and the Pursuit of Profit*, New York: Vintage.

Poe, E. A. (1845) 'The purloined letter', reprinted in *The Complete Tales and Poems of Edgar Allan Poe*, London: Penguin, pp. 208–22.

Rappaport, A. (1998) *Creating Shareholder Value*, 2nd edn, New York: Free Press.

Robinson, J. W. (2001) *Jack Welch on Leadership: Executive Lessons of the Master CEO*, New York: Crown.

Slater, R. (1993) *The New GE*, New York: McGraw Hill.

—— (1999) *Jack Welch and the GE Way*, New York: McGraw Hill.

—— (2000) *The GE Way Fieldbook*, New York: McGraw Hill.

—— (2003) *29 Leadership Secrets from Jack Welch*, New York: McGraw Hill.

Soros, G. (1987) *The Alchemy of Finance*, Hoboken, NJ: John Wiley & Sons.

Standard & Poor's (S&P) (2002) *Spotlight on General Electric Capital Corp.: How One Finance Company is Evaluated*, Analyst: E.Richard Schmidt, 6 June 2002, New York: Standard & Poor's.

Stern, J., G. Stuart, and D. Chew (1995) 'The EVA™ financial management system', *Journal of Applied Corporate Finance* 8 (2): 32–46.

Strebel, P. (2003) *Trajectory Management: Leading a Business Over Time*, Chichester: John Wiley & Sons.

Tichy, N. (1999) 'The teachable point of view', *Harvard Business Review*, March–April 1999: 82–3.

Tichy, N. M. and N. Cardwell (2002) *The Cycle of Leadership: How Great Leaders Teach Their Companies to Win*, New York: Harper Business.

Tichy, N. M. and S. Sherman (1993) *Control Your Destiny or Someone Else Will*, New York: Harper Business.

Ulrich, D., S. Kerr and R. Ashkenas (2002) *The GE Work-Out*, New York: McGraw-Hill.

Welch, J. (2001) *Jack: What I've Learnt Leading a Great Company and Great People*, with John A. Byrne, London: Headline.

Williams, K., J. Williams and D. Thomas (1983) *Why are the British Bad at Manufacturing?* London: Routledge & Kegan Paul.

Williams, K., C. Haslam and J. Williams (1993) 'The myth of the moving assembly line', *Business History Review*, 35 (3): 66–87.

Womack, J. P., D. T. Jones and D. Roos (1990) *The Machine That Changed the World*, New York: Rawson Associates.

## APPENDIX

***Table C3.1*** *GE: the scale and significance of dividends*

| | *Total dividend paid* | *Dividend payout (as a % net income)* | *Dividend payout for the S&P 500 (as a % of net income)* | *Dividend per share (adjusted for stock split and in 2003 prices)* | *Dividend yield* | *Dividends as a % of total shareholder return per share* | *Stock price change as a % of total shareholder return per share* |
|---|---|---|---|---|---|---|---|
| | $ million | % | % | $ | % | % | % |
| **1980** | 670 | 43.7 | 40.5 | 0.13 | 5.6 | | |
| **1981** | 715 | 43.4 | 42.2 | 0.13 | 5.2 | 72.2 | 27.8 |
| **1982** | 760 | 42.0 | 52.5 | 0.13 | 4.3 | 20.2 | 79.8 |
| **1983** | 852 | 42.1 | 48.4 | 0.14 | 3.6 | 13.3 | 86.7 |
| **1984** | 930 | 40.9 | 43.4 | 0.15 | 3.8 | 126.7 | −26.7 |
| **1985** | 1,020 | 43.5 | 52.8 | 0.16 | 3.5 | 20.2 | 79.8 |
| **1986** | 1,058 | 43.4 | 59.7 | 0.16 | 3.0 | 16.9 | 83.1 |
| **1987** | 1,177 | 41.0 | 54.6 | 0.17 | 2.5 | 9.7 | 90.3 |
| **1988** | 1,263 | 38.9 | 49.2 | 0.18 | 3.2 | 100.0 | 0.0 |
| **1989** | 1,479 | 39.0 | 48.9 | 0.21 | 3.0 | 16.0 | 84.0 |
| **1990** | 1,678 | 39.0 | 55.0 | 0.22 | 3.1 | 25.2 | 74.8 |
| **1991** | 1,780 | 68.2 | 72.7 | 0.23 | 3.1 | 92.2 | 7.8 |
| **1992** | 1,925 | 42.0 | 63.4 | 0.25 | 2.8 | 15.6 | 84.4 |
| **1993** | 2,153 | 51.6 | 56.0 | 0.27 | 2.7 | 18.6 | 81.4 |
| **1994** | 2,462 | 53.8 | 42.7 | 0.30 | 2.9 | 41.2 | 58.8 |
| **1995** | 2,770 | 42.8 | 45.2 | 0.33 | 2.7 | 14.7 | 85.3 |
| **1996** | 3,050 | 42.9 | 37.0 | 0.36 | 2.1 | 7.2 | 92.8 |
| **1997** | 3,411 | 43.0 | 37.6 | 0.40 | 1.7 | 5.9 | 94.1 |
| **1998** | 3,913 | 44.0 | 38.4 | 0.46 | 1.4 | 5.1 | 94.9 |
| **1999** | 4,587 | 44.8 | 54.9 | 0.52 | 1.1 | 3.7 | 96.3 |
| **2000** | 5,401 | 44.5 | 32.2 | 0.59 | 1.1 | 7.2 | 92.8 |
| **2001** | 6,358 | 47.9 | 72.4 | 0.67 | 1.6 | 100.0 | 0.0 |
| **2002** | 7,157 | 51.6 | 168.3 | 0.73 | 2.3 | 100.0 | 0.0 |
| **2003** | 7,643 | 51.7 | | 0.77 | 2.8 | 100.0 | 0.0 |

*Source*: GE Annual Report and Accounts and 10K, various years, Compustat

*Note*: The table includes a correction for share splits. Treasury shares excluded from all calculations. The data for the S&P500 is based on the annual constituents ie those 500 companies that comprise the S&P 500 in any particular year; this data was derived by the authors from Compustat

*Table C3.2* *GE market value and P/E ratio*

| | *Average stock price per share during year* | *Market capitalization, based on average stock value in year* | *P/E ratio based on average stock price for year* | *S&P 500 average P/E* |
|---|---|---|---|---|
| | $ | $ million | ratio | ratio |
| 1980 | 53.8 | 12,044 | 8.0 | 8.1 |
| 1981 | 60.5 | 13,780 | 8.3 | 8.4 |
| 1982 | 77.5 | 17,657 | 9.7 | 9.8 |
| 1983 | 52.2 | 23,726 | 11.7 | 11.0 |
| 1984 | 54.0 | 24,563 | 10.8 | 9.5 |
| 1985 | 64.8 | 29,524 | 12.6 | 12.6 |
| 1986 | 77.6 | 35,389 | 14.2 | 15.7 |
| 1987 | 52.6 | 47,461 | 16.3 | 15.6 |
| 1988 | 43.1 | 38,904 | 11.5 | 10.8 |
| 1989 | 54.1 | 48,971 | 12.4 | 13.7 |
| 1990 | 62.8 | 54,788 | 12.7 | 15.0 |
| 1991 | 65.6 | 56,654 | 21.5 | 22.5 |
| 1992 | 80.1 | 68,541 | 14.5 | 21.4 |
| 1993 | 93.9 | 80,190 | 18.6 | 20.1 |
| 1994 | 50.3 | 85,831 | 18.2 | 15.2 |
| 1995 | 61.5 | 102,490 | 15.6 | 16.7 |
| 1996 | 87.8 | 144,411 | 19.8 | 17.2 |
| 1997 | 62.3 | 203,221 | 24.8 | 21.5 |
| 1998 | 86.5 | 282,865 | 30.4 | 24.9 |
| 1999 | 126.9 | 416,764 | 38.9 | 28.7 |
| 2000 | 51.1 | 507,377 | 39.8 | 29.5 |
| 2001 | 39.1 | 387,856 | 28.3 | 57.9 |
| 2002 | 31.6 | 315,248 | 22.3 | 103.2 |
| 2003 | 26.9 | 270,295 | 18.0 | |

*Source*: GE Annual Report and Accounts and 10K, various years; Annual Abstract of the USA, and Compustat

*Notes*: Treasury shares excluded from all calculations. Some 2002 data is derived. (Average market values used.) Note that the 2002 S&P 500 P/E ratio is distorted by large write downs at AOL TimeWarner

*Table C3.3 GE Consolidated sales revenue (turnover) and contribution from main Industrial and Capital Services divisions*

| | GE total sales | GE Industrial sales | GE Capital sales | GE Industrial sales as a % of company total | GE Capital sales as a % of company total |
|---|---|---|---|---|---|
| | $ million | $ million | $ million | % | % |
| 1980 | 24,959 | 24,959 | 931 | 96.4 | 3.6 |
| 1981 | 27,240 | 27,240 | 1,074 | 96.2 | 3.8 |
| 1982 | 26,500 | 26,500 | 1,279 | 95.4 | 4.6 |
| 1983 | 26,797 | 26,797 | 1,550 | 94.5 | 5.5 |
| 1984 | 27,947 | 27,947 | 1,874 | 93.7 | 6.3 |
| 1985 | 28,285 | 28,285 | 2,302 | 92.5 | 7.5 |
| 1986 | 35,211 | 35,211 | 2,991 | 92.2 | 7.8 |
| 1987 | 39,315 | 39,315 | 3,980 | 90.8 | 9.2 |
| 1988 | 50,089 | 40,292 | 10,655 | 79.1 | 20.9 |
| 1989 | 54,574 | 42,650 | 12,945 | 76.7 | 23.3 |
| 1990 | 58,414 | 44,879 | 14,774 | 75.2 | 24.8 |
| 1991 | 60,236 | 45,227 | 16,399 | 73.4 | 26.6 |
| 1992 | 57,073 | 40,254 | 18,440 | 68.6 | 31.4 |
| 1993 | 60,562 | 40,359 | 22,137 | 64.6 | 35.4 |
| 1994 | 60,109 | 42,498 | 19,875 | 68.1 | 31.9 |
| 1995 | 70,028 | 46,181 | 26,492 | 63.5 | 36.5 |
| 1996 | 79,179 | 49,565 | 32,713 | 60.2 | 39.8 |
| 1997 | 90,840 | 54,515 | 39,931 | 57.7 | 42.3 |
| 1998 | 100,469 | 56,026 | 48,694 | 53.5 | 46.5 |
| 1999 | 111,630 | 60,944 | 55,749 | 52.2 | 47.8 |
| 2000 | 129,853 | 69,497 | 66,177 | 51.2 | 48.8 |
| 2001 | 125,913 | 74,037 | 58,353 | 55.9 | 44.1 |
| 2002 | 131,698 | 79,049 | 58,187 | 57.6 | 42.4 |
| 2003 | 134,187 | 78,841 | 64,279 | 55.1 | 44.9 |

*Source*: GE Annual Report and Accounts and 10K, various years

*Note*: GE began consolidating GE Capital in 1988. Prior to 1988, GE Consolidated sales in the table are calculated as the sum of the GE Industrial and GE Capital totals. After 1988, the divisional totals will not necessarily sum to the GE Consolidated totals due to intra-company transactions

**Table C3.4** *Growth of sales vs. growth of profits in GE and its main divisions*

| | *GE Consolidated* | | *GE Industrial* | | *GE Capital* | |
|---|---|---|---|---|---|---|
| | *Growth in sales* | *Growth in net income* | *Growth in sales* | *Growth in net income* | *Growth in sales* | *Growth in net income* |
| | % | % | % | % | % | % |
| **1981** | 9.1 | 9.1 | 9.1 | 7.9 | 15.4 | 23.5 |
| **1982** | –2.7 | 10.0 | –2.7 | 6.8 | 19.1 | 44.4 |
| **1983** | 1.1 | 11.4 | 1.1 | 8.7 | 21.2 | 32.2 |
| **1984** | 4.3 | 12.6 | 4.3 | 11.3 | 20.9 | 21.4 |
| **1985** | 1.2 | 2.5 | 1.2 | –1.4 | 22.8 | 25.5 |
| **1986** | 24.5 | 6.7 | 24.5 | 3.4 | 29.9 | 22.0 |
| **1987** | 11.7 | 17.0 | 11.7 | 18.9 | 33.1 | 9.5 |
| **1988** | 27.4 | 16.2 | 2.5 | 9.9 | 167.7 | 42.8 |
| **1989** | 9.0 | 16.3 | 5.9 | 15.9 | 21.5 | 17.6 |
| **1990** | 7.0 | 9.2 | 5.2 | 6.5 | 14.1 | 18.0 |
| **1991** | 3.1 | –38.7 | 0.8 | –57.0 | 11.0 | 14.8 |
| **1992** | –5.3 | 79.2 | –11.0 | 133.8 | 12.4 | 19.3 |
| **1993** | 6.1 | –8.7 | 0.3 | –22.3 | 20.0 | 20.5 |
| **1994** | –0.7 | 9.5 | 5.3 | 52.7 | –10.2 | –50.4 |
| **1995** | 16.5 | 39.1 | 8.7 | 8.6 | 33.3 | 169.5 |
| **1996** | 13.1 | 10.8 | 7.3 | 7.3 | 23.5 | 16.6 |
| **1997** | 14.7 | 12.7 | 10.0 | 10.8 | 22.1 | 15.6 |
| **1998** | 10.6 | 13.3 | 2.8 | 11.2 | 21.9 | 16.6 |
| **1999** | 11.1 | 15.3 | 8.8 | 14.1 | 14.5 | 17.0 |
| **2000** | 16.3 | 18.8 | 14.0 | 20.2 | 18.7 | 16.9 |
| **2001** | –3.0 | 7.5 | 6.5 | 9.6 | –11.8 | 4.3 |
| **2002** | 4.6 | 3.2 | 6.8 | 27.1 | –0.3 | –33.3 |
| **2003** | 1.9 | 6.3 | –0.3 | –27.8 | 10.5 | 105.3 |

|  |  |  |  |  |  |  |
|---|---|---|---|---|---|---|
| Average annual growth 1980–2003 | 7.9 | 12.1 | 5.3 | 12.0 | 23.1 | 25.6 |
| Average annual growth 1980–90 | 9.3 | 11.1 | 6.3 | 8.8 | 36.6 | 25.7 |
| Average annual growth 1990–2003 | 6.9 | 12.7 | 4.7 | 13.9 | 12.8 | 25.1 |

*Source*: GE Annual Report and Accounts and 10K, various years

*Notes*: GE began consolidating GE Capital in 1988. Prior to 1988, GE Consolidated sales in the table are calculated as the sum of the GE Industrial and GE Capital totals. GE Industrial owns nearly all the shares in GE Capital and therefore consolidates the net income. To avoid double counting, the above calculation deducts GE Capital's contribution to GE Industrial's net income

**Table C3.5** *GE: real sales and net income (all values in 2003 prices)*

| | *Real sales* | | | *Real net income* | | |
|---|---|---|---|---|---|---|
| | *GE Consolidated* | *GE Industrial* | *GE Capital* | *GE Consolidated* | *GE Industrial* | *GE Capital* |
| | $ million | $ million | $ million | $ million | $ million | $ million |
| **1980** | 58,856 | 55,753 | 3,103 | 3,382 | 3,125 | 257 |
| **1981** | 58,775 | 55,166 | 3,609 | 3,346 | 3,058 | 288 |
| **1982** | 54,232 | 50,534 | 3,698 | 3,465 | 3,074 | 391 |
| **1983** | 53,118 | 49,516 | 3,601 | 3,740 | 3,239 | 501 |
| **1984** | 54,708 | 49,512 | 5,196 | 4,039 | 3,456 | 583 |
| **1985** | 54,877 | 48,370 | 6,507 | 3,995 | 3,288 | 706 |
| **1986** | 68,848 | 59,091 | 9,757 | 4,182 | 3,336 | 846 |
| **1987** | 76,935 | 63,624 | 13,311 | 4,717 | 3,824 | 893 |
| **1988** | 77,942 | 62,697 | 16,580 | 5,269 | 4,043 | 1,226 |
| **1989** | 81,032 | 63,327 | 19,221 | 5,849 | 4,472 | 1,376 |
| **1990** | 82,290 | 63,223 | 20,813 | 6,062 | 4,521 | 1,541 |
| **1991** | 81,436 | 61,145 | 22,171 | 3,564 | 1,866 | 1,698 |
| **1992** | 74,913 | 52,836 | 24,204 | 6,202 | 4,234 | 1,968 |
| **1993** | 77,177 | 51,431 | 28,210 | 5,499 | 3,196 | 2,303 |
| **1994** | 74,658 | 52,785 | 24,686 | 5,870 | 4,757 | 1,113 |
| **1995** | 84,609 | 55,797 | 32,008 | 7,942 | 5,024 | 2,918 |
| **1996** | 92,970 | 58,198 | 38,411 | 8,548 | 5,240 | 3,308 |
| **1997** | 104,263 | 62,571 | 45,832 | 9,415 | 5,678 | 3,737 |
| **1998** | 113,499 | 63,292 | 55,009 | 10,502 | 6,213 | 4,288 |
| **1999** | 123,393 | 67,366 | 61,624 | 11,846 | 6,935 | 4,911 |
| **2000** | 138,817 | 74,294 | 70,745 | 13,614 | 8,064 | 5,550 |
| **2001** | 130,898 | 76,968 | 60,663 | 14,226 | 8,594 | 5,631 |
| **2002** | 134,595 | 80,788 | 59,467 | 14,429 | 10,738 | 3,690 |
| **2003** | 134,187 | 78,841 | 64,279 | 15,002 | 7,587 | 7,415 |

*Source*: GE Annual Report and Accounts and 10K, various years

*Notes*: GE began consolidating GE Capital in 1988. Prior to 1988, GE Consolidated sales in the table are calculated as the sum of the GE Industrial and GE Capital totals. GE Industrial owns nearly all the shares in GE Capital and therefore consolidates the net income. To avoid double counting, the above calculation deducts GE Capital's contribution to GE Industrial's net income

**Table C3.6** *GE Industrial division real sales by business segment (in real 2002 prices)*

| | *Aircraft engines* | *Aerospace* | *Consumer products* | *Major appliances/ appliances* | *Industrial products/ systems/ industrial* | *Natural resources* | *NBC/ broad-casting* | *Power systems/ power generation* | *Technical systems/ technical products and services* | *Services and materials/ materials/ plastics* | *Other* | *Corporate items and eliminations* | *TOTAL* |
|---|---|---|---|---|---|---|---|---|---|---|---|---|---|
| | $ million | $ million | $ million | $ million | $ million | $ million | $ million | $ million | $ million | $ million | $ million | $ million | $ million |
| **1980** | 5,710 | | 13,558 | | 9,439 | 2,990 | | 12,061 | 6,628 | 4,419 | | 481 | 55,287 |
| **1981** | 5,711 | | 12,853 | | 8,893 | 3,397 | | 11,361 | 7,465 | 4,681 | | 333 | 54,695 |
| **1982** | 5,744 | | 10,960 | | 7,339 | 2,926 | | 11,086 | 7,510 | 4,209 | | 357 | 50,131 |
| **1983** | 6,183 | | 11,246 | | 6,984 | 2,842 | | 10,235 | 6,766 | 3,535 | | 454 | 48,246 |
| **1984** | 6,439 | | 6,441 | 6,299 | 6,791 | 1,051 | | 10,004 | 7,901 | 3,654 | | 585 | 49,164 |
| **1985** | 7,704 | | 5,750 | 6,025 | 6,670 | | | 8,950 | 8,319 | 3,910 | | 601 | 47,931 |
| **1986** | 9,678 | 6,940 | 7,314 | 6,714 | 6,727 | | 2,967 | 8,300 | 5,078 | 3,753 | 1,262 | 348 | 59,080 |
| **1987** | 10,677 | 8,295 | 7,948 | 7,442 | 7,420 | | 4,989 | 7,874 | 5,786 | 4,337 | 134 | –2,030 | 62,873 |
| **1988** | 9,824 | 8,099 | | 8,017 | 10,703 | | 5,514 | 7,283 | 6,717 | 5,364 | 597 | –2,239 | 59,880 |
| **1989** | 9,926 | 7,640 | | 8,129 | 10,210 | | 4,906 | 7,418 | 6,574 | 7,129 | 461 | –2,047 | 60,347 |
| **1990** | 10,372 | 7,704 | | 7,830 | 9,661 | | 4,441 | 7,965 | 6,564 | 7,091 | 377 | –1,918 | 60,085 |
| **1991** | 10,403 | 7,014 | | 7,179 | 9,124 | | 4,110 | 8,145 | 6,880 | 6,219 | 356 | –1,546 | 57,883 |
| **1992** | 9,421 | | | 6,815 | 8,831 | | 4,300 | 8,146 | 5,976 | 6,205 | 2,236 | –462 | 51,469 |
| **1993** | 8,168 | | | 6,896 | 9,160 | | 3,851 | 8,307 | 5,181 | 6,259 | 2,536 | –258 | 50,100 |
| **1994** | 6,913 | | | 7,217 | 11,380 | | 4,066 | 7,178 | 5,184 | 6,873 | 2,841 | –236 | 51,419 |
| **1995** | 7,177 | | | 6,983 | 11,998 | | 4,612 | 7,703 | 5,207 | 7,823 | 3,186 | –337 | 54,353 |
| **1996** | 7,208 | | | 7,292 | 11,909 | | 5,984 | 8,300 | 5,367 | 7,445 | 3,555 | –368 | 56,692 |
| **1997** | 8,720 | | | 7,541 | 12,247 | | 5,761 | 8,380 | 5,498 | 7,485 | 3,985 | 1,334 | 60,951 |
| **1998** | 11,328 | | | 6,183 | 12,349 | | 5,798 | 9,316 | 5,858 | 7,299 | 848 | –1,504 | 57,477 |
| **1999** | 11,369 | | | 6,106 | 12,442 | | 6,235 | 10,817 | 7,390 | 7,474 | 667 | –1,660 | 60,839 |
| **2000** | 11,225 | | | 6,131 | 12,338 | | 7,078 | 15,476 | 8,242 | 8,098 | 538 | –2,161 | 66,965 |
| **2001** | 11,537 | | | 5,886 | 11,798 | | 5,844 | 20,474 | 9,128 | 7,161 | 451 | –2,938 | 69,341 |
| **2002** | 11,141 | | | 6,072 | 12,139 | | 7,149 | 22,926 | 9,266 | 7,651 | 4,331 | –2,833 | 77,842 |

*Source*: GE Annual Report and Accounts and 10K, various years

Notes: The TOTAL column may not equal the totals from the income statement due to the method used to calculate GE Capital's income and (less so) corporate reshuffling. Some totals are derived. The data in this table covers 1980 to 2002. It has not been possible to include comparable, consistent data for 2003 due to a reclassification of the business segments in GE's 2003 accounts

**Table C3.7** *GE performance: ROCE and ROE*

| | *ROCE (using income before interest and tax)* % | | | *ROCE (using net income)* % | | | *ROE* % | | |
|---|---|---|---|---|---|---|---|---|---|
| | *GE Consolidated* | *GE Industrial* | *GE Capital* | *GE Consolidated* | *GE Industrial* | *GE Capital* | *GE Consolidated* | *GE Industrial* | *GE Capital* |
| **1980** | 27.6 | 28.1 | 25.9 | 11.4 | 14.0 | 3.5 | 18.5 | 9.9 | 12.4 |
| **1981** | 28.5 | 27.5 | 31.5 | 11.0 | 13.6 | 3.7 | 18.1 | 18.7 | 13.2 |
| **1982** | 26.0 | 25.4 | 27.5 | 10.9 | 13.2 | 4.5 | 17.8 | 18.1 | 16.0 |
| **1983** | 25.5 | 26.1 | 24.1 | 11.3 | 13.4 | 5.6 | 18.0 | 18.0 | 17.5 |
| **1984** | 25.6 | 25.9 | 24.8 | 11.3 | 13.7 | 5.5 | 18.1 | 18.2 | 17.6 |
| **1985** | 25.3 | 25.6 | 24.7 | 10.5 | 12.6 | 5.8 | 16.8 | 16.6 | 17.9 |
| **1986** | 21.9 | 21.4 | 23.2 | 8.7 | 9.9 | 5.8 | 16.5 | 16.4 | 16.9 |
| **1987** | 23.7 | 17.3 | 35.7 | 8.5 | 10.6 | 4.6 | 17.7 | 18.9 | 13.9 |
| **1988** | 24.6 | 21.9 | 25.2 | 8.7 | 11.0 | 3.8 | 18.3 | 19.0 | 16.4 |
| **1989** | 28.6 | 25.2 | 29.4 | 9.2 | 12.2 | 3.9 | 18.9 | 20.3 | 15.3 |
| **1990** | 27.4 | 27.6 | 26.0 | 8.7 | 13.0 | 3.6 | 19.8 | 21.6 | 16.0 |
| **1991** | 26.7 | 26.5 | 24.6 | 5.1 | 5.3 | 3.8 | 12.2 | 9.9 | 16.2 |
| **1992** | 22.6 | 25.6 | 22.4 | 8.1 | 12.7 | 3.8 | 20.1 | 22.1 | 16.9 |
| **1993** | 17.1 | 23.8 | 15.0 | 5.5 | 9.5 | 3.0 | 16.7 | 16.7 | 16.7 |
| **1994** | 14.4 | 28.7 | 10.0 | 5.0 | 13.4 | 1.2 | 17.9 | 22.5 | 9.6 |
| **1995** | 13.8 | 32.6 | 9.8 | 5.3 | 14.6 | 2.3 | 22.2 | 24.7 | 18.9 |
| **1996** | 12.9 | 35.4 | 9.0 | 5.0 | 15.6 | 2.2 | 23.4 | 26.5 | 19.7 |
| **1997** | 12.9 | 36.0 | 9.0 | 5.4 | 16.5 | 2.4 | 23.8 | 28.8 | 18.9 |
| **1998** | 12.9 | 39.1 | 8.9 | 5.2 | 16.5 | 2.4 | 23.9 | 28.7 | 19.2 |
| **1999** | 12.4 | 39.1 | 8.5 | 5.2 | 16.7 | 2.4 | 25.2 | 28.2 | 21.9 |
| **2000** | 12.4 | 39.4 | 8.5 | 5.2 | 17.1 | 2.4 | 25.2 | 27.5 | 22.6 |
| **2001** | 12.1 | 43.4 | 7.8 | 5.4 | 18.8 | 2.4 | 25.0 | 31.5 | 18.9 |
| **2002** | 8.4 | 43.0 | 4.6 | 4.1 | 23.1 | 1.1 | 22.2 | 39.2 | 9.8 |
| **2003** | 7.8 | 31.4 | 5.5 | 3.8 | 12.3 | 2.1 | 18.9 | 22.4 | 16.4 |
| Average 1980–2003 | 14.5 | 30.7 | 10.0 | 5.7 | 14.0 | 2.4 | 20.6 | 24.9 | 17.0 |

*Source*: GE Annual Report and Accounts and 10K, various years

*Note*: Prior to 1988, GE Consolidated equity is the sum of the two divisions. GE Industrial equity excludes its equity holding in GE Capital Services. GE Industrial income excludes the contribution of GE Capital. GE Industrial owns nearly all the shares in GE Capital and therefore consolidates the net income. To avoid double counting, the above calculation deducts GE Capital's contribution to GE Industrial's net income. The 1980–2003 average is a weighted average

*Table C3.8* GE ROS

| | Pre-tax ROS | | | Net ROS | | |
|---|---|---|---|---|---|---|
| | GE Consolidated | GE Industrial | GE Capital | GE Consolidated | GE Industrial | GE Capital |
| | % | % | % | % | % | % |
| **1980** | 9.5 | 9.4 | 10.2 | 5.7 | 5.6 | 8.3 |
| **1981** | 9.2 | 9.1 | 9.8 | 5.7 | 5.5 | 8.0 |
| **1982** | 9.7 | 9.5 | 11.5 | 6.4 | 6.1 | 10.6 |
| **1983** | 10.6 | 10.1 | 16.4 | 7.0 | 6.5 | 13.9 |
| **1984** | 10.9 | 10.7 | 12.1 | 7.4 | 7.0 | 11.2 |
| **1985** | 11.0 | 11.0 | 11.1 | 7.3 | 6.8 | 10.9 |
| **1986** | 9.0 | 10.7 | −1.0 | 6.1 | 5.6 | 8.7 |
| **1987** | 6.7 | 5.5 | 12.5 | 6.1 | 6.0 | 6.7 |
| **1988** | 9.4 | 8.6 | 9.6 | 6.8 | 6.4 | 7.4 |
| **1989** | 10.5 | 10.2 | 8.8 | 7.2 | 7.1 | 7.2 |
| **1990** | 10.5 | 9.9 | 9.4 | 7.4 | 7.2 | 7.4 |
| **1991** | 10.7 | 9.7 | 10.1 | 4.4 | 3.1 | 7.7 |
| **1992** | 11.0 | 9.2 | 11.0 | 8.3 | 8.0 | 8.1 |
| **1993** | 10.9 | 7.6 | 12.0 | 7.1 | 6.2 | 8.2 |
| **1994** | 14.4 | 11.4 | 14.8 | 7.9 | 9.0 | 4.5 |
| **1995** | 13.9 | 11.1 | 13.3 | 9.4 | 9.0 | 9.1 |
| **1996** | 13.6 | 11.2 | 12.4 | 9.2 | 9.0 | 8.6 |
| **1997** | 12.3 | 10.3 | 11.1 | 9.0 | 9.1 | 8.2 |
| **1998** | 13.4 | 12.4 | 10.6 | 9.3 | 9.8 | 7.8 |
| **1999** | 14.0 | 12.8 | 10.9 | 9.6 | 10.3 | 8.0 |
| **2000** | 14.2 | 13.6 | 10.7 | 9.8 | 10.9 | 7.8 |
| **2001** | 15.6 | 15.3 | 11.9 | 10.9 | 11.2 | 9.3 |
| **2002** | 14.3 | 18.2 | 7.8 | 10.7 | 13.3 | 6.2 |
| **2003** | 14.8 | 11.7 | 14.3 | 11.2 | 9.6 | 11.5 |

*Source*: Annual report and accounts, and SEC 10K

*Notes*: GE began consolidating GE Capital in 1988. GE Industrial owns nearly all the shares in GE Capital and therefore consolidates the net income. Pre-1988, GE Consolidated sales is calculated as the summation of both GE Industrial and GE Capital Services totals. To avoid double counting, the above calculation deducts GE Capital's contribution to GE Industrial's net income

*Table C3.9* *The scale of GE's cashflows*

| | *GE cashflow from operations* | *GE cashflow as a % of sales* | *GE cashflow from operations as a % of GE sales* | *GE Industrial cashflow from operations as a % of GEI sales* | *GECS cashflow from operations as a % of GECS sales* |
|---|---|---|---|---|---|
| | $ million (real 2003 prices) | % | % | % | % |
| **1980** | 5,225 | 12.3 | 8.9 | 9.4 | |
| **1981** | 5,330 | 13.6 | 9.1 | 9.7 | |
| **1982** | 5,595 | 13.4 | 10.3 | 11.1 | |
| **1983** | 5,712 | 14.9 | 10.8 | 11.5 | |
| **1984** | 5,120 | 16.3 | 9.4 | 10.3 | |
| **1985** | 5,712 | 13.3 | 10.4 | 11.8 | |
| **1986** | 5,647 | 28.8 | 8.2 | 9.6 | |
| **1987** | 5,026 | 15.0 | 6.5 | 7.9 | |
| **1988** | 11,051 | 49.1 | 14.2 | 9.0 | 32.8 |
| **1989** | 9,834 | 43.7 | 12.1 | 11.2 | 16.1 |
| **1990** | 12,729 | 50.3 | 15.5 | 9.0 | 36.3 |
| **1991** | 10,136 | 51.6 | 12.4 | 8.9 | 24.2 |
| **1992** | 13,453 | 50.3 | 18.0 | 13.2 | 29.0 |
| **1993** | 12,982 | 53.8 | 16.8 | 13.1 | 24.6 |
| **1994** | 16,634 | 67.9 | 22.3 | 14.3 | 42.5 |
| **1995** | 18,058 | 77.6 | 21.3 | 13.1 | 38.0 |
| **1996** | 20,960 | 68.5 | 22.5 | 18.3 | 29.9 |
| **1997** | 16,344 | 57.5 | 15.7 | 17.1 | 15.6 |
| **1998** | 21,871 | 81.9 | 19.3 | 17.9 | 22.5 |
| **1999** | 27,185 | 76.9 | 22.0 | 19.3 | 26.6 |
| **2000** | 24,256 | 69.7 | 17.5 | 22.2 | 14.0 |
| **2001** | 33,470 | 74.8 | 25.6 | 23.2 | 30.2 |
| **2002** | 30,137 | 102.0 | 22.4 | 12.8 | 36.1 |
| **2003** | 30,289 | 85.0 | 22.6 | 16.4 | 33.4 |

*Source*: GE Annual Report and Accounts and 10K, various years

*Note*: Prior to 1988, GE did not consolidate GE Capital results and cash-flow information was not separately disclosed

**Table C3.10** *GE pre-tax and net income and contribution by main division (Industrial and Capital)*

| | *Pre-tax income* | | | | | *Net income* | | | | |
|---|---|---|---|---|---|---|---|---|---|---|
| | *GE Consolidated* | *GE Industrial* | | *GE Capital* | | *GE Consolidated* | *GE Industrial* | | *GE Capital* | |
| | $ million | $ million | % | $ million | % | $ million | $ million | % | $ million | % |
| **1980** | 2,493 | 2,352 | 94.3 | 141 | 5.7 | 1,514 | 1,399 | 92.4 | 115 | 7.6 |
| **1981** | 2,660 | 2,486 | 93.5 | 174 | 6.5 | 1,652 | 1,510 | 91.4 | 142 | 8.6 |
| **1982** | 2,753 | 2,530 | 91.9 | 223 | 8.1 | 1,817 | 1,612 | 88.7 | 205 | 11.3 |
| **1983** | 3,033 | 2,713 | 89.4 | 320 | 10.6 | 2,024 | 1,753 | 86.6 | 271 | 13.4 |
| **1984** | 3,356 | 3,002 | 89.5 | 354 | 10.5 | 2,280 | 1,951 | 85.6 | 329 | 14.4 |
| **1985** | 3,540 | 3,116 | 88.0 | 424 | 12.0 | 2,336 | 1,923 | 82.3 | 413 | 17.7 |
| **1986** | 3,689 | 3,750 | 101.7 | −61 | −1.7 | 2,492 | 1,988 | 79.8 | 504 | 20.2 |
| **1987** | 3,207 | 2,199 | 68.6 | 1,008 | 31.4 | 2,915 | 2,363 | 81.1 | 552 | 18.9 |
| **1988** | 4,721 | 3,484 | 77.2 | 1,027 | 22.8 | 3,386 | 2,598 | 76.7 | 788 | 23.3 |
| **1989** | 5,703 | 4,354 | 79.3 | 1,138 | 20.7 | 3,939 | 3,012 | 76.5 | 927 | 23.5 |
| **1990** | 6,147 | 4,451 | 76.1 | 1,395 | 23.9 | 4,303 | 3,209 | 74.6 | 1,094 | 25.4 |
| **1991** | 6,436 | 4,397 | 72.6 | 1,657 | 27.4 | 2,636 | 1,380 | 52.4 | 1,256 | 47.6 |
| **1992** | 6,273 | 3,702 | 64.5 | 2,035 | 35.5 | 4,725 | 3,226 | 68.3 | 1,499 | 31.7 |
| **1993** | 6,575 | 3,086 | 53.8 | 2,648 | 46.2 | 4,315 | 2,508 | 58.1 | 1,807 | 41.9 |
| **1994** | 8,661 | 4,848 | 62.2 | 2,949 | 37.8 | 4,726 | 3,830 | 81.0 | 896 | 19.0 |
| **1995** | 9,737 | 5,112 | 59.2 | 3,520 | 40.8 | 6,573 | 4,158 | 63.3 | 2,415 | 36.7 |
| **1996** | 10,806 | 5,527 | 57.7 | 4,048 | 42.3 | 7,280 | 4,463 | 61.3 | 2,817 | 38.7 |
| **1997** | 11,179 | 5,591 | 55.8 | 4,422 | 44.2 | 8,203 | 4,947 | 60.3 | 3,256 | 39.7 |
| **1998** | 13,477 | 6,952 | 57.4 | 5,161 | 42.6 | 9,296 | 5,500 | 59.2 | 3,796 | 40.8 |
| **1999** | 15,577 | 7,828 | 56.2 | 6,096 | 43.8 | 10,717 | 6,274 | 58.5 | 4,443 | 41.5 |
| **2000** | 18,446 | 9,430 | 57.0 | 7,104 | 43.0 | 12,735 | 7,543 | 59.2 | 5,192 | 40.8 |
| **2001** | 19,701 | 11,355 | 62.0 | 6,966 | 38.0 | 13,684 | 8,267 | 60.4 | 5,417 | 39.6 |
| **2002** | 18,891 | 14,423 | 76.0 | 4,547 | 24.0 | 14,118 | 10,507 | 74.4 | 3,611 | 25.6 |
| **2003** | 19,904 | 9,234 | 46.4 | 9,212 | 46.2 | 15,002 | 7,587 | 50.6 | 7,415 | 49.4 |

*Source*: GE Annual Report and Accounts and 10K, various years

*Notes*: GE began consolidating GE Capital in 1988. Pre-1988, GE Consolidated sales is calculated as the summation of both GE Industrial and GE Capital totals. GE Industrial owns nearly all the shares in GE Capital and therefore consolidates the net income. To avoid double counting, the above calculation deducts GE Capital's contribution to GE Industrial's net income. Divisional totals will not sum to consolidated totals due to intra-company transactions. In particular, all 'below the line' adjustments in the accounts which cannot be attributed to any division occur between the pre-tax and net income stage. There are significant changes or events in both GE Industrial and Capital between 2000 and 2002: in GE Capital a decline in profits in 2001 was caused by the sale of Paine Webber and in 2002 from problems in the insurance business. Most of the change in GE Industrial is a result of the power-systems division

**Table C3.11** *GE: growth in real net (post-tax) income and contribution of GE Industrial and GE Capital*

| | *Real net income* | | | *% Share of real net income* | | *Annual increase/decrease in real net income* | | |
|---|---|---|---|---|---|---|---|---|
| | *GE Consolidated* | *GE Industrial* | *GE Capital* | *GE Industrial* | *GE Capital* | *GE Consolidated* | *GE Industrial* | *GE Capital* |
| | $ million | $ million | $ million | % | % | % | % | % |
| **1980** | 3,382 | 3,125 | 257 | 92.4 | 7.6 | | | |
| **1981** | 3,346 | 3,058 | 288 | 91.4 | 8.6 | –1.1 | –2.1 | 11.9 |
| **1982** | 3,465 | 3,074 | 391 | 88.7 | 11.3 | 3.6 | 0.5 | 35.9 |
| **1983** | 3,740 | 3,239 | 501 | 86.6 | 13.4 | 7.9 | 5.4 | 28.1 |
| **1984** | 4,039 | 3,456 | 583 | 85.6 | 14.4 | 8.0 | 6.7 | 16.4 |
| **1985** | 3,995 | 3,288 | 706 | 82.3 | 17.7 | –1.1 | –4.9 | 21.2 |
| **1986** | 4,182 | 3,336 | 846 | 79.8 | 20.2 | 4.7 | 1.5 | 19.8 |
| **1987** | 4,717 | 3,824 | 893 | 81.1 | 18.9 | 12.8 | 14.6 | 5.6 |
| **1988** | 5,269 | 4,043 | 1,226 | 76.7 | 23.3 | 11.7 | 5.7 | 37.3 |
| **1989** | 5,849 | 4,472 | 1,376 | 76.5 | 23.5 | 11.0 | 10.6 | 12.3 |
| **1990** | 6,062 | 4,521 | 1,541 | 74.6 | 25.4 | 3.6 | 1.1 | 12.0 |
| **1991** | 3,564 | 1,866 | 1,698 | 52.4 | 47.6 | –41.2 | –58.7 | 10.2 |
| **1992** | 6,202 | 4,234 | 1,968 | 68.3 | 31.7 | 74.0 | 127.0 | 15.9 |
| **1993** | 5,499 | 3,196 | 2,303 | 58.1 | 41.9 | –11.3 | –24.5 | 17.0 |
| **1994** | 5,870 | 4,757 | 1,113 | 81.0 | 19.0 | 6.7 | 48.8 | –51.7 |
| **1995** | 7,942 | 5,024 | 2,918 | 63.3 | 36.7 | 35.3 | 5.6 | 162.2 |
| **1996** | 8,548 | 5,240 | 3,308 | 61.3 | 38.7 | 7.6 | 4.3 | 13.4 |
| **1997** | 9,415 | 5,678 | 3,737 | 60.3 | 39.7 | 10.1 | 8.4 | 13.0 |
| **1998** | 10,502 | 6,213 | 4,288 | 59.2 | 40.8 | 11.5 | 9.4 | 14.7 |
| **1999** | 11,846 | 6,935 | 4,911 | 58.5 | 41.5 | 12.8 | 11.6 | 14.5 |
| **2000** | 13,614 | 8,064 | 5,550 | 59.2 | 40.8 | 14.9 | 16.3 | 13.0 |
| **2001** | 14,226 | 8,594 | 5,631 | 60.4 | 39.6 | 4.5 | 6.6 | 1.5 |
| **2002** | 14,429 | 10,738 | 3,690 | 74.4 | 25.6 | 1.4 | 24.9 | –34.5 |
| **2003** | 15,002 | 7,587 | 7,415 | 50.6 | 49.4 | 4.0 | –29.3 | 100.9 |
| **Average annual growth %** | | | | | | 8.3 | 8.2 | 21.3 |

*Source*: GE Annual Report and Accounts and 10K, various years

*Notes*: GE began consolidating GE Capital in 1988. Pre-1988, GE Consolidated sales is calculated as the summation of both GE Industrial and GE Capital totals. GE Industrial owns nearly all the shares in GE Capital and therefore consolidates the net income. To avoid double counting, the above calculation deducts GE Capital's contribution to GE Industrial's net income. Divisional totals will not sum to consolidated totals due to intra-company transactions

**Table C3.12** *The significance of sales revenue from services in GE, 1992–2003*

| | *GE total sales* | *GE Industrial sales* | *GE Industrial-sales of services* | *Sales of services in GE Industrial as a % of all GE Industrial sales* | *GE Capital sales* | *GE Capital sales of services* | *Sales of services in GE Capital as a % of all GE Capital sales* | *GE Industrial gross margin on sale of goods* | *GE Industrial gross margin on the sale of services* |
|---|---|---|---|---|---|---|---|---|---|
| | $million | $million | $million | % | $million | $million | % | % | % |
| **1992** | 57,073 | 40,254 | 8,348 | 20.7 | 18,440 | | | 25.2 | 24.7 |
| **1993** | 60,562 | 40,359 | 8,289 | 20.5 | 22,137 | | | 23.4 | 23.6 |
| **1994** | 60,109 | 42,498 | 8,863 | 20.9 | 19,875 | | | 26.0 | 29.2 |
| **1995** | 70,028 | 46,181 | 9,836 | 21.3 | 26,492 | 26,025 | 98.2 | 26.7 | 31.0 |
| **1996** | 79,179 | 49,565 | 11,923 | 24.1 | 32,713 | 30,787 | 94.1 | 28.1 | 29.3 |
| **1997** | 90,840 | 54,515 | 12,893 | 23.7 | 39,931 | 35,309 | 88.4 | 25.8 | 27.4 |
| **1998** | 100,469 | 56,026 | 15,170 | 27.1 | 48,694 | 41,320 | 84.9 | 31.3 | 29.2 |
| **1999** | 111,630 | 60,944 | 16,600 | 27.2 | 55,749 | 47,009 | 84.3 | 31.9 | 29.4 |
| **2000** | 129,853 | 69,497 | 18,380 | 26.4 | 66,177 | 56,769 | 85.8 | 32.2 | 30.5 |
| **2001** | 125,913 | 74,037 | 18,961 | 25.6 | 58,353 | 54,726 | 93.8 | 33.9 | 28.0 |
| **2002** | 131,698 | 79,049 | 21,360 | 27.0 | 58,187 | 54,891 | 94.3 | 30.8 | 33.3 |
| **2003** | 134,187 | 78,841 | 22,675 | 28.8 | 64,279 | 61,356 | 96.5 | 26.5 | 36.9 |

*Source*: GE Annual Report and Accounts, various years

*Note*: All values in this table are nominal

**Table C3.13** *Major acquisitions by GE, 2002–4*

| *Date (of completion of deal, or announcement)* | *Business acquired* | *Cost/method of payment (where disclosed)* |
|---|---|---|
| January 2002 | Real estate and asset based lending businesses from DaimlerChrysler Services | $1.2 billion cash |
| April 2002 | Telemundo Communications Group, Spanish language TV network, from a private consortium (including Sony) | $2.7 billion ($2 billion cash plus debt repayment) |
| May 2002 | Enron Wind | |
| October 2002 | Deutsche Financial Services commercial inventory financing business from Deutsche Bank | $2.9 billion (cash plus debt repayment) |
| November 2002 | ABB's structured finance business | $2.4 billion |
| December 2002 | Bravo, film and arts network, from Cablevision Systems | $1.25 billion |
| February 2003 | First National, consumer credit arm of UK bank Abbey National | $1.3 billion |
| August 2003 | US commercial lending business of Dutch insurer Aegon (Transamerica Finance) | $5.4 billion ($1 billion plus repayment of debt) |
| October 2003 | Vivendi Universal entertainment assets | $14 billion approx (mix of debt reduction and equity) |
| October 2003 | Instrumentarium, Finnish healthcare technology | $2 billion |
| October 2003 | Amersham, UK healthcare technology | $9.5 billion (all stock transaction) |
| December 2003 | IKON, business equipment leasing unit | $1.5 billion |
| May 2004 | Leases and secured loans from Boeing Capital ($2 billion total) | |
| spring 2004 | InVision Technologies, baggage screening equipment for airports | $0.9 billion |
| August 2004 | Deltabank, Moscow-based Russian consumer bank | |

| | | |
|---|---|---|
| September 2004 | CrossCountry Energy, interstate natural gas pipeline infrastructure (from Enron) | $2.45 billion (including debt), as a joint venture with Southern Union |
| November 2004 | Edwards Systems Technology, fire detection systems (from SPX Corp) | $1.395 billion cash |
| November 2004 | CitiCapital's Transportation Financial Services Group, a subsidiary of Citigroup | $4.4 billion approx cash |
| November 2004 | Ionics, water technology and services | $1.1 billion cash (plus $200 million debt) |
| **Total number of deals disclosed on the GE acquisitions/growth platform web site** | | |
| 2002 | 39 | |
| 2003 | 24 | |
| 2004 | 4 (up to July 2004) | |

*Source*: GE web site www.ge.com/en/company/investor/acquisitions.htm (accessed 1May 2004 and 17 April 2005)

*Note*: In April 2005, the website lists information on 'growth platforms'; previously these were termed 'acquisitions'. This web page does not list all of GE's acquisitions, nor does it always disclose the financial term. The summary data in the final row lists deals disclosed up to July 2004, after which no further information was available (last accessed 17 April 2005). Deals are generally included above when they are concluded

**Table C3.14** *GE: scale of acquisitions, as measured by cash flows (in real 2003 prices)*

| | *Total cash inflow* | *Of which, cash from operations* | *Of which, other sources of cash* | *Cash applied to acquisitions* | | |
|---|---|---|---|---|---|---|
| | | | | *Total* | *Of which, cash for GE Industrial acquisitions* | *Of which, cash for GE Capital acquisitions* |
| | $ million | $ million | $ million | $million | $million | $million |
| **1980** | 7,233 | 5,225 | 2,008 | | | |
| **1981** | 7,993 | 5,330 | 2,663 | | | |
| **1982** | 7,292 | 5,595 | 1,697 | | | |
| **1983** | 7,907 | 5,712 | 2,195 | | | |
| **1984** | 8,901 | 5,120 | 3,781 | | | |
| **1985** | 7,278 | 5,712 | 1,566 | | | |
| **1986** | 19,848 | 5,647 | 14,201 | | | |
| **1987** | 11,577 | 5,026 | 6,551 | | | |
| **1988** | 38,279 | 11,051 | 27,228 | 5,452 | 4,611 | 842 |
| **1989** | 35,433 | 9,834 | 25,600 | 2,762 | 1,127 | 1,635 |
| **1990** | 41,425 | 12,729 | 28,696 | 6,473 | 183 | 6,290 |
| **1991** | 42,050 | 10,136 | 31,914 | 5,096 | 1,261 | 3,834 |
| **1992** | 37,714 | 13,453 | 24,262 | 2,642 | 0 | 2,642 |
| **1993** | 41,500 | 12,982 | 28,519 | 2,663 | 0 | 2,663 |
| **1994** | 50,669 | 16,634 | 34,036 | 3,237 | 714 | 2,523 |
| **1995** | 65,668 | 18,058 | 47,610 | 6,816 | 288 | 6,528 |
| **1996** | 63,666 | 20,960 | 42,706 | 6,477 | 1,317 | 5,159 |
| **1997** | 59,924 | 16,344 | 43,580 | 6,020 | 1,636 | 4,384 |
| **1998** | 92,965 | 21,871 | 71,094 | 21,024 | 1,644 | 19,380 |
| **1999** | 94,848 | 27,185 | 67,663 | 12,882 | 1,762 | 11,120 |
| **2000** | 96,761 | 24,256 | 72,505 | 2,493 | 1,236 | 1,257 |
| **2001** | 97,867 | 33,470 | 64,397 | 12,921 | 1,493 | 11,428 |
| **2002** | 137,332 | 30,137 | 107,196 | 22,045 | 9,149 | 12,896 |
| **2003** | 114,104 | 30,289 | 83,815 | 14,407 | 3,870 | 10,537 |
| **Total 1980–2003** | 1,188,236 | 352,754 | 835,482 | 143,663 | 40,544 | 103,119 |

*Source*: GE Annual Report and Accounts and 10K, various years

*Notes*: Prior to 1988, GE did not consolidate GE Capital results. Between 1980 and 1986, GE did not reveal/disaggregate cash applied to acquisitions. Acquisitions exclude purchases made through transfer of shares

**Table C3.15** *GE: contributions to and holidays from the employee pension fund (in real 2002 prices)*

| | *GE net income* | *Pension fund surplus* | *Pension fund spend (in years with a net contribution)* | *Pension fund holiday (in years with no contribution)* | *Pension fund contribution/ holiday as % of net income* |
|---|---|---|---|---|---|
| | $million | $million | $ million | $ million | % |
| **1980** | 3,294 | 300 | 879 | | 26.7 |
| **1981** | 3,259 | 509 | 874 | | 26.8 |
| **1982** | 3,375 | 1,847 | 873 | | 25.9 |
| **1983** | 3,643 | 3,017 | 981 | | 26.9 |
| **1984** | 3,935 | 4,582 | 1,041 | | 26.5 |
| **1985** | 3,891 | 8,694 | 723 | | 18.6 |
| **1986** | 4,074 | 2,200 | 234 | | 5.7 |
| **1987** | 4,595 | 3,908 | 39 | | 0.9 |
| **1988** | 5,133 | 5,813 | | 344 | 6.7 |
| **1989** | 5,697 | 6,852 | | 349 | 6.1 |
| **1990** | 5,905 | 8,483 | | 522 | 8.8 |
| **1991** | 3,472 | 7,687 | | 917 | 26.4 |
| **1992** | 6,041 | 7,934 | | 749 | 12.4 |
| **1993** | 5,357 | 4,638 | | 706 | 13.2 |
| **1994** | 5,718 | 7,389 | | 695 | 12.2 |
| **1995** | 7,736 | 5,503 | | 820 | 10.6 |
| **1996** | 8,327 | 7,035 | | 811 | 9.7 |
| **1997** | 9,172 | 7,563 | | 370 | 4.0 |
| **1998** | 10,230 | 17,470 | | 1,118 | 10.9 |
| **1999** | 11,540 | 26,619 | | 1,486 | 12.9 |
| **2000** | 13,262 | 22,100 | | 1,816 | 13.7 |
| **2001** | 13,862 | 14,773 | | 2,122 | 15.3 |
| **2002** | 14,118 | 4,545 | | 1,556 | 11.0 |

*Source*: GE Annual Report and Accounts, various years

**Table C3.16** *The relationship between capital employed and sales in GE Consolidated (in real 2003 prices)*

| | *Capital employed* | *Sales revenues* | *Capital employed per $ of sales* | *Annual growth in capital employed* | *Annual growth in sales* |
|---|---|---|---|---|---|
| | $ million | $ million | $ | % | % |
| **1980** | 41,350 | 58,856 | 0.70 | | |
| **1981** | 42,411 | 58,775 | 0.72 | 2.6 | –0.1 |
| **1982** | 41,219 | 54,232 | 0.76 | –2.8 | –7.7 |
| **1983** | 43,032 | 53,118 | 0.81 | 4.4 | –2.1 |
| **1984** | 43,813 | 54,708 | 0.80 | 1.8 | 3.0 |
| **1985** | 45,201 | 54,877 | 0.82 | 3.2 | 0.3 |
| **1986** | 58,050 | 68,848 | 0.84 | 28.4 | 25.5 |
| **1987** | 62,985 | 76,935 | 0.82 | 8.5 | 11.8 |
| **1988** | 172,514 | 77,942 | 2.21 | 173.9 | 1.3 |
| **1989** | 190,566 | 81,032 | 2.35 | 10.5 | 4.0 |
| **1990** | 216,781 | 82,290 | 2.63 | 13.8 | 1.6 |
| **1991** | 227,478 | 81,436 | 2.79 | 4.9 | –1.0 |
| **1992** | 253,164 | 74,913 | 3.38 | 11.3 | –8.0 |
| **1993** | 320,505 | 77,177 | 4.15 | 26.6 | 3.0 |
| **1994** | 241,559 | 74,658 | 3.24 | –24.6 | –3.3 |
| **1995** | 275,516 | 84,609 | 3.26 | 14.1 | 13.3 |
| **1996** | 319,846 | 92,970 | 3.44 | 16.1 | 9.9 |
| **1997** | 348,936 | 104,263 | 3.35 | 9.1 | 12.2 |
| **1998** | 402,098 | 113,499 | 3.54 | 15.2 | 8.9 |
| **1999** | 447,899 | 123,393 | 3.63 | 11.4 | 8.7 |
| **2000** | 467,172 | 138,817 | 3.37 | 4.3 | 12.5 |
| **2001** | 514,620 | 130,898 | 3.93 | 10.2 | –5.7 |
| **2002** | 587,899 | 134,595 | 4.37 | 14.2 | 3.3 |
| **2003** | 647,483 | 134,187 | 4.82 | 10.1 | –0.3 |

*Source*: GE Annual Report and Accounts and 10K, various years

Table C3.17 *GE: changes in balance-sheet structure*

| | *GE Consolidated breakdown of capital employed* | | *Equity as a % of long term capital in* | |
|---|---|---|---|---|
| | *Debt as a % of total capital* | *Equity as a % of total capital* | *GE Industrial* | *GE Capital* |
| **1980** | 55.7 | 44.3 | 44.3 | 10.0 |
| **1981** | 56.4 | 43.6 | 43.6 | 9.1 |
| **1982** | 52.8 | 47.2 | 47.2 | 10.0 |
| **1983** | 51.6 | 48.4 | 48.4 | 9.9 |
| **1984** | 49.2 | 50.8 | 50.8 | 8.7 |
| **1985** | 47.4 | 52.6 | 52.6 | 9.0 |
| **1986** | 56.3 | 43.7 | 43.7 | 5.6 |
| **1987** | 57.7 | 42.3 | 42.3 | 6.5 |
| **1988** | 83.3 | 16.7 | 44.7 | 6.4 |
| **1989** | 83.7 | 16.3 | 47.4 | 6.7 |
| **1990** | 85.9 | 14.1 | 46.8 | 5.9 |
| **1991** | 87.1 | 12.9 | 44.3 | 6.1 |
| **1992** | 87.8 | 12.2 | 48.8 | 5.7 |
| **1993** | 89.7 | 10.3 | 50.5 | 5.1 |
| **1994** | 86.4 | 13.6 | 51.9 | 6.1 |
| **1995** | 87.0 | 13.0 | 53.1 | 6.9 |
| **1996** | 88.6 | 11.4 | 51.9 | 6.3 |
| **1997** | 88.7 | 11.3 | 51.1 | 6.7 |
| **1998** | 89.1 | 10.9 | 52.1 | 6.5 |
| **1999** | 89.5 | 10.5 | 51.5 | 5.9 |
| **2000** | 88.4 | 11.6 | 52.2 | 6.2 |
| **2001** | 88.9 | 11.1 | 50.0 | 6.7 |
| **2002** | 88.9 | 11.1 | 50.8 | 7.5 |
| **2003** | 87.8 | 12.2 | 56.8 | 8.2 |

*Source*: GE Annual Report and Accounts and 10K, various years

*Notes*: Shareholder equity excludes treasury shares. From 1988 onwards, reserves of insurance affiliates are classified as long-term debt

**Table C3.18** *The composition of capital employed in GE Industrial and GE Capital (in real 2003 prices)*

| | *GE Consolidated* | | | *GE Industrial* | | | *GE Capital* | | |
|---|---|---|---|---|---|---|---|---|---|
| | *Long-term liabilities* | *Current liabilities* | *Equity* | *Long-term liabilities* | *Current liabilities* | *Equity* | *Long-term liabilities* | *Current liabilities* | *Equity* |
| **1980** | 11,399 | 30,426 | 18,317 | 6,074 | 16,959 | 16,237 | 5,325 | 13,467 | 2,080 |
| **1981** | 11,910 | 33,762 | 18,486 | 6,238 | 17,688 | 16,311 | 5,673 | 16,074 | 2,175 |
| **1982** | 12,401 | 31,276 | 19,447 | 6,224 | 15,547 | 17,008 | 6,177 | 15,729 | 2,439 |
| **1983** | 12,310 | 36,079 | 20,825 | 6,153 | 16,054 | 17,961 | 6,157 | 20,025 | 2,864 |
| **1984** | 13,502 | 42,667 | 22,275 | 6,289 | 15,249 | 18,955 | 7,212 | 27,418 | 3,320 |
| **1985** | 14,431 | 46,851 | 23,777 | 6,172 | 15,252 | 19,840 | 8,260 | 31,599 | 3,937 |
| **1986** | 22,953 | 95,048 | 25,356 | 13,461 | 19,234 | 20,336 | 9,492 | 75,814 | 5,019 |
| **1987** | 28,816 | 100,428 | 26,670 | 15,809 | 20,506 | 20,229 | 13,006 | 79,922 | 6,441 |
| **1988** | 31,495 | 112,285 | 28,734 | 15,621 | 19,884 | 21,236 | 24,574 | 84,548 | 7,499 |
| **1989** | 32,878 | 126,670 | 31,018 | 14,648 | 19,825 | 22,006 | 26,600 | 99,399 | 9,011 |
| **1990** | 39,191 | 147,049 | 30,541 | 13,861 | 20,913 | 20,915 | 33,085 | 119,427 | 9,626 |
| **1991** | 40,818 | 157,345 | 29,314 | 16,629 | 20,278 | 18,826 | 34,483 | 127,827 | 10,488 |
| **1992** | 45,504 | 176,868 | 30,792 | 14,262 | 18,048 | 19,131 | 40,557 | 150,606 | 11,661 |
| **1993** | 67,330 | 220,266 | 32,909 | 14,336 | 17,917 | 19,134 | 63,838 | 192,204 | 13,774 |
| **1994** | 84,787 | 123,998 | 32,774 | 14,344 | 15,994 | 21,124 | 81,000 | 98,103 | 11,650 |
| **1995** | 113,188 | 126,554 | 35,774 | 14,062 | 17,481 | 20,340 | 109,961 | 99,006 | 15,434 |
| **1996** | 133,362 | 149,938 | 36,546 | 13,910 | 19,906 | 19,784 | 130,959 | 119,307 | 16,762 |
| **1997** | 134,926 | 174,483 | 39,527 | 14,734 | 23,129 | 19,740 | 133,568 | 139,795 | 19,786 |
| **1998** | 159,510 | 198,666 | 43,923 | 15,940 | 24,492 | 21,637 | 157,882 | 162,466 | 22,285 |
| **1999** | 180,637 | 220,220 | 47,042 | 17,042 | 27,202 | 24,579 | 178,997 | 179,916 | 22,462 |
| **2000** | 206,556 | 206,639 | 53,977 | 17,798 | 31,669 | 29,366 | 204,716 | 166,894 | 24,611 |
| **2001** | 207,132 | 250,494 | 56,994 | 18,530 | 38,553 | 27,273 | 205,403 | 207,204 | 29,722 |
| **2002** | 288,161 | 234,631 | 65,108 | 19,029 | 43,932 | 27,366 | 287,319 | 175,544 | 37,741 |
| **2003** | 312,048 | 256,255 | 79,180 | 27,816 | 32,453 | 33,872 | 303,505 | 205,713 | 45,308 |
| **% change 1980–2003** | **2,638** | **742** | **332** | **358** | **91** | **109** | **5,599** | **1,427** | **2,079** |

*Source*: GE Annual Report and Accounts and 10K, various years

*Notes*: GE began consolidating GE Capital in 1988. Pre-1988, GE Consolidated sales is calculated as the summation of both GE Industrial and GE Capital totals. GE Industrial owns nearly all the shares in GE Capital and therefore consolidates the net income. To avoid double counting, the above calculation deducts GE Capital's contribution to GE Industrial's net income. Divisional totals will not sum to consolidated totals due to intra-company transactions

# Index